D1312252

Oracle Press™

OCA Oracle9*i* Associate DBA Certification Exam Guide

Jason S. Couchman
Sudheer N. Marisetti

McGraw-Hill/Osborne

New York   Chicago   San Francisco
Lisbon   London   Madrid   Mexico City   Milan
New Delhi   San Juan   Seoul   Singapore   Sydney   Toronto

McGraw-Hill/Osborne
2600 Tenth Street
Berkeley, California 94710
U.S.A.

To arrange bulk purchase discounts for sales promotions, premiums, or fund-raisers, please contact **McGraw-Hill**/Osborne at the above address. For information on translations or book distributors outside the U.S.A., please see the International Contact Information page immediately following the index of this book.

OCA Oracle9*i* Associate DBA Certification Exam Guide

Copyright © 2002 by The McGraw-Hill Companies, Inc. (Publisher). All rights reserved. Printed in the United States of America. Except as permitted under the Copyright Act of 1976, no part of this publication may be reproduced or distributed in any form or by any means, or stored in a database or retrieval system, without the prior written permission of Publisher.

Oracle is a registered trademark and Oracle8i and Oracle9i are trademarks or registered trademarks of Oracle Corporation.

1234567890 DOC DOC 0198765432
Book p/n 0072225378 and CD p/n 0072225386
parts of
ISBN 0-07-222536-X

Publisher
    Brandon A. Nordin

Vice-President & Associate Publisher
    Scott Rogers

Acquisitions Editor
    Lisa McClain

Project Editor
    Julie M. Smith

Acquisitions Coordinator
    Athena Honore

Technical Editors
    Aradhana Puri
    Divya Sandeep
    Trevor Davies

Cover Series Design
    Damore Johann Design, Inc.

Composition and Indexing
    MacAllister Publishing Services, LLC

This book was composed with QuarkXPress™.

Information has been obtained by Publisher from sources believed to be reliable. However, because of the possibility of human or mechanical error by our sources, Publisher, or others, Publisher does not guarantee the accuracy, adequacy, or completeness of any information included in this work and is not responsible for any errors or omissions or the results obtained from the use of such information.

    Oracle Corporation does not make any representations or warranties as to the accuracy, adequacy or completeness of any information contained in this work, and is not responsible for any errors or omissions.

To my wife Stacy
—Jason Couchman

To my wife Sujani and my sons, Rahath and Rishabh
—Sudheer Marisetti

About the Authors

Jason S. Couchman

Jason S. Couchman is a database consultant and the author of *Oracle8i Certified Professional DBA Certification Exam Guide*, also from Oracle Press. He is a regular presenter on Oracle and OCP at international Oracle user conferences and meetings. His work has been published by *Oracle Magazine*, Harvard Business School Publishing, and Gannett Newspapers, among others.

Sudheer N. Marisetti

Sudheer N. Marisetti is a database, Unix, and Web administrator and president of Abacus Concepts Inc., a New Jersey-based consulting firm specializing in designing, building, and maintaining database systems. He is an adjunct faculty member at Columbia University teaching advanced Oracle administration classes. He holds a master's degree in electrical engineering.

OracleCertified Professional

About the Oracle Certification Program

The expertise of Oracle database administrators (DBAs) is integral to the success of today's increasingly complex system environments. The best DBAs operate primarily behind the scenes, looking for ways to fine tune day-to-day performance to prevent unscheduled crises and hours of expensive downtime. They know they stand between optimal performance and a crisis that could bring a company to a standstill. Knowing that reaching that level of expertise often takes years, the Oracle Certification Program Database Administrator Track now provides DBAs three tiers of certification to demonstrate with tangible evidence the level of their skills with the Oracle database. These tiers are the Oracle Certified Associate (OCA), Oracle Certified Professional (OCP), and Oracle Certified Master (OCM).

The Oracle Certification Program was developed by Oracle to recognize technical professionals who can demonstrate a specific depth of knowledge using Oracle technologies according to a rigorous standard established by Oracle. The OCA is an apprentice skill level certification that will give the beginning IT professional recognition for their foundation of knowledge and will help in differentiating them from others without credentials. Obtaining the OCA credential is the first step toward reaching the OCP and OCM tiers of the DBA certification track. By earning professional certification, you can translate the impressive knowledge and skill you have worked so hard to accumulate into a tangible credential that can lead to greater job security or more challenging, better-paying opportunities.

Oracle Certified Associates are eligible to receive use of the Oracle Certified Associate logo and a certificate for framing.

Requirements for OCA Certification

To become an Oracle Certified Associate Database Administrator for the Oracle9i track, you must pass two tests. These exams cover knowledge of the essential aspects of the SQL language and Oracle administration. The certification process requires that you pass the following two exams:

- Introduction to Oracle9i: SQL (1Z0-007)
- Oracle9i Database: Fundamentals I (1Z0-031)

If you fail a test, you must wait at least 30 days before you retake that exam. You may attempt a particular test up to three times in a twelve-month period.

Recertification

Oracle announces the requirements for upgrading your certification based on the release of new products and upgrades. Oracle will give six months' notice announcing when an exam version is expiring.

Exam Format

The computer-based exams are multiple-choice tests, usually consisting of 50-65 questions that must be completed in 90-120 minutes. With the introduction of the OCA track, Oracle is now offering the SQL Exam (1Z0-007) in either online or proctored formats. Please make sure to visit www.oracle.com/education/certification for details and for updates on the most recent specifications for the exams.

Contents

ACKNOWLEDGMENTS xv
PREFACE xvii
INTRODUCTION xix

PART I
Preparing for OCA DBA Exam 1:
Introduction to SQL

1 Overview of Oracle Databases **5**
Overview of Oracle 7
    Theoretical and Physical Aspects of Relational Databases 7
    Oracle's RDBMS and ORDBMS Implementations 11
    Usage and Benefits of PL/SQL 17
Writing Basic SQL Statements 20
    Capabilities of SQL select Statements 20
    Executing select Statements 25
    Differentiating Between SQL and SQL*Plus Commands 38
Chapter Summary 48
Two-Minute Drill 48
Fill-in-the-Blank Questions 50
Chapter Questions 50
Fill-in-the-Blank Answers 53
Answers to Chapter Questions 53

2 Limiting, Sorting, and Manipulating Return Data **55**
    Restricting and Sorting Row Data 56
        Sorting Return Data with the order by Clause 56
        Limiting Return Data with the where Clause 61
    Using Single-Row Functions 67
        Various Single-Row Functions Explained 67
        Using Functions in select Statements 73
        Date Functions 81
        Conversion Functions 86
    Chapter Summary 90
    Two-Minute Drill 90
    Fill-in-the-Blank Questions 91
    Chapter Questions 91
    Fill-in-the-Blank Answers 94
    Answers to Chapter Questions 94

3 Advanced Data Selection in Oracle **97**
    Displaying Data from Multiple Tables 98
        The Keys to Table Joins 99
        select Statements That Join Data from More Than One Table 99
        Creating Outer Joins 109
        Joining a Table to Itself 118
    Group Functions and Their Uses 122
        Identifying and Using Group Functions 122
        Using the group by Clause 126
        Excluding group Data with having 133
    Chapter Summary 135
    Two-Minute Drill 135
    Fill-in-the-Blank Questions 138
    Chapter Questions 138
    Fill-in-the-Blank Answers 140
    Answers to Chapter Questions 140

4 Subqueries **143**
    Using Subqueries 144
        Understanding and Defining Subqueries 145
        Listing and Writing Different Types of Subqueries 150
        Writing Multiple-Column Subqueries 156
        NULL Values and Subqueries 158
        Subqueries in a from Clause 161
    Producing Readable Output with SQL*Plus 165
        Entering Variables 165
        Customizing SQL*Plus Environments 173

Producing Readable Output 181
Creating and Executing Scripts. 187
Saving Customizations. 188
Chapter Summary. 190
Two-Minute Drill 191
Fill-in-the-Blank Questions. 193
Chapter Questions 193
Fill-in-the-Blank Answers 197
Answers to Chapter Questions 197

5 Creating Oracle Database Objects **201**
Creating the Tables of an Oracle Database 202
Describing Tables 203
Creating Tables 205
Datatypes and Column Definitions 211
Altering Table Definitions 219
Dropping, Renaming, and Truncating Tables 224
Including Constraints 227
Describing Constraints. 228
Creating and Maintaining Constraints 232
Chapter Summary. 248
Two-Minute Drill 248
Fill-in-the-Blank Questions. 251
Chapter Questions 251
Fill-in-the-Blank Answers 255
Answers to Chapter Questions 255

6 Manipulating Oracle Data **259**
Adding New Rows to a Table. 260
Making Changes to Existing Row Data. 267
Deleting Data from the Oracle Database. 270
Merging Data in Oracle Tables 273
The Importance of Transaction Control 279
Chapter Summary. 285
Two-Minute Drill 286
Fill-in-the-Blank Questions. 287
Chapter Questions 287
Fill-in-the-Blank Answers 289
Answers to Chapter Questions 289

7 Creating Other Database Objects in Oracle **291**
Creating Views 292
Creating Simple Views. 293
Creating Views That Enforce Constraints. 301

Creating Complex Views 305
Modifying and Removing Views. 310
Other Database Objects 313
Overview of Other Database Objects 314
Using Sequences 315
Using Indexes 322
Using Public and Private Synonyms. 331
Chapter Summary. 335
Two-Minute Drill 336
Fill-in-the-Blank Questions. 339
Chapter Questions 339
Fill-in-the-Blank Answers 343
Answers to Chapter Questions 343

8 **User Access Control in Oracle** **347**
Creating Users. 348
Granting and Revoking Object Privileges. 356
Using Roles to Manage Database Access. 365
Chapter Summary. 372
Two-Minute Drill 372
Fill-in-the-Blank Questions. 374
Chapter Questions 374
Fill-in-the-Blank Answers 376
Answers to Chapter Questions 376

PART II
OCA Oracle9i SQL Practice Exams

9 **OCA Exam 1: Introduction to SQL** **381**
Practice Exam 1 382
Practice Exam 2 401
Practice Exam 3 417
Answers to Practice Exam 1 439
Answers to Practice Exam 2 452
Answers to Practice Exam 3 464

PART III
Preparing for OCA Database Administration
Fundamentals I Exam

10 **Basics of the Oracle Database Architecture** **483**
Oracle Architectural Components. 484
Oracle Server Architecture. 485
Reading Data from Disk for Users: The Server Process 487

Structures That Connect Users to Oracle Servers 490
Stages in Processing Queries, Changes, and commits 493
Getting Started with the Oracle Server 500
Common Database Administrative Tools 500
The OUI 502
Setting Up Password File Authentication 509
Using OEM Components.................................. 516
Managing an Oracle Instance............................... 521
Creating and Managing Initialization Parameter File 521
Configuring OMF 527
Starting an Instance 531
Monitoring the Use of Diagnostic Files 539
Creating an Oracle Database 543
Prerequisites for Database Creation 543
Creating Databases Using the Database Configuration Assistant ... 549
Creating a Database Manually........................... 552
Chapter Summary....................................... 556
Two-Minute Drill 556
Fill-in-the-Blank Questions.............................. 561
Chapter Questions 562
Fill-in-the-Blank Answers 565
Answers to Chapter Questions 565

11 Managing the Physical Database Structure **569**
Data Dictionary Content and Usage........................ 570
Constructing the Data Dictionary Views 571
Key Data Dictionary Components and Contents 574
Querying the Data Dictionary 581
Maintaining Control Files................................ 585
How Control Files Are Used 585
Examining Control File Contents 588
Managing Control Files with Oracle-Managed Files............ 592
Obtaining Information about Control Files.................. 595
Multiplexing Control Files 599
Maintaining Redo Log Files 601
The Purpose and Structure of Online Redo Logs 601
Controlling Log Switches and Checkpoints 605
Multiplexing and Maintaining Redo Log Files 608
Managing Online Redo Log Files with OMF 611
Chapter Summary....................................... 613
Two-Minute Drill 613
Chapter Questions 618
Answers to Chapter Questions 620

12 Managing Tablespaces and Datafiles 623
   Describing the Logical Structure of the Database 624
      Creating Tablespaces 631
      Changing Tablespace Size 637
      Allocating Space for Temporary Segments 640
      Temporary Segments in Permanent Tablespaces.............. 640
      Changing Tablespace Status.................................. 645
      Changing Tablespace Storage Settings 648
      Oracle-Managed Files (OMF)................................. 652
   Chapter Summary... 655
   Two-Minute Drill 655
   Fill-in-the-Blank Questions...................................... 658
   Chapter Questions 658
   Fill-in-the-Blank Answers 660
   Answers to Chapter Questions 660

13 Storage Structures and Undo Data 663
   Storage Structures and Relationships 664
      Different Segment Types and Their Uses...................... 665
      Controlling the Use of Extents by Segments 673
      Using Block Space Utilization Parameters 682
      Obtaining Information about Storage Structures................ 686
   Managing Undo Data... 689
      The Purpose of Undo Segments............................. 689
      Implementing Automatic Undo Management 693
      Creating and Configuring Undo Segments Manually 698
      Obtaining Information about Undo Data...................... 708
   Chapter Summary.. 709
   Two-Minute Drill 709
   Fill-in-the-Blank Questions...................................... 712
   Chapter Questions 712
   Fill-in-the-Blank Answers 715
   Answers to Chapter Questions 715

14 Managing Database Objects 717
   Managing Tables... 718
      Various Methods of Storing Data 719
      Distinguishing Oracle Datatypes 724
      Extended and Restricted ROWIDs 728
      Structure of Data Blocks and Rows 731
      Creating Permanent and Temporary Tables................... 733
      Managing Storage Structures in a Table 740
      Reorganizing, Truncating, and Dropping Tables 744
      Dropping Unused Columns from Tables 750

Managing Indexes 753
    Different Index Types and Their Uses 754
    Creating B-Tree and Bitmap Indexes 761
    Reorganizing Indexes 765
    Dropping Indexes 770
    Getting Index Information from the Data Dictionary 771
    Monitoring Use of Indexes. 773
Managing Data Integrity 777
    Implementing Data Integrity Constraints 777
    Maintaining Integrity Constraints 784
    Obtaining Constraint Information from Oracle 788
Chapter Summary. 790
Two-Minute Drill 791
Fill-in-the-Blank Questions. 794
Chapter Questions 794
Fill-in-the-Blank Answers 799
Answers to Chapter Questions 799

15 Managing Database Users **803**
Managing Users 804
    Creating New Database Users 804
    Altering and Dropping Existing Users 810
    Monitoring Information about Existing Users 815
Managing Password Security and Resources 817
    Controlling Resource Use with Profiles 818
    Administering Profiles 822
    Administering Passwords Using Profiles. 826
    Obtaining Profile Information from the Data Dictionary 831
Managing Privileges 833
    Identifying System and Object Privileges 834
    Granting and Revoking Privileges 840
    Identifying Audit Capabilities. 845
Managing Roles 853
    Creating and Modifying Roles 853
    Controlling Availability of Roles. 856
    Removing Roles. 860
    Using Predefined Roles 861
    Displaying Role Information from the Data Dictionary 863
Chapter Summary. 864
Two-Minute Drill 865
Fill-in-the-Blank Questions. 871
Chapter Questions 871
Fill-in-the-Blank Answers 875
Answers to Chapter Questions 875

PART IV

OCA Oracle9i DBA Fundamentals I Practice Exams

16 OCA Database Administration Fundamentals I **881**

Practice Exam 1 882

Practice Exam 2 900

Practice Exam 3 916

Answers to Practice Exam 1 936

Answers to Practice Exam 2 949

Answers to Practice Exam 3 963

A Globalization Support **979**

Choosing a Database and a National Character Set for a Database . 981

Specifying Language-Dependent Behavior. 982

NLS Parameters 983

Obtaining Information about Globalization Support Usage 984

Index **987**

Acknowledgments

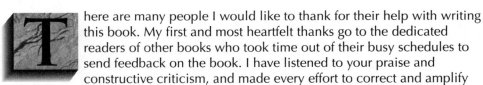

here are many people I would like to thank for their help with writing this book. My first and most heartfelt thanks go to the dedicated readers of other books who took time out of their busy schedules to send feedback on the book. I have listened to your praise and constructive criticism, and made every effort to correct and amplify my work based on the points you made. Next, a note of gratitude to the folks at Oracle who made the book possible. Ulrike Schwinn and Jim DiIanni have both been loyal associates, colleagues, and friends during my ongoing effort to help 110,000-plus readers get Oracle certified. Thanks also to Oracle University for its feedback and assistance with the overall direction for the OCP DBA track. As always, thanks to the fine folks at Osborne and MacAllister Publishing Services for their hard work in assembling the manuscript into a finished product.

This book is dedicated to my wife, Stacy, who makes every part of my life better. Stacy, I strive to be a better husband to you, and to help you grow as a person. As you take this next step in your life from student to professional, I want you to know that I support you wholeheartedly and will do everything in my power to keep our marriage strong and solid—especially when you have to work late! I love you.

—*Jason Couchman*

I wish to thank Jason for giving me an opportunity to coauthor this book with him. Working with him on this book and the guidance he provided me were invaluable. I thank all the folks at Osborne/McGraw-Hill in helping us complete this book. I also thank Oracle Corporation for reviewing each chapter and providing valuable feedback. I thank all my previous, current, and future students, whose interaction was invaluable in building my technical expertise.

I thank my good friend Ravi Kadeermangalan, whose support and advice helped me in my life and in writing this book. I am fortunate to have such a friend. Most of all I am indebted to my beloved wife, Sujani "Puppala" Marisetti, who held the fort and kept our two active kids occupied while I toiled on this book during the weekends and nights. Without her patience, support, and affection I would not have traveled so far in my life.

For your comments, I can be reached at smarisetti@yahoo.com.

—Sudheer Marisetti

Preface

Jason's interest in Oracle certification began in 1996 when he read about the Oracle DBA certificate offered by the Chauncey Group. He found it difficult to prepare for that certification exam for two reasons. First, there was an absence of practice questions readily available. Second, preparation for the exam involved reviewing six or seven different manuals and Oracle Press books, none of which were particularly suited to the task. Judging from the response to the proliferation of titles now available in the Oracle Certified Professional (OCP) Exam Guide Series from Oracle Press, it would seem others have had similar experiences.

This book is divided into four units, the first containing preparatory material for the Introduction to Oracle9i SQL exam, part of the Oracle9i OCA DBA certification track. The first unit has eight chapters, each containing several discussions that focus on a particular topic or subtopic objective listed by the Oracle Certification Program Oracle9i Certified Database Associate Track Candidate Guide for the SQL exam. (For a complete listing of all the topics tested for this exam, see Chapter 1.) These discussions are followed by a For Review section, each listing the three or four most important concepts for you to retain from the discussion. After the review, you'll see two to six exercise questions in exam-based multiple choice or short answer format. Following the questions you will find an answer key for those questions, which should help you master the material even more quickly. Thus, with this book you're never more than a few pages away from demonstrating what you've learned about Oracle9i DBA topics for the OCA exams.

At the end of each chapter, you will find a short Summary of what was covered in the chapter, followed by a Two-Minute Drill. The Two-Minute Drill contains another bulleted list of fast facts to review, or crib notes for the days leading up to your OCA exam. The chapters conclude with 5 to 20 short answer and exam-based multiple choice questions designed to help you further test your understanding of the materials you learned in the chapter.

The second unit consists of one chapter containing three full-length practice exams. Each test contains exam-based multiple choice and scenario-based questions that are designed to help you strengthen your test-taking skills for the OCA exams. You will also find answers and in-depth explanations for every question in the practice exams in the back of that chapter, along with a reference back to the exam topic and subtopic objectives from the OCA Candidate Guide. This feature should help you determine your areas requiring further improvement with pinpoint accuracy.

Units three and four of the book are structured similarly to units one and two, respectively, but cover the Oracle9i Fundamentals I exam. The third unit consists of six chapters, each containing several discussions that focus on a particular topic or subtopic objective listed by the Oracle Certification Program Oracle9i Certified Database Associate Track Candidate Guide for the Fundamentals I exam. (For a complete listing of all the topics tested for this exam, see Chapter 10.) The fourth unit consists of one chapter containing three full-length practice exams for preparation for the Fundamentals I exam.

Finally, a note about updates and errata. Because OCA covers such vast ground in a short time, this has become a living text. If you feel you have encountered difficulties due to errors, you can check out www.OraclePressBooks.com to find the latest errata.

Good luck!

Introduction

The Oracle Certification Program for DBAs from Oracle Corporation is a great opportunity for you to demonstrate your expertise on the use of Oracle database software. Now consisting of three tiers of certification depending on mastery level, it represents the culmination of many people's requests for objective standards in Oracle database administration, one of the hottest markets in the software field. The presence of these certifications on the market indicates an important reality about Oracle as a career path. Oracle is mature, robust, and stable for enterprisewide information management. However, corporations facing a severe shortage of qualified Oracle professionals need a measurement for Oracle expertise.

The OCA certification tier for DBAs is the entry-level credential and consists of two tests in the following areas of Oracle9i: SQL and DBA Fundamentals I, with the current content of those exams covering Oracle through Oracle9i. As of this printing, each test consists of about 60 multiple choice questions pertaining to the recommended usage of Oracle databases. You have about 90 minutes to take each exam. Obtaining certification for the Oracle9i OCA tier of the DBA track is contingent on taking and passing *both* examinations. This book will help you prepare for both the Introduction to Oracle9i SQL exam and DBA Fundamentals I exam.

Why Get Certified?

If you are just starting out as an Oracle professional, you may wonder, "Why should I get certified?" The Oracle Certification Program provides an industry recognized benchmark of your skills and the credential can provide instant prestige on your résumé. While no one is saying you don't know Oracle without this certification on your résumé, the recognized credential will help you prove how well you *do* know Oracle without undergoing a technical interview. We started asking ourselves about the value of Oracle certification when it began to emerge and were surprised to find out that, after years of using Oracle, developing Oracle applications, and administering Oracle databases for Fortune 500 companies, there were a lot of things about Oracle we *didn't* know. And the only reason we know them now is because we took the time and effort to become certified.

If you're looking for another reason to become certified in Oracle, consider the experience of computer professionals with Novell NetWare experience in the late 1980s and early 1990s. Back then, it seemed that anyone with even a little experience in Novell could count on a fantastic job offer. Then Novell introduced its CNE/CNA programs. At first, employers were okay with hiring Novell professionals whether they had a certificate or not. As time went on, however, employers no longer asked for computer professionals with Novell NetWare *experience*; they asked for CNEs and CNAs. A similar phenomenon can be seen in the arena of Microsoft Windows NT, where the MCSE has already become the standard by which those professionals are measuring their skills. Furthermore, with the latest economic downturn in the technology-driven U.S. economy comes the possibility of involuntary information technologies (IT) job changes. If you want to stay competitive in the field of Oracle database administration or development through those changes, your real question shouldn't be *whether* you should become certified, but *when*.

If you are not in the field of Oracle development or database management, or if you want to advance your career using Oracle products, there has never been a better time to do so. With the introduction of the three tiers, OCA, OCP, and OCM, the certification program is ideal for anyone newly entering the industry and focusing on Oracle. By providing a certification level, OCA, that is appropriate for junior Oracle team members, this program provides a clear path of advancement to the more advanced skill sets of the OCP and OCM. The Oracle Certification Program is already altering the playing field for DBAs and developers by changing the focus of the Oracle skill set from "How many years have you used it?" to "Do you know *how* to use it?" That shift benefits organizations using Oracle as much as it benefits the professionals who use Oracle because the emphasis is on *skills*, not attrition.

Managers who are faced with the task of hiring Oracle professionals can breathe a sigh of relief with the debut of the multiple tiers as well. By seeking professionals who are certified at a specific level, managers can spend less time trying to determine if the candidate possesses the needed Oracle skills for the job, and spend more time assessing the candidate's work habits and compatibility with the team.

TIP
You can find the exam objectives tested on the OCA SQL exam and DBA Fundamentals I exam at the beginning of Chapters 1 and 10, respectively.

How Should You Prepare for the Exam?

If you spend your free time studying things like the feature that permits Oracle to remove database files after you issue the DROP TABLESPACE command, you are probably ready to take the OCA exams now. For the rest of us, Oracle and other companies offer classroom- and computer-based training options to learn Oracle. Now users have another option—this book! By selecting this book, you demonstrate two excellent characteristics—that you are committed to a superior career using Oracle products and that you care about preparing for the exam correctly and thoroughly. And by the way, the feature that permits Oracle to remove database files after you drop a tablespace is the Oracle-Managed Files feature, and it is tested heavily on the OCA Oracle9i DBA Fundamentals I exam. That fact, along with thousands of others, is covered extensively in this book to help you prepare for, and pass, the OCA exams.

DBA Certification Past and Present

Oracle certification started in the mid-1990s with the involvement of the Chauncey Group International, a division of the Educational Testing Service. With the help of many Oracle DBAs, Chauncey put together an objective, fact-based, and scenario-based examination on Oracle database administration. This test did an excellent job of measuring knowledge of Oracle7, versions 7.0 to 7.2. Consisting of 60 questions, Chauncey's exam covered several different topic areas, including backup and recovery, security, administration, and performance tuning, all in one test.

The next step that the Oracle Corporation took was to move DBA certification ahead with the advent of OCP (formerly the Oracle Certified Professional). Their core DBA certification consisted of four tests, each about 60 questions in length. By quadrupling the number of questions you had to answer, Oracle required that you have an unprecedented depth of knowledge in Oracle database administration. Oracle has also committed to including scenario-based questions on the OCP examinations, and preparation material for these new questions is included in this book as well. Scenario-based questions require you to not only know the facts about Oracle, but also to understand how to apply those facts in real-life situations.

With the release of the Oracle9*i* exams, Oracle has moved its certification program forward again by recognizing the industry need for certified professionals at all skill levels from the entry-level OCA, to the experienced OCP-level expert, to the enterprise-leading OCM. To become an OCA, a candidate must pass the following exams:

- Introduction to Oracle9*i*: SQL (1Z0-007)

- Oracle9*i* Database: Fundamentals I (1Z0-031)

After obtaining OCA status and gaining more skill and ability through hands-on job experience and training, the upwardly mobile Oracle professional may reach the OCP status by passing these two exams:

- Oracle9*i* Database: Fundamentals II (1Z0-032)

- Oracle9*i* Database: Performance Tuning (1Z0-033)

The top OCM tier is the culmination of years of experience and continual training. To reach this point you must first reach the OCA and OCP levels, take two additional advanced level Oracle University classes, and pass a practicum test administered by Oracle. As with all achievements, this one starts with taking the first step of getting your OCA.

Oracle's final contribution to the area of Oracle certification is a commitment to reviewing and updating the material presented in the certification exams. Oracle-certified DBAs will be required to maintain their certification by retaking the certification exams periodically, meaning that those who certify will stay on the cutting edge of the Oracle database better than those who do not.

The Next Steps

Next, let's examine the test interface you will encounter on exam day. Figure I-1 contains a diagram of the actual test graphical user interface (GUI). The top of the interface tells you how much time has elapsed and the number of questions you have answered. You can use the checkbox in the upper left-hand corner of the interface to mark questions you would like to review later. In the main window of the interface you'll find the actual exam question, along with the choices. Generally, the interface enables the user to select only one answer (unless the question specifically directs you to select more answers). In this case, the interface will enable you to select only as many answers as the question requests. After answering

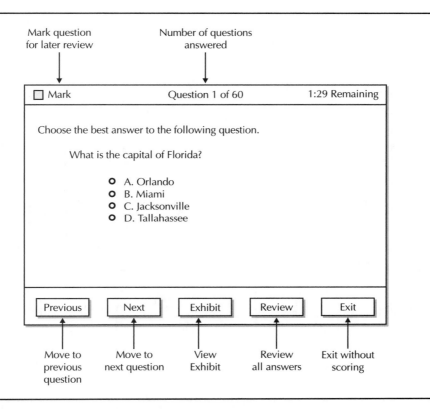

FIGURE I-1. *Sylvan Prometric exam interface illustration*

a question, or marking the question for later review, the candidate can move onto the next question by clicking the appropriate button in the lower left-hand corner. To return to the previous question on the exam, hit the Previous button over to the left.

The final point feature to cover is the Exhibit button. In some cases, you may require the use of an exhibit consisting of extra information from the database, which is useful in answering a question. If the question does not require the use of an exhibit, the button will be grayed out.

Once you've completed all questions on the exam, the Sylvan Prometric interface will display a listing of all the answers you selected, shown in Figure I-2. The questions you marked for later review will be highlighted, and the interface will guide you through a review of all those questions you marked. You can review individual questions or simply have Sylvan Prometric grade your exam.

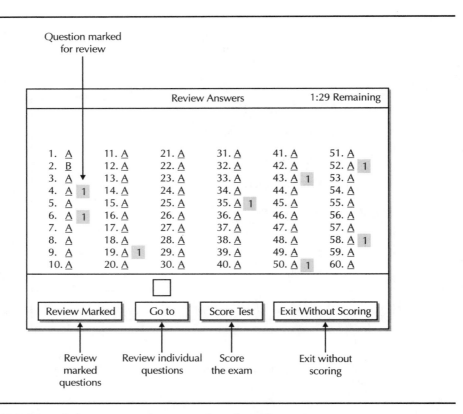

FIGURE I-2. *Sylvan Prometric answer interface illustration*

The assessment test indicates your performance by means of a grade window, such as the one displayed in Figure I-3. You will be shown a section-by-section breakdown of how you did according to the topics covered on the exam, as published in the Candidate Guide from Oracle. Finally, a bar graph indicates where your performance falls in comparison to the maximum score possible on the exam. The exam reports your score immediately after you exit the exam, so you will know right then whether you pass or not in a similar fashion as the assessment test. Both interfaces offer you the ability to print a report of your score.

With the introduction of the OCA track, Oracle is now also offering the SQL Exam (1Z0-007) online as well as in the proctored format. Please make sure to visit www.oracle.com/education/certification for details about taking that exam online.

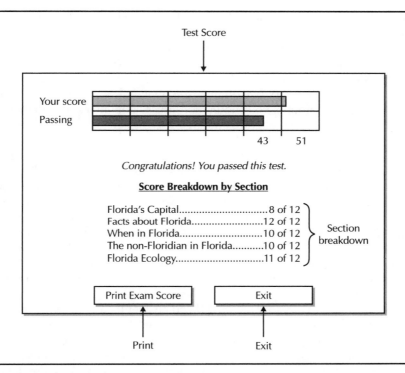

FIGURE I-3. *Sylvan Prometric score interface illustration*

Strategies for Improving Your Score

When OCP exams were first released, the score range for each exam was between 200 and 800. However, Oracle has moved away from scaling the exam score and has experimented lately with reporting only a raw score of the number of questions you answered correctly. The bottom line is still the same. Because there are typically 60 questions on an exam, you want to make sure you get at least 75 percent, or 45 of the questions right, in order to pass. Be sure to check www.oracle.com/education/ certification for the latest information on passing scores—Oracle routinely publishes new versions of exams and passing scores may vary across versions. Additionally, the Fundamentals I exam has both Basic and Mastery sections with different passing percentages. Given the recent use of questions with two or even three correct answers on exams, you need to be careful to select *all* correct answer choices on a question or else you may not get full credit for a correct answer. *There is no penalty for wrong answers.*

Some preliminary items are now identified for you to take the exams. The first tip is, *don't wait until you're the world's foremost authority on Oracle to take the OCA Exams.* If your OCP exam is scaled as it was when the exams were first released, the passing score for most exams is approximately 650. You have to get 45 to 50 questions right, or about 75 to 80 percent of the exam. So, if you are getting about four questions right out of five on the assessment test or in the chapters (more on chapter format in a minute), you should consider taking the exams. Remember, you're certified if you pass with approximately 77 to 96 percent of the correct answers.

Second, if you can't answer the question within 30 seconds, mark it with the check box in the upper left-hand corner of the OCP interface for review later. The most significant difference between the actual interface and the assessment test interface is a special screen appearing after you answer all the questions. This screen displays all your answers, along with a special indicator next to the questions you marked for review. This screen also offers a button for you to click in order to review the questions you marked. You should use this feature extensively. If you spend only 30 seconds answering each question in your first pass on the exam, you will have at least an hour to review the questions you're unsure of, with the added bonus of knowing you answered all the questions that were easiest to you first.

Third, *there is no penalty for guessing.* If you answer the question correctly, your score goes up; if not, your score does not change. If you can eliminate any choices on a question, you should take the chance in the interest of improving your score. In some questions, the exam requires you to specify two or even three choices; this can work in your favor, meaning you need to eliminate fewer choices to get the question right.

A Note about Updates and Errata

You can typically find related information such as posted updates, corrections, and amplifications for all Oracle Press books on www.OraclePressBooks.com. Check back on this site often, as new issues arise all the time in the pursuit of OCA. Good luck with OCA and best wishes for your Oracle career!

PART
I

Preparing for OCA DBA Exam 1: Introduction to SQL

Part I

Oracle9*i* Introduction to SQL Exam Objectives

The first exam in the OCP DBA and Developer tracks covers fundamental usage of the SQL programming language for interacting with the Oracle9*i* database. The following list identifies all OCP objectives for this exam as of this printing. This information comes from the OCP Candidate Guide published for this exam by Oracle Corporation. This candidate guide is online at www.oracle.com/education/certification:

1. Writing Basic SQL `Select` Statements
   - 1.1   List capabilities of SQL `select` statements
   - 1.2   Execute a basic `select` statement
   - 1.3   Differentiate between SQL and SQL*Plus commands

2. Restricting and Sorting Data
   - 2.1   Limit the rows retrieved by a query
   - 2.2   Sort the rows retrieved by a query

3. Single-Row Functions
   - 3.1   Describe various types of functions available in SQL
   - 3.2   Use character, number, and date functions in select statements
   - 3.3   Use conversion functions

4. Displaying Data from Multiple Tables
   - 4.1   Write `select` statements to access data from more than one table using equality and nonequality joins
   - 4.2   View data that generally does not meet a join condition by using outer joins
   - 4.3   Join a table to itself using a self-join

5. Aggregating Data Using Group Functions
   - 5.1   Identify the available group functions
   - 5.2   Use group functions
   - 5.3   Group data using the `group by` clause
   - 5.4   Include or exclude grouped rows using the `having` clause

6. Subqueries
   - 6.1   Describe the types of problems that subqueries can solve
   - 6.2   Define subqueries

6.3   List the types of subqueries
6.4   Write single-row and multiple-row subqueries

7. Producing Readable Output with SQL*Plus
   7.1   Produce queries that require a substitution variable
   7.2   Produce more readable output
   7.3   Create and execute script files

8. Manipulating Data
   8.1   Describe each DML statement
   8.2   Insert rows in a table
   8.3   Update rows in a table
   8.4   Delete rows in a table
   8.5   Merge rows in a table
   8.6   Control transactions

9. Creating and Managing Tables
   9.1   Describe the main database objects
   9.2   Create tables
   9.3   Describe the datatypes that can be used when specifying column
         definitions
   9.4   Alter table definitions
   9.5   Drop, rename, and truncate tables

10. Including Constraints
    10.1 Describe constraints
    10.2 Create and maintain constraints

11. Creating Views
    11.1 Describe a view
    11.2 Create, alter, and drop a view
    11.3 Retrieve data through a view
    11.4 Insert, update, and delete data through a view
    11.5 Create and use an inline view
    11.6 Perform top-N analysis

12. Creating Other Database Objects
    12.1 Create, maintain, and use sequences
    12.2 Create and maintain indexes
    12.3 Create private and public synonyms

13. Controlling User Access
    13.1 Create users
    13.2 Create roles to ease setup and maintenance of the security model
    13.3 Use the `grant` and `revoke` statements

CHAPTER
1

Overview of
Oracle Databases

n this chapter, you will learn about and demonstrate knowledge in the following areas:

- Overview of Oracle databases
- Selecting data from Oracle

The first exam in the OCP series covers your understanding of basic areas of database usage and design. Every Oracle user, developer, and DBA should have complete mastery in these areas before moving into other test areas. This unit assumes little or no prior knowledge of Oracle on your part in order to help you go from never having used Oracle to having enough expertise in the Oracle server product to maintain and enhance existing applications and develop small new ones. This chapter will introduce Oracle and cover the basic aspects of data retrieval from the Oracle database.

This chapter covers material comprising approximately 8 percent of the test content of OCP Exam 1.

Try Following along on Your Own Database! As we move through the chapter, you will see examples of SQL statements issued on an Oracle database. For the most part, you can follow along with most of these examples on your own working database if you want. If the following instructions below look like a foreign language to you, show this page to your Oracle DBA and ask for his or her help:

1. On the command line of your machine hosting Oracle, change the directory to $ORACLE_HOME/rdbms/admin.

2. Log into Oracle as a privileged user, such as SYSTEM, who is allowed to create other users.

3. Issue the command @utlsampl.sql. This command runs the utlsampl.sql script, which creates objects owned by the user SCOTT/TIGER that we will use in the examples throughout the rest of the book.

4. If you're more experienced with Oracle and want to specify your own username and password instead of using SCOTT/TIGER, you can run the demobld.sql script found in $ORACLE_HOME/sqlplus/demo while logged into Oracle as a user other than SCOTT.

TIP
Some of the more trivial examples in the chapter may use tables not created by utlsampl.sql. These examples are noted in the text. No script is available for creating those examples. If you want to

use these tables, you have to create them yourself.
Instructions for creating tables appear in Chapter 5.

Overview of Oracle

This section covers the following topics as an overview of the Oracle database:

- Theoretical and physical aspects of relational databases
- Oracle's RDBMS and ORDBMS implementations
- Usage and benefits of PL/SQL

Welcome to the world of Oracle databases. Although this section is not associated with an official exam objective, it covers a great deal of the introductory material you may find helpful in order to get started with Oracle in preparation for using query operations to obtain data from the database. Many readers who have never used Oracle before find this material helpful in order to get the big picture of Oracle software before digging into the nitty-gritty. If you're one of those readers, then read on! Even if you're already a whiz at using Oracle SQL, you still might want to skim the material in this discussion before moving on, especially if you've never had an overview of Oracle software before. We'll first talk about several basic aspects regarding theoretical and physical aspects of relational databases, as well as Oracle's RDBMS and ORDBMS implementations. The use and benefits of PL/SQL—Oracle's own language for developing database applications that are stored and executed directly inside the Oracle database—will be explained as well.

Theoretical and Physical Aspects of Relational Databases

Oracle finds its roots in relational database theory, as conceived by E. F. Codd in the 1950s, and extends those theories into an infinite variety of directions, such as data warehousing, online transaction processing, and Web-enabled applications. Undoubtedly, the popularity of this software is part of the reason you are reading this book. This book has the answers to your questions about what an Oracle database is, how it works, and what you can do with it, all of which you'll need to know in order to pass the Introduction to SQL exam.

Software-development companies have taken many different approaches to information management. In years gone by, the more popular software packages for data storage and retrieval focused on flat-file systems as the storage means of choice while simultaneously requiring you to define how information is stored and retrieved, using a programming language such as COBOL. Some early breeds of flat-file systems included hierarchical storage systems, where data records were stored in a hierarchy similar to the hierarchical directory structure you might see on your PC's hard drive in Windows Explorer. These applications ran on mainframes, and brand names of these older data-management packages included IMS from IBM and IDMS from Computer Associates. The language most often used to develop mechanisms to add or manage data in those systems was COBOL.

Those older flat-file systems were great for certain tasks, such as defining parent/child relationships. A parent/child relationship might include the relationship of salespeople within a food service distribution company to the company's customers. Another parent/child relationship might be the tracking number for an invoice as it relates to product line items on the customer's order from that food service distribution company. However, one drawback to flat-file systems stems from the fact that a parent/child relationship cannot model every possible type of data relationship. Within the food service company example, a customer's order may list many different products. Each of those products themselves will probably appear on many different orders. In this case of a "many products to many orders" relationship, which way should the hierarchy be designed? What should be the parent and what should be the child? The usual solution was to create two separate hierarchies—one with product as parent, the other with order as parent. Unfortunately, this often meant maintaining much of the same information in two (or more) places, creating redundant data. Keeping data content consistent across multiple places where it is kept makes storage and retrieval complex. Another shortcoming of hierarchical databases using flat-file systems is that they are not easily adaptable to changing business needs. If the food service distributor creates a new sales system that calls for joint ownership of customer accounts by multiple salespeople, the hierarchical database needs to be redesigned.

Motivated by dissatisfaction with the cumbersome characteristics of hierarchical flat-file databases, E. F. Codd, a computer scientist working for IBM in the 1950s, developed an alternative: the *relational* model. Instead of storing data in hierarchies, Codd proposed storing related data items, such as control numbers and ordered products, in tables. If the tables were designed according to a few simple principles, they were both intuitive and extremely efficient in storing data, as Codd discovered. A single data item could be stored in only one place. Over time, many software makers recognized the significance of Codd's work and began developing products that adhered to Codd's model. Since the 1980s, virtually all database software products (including Oracle's) conform to the relational model.

Central to the success of the relational model is the use of a relational database management system, or *RDBMS*, for storing, retrieving, and manipulating data in a database. Earlier products required organizations to have many COBOL programmers on staff to code mechanisms for managing data-retrieval routines that interact directly with the files of the database. In contrast, the RDBMS handles these tasks automatically using a functional programming language called *SQL* (pronounced either *sequel* or as the letters spelled out). SQL stands for *structured query language,* and it allows users to request the data they want according to strict comparison criteria. For example, if we wanted to look at an employee ID number and salary information for an employee named SMITH, the following code block shows a SQL statement that would help us do so:

```
SQL> SELECT EMPNO, ENAME, SAL FROM EMP
  2  WHERE ENAME = 'SMITH';
```

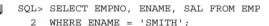

TIP
The preceding block was taken directly from SQL*Plus, a tool Oracle provides for interacting with the Oracle database. The "2," which indicates that you are typing in the second line, is written automatically by SQL*Plus. As such, you do not actually need to type "2" yourself. For now, don't worry about what this SQL statement actually does or what the results would be, just understand that it is an example of a SQL statement.

Behind the scenes, an RDBMS translates this statement into a series of operations that retrieve the actual data from a file somewhere on the machine hosting your database. This step is called *parsing.* After parsing is complete, the RDBMS executes the series of operations to complete the requested action. That series of operations may involve some or all of the following tasks, listed below in no particular order:

■ Implicit datatype conversion

■ Index lookups (if appropriate) for faster response time

■ Disk reads or disk writes

■ Filtering table data according to search criteria

■ Sorting and formatting data returned

TIP
An index is a special database object that can be used to enhance performance of certain RDBMS operations. A datatype is literally a definition of the type of data being stored in the table's column. You'll learn more about both these topics in later chapters.

RDBMS vs. Flat-File System Quick Reference

Table 1-1 shows a quick comparison of flat-file systems to relational database management systems.

For Review

1. Understand the tasks an RDBMS completes behind the scenes when users request certain pieces of data.

2. Be sure you can describe the features, advantages, and disadvantages of flat-file systems and relational database management systems.

Exercises

1. **You are exploring theoretical aspects of the Oracle RDBMS. Which of the following choices identifies an aspect of data management that the Oracle RDBMS does not handle on your behalf?**

   A. Datatype conversion

   B. Disk reads

   C. Sorting and formatting return data

   D. Defining required information via SQL

2. **You are evaluating the use of Oracle to replace legacy pre-relational systems in your organization. In comparison to the Oracle RDBMS, which of the following aspects of prerelational database systems did those systems handle as well as their relational counterpart?**

   A. Many-to-many data relationships

   B. Parent-child relationships

   C. Adaptability to changing business needs

   D. Data manipulation

3. **What is the name of the scientist who first conceptualized the use of relational database management systems?** _____

Answer Key
1. D 2. B 3. E. F. Codd

Task	FlatFile System	RDBMS
Handles parent/child data relationships?	Yes	Yes
Handles other types of data relationships?	Not well	Yes
Handles data manipulation easily?	No	Yes
Easily adaptable to changing business needs?	No	Yes
Handles data retrieval easily?	Sometimes	Yes
Handles data retrieval quickly?	Sometimes	Sometimes

TABLE 1-1.   *Comparing Relational Databases to Other Data Management Systems*

Oracle's RDBMS and ORDBMS Implementations

Although every relational database offers an RDBMS that accepts basically the same types of SQL statements, not all databases have the same components. An Oracle database is considerably more complicated than some other PC-based databases you may have seen, such as Microsoft Access or even SQL Server. The components of an Oracle database are broken into three basic areas, corresponding to the three basic areas of host machines that run Oracle databases. In this section, pay close attention to how each component in each part of the Oracle database interacts with a component in another part. Figure 1-1 illustrates the various elements of the Oracle database, which are tested thoroughly on OCP Database Administration Fundamentals I exam (1Z0-022). The components are as follows:

- **Memory**   The Oracle System Global Area (SGA), sometimes also called the Shared Global area because this allocation of memory is shared between all users of the Oracle database.

- **Disk**   Oracle datafiles, redo logs, control files, password files, and parameter files. These files contain the stored data of the Oracle database.

- **Processes**   Threads in the `oracle.exe` background process (Windows) or individual processes (UNIX) and the server process. These processes do all the behind-the-scenes work to keep the Oracle database functioning properly.

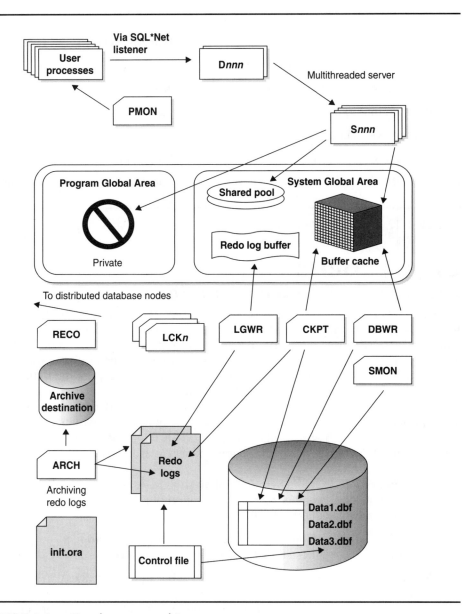

FIGURE 1-1. *Oracle server architecture*

Oracle SGA

Oracle's memory component, the SGA, consists of several elements, each of which is designed for a specific purpose.

Buffer Cache   The buffer cache stores Oracle data in memory for users to view or change. In this way, users never make changes directly to disk files. Instead, Oracle reads the appropriate data into memory for the user process to change, and it writes the changes back to disk at some point later. The buffer cache follows a modified least-recently used (LRU) algorithm to determine when data in this area can be eliminated when more space is needed in the buffer cache to make room for user data requested. The information in the buffer cache is shared among all concurrent users connected to the Oracle database.

Log Buffer   The log buffer stores special information called *redo*, which helps Oracle reconstruct data changes in the event of a system failure. Redo information is written to the log buffer by users making data changes and is stored in the log buffer until Oracle can write the redo information to disk.

Shared Pool   The shared pool stores many items that are "mission critical" to the operation of your Oracle database. Components of the shared pool include the library cache, for storing parsed SQL statements for reuse by other users; the dictionary or row cache, for storing Oracle data dictionary information in memory where it can be accessed quickly; and latches and other database-control mechanisms.

TIP
The Oracle data dictionary is a set of information stored in Oracle that tells you all kinds of important things about your database. The data dictionary is used frequently by users and Oracle processes alike, so it is important for overall database performance to store dictionary information in memory whenever possible. Hence, you can see the need for the dictionary cache in your shared pool.

Large Pool   The fourth and less frequently used component of Oracle's SGA is the large pool, which is a large memory allocation area used to support Oracle backup and restore operations, I/O server processes, and session memory for the shared server. Introduced in Oracle8, this component is optional for Oracle database operation.

Other Memory Areas   There are other components to the SGA in Oracle8i and later versions, such as the Java pool and large pool, that are not shown in Figure 1-1. The items not included in this discussion and/or the figure are excluded because a detailed examination of these topics is not necessary for passing the OCP exam on SQL. This figure and the current discussion are merely meant to give you the larger picture of Oracle before digging into a meaningful discussion of SQL queries.

Oracle Disk Components

The Oracle disk components store all kinds of vital information in your Oracle database. You cannot run Oracle without having all your disk components (except password files) in their proper places.

Datafiles   This mandatory disk component is used for storing Oracle dictionary and application database objects. These components often grow extremely large in size. Information in the buffer cache and the dictionary cache in memory comes from datafiles on disk. Every Oracle database has at least one datafile (but usually more). Datafiles store Oracle data. If you create a table in Oracle and populate it with rows, Oracle places the table and the rows in a datafile. Each datafile can be associated with only one database.

Redo Logs   This mandatory disk component is used for storing redo information on disk. Information from the log buffer in memory eventually gets written here. This component is meant to record all changes made to data in your Oracle database. These logs are critical for recovery of data in the event of a database failure.

Control Files   This mandatory disk component is used for storing vital information about the location of Oracle disk components on the host system. The physical locations of both datafiles and redo logs in the server's file system are stored in your control file. There can be one or many control files in an Oracle database. If there is more than one control file, each will be an identical copy. Oracle reads the control files every time you start the database and updates the control files when redo logs or datafiles are added or moved.

Password Files   This optional disk component is used for securing privileged user connection information to allow the database to be managed remotely via Enterprise Manager, Oracle's database-management tool. It also controls the number of the privileged system-management connections that can be made to the database at the same time. Without a password file, you may only administer your database by connecting directly to the machine hosting the Oracle database and using management tools such as SQL*Plus directly from the host machine.

Parameter Files   This mandatory disk component is used for configuring how Oracle operates while it is running. To start the database instance, Oracle must read the parameter file to determine what the configuration parameters are for that instance. A parameter file contains many parameters and their set values. Oracle reads the parameter file when you start the database. Some Oracle professionals refer to the parameter file as the `init.ora` file. You may maintain one or many parameter files for a database, corresponding to different instance configurations you may want to implement at various times.

Oracle Server and Background Processes

The final component of Oracle to be covered is the set of elements that comprise Oracle on your host system's CPU. The Oracle server process reads data from datafiles into the buffer cache on behalf of user processes. It can either be shared between multiple users or be dedicated to one user. The Oracle database also has one background process in Windows environments—`oracle.exe`. If you hit CTRL-ALT-DELETE on your system hosting the Oracle database, click the Task Manager button to bring up the Task Manager, and then click on the Processes tab, you will see this process running on your Windows machine. In Windows, this process has many threads that handle other important activities your database is engaged in at all times in the background. If you want to find information in Windows about services setup for use with Oracle software, you can look in Start | Settings | Control Panel. For NT, the Services icon lists all the Windows services available on the machine. For Windows 2000, you can double-click the Administrative Tools icon to find the Services icon. On UNIX machines, Oracle consists of multiple background processes. If the database is running on a UNIX machine, you can usually see its background processes if you issue the command `ps -fu oracle` on your UNIX command line.

What an ORDBMS Is

As object-oriented programming has gained popularity, Oracle has adjusted its relational database-management paradigm to include support for object-relational database design. This methodology incorporates the best features of object programming with the best features of relational programming and allows the developer to draw from both when designing a system in Oracle. Two important features supported on the object side include:

- Permitting users to define the structure of the data they wish to store

- Allowing users to define programmatic methods for manipulating that data and associating those methods directly to the data stored

For Review

Know the three components of the Oracle database, and be able to name each of the elements in each component.

Exercises

1. **You are examining the components of an Oracle database. Which of the following choices identifies an aspect of Oracle that resides on the disk of the machine hosting the Oracle database?**

   A. SGA

   B. Datafile

   C. Background process

   D. Java pool

2. **You are interested in seeing Oracle running on your Windows-based host machine. In which of the following areas would you look?**

   A. Control Panel | Services Icon

   B. Desktop

   C. Windows Explorer

   D. Start Menu

3. **You are interested in seeing Oracle running on your UNIX machine. Which of the following commands might you use?**

   A. ls

   B. grep

   C. ps

   D. df

Answer Key

1. B. 2. A. 3. C.

Usage and Benefits of PL/SQL

How to write programs in PL/SQL is no longer a topic being tested on the OCP Introduction to SQL exam. Nevertheless, it is worth your time as an Oracle professional to know about the existence of PL/SQL and its usage and benefits. PL/SQL is Oracle's own language for developing database applications. In addition to supporting all SQL operations that Oracle SQL supports, PL/SQL adds programming language extensions such as conditional statement processing, loops, variables, cursor operations, abstract datatypes, modularization, encapsulation, overloading, and more. The following bullets list frequently cited reasons why PL/SQL developers use the language:

- *PL/SQL is easy to learn and use.* Professionals with even a modest programming background can usually pick up PL/SQL syntax before too long and develop programs of moderate complexity without much effort. Professionals without a programming background can learn PL/SQL with more effort spent learning basic constructs, such as variable declaration, conditional statement processing, and so on.

- *PL/SQL is stored in the Oracle database, dramatically improving performance.* This means that you only have to compile the code into the Oracle database to make that code available to every user on the system. There is no need for an extended deployment as with traditional client/server applications. The result is code that runs quickly and works natively with your Oracle data.

- *PL/SQL integrates well with the Oracle database.* No special command syntax is needed to perform SQL operations involving data in the Oracle database. No colons, question marks, or other odd characters are required to prefix variables as in other languages. One exception to this rule relates to trigger development, which is a hybrid between a database object and PL/SQL.

- *PL/SQL is especially adept at processing large blocks of data.* Oracle PL/SQL provides a special construct called a `cursor for` loop, which allows you to query several rows of table data and then process through each row of that data in an iterative fashion. This feature allows you to process large amounts of data in bulk.

- *PL/SQL comes with lots of Oracle-supplied code to assist in performing tasks.* Oracle distributes several packages of PL/SQL code with every database shipped. This code enables you to perform highly specialized operations, such as file input/output, or I/O, retrieving Web pages into your database, job scheduling, dynamic SQL, interprocess communication, resource management, and much more. You can refer to these Oracle-supplied packages just like any other PL/SQL program.

■ *PL/SQL supports named and anonymous programs.* There are many different types of named programs you can develop in PL/SQL, including stored procedures, functions, and packages. These code blocks are actually compiled and stored in the database and are available for later use. You can also write anonymous programs, which are compiled at the time you submit the code for execution, executed, but not stored in the database.

■ *PL/SQL can be integrated into database tables via triggers.* Oracle integrates PL/SQL programmatic activity into database tables via triggers. This feature allows you to develop applications that use complex business rules for regulating data inside the database, thus reducing the potential for corrupt or inappropriate data from users.

■ *PL/SQL supports encapsulation and modularization. Encapsulation* involves using one named PL/SQL program to call another named PL/SQL program. *Modularization* involves breaking down a large task into several smaller components and then writing named PL/SQL programs to handle those smaller tasks. The result is code that's easier to read and maintain.

■ *PL/SQL supports overloading. Overloading* occurs when you have a package containing procedures or functions with the same name that accept different variables of different datatypes. When you call the overloaded procedure, Oracle dynamically decides which version of the procedure to use based on the datatype of the variable you pass.

■ *PL/SQL allows programmers to package their Oracle code.* Oracle PL/SQL supports a construct called a *package.* This feature allows you to logically group several procedures or functions that work together into one single construct. Procedures grouped together using packages perform better than they would individually because all procedures in the package will be loaded into memory as soon as one of the procedures is referenced. In contrast, stand-alone procedures are only loaded into memory when called. This reduces the overhead Oracle requires for memory management, thus improving performance.

■ *PL/SQL supports advanced datatypes.* PL/SQL gives users the ability to define abstract datatypes, such as records, allowing you some object-oriented flexibility in your procedural code. PL/SQL also offers table constructs for variable definition and use, approximating the use of arrays. Finally, PL/SQL allows you to declare REF datatypes, which gives PL/SQL the ability to use datatypes similar to pointers in C and C++.

■ *PL/SQL code is portable.* You can write a PL/SQL program on an Oracle database running on Solaris and then move the program to Oracle running on Windows 2000 or some other operating system without rewriting the program.

For Review

Be sure you understand the benefits of PL/SQL programming at a conceptual level as part of the Oracle database. However, OCP Exam 1 no longer tests your knowledge of how to develop PL/SQL applications, so a conceptual level is sufficient at this point.

Exercises

1. **You develop a PL/SQL package for use with Oracle. Which of the following choices identifies where that code is stored?**

   A. As an executable file on the host system

   B. As uncompiled code in the database

   C. As compiled code in the database

   D. As a flat file, sent to the database when you want to run the program

2. **You want to develop a PL/SQL package containing different procedures with the same name but different variable datatypes. What is the name of the PL/SQL feature that allows this?**

   A. Packaging.

   B. Overloading.

   C. Encapsulation.

   D. This functionality is not possible in PL/SQL.

3. **What is the name of the special loop that makes PL/SQL especially adept at processing large numbers of data records?** _____

Answer Key

1. C. 2. B. 3. The `cursor for` loop.

Writing Basic SQL Statements

This section will cover the following areas related to selecting rows:

- Capabilities of SQL `select` statements

- Executing `select` statements

- Differentiating between SQL and SQL*Plus commands

Now, let's dig in and start your approach to Oracle systems. This section maps directly to objectives on the OCP exam, and in the section you will learn what SQL provides you in the Oracle working environment. You'll also cover how to develop the all-important `select` statement, used for obtaining data from Oracle. You will even learn how to distinguish SQL commands from SQL*Plus commands. This skill becomes increasingly important as you use SQL*Plus for developing and running queries and because there are certain SQL*Plus commands you must know for passing the OCP exam.

Capabilities of SQL `select` Statements

If you've already developed SQL code for other database applications, you're in for some good news. Oracle SQL complies with the industry-accepted standards, such as ANSI SQL92. But before exploring SQL `select` statements in detail, consider the following overview of all the statement categories available in SQL and their associated usage:

- **`select`** Used for data retrieval and query access. Many developers consider this statement to be part of data manipulation language (DML) operations against the database. However, Oracle does not. When OCP refers to DML statements, you should make a mental note that Oracle is not referring to the `select` command.

- **`insert`, `update`, `delete`** Used for DML operations against the Oracle database, including adding new records, changing existing records, and removing records, respectively.

- **`create`, `alter`, `drop`** Used for data definition language (DDL) operations against the Oracle database, including adding, modifying, and removing database objects such as tables, indexes, sequences, and so on, respectively.

- **`commit`, `rollback`, `savepoint`** Used for transaction-control activities inside a user's session, including saving changes, discarding changes, and marking logical breakpoints within the transaction, respectively.

- **grant, revoke**   Used for data control language (DCL) operations against your Oracle database, where you might need to control user access to data.

Getting Started: SQL*Plus

Many developers, designers, DBAs, and power users begin their experience with Oracle using an existing Oracle application in an organization. The first tool many people see for selecting data directly from the Oracle relational database management system is SQL*Plus. When users first start SQL*Plus, in most cases, they must enter their Oracle username and password in order to begin a session with the Oracle database. There are some exceptions to this rule that use the password authentication provided with the operating system. The following example shows how you might begin a session with Oracle on the UNIX command line if the database is present on the UNIX machine you are connected to:

```
$/home/oracle> sqlplus scott/tiger
```

TIP
*From Windows, you can execute the above command at a DOS prompt to run the command-line version of SQL*Plus. Or, you can click on Start | Programs | Oracle ORACLE_HOME | Application Development | SQL*Plus to run the GUI version of SQL*Plus. On most systems, ORACLE_HOME will be replaced with the name of the Oracle software home location, such as OraHome1.*

Alternately, if you want to connect to an Oracle database not present on the machine you are currently connected to, you might issue the sqlplus command with a specified database name tacked onto the end of your username and password, as you'll see in the code block following this paragraph. That extra @orcl tacked onto the end of your username and password tells the operating system the name of the Oracle database you want to connect to. Here's the example:

```
$/home/oracle> sqlplus scott/tiger@orcl
```

TIP
*For our purposes in this book, we'll assume that the Oracle database you want to connect to is present on the same machine where you'll be running SQL*Plus.*

Whenever you log into Oracle via SQL*Plus, you create a session with the database. A *session* is an interactive runtime environment similar to a command-line environment, such as UNIX or DOS, in which you enter commands to retrieve data. Oracle performs a series of activities to obtain the data you ask for based on the SQL command you enter. The session starts as soon as you log into Oracle, and ends when you log out. Think of it as a conversation, which in turn implies *language*. Remember, you communicate with Oracle using the structured query language, SQL, to obtain the information you need.

TIP
To connect to the database, you must be granted permission to do so—simply having a user ID and password isn't enough. For more information on permissions, see Chapter 8.

SQL is a *functional* programming language, which means that you specify the types of things you want to see happen in terms of the results you want. You define the result you want, and Oracle determines how to get it for you. Take another look at the `select` statement I showed you earlier:

```
SQL> SELECT EMPNO, ENAME, SAL FROM EMP
  2   WHERE ENAME = 'SMITH';
```

The first point you should understand about SQL statements is that they can be entered across multiple lines. Our statement above contains two lines of keywords and text string expressions. However, notice also that we did not split any keywords across two lines—this is not permitted in Oracle. Finally, SQL statements are not case-sensitive. Thus, the following statement is logically equivalent to the one shown above:

```
SQL> select empno, ename, sal from emp
  2   where ename = 'SMITH';
```

NOTE
While column names, table names, and keywords (such as select, from, *and* where) *are not case-sensitive, text strings like SMITH, appearing in the code sample above in single-quotes, are case-sensitive. This is because Oracle stores the text exactly as you type it, so if you typed SMITH in uppercase when you stored that string in the EMP table, then that is exactly what Oracle stored.*

Sometimes text strings are called literals for this reason—they are literally what you entered.

Now let's look at the content of the SQL statement. This statement asks Oracle to provide data from the EMP table, where the value in a certain column called ENAME equals SMITH. We don't care how Oracle gets it, just as long as Oracle returns only the record from table EMP we asked for. Contrast this approach to other languages you may have heard about or programmed in, such as C++ and COBOL. These languages are often referred to as *procedural* or *iterative* programming languages because the code written in these languages implies an end result by explicitly defining the *process* for obtaining the result. The following block of code from an imaginary procedural programming language similar to C illustrates how the same function may be handled by explicitly defining the means to the end:

```
Include <stdio.h>
Include <string.h>
Include <rdbms.h>

Int *empno;
Char *statement;

Type emp_rec is record (
Int             empno;
Char[10]        emp_name;
Int             sal; )

Void main() {
  login_to_oracle(scott,tiger);
  Access_table(emp);
  Open(statement.memaddr);
  Strcpy("SELECT EMPNO, ENAME, SAL FROM EMP WHERE
          ENAME = 'SMITH'",statement.text);
  parse(statement);
  execute(statement);
  for (I=1,I=statement.results,I+1)
    fetch(statement.result[I],emp_rec);
    printf(emp_rec);

  close(statement.memaddr);
  }
```

Of course, this C-like block of code will not compile anywhere but in your imagination, but the point of the example is clear—other languages make you define the process, whereas SQL lets you define the result.

For Review

What is SQL? What is SQL capable of? How does SQL compare to other programming languages you might use, such as Java and C?

Exercises

1. You are determining which type of SQL statement to use in your Oracle database. Which of the following choices identifies the type of statement you would use when trying to obtain data from the database?

    A. `select`

    B. `update`

    C. `insert`

    D. `delete`

2. Which of the following choices identifies a functional programming language?

    A. C

    B. Java

    C. COBOL

    D. SQL

3. Identify a command that is part of SQL's data control language (DCL).

    _____

4. Identify a command that is part of SQL's data manipulation language (DML). _____

5. Identify a command that is part of SQL's data definition language (DDL).

    _____

Answer Key

1. A. **2.** D. **3.** B. `grant` or `revoke` **4.** `update`, `delete`, or `insert`. Oracle does not consider `select` to be part of DML. **5.** `create`, `alter`, `drop`

Executing `select` Statements

The most common type of SQL statement executed in most database environments is the `select` statement, which queries a table in the database for requested data. Tables in Oracle are similar in concept to spreadsheets (but not necessarily similar to the table in your kitchen!). Examine the following code block, where you see a `select` statement in the context of a session with Oracle:

```
$/home/oracle> sqlplus scott/tiger
SQL*Plus: Release 8.1.7.0.0 - Production on Fri July 06 18:53:11 2001
Copyright (c) Oracle Corporation 1979, 2000.  All rights reserved.
Connected to: Oracle9i Release 9.0.1.0.0
With the partitioning option
JServer Release 9.0.1.0.0 Production
SQL> select * from emp;
    EMPNO ENAME     JOB         MGR HIREDATE    SAL COMM DEPTNO
--------- -------- --------- ----- --------- ---- ---- ------
     7369 SMITH     CLERK      7902 17-DEC-80  800           20
     7499 ALLEN     SALESMAN   7698 20-FEB-81 1600  300      30
     7521 WARD      SALESMAN   7698 22-FEB-81 1250  500      30
     7566 JONES     MANAGER    7839 02-APR-81 2975           20
     7654 MARTIN    SALESMAN   7698 28-SEP-81 1250 1400      30
     7698 BLAKE     MANAGER    7839 01-MAY-81 2850           30
     7782 CLARK     MANAGER    7839 09-JUN-81 2450           10
     7788 SCOTT     ANALYST    7566 19-APR-87 3000           20
     7839 KING      PRESIDENT       17-NOV-81 5000           10
     7844 TURNER    SALESMAN   7698 08-SEP-81 1500    0      30
     7876 ADAMS     CLERK      7788 23-MAY-87 1100           20
     7900 JAMES     CLERK      7698 03-DEC-81  950           30
     7902 FORD      ANALYST    7566 03-DEC-81 3000           20
     7934 MILLER    CLERK      7782 23-JAN-82 1300           10
14 rows selected.
```

TIP
The last part of the code block is where Oracle tells you how many rows it obtained from the database table in response to your SQL command. Later code blocks in this book omit that part to conserve space. You can tell SQL*Plus not to display row count information as well using the `set feedback off` *command. We'll talk more about SQL*Plus commands later in the chapter.*

The first part, containing the copyright information, is a welcome message from SQL*Plus. If you wanted, you could suppress this information in your call to SQL*Plus from the operating system command line by entering sqlplus -s and pressing ENTER, where the -s extension indicates SQL*Plus should run in silent mode. This is sometimes useful for batch programs that write output to an automated feed file where you don't want a lot of extraneous junk in the feed because an error will result. We'll explore some other SQL*Plus commands that help you control the appearance of your output later in the chapter. The bold line in the block illustrates a simple SQL select statement. In essence, you're asking Oracle to return all data from all columns in the EMP table. Oracle replies with the contents of the EMP table. The main components of a select statement are listed next, and *both* are required in every select statement you issue on the database:

- **The select, or *column*, clause**   This clause contains columns or expressions containing data you want to see, separated by commas. The preceding query uses a *wildcard* (*) character, indicating we want data from every column in the table.

- **The from, or *table*, clause**   This clause tells Oracle what table to get the data from.

TIP
*Always use a semicolon (;) to end SQL statements when entering them directly into SQL*Plus. You can use a slash(/) in some situations, such as for SQL*Plus batch scripts, but be careful—a slash at the end of a SQL statement already ended with a semicolon makes the statement run twice!*

A Note about Columns and Datatypes

Tables in the Oracle database are comprised of columns, each storing a unit of information for the row. These units taken together across a single row comprise a record stored in the table. Review the first record in the preceding code block for EMPNO 7369, which is listed here:

```
    EMPNO ENAME     JOB          MGR HIREDATE   SAL COMM DEPTNO
--------- -------- ---------   ----- --------- ---- ---- ------
     7369 SMITH     CLERK       7902 17-DEC-80  800          20
```

Each column identifies an aspect of this unique employee. EMPNO identifies his employee number, ENAME identifies his name, and so on. The information stored in each column of the table for this fellow must correspond to the datatype defined for that column. For example, column EMPNO is defined as a NUMBER column, meaning that only numbers of a certain size can be stored for records in that column. No text, date, or nonnumerical information can be stored in EMPNO, because doing so would violate the column's stated datatype. I'll refer to a column's datatype frequently throughout the rest of the book, so it's worth your time to master this fundamental concept. The column datatypes permitted in Oracle tables that we'll work with most frequently are listed here:

- **NUMBER**   A datatype used for storing numerical data. No dashes, text, or other nonnumerical information are allowed in columns of this datatype.

- **DATE**   A datatype used for storing date information. Internally, Oracle stores dates as numbers, which it can then convert into any DATE format you want. By default, DATE information is displayed in DD-MON-YY format (for example, 25-DEC-79).

- **VARCHAR2**   A datatype used for storing text data. Any text character (including special characters, numbers, dashes, and so on) can be stored in a VARCHAR2 column.

- **CHAR**   A datatype used for storing text data. Any text character (including special characters, numbers, dashes, and so on) can be stored in a CHAR column, padded with spaces so that the text stored in the CHAR column fills the entire length available. Thus, the name SMITH would take up ten spaces in a column declared as CHAR(10), even though the name itself is only five characters long, with the other five characters occupied by blank spaces.

TIP
The main difference between VARCHAR2 and CHAR columns is the amount of space required for storing text data, which is greater for CHAR columns than for VARCHAR2 columns. This is because CHAR columns have a fixed length and always store the same number of bytes, whereas VARCHAR2 has a variable length and only contains the number of bytes you provide it.

Datatypes for storing other types of information exist in Oracle; however, there aren't as many of them as you might encounter in database products from other vendors. For example, Oracle has no currency datatype. Monetary values are treated simply as numbers, and as such they can be stored in a column defined as the NUMBER datatype.

TIP
Another datatype we'll observe from time to time in the book is the ROWID datatype. This is a special datatype used by Oracle to format the information used to display the physical location of the row on disk.

The "Schema" of Things

Take a look at the following code block:

```
SQL> select empno, ename, sal
  2  from scott.emp;
    EMPNO ENAME           SAL
--------- ---------- ---------
     7369 SMITH           800
     7499 ALLEN          1600
     7521 WARD           1250
     7566 JONES          2975
     7654 MARTIN         1250
     7698 BLAKE          2850
     7782 CLARK          2450
     7788 SCOTT          3000
     7839 KING           5000
     7844 TURNER         1500
     7876 ADAMS          1100
     7900 JAMES           950
     7902 FORD           3000
     7934 MILLER         1300
```

Notice anything different about the way table EMP is referenced in this table clause? It has the name of the owner, SCOTT, prefixed to it. Oracle developers and DBAs refer to the concept of referencing the table owner as well as the table itself as a *schema*. If you create a database object such as a table, this object belongs to you. It is part of your schema. The identity you use when you log into your database to run `demobld.sql` determines the schema that all those tables will belong to.

When the table you reference in a query isn't prefixed with the schema it belongs to, Oracle assumes the table exists in your schema and tries to query it. If the table doesn't exist in your schema, you must prefix the table name with the schema information, separating the schema owner from the table name with a period.

TIP
A schema is a logical grouping of database objects
based on the user who owns the objects.

Prefixing Columns with Table Names

The same aliasing concept works in the column clause, too—you can prefix the
column name with the table name separated by a dot (.) in the table clause for your
query. Make sure you understand how to specify a schema owner, the table name,
and the column name in a select statement in SQL*Plus. The following code
block demonstrates the most formal usage for prefixing with appropriate schema
and table information:

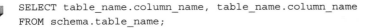

```
SELECT table_name.column_name, table_name.column_name
FROM schema.table_name;
```

Arithmetic and Table Data

Oracle lets you perform arithmetic operations on your numeric table data as well.
The operators used in Oracle are the same as in daily use (+ for addition, − for
subtraction, * for multiplication, and / for division). Say, for example, you are
performing a simple annual review that involves giving each user a cost-of-living
increase in the amount of 8 percent of his or her salary. The process involves
multiplying each person's salary by 1.08. Oracle makes the work easy if you use
arithmetic expressions, as shown here:

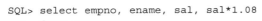

```
SQL> select empno, ename, sal, sal*1.08
  2  from emp;
    EMPNO ENAME           SAL  SAL*1.08
--------- ---------- --------- ---------
     7369 SMITH           800       864
     7499 ALLEN          1600      1728
     7521 WARD           1250      1350
     7566 JONES          2975      3213
     7654 MARTIN         1250      1350
     7698 BLAKE          2850      3078
     7782 CLARK          2450      2646
     7788 SCOTT          3000      3240
     7839 KING           5000      5400
     7844 TURNER         1500      1620
     7876 ADAMS          1100      1188
     7900 JAMES           950      1026
     7902 FORD           3000      3240
     7934 MILLER         1300      1404
```

Operator Precedence

There's usually at least one question on OCP dealing with operator precedence—that high-school math concept regarding which calculation to do first. An easy way to remember operator precedence in mathematics is to use the acronym PEMDAS. You can remember PEMDAS using the mnemonic "Please Excuse My Dear Aunt Sally." PEMDAS stands for parentheses, exponents, multiplication *and* division, addition *and* subtraction. Here are some examples of PEMDAS in action:

- 2 + 6 / 2 equals 5
- (2 + 6) / 2 equals 4
- 2 / 10 + 36 * (84 − 6) is 2808.2
- 2 / 10 + 36 * 84 − 6 is 3018.2.

2 + 2 and the DUAL Table

As mentioned earlier, every `select` statement must have a column clause and a table clause. However, you might not always want to perform arithmetic calculations on data from an actual table. Say, for example, you simply want to add 2 + 2. Conveniently, the column clause in a `select` statement needn't contain actual column names. It can contain fixed numbers or other types of expressions instead. But what about the table clause? Because you're using fixed numbers, you don't want data from a real table. So why not use a fake one? You can use a special table called *DUAL* to fill in the table clause without Oracle actually using its data. Take a look at the following block:

```
SQL> select 2 + 2 from dual;
     2+2
---------
       4
```

The DUAL table consists of one column, called *DUMMY*, containing one value, X. Execute a `select * from DUAL` statement and see for yourself that there is no meaningful data stored here. It simply exists as a SQL construct to support the requirement of a table specification in the `from` clause. The DUAL table is owned by the Oracle built-in user SYS. We can also use the DUAL table in our understanding of schemas. The following example shows you how to obtain the username you used when you logged into Oracle:

```
SQL> select user from dual;
USER
-----
SCOTT
```

Handling NULL Values

Sometimes a query for information produces a nothing result. In database terms, *nothing* is called *NULL*. In set theory, the mathematical foundation for relational databases, NULL represents the value of an empty dataset, or a dataset containing no values. Put another way, NULL is *not* the blank character displayed when you hit the spacebar, nor is it somehow equivalent to zero! NULL is the *absence of information*. Unless specified otherwise, a column in a table is designed to accommodate the placement of nothing into the column. An example of retrieving NULL is listed in the MGR column of the following code block on EMPNO 7839:

```
SQL> select empno, ename, mgr
  2  from emp;
    EMPNO ENAME            MGR
--------- ---------- ---------
     7369 SMITH           7902
     7499 ALLEN           7698
     7521 WARD            7698
     7566 JONES           7839
     7654 MARTIN          7698
     7698 BLAKE           7839
     7782 CLARK           7839
     7788 SCOTT           7566
     7839 KING
     7844 TURNER          7698
     7876 ADAMS           7788
     7900 JAMES           7698
     7902 FORD            7566
     7934 MILLER          7782
```

However, there are times when you may want to substitute a value in place of NULL. Oracle provides this functionality with a special function, called `nvl( )`. Assume that you do not want to see blank spaces for manager information. Instead, you want the output of the query to contain a zero where a NULL value is listed. The query in the following code block illustrates how you can obtain the desired result:

```
SQL> select empno, ename, nvl(mgr,0)
  2  from emp;
    EMPNO ENAME      NVL(MGR,0)
--------- ---------- ----------
     7369 SMITH           7902
     7499 ALLEN           7698
     7521 WARD            7698
     7566 JONES           7839
```

```
7654 MARTIN          7698
7698 BLAKE           7839
7782 CLARK           7839
7788 SCOTT           7566
7839 KING               0
7844 TURNER          7698
7876 ADAMS           7788
7900 JAMES           7698
7902 FORD            7566
7934 MILLER          7782
```

The basic syntax for nvl ( ) is NVL (*column_name, value_if_null*).
Notice that the column specified in nvl ( ) contains an actual value. That value is
what Oracle returns; when the column is NULL, the special string is returned. The
nvl ( ) function can be used on columns of all datatypes, but remember this: *The
value specified to be returned if the column value is NULL must be the same
datatype as the column specified.*

The distinct Keyword

If you look back at the code block that lists all the employees in the EMP table,
you'll notice something interesting in the JOB column. Many of the employees have
the same job title. Sometimes, you might have a situation where you want to see
only the unique values for a column that you know contains many repeated values.
In order to do so, Oracle offers the distinct keyword. To obtain the unique values
for a column containing duplicates, you simply precede the column reference with
the distinct keyword in your column clause, like this:

```
SQL> select distinct job
  2  from emp;
JOB
---------
ANALYST
CLERK
MANAGER
PRESIDENT
SALESMAN
```

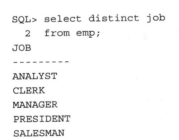

TIP
*In order for the distinct keyword to work, it must
appear directly after the select keyword in your
SQL query.*

When more than one column name appears after the distinct keyword in a select statement, then Oracle attempts to identify all the distinct combinations of values in those columns named. Take a look at an example:

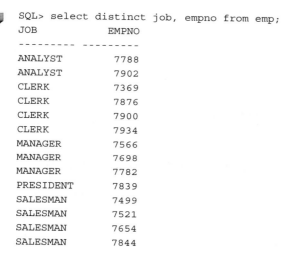

```
SQL> select distinct job, empno from emp;
JOB            EMPNO
---------    ---------
ANALYST         7788
ANALYST         7902
CLERK           7369
CLERK           7876
CLERK           7900
CLERK           7934
MANAGER         7566
MANAGER         7698
MANAGER         7782
PRESIDENT       7839
SALESMAN        7499
SALESMAN        7521
SALESMAN        7654
SALESMAN        7844
```

Changing Output Headings with Aliases

In every result set Oracle returns in response to your SQL select commands, Oracle creates headings for each column so that you know what the data is. By default, Oracle reprints the column name exactly as you defined it in the select statement, including functions if there are any. Unfortunately, this method often leaves you with a bad description of the column data. Oracle truncates the expression to fit a certain width corresponding to the datatype of the column returned, making the problem even worse. Fortunately, you can use *aliases* in your column clause to solve this problem. In a column alias, you give the column another name that Oracle uses when the select statement results are displayed. This feature gives you the ability to fit more descriptive names into the space allotted. Here's an example:

```
SQL> select empno, ename, nvl(mgr,0) as mgr
  2  from emp;
    EMPNO ENAME            MGR
--------- ---------- ---------
     7369 SMITH           7902
     7499 ALLEN           7698
     7521 WARD            7698
     7566 JONES           7839
     7654 MARTIN          7698
```

```
7698 BLAKE          7839
7782 CLARK          7839
7788 SCOTT          7566
7839 KING              0
7844 TURNER         7698
7876 ADAMS          7788
7900 JAMES          7698
7902 FORD           7566
7934 MILLER         7782
```

TIP
You can omit the as *keyword in the column alias
and still wind up with substantially the same result.*

Column aliases are useful for adding meaningful headings to output from SQL queries. Aliases can be specified in two ways: either by naming the alias after the column specification separated by a space or by using of the as keyword to mark the alias more clearly. Here's the general rule:

```
SQL> -- SELECT column_name_or_operation alias, ...;
SQL> SELECT nvl(mgr,0) MGR
  2  FROM EMP;
```

or

```
SQL> -- SELECT column_name_or_operation  AS alias, ...;
SQL> SELECT nvl(mgr,0) AS MGR
  2  FROM EMP;
```

You don't need to specify a function in order to use an alias. For example, if you simply wanted to change the column heading for the MGR column to something more descriptive, you could do so using a column alias. The SQL statement might look something like select mgr as "Manager Code" from emp.

Putting Columns Together with Concatenation

You can also glue together column data to produce more interesting or readable output. This is called *concatenation*. The concatenation operator is two pipe characters put together: ||. You can also use the concat( ) operation, passing it the two column names. In the following example, the ENAME column is concatenated with a text expression and the JOB column using both available methods to produce a meaningful result:

```
SQL> select ename || ', who is the ' ||
  2  concat(job,' for the company')
```

```
 3   as "Name and Role"
 4   from emp;
Name and Role
-------------------------------------------------
SMITH, who is the CLERK for the company
ALLEN, who is the SALESMAN for the company
WARD, who is the SALESMAN for the company
JONES, who is the MANAGER for the company
MARTIN, who is the SALESMAN for the company
BLAKE, who is the MANAGER for the company
CLARK, who is the MANAGER for the company
SCOTT, who is the ANALYST for the company
KING, who is the PRESIDENT for the company
TURNER, who is the SALESMAN for the company
ADAMS, who is the CLERK for the company
JAMES, who is the CLERK for the company
FORD, who is the ANALYST for the company
MILLER, who is the CLERK for the company
```

TIP

Use column aliases to name your concatenated column to make the output more readable and meaningful.

For Review

1. Understand the two components of `select` statements and what a schema is.

2. Know how to perform arithmetic on selected columns and on numeric expressions in Oracle and know what the DUAL table is.

3. Know both methods used for concatenating columns and how to define column aliases. Also, know what the `distinct` keyword is and how it is used.

4. Be able to define what NULL means in the context of Oracle SQL and how to use the `nvl ( )` function.

5. Be sure you understand the correct operator precedence using the acronym PEMDAS.

Exercises

1. You are identifying a table for use in your `select` clause that was not created by you. Which of the following choices identifies the reference that must be included in your `select` statement so that Oracle knows where to look for the information?

   A. Alias

   B. Schema

   C. Expression

   D. Session

2. Use the following code block to answer this question:

```
SQL> select empno, ename, mgr
  2  from emp;
     EMPNO ENAME           MGR
--------- ---------- ---------
      7369 SMITH          7902
      7499 ALLEN          7698
      7521 WARD           7698
      7566 JONES          7839
      7654 MARTIN         7698
      7698 BLAKE          7839
      7782 CLARK          7839
      7788 SCOTT          7566
      7839 KING
      7844 TURNER         7698
      7876 ADAMS          7788
      7900 JAMES          7698
      7902 FORD           7566
      7934 MILLER         7782
SQL> select empno, ename, nvl(mgr,'none') as mgr
  2  from emp;
```

   Which of the following choices describes what Oracle will return as the output in the MGR column for KING's record from this query?

   A. Oracle returns NULL in the MGR column for KING's record.

   B. Oracle returns MGR in the MGR column for KING's record.

   C. Oracle returns NONE in the MGR column for KING's record.

   D. Oracle returns an error.

3. You are concatenating information from two columns in an SQL query. Which of the following choices best identifies the special character required for this operation?

   A. @

   B. #

   C. ||

   D. /

4. Provide the name of the table containing no meaningful information that can be used to fulfill the table clause requirement for `select` statements when you perform arithmetic operations on fixed numeric expressions:

   _____

5. You may use the contents from the standard EMP table used in this discussion to answer the following question. You are attempting to calculate 20 percent of the salary and commission for all employees of the company. Which of the following SQL statements would be appropriate for the task?

   A. `select empno, ename, sal/20, comm/20 from emp;`

   B. `select empno, ename, sal*20, comm*20 from emp;`

   C. `select empno, ename, sal/.20, comm/.20 from emp;`

   D. `select empno, ename, sal*.20, comm*.20 from emp;`

6. You may use the contents of the following code block to answer this question:

```
SQL> select * from dept;
    DEPTNO DNAME          LOC
    ------ -------------- -------------
        10 ACCOUNTING     NEW YORK
        20 RESEARCH       DALLAS
        30 SALES          CHICAGO
        40 OPERATIONS     BOSTON
```

   You issue the following statement in Oracle: `select distinct dname, loc from dept`. Which of the following choices correctly describes the result Oracle will return?

    A. Oracle returns the distinct combinations of values from DNAME and LOC.

    B. Oracle returns only three distinct values from DNAME in the DEPT table.

    C. Oracle returns only the distinct values from the DEPTNO column.

    D. Oracle returns the contents of all four records from the table.

Answer Key

1. B. 2. D. Remember, the datatype in the nvl ( ) function must match the datatype for the column. **3.** C. **4.** DUAL. **5.** D. **6.** A.

Differentiating Between SQL and SQL*Plus Commands

Although the SQL*Plus work environment works well when you don't make mistakes, it is unforgiving to the fat-fingered once you have pressed ENTER to move to the next input line. So far, this limitation hasn't presented much difficulty because our queries haven't been long. However, as the queries you write get more and more complicated, you will grow frustrated. SQL*Plus does allow some correction of entered statements with a special command called change, abbreviated as c. Consider the following example, which illustrates this point:

```
SQL> SELECT empno, ename, NVL(mgr,'none') mgr,
  2  hiredate, sal, comm, deptno
  3  FROM EMP;
SELECT empno, ename, NVL(mgr,'none') mgr,
                          *
ERROR at line 1:
ORA-01722: invalid number
SQL> 1
1* SELECT empno, ename, NVL(mgr,'none') mgr,
SQL> c/'none'/0
1* SELECT empno, ename, NVL(mgr,0) mgr,
SQL> /
    EMPNO ENAME      JOB         MGR HIREDATE   SAL COMM DEPTNO
--------- -------- --------- ----- --------- ---- ---- ------
     7369 SMITH      CLERK      7902 17-DEC-80  800          20
     7499 ALLEN      SALESMAN   7698 20-FEB-81 1600  300      30
```

```
7521 WARD       SALESMAN   7698 22-FEB-81 1250  500      30
7566 JONES      MANAGER    7839 02-APR-81 2975           20
7654 MARTIN     SALESMAN   7698 28-SEP-81 1250 1400      30
7698 BLAKE      MANAGER    7839 01-MAY-81 2850           30
7782 CLARK      MANAGER    7839 09-JUN-81 2450           10
7788 SCOTT      ANALYST    7566 19-APR-87 3000           20
7839 KING       PRESIDENT     0 17-NOV-81 5000           10
7844 TURNER     SALESMAN   7698 08-SEP-81 1500    0      30
7876 ADAMS      CLERK      7788 23-MAY-87 1100           20
7900 JAMES      CLERK      7698 03-DEC-81  950           30
7902 FORD       ANALYST    7566 03-DEC-81 3000           20
7934 MILLER     CLERK      7782 23-JAN-82 1300           10
```

In this example, the `select` statement contains a datatype mismatch error in the `nvl( )` function. Oracle notices the error and alerts you to it with the `ORA-01722` error message.

Other error messages that may be produced include the following:

`ORA-00904: invalid column name`

This error indicates that the column you referenced does not exist or was misspelled or misplaced. To resolve this problem, you need to check for typos in your column clause and verify that the column actually exists in the table. Sometimes, a column name may include nonalphanumeric characters, such as underscores, designed to separate two words. Thus, the column name EMPNO is not the same as EMP_NO, even though conceptually they mean about the same thing.

`ORA-00923: FROM keyword not found where expected`

This error indicates that the `from` keyword was not included or was misspelled. Sometimes this error occurs when you put a comma after the last column listed in your select clause (that is, `select empno, ename, from emp`), so watch out for that common mistake.

`ORA-00942: table or view does not exist`

This error indicates that the table or view typed in does not exist. Usually, the `ORA-00942` error message indicates a typo in the name of the table or view, or that the schema owner was not specified in front of the table name. This error is fixed either by correcting the typing problem or by adding the schema owner onto the front of the table name. (An alternative solution for the latter case involves creating synonyms for tables that are accessible to other users. This solution is discussed later in the book.)

In any case, the method used to correct the typing problem is to first type the line number containing the error to activate that line for editing. In the preceding example, we did so by typing the number 1, shown in bold. Then we used the change command, also shown in bold, observing the proper syntax:

```
c/old_value/new_value
```

After the change is made to the *first* appearance of *old_value* in the current line, Oracle redisplays the current line with the change made. Note that the change will be made to the first appearance of *old_value* only. If the change must be made to a specific place in the line, more characters can be added to the *old_value* parameter, as appropriate. Finally, the corrected text can be reexecuted by entering a slash (/) at the prompt, as indicated, or by entering the command run on the SQL*Plus command line.

TIP
*If you ever get confused about the difference between the use of the slash and semicolon, remember that the slash command reruns the code currently in your SQL*Plus operating buffer, whereas the semicolon is used to end a SQL statement you type into the buffer.*

Using a Text Editor

Oracle makes provisions for you to use your favorite text editor to edit the statement created in afiedt.buf, the file in which SQL*Plus stores the most recently executed SQL statement. You simply type edit (abbreviated ed). This action causes Oracle to bring up the SQL statement from afiedt.buf into the operating system's default text editor. On UNIX systems, that text editor is usually VI or EMACS, whereas Windows environments use Notepad. To change the text editor used, issue the define _editor='youreditor' statement on the SQL*Plus prompt.

TIP
*You can also define your text editor in the SQL*Plus GUI interface using the Tools | Environment menu option.*

Using a text editor rather than the line editor native to SQL*Plus offers many benefits. By using a text editor you know well, you can create a familiarity with SQL*Plus that is useful for adapting to the application. Also, it is helpful with large queries to have the entire block of code in front of you and immediately accessible.

Writing SQL Commands in Scripts

You can write entire queries in a text editor first and then load the queries into SQL*Plus if you want to. When you do this, try to remember to save the script with a .sql extension so that SQL*Plus can identify it easily. Two commands are available to load the file into SQL*Plus. The first is get. The get command opens the text file specified and places the contents in afiedt.buf. Once the script is loaded, you can execute the command using the slash (/) command. Alternatively, you can use the @ or start command, which loads SQL statements from the named file into afiedt.buf and executes them in one step. The methods are shown in the following example, with a script called select_emp.sql:

```
$/home/oracle> sqlplus scott/tiger
SQL*Plus: Release 8.1.7.0.0 - Production on Fri Jul 06 18:53:11 2001
Copyright (c) Oracle Corporation 1979, 2000.  All rights reserved.
Connected to Oracle9i Release 9.0.1.0.0
With the partitioning option
JServer Release 9.0.1.0.0 - Production
SQL> GET select_emp
SELECT * FROM emp
SQL> /
```

EMPNO	ENAME	JOB	MGR	HIREDATE	SAL	COMM	DEPTNO
7369	SMITH	CLERK	7902	17-DEC-80	800		20
7499	ALLEN	SALESMAN	7698	20-FEB-81	1600	300	30
7521	WARD	SALESMAN	7698	22-FEB-81	1250	500	30
7566	JONES	MANAGER	7839	02-APR-81	2975		20
7654	MARTIN	SALESMAN	7698	28-SEP-81	1250	1400	30
7698	BLAKE	MANAGER	7839	01-MAY-81	2850		30
7782	CLARK	MANAGER	7839	09-JUN-81	2450		10
7788	SCOTT	ANALYST	7566	19-APR-87	3000		20
7839	KING	PRESIDENT		17-NOV-81	5000		10
7844	TURNER	SALESMAN	7698	08-SEP-81	1500	0	30
7876	ADAMS	CLERK	7788	23-MAY-87	1100		20
7900	JAMES	CLERK	7698	03-DEC-81	950		30
7902	FORD	ANALYST	7566	03-DEC-81	3000		20
7934	MILLER	CLERK	7782	23-JAN-82	1300		10

```
SQL> @select_emp
SELECT * FROM emp
```

EMPNO	ENAME	JOB	MGR	HIREDATE	SAL	COMM	DEPTNO
7369	SMITH	CLERK	7902	17-DEC-80	800		20
7499	ALLEN	SALESMAN	7698	20-FEB-81	1600	300	30
7521	WARD	SALESMAN	7698	22-FEB-81	1250	500	30
7566	JONES	MANAGER	7839	02-APR-81	2975		20
7654	MARTIN	SALESMAN	7698	28-SEP-81	1250	1400	30

7698 BLAKE	MANAGER	7839 01-MAY-81 2850		30
7782 CLARK	MANAGER	7839 09-JUN-81 2450		10
7788 SCOTT	ANALYST	7566 19-APR-87 3000		20
7839 KING	PRESIDENT	17-NOV-81 5000		10
7844 TURNER	SALESMAN	7698 08-SEP-81 1500	0	30
7876 ADAMS	CLERK	7788 23-MAY-87 1100		20
7900 JAMES	CLERK	7698 03-DEC-81 950		30
7902 FORD	ANALYST	7566 03-DEC-81 3000		20
7934 MILLER	CLERK	7782 23-JAN-82 1300		10

TIP
The "at" (@) sign in front of your SQL script name in the code block above serves a different purpose than the @ in front of the database name we saw in an earlier example when we started SQL*Plus on the command line. Be sure you don't confuse the two forms of usage.

Notice that the .sql extension was left off the end of the filename in the line with the get command. SQL*Plus assumes that all scripts containing SQL statements will have the .sql extension, so it can be omitted in the get and the @ commands. You can store SQL commands in text files with other extensions, such as .txt and .lst, but if you do, you have to specify the full filename, including the extension, in the get command. Notice also that after the file is brought in using get, it can then be executed using the slash (/) command. Later in that same code block, we use the @ command to read the same file into afiedt.buf. The contents of the buffer are executed in the same step, which eliminates the need for entering the slash (/) command. Again, we omit the .sql extension. Finally, if you don't specify the path when typing the filename for the get or @ command, Oracle assumes the file is in whatever directory you were in when you started running SQL*Plus.

TIP
When typing SQL statements in a script that you intend to execute in SQL*Plus, do not put a semicolon (;) at the end of these SQL statements. Instead, put a slash (/) character as the first character on the last line in the script. Do this if you encounter problems where Oracle says it encountered an invalid character (the semicolon) in your script.

Other SQL*Plus Commands to Know

The rest of this discussion focuses on identifying other important commands you should know in SQL*Plus, both for your job and for passing the OCP exam. Let's now take a look at explanations for important SQL*Plus commands to know about.

DESCRIBE tablename   This command returns a description of *tablename*, including all columns in that table, the datatype for each column, and an indication of whether the column permits storage of NULL values. If you experience ORA-00904 errors, this command is used for determining the names of columns in the table you referenced. This command is synonymous with its abbreviation, desc. Here's an example:

```
SQL> describe emp
Name                              Null?    Type
-----------------------------     -------- ------------
EMPNO                             NOT NULL NUMBER(4)
ENAME                                      VARCHAR2(10)
JOB                                        VARCHAR2(9)
MGR                                        NUMBER(4)
HIREDATE                                   DATE
SAL                                        NUMBER(7,2)
COMM                                       NUMBER(7,2)
DEPTNO                                     NUMBER(2)
```

LIST   This command is used to list the contents of the current SQL*Plus working buffer, organized by line number. SQL*Plus buffers the last SQL command you issued. If you haven't entered a SQL command yet, the SP2-0223: No lines in SQL buffer error message is displayed. The current line available for editing and other changes is indicated by an asterisk next to the line number. Here's an example:

```
SQL> select empno, ename
  2   from emp
  3   where empno < 7700;
    EMPNO ENAME
--------- ----------
     7369 SMITH
     7499 ALLEN
     7521 WARD
     7566 JONES
     7654 MARTIN
     7698 BLAKE
6 rows selected.
SQL> list
```

```
1  select empno, ename
2  from emp
3* where empno < 7700
```

DEL number   This command deletes line *number* from the SQL*Plus working buffer (not *number* lines!). Each line in the buffer is preceded by a line number, and the last line in the buffer has an asterisk (*) next to the line number. If you want to delete multiple lines, list each line to be removed separated by a space. Here's an example:

```
SQL> del 3
SQL> list
  1  select empno, ename
  2* from emp
```

APPEND string   This command adds *string* specified to the current line. Blank spaces are permitted in the string, and a leading blank space should be included if the current string already has information in it. The current line is indicated with an asterisk (*) in the output of the append command. See the following append command for displaying current line information along with the contents of the SQL*Plus working buffer:

```
SQL> append  where empno < 7700
  2* from emp where empno < 7700
```

CLEAR BUFFER   This command clears the contents of the SQL*Plus buffer. Here's an example:

```
SQL> clear buffer
Buffer cleared
```

INPUT   When entered at the SQL prompt, this command enables you to add contents to your SQL*Plus operating buffer at the current line. If the buffer was cleared, you start at the first line. If the buffer has something in it, you start at the beginning of a new line at the end of the buffer. Here's an example:

```
SQL> input
  1  select ename, sal
  2  from emp
  3  where empno < 7600;
ENAME           SAL
---------- ---------
SMITH           800
ALLEN          1600
```

```
WARD            1250
JONES           2975
```

TIP
The append command is different from the `input`
command because `append` *allows you to specify*
the string you want to append, while `input` *is*
specified by itself so that you can enter the string
you want added on the next line.

RUN   This command executes the contents of the SQL*Plus buffer. Here's an example:

```
SQL> run
  1  select ename, sal
  2  from emp
  3* where empno < 7600
ENAME             SAL
---------- ---------
SMITH             800
ALLEN            1600
WARD             1250
JONES            2975
```

number string   When a number is entered in SQL*Plus followed by a string of characters, SQL*Plus adds the *string* you specify to the operating buffer as the line *number* you indicated. If the line number already exists, Oracle replaces it. If the line number indicated is not contiguous with the existing lines in the buffer, SQL*Plus adds the string as the last line number in the buffer. Here's an example:

```
SQL> 6 new line being added
SQL> list
  1  select ename, sal
  2  from emp
  3  where empno < 7600
  4* new line being added
SQL> 2 from jason.emp
SQL> list
  1  select ename, sal
  2  from jason.emp
  3  where empno < 7600
  4* new line being added
```

SPOOL {filename|OFF|OUT}   This command writes all output shown in SQL*Plus following issuance of the `spool filename` command to a text file identified by `filename`. If no filename extension is specified, SQL*Plus appends the `.1st` extension. When the `off` or `out` keyword is specified, spooling SQL*Plus output to a file is turned off. Here's an example:

```
SQL> spool jason.out
SQL> select ename, sal
  2  from emp
  3  where empno < 7600;
ENAME             SAL
---------- ---------
SMITH             800
ALLEN            1600
WARD             1250
JONES            2975
SQL> spool off
SQL> exit
C:\WINDOWS> type jason.out
SQL> select ename, sal
  2  from emp
  3  where empno < 7600;
ENAME             SAL
---------- ---------
SMITH             800
ALLEN            1600
WARD             1250
JONES            2975
SQL> spool off
```

SAVE filename   This command places the contents of your SQL*Plus buffer into a text file called `filename`. If no filename extension is specified, SQL*Plus appends `.sql`.

EXIT   This command exits the SQL*Plus interface and returns to the operating system.

> **TIP**
> *You can see where having the ability to edit your SQL commands using your favorite text editor is a handy feature of SQL*Plus that makes it possible to avoid learning all the commands of SQL*Plus. Nevertheless, be sure you understand the basics of entering SQL using SQL*Plus before taking the OCP exam.*

For Review

1. Be sure you know the two mechanisms available for entering and modifying SQL statements within SQL*Plus.

2. Know how to use the `edit` command in the SQL*Plus command line and how to load and run the contents of SQL scripts into SQL*Plus.

3. Understand how to use the other SQL*Plus commands identified in this section.

Exercises

1. **You are modifying a text string on line 3 of your SQL*Plus buffer. Which of the following choices best identifies the method you must use if the `edit` command is used?**

   A. Modify the code block using your favorite text editor.

   B. First refer to the line number; then use the `change` command.

   C. First delete the line using the `del` command; then refer to the line number.

   D. Load the SQL you intend to modify using the `input` command.

2. **You would like to list the columns found in an Oracle table. Which of the following SQL*Plus commands are useful for this purpose?**

   A. `get`

   B. `input`

   C. `describe`

   D. `spool`

3. **This command displays the contents of your SQL*Plus buffer:** _____ _____

4. **This is the name of the file Oracle stores the contents of your SQL*Plus buffer in:** _____

Answer Key
1. A. 2. C. 3. `list` 4. `afiedt.buf`

Chapter Summary

This chapter ambitiously takes you from an introduction to the Oracle database through some basic techniques used in `select` statements. You learned about the theory behind relational database systems such as Oracle's and how they differ from earlier systems for data storage and retrieval. The concept of a table was presented, along with common Oracle datatypes used in those tables. The chapter also described the basic architecture of an Oracle database system and covered such factors as what an object-relational RDBMS is and some of the features for developing code in Oracle's proprietary programming language, PL/SQL. You then focused your attention on the use of `select` statements. We discussed the use of the column and table clauses as well.

Two-Minute Drill

- Data is retrieved from Oracle using `select` statements.

- The syntax for a `select` statement consists of `select ... from ...;`.

- Expressions appearing after the keyword `select` are part of the column clause, and are usually the names of columns from the table storing the data you wish to retrieve.

- Expressions appearing after the `from` keyword are part of the table clause, and are usually the names of tables you want to retrieve data from.

- When you're entering a `select` statement from the prompt using SQL*Plus, a semicolon (;) at the end of the statement or a slash (/) at the beginning of the first empty line appearing after the statement in your operating buffer must be used to terminate the statement.

- Arithmetic operations can be used to perform math operations on data selected from a table or on numbers using the DUAL table.

- The DUAL table is a table with one column and one row used to fulfill the syntactic requirements of SQL `select` statements.

- Values in columns for particular rows may be empty (NULL).

- If a column contains a NULL value, you can use the `nvl( )` function to return meaningful information instead of an empty field.

- Aliases can be used in place of the actual column name or to replace the appearance of the function name in the header.

- Output from two columns can be concatenated together using a double pipe (||). Alternately, the `concat( )` function can be used for this purpose.

■ SQL commands can be entered directly into SQL*Plus on the command line.

■ You can edit mistakes in SQL*Plus with the `change` command. If a mistake is made, the `change (c/old/new)` command is used.

■ Alternatively, the `edit (ed)` command can be used to make changes in your favorite text editor.

■ You can specify your favorite text editor by issuing the `define _editor` command at the prompt.

■ Use the acronym PEMDAS to remember the correct order for operator precedence.

■ There are a host of commands available in SQL*Plus that are not part of Structured Query Language to be aware of. A few to pay close attention to include

■ `get` for retrieving SQL scripts into SQL*Plus

■ `run` for executing retrieved SQL scripts

■ `@` for getting and running a script in one operation

■ `describe` for listing the columns in a particular table, along with their datatypes

■ `spool` for telling SQL*Plus to write the contents of your session to a file

Fill-in-the-Blank Questions

1. This term refers to a logical grouping of tables according to the user who created the tables: _____

2. When you want to perform an operation on two expressions, you can query this table: _____

3. A command-line tool you will use frequently to access Oracle is called: _____

4. The function whose work is performed by placing two pipe characters (||) together is called: _____

5. The Oracle component handling the actual obtainment of data you request is called: _____

6. The command set you request data from Oracle with is called: _____

Chapter Questions

1. **You are formulating queries in SQL*Plus. Which of the following statements correctly describes how to specify a column alias?**

   A. Place the alias at the beginning of the statement to describe the table.

   B. Place the alias after each column, separated by a space, to describe the column.

   C. Place the alias after each column, separated by a comma, to describe the column.

   D. Place the alias at the end of the statement to describe the table.

2. **You wish to use a function in your column clause of a SQL statement. The nvl ( ) function accomplishes which of the following tasks?**

   A. Assists in the distribution of output across multiple columns

   B. Enables you to specify alternate output for non-NULL column values

   C. Enables you to specify alternate output for NULL column values

   D. Nullifies the value of the column output

3. **Output from a table called PLAYS with two columns, PLAY_NAME and AUTHOR, is shown next. Which of the following SQL statements produced it?**

```
PLAY_TABLE
------------------------------------
"Midsummer Nights Dream", SHAKESPEARE
"Waiting For Godot", BECKETT
"The Glass Menagerie", WILLIAMS
```

   A. select PLAY_NAME|| AUTHOR from PLAYS;

   B. select PLAY_NAME, AUTHOR from PLAYS;

   C. select PLAY_NAME||', ' || AUTHOR from PLAYS;

   D. select PLAY_NAME||', ' || AUTHOR play_table from PLAYS;

4. **You are configuring your SQL*Plus working environment. Issuing the define _editor='emacs' will produce which of the following outcomes?**

   A. The EMACS editor will become the SQL*Plus default text editor.

   B. The EMACS editor will start running immediately.

   C. The EMACS editor will no longer be used by SQL*Plus as the default text editor.

   D. The EMACS editor will be deleted from the system.

5. **You are using SQL*Plus to execute some math functions. What is the appropriate table to use when performing arithmetic calculations on values defined within the select statement (not pulled from a table column)?**

   A. EMP

   B. The table containing the column values

   C. DUAL

   D. An Oracle-defined table

6. You wish to use SQL*Plus to connect to the Oracle database. Which of the following choices does not indicate a component you must specify when logging into Oracle?

   A. The `sqlplus` keyword

   B. The username

   C. The password

   D. The database name

7. Review the following output from a SQL*Plus session:

```
Name                            Null?    Type
------------------------------- -------- ------------
SYMPTOM                         NOT NULL VARCHAR2(10)
CAUSE                                    VARCHAR2(10)
TREATMENT                                VARCHAR2(9)
```

Which of the following keywords likely produced the output above?

   A. `describe`

   B. `get`

   C. `run`

   D. `spool`

Fill-in-the-Blank Answers

1. Schema

2. DUAL

3. SQL*Plus

4. concat( )

5. RDBMS or relational database management system

6. SQL or structured query language

Answers to Chapter Questions

1. B. Place the alias after each column, separated by a space, to describe the column.

Explanation   Aliases do not describe tables; they describe columns, which eliminates choices A and D. Commas are needed between each column appearing in the column clause of the `select` statement. If a column alias appeared after a column, Oracle would either select the wrong column name, based on information provided in the alias, or return an error.

2. C. Enables you to specify alternate output for NULL column values

Explanation   The `nvl( )` function is a simple `if-then` operation that tests column value output to see whether it is NULL. If it is, `nvl( )` substitutes the specified default value for the NULL value. Because this function only operates on one column per call to `nvl( )`, choice A is incorrect. Choice B is incorrect because it is the logical opposite of choice C. Choice D is incorrect because `nvl( )` is designed to substitute actual values for situations where NULL is present, not nullify data.

3. D. `select PLAY_NAME||', ' || AUTHOR play_table from PLAYS;`

Explanation   This question illustrates the need to read carefully. Because the output specified for the question contains a column alias for the output of the statement, choice D is the only one that is correct, even though choice C also performs the correct calculation. Choice A is incorrect because it specifies an inaccurate concatenation method, and choice B is wrong because it doesn't specify concatenation at all.

4. A. The emacs editor will become the SQL*Plus default text editor.

Explanation   The define _editor statement is designed to define the default text editor in SQL*Plus. Changing the definition will not start or stop the editor specified from running, which eliminates choices B and D. Choice C is the logical opposite of choice A and is therefore incorrect.

5. C. DUAL

Explanation   When all data to be processed by the query is present in the statement, and no data will be pulled from the database, users typically specify the DUAL table to fulfill the syntactic requirements of the from clause.

6. D. The database name

Explanation   You needn't specify the name of the database you wish to connect to. If this information is omitted, then Oracle assumes you want to connect to the local database called ORCL on your machine. All other choices identify a component required for connecting to the Oracle database.

7. A. describe

Explanation   The describe command produces a listing of all columns in a table, along with their associated datatypes. Choice B is incorrect because get merely loads the contents of a script into SQL*Plus memory. Choice C is incorrect because run executes a script that has already been loaded into SQL*Plus memory. Finally, choice D is incorrect because the spool command is used for writing the commands from a SQL*Plus session issued after the spool command to flat file.

CHAPTER
2

Limiting, Sorting, and Manipulating Return Data

n this chapter, you will learn about and demonstrate knowledge in the following areas:

- Restricting and sorting row data
- Using single-row functions

This chapter will build on the concepts you learned in Chapter 1 with respect to selecting data from Oracle. In this chapter, we'll discuss how to limit the data selected from the Oracle database and how to tell Oracle to return the data in a specific order. We'll also discuss how to use a category of functions called *single-row* functions to manipulate the results of your queries in a variety of ways. This chapter covers important material comprising 16 percent of the test content of OCP Exam 1.

Restricting and Sorting Row Data

This section will cover the following areas related to restricting and sorting row data:

- Sorting return data with the `order by` clause
- Limiting return data with the `where` clause

Obtaining all output from a table is great, but usually you must be more selective in choosing output. Most database applications contain a lot of data. How much data can a database contain? Some applications contain tables with a million rows or more, and the most recent release of Oracle9*i* will store over 512 petabytes (512 × 1,024⁵ bytes) of data. Of course, this is only a theoretical limit. The real amount of data you can store with Oracle depends on how much disk space you give Oracle to use, but, needless to say, manipulating vast amounts of data like that requires you to be careful. Always ask for *exactly* what you want, and no more. This section tells you how.

Sorting Return Data with the `order by` Clause

Notice that Oracle does not return data requested in a particular order on any particular column, either numeric or alphabetical. According to the fundamentals of relational database theory, a table is by definition an *unordered* set of row data. That's fine for the ivory tower, but it's not always useful in real-world situations. Oracle enables you to order the output from `select` statements using the `order by` clause. This clause can impose a sort order on one or more columns in ascending *or* descending order in each of the columns specified. If more than one expression is specified for a sort order, then Oracle sorts in the order of data appearing in the first expression. If the first expression has duplicates, Oracle sorts in the order of data appearing in the second expression, and so on. The `order by` clause usually appears last in the Structured Query Language (SQL) statement, and the general syntax for the `order by` clause is to include both the clause and the column(s) or column alias(es) by which Oracle will order the results, each optionally followed by a special clause defining the direction of the order (`asc` for ascending and `desc` for descending). The default value is `asc`, and here is an example:

```
SQL> select empno, ename, sal
  2   from emp
  3   order by ename asc;
    EMPNO ENAME             SAL
--------- ---------- ---------
     7876 ADAMS            1100
     7499 ALLEN            1600
     7698 BLAKE            2850
     7782 CLARK            2450
     7902 FORD             3000
     7900 JAMES             950
     7566 JONES            2975
     7839 KING             5000
     7654 MARTIN           1250
     7934 MILLER           1300
     7788 SCOTT            3000
     7369 SMITH             800
     7844 TURNER           1500
     7521 WARD             1250
```

An example of sorting output in descending order using the `desc` keyword is shown here:

```
SQL> select * from emp
  2   order by ename desc;

EMPNO ENAME      JOB        MGR  HIREDATE    SAL  COMM  DEPTNO
------ ---------- ---------- ----- --------- ----- ----- -------
 7521 WARD       SALESMAN   7698 22-FEB-81 1250   500      30
 7844 TURNER     SALESMAN   7698 08-SEP-81 1500     0      30
 7369 SMITH      CLERK      7902 17-DEC-80  800             20
 7788 SCOTT      ANALYST    7566 19-APR-87 3000             20
 7934 MILLER     CLERK      7782 23-JAN-82 1300             10
 7654 MARTIN     SALESMAN   7698 28-SEP-81 1250  1400      30
 7839 KING       PRESIDENT       17-NOV-81 5000             10
 7566 JONES      MANAGER    7839 02-APR-81 2975             20
```

```
 7900  JAMES      CLERK      7698  03-DEC-81   950                30
 7902  FORD       ANALYST    7566  03-DEC-81  3000                20
 7782  CLARK      MANAGER    7839  09-JUN-81  2450                10
 7698  BLAKE      MANAGER    7839  01-MAY-81  2850                30
 7499  ALLEN      SALESMAN   7698  20-FEB-81  1600       300      30
 7876  ADAMS      CLERK      7788  23-MAY-87  1100                20
```

TIP
When NULL data appears in a column that Oracle is attempting to sort in ascending order, Oracle lists the NULL records at the end of the list. When sorting in descending order, Oracle places the NULL data at the top of the list.

The order by clause can be useful in simple reporting. It can be applied to columns that are NUMBER, text (VARCHAR2 and CHAR), and DATE datatypes. You can even use numbers to positionally indicate the column where Oracle should order the output from a statement. For example, if you issue a statement similar to the one in the following code block, the order for the output will be as shown (the number 2 indicates that the second column specified in the statement should be used to define the order in the output):

```
SQL> select empno, ename from emp
  2 order by 2 desc;
 EMPNO ENAME
------ --------
  7521 WARD
  7844 TURNER
  7369 SMITH
  7788 SCOTT
  7934 MILLER
  7654 MARTIN
  7839 KING
  7566 JONES
  7900 JAMES
  7902 FORD
  7782 CLARK
  7698 BLAKE
  7499 ALLEN
  7876 ADAMS
SQL> select ename, empno from emp
  2  order by 2 desc;
ENAME       EMPNO
---------  ------
```

```
MILLER      7934
FORD        7902
JAMES       7900
ADAMS       7876
TURNER      7844
KING        7839
SCOTT       7788
CLARK       7782
BLAKE       7698
MARTIN      7654
JONES       7566
WARD        7521
ALLEN       7499
SMITH       7369
```

TIP
You can also sort by column alias.

Here's an even more complex example:

```
SQL> select ename, deptno, sal
  2    from emp
  3    order by 2 asc, 3 desc;
ENAME        DEPTNO        SAL
---------- --------- ---------
KING             10       5000
CLARK            10       2450
MILLER           10       1300
SCOTT            20       3000
FORD             20       3000
JONES            20       2975
ADAMS            20       1100
SMITH            20        800
BLAKE            30       2850
ALLEN            30       1600
TURNER           30       1500
WARD             30       1250
MARTIN           30       1250
JAMES            30        950
```

For Review

1. Know how to put row data returned from a `select` statement in order and know the various sort orders (ascending and descending) that can be used with this option. Know also that Oracle can sort based on multiple columns.

2. Be sure you understand both the positional and named ways to specify the column on which the sort order should be defined.

Exercises

1. Which of the choices below identifies the `order by` clause that produces the following output?

```
EMPNO ENAME         MGR
-------- ---------- ---------
    7369 SMITH      7902
    7566 JONES      7839
    7782 CLARK      7839
    7698 BLAKE      7839
    7876 ADAMS      7788
    7934 MILLER     7782
    7499 ALLEN      7698
    7654 MARTIN     7698
    7521 WARD       7698
    7900 JAMES      7698
    7844 TURNER     7698
    7788 SCOTT      7566
    7902 FORD       7566
```

   A. `order by empno asc`

   B. `order by ename desc`

   C. `order by hiredate asc`

   D. `order by mgr desc`

2. You are sorting data in a table in your `select` statement in descending order. The column you are sorting on contains NULL records. Where will the NULL records appear?

   A. At the beginning of the list

   B. At the end of the list

   C. In the middle of the list

   D. At the same location they are listed in the unordered table

3. Identify the default sort order used by Oracle when no sort order is specified: _____

4. **The results from an SQL query are shown here:**

```
DEPTNO DNAME            LOC
-------- -------------- -------------
      10 ACCOUNTING      NEW YORK
      40 OPERATIONS      BOSTON
      20 RESEARCH        DALLAS
      30 SALES           CHICAGO
```

Which of the following SQL statements could not have produced this output?

A. select deptno, dname, loc from dept order by 2 asc, 1 asc, 3 desc;

B. select deptno, dname, loc from dept order by 3 asc;

C. select deptno, dname, loc from dept order by 2 asc;

D. select deptno, dname, loc from dept order by 2 asc, 3 desc, 1 desc;

Answer Key

1. D. 2. A. 3. Ascending. 4. B.

Limiting Return Data with the where Clause

The where clause in Oracle select statements is where things really become interesting. This important clause in select statements enables you to single out a few rows from hundreds, thousands, or even millions like it. The where clause operates on a basic principle of comparison and must follow the select and from clauses in the SQL statement. Here's an example:

```
SQL> select * from emp
  2  where empno = 7844;
EMPNO ENAME     JOB        MGR HIREDATE    SAL  COMM  DEPTNO
------ --------- --------- ----- --------- ----- ----- -------
 7844 TURNER    SALESMAN  7698 08-SEP-81  1500     0      30
```

Assuming the EMPNO column contains all unique values, instead of pulling all rows from EMP, Oracle pulls just one row for display. To determine which row to display, the where clause performs a comparison operation as specified by the query. In this case, the comparison is an equality operation: `where empno = 7844`. However, equality is not the only means by which Oracle can obtain data. Some other examples of comparisons are demonstrated in Table 2-1. Every comparison between two values in Oracle boils down to one or more of the operations from that table.

`x = y`	Comparison to see if x is equal to y.
`x > y`	Comparison to see if x is greater than y.
`x >= y`	Comparison to see if x is greater than or equal to y.
`x < y`	Comparison to see if x is less than y.
`x <= y`	Comparison to see if x is less than or equal to y.
`x <> y, x != y,` `x ^= y`	Comparison to see if x is not equal to y.
`like`	A special comparison used in conjunction with search wildcards. Two wildcards exist in Oracle. The first, percent (`%`), is for multiple characters, as in `'%ORA%'` for all columns or rows containing string ORA. The second, underscore (`_`), is used for single-character substitution, as in `'OR_CLE'` for all strings where the user may have mistyped I instead of A. An example might be `select ename from emp where ename is like 'S%'`.
`soundex`	A special function used to introduce "fuzzy logic" into text-string comparisons by enabling equality based on similarly spelled words.
`between`	A range comparison operation that enables operations on dates, numbers, and characters that are similar to the following numeric comparison: y is between x and z. An example might be `select * from emp where sal is between 300 and 500`.
`in (set)`	A special comparison that enables you to specify multiple equality statements by defining a set of values, any of which the value can be equal to. An example of its usage would be `select * from emp where deptno in (10,20,30)`.

TABLE 2-1.   *Comparison Operations in Oracle*

You can also use the `where` clause and the `order` by clause together in the same statement. The following code block shows an example of all the data from EMP for sales persons in order of the highest salary to the lowest:

```
SQL> select ename, empno, sal
  2   from emp
  3   where job = 'SALESMAN'
  4   order by sal desc;
ENAME           EMPNO       SAL
----------   ---------   ---------
ALLEN           7499       1600
TURNER          7844       1500
WARD            7521       1250
MARTIN          7654       1250
```

Getting Even More Selective

Multiple comparisons can be placed together using the list of operations given in Table 2-2. The operator is listed along with the result that is required to fulfill the criteria based on the presence of this operator. For example, the and keyword can be used to join two comparisons together, forcing Oracle to return only the rows that fulfill both criteria. In contrast, the or keyword enables a much looser joining of two comparisons, enabling Oracle to return records that fulfill one criteria or the other. In this case, if a record fulfills the criteria of both comparisons, Oracle will return the record as well.

x and y	Both comparisons in x and y must be true.
x or y	One comparison in x or y must be true.
not x	The logical opposite of x.
x is NULL	This returns TRUE if the value is NULL. This operator resolves the problem where comparing variable x to NULL produces a NULL result rather than TRUE. An example might be `select ename from emp where mgr is null`.

TABLE 2-2. *Keywords for Joining Comparisons Together*

The OCP exam may or may not contain a question covering the order of precedence between operators in a `where` clause of a `select` statement. The order in which Oracle resolves operators in a `where` clause is as follows:

1. First, Oracle resolves comparison operators.

2. Next, Oracle resolves all `and` operators as a single unit.

3. After that, Oracle resolves all `or` operators as separate units.

4. Finally, Oracle resolves all `not` reversers. You can force a different resolution priority using parentheses.

More Examples

Let's look at a more complex example of a query that uses a where clause so that we can see some other comparison operations and the keywords from Table 2-2 in action. Let's say we want to obtain information on all the employees at our company who make more than $900 per year and also have a last name between QUENTIN and ZYRYRAB. The following code block illustrates how to execute this query:

```
SQL> select empno, ename, sal
  2   from emp
  3   where sal > 900
  4   and ename between 'QUENTIN' and 'ZYRYRAB';
     EMPNO ENAME            SAL
--------- ---------- ---------
      7521 WARD           1250
      7788 SCOTT          3000
      7844 TURNER         1500
```

Perhaps you noticed that the output above doesn't list KING, the president of the company. We know from earlier examples and from Chapter 1 that KING makes more money than SCOTT, WARD, or TURNER, and yet he's not listed among the output. There's a simple reason for this. KING's last name doesn't fall between QUENTIN and ZYRYRAB alphabetically, and because we used the AND operation to concatenate the two comparison criteria, KING was excluded.

So, let's take a look at another example of output where we see the employees that make more than $900 or if their names fall between QUENTIN and ZYRYRAB alphabetically:

```
SQL> select empno, ename, sal
  2   from emp
  3   where sal > 900
  4   OR ename between 'QUENTIN' and 'ZYRYRAB';
     EMPNO ENAME            SAL
```

```
---------  ----------  ---------
    7369 SMITH              800
    7499 ALLEN            1600
    7521 WARD             1250
    7566 JONES            2975
    7654 MARTIN           1250
    7698 BLAKE            2850
    7782 CLARK            2450
    7788 SCOTT            3000
    7839 KING             5000
    7844 TURNER           1500
    7876 ADAMS            1100
    7900 JAMES             950
    7902 FORD             3000
    7934 MILLER           1300
```

As we can see from the output above, we weren't at all selective in our output because apparently everyone in the company falls within the criteria given. In other words, every employee of our company EITHER makes more than $900 or has a last name that falls alphabetically between QUENTIN and ZYRYRAB.

Finally, let's look at an example using the not operator to see how this "reverser" can potentially change the output of a query:

```
SQL> select empno, ename, sal
  2  from emp
  3  where sal > 900
  4  OR ename NOT between 'QUENTIN' and 'ZYRYRAB';
   EMPNO ENAME             SAL
---------  ----------  ---------
    7499 ALLEN            1600
    7521 WARD             1250
    7566 JONES            2975
    7654 MARTIN           1250
    7698 BLAKE            2850
    7782 CLARK            2450
    7788 SCOTT            3000
    7839 KING             5000
    7844 TURNER           1500
    7876 ADAMS            1100
    7900 JAMES             950
    7902 FORD             3000
    7934 MILLER           1300
```

Did you notice who's not listed in the output above? SMITH, whose name is between QUENTIN and ZYRYRAB, is not listed. Thus, you can see how this reverser can eliminate records that would otherwise appear in the set. However, be careful with your use of the not keyword. You can include it in contexts where it would appear with other keywords, but not in front of symbols or expressions. For example, using where empno is not null is acceptable in Oracle SQL, but using where sal not > 900 would result in an error.

TIP

A substantial portion of the OCP exam on SQL rides on your ability to formulate queries with where clauses. Thus, it is important that you practice this ability.

For Review

1. Be able to define what a where clause is as well as the principle of comparison that the clause operates on in order to determine the data to return to the user.

2. Know all the operations available that can assist in the purpose of comparison. Also, be sure you know which operations enable you to specify more than one comparison in the where clause.

Exercises

1. You are defining an SQL statement to return a limited number of rows based on specific criteria. Which of the following choices identifies the clause you will use to define the search criteria?

    A. select

    B. from

    C. where

    D. order by

2. The principle that the search criteria available within SQL select statements operate on is _____.

3. The operation used when you want to determine whether a NULL value appears in a column (two words) is _____.

4. You want to obtain data from the ORDERS table, which contains three columns: CUSTOMER, ORDER_DATE, and ORDER_AMT. Which of the

following choices identifies how you would formulate the `where` clause in a query against the ORDERS table when you want to see orders for customer LESLIE that exceed 2,700?

A. `where customer = 'LESLIE';`

B. `where customer = 'LESLIE' and order_amt < 2700;`

C. `where customer = 'LESLIE' or order_amt > 2700;`

D. `where customer = 'LESLIE' and order_amt > 2700;`

Answer Key

1. C. **2.** Comparison. **3.** `is NULL` **4.** D.

Using Single-Row Functions

This section will cover the following areas related to using single-row functions:

- Explanations of various single-row functions
- Using functions in `select` statements
- Date functions
- Conversion functions

Dozens of functions are available in Oracle that can be used for many purposes. Some functions in Oracle are designed to alter the data returned by a query, such as the `nvl( )` function already presented. The functions in this category are designed to work on columns of any datatype to return information in different ways. Other single-row functions operate on only one or two datatypes. This section will explain the use of various important single-row functions in the Oracle database. Single-row functions are those designed to operate on individual column records in a row, for every row returned in the result set. You'll also see how these functions are used in SQL commands. Date and conversion functions will be covered in some detail as well.

Various Single-Row Functions Explained

Functions are similar to comparison operators in that they manipulate data items and return a result. The difference is that functions can usually do more complex things than simple comparisons. Several different types of functions exist and they include the following:

- Text functions that perform operations on alphanumeric text strings

- Arithmetic functions that perform operations on numbers

- List functions that perform operations on lists of values

- Other functions, such as decode ( ), that perform important or unique operations

Text Functions

Several functions in Oracle manipulate text strings. These functions are similar in concept to nvl ( ) and decode ( ) in that they can perform a change on a piece of data, but the functions in this family can change only VARCHAR2 and CHAR data. Here are some examples:

- **lpad(x,y[,z]) and rpad(x,y[,z])**   Return data in string or column x padded on the left or right side, respectively, to width y. The optional value z indicates the character(s) that lpad ( ) or rpad ( ) use to pad the column data. If no character z is specified, a space is used.

- **lower(x), upper(x), and initcap(x)**   Return data in string or column x in lowercase or uppercase characters, respectively, or change the initial letter in the data from column x to a capital letter.

- **length(x)**   Returns the number of characters in string or column x.

- **substr(x,y[,z])**   Returns a substring of string or column x, starting at the character in position number y to the end, which is optionally defined by the character appearing in position z of the string. For example, substr('ABCDEFG',3,4) returns CDEF.

- **instr(x,y)**   Determines whether a substring y given can be found in string x. For example, instr('CORPORATE FLOOR','OR') returns 2.

The trim( ) Function   A single-row function called trim( ) behaves like a combination of ltrim( ) and rtrim( ). The trim( ) function accepts a string describing the data you would like to trim from a column value using the following syntax: trim([[keyword]'x' from] column). Here keyword is replaced by leading, trailing, or both, or it's omitted. Also, x is replaced with the character to be trimmed, or it's omitted. If x is omitted, Oracle assumes it must trim whitespace. Finally, column is the name of the column in the table to be trimmed. Note that trim( ) only removes trailing or leading instances of the character specified. If that character appears somewhere in the string, `trim( )` will not remove it. The following code block illustrates the use of `trim( )`:

```
SQL> select col_1,
  2   trim(both '_' from col_1) as trimmed
  3   from example;
LASTNAME TRIMMED
-------- ---------
__thr_    thr
@_593__   @_593
Booga__   Booga
```

Another example appears here:

```
SQL> select trim(0 from 000004439094000)
  2   as example
  3   from dual;
EXAMPLE
-------
4439094
```

TIP
The table used in the previous code block is not created by `utlsampl.sql` or `demobld.sql` and will not exist in your database unless you create and populate it yourself. It's a really trivial example, though, and you're time will be better spent focusing on how to formulate `where` clauses, but if you must recreate the example, instructions for creating tables and adding data to them appear in Chapter 5.

Arithmetic Functions

Other functions are designed to perform specialized mathematical functions, such as those used in scientific applications such as sine and logarithms. These operations are commonly referred to as *arithmetic* or *number operations*. The functions falling into this category are listed next. These functions are not all that is available in Oracle, but rather they are the most commonly used ones that will likely appear on OCP Exam 1:

- **abs(x)**   Obtains the absolute value for a number. For example, the absolute value of −1 is 1, whereas the absolute value of 6 is 6.

- **round(x,y)** Rounds x to the decimal precision of y. If y is negative, it rounds to the precision of y places to the left of the decimal point. For example, round(134.345,1) = 134.3, round(134.345,0) = 134, round(134.345,-1) = 130. This can also be used on DATE columns.

- **ceil(x)** Similar to executing round on an integer (for example, round(x,0)), except ceil always rounds up. For example, ceil(1.4) = 2. Note that rounding up on negative numbers produces a value closer to zero (for example, ceil(-1.6) = −1, not −2).

- **floor(x)** Similar to ceil, except floor always rounds down. For example, floor(1.6) = 1. Note that rounding down on negative numbers produces a value further away from zero (for example, floor(-1.6) = −2, not −1).

- **mod(x,y)** The modulus of x, defined in long division as the integer remainder when x is divided by y until no further whole number can be produced. For example, mod(10,3) = 1, and mod(10,2) = 0.

- **sign(x)** Displays an integer value corresponding to the sign of x: 1 if x is positive, −1 if x is negative.

- **sqrt(x)** The square root of x.

- **trunc(x,y)** Truncates x to the decimal precision of y. If y is negative, it truncates to y number of places to the left of the decimal point. This can also be used on DATE columns.

- **vsize(x)** The storage size in bytes for value x.

TIP
All arithmetic functions containing a NULL value passed in as input will return NULL as the result.

List Functions

The final category of number functions discussed here is the set of list functions. These functions are actually used for many different datatypes, including CHAR, VARCHAR2, NUMBER, and DATE. Let's now take a look at the list functions available in Oracle:

- **greatest(x,y, . . .)** Returns the highest value from the list of text strings, numbers, or dates (x, y . . .).

- **least(x,y, . . .)** Returns the lowest value from the list of text strings, numbers, or dates (x, y . . .).

TIP
If you're a little confused after reading about all these functions because you don't know how their output would look in SQL*Plus, don't worry. We're going to look at some examples in the next discussion.

The `decode ( )` Function

One commonly used single-row function merits a separate explanation. It is `decode ( )`. The `decode ( )` function works on the same principle as the `if-then-else` statement does in many common programming languages, including PL/SQL. You can pass a variable number of values into the call to the `decode ( )` function, which will appear in the column clause of your `select` statement. Your first item will always be the name of the column you want to decode. Next, you identify the first specific value Oracle should look for in that column. After that, you pass in the substitute you want Oracle to return if the first specific value is encountered. From there, you can then define as many specific value-substitute pairs as you would like. Once all value-substitute pairs have been defined, you can optionally specify a default value that Oracle will return if the column value doesn't match a specified value. Take a look at the following code block to get a better idea of how this works:

```
SELECT decode(column_name,
              value1, substitute1,
              value2, substitute2,
              ... ,
              return_default)
FROM ... ;
```

The `decode ( )` function enables a powerful transformation of data from one value to another. Some examples of `decode ( )` in action will appear shortly. This function is presented first because, like `nvl ( )`, `decode ( )` can operate on virtually every datatype in Oracle. From this point on, all functions described have limitations on the datatypes that they can perform their operations on. Let's look at an example:

```
SQL>  select ename, decode(deptno, 10, 'Accounting',
  2     20, 'Research',
  3     30, 'Sales',
  4     40, 'Operations', 'Other') Department
  5  from emp
```

```
6  order by department;
ENAME      DEPARTMENT
---------- ----------
CLARK      Accounting
KING       Accounting
MILLER     Accounting
SMITH      Research
ADAMS      Research
FORD       Research
SCOTT      Research
JONES      Research
ALLEN      Sales
BLAKE      Sales
MARTIN     Sales
JAMES      Sales
TURNER     Sales
WARD       Sales
```

For Review

1. Be sure you can identify the character, math, and date functions available in SQL, as shown in this discussion. Know the two functions that enable you to transform column values regardless of the datatype.

2. Know how to use the `trim( )` function.

3. Understand the list functions presented in this discussion that perform operations on specified sets of information.

Exercises

1. **The result of a math function is −97, and the information passed into that function was −97.342. Which of the following choices identifies the single-row function that could have produced this output?**

   A. `abs( )`

   B. `ceil( )`

   C. `mod( )`

   D. `sqrt( )`

2. **You want to determine the size in bytes of a particular column value. Which of the following single-row functions might be useful for doing so?**

   A. `vsize( )`

   B. `trunc( )`

    C. trim( )

    D. greatest( )

3. **Which of the single-row functions covered in this discussion operates in a way similar to an** if-then-else **expression?**

    _____

Answer Key

1. B. **2.** A. **3.** decode( )

Using Functions in select Statements

Let's take a look at the functions introduced in the last discussion in action. The first example details the use of the decode( ) function. Assume that you select data from the EMP table. The data in the JOB column identifies the role each employee performs for the company. Instead of displaying the job title, the following code block lets you write out a verb that describes the employee's role so that you know that no slackers exist in the company:

```
SQL> select ename || ' does the ' ||
  2  decode(job, 'ANALYST','analyzing','CLERK','filing',
  3  'MANAGER','managing','PRESIDENT','bossing around',
  4  'SALESMAN','golfing','goofing off') as functions
  5  from emp;
FUNCTIONS
---------------------------------
SMITH does the filing
ALLEN does the golfing
WARD does the golfing
JONES does the managing
MARTIN does the golfing
BLAKE does the managing
CLARK does the managing
SCOTT does the analyzing
KING does the bossing around
TURNER does the golfing
ADAMS does the filing
JAMES does the filing
FORD does the analyzing
MILLER does the filing
```

This decode ( ) command has 12 variables. The first is the name of the column to be decoded and must always be present. The next two variables identify, respectively, a value that could be found in the JOB column (ANALYST, in this case) and what decode ( ) should substitute if the value is found. This matching of potential values with appropriate substitutes continues until you identify all the cases you would like to decode. The last variable, which is optional, is used for the default substitute value.

Text Function Examples

Now let's look at some text (character) function examples. The first of these examples is for rpad ( ) and lpad ( ). As shown in the following code, these two functions can be used to place additional filler characters on the right and left sides of data in a column out to a specified column width:

```
SQL> select ename || ' does the ' ||
  2  RPAD(decode(job, 'ANALYST','analyzing','CLERK','filing',
  3  'MANAGER','managing','PRESIDENT','bossing around',
  4  'SALESMAN','golfing','goofing off'), 10, '-') as functions
  5  from emp
  6  where empno < 7600;
FUNCTIONS
------------------------------
SMITH does the filing----
ALLEN does the golfing---
WARD does the golfing---
JONES does the managing--
```

TIP
This example also illustrates another important principle—the output from one SQL function can be used as input for another!

Some of the simpler character functions are shown next. The following examples show single-row functions that are sometimes referred to as "case translators" because they perform a simple translation of case based on the text string passed:

```
SQL> SELECT lower(ename) as one,
  2  upper(ename) as two,
  3  initcap(ename) as three
  4  FROM emp;
ONE          TWO           THREE
---------- ---------- ----------
```

```
smith        SMITH        Smith
allen        ALLEN        Allen
ward         WARD         Ward
jones        JONES        Jones
martin       MARTIN       Martin
blake        BLAKE        Blake
clark        CLARK        Clark
scott        SCOTT        Scott
king         KING         King
turner       TURNER       Turner
adams        ADAMS        Adams
james        JAMES        James
ford         FORD         Ford
miller       MILLER       Miller
```

Another straightforward and useful character function is the `length( )` function, which returns the length of a text string:

```
SQL> select ename, length(ename) as length
  2  from emp;
ENAME          LENGTH
---------   ---------
SMITH              5
ALLEN              5
WARD               4
JONES              5
MARTIN             6
BLAKE              5
CLARK              5
SCOTT              5
KING               4
TURNER             6
ADAMS              5
JAMES              5
FORD               4
MILLER             6
```

TIP

If the string includes spaces, double quotes, or other special characters, all those special characters are counted as part of the length of the string.

Another extraordinarily useful function related to character strings is the `substr( )` function. This function is commonly used to extract data from a longer text string. The `substr( )` function takes as its first variable the full text string to be searched. The second variable contains an integer that designates the character number at which the substring should begin. The third parameter is optional and specifies how many characters to the right of the start of the substring will be included in the substring. By default, it will include all the characters until the end of the string. Observe the following output to understand the effects of omitting the third parameter:

```
SQL> select ename, substr(ename,2,3)
  2  from emp;
ENAME       SUB
---------   ---
SMITH       MIT
ALLEN       LLE
WARD        ARD
JONES       ONE
MARTIN      ART
BLAKE       LAK
CLARK       LAR
SCOTT       COT
KING        ING
TURNER      URN
ADAMS       DAM
JAMES       AME
FORD        ORD
MILLER      ILL
SQL> select ename, substr(ename,2)
  2  from emp;
ENAME       SUBSTR(EN
---------   ---------
SMITH       MITH
ALLEN       LLEN
WARD        ARD
JONES       ONES
MARTIN      ARTIN
BLAKE       LAKE
CLARK       LARK
SCOTT       COTT
KING        ING
TURNER      URNER
ADAMS       DAMS
JAMES       AMES
FORD        ORD
MILLER      ILLER
```

Arithmetic Function Examples

The number (math) functions are frequently used in scientific applications. The first function detailed here is the abs ( ) function, or *absolute value* function, which calculates how far away from zero the parameter passed lies on the number line:

```
SQL> SELECT ABS(25), ABS(-12) FROM DUAL;
ABS(25) ABS(-12)
------- --------
     25       12
```

The next single-value function is the ceil ( ) function, which automatically rounds the number passed as its parameter up to the next highest integer:

```
SQL> SELECT CEIL(123.323), CEIL(45),
  2  CEIL(-392), CEIL(-1.12) FROM DUAL;
CEIL(123.323) CEIL(45) CEIL(-392) CEIL(-1.12)
------------- -------- ---------- -----------
          124       45       -392          -1
```

The next single-value function is the floor ( ) function. The floor ( ) function is the opposite of ceil ( ), because it rounds the value passed down to the next lowest integer:

```
SQL> SELECT FLOOR(123.323), FLOOR(45), FLOOR(-392),
  2  FLOOR(-1.12) FROM DUAL;
FLOOR(123.323) FLOOR(45) FLOOR(-392) FLOOR(-1.12)
-------------- --------- ----------- ------------
           123        45        -392           -2
```

The next function covered in this section is related to long division. The function is called mod ( ), and it returns the remainder (or *modulus*) for a number and its divisor:

```
SQL> SELECT MOD(12,3), MOD(55,4) FROM DUAL;
MOD(12,3)   MOD(55,4)
---------   ---------
        0           3
```

After that, look at round ( ). This important function enables you to round a number off to a specified precision:

```
SQL>
SELECT ROUND(123.323,2), ROUND(45,1),
  2  ROUND(-392,-1), ROUND (-1.12,0) FROM DUAL;
```

```
ROUND(123.323,2) ROUND(45,1) ROUND(-392,-1) ROUND(-1.12,0)
---------------- ----------- -------------- --------------
         123.32          45           -390             -1
```

The next function is called `sign( )`. It assists in identifying whether a number is positive or negative. If the number passed is positive, `sign( )` returns 1, and if the number is negative, `sign( )` returns −1. If the number is zero, `sign( )` returns 0:

```
SQL> SELECT SIGN(-1933), SIGN(55), SIGN(0) FROM DUAL;
SIGN(-1933) SIGN(55) SIGN(0)
----------- -------- -------
         -1        1       0
```

The next example is the `sqrt( )` function. It is used to derive the square root for a number:

```
SQL> SELECT SQRT(34), SQRT(9) FROM DUAL;
SQRT(34) SQRT(9)
-------- -------
5.830951       3
```

The next single-value number function is called `trunc( )`. Similar to `round( )`, `trunc( )` truncates a value passed into it according to the precision that is also passed in:

```
SQL> SELECT TRUNC(123.232,2), TRUNC(-45,1),
  2  TRUNC(392,-1), TRUNC(5,0) FROM DUAL;
TRUNC(123.232,2) TRUNC(-45,1) TRUNC(392,-1) TRUNC(5,0)
---------------- ------------ ------------- ----------
          123.23          -45           390          5
```

The final single-row operation that is covered in this section is the `vsize( )` function. This function is not strictly for numeric datatypes. The `vsize( )` function gives the size in bytes of any value for VARCHAR2, CHAR, NUMBER, DATE, ROWID, and other column datatypes:

```
SQL> SELECT VSIZE(384838), VSIZE('ORANGE_TABBY'),
  2  VSIZE(sysdate) FROM DUAL;
VSIZE(384838) VSIZE('ORANGE_TABBY') VSIZE(SYSDATE)
------------- --------------------- --------------
            4                    12              8
```

For Review

I. Be sure you understand the purpose of the decode ( ) statement and that it accepts all the common Oracle datatypes. Make sure you can set up a call to this function correctly.

2. Know how to use the text functions. Also make sure you understand how to combine two functions using the output of one function as input for the other.

3. Understand the use of the math functions. Be sure you know how to utilize them on real columns and how to use them on fixed expressions using the DUAL table.

Exercises

I. Use the following output to answer this question (assume that the information shown comes from the EMP table we've been using in the chapter).

```
ENAME
----------
SMITH-dog-
ALLEN-dog-
WARD-dog-d
JONES-dog-
MARTIN-dog
BLAKE-dog-
CLARK-dog-
SCOTT-dog-
KING-dog-d
TURNER-dog
ADAMS-dog-
JAMES-dog-
FORD-dog-d
MILLER-dog
```

Which of the following choices identifies the SQL statement that produced this output?

A. select trim(trailing '-dog' from ename) as ename from emp;

B. select rpad(ename, 10, '-dog') as ename from emp;

C. select substr(ename, 1, 10) as ename from emp;

D. select lpad(ename, 10, '-dog') as ename from emp;

2. Use the following code block to answer the question:

```
SQL> select _____(-45) as output from dual;
OUTPUT
------
   -45
```

Which of the following choices identifies a single-row function that could not have produced this output?

A. abs ( )

B. ceil ( )

C. floor ( )

D. round ( )

3. For a certain row in a table, a VARCHAR2 column contains the value SMITHY, padded to the right with seven spaces by the application. When the length ( ) function processes that column value, what will be the value returned?

A. 5

B. 6

C. 12

D. 13

4. You issue the following statement in SQL*Plus:

```
SQL> select ceil(-97.342),
   2   floor(-97.342),
   3   round(-97.342,0),
   4   trunc(-97.342)
   5   from dual;
```

Which of the following choices identifies the function that will not return −97 as the result?

A. ceil ( )

B. floor ( )

C. round ( )

D. trunc ( )

5. You issue the following statement in SQL*Plus:

```
SQL> select ceil(256.342),
   2   floor(256.342),
   3   round(256.342,0),
   4   trunc(256.342)
   5   from dual;
```

Which of the following choices identifies the function that will not return 256 as the result?

A. `ceil( )`

B. `floor( )`

C. `round( )`

D. `trunc( )`

Answer Key

1. B. **2.** A. **3.** D. **4.** B. Ceil( ) returns −97 because −97 is closer to 0 and is therefore greater than −98. **5.** A.

Date Functions

You may not see this listed as an official objective on the OCP 9i SQL Candidate Guide, but understanding date functions is crucial for your use of the Oracle database. Thus, I like to cover it as a separate topic. To start our discussion of date functions, you should be aware that a special keyword can be specified to give Oracle users the current date. This keyword is `sysdate`. In the same way you calculated simple arithmetic earlier in the chapter using the DUAL table, so too can you execute a `select` statement using `sysdate` to produce the current date. Here's an example:

```
SQL> SELECT sysdate FROM DUAL;
SYSDATE
---------
15-MAR-01
```

TIP

The DATE information you obtain when using the keyword `sysdate` *is the date according to the server hosting the Oracle database. Therefore, the date information returned could differ from the date information for your client PC.*

Now for a note about the format. Typically, Oracle by default displays date information either in DD-MON-YY format or DD-MON-YYYY format. Thus, DD stands for a two-digit date (01 for the first day of the month, 02 for the second, and so on), while MON is a three-character abbreviation for the month of the year (JAN for January, FEB for February, and so on). YY or YYYY stands for a two- or four-digit year. If you use Oracle in your organization and you retrieve `sysdate` information in a format other than the ones described, don't panic! Chances are, your DBA or someone else in the organization has altered Oracle to display date information in some nondefault format. We'll discuss ways to apply other format masks to Oracle date information shortly.

Some Available Date Functions

The date functions available in Oracle can operate on columns of the DATE datatype. The date functions available in Oracle are very useful for executing well-defined operations on DATE data in a table or on constant values. Make sure you understand these functions for the OCP exam. The functions that can be used on DATE columns are as follows, along with their definitions:

- **add_months (x, y)** Returns a date corresponding to date x plus y months.

- **last_day (x)** Returns the date of the last day of the month that contains date x.

- **months_between (x, y)** Returns a number of months between dates x and y. If date x is earlier than y, the result is negative; otherwise, the result is positive. If dates x and y contain the same day of different months, the result is an integer; otherwise, the result is a decimal.

- **new_time (x, y, z)** Returns the current date and time for date x in time zone y as it would be in time zone z.

- **next_day (x)** Identifies the name of the next day from the given date, x.

Let's look at date information and the associated functions in more detail. As mentioned earlier, Oracle stores dates as integers, representing the number of days since the beginning of the Julian calendar. This method enables easy format changes and inherent millennium compliance. The first function is the `add_months ( )` function. This function takes as input a date and a number of months to be added. Oracle then returns the new date, which is the old date plus the number of months:

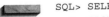

```
SQL> SELECT ADD_MONTHS('15-MAR-00',26)
  2    FROM DUAL;
ADD_MONTHS('15
--------------
   15-MAY-02
```

The next function, `last_day( )`, helps to determine the date for the last day in the month for the date given:

```
SQL> SELECT LAST_DAY('15-MAR-00') FROM DUAL;
LAST_DAY('15-M
--------------
     31-MAR-00
```

The next date function determines the number of months between two different dates. The name of the function is `months_between( )`. The syntax of this command is tricky, so it will be presented here. The syntax of this command is `months_between(x, y)`, and the return value for this function is x-y:

```
SQL> SELECT MONTHS_BETWEEN('26-JUN-99','15-MAR-00') FROM DUAL;
MONTHS_BETWEEN
--------------
     8.6451613
```

TIP

In general, you should try to specify the values passed into `months_between( )`, *such that the first value is larger than the second. If you pass a second value that is greater than the first, a negative number will be returned.*

The last example of a date function is `new_time( )`. It accepts three parameters—the first being a date and time, the second being the time zone the first parameter belongs in, and the last parameter being the time zone you would like to convert to. Each time zone is abbreviated in the following way: *X*ST or *X*DT, where *S* and *D* stands for standard and daylight saving time, respectively, and *X* stands for the first letter of the time zone (for example, *A*tlantic, *B*ering, *C*entral, *E*astern, *H*awaii, *M*ountain, *N*ewfoundland, *P*acific, or *Y*ukon). This function has two exceptions: Greenwich mean time is indicated by GMT, whereas Newfoundland standard time does not use daylight saving. Take a look at the following example:

```
SQL> ALTER SESSION
  2  SET NLS_DATE_FORMAT = 'DD-MON-YYYY HH24:MI:SS';
Session altered.
SQL> SELECT NEW_TIME('15-MAR-1999 14:35:00','AST','GMT')
  2  FROM DUAL;
NEW_TIME('15-MAR-199
--------------------
15-MAR-1999 18:35:00
```

None of the queries used to demonstrate the date functions have required that much precision so far, except for this one. In order to demonstrate the full capability of Oracle in the new_time ( ) function, we altered the format Oracle uses to displays date information, also known as the National Language Set (NLS) date format. The alter session set NLS_DATE_FORMAT command can be used to display the full date and time for the query. The next discussion contains information you may find useful in defining date format masks for NLS_DATE_FORMAT.

Date Arithmetic

Oracle stores date information internally as a number, so you can perform arithmetic on dates as though they were numbers too. You can add numbers to or subtract numbers from a date in order to determine a new date value. For example, if you wanted to determine when an employee's 180-day evaluation should take place based on the employee's hire date, you could issue the following query:

```
SQL> select hiredate + 180 as "Review Date"
  2  from emp
  3  where ename = 'TURNER';
Review Da
---------
07-MAR-82
```

Alternately, you could subtract two dates to find the number of weeks between those days if you wanted to determine how many weeks on the job a particular employee had with the company. The following example shows how:

```
SQL> select ename, (sysdate-hiredate)/7 as "Weeks at Work"
  2  from emp
  3  where ename = 'TURNER';
ENAME       Weeks at Work
----------  -------------
TURNER          4176.485
```

For Review

1. Understand that dates are stored as numbers in Oracle to enable the database to display the date information into multiple formats.

2. Know that the date format is defined by the alter session set nls_date_format command.

3. Be able to identify and use the date functions described in this section to return information about dates. Also know that only the `months_between( )` function returns information in a datatype other than DATE.

Exercises

1. You issue the following query in Oracle:

```
SQL> select sysdate from dual;
SYSDATE
--------------------------------
THURSDAY, MARCH 15 2001 10:35AM
```

Which format mask was used for generating this output?

A. DD, MONTH DAY RRRR HH:MI

B. DAY, MONTH DD YYYY HH:MIAM

C. DAY, MON DD RR HH:MIAM

D. MONTH, DAY DD YYYY HH24:MI

2. You issue the following query in Oracle:

```
SQL> select months_between('15-MAR-83', '15-MAR-97') from dual;
```

What will Oracle return?

A. 14

B. −14

C. 168

D. −168

3. Which command is used for adjusting your date format for the duration of your connection with Oracle (two words)? _____

Answer Key

1. B. This question was a little tricky—we'll cover date format conventions in the next discussion of the chapter. **2.** D. **3.** `alter session`

Conversion Functions

Conversion functions are designed to convert data from one datatype format to another. These functions do not actually modify the stored data in the table itself; they just return the converted values to the SQL*Plus session. Figure 2-1 displays how information can get converted from one datatype to another using various functions. Several different conversion functions are available in the Oracle database, as listed here:

- **to_char(x)** Converts the value x to a character or converts a date to a character string using formatting conventions (see "Date-Formatting Conventions" subtopic below).

- **to_number(x)** Converts nonnumeric value x to a number.

- **to_date(x[,y])** Converts the nondate value x to a date using the format specified by y.

- **to_multi_byte(x)** Converts the single-byte character string x to multibyte characters according to national language standards.

- **to_single_byte(x)** Converts the multibyte character string x to single-byte characters according to national language standards.

- **chartorowid(x)** Converts the string of characters x into an Oracle ROWID.

- **rowidtochar(x)** Converts the ROWID value into the string of characters x of VARCHAR2 datatype.

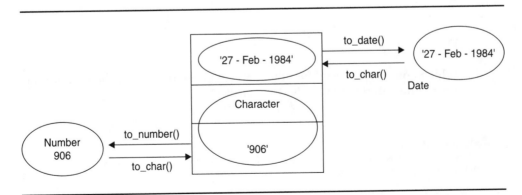

FIGURE 2-1. *Converting data of different types*

- **hextoraw(x)**   Converts the hexadecimal (base-16) value x into a raw (binary) format.

- **rawtohex(x)**   Converts the raw (binary) value x into a hexadecimal (base-16) format.

- **convert(x[,y[,z]])**   Executes a conversion of alphanumeric string x from the current character set (optionally specified as z) to the one specified by y.

- **translate(x,y,z)**   Executes a simple value conversion for character or numeric string x into something else based on the conversion factors y and z.

Date-Formatting Conventions

You can use the to_char( ) function to convert DATE column information into a text string. The format is to_char(column_name, 'date_format_mask'). Some of the most popular format masks available in Oracle include the following:

- **DD**   Shows the two-digit date.

- **DAY**   Shows the day spelled out.

- **MON**   Shows a three-letter month abbreviation, such as MAR for March.

- **MONTH**   Shows the month spelled out.

- **YY**   Shows the two-digit year (not millennium-compliant).

- **YYYY**   Shows the four-digit year (not millennium-compliant).

- **RR**   Shows the two-digit year (millennium-compliant).

- **RRRR**   Shows the four-digit year (millennium-compliant).

- **HH**   Shows the two-digit hour in A.M./P.M. format (must be used with the MIAM mask, explained later).

- **HH24**   Shows the two-digit hour in 24-hour format (cannot be used with the MIAM mask).

- **MI**   Shows the two-digit minute (use with HH24 mask).

- **MIAM**   Shows the two-digit minute in A.M./P.M. format (do not use with the HH24 mask).

- **SS**   Shows the two-digit second.

TIP
Oracle stores hour and minute information as well as the day, month, and year for a DATE column. Therefore, if you want to compare dates, you need to adjust your expectations about what you're actually comparing or else you will often have problems because the times won't match on dates that are otherwise the same. Use the `trunc( )` *function to avoid this problem.*

Demonstrating Single-Row Functions, Continued

This section illustrates the most commonly used procedures for converting data in action. These are the `to_char( )`, `to_number( )`, and `to_date( )` functions. We'll first examine the `to_char( )` function.

In the example of `new_time( )`, the date function described earlier, the `alter session set nls_date_format` statement was used to demonstrate the full capabilities of Oracle in both storing date information and converting dates and times from one time zone to another. That exercise could have been accomplished with the `to_char( )` conversion function as well. Using `to_char( )` in this manner saves you from converting `nls_date_format`, which, once executed, is in effect for the rest of your session, or until you execute another `alter session set nls_date_format` statement. Rather than using this method, you may want to opt for the less permanent option offered by the `to_char( )` function, as shown here:

```
SQL> SELECT TO_CHAR(NEW_TIME(TO_DATE('15-MAR-2000 14:35:00',
  2  'DD-MON-YYYY HH24:MI:SS'),'AST','GMT'))
  3  FROM DUAL;
NEXT_DAY('15-MAR-200
--------------------
15-MAR-2000 18:35:00
```

Note that this example also uses the `to_date( )` function, another conversion function in the list to be discussed. The `to_date( )` function is very useful for converting numbers, and especially character strings, into properly formatted DATE fields.

The next function to consider is `to_number( )`, which converts text or date information into a number:

```
SQL> SELECT TO_NUMBER('49583') FROM DUAL;
TO_NUMBER('49583')
```

```
-----------------
         49583
```

Although not much difference appears to exist between the output of this query and the string that was passed, the main difference is the underlying datatype. Even so, Oracle is intelligent enough to convert a character string consisting of all numbers before performing an arithmetic operation using two values of two different datatypes, as shown in the following code:

```
SQL> SELECT '49583' + 34 FROM DUAL;
'49583'+34
----------
     49617
```

For Review

1. Be sure you can identify the datatype-conversion functions. Also, know which of the functions are most commonly used.

2. Understand the situations where Oracle performs an implicit datatype conversion.

Exercises

1. **You want to use a format mask for date information in Oracle. In which of the following situations is this format mask not appropriate?**

   A. `to_date( )`

   B. `to_char( )`

   C. `alter session set nls_date_format`

   D. `to_number( )`

2. **State the reason why using `to_number( )` to convert a numeric text string into an actual number is unnecessary in the Oracle database (three words):** _____

Answer Key
1. D. 2. Implicit datatype conversion.

Chapter Summary

This chapter adds to your understanding of how to query data in the Oracle database by building on what you learned about `select` statements in Chapter 1. We discussed the use of the comparison clause via the `where` keyword to restrict the data Oracle returns. Then we discussed the use of the `order by` clause to place return data in a specific order based on whatever criteria we want to use. The chapter wrapped up the intermediate coverage of queries by introducing a multitude of single-row functions that you can use to manipulate the data Oracle returns.

Two-Minute Drill

- The `order by` clause in a `select` statement is a useful clause for incorporating a sort order into the output of a file.

- The sort orders that can be used are `ascending` and `descending`, abbreviated as `asc` and `desc`, respectively. The order is determined by the column identified in the `order by` clause. The default is `asc`.

- The `where` clause is used in SQL queries to limit the data returned by a query.

- The `where` clauses contain comparison operations that determine whether a row will be returned by a query.

- The logical comparison operations include =, >, >=, <, <, <=, <>, !=, and ^=.

- In addition to the logical operations, a comparison operation, called `like`, can be used for pattern matching. The % and _ characters are used to designate wildcards.

- The range operation is called `between`.

- The fuzzy logic operation is called `soundex`.

- The `where` clause can contain one or more comparison operations linked together by using `and` or `or` and preceded by `not`.

- SQL functions are broken down into character functions, number functions, and date functions. Be sure you know how to use these functions for the OCP exam.

- Several conversion functions are available for transforming data from text to numeric datatypes and back, numbers to dates and back, text to ROWID and back, and so on.

Fill-in-the-Blank Questions

1. The `order` by clause lists output in this `order` by default:
   _____

2. Finish the sentence: The `where` clause works on the premise of
   _____ one value to another.

3. Two or more `where` clause criteria can be joined together using this
   keyword to force Oracle to return data only if both criteria are met:
   _____

4. This indicates that two values are compared to each other, yielding a TRUE
   or FALSE result: _____

5. This keyword is considered a reverser because it negates the Boolean result
   of the comparison it precedes: _____

Chapter Questions

1. **You are writing `select` statements in a SQL*Plus session against the
   Oracle database. Which of the following statements contains an error?**

   A. `select * from EMP where EMPNO = 493945;`

   B. `select EMPNO from EMP where EMPNO = 493945;`

   C. `select EMPNO from EMP;`

   D. `select EMPNO where EMPNO = 56949 and ENAME =
   'SMITH';`

2. **You are using single-row functions in a `select` statement. Which function
   can best be categorized as similar in function to an `if-then-else`
   statement?**

   A. `sqrt ( )`

   B. `decode ( )`

   C. `new_time ( )`

   D. `rowidtochar ( )`

3. You want to use single-row functions in your SQL statements. Which three of the following are number functions? (Choose three of the four.)

   A. `sinh( )`

   B. `to_number( )`

   C. `sqrt( )`

   D. `round( )`

4. You are using SQL*Plus to retrieve data from an Oracle database. Which of the following is a valid SQL statement?

   A. `select to_char(nvl(sqrt(59483), '0')) from dual;`

   B. `select to_char(nvl(sqrt(59483), 'INVALID')) from dual;`

   C. `select (to_char(nvl(sqrt(59483), '0')) from dual;`

   D. `select to_char(nvl(sqrt(59483), 'TRUE')) from dual;`

5. You want to utilize an `order by` clause in your `select` statement. Which of the following keywords are used in `order by` clauses? (Choose two.)

   A. `abs`

   B. `asc`

   C. `desc`

   D. `disc`

6. You are formulating SQL statements in a SQL*Plus session. Which of the following statements are *not* true about `order by` clauses?

   A. The ascending or descending order can be defined with the `asc` or `desc` keyword.

   B. Only one column can be used to define the sort order in an `order by` clause.

   C. Multiple columns can be used to define sort order in an `order by` clause.

   D. Columns can be represented by numbers indicating their listed order in the `select` clause within `order by`.

7. **The following SQL statement was taken from a SQL*Plus session:**

```
select decode(EMPNO, 58385, 'INACTIVE', 'ACTIVE') empno
from EMP
where substr(ENAME,1,1) > to_number('S')
and EMPNO > 02000
order by EMPNO desc, ENAME asc;
```

Which of the following lines in the `select` statement shown in the previous code block contain an error?

A. `select decode(EMPNO, 58385, 'INACTIVE', 'ACTIVE') empno`

B. `from EMP`

C. `where substr(ENAME,1,1) > to_number('S')`

D. `and EMPNO > 02000`

E. `order by EMPNO desc, ENAME asc;`

F. No errors in this statement

Fill-in-the-Blank Answers

1. ascending

2. Comparing

3. and

4. Boolean

5. not

Answers to Chapter Questions

1. D. select EMPNO where EMPNO = 56949 and ENAME = 'SMITH';

Explanation This statement has no from clause. Although a select statement can be issued without a where clause, no select statement can be executed without a from clause specified. For that reason, the DUAL table exists to satisfy the from clause in situations where you define all the data needed within the statement.

2. B. decode ( )

Explanation The decode ( ) function acts like an if-then-else clause in your SQL statements. Choice A is incorrect because sqrt ( ) produces the square root of a number. Choice C is incorrect because the new_time ( ) function returns a new time based on values specified in the call to that function. Finally, choice D is incorrect because rowidtochar ( ) is a function that converts ROWID information to CHAR information.

3. A, C, and D. sinh ( ), sqrt ( ), and round ( )

Explanation The only nonnumber function in this list is the to_number ( ) function, which is a conversion operation. Several questions of this type appear throughout the OCP exams, and for these types of questions you must choose multiple answers.

4. A. select to_char(nvl(sqrt(59483), '0')) from dual;

Explanation Functions such as these can be used in conjunction with one another. Although usually the datatype of the value inserted if the column value is NULL and the column specified for `nvl ( )` must match, Oracle performs many datatype conversions implicitly, such as this one.

5. B and C. `asc` and `desc`

Explanation   Information returned from Oracle in a query that uses the `order by` clause can be returned either in ascending or descending order, as indicated by the keywords in choices B and C. The `abs ( )` function is the absolute value function, which eliminates choice A. The `disc ( )` function is not an actual option either, thus eliminating choice D.

6. B. Only one column can be used to define the sort order in an `order by` clause.

Explanation   Notice, first, that a logical difference exists between choices B and C, meaning you can eliminate one of them on principle. Multiple columns can be used to define order in `order by` statements, thereby eliminating choice C automatically. Choice A is incorrect because you can use `asc` or `desc` to specify ascending or descending order in your `order by` clause. Finally, choice D is incorrect because you can use numbers to represent the column you want to place an order on, based on how the columns are listed in the `select` statement.

7. C. `where substr(ENAME,1,1) > to_number('S')`

Explanation   Characters that are alphabetic, such as *S*, cannot be converted into numbers. When this statement is run, it will produce an error on this line. The other lines in this query are correct as composed.

CHAPTER
3

Advanced Data
Selection in Oracle

n this chapter, you will learn about and demonstrate knowledge in the following areas:

- Displaying data from multiple tables
- Group functions and their uses

This chapter will take you to a fairly sophisticated level of understanding how to query data in Oracle. First, we will cover how you can write `select` statements to access data from more than one table. You will also learn how to create joins that display data from different tables even when the information in the two tables does not correspond completely. The chapter discusses how to create and use table self-joins as well. After discussing table joins, the chapter introduces the `group by` clause used in `select` statements and group functions. This clause allows you to treat entire columns of data as a single unit for operation.

The material in this chapter comprises 18 percent of OCP Exam 1.

NOTE
Like Chapters 1 and 2, this chapter also uses the standard demo tables created by `utlsampl.sql` or `demobld.sql`. However, this chapter also uses trivial and not-so-trivial examples from other tables. For nontrivial examples, I've included commands that will create and populate the table used. Because it's so important that you practice your use of Oracle as much as possible for OCP, I don't provide scripts to automatically generate the objects for you.

Displaying Data from Multiple Tables

This section will cover the following areas related to displaying data from multiple tables:

- Using `select` statements to join data from more than one table
- Creating outer joins
- Joining a table to itself

The typical database contains many tables. Some smaller databases may have only a dozen or so tables, whereas other databases may have hundreds or even thousands. The common factor, however, is that few databases have just one table containing everything you need. Therefore, you usually have to draw data from multiple tables together in a meaningful way. To show data from multiple tables in one query, Oracle allows you to perform *table joins*. Here are the two rules you need to remember for table joins. Data from two (or more) tables can be joined, if the same column (under the same or a different name) appears in *both* tables, and the column is the primary key (or part of that key) in *one* of the tables.

TIP
At least one column must be shared between two tables for you to join the two tables in a `select` *statement, and that column must be a primary key (or part of the key) in at least one of the tables.*

The Keys to Table Joins

Having a common column in two tables implies a relationship between the two tables. The nature of that relationship is determined by which table uses the column as a primary key. This begs the question, what is a primary key? A *primary key* is a column in a table used for identifying the uniqueness of each row in a table. The table in which the column appears as a primary key is referred to as the *parent table* in this relationship (sometimes also called the *master table*), whereas the column that references the other table in the relationship is often called the *child table* (sometimes also called the *detail table*). The common column appearing in the child table is referred to as a *foreign key*. Figure 3-1 demonstrates how the relationship may work in a database.

`select` Statements That Join Data from More Than One Table

Recall from Chapters 1 and 2 that a `select` statement can have three parts: the `select` clause, the `from` clause, and the `where` clause. That final clause, the `where` clause, contains comparison operators that filter out the unwanted data from what you want to see. To join data from one table to another, you must compare the data in the common column from one table to that same column in the other table in the `where` clause.

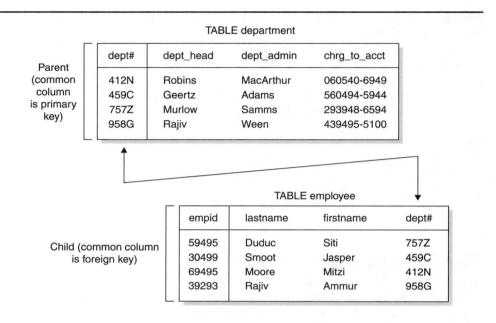

FIGURE 3-1. *Parent and child tables*

Oracle Join Syntax

Let's look at an example of a join statement using the Oracle traditional syntax, where we join the contents of the EMP and DEPT tables together to obtain a listing of all employees, along with the names of the departments they work for:

```
SQL> select e.ename, e.deptno, d.dname
  2  from emp e, dept d
  3  where e.deptno = d.deptno;
ENAME         DEPTNO DNAME
---------- --------- --------------
SMITH            20 RESEARCH
ALLEN            30 SALES
WARD             30 SALES
JONES            20 RESEARCH
MARTIN           30 SALES
BLAKE            30 SALES
CLARK            10 ACCOUNTING
SCOTT            20 RESEARCH
KING             10 ACCOUNTING
```

```
TURNER              30 SALES
ADAMS               20 RESEARCH
JAMES               30 SALES
FORD                20 RESEARCH
MILLER              10 ACCOUNTING
```

Note the many important components in this table join. Listing two tables in the `from` clause clearly indicates that a table join is taking place. Note also that each table name is followed by a letter: E for EMP or D for DEPT. This demonstrates an interesting concept—just as columns can have aliases, so too can tables. The aliases serve an important purpose—they prevent Oracle from getting confused about which table to use when listing the data in the DEPTNO column. Remember, EMP and DEPT both have a column named DEPTNO. Look what happens when we don't use aliases:

```
SQL> select ename, deptno, dname
  2  from emp, dept
  3  where deptno = deptno;
where deptno = deptno
              *
ERROR at line 3:
ORA-00918: column ambiguously defined
```

You can also avoid ambiguity in table joins by prefixing references to the columns with the table names, but this often requires extra coding. You can also give the column two different names, but then you might forget that the relationship exists between the two tables. It's just better to use aliases! Notice something else, though. Neither the alias nor the full table name needs to be specified for columns appearing in only one table. Take a look at another example:

```
SQL> select ename, emp.deptno, dname
  2  from emp, dept
  3  where emp.deptno = dept.deptno;
ENAME           DEPTNO DNAME
---------- --------- --------------
SMITH               20 RESEARCH
ALLEN               30 SALES
WARD                30 SALES
JONES               20 RESEARCH
MARTIN              30 SALES
BLAKE               30 SALES
CLARK               10 ACCOUNTING
SCOTT               20 RESEARCH
KING                10 ACCOUNTING
TURNER              30 SALES
```

```
ADAMS            20 RESEARCH
JAMES            30 SALES
FORD             20 RESEARCH
MILLER           10 ACCOUNTING
```

Cartesian Products

Notice also that our `where` clause includes a comparison on DEPTNO linking data in EMP to that of DEPT. Without this link, the output would have included all data from EMP and DEPT, jumbled together in a mess called a *Cartesian product*. Cartesian products are big, meaningless listings of output that are nearly never what you want. They are formed when you omit a join condition in your SQL statement, which causes Oracle to join all rows in the first table to all rows in the second table. Let's look at a simple example in which we attempt to join two tables, each with three rows, using a `select` statement with no `where` clause, resulting in output with nine rows:

```
SQL> select a.col1, b.col_2
  2  from example_1 a, example_2 b;
     COL1 COL_2
--------- ---------------------------
        1 one
        2 one
        3 one
        1 two
        2 two
        3 two
        1 three
        2 three
        3 three
```

TIP
This table isn't created by `utlsampl.sql` *or* `demobld.sql`. *It's a trivial example, so unless you want to get some experience creating and populating tables, don't bother trying to execute the query on Oracle. If you want some experience on your own database, run the* `select` *statement on EMP and DEPT from the previous example, but leave off the* `where` *clause.*

You must always remember to include join conditions in join queries to avoid Cartesian products. But take note of another important fact. Although you learned in Chapter 2 that `where` clauses can contain comparison operations other than equality, to avoid Cartesian products, *you must always use equality operations in a comparison joining data from two tables.* If you want to use another comparison operation, you must first join the information using an equality comparison and then perform the other comparison somewhere else in the `where` clause. This is why table join operations are also sometimes referred to as *equijoins.* Take a look at the following example that shows proper construction of a table join, where the information being joined is compared further using a nonequality operation to eliminate the employees from accounting:

```
SQL> select ename, emp.deptno, dname
  2   from emp, dept
  3   where emp.deptno = dept.deptno
  4   and dept.deptno > 10;
ENAME          DEPTNO DNAME
---------- --------- --------------
SMITH              20 RESEARCH
ALLEN              30 SALES
WARD               30 SALES
JONES              20 RESEARCH
MARTIN             30 SALES
BLAKE              30 SALES
SCOTT              20 RESEARCH
TURNER             30 SALES
ADAMS              20 RESEARCH
JAMES              30 SALES
FORD               20 RESEARCH
```

ANSI/ISO Join Syntax

 In Oracle9i, Oracle introduces strengthened support for ANSI/ISO join syntax. To join the contents of two tables together in a single result according to that syntax, we must include a `join tablename on join_condition` in our SQL statement. If we wanted to perform the same table join as before using this new syntax, our SQL statement would look like the following:

```
SQL> select ename, emp.deptno, dname
  2   from emp join dept
  3   on emp.deptno = dept.deptno;
ENAME          DEPTNO DNAME
---------- --------- --------------
SMITH              20 RESEARCH
ALLEN              30 SALES
WARD               30 SALES
JONES              20 RESEARCH
```

```
MARTIN          30 SALES
BLAKE           30 SALES
CLARK           10 ACCOUNTING
SCOTT           20 RESEARCH
KING            10 ACCOUNTING
TURNER          30 SALES
ADAMS           20 RESEARCH
JAMES           30 SALES
FORD            20 RESEARCH
MILLER          10 ACCOUNTING
```

Note how different this is from Oracle syntax. First, ANSI/ISO syntax separates join comparisons from all other comparisons by using a special keyword, on, to indicate what the join comparison is. You can still include a where clause in your ANSI/ISO-compliant join query, the only difference is that the where clause will contain only those additional conditions you want to use for filtering your data. You also do not list all your tables being queried in one from clause. Instead, you use the join clause directly after the from clause to identify the table being joined.

TIP
Never combine Oracle's join syntax with ANSI/ISO's join syntax! Also, there are no performance differences between Oracle join syntax and ANSI/ISO join syntax.

How Many Comparisons Do You Need?

When using Oracle syntax for table joins, a query on data from more than two tables must contain the right number of equality operations to avoid a Cartesian product. To avoid confusion, use this simple rule: If the number of tables to be joined equals *N*, include at least *N–1* equality conditions in the select statement so that each common column is referenced at least once. Similarly, if you are using the ANSI/ISO syntax for table joins, you need to use *N–1* join tablename on join_condition clauses for every *N* tables being joined.

TIP
For N joined tables using Oracle or ANSI/ISO syntax for table joins, you need at least N–1 equijoin conditions in the where clause of your select statement or N–1 join tablename on join_condition clauses in order to avoid a Cartesian product, respectively.

Natural Joins

One additional type of join you need to know about for OCP is the natural join. A natural join is a join between two tables where Oracle joins the tables according to the column(s) in the two tables sharing the same name (naturally!). Natural joins are executed whenever the `natural` keyword is present. Let's look at an example. Recall our use of the EMP and DEPT tables from our discussion above. Let's take a quick look at the column listings for both tables:

```
SQL> describe emp
Name                             Null?      Type
-------------------------------  ---------  ------------
EMPNO                            NOT NULL   NUMBER(4)
ENAME                                       VARCHAR2(10)
JOB                                         VARCHAR2(9)
MGR                                         NUMBER(4)
HIREDATE                                    DATE
SAL                                         NUMBER(7,2)
COMM                                        NUMBER(7,2)
DEPTNO                                      NUMBER(2)
SQL> describe dept
Name                             Null?      Type
-------------------------------  ---------  ------------
DEPTNO                           NOT NULL   NUMBER(2)
DNAME                                       VARCHAR2(14)
LOC                                         VARCHAR2(13)
```

As you can see, DEPTNO is the only column in common between these two tables, and appropriately enough, it has the same name in both tables. This combination of facts makes our join query of EMP and DEPT tables a perfect candidate for a natural join. Take a look and see:

```
SQL> select ename, deptno, dname
  2  from emp natural join dept;
ENAME          DEPTNO DNAME
----------     ------- --------------
SMITH              20 RESEARCH
ALLEN              30 SALES
WARD               30 SALES
JONES              20 RESEARCH
MARTIN             30 SALES
BLAKE              30 SALES
CLARK              10 ACCOUNTING
SCOTT              20 RESEARCH
KING               10 ACCOUNTING
TURNER             30 SALES
```

```
ADAMS            20 RESEARCH
JAMES            30 SALES
FORD             20 RESEARCH
MILLER           10 ACCOUNTING
```

We can see that natural joins allow you to greatly simplify your join queries by eliminating table aliases and join comparisons. This is because Oracle assumes the column with the same name in both tables is the one to use for the join comparison. If multiple columns in the tables have the same name, Oracle incorporates join comparisons for all the common columns. We can see where natural joins can aid greatly in consolidating the contents of a `where` clause in your queries to include only filter criteria. Let's look at an example:

```
SQL> select ename, deptno, dname
  2  from emp natural join dept
  3  where dept.loc = 'NEW YORK';
ENAME           DEPTNO DNAME
---------- --------- --------------
CLARK           10 ACCOUNTING
KING            10 ACCOUNTING
MILLER          10 ACCOUNTING
```

Cartesian Products: An ANSI/ISO Perspective

In some cases, you might actually want to retrieve a Cartesian product, particularly in financial applications where you have a table of numbers that needs to be cross-multiplied with another table of numbers for statistical analysis purposes. ANSI/ISO makes a provision in its syntax for producing Cartesian products through the use of a *cross-join*. A cross-join is produced when you use the `cross` keyword in your ANSI/ISO-compliant join query. Recall from a previous example that we produced a Cartesian product by omitting the `where` clause when joining two sample tables, each containing three rows, to produce nine rows of output. We can produce this same result in ANSI/ISO SQL by using the `cross` keyword, as shown here in bold:

```
SQL> select col1, col_2
  2  from example_1 cross join example_2;
     COL1 COL_2
-------- ----------------------------
       1 one
       2 one
       3 one
       1 two
       2 two
       3 two
       1 three
```

```
2 three
3 three
```

For Review

1. A *table join* is a type of query that obtains data from two or more tables based on common information in both tables.

2. In order to join data from two tables, you must have a common column in both tables, and that column must be a primary key in *one* of the tables.

3. You must use equality comparisons in the `where` clause joining data between two tables. Nonequality comparisons usually result in Cartesian products.

4. To know how many comparisons to include in a join statement, remember this formula: For *N* tables, use *N–1* equality comparisons.

5. Be sure you know what natural joins and cross-joins are for OCP.

Exercises

1. **Two tables, PRODUCT and STORAGE_BOX, exist in a database. Individual products are listed in the table by unique ID number, product name, and the box a particular product is stored in. Individual storage boxes (identified by number) listed in the other table can contain many products, but each box can be found in only one location. Which of the following statements will correctly display the product ID, name, and box location of all widgets in this database?**

   A. `select p.prod_id, p.prod_name, b.box_loc from product p, storage_box b where p.prod_id = b.prod_id and prod_name = 'WIDGET';`

   B. `select p.prod_id, p.prod_name, b.box_loc from product p, storage_box b where prod_name = 'WIDGET';`

   C. `select p.prod_id, p.prod_name, b.box_loc from product p, storage_box b where p.stor_box_num = b.stor_box_num and p.prod_name = 'WIDGET';`

   D. `select prod_id, prod_name, box_loc from product, storage_box where stor_box_num = stor_box_num and prod_name = 'WIDGET';`

2. You want to join information from three tables as part of developing a report. The tables are EMP, DEPT, and SALGRADE. Only records corresponding to employee, department location, and salary range are required for employees in grades 10 and higher for the organization. How many comparison operations are required for this query?

   A. Two

   B. Three

   C. Four

   D. Five

3. You wish to join the contents of two tables, PRODUCT and STORAGE, to list the location of all boxes. PRODUCT has three columns, ID, NAME, and BOX#. STORAGE has two columns, BOX# and LOC. Which of the following choices will not give the desired result?

   A. `select product.id, product.name, storage.loc from product, storage where product.box# = storage.box#;`

   B. `select product.id, product.name, storage.loc from product join storage on product.box# = storage.box#;`

   C. `select product.id, product.name, storage.loc from product natural join storage on product.box# = storage.box#;`

   D. `select product.id, product.name, storage.loc from product natural join storage;`

4. What is the name of the result when a join statement lacks a where clause (two words)? _____. What ANSI/ISO keywords can be used to obtain this type of result? _____.

Answer Key

1. C. 2. B. Remember, you must include two equality comparisons to form the join properly, plus an additional filtering comparison to get only records where salary grade is greater than 10. 3. C. 4. Cartesian product, `cross-join`

Creating Outer Joins

Outer joins extend the capacity of Oracle queries to include handling of situations where you want to see information from tables even when no corresponding records exist in the common column. You can see a graphical representation of outer joins in Figure 3-2. For the purposes of this demonstration, let's issue the following statement in our SQL*Plus session:

```
SQL> update emp set deptno = NULL where ename = 'KING';
1 row updated.
```

TIP
We'll talk more about update *statements in Chapter 6.*

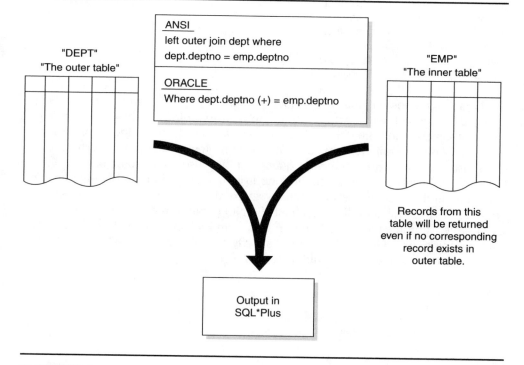

FIGURE 3-2. *Outer joins*

In effect, we're telling Oracle that because KING is the company president, he is no longer reporting to his old department number. Now look at what happens when we try to join the EMP table to the DEPT table using the common DEPTNO column:

```
SQL> select e.ename, e.deptno, d.dname
  2  from dept d, emp e
  3  where d.deptno = e.deptno;
ENAME          DEPTNO DNAME
---------- --------- --------------
SMITH              20 RESEARCH
ALLEN              30 SALES
WARD               30 SALES
JONES              20 RESEARCH
MARTIN             30 SALES
BLAKE              30 SALES
CLARK              10 ACCOUNTING
SCOTT              20 RESEARCH
TURNER             30 SALES
ADAMS              20 RESEARCH
JAMES              30 SALES
FORD               20 RESEARCH
MILLER             10 ACCOUNTING
```

Notice someone missing? KING does not appear in the output because he isn't assigned to a department anymore. When no corresponding information exists in the common column from either table, the join statement ignores the record from that table. An outer join query would solve this problem. Outer joins return rows that satisfy the join condition in your query, but they also return some or all rows from one of the tables, even when the rows from that table don't satisfy the join condition. In this case, we want Oracle to return KING's record even though KING doesn't satisfy the join condition on the DEPTNO column shared by the EMP and DEPT tables. To force the query to return data from EMP even when there is no corresponding record in DEPT, you must specify an *outer join* operation. Let's look at how such a join operation would be written:

```
SQL> select e.ename, e.deptno, d.dname
  2  from dept d, emp e
  3  where d.deptno (+) = e.deptno;
ENAME          DEPTNO DNAME
---------- --------- --------------
SMITH              20 RESEARCH
ALLEN              30 SALES
WARD               30 SALES
JONES              20 RESEARCH
```

```
MARTIN              30 SALES
BLAKE               30 SALES
CLARK               10 ACCOUNTING
SCOTT               20 RESEARCH
KING
TURNER              30 SALES
ADAMS               20 RESEARCH
JAMES               30 SALES
FORD                20 RESEARCH
MILLER              10 ACCOUNTING
```

By using outer join statements, we can get KING listed in the result, even though he is outside the join criteria specified by the query. Notice the use of the (+) marker (in bold) after the reference to the DEPTNO column in the DEPT table; this is called the *outer join operator*. This marker denotes which table can have NULL data corresponding to non-NULL values in the column values from the other table. The outer join marker is on the side of the DEPT table, meaning that data in the EMP table can correspond either to values in DEPT or to NULL if there is no corresponding value in the DEPT table. Had the order been reversed, such that the outer join operator appears next to the column reference in EMP, then values from DEPT with or without corresponding values in EMP would have been listed. Take a look at the following code block to see what I mean:

```
SQL> select e.ename, e.deptno, d.dname
  2  from dept d, emp e
  3 where d.deptno = e.deptno (+);
ENAME            DEPTNO DNAME
---------- --------- --------------
MILLER              10 ACCOUNTING
CLARK               10 ACCOUNTING
SMITH               20 RESEARCH
SCOTT               20 RESEARCH
ADAMS               20 RESEARCH
FORD                20 RESEARCH
JONES               20 RESEARCH
ALLEN               30 SALES
JAMES               30 SALES
TURNER              30 SALES
BLAKE               30 SALES
MARTIN              30 SALES
WARD                30 SALES
                       OPERATIONS
```

TIP
Be careful where you place the (+) symbol for outer joins—if it appears next to the column reference for the wrong table in the join comparison, your result set will contain unexpected data.

ANSI/ISO Syntax for Outer Joins

| Oracle**9i** |
| and higher |

Oracle9i extends its compliance with ANSI/ISO by supporting that standard's requirements for outer join syntax and semantics. As with the syntax for standard join operations, the syntax for outer joins in ANSI/ISO seeks to separate the join conditions from the rest of the comparison operations in the where clause of your SQL query. Let's take another look at the query from earlier, where we managed to include KING's record in the output even though he wasn't assigned to a department. For reference, both versions of the query are shown below:

```
SQL> -- earlier version with outer join operator
SQL> -- select e.ename, e.deptno, d.dname
SQL> -- from dept d, emp e
SQL> -- where d.deptno (+) = e.deptno;
SQL>
SQL> -- ANSI/ISO version
SQL> select e.ename, e.deptno, d.dname
  2  from emp e left outer join dept d
  3  on d.deptno = e.deptno;
ENAME          DEPTNO DNAME
---------- --------- --------------
MILLER             10 ACCOUNTING
CLARK              10 ACCOUNTING
FORD               20 RESEARCH
ADAMS              20 RESEARCH
SCOTT              20 RESEARCH
JONES              20 RESEARCH
SMITH              20 RESEARCH
JAMES              30 SALES
TURNER             30 SALES
BLAKE              30 SALES
MARTIN             30 SALES
WARD               30 SALES
ALLEN              30 SALES
KING
```

Let's look at the code shown in bold above in more detail. We can see that the keywords left outer precede the join keyword to signify this is an outer join. Thus, we can see how ANSI/ISO introduces the convention of bidirectionality in outer joins. Earlier, we placed the (+) symbol next to D.DEPTNO on the left side of the join comparison. This signifies to Oracle that records from EMP could be returned even if there were no corresponding record in DEPT. ANSI/ISO replaces the outer join operator with the `left outer join` *tablename* clause. We specify DEPT as the table name in this clause in the same way that we placed the outer join symbol next to D.DEPTNO referenced in the join comparison.

But what if we want to return records from DEPT even if there are no corresponding records in EMP? We can also specify a right join that produces results similar to another earlier query, where we moved the outer join operator to the other side. For reference, both versions of the query are shown below:

```
SQL> -- Earlier version of outer join
SQL> -- select e.ename, e.deptno, d.dname
SQL> -- from dept d, emp e
SQL> -- where d.deptno = e.deptno (+);
SQL>
SQL> -- ANSI/ISO version
SQL> select e.ename, e.deptno, d.dname
SQL> from emp e right outer join dept d
SQL> on d.deptno = e.deptno;
ENAME           DEPTNO DNAME
---------- --------- --------------
SMITH           20 RESEARCH
ALLEN           30 SALES
WARD            30 SALES
JONES           20 RESEARCH
MARTIN          30 SALES
BLAKE           30 SALES
CLARK           10 ACCOUNTING
SCOTT           20 RESEARCH
TURNER          30 SALES
ADAMS           20 RESEARCH
FORD            20 RESEARCH
MILLER          10 ACCOUNTING
JAMES           30 SALES
                   OPERATIONS
```

As you can see above, the right outer join allows us to alter the returned data without making too many drastic changes. We simply substitute the keyword `right` for `left`, and Oracle handles the rest.

TIP
There is no default outer join option. If you omit the left *or* right *keywords from the* outer join *clause, then Oracle returns an error saying the SQL command was not properly ended. You must identify to Oracle whether the outer join is a left join or a right join.*

Full Outer Joins

Oracle**9i**
and higher
Oracle9i also makes it possible for you to easily execute a full outer join, including all records from the tables that would have been displayed if you had used both the left outer join or right outer join clauses. Let's take a look at an example:

```
SQL> select e.ename, e.deptno, d.dname
  2 from emp e full outer join dept d
  3 on d.deptno = e.deptno;
ENAME          DEPTNO DNAME
---------- --------- --------------
MILLER             10 ACCOUNTING
CLARK              10 ACCOUNTING
FORD               20 RESEARCH
ADAMS              20 RESEARCH
SCOTT              20 RESEARCH
JONES              20 RESEARCH
SMITH              20 RESEARCH
JAMES              30 SALES
TURNER             30 SALES
BLAKE              30 SALES
MARTIN             30 SALES
WARD               30 SALES
ALLEN              30 SALES
KING
                      OPERATIONS
```

TIP
Never combine the Oracle outer join syntax with the ANSI/ISO join syntax!

Concluding This Lesson

Because we have made a change to KING's record in the EMP table for our sample data, we want to discard those changes using the following command:

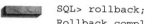

```
SQL> rollback;
Rollback complete.
```

TIP

You'll learn more about the `rollback` *command in Chapter 6.*

For Quick Reference

For quick reference, Table 3-1 shows a listing of outer join where clauses using Oracle syntax and the ANSI/ISO equivalents using fictitious tables A and B.

For Review

1. Understand that an outer join accommodates the situation in which you want to display data in a join statement where records from one table don't necessarily all have corresponding records in the other.

2. (+) is the special character used to denote outer joins, however, remember that it's an Oracle convention. Remember the importance of where you

---

Oracle Outer Join Syntax	ANSI/ISO Equivalent
`from tab_a a, tab_b b` `where a.col_1 (+) = b.col_1`	`from tab_a a left outer join` `tab_b b on a.col_1 = b.col_1`

`from tab_a a, tab_b b`
`where a.col_1 = b.col_1 (+)`
	`from tab_a a right outer`
	`join tab_b b on a.col_1 =`
	`b.col_1`

`from tab_a a, tab_b b`
`where a.col_1 (+) = b.col_1`
`and b.col_2 = 'VALUE'`
	`from tab_a a left outer join`
	`tab_b b on a.col_1 = b.col_1`
	`and b.col_2 = 'VALUE'`

TABLE 3-1. *Oracle Outer Join Syntax and ANSI/ISO Equivalent*

place the outer join operator—it tells Oracle which table in the join can have NULL records corresponding to values from the other table.

3. Oracle's adopting ANSI/ISO conventions for join operations, using the clauses [left|right] outer join *tablename* on *join_condition*, where *tablename* is the name of the table being joined and *join_condition* is the comparison used to join the data.

4. Oracle9i introduces the possibility of executing a full outer join to include records from both tables that would be returned by combining results from left and right outer joins. To do so, use the clause full outer join *tablename* on *join_condition*.

Exercises

1. Identify the Oracle syntax symbol used for outer join operations: _____. Identify the equivalent ANSI/ISO outer join clause: _____.

2. You are defining an outer join statement. Which of the following choices is true concerning outer join statements?

   A. Because outer join operations permit NULL values from one of the tables, you do not have to specify equality comparisons to join those tables.

   B. In outer join statements on tables A and B, you specify the right outer join when you want all of table A's rows, even when no corresponding record exists in table B.

   C. In outer join statements on tables A and B, you specify the left outer join when you want all of table B's rows, even when no corresponding record exists in table A.

   D. Even though outer join operations permit NULL values from one of the tables, you still need to specify equality comparisons to join those tables.

3. Two tables, PRODUCT and STORAGE_BOX, exist in a database. Individual products are listed in the table by unique ID number, product name, and the box a particular product is stored in. Individual storage boxes (identified by number) listed in the other table can contain many products, but the box can be found in only one location. Which of the following statements will correctly display the product ID, name, and box location of all widgets in this database that have or have not been assigned to a storage box?

A. select p.prod_id, p.prod_name, b.box_loc from product p left outer join storage_box b on p.stor_box_num = b.stor_box_num where p.prod_name = 'WIDGET' (+);

B. select p.prod_id, p.prod_name, b.box_loc from product p left outer join storage_box b on p.stor_box_num = b.stor_box_num where p.prod_name = 'WIDGET';

C. select p.prod_id, p.prod_name, b.box_loc from product p right outer join storage_box b where b.stor_box_num = p.stor_box_num (+) and p.prod_name = 'WIDGET';

D. select p.prod_id, p.prod_name, b.box_loc from product p full outer join storage_box b on p.stor_box_num = b.stor_box_num where b.stor_box_num is NULL;

4. You issue the following command in Oracle:

```
SQL> select e.ename, a.street_address, a.city, a.state, a.post_code
  2  from emp e, addr a
  3  where e.empno = a.empno (+)
  4  and a.state = 'TEXAS';
```

Which of the following choices shows the ANSI/ISO equivalent statement?

A. select e.ename, a.street_address, a.city, a.state, a.post_code from emp e outer join addr a on e.empno = a.empno where a.state = 'TEXAS';

B. select e.ename, a.street_address, a.city, a.state, a.post_code from emp e left outer join addr a on e.empno = a.empno and a.state = 'TEXAS';

C. select e.ename, a.street_address, a.city, a.state, a.post_code from emp e right outer join addr a on e.empno = a.empno and a.state = 'TEXAS';

D. select e.ename, a.street_address, a.city, a.state, a.post_code from emp e right outer join addr a where e.empno = a.empno (+) and a.state = 'TEXAS';

5. **Examine the following output from SQL*Plus:**

```
PRODUCT.ID  PRODUCT.NAME  BOX.LOCATION
----------  ------------  ------------
578-X       WIDGET        IDAHO
                          TENNESSEE
456-Y       WIDGET
```

Which of the following choices identify the type of query that likely produced this result?

A. Full outer join

B. Left outer join

C. Right outer join

D. Equijoin

Answer Key
1. (+), [left|right] outer join tablename on join_condition **2.** D. **3.** B. **4.** C. **5.** A.

Joining a Table to Itself

In special situations, it may be necessary for you to perform a join using only one table. What you are really doing is using two copies of the table to join the data in the table to itself. This SQL programming technique is known as a table *self-join*. This task can be useful in cases where there is a possibility that some slight difference exists between two rows that would otherwise be duplicate records. If you want to perform a self-join on a table, use table aliases to specify the same table so that Oracle understands that a self-join is being performed. This lesson illustrates proper use of a self-join to show how to employ the technique properly. To follow along in your Oracle database, issue the following command:

```
SQL> insert into emp values (7903, 'FORD', 'ANALYST', '7566',
  2  '03-DEC-81', 3000, null, 10);
1 row created.
```

TIP
You'll see more examples of using the insert *command in Chapter 6.*

In this case, we've added a new record to table EMP for employee FORD, who is already an employee of the company. Everything about this user is the same, except for her employee number. Once we realize our mistake, we can issue the following simple query to obtain the duplicate records:

```
SQL> select * from emp where ename = 'FORD';
EMPNO ENAME      JOB  MGR HIREDATE   SAL COMM DEPTNO
----- ----- ------- ---- --------- ---- ---- ------
 7902 FORD  ANALYST 7566 03-DEC-81 3000        20
 7903 FORD  ANALYST 7566 03-DEC-81 3000        20
```

This simple query works fine for this uncomplicated example, but let's make it more complex. Let's pretend that the EMP table stores values for a company with hundreds of employees named FORD, each working in different jobs and under different managers. In this case, we might use the following query to guarantee that the instances of FORD we get are the ones we want:

```
SQL> select e.empno, e.ename, e.job
  2  from emp e, emp e2
  3  where e.empno <> e2.empno
  4  and e.ename = e2.ename
  5  and e.job = e2.job
  6  and e.mgr = e2.mgr;
    EMPNO ENAME        JOB         MGR
--------- ---------- --------- ----
     7903 FORD         ANALYST     7566
     7902 FORD         ANALYST     7566
```

This query says, "OK, Oracle, give me the records for users named FORD who have different employee numbers, but filter out the FORDs working in different jobs for different managers." As you can see, self-joins can be useful for obtaining nearly duplicate records in the event some error occurs. Situations where this might be useful include the following:

- Batch jobs that incorrectly load lots of duplicate records
- Situations where users enter nearly duplicate records by mistake
- Any instance where a record nearly identical to a record already in the table may have been entered

Some Self-Join Caveats

Here's a final note of caution. Although powerful and useful for identifying duplicate records, self-joins should be run with extreme caution because of two important factors. First, self-joins often take a long time to process and can cause performance issues for other users on the database. This is because Oracle must read all table data twice sequentially. Second, because the required number of equality operations is at least *two* in the situation of self-joins (one to join the table to itself and the other to distinguish the duplication), Cartesian products can result when you don't formulate your where clause properly. Without a proper comparison operation set up in the where clause, you may wind up with many copies of every row in the table returned, which will certainly run for a long time and produce a lot of unnecessary output.

TIP
The number of equality operations usually needed in the where clause of a self-join of a table to itself should be two or more—one to join the table to itself and the other to distinguish the duplicates.

In Conclusion

To wrap up this lesson, let's once again make sure that the changes we made to the demo tables are not saved. To do this, issue the following command:

```
SQL> rollback;
Rollback complete.
```

TIP
Once again, you'll learn more about the rollback command in Chapter 6.

For Review

1. Know what a self-join is and how one is formulated and used.

2. When using a self-join, remember that you need enough comparison operations in the where clause to join the table to itself and distinguish the duplicate records.

3. Understand the slow performance and Cartesian product issues that may arise from the use of self-joins.

Exercises

1. **A multinational Fortune 500 company uses internal testing to determine employee promotability and job placement. Tests are offered at multiple locations. Employees are permitted to take tests for any job they want to apply for, with one restriction: An employee may take a specific exam for a corresponding job position only once per year. Recently, Human Resources discovered that some employees were circumventing this restriction by taking the same exam in different test locations. Which of the following queries might be useful in identifying employees who have circumvented this restriction?**

   A.
   ```
   select a.ename, a.test_name, a.test_date,
   a.location b.test_date, b.location from tests a,
   tests b where a.ename = b.ename and a.test_name =
   b.test_name and a.location = b.location and
   trunc(a.test_date) > trunc(sysdate-365) and
   trunc(b.test_date) > trunc(sysdate-365);
   ```

   B.
   ```
   select a.ename, a.test_name, a.test_date,
   a.location b.test_date, b.location from tests a,
   tests b where a.ename <> b.ename and a.test_name =
   b.test_name and a.location = b.location and
   trunc(a.test_date) > trunc(sysdate-365) and
   trunc(b.test_date) > trunc(sysdate-365);
   ```

   C.
   ```
   select a.ename, a.test_name, a.test_date,
   a.location b.test_date, b.location from tests a,
   tests b where a.ename = b.ename and a.test_name <>
   b.test_name and a.location = b.location and
   trunc(a.test_date) > trunc(sysdate-365) and
   trunc(b.test_date) > trunc(sysdate-365);
   ```

   D.
   ```
   select a.ename, a.test_name, a.test_date,
   a.location b.test_date, b.location from tests a,
   tests b where a.ename = b.ename and a.test_name =
   b.test_name and a.location <> b.location and
   a.test_date > trunc(sysdate-365) and b.test_date >
   trunc(sysdate-365);
   ```

2. **Identify a general concern related to the use of self-joins on the Oracle database:** _____

3. **Identify a problem with self-joins resulting from malformed where clauses (two words):** _____

Answer Key
1. D. 2. Performance. 3. Cartesian products.

Group Functions and Their Uses

This section will cover the following topics related to group functions and their uses:

- Identifying and using group functions

- Using the group by clause

- Excluding group data with the having clause

Group functions allow you to perform data operations on several values in a column of data as though the column were one collective group of data. These functions are also called *group-by functions* because they are often used in a special clause of select statements, called the group by clause. A more complete discussion of the group by clause appears later in this section. This discussion also describes how to use the having clause in group by clauses, which can act as a where clause within a where clause.

Identifying and Using Group Functions

Sometimes, you may want to treat the data in a column as if it were a list of items to be manipulated as a group. Think about the contents of the EMP table. Let's say you want to obtain the average salary for employees in the company. The formula for averaging numbers is to add all the numbers in the list together and then divide by the number of elements in that list. Group functions are useful for this sort of activity because, unlike single-row functions, group functions can operate on column data in several rows at a time. Here's a list of the available group functions:

- **avg(x)**   Averages all *x* column values returned by the select statement

- **count(x)**   Counts the number of non-NULL values returned by the select statement for column *x*

- **max(x)**   Determines the maximum value in column *x* for all rows returned by the select statement

- **min(x)**   Determines the minimum value in column *x* for all rows returned by the select statement

- **stddev(x)**   Calculates the standard deviation for all values in column *x* in all rows returned by the select statement

- **sum(x)**   Calculates the sum of all values in column *x* in all rows returned by the `select` statement
- **Variance(x)**   Calculates the variance for all values in column *x* in all rows returned by the `select` statement

Group Functions in Action

Let's take a closer look at the grouping functions. The `avg( )` function takes the values for a single column on all rows returned by the query and calculates the average value for that column. Based on EMP, the `avg( )` function on the SAL column produces the following result:

```
SQL> select avg(sal) from emp;
 AVG(SAL)
---------
2073.2143
```

The second grouping function listed is `count( )`. This function is bound to become the cornerstone of any Oracle professional's repertoire. The `count( )` function returns a row count for the table, given certain column names, `select` criteria, or both. Note that the fastest way to execute `count( )` is to pass a value that resolves quickly in the SQL processing mechanism. Some values that resolve quickly are integers and the ROWID pseudocolumn. Here's an example:

```
SQL> SELECT COUNT(*), -- Slow
  2    COUNT(1), -- Fast
  3    COUNT(rowid) -- Fast
  4  FROM EMP;

COUNT(*)   COUNT(1) COUNT(rowid)
--------   -------- ------------
      14         14           14
```

TIP
The `count(expr)` *function returns the number of rows in the table with a non-NULL value in the column you are counting. In other words, if you specify a column for the* `count( )` *function, and a row for that column contains a NULL value, then the row won't be counted. Many users of Oracle avoid this problem by using* `count(ROWID)`. *It's faster than* `count(*)`, *and every row in a table will have a ROWID value.*

The asterisk (*) in the previous query is a wildcard variable that indicates all columns in the table. For better performance, this wildcard should not generally be used because the Oracle SQL processing mechanism must first resolve all column names in the table—a step that is unnecessary if you're simply trying to count rows. Notice that one of these examples uses the special pseudocolumn ROWID, which is a special value that uniquely identifies each row. Each row in a table has one unique ROWID.

TIP
Do not use count (*) to determine the number of rows in a table. Use count (1) or count (ROWID) instead. These options are faster because they bypass some unnecessary operations in Oracle's SQL processing mechanism.

The next pair of grouping functions to be covered is the max ( ) and min ( ) functions. The max ( ) function determines the largest value for the column passed, whereas min ( ) determines the smallest value for the column passed, as shown here:

```
SQL> select max(sal), min(sal) from emp;
 MAX(SAL)   MIN(SAL)
--------- ---------
     5000       800
```

You can combine group functions with single-row functions as well. The following example shows how:

```
SQL> select to_char(max(hiredate),'DD-MON-YYYY') "Newest",
  2   to_char(min(hiredate),'DD-MON-YYYY') "Oldest"
  3  from emp;
Newest      Oldest
----------- -----------
23-MAY-1987 17-DEC-1980
```

The final group function, sum ( ), is used commonly in simple accounting reports. The sum ( ) function gives the total of all values in a column. Here's an example:

```
SQL> select sum(sal) from emp;
 SUM(SAL)
---------
    29025
```

In general, the group functions operate on columns of datatypes NUMBER and DATE because many of the functions they represent in mathematics are numeric operations. It makes little sense to take the standard deviation for a set of 12 words, unless the user wants to take the standard deviation of the length of those words by combining the use of the `length( )` function with the `stddev( )` function. A few notable exceptions to this general rule exist, though. The first exception is the `count( )` function. The `count( )` function operates on a column of any datatype. The other exceptions are `max( )` and `min( )`, which operate on many different Oracle datatypes in addition to NUMBER and DATE.

Group Functions Ignore Null Values!

Group functions ignore NULL values by default. To force Oracle group functions not to ignore NULL values, you can use the `nvl( )` function. For example, let's look at the results of a group function when NULL values are present in the column with and without use of the `nvl( )` function:

```
SQL> select avg(comm) from emp;
AVG(COMM)
---------
      550
SQL> select avg(nvl(comm,0)) from emp;
AVG(NVL(COMM,0))
----------------
      157.142857
```

For Review

1. Know what the group functions are and how they are used in simple `select` statements.

2. Understand specifically how to use the `count( )` function and why using `count(ROWID)` or `count(1)` might be a better idea than using `count(*)`.

3. Understand that group functions ignore NULL values by default, but can be forced not to ignore NULL values through the use of the `nvl( )` function.

Exercises

1. **A table containing all 1,232,432 customer orders for the last year has a column, TOTAL, that lists the total amount spent by the customers on their orders. You issue the following command to obtain gross sales for the year:**

`select sum(total) from customers`. Which of the following choices identifies the number of rows that will appear in the output?

A. 1

B. 2

C. 500

D. 1,232,432

2. The standard EMP table we have worked with so far in the book contains 14 records corresponding to employees of the corporation. One of those records has a NULL value stored in the MGR column. You issue the following command on that table: `select count(mgr) from emp;`. Which of the following choices identifies the result Oracle will return?

A. 11

B. 12

C. 13

D. 14

3. Identify the type of value that group functions ignore by default: _____. Name the single-row function that can be used in conjunction with group functions to force group functions not to ignore that type of value: _____.

Answer Key
1. A. 2. C. 3. NULL, nvl ( )

Using the group by Clause

So far, you've seen examples of using group functions by themselves in the column clause of your query. This use is well and good, but sometimes it gives more meaning to the output of a `select` statement to collect data into logical groupings in combination with group functions. For example, let's say you want a listing of the different job roles in the corporation, along with the number of employees who fill those roles. For our small company, you could simply list all the information in the EMP table and count by hand. However, that process wouldn't work in a larger organization. Instead, you might want to use a `select` statement with a group function such as count ( ) to produce a meaningful listing of information. Let's try it out:

```
SQL> select job, count(job)
  2  from emp;
SQL> select job, count(job)
            *
ERROR at line 1:
ORA-00937: not a single-group group function
```

What happened? Well, we forgot something. Oracle expects group functions to produce one line of output for all rows in the table whose column you specify. In this case, Oracle became confused when we told it to list the individual values for the JOB column by including a reference to JOB in the column clause, too. The solution is to include a group by clause, which in effect tells Oracle to list each *distinct* value for JOB and then count the number of times that value appears in the EMP table. Let's take another look:

```
SQL> select job, count(job)
  2  from emp
  3  group by job;
JOB         COUNT(JOB)
---------   ----------
ANALYST              2
CLERK                4
MANAGER              3
PRESIDENT            1
SALESMAN             4
```

TIP

All columns in the column clause of your select statement that are not in a group function must be listed in the group by clause. However, a column listed in the group by clause needn't appear in the column clause.

Perfect! The group by clause in this example saves you from performing a great deal of work by hand. Instead, Oracle shoulders most of the work and shows only the results you need. The group by clause works well in many situations where you want to report calculations on data according to groups or categories.

Now let's consider a more complex example. Suppose you want a list of our company's average salary for a given job within a department. You already saw what happens when the group by clause is left out entirely. But there's something else we need to be careful about. Take a look at a first stab for developing a group by query that satisfies our requirements:

```
SQL> select deptno, avg(sal), job
  2  from emp
  3  group by deptno;
select deptno, avg(sal), job
                         *
ERROR at line 1:
ORA-00979: not a GROUP BY expression
```

When you use a group by clause in your query, all the nongroup expressions in the column clause of the query must appear before the grouped expression in the column clause. Put another way, *no nongroup expression can appear after the group expression in the column clause*. To solve the problem, we can remove the JOB column from the column clause entirely. However, that won't give us the output we need. Instead, we must first rearrange the nongroup expressions in the column clause to appear in front of the group function and then add the JOB column to the group by clause. This way, Oracle knows how to evaluate the aggregate columns in the select statement that are part of the grouping expression. The solution is shown here:

```
SQL> select deptno, job, avg(sal)
  2  from emp
  3  group by deptno, job;
DEPTNO JOB         AVG(SAL)
--------- --------- ---------
       10 CLERK         1300
       10 MANAGER       2450
       10 PRESIDENT     5000
       20 ANALYST       3000
       20 CLERK          950
       20 MANAGER       2975
       30 CLERK          950
       30 MANAGER       2850
       30 SALESMAN      1400
```

Notice something else about this output—the records are listed in order based on the contents of the DEPTNO column. This is because DEPTNO appears first in the group by clause. If we listed JOB first, the output would be alphabetized by job, as shown here:

```
SQL> select deptno, job, avg(sal)
  2  from emp
```

```
  3   group by job, deptno;
     DEPTNO JOB            AVG(SAL)
  --------- --------- ---------
        20 ANALYST          3000
        10 CLERK            1300
        20 CLERK             950
        30 CLERK             950
        10 MANAGER          2450
        20 MANAGER          2975
        30 MANAGER          2850
        10 PRESIDENT        5000
        30 SALESMAN         1400
```

You can use order by clauses with group by clauses as well—it's actually fairly common to do so. Take a look at the following output, where we've created some additional meaning by ordering the output such that the highest average salaries are listed at the top, so we can figure out which departments and jobs pay the most:

```
SQL> select deptno, job, avg(sal)
  2   from emp
  3   group by deptno, job
  4   order by 3 desc;
     DEPTNO JOB            AVG(SAL)
  --------- --------- ---------
        10 PRESIDENT        5000
        20 ANALYST          3000
        20 MANAGER          2975
        30 MANAGER          2850
        10 MANAGER          2450
        30 SALESMAN         1400
        10 CLERK            1300
        20 CLERK             950
        30 CLERK             950
```

TIP

When you're using an order by clause with a group by clause, the order in which you list columns in the group by clause doesn't matter— the order of output is dictated by the order by clause.

OLAP Features in Oracle

Some features for query processing in Oracle include the use of online analytical processing (OLAP) operations in your database. These features are useful for data warehousing and data mart applications used for supporting business decision-making processes. The first of these new operations is a performance enhancement to a specific type of query, called a *top-N* query. We discuss top-N queries more extensively later in the book. The other two new operations make it possible to perform certain OLAP operations in a group by clause. These two operations are cube and rollup. Let's look at each in more detail.

rollup   This group by operation is used to produce subtotals at any level of aggregation needed. These subtotals then "roll up" into a grand total, according to items listed in the group by expression. The totaling is based on a one-dimensional data hierarchy of grouped information. For example, let's say we wanted to get a payroll breakdown for our company by department and job position. The following code block would give us that information:

```
SQL> select deptno, job, sum(sal) as salary
  2   from emp
  3   group by rollup(deptno, job);
   DEPTNO JOB             SALARY
--------- ---------- ----------
       10 CLERK            1300
       10 MANAGER          2450
       10 PRESIDENT        5000
       10                  8750
       20 ANALYST          6000
       20 CLERK            1900
       20 MANAGER          2975
       20                 10875
       30 CLERK             950
       30 MANAGER          2850
       30 SALESMAN         5600
       30                  9400
                          29025
```

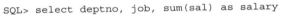

TIP
Notice that NULL values in the output of rollup *operations typically mean that the row contains subtotal or grand total information. If you want, you can use the* nvl ( ) *function to substitute a more meaningful value.*

cube   This is an extension, similar to `rollup`. The difference is that `cube` allows you to take a specified set of grouping columns and create subtotals for all possible combinations of them. The `cube` operation calculates all levels of subtotals on horizontal lines across spreadsheets of output and creates cross-tab summaries on multiple vertical columns in those spreadsheets. The result is a summary that shows subtotals for every combination of columns or expressions in the `group by` clause, which is also known as *n-dimensional cross-tabulation*. In the following example, notice how `cube` not only gives us the payroll breakdown of our company by DEPTNO and JOB, but it also gives us the breakdown of payroll by JOB across all departments:

```
SQL>  select deptno, job, sum(sal) as salary
  2   from emp
  3   group by cube(deptno, job);
DEPTNO JOB              SALARY
-------- --------- ---------
    10 CLERK          1300
    10 MANAGER        2450
    10 PRESIDENT      5000
    10                8750
    20 ANALYST        6000
    20 CLERK          1900
    20 MANAGER        2975
    20               10875
    30 CLERK           950
    30 MANAGER        2850
    30 SALESMAN       5600
    30                9400
       ANALYST        6000
       CLERK          4150
       MANAGER        8275
       PRESIDENT      5000
       SALESMAN       5600
                     29025
```

For Review

1. Know that the use of a group function in combination with a nongroup expression in the column clause requires using the group by clause. All nongroup expressions must be listed before the group expression.

2. Understand the relationship between the order in which columns are listed in the group by expression and the order in which Oracle will list records in

the output. Also, know that when an order by clause is used, it overrides the order set by the group by clause.

3. Be sure you can identify the situations in which statements containing the group by clause return errors as well as how to resolve those errors.

4. Know how to use OLAP functionality provided by cube and `rollup` in the group by clause. Also, know that without this functionality, you would have to develop long multiple queries whose output is joined by `union all` operations (don't worry about what a `union all` operation is; just be sure you can identify it as an alternative to the OLAP functions described in this section).

Exercises

1. **You are developing a query on the PROFITS table that stores profit information by company region, product type, and quarterly time period. Which of the following SQL statements will display a cross-tabulation of output showing profits by region, product type, and time period?**

    A. `select region, prod_type, time, sum(profit) from profits group by region, prod_type, time;`

    B. `select region, prod_type, time from profits group by rollup (region, prod_type, time);`

    C. `select region, prod_type, time from profits group by cube (region, prod_type, time);`

    D. `select region, prod_type, time, sum(profit) from profits group by cube (region, prod_type, time);`

2. **Which of the following choices identifies a group by query that will not result in an error from Oracle when run against the database?**

    A. `select deptno, job, sum(sal) from emp group by job, deptno;`

    B. `select sum(sal), deptno, job from emp group by job, deptno;`

    C. `select deptno, job, sum(sal) from emp;`

    D. `select deptno, sum(sal), job from emp group by job, deptno;`

3. **Review the following SQL statement:**

```
SQL> select a.deptno, a.job, b.loc, sum(a.sal)
  2  from emp a, dept b
  3  where a.deptno = b.deptno
  4  group by a.deptno, a.job, b.loc
  5  order by sum(a.sal);
```

Which of the following choices identifies the column upon which the order of output from this query will be returned?

A. A.DEPTNO

B. A.JOB

C. B.LOC

D. sum(A.SAL)

4. **Without the OLAP functionality built into group by statements, you would need to develop multiple SQL queries whose output is joined by these types of statements (two words):**

_____

Answer Key

1. D. 2. A. 3. D. 4. union all

Excluding group Data with having

Once the data is grouped using the group by statement, it is sometimes useful to _weed out_ unwanted data. For example, let's say we want to list the average salary paid to employees in our company, broken down by department and job title. However, for this query, we only care about departments and job titles where the average salary is over $2000. In effect, we want to put a where clause on the group by clause to limit the results we see to departments and job titles where the average salary equals $2001 or higher. This effect can be achieved with the use of a special clause called the having clause, which is associated with group by statements. Take a look at an example of this clause:

```
SQL> select deptno, job, avg(sal)
  2  from emp
  3  group by deptno, job
  4  having avg(sal) > 2000;
   DEPTNO JOB        AVG(SAL)
```

```
--------- --------- ---------
    10 MANAGER       2450
    10 PRESIDENT     5000
    20 ANALYST       3000
    20 MANAGER       2975
    30 MANAGER       2850
```

Consider the output of this query for a moment. First, Oracle computes the average for every department and job title in the entire company. Then, the `having` clause eliminates departments and titles whose constituent employees' average salary is $2000 or less. This selectivity cannot easily be accomplished with an ordinary `where` clause, because the `where` clause selects individual rows, whereas this example requires that groups of rows be selected. In this query, you successfully limit output on the `group by` rows by using the `having` clause.

TIP
There is no specific order that the `having` and `group by` clauses must appear in. A `having` clause can appear before the `group by` clause in the query. However, it is logical that the `group by` appear first in the SQL statement.

For Review

1. Know what the `having` clause is and the function that it serves.

2. Know that referencing the group expression in the `having` clause allows Oracle to filter data based on known or derived criteria.

Exercises

1. **You are developing a query on the PROFITS table that stores profit information by company region, product type, and quarterly time period. Which of the following choices identifies a query that will obtain the average profits greater than $100,000 by product type, region, and time period?**

   A. `select region, prod_type, period, avg(profit) from profits where avg(profit) > 100000 group by region, prod_type, period;`

   B. `select region, prod_type, period, avg(profit) from profits where avg(profit) > 100000 order by region, prod_type, period;`

C. `select region, prod_type, period, avg(profit) from profits group by region, prod_type, period having avg(profit) > 100000;`

D. `select region, prod_type, period, avg(profit) from profits group by region, prod_type, period having avg(profit) < 100000;`

2. **A having clause can act like this type of clause inside group by expressions:** _____

Answer Key

1. C. **2.** where

Chapter Summary

This chapter covered a lot of territory. You learned a great deal about advanced selection of data in SQL*Plus. We discussed how to join data in multiple tables into one output result using the premise that two tables with a common column can be used in a join operation. We discussed how to create equijoins, which are joins where the data from one table only appears if a corresponding record can be found in the other table. From there, we covered how to formulate outer joins, where the corresponding record requirement between tables isn't enforced as strictly. We learned how to join data from one table to itself using the self-join process as well. From there, we moved onto discuss group expressions and group by operations. We covered the use of the `having` clause, as well as the use of OLAP expressions like `cube` and `rollup`.

Two-Minute Drill

- `Select` statements that obtain data from more than one table and merge the data together are called *joins*.

- In order to join data from two tables, a common column must exist.

- A common column between two tables can create a foreign key, or *link*, from one table to another. This condition is especially true if the data in one of the tables is part of the primary key—the column that defines uniqueness for rows on a table.

- A foreign key can create a parent/child relationship between two tables.

- One type of join is the inner join, or *equijoin*. An equijoin operation is based on an equality operation linking the data in common columns of two tables.

- When joining tables using Oracle syntax, a join comparison on the common columns in the tables must be included in the `where` clause of the query.

- When joining tables using ANSI/ISO syntax, the `join tablename` on `join_comparison` clause must be used. The join comparison operation is thus kept separate from other filter comparisons that might otherwise appear in the `where` clause.

- ANSI/ISO and Oracle syntax for joins is logically equivalent. There is no performance advantage for using one over the other. However, ANSI/ISO and Oracle syntax for joins cannot be used together in the same SQL query.

- Another type of join is the outer join. An outer join returns data in one table even when there is no data in the other table. The "other" table in the outer join operation is called the *outer table*.

- The common column that appears in the outer table of the join must have a special marker next to it in the comparison operation of the `select` statement that creates the table.

- The Oracle-syntax outer join symbol is "(+)", which is equivalent to the ANSI/ISO [left|right] outer join clause. Whether the outer join is a left join or a right join depends on where the outer join symbol is placed.

- If the column name is the same in both tables, the common column in both tables used in Oracle-syntax join operations must be preceded either with a table alias that denotes the table in which the column appears or the entire table name.

- The data from a table can be joined to itself. This technique is useful in determining whether there are rows in the table that have slightly different values but are otherwise duplicate rows. This is called a *self-join* operation.

- Table aliases must be used in self-join `select` statements.

- A Cartesian product is formed when you omit a join comparison from your Oracle-syntax join statement, or when you use the `cross join` keywords in ANSI/ISO syntax.

- A natural join can be used to simplify join operations. Natural joins are possible in ANSI/ISO syntax when all common columns between joined tables have the same name. Use the `natural` keyword to specify to Oracle to execute a natural join. You do not need to specify a join comparison in order to execute a natural join.

- Data output from table `select` statements can be grouped together according to criteria set by the query.

- The `group by` clause assists you in grouping data together.

- Several grouping functions are available that allow you to perform operations on data in a column as though the data were logically one variable.

- The grouping functions are `max( )`, `min( )`, `sum( )`, `avg( )`, `stddev ( )`, `variance( )`, and `count( )`.

- These grouping functions can be applied to the column values for a table as a whole or for subsets of column data for rows returned in `group by` statements.

- Data in a `group by` statement can be excluded or included based on a special set of where criteria defined specifically for the group in a `having` clause.

- The data used to determine the `having` clause can be specified at runtime by the query.

- NULL values are ignored by group functions. To force group functions not to ignore NULL values, use the `nvl( )` function.

Fill-in-the-Blank Questions

1. This SQL command allows you to aggregate data using column functions (two words): _____

2. This phrase describes the result of a join operation on two or more tables when the `where` clause is poorly defined:

   _____

3. This SQL keyword extends the functionality of a grouping expression to act as a `where` clause within a `where` clause: _____

4. This type of constraint in Oracle is used for defining a relationship between two tables so that join operations can be executed:

   _____

Chapter Questions

1. **You want to specify a group expression in SQL*Plus. Which of the following is not a group function?**

   A. `avg ( )`

   B. `sqrt ( )`

   C. `sum ( )`

   D. `max ( )`

2. **You are selecting data from multiple tables in Oracle with the intent of merging the results together. In order to perform an inner join, which criteria must be true?**

   A. The common columns in the join do not need to have shared values.

   B. The tables in the join need to have common columns.

   C. The common columns in the join may or may not have shared values.

   D. The common columns in the join must have shared values.

3. **A user is setting up a join operation between tables EMPLOYEE and DEPT. There are some employees in the EMPLOYEE table that the user wants returned by the query, but the employees are not assigned to department heads yet. Which select statement is most appropriate for this user?**

   A. `select e.empid, d.head from EMPLOYEE e, dept d;`

B. `select e.empid, d.head from EMPLOYEE e, dept d`
`where e.dept# = d.dept#;`

C. `select e.empid, d.head from EMPLOYEE e, dept d`
`where e.dept# = d.dept# (+);`

D. `select e.empid, d.head from EMPLOYEE e, dept d`
`where e.dept# (+) = d.dept#;`

4. **You are developing group expressions in Oracle. Which of the following uses of the `having` clause are appropriate? (Choose three.)**

   A. To put returned data into sorted order

   B. To exclude certain data groups based on known criteria

   C. To include certain data groups based on unknown criteria

   D. To include certain data groups based on known criteria

5. **You are developing table join statements in Oracle and wish to do so properly. Which of the following statements indicates the proper definition of a Cartesian product?**

   A. A group function

   B. The result of a join `select` statement with no `where` clause

   C. The result of fuzzy logic

   D. A special feature of Oracle server

6. **You develop the following SQL statement containing a group expression. Which line in the following `select` statement, when removed from the statement, will correct the error?**

   ```
   select deptno, avg(sal)
   from emp
   group by empno;
   ```

   A. `select deptno, avg(sal)`

   B. `from EMP`

   C. `group by empno;`

   D. There are no errors in this statement, therefore no clauses should be removed.

Fill-in-the-Blank Answers

1. group by

2. Cartesian product.

3. having

4. Foreign key.

Answers to Chapter Questions

1. B. sqrt ( )

Explanation Square root operations are performed on one column value. Choice A is incorrect because avg ( ) is a group function that accepts a set of data and returns the average. Choice C is incorrect because the sum ( ) function is a group function that returns the sum of a set of numbers. Finally, choice D is incorrect because max ( ) is a group function that accepts a set of numbers and returns the highest value.

2. B. The tables in the join need to have common columns.

Explanation It is possible that a join operation will produce no return data, just as it is possible for any select statement not to return any data. Choices A, C, and D represent the spectrum of possibilities for shared values that may or may not be present in common columns. However, joins themselves are not possible without two tables having common columns.

3. C. select e.empid, d.head from EMPLOYEE e, dept d where
   e.dept# = d.dept# (+);

Explanation Choice C details the outer join operation most appropriate to this user's needs. The outer table in this join is the DEPT table, as identified by the (+) marker next to the DEPT# column in the comparison operation that defines the join. Each of the other choices incorrectly identifies the location of the outer join operator, or else contains some other error.

4. B, C, and D. To exclude certain data groups based on known criteria, to include certain data groups based on unknown criteria, *and* to include certain data groups based on known criteria

Explanation All exclusion or inclusion of grouped rows is handled by the having clause of a select statement. Choice A is not an appropriate answer because sort order is given in a select statement by the order by clause.

5. B. The result of a join `select` statement with no `where` clause

Explanation   A Cartesian product is the resultant dataset from a `select` statement in which all data from both tables is returned. Some potential causes of a Cartesian product include not specifying a `where` clause for the join `select` statement.

6. C. `group by empno;`

Explanation   Because the EMPNO column does not appear in the original list of columns to be displayed by the query, it cannot be used in a `group by` statement. This question confuses many readers who believe that the ordering of the column references in the column clause is really at fault. To avoid being confused by this thought, remember that if you removed the `group by` expression, the query would execute correctly, while if you removed the column clause the query would still fail.

CHAPTER
4

Subqueries

n this chapter, you will learn about and demonstrate knowledge in the following areas:

- Using subqueries
- Producing readable output from SQL*Plus

This chapter concludes the required coverage of topics related to Oracle data selection. First, we will discuss how to use subqueries in your select statements. You will learn both about straightforward subqueries and about multiple-column subqueries. Finally, this chapter will cover how to specify special formatting in order to use SQL*Plus as a reporting tool. The material in this chapter will complete your knowledge of data selection and comprises 10 percent of OCP Exam 1.

TIP
Of these two subject areas, the topic of subqueries is covered in more detail on the OCP exams. You might want to limit your review of producing readable output to understanding how to use substitution variables and simply use the rest of the information for reference.

Using Subqueries

This section will cover the following topics related to using subqueries:

- Understanding and defining subqueries
- Listing and writing different types of subqueries
- Multiple-column subqueries
- NULL values in subqueries
- Subqueries in a `from` clause

A *subquery* is a "query within a query." In other words, a subquery is a `select` statement nested within a `select` statement, designed to limit the selected output of the parent query by producing an intermediate result set of some sort. There are several different ways to include subqueries in SQL statements' `where` clauses. We'll talk in this section about the types of problems subqueries can solve, how to develop subqueries, the different subquery types, and how to write single-row and multiple-row subqueries.

TIP
Some of the topics we'll cover here go into slightly further detail than what you might see on the OCP exams. We recommend working through the material so that you understand subqueries thoroughly in order to do well not just on the exam, but in your career as an Oracle professional.

Understanding and Defining Subqueries

Subqueries can be used to obtain values for parent `select` statements when specific search criteria isn't known. To do so, the `where` clause in the parent `select` statement must have a comparison operation where the unknown value being compared is determined by the result of the subquery. The inner subquery executes once, right before the main outer query executes. The subquery returns its results to the main outer query. Consider the following example, where we search for the name, department number, and salary information for employees working in New York. The known criterion is that the employees work in New York. However, without looking at the DEPT table, we won't know which department number corresponds to the New York office. Let's look at how we might obtain the desired result using a join statement:

```
SQL> select ename, emp.deptno, sal
  2  from emp join dept on emp.deptno = dept.deptno
  3. where dept.loc = 'NEW YORK';
ENAME          DEPTNO        SAL
---------- --------- ---------
CLARK             10       2450
KING              10       5000
MILLER            10       1300
```

Now, let's take a look at how a subquery can help us out:

```
SQL>  select ename, deptno, sal
  2      from emp
  3      where deptno =
  4       ( select deptno
  5         from dept
  6         where loc = 'NEW YORK' );
ENAME          DEPTNO        SAL
---------- --------- ---------
CLARK             10       2450
KING              10       5000
MILLER            10       1300
```

TIP
*Subqueries must appear inside parentheses, or else
Oracle will have trouble distinguishing the
subquery from the parent query. You should also
make sure to place subqueries on the right side of
the comparison operator.*

The highlighted portion of the SQL statement is the subquery. Notice how the parent query requires the subquery to resolve itself for the DEPTNO value corresponding to the New York office. When this `select` statement is submitted, Oracle will process the subquery *first* in order to resolve all unknown search criteria and then feed that resolved criteria to the outer query. The outer query then can resolve the dataset it is supposed to return.

Consider also that the preceding example uses an equality comparison to connect the parent query to the subquery. This is the most commonly used method for connecting subqueries to their parents, but it isn't the only one. You could use many of the other comparison operations, such as <, >, <=, <>, and >=. You can also use the `in` comparison, which is similar to the `case` statement offered in many programming languages, because resolution can be established based on the parent column's equality with any element in the group. Let's take a look at an example:

```
SQL> select ename, job, sal
  2  from emp
  3  where deptno in
  4  ( select deptno
  5    from dept
  6    where dname in
  7    ('ACCOUNTING', 'SALES'));
ENAME       JOB            SAL
---------- --------- ---------
ALLEN       SALESMAN      1600
WARD        SALESMAN      1250
MARTIN      SALESMAN      1250
BLAKE       MANAGER       2850
CLARK       MANAGER       2450
KING        PRESIDENT     5000
TURNER      SALESMAN      1500
JAMES       CLERK          950
MILLER      CLERK         1300
```

Another way of including a subquery in the `where` clause of a `select` statement is to use the `exists` clause. This clause enables you to test for the existence of rows in the results of a subquery, and its logical opposite is not exists. When you specify the exists operation in a where clause, you must include a subquery that satisfies the exists operation. If the subquery returns data, the exists operation returns TRUE, and a record from the parent query will be returned. If not, the exists operation returns FALSE, and no record for the parent query will be returned. Let's look at an example in which we obtain the same listing of employees working in the New York office, only this time, we use the exists operation:

```
SQL> select e.ename, e.job, e.sal
  2  from emp e
  3  where exists
  4    ( select d.deptno
  5      from dept d
  6      where d.loc = 'NEW YORK'
  7      and d.deptno = e.deptno);
ENAME       JOB          SAL
----------  ----------  ----------
CLARK       MANAGER        2450
KING        PRESIDENT      5000
MILLER      CLERK          1300
```

Notice something very interesting about this subquery example. We used table aliases in both the parent query and the subquery to create a *correlated subquery*. Oracle performs a correlated subquery when the subquery references a column from a table referred to in the parent statement. A correlated subquery is evaluated once for each row processed by the parent statement. Correlated subqueries are used to affect row-by-row processing. Each subquery is executed once for every row produced by the outer query. This technique enables us to "jump" from the subquery to the parent level in order to perform incredibly complex, almost counterintuitive, processing that necessarily must involve some discussion of a programming concept known as *variable scope*.

Variable scope refers to the availability or "viewability" of data in certain variables at certain times. Sometimes a variable has a *local* scope. That is to say that the variable can only be seen when the current block of code is being executed. You can consider the columns in subquery comparison operations to be variables whose scope is *local* to the query. There is also *global* scope. In addition to a variable having local scope within the subquery where it appears, the variable also has *global* scope, meaning that it is available in all subqueries to that query. In the previous example, all variables or columns named in comparison operations in the outermost select operation are local to that operation and global to all the nested subqueries.

TIP
You've only seen some simple examples, but you should know that subqueries can be nested inside other subqueries to a surprisingly deep level – up to 255 subqueries in a single `select` statement! Subqueries are also the topic of many OCP questions, so you should make sure you have plenty of experience writing them before taking the exam —and make sure you know the subquery discussions in this book cold!

We can use many different types of functions in subqueries. In general, whatever functions are permitted in a parent query are also permitted in a subquery. For example, to obtain a listing of employees earning the minimum salary for a company might ordinarily present a small problem, especially if that minimum salary is an unknown value. You can solve this problem by using a group function in your subquery to obtain the unknown value, then use the parent query to search the EMP table for all employees whose salary is that value. The following code block shows the SQL:

```
SQL> select empno, ename, sal
  2  from emp
  3  where sal = (select min(sal) from emp);
     EMPNO ENAME               SAL
---------- ---------- ----------
      7369 SMITH               800
```

For Review

1. Know what a subquery is as well as when you might want to incorporate a subquery into a database `select` statement.

2. Be sure you can identify and give examples of how to write subqueries that are linked to their parent query by means of equality comparison, the `in` comparison, and the `exists` comparison.

Exercises

1. The company has an employee expense application with two tables. One table, called EMP, contains all employee data. The other, called EXPENSE, contains expense vouchers submitted by every employee in the company. Which of the following queries will obtain the employee ID and name for

those employees who have submitted expenses whose total value exceeds their salary?

A. `select e.empno, e.ename from emp e where e.sal < (select sum(x.vouch_amt) from expense x) and x.empno = e.empno;`

B. `select e.empno, e.ename from emp e where e.sal < (select x.vouch_amt from expense x where x.empno = e.empno);`

C. `select e.empno, e.ename from emp e where sal < (select sum(x.vouch_amt) from expense x where x.empno = e.empno);`

D. `select e.empno, e.ename from emp e where exists (select sum(x.vouch_amt) from expense x where x.empno = e.empno);`

2. **Take a look at the following statement:**

```
SQL>  select ename
  2     from emp
  3     where empno in
  4       ( select empno
  5          from expense
  6          where vouch_amt > 10000 );
```

Which of the following choices identifies a SQL statement that will produce the same output as the preceding, rewritten to use the `exists` operator?

A. `select e.ename from emp e where exists (select x.empno from expense x where x.vouch_amt > 10000) and x.empno = e.empno;`

B. `select e.ename from emp e where exists (select x.empno from expense x where x.vouch_amt > 10000 and x.empno = e.empno);`

C. `select e.ename from emp e where x.empno = e.empno and exists (select x.empno from expense x where x.vouch_amt > 10000);`

D. `select e.ename from emp e, expense x where x.empno = e.empno and x.vouch_amt > 10000 and exists (select x.empno from expense x where x.vouch_amt > 10000);`

3. In order to jump levels in nested subqueries, the availability of data from the parent query is often useful. Therefore, the variables from the parent query are said to be _____ in scope.

Answer Key
1. C. 2. B. 3. Global.

Listing and Writing Different Types of Subqueries

The following list identifies several different types of subqueries you may need to understand and use on the OCP exam:

- **Single-row subqueries**   The main query expects the subquery to return only one value.

- **Multirow subqueries**   The main query can handle situations where the subquery returns more than one value.

- **Inline views**   A subquery in a from clause used for defining an intermediate result set to query from. These types of subqueries will be discussed later in the chapter.

- **Multiple-column subqueries**   A subquery that contains more than one column of return data in addition to however many rows are given in the output. These types of subqueries will be discussed later in the chapter.

Writing Single-Row Subqueries

Check out the following example, which should look familiar:

```
SQL>  select ename, deptno, sal
   2    from emp
   3    where deptno =
   4     ( select deptno
   5       from dept
   6       where loc = 'NEW YORK' );
ENAME          DEPTNO        SAL
---------- --------- ---------
CLARK              10       2450
KING               10       5000
MILLER             10       1300
```

Believe it or not, this is a single-row subquery. Why, you ask? Because, although the resulting set of data contains multiple rows of output from the EMP table, the subquery on the DEPT table to derive the output from EMP returns only one row of data. If you don't believe me, check out the following code block and see for yourself:

```
SQL> select deptno
  2  from dept
  3  where loc = 'NEW YORK';
   DEPTNO
---------
      10
```

Sure enough, there's only one column returned from one row of data by this query. Sometimes, single-row subqueries are also referred to as *scalar subqueries*. What makes the difference between whether a subquery can handle a single value or multiple values has to do with the comparison operation used for linking the parent query to the subquery. Notice in this situation that we used an equal sign. Therefore, we can generalize a simple rule: *When subqueries are linked to the parent by equality comparisons, the parent query expects only one row of data from the subquery.* Therefore, parent queries with subqueries linked by equality comparison operations are single-row subqueries.

TIP
Other comparison operations that indicate single-row subqueries include <, >, <=, >, and <>.

Writing Multirow Subqueries
Check out what happens when a parent query gets more than it bargained for:

```
SQL> select ename, job, sal
  2  from emp
  3  where deptno =
  4  (select deptno
  5  from dept
  6  where dname in ('ACCOUNTING','SALES'));
   (select deptno
      *
ERROR at line 4:
ORA-01427: single-row subquery returns more than one row
```

To solve the problem that arises in this example, you must transform the single-row subquery into a multirow subquery. How, you ask? You should transform the equality comparison that links the subquery to its parent into a comparison operation that handles multiple rows of output from the subquery—an operation such as `in` (shown in bold in the following example):

```
SQL> select ename, job, sal
  2  from emp
  3  where deptno in
  4  (select deptno
  5  from dept
  6  where dname in ('ACCOUNTING','SALES'));
ENAME      JOB            SAL
---------- --------- ---------
ALLEN      SALESMAN      1600
WARD       SALESMAN      1250
MARTIN     SALESMAN      1250
BLAKE      MANAGER       2850
CLARK      MANAGER       2450
KING       PRESIDENT     5000
TURNER     SALESMAN      1500
JAMES      CLERK          950
MILLER     CLERK         1300
```

having Clauses and Subqueries

The `having` clause can use subqueries, too. Let's say you want to look at the average salaries of people in the company, broken out by department and job title again. This time, however, you only want to see departments and job titles where the average salary is higher than what the company is paying MARTIN, a salesman. There's just one small problem—you don't remember what MARTIN's salary is. We know that subqueries are useful when you need valid data that you don't know the value of, but you do know how to obtain it. You'll see how to use subqueries with the `having` clause in the following example:

```
SQL> select deptno, job, avg(sal)
  2  from emp
  3  group by deptno, job
  4  having avg(sal) >
  5    ( select sal
  6      from emp
  7      where ename = 'MARTIN');
  DEPTNO JOB        AVG(SAL)
--------- --------- ---------
      10 CLERK         1300
```

```
10  MANAGER        2450
10  PRESIDENT      5000
20  ANALYST        3000
20  MANAGER        2975
30  MANAGER        2850
30  SALESMAN       1400
```

TIP

The order *by clause can be used in a query that uses subqueries, but this clause must appear in the outermost query only. The subquery cannot have the* order *by clause defined for it.*

The with **Clause and Subqueries**

Oracle**9i** and higher   Sometimes complex queries may need to process the same subquery several times, once for each row obtained by the main query. This situation causes a great deal of processing overhead for Oracle, which could slow down the database's ability to provide you with the result requested quickly. Rather than force repeated processing of the subquery, Oracle9i provides you with the with clause that lets you factor out the subquery, give it a name, then reference that name multiple times within the original complex query. This technique lets the optimizer choose how to deal with the subquery results. The optimizer may perform either of the following. It might create a temporary table and query that table, and you'll learn more about temporary tables in Chapter 5. Alternately, the Oracle optimizer might rewrite the subquery using an inline view, and you'll learn about inline views later in this chapter. For example, the following query joins two tables and computes the aggregate sum of salaries redundantly, creating additional performance overhead, in order to list the sum of salaries for departments comprising more than ⅓ of the firm's annual salary budget. The bold text represents the parts of the query that are repeated:

```
SQL> select dname, sum(sal) as dept_total
  2  from emp, dept
  3  where emp.deptno = dept.deptno
  4  group by dname having sum(sal) >
  5  (select sum(sal)*1/3
  6   from emp, dept
  7   where emp.deptno = dept.deptno)
  8  order by sum(sal) desc;
DNAME                DEPT_TOTAL
-------------------- ----------
RESEARCH                  10875
```

You can improve the performance of this query by having Oracle9i execute the subquery only once, then simply letting Oracle9i reference it at the appropriate points in the main query. The following code block gives a better logical idea of the work Oracle must perform to give you the result. In it, the bold text represents the common parts of the subquery that are performed only once, and the places where the subquery is referenced:

```
SQL> with summary as
  2  (select dname, sum(sal) as dept_total
  3   from emp, dept
  4   where emp.deptno = dept.deptno
  5   group by dname)
  6  select dname, dept_total
  7  from summary
  8  where dept_total >
  9  (select sum(dept_total) * 1/3
 10   from summary)
 11  order by dept_total desc;
DNAME                   DEPT_TOTAL
-------------------- ----------
RESEARCH                  10875
```

For Review

1. Know what the four different types of subqueries are. Also, be sure you can write and understand examples of single-row and multirow subqueries.

2. Know what happens when a parent query expecting a subquery to return only one row receives more than one row from the subquery.

3. Know that you can substitute the in operator for equality or other single-row comparison operations in order to let the parent query support multiple rows returned.

4. Understand the use of the with clause to minimize redundancy in defining steps to be performed in subqueries.

Exercises

1. Use the following code block to answer the question:

```
SQL> select deptno, job, avg(sal)
  2  from emp
  3  group by deptno, job
  4  having avg(sal) >
  5    ( select sal
```

```
6        from emp
7        where ename = 'MARTIN');
```

Which of the following choices identifies the type of subquery used in the preceding statement?

A. A single-row subquery

B. A multirow subquery

C. A `from` clause subquery

D. A multicolumn subquery

2. **The company's sales database has two tables. The first, PROFITS, stores the amount of profit made on products sold by the different corporate regions in different quarters. The second, REGIONS, stores the name of each departmental region, the headquarter location for that region, and the name of the region's vice president. Which of the following queries will obtain total profits on toys for regions headed by SMITHERS, FUJIMORI, and LAKKARAJU?**

A. `select sum(profit) from profits where region in (select region from regions where reg_head in ('SMITHERS', 'FUJIMORI', 'LAKKARAJU')) and product = 'TOYS';`

B. `select sum(profit) from profits where region in (select region from regions where reg_head in ('SMITHERS', 'FUJIMORI', 'LAKKARAJU') and product = 'TOYS');`

C. `select sum(profit) from profits where region = (select region from regions where reg_head in ('SMITHERS', 'FUJIMORI', 'LAKKARAJU')) and product = 'TOYS';`

D. `select sum(profit) from profits where region in (select region from regions where reg_head = ('SMITHERS', 'FUJIMORI', 'LAKKARAJU')) and product = 'TOYS';`

3. **Provide the name of the operator used for transforming single-row subqueries returning more than one row into a subquery capable of handling multiple rows returned to the main query:**

_____

4. The following code block shows a query containing a subquery:

```
SQL> select dname, avg(sal) as dept_avg
  2  from emp, dept
  3  where emp.deptno = dept.deptno
  4  group by dname having avg(sal) >
  5  (select avg(sal) * 1/4
  6   from emp, dept
  7   where emp.deptno = dept.deptno)
  8  order by avg(sal);
```

Which of the following choices identifies a clause you might use to redefine this query to remove redundancy of group function execution in the subquery and in the main query?

A. group by

B. order by

C. with

D. having

Answer Key
1. A. 2. A. 3. In 4. C.

Writing Multiple-Column Subqueries

Notice that in all the prior examples, regardless of whether one row or multiple rows were returned from the subquery, each of those rows contained only one column's worth of data to compare at the main query level. The main query can be set up to handle multiple columns in each row returned, too. To evaluate how to use multiple-column subqueries, let's consider an example. Let's say we want to find out the highest-paid employee in each department. Check out the following code block to see how we might perform this task:

```
SQL> select deptno, ename, job, sal
  2  from emp
  3  where (deptno, sal) in
  4   (select deptno, max(sal)
  5    from emp
  6    group by deptno);
```

```
DEPTNO ENAME        JOB            SAL
-------- ---------- ---------- ----------
    10 KING        PRESIDENT       5000
    20 SCOTT       ANALYST         3000
    20 FORD        ANALYST         3000
    30 BLAKE       MANAGER         2850
```

A couple of noteworthy points need to be made concerning multiple-column subqueries and syntax. For multiple-column subqueries only, you must enclose the multiple columns requested in the main query in parentheses; otherwise, the query will result in an "invalid relational operator" error. Also, your column references in both the main query's `where` clause and the subquery must match positionally—in other words, because DEPTNO is referenced first in the main query, it must be selected first in the subquery.

For Review

Be sure you understand the syntax and semantics of multiple-column subqueries.

Exercises

1. **The database for an international athletic competition consists of one table, ATHLETES, containing contestant name, age, and represented country. To determine the youngest athlete representing each country, which of the following queries could be used?**

   A. `select name, country, age from athletes where (country, age) in (select min(age), country from athletes group by country);`

   B. `select name, country, age from athletes where (country, age) in (select country, min(age) from athletes) group by country;`

   C. `select name, country, age from athletes where age in (select country, min(age) from athletes group by country);`

   D. `select name, country, age from athletes where (country, age) in (select country, min(age) from athletes group by country);`

2. **You are developing a multiple-column subquery on an Oracle database. Which of the following statements is true about SQL statements containing multiple-column subqueries?**

   A. The parent query must use a single-column subquery.

   B. The order of multiple columns being referenced in the where clause must match the column order in the subquery.

   C. The parent query must use an inline view, or else the query must be rewritten.

   D. The parent query must contain a group by expression in order to obtain the correct result.

Answer Key
1. D. 2. B.

NULL Values and Subqueries

If you're planning to follow along on your own EMP table built by demobld.sql, you need to execute the following statement for this lesson to flow properly:

```
SQL> update emp set deptno = null where ename = 'KING';
1 row updated.
```

TIP
You'll learn more about update statements in Chapter 6.

Now, review the following code block, where we rerun the multiple-column subquery from the previous example:

```
SQL> select deptno, ename, job, sal
  2  from emp
  3  where (deptno, sal) in
  4    ( select deptno, max(sal)
  5      from emp
  6      group by deptno);
  DEPTNO ENAME      JOB           SAL
--------- ---------- --------- ---------
      10 CLARK      MANAGER        2450
```

```
20 SCOTT      ANALYST      3000
20 FORD       ANALYST      3000
30 BLAKE      MANAGER      2850
```

Notice someone missing from the output? Even though KING is still listed in the EMP table, he is no longer the highest-paid employee in his department. That's strange, especially when we review the output from the subquery in our example:

```
DEPTNO   MAX(SAL)
-------- ---------
      10      2450
      20      3000
      30      2850
              5000
```

You can see that KING was listed among the highest paid in his respective department. However, notice that his department is set to NULL. If you're thinking that the problem must have something to do with how subqueries handle NULL values, you're right. Unfortunately, the subquery only returns non-NULL values to the parent query. Therefore, we don't see KING listed in the output from that main query. In order to ensure that your queries don't miss any NULL values, you should rewrite them in such a way that they don't use the group by expression. This step can be done using a correlated subquery, as demonstrated in the following code block:

```
SQL> select e.deptno, e.ename, e.job, e.sal
  2  from emp e
  3  where e.sal =
  4  (select max(e2.sal)
  5    from emp e2
  6*  where nvl(e.deptno,99) = nvl(e2.deptno,99));
DEPTNO ENAME      JOB           SAL
-------- ---------- --------- ---------
      30 BLAKE      MANAGER      2850
      10 CLARK      MANAGER      2450
      20 SCOTT      ANALYST      3000
         KING       PRESIDENT    5000
      20 FORD       ANALYST      3000
```

Notice something interesting about this query? The use of the nvl ( ) function in the subquery substitutes the value 99 for NULL on KING's record. This is an arbitrary value picked simply because it wasn't already in use as a department number. However, you're probably wondering why the output doesn't display 99 in the DEPTNO column for KING. The reason is because the subquery is not actually returning a value for DEPTNO to the parent query—it only returns the maximum salary for that department! We use `nvl ( )` in the subquery only so we have a non-NULL value to compare E.DEPTNO and E2.DEPTNO in the subquery. Because the department number for KING's record is still NULL, that is what the parent query displays.

TIP

When writing queries that use subqueries, remember that certain operations, such as group by, may return NULL values and that NULL values are ignored by subqueries when the subquery returns its dataset to the main query. If you need to include NULL values in your output, experiment with rewriting the query in other ways.

In Conclusion

Remember to discard the change to KING's record in the EMP table when you're done:

```
SQL> rollback;
Rollback complete.
```

For Review

Be sure you understand that certain operations, such as group by, may generate NULL values, which are ignored by subqueries when the dataset is returned to the main query. Know how to rewrite a subquery if you need to handle NULL values.

Exercises

1. Subqueries ignore this value by default: _____

2. Use the output in the code block to answer the following question:

```
SQL> select e.deptno, e.ename, e.job, e.sal
  2  from emp e
  3  where e.sal =
  4  (select max(e2.sal)
  5  from emp e2
  6* where nvl(e.deptno,99) = nvl(e2.deptno,99));
DEPTNO ENAME        JOB          SAL
-------- ---------- --------- ---------
    30 BLAKE        MANAGER        2850
```

```
10  CLARK      MANAGER        2450
20  SCOTT      ANALYST        3000
    KING       PRESIDENT      5000
20  FORD       ANALYST        3000
```

In order to display a value of 99 in the DEPTNO column in the preceding return set, which of the following SQL statements might be appropriate?

A. `select nvl(e.deptno,99), e.ename, e.job, e.sal from emp e where (e.deptno, e.sal) =(select max(e2.sal) from emp e2 where nvl(e.deptno,99) = nvl(e2.deptno,99));`

B. `select nvl(e.deptno,99), e.ename, e.job, e.sal from emp e where e.sal =(select max(e2.sal) from emp e2 where nvl(e.deptno,99) = nvl(e2.deptno,99));`

C. `select nvl(e.deptno,99), e.ename, e.job, e.sal from emp e where (e.deptno, e.sal) =(select e2.deptno, max(e2.sal) from emp e2 where nvl(e.deptno,99) = nvl(e2.deptno,99));`

D. `select nvl(e.deptno,99), e.ename, e.job, e.sal from emp e where (e.deptno, e.sal) =(select e2.deptno, max(e2.sal) from emp e2 where nvl(e.deptno,99) = nvl(e2.deptno,99) group by e2.deptno);`

Answer Key
1. NULL. 2. B.

Subqueries in a `from` Clause

If you're planning to follow along on your own EMP table built by `demobld.sql`, you need to execute the following statement for this lesson to flow properly:

```
SQL> update emp set deptno = null where ename = 'KING';
1 row updated.
```

TIP
You'll learn more about `update` statements in Chapter 6.

You can also write subqueries that appear in your `from` clause. Writing subqueries in the `from` clause of the main query can be a handy way to collect an intermediate set of data that the main query treats as a table for its own query-access purposes. This subquery in the `from` clause of your main query is called an *inline view*. You must enclose the query text for the inline view in parentheses and also give a label for the inline view so that columns in it can be referenced later. The subquery can be a `select` statement that utilizes joins, the `group` by clause, or the `order` by clause. The following code block shows you a very simple example of using an inline view that accomplishes the same result as a regular table join. In the following code block, the query in parenthesis is given an alias, SUBQ. SUBQ contains an inline view listing the DEPTNO information for the New York and Dallas locations. The main query uses this information to determine which employees work in those locations:

```
SQL> select e.ename, subq.loc
  2  from emp e,
  3    ( select deptno, loc
  4      from dept
  5      where loc in ('NEW YORK', 'DALLAS')) subq
  6  where e.deptno = subq.deptno;
ENAME        LOC
---------- -------------
SMITH        DALLAS
JONES        DALLAS
CLARK        NEW YORK
SCOTT        DALLAS
ADAMS        DALLAS
FORD         DALLAS
MILLER       NEW YORK
```

TIP

In some cases, the columns referenced in your inline view might call single-row or group functions. This is permitted; however, if you want to refer to those columns in the main query's where clause, you will need to supply column aliases for that column in the inline view, in addition to supplying a table alias for the entire inline view.

Inline Views and Top-N Queries

Top-N queries use inline views and are handy for displaying a short list of table data, based on "greatest" or "least" criteria. For example, let's say that profits for our company were exceptionally strong this year, and we want a list of the three lowest-paid employees in our company so that we could give them a raise. A top-N query would be useful for this purpose. Take a look at a top-N query that satisfies this business scenario:

```
SQL> select ename, job, sal, rownum
  2  from (select ename, job, sal from emp
  3           order by sal)
  4  where rownum <=3;
ENAME        JOB              SAL     ROWNUM
----------   ---------   ---------   ---------
SMITH        CLERK            800          1
JAMES        CLERK            950          2
ADAMS        CLERK           1100          3
```

You need to know two important things about top-N queries for OCP. The first is their use of the inline view to list all data in the table in sorted order. The second is their use of ROWNUM—a virtual column identifying the row number in the table—to determine the top number of rows to return as output. Conversely, if we have to cut salaries based on poor company performance and want to obtain a listing of the highest-paid employees, whose salaries will be cut, we would reverse the sort order inside the inline view, as shown here:

```
SQL> select ename, job, sal, rownum
  2  from (select ename, job, sal from emp
  3           order by sal desc)
  4  where rownum <=3;
ENAME        JOB              SAL     ROWNUM
----------   ---------   ---------   ---------
KING         PRESIDENT       5000          1
SCOTT        ANALYST         3000          2
FORD         ANALYST         3000          3
```

TIP
Inline views support the use of the `order by` *clause. However, they are the only view in Oracle that does so. Other types of views that you will learn about in Chapter 7 do not support the use of the* `order by` *clause.*

In Conclusion

Remember to discard the change to KING's record in the EMP table when you're done:

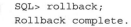

```
SQL> rollback;
Rollback complete.
```

For Review

1. Understand the syntax and semantics of creating basic inline views. Be able to remember that inline views are the only views in Oracle that support the use of the order by clause.

2. Know what a top-N query is and how to use an inline view to create one. Also, be sure you understand the use of ROWNUM in these types of queries.

Exercises

1. **This is the name of the pseudo-column often utilized for obtaining information for top-N queries:** _____

2. **Your company's sales database contains one table, PROFITS, which stores profits listed by product name, sales region, and quarterly time period. If you wanted to obtain a listing of the five best-selling products in company history, which of the following SQL statements would you use?**

   A. `select p.prod_name, p.profit from (select prod_name, profit from profits order by profit desc) where rownum <= 5;`

   B. `select p.prod_name, p.profit from (select prod_name, sum(profit) from profits group by prod_name order by sum(profit) desc) subq where p.prod_name = subq.prod_name;`

   C. `select prod_name, profit from (select prod_name, sum(profit) from profits group by prod_name order by sum(profit) desc) where rownum <=5;`

   D. `select prod_name, profit from (select prod_name, sum(profit) from profits order by sum(profit) desc) where rownum <=5;`

Answer Key

1. ROWNUM. **2.** C. Remember, you must account for the fact that the profits for the same products will appear once for each quarter.

Producing Readable Output with SQL*Plus

This section will cover the following topics related to using runtime variables:

- Entering variables

- Customizing SQL*Plus environments

- Producing readable output

- Creating and executing scripts

- Saving customizations

SQL*Plus is a powerful tool that can be used interactively to enter commands, as demonstrated so far throughout the book, or silently through batch processing and reporting. It is on this second topic thatwe will focus considerable attention in the next section. In this section, you will learn more about how entering variables into statements in SQL*Plus, customizing your work environment, producing readable output for reporting, creating and executing scripts, and saving your environment customizations.

TIP

*At any point in SQL*Plus operation, you can enter the* help SQLPLUS_command *command, and SQL*Plus will give you more information about use of that command.*

Entering Variables

In order to prepare for OCP, you should spend a little extra time on this topic, and treat the rest of the other topics in this section as background or reference material. Thus, if you've already been working with SQL for a while, you'll have less work to do in preparation for OCP. Let's say you have to pull up data for several different employees manually for the purpose of reviewing some aspect of their data. The following example shows how you've learned to do it so far:

```
SQL> select ename, job, deptno, sal
  2  from emp
  3  where empno = 7844;
ENAME       JOB         DEPTNO      SAL
----------  ----------  ----------  ----------
TURNER      SALESMAN        30      1500
```

Now, let's say you wanted to pull up the same data for KING, whose employee number is 7839. You've seen how to edit SQL commands in SQL*Plus and how to reexecute them using the slash (/) command. In light of these facts, you could edit the SQL statement with either the change or edit command to change the EMPNO information and then reissue the command. However, let's face it, you'll have to do a lot of typing and mouse clicking, and all that work is tedious. First, you have to open the text editor; then you have to find the text to change, modify it, and then save it to the SQL*Plus buffer—all before you reexecute the command. An easier way exists. Take a look at the following code block:

```
SQL> select ename, job, deptno, sal
  2  from emp
  3  where empno = &empno;
Enter value for empno: 7844
old   3: where empno = &empno
new   3: where empno = 7844
ENAME       JOB         DEPTNO      SAL
----------  ----------  ----------  ----------
TURNER      SALESMAN        30      1500
```

Now, all you have to do is issue the slash command and then enter a new employee number every time you want to see this information from the EMP table, as shown here:

```
SQL> /
Enter value for empno: 7839
old   3: where empno = &empno
new   3: where empno = 7839
ENAME       JOB         DEPTNO      SAL
----------  ----------  ----------  ----------
KING        PRESIDENT       10      5000
```

You can repeat this activity as often as you want until you enter a new SQL statement, which is great when you have repetitive SQL operations that you need to execute. Notice two important things about this output. First, notice the ampersand (&) preceding the reference to EMPNO in the where clause. This ampersand indicates to Oracle that you want to specify a value for that column before Oracle processes the query. This combination of ampersand and column identifier creates a *lexical substitution variable*. Second, Oracle shows you the line as it appeared in the buffer and then shows you the value you substituted. This presentation lets you know what data was changed by your input.

TIP
You can also use the double-ampersand (&&) keyword in Oracle to define variable values in SQL*Plus. The && keyword has an advantage over & in that && will preserve the value you define for the variable after you define it the first time you execute the statement, whereas & will prompt you to specify a value every time you execute the statement.

If you don't want to use the ampersand to create the substitution variable, the input can be changed with the set define command at the SQL prompt in SQL*Plus. You can reexecute the statement containing a runtime variable declaration by using the slash (/) command at the prompt in SQL*Plus. The following code block illustrates this:

```
SQL> set define ?
SQL> select ename, job, deptno, sal
  2  from emp
  3  where empno = ?empno;
Enter value for empno: 7839
old   3: where empno = ?empno
new   3: where empno = 7839
ENAME       JOB           DEPTNO       SAL
---------- --------- --------- ---------
KING        PRESIDENT       10      5000
SQL> /
Enter value for empno: 7844
old   3: where empno = ?empno
new   3: where empno = 7844
ENAME       JOB           DEPTNO       SAL
---------- --------- --------- ---------
TURNER      SALESMAN        30      1500
```

Now, for your own sanity, go ahead and switch back to the default:

```
SQL> set define &
```

TIP
You can find more information about the set define command in the "Customizing SQL*Plus Environments" discussion appearing later in this chapter.

Defining lexical substitution variables that handle text information is done slightly differently. Because text information must appear within single quotes in SQL queries in Oracle, you must therefore define the lexical substitution variable inside single-quotes as well. Also, remember that Oracle stores the text information literally as you typed it when the data was first added to Oracle, so pay attention to issues like spaces between words, case sensitivity, and so on. The following code block illustrates how to set up lexical substitution variables for text data:

```
SQL> select empno, deptno, sal
  2   from emp
  3   where ename = '&empname';
Enter value for empname: SMITH
old   3: where ename = '&empname'
new   3: where ename = 'SMITH'
    EMPNO     DEPTNO         SAL
---------- ---------- ----------
     7369         20         800
```

Finally, setting up lexical substitution variables that accommodate date information should be enclosed in single-quotes. The data entered should conform to whatever date format mask is used by Oracle to display data. The following code block illustrates both how to discover the format mask being used and how to enter it properly in a lexical substitution variable:

```
SQL> select ename, job, sal
  2   from emp where hiredate = '&startdate';
Enter value for startdate: 23-JAN-82
old   2: from emp where hiredate = '&startdate'
new   2: from emp where hiredate = '23-JAN-82'
ENAME      JOB             SAL
---------- --------- ----------
MILLER     CLERK          1300
SQL> /
```

```
Enter value for startdate: 23-jan-82
old    2: from emp where hiredate = '&startdate'
new    2: from emp where hiredate = '23-jan-82'
ENAME      JOB              SAL
---------- --------- ----------
MILLER     CLERK           1300
```

Automatic Definition of Runtime Variables

In some cases, it may not be useful to enter new values for a runtime variable every time the statement executes. For example, assume you must perform some onerous reporting process weekly for every person in a company. A great deal of value is added to the process by having a variable that can be specified at runtime because you can then simply execute the same statement over and over again with new EMPNO values each time. However, even this improvement does not streamline the process as much as one might like. Instead of running the statement over and over again with new values specified each time, you could create a script similar to the following:

```
------------------------
--  empinfo.sql -
--  This script selects information
--  from EMP and returns it to
--  the user
------------------------
define var_empno = 7844
select ename, job, deptno, sal
from emp
where empno = &var_empno;
undefine var_empno
define var_empno = 7839
select ename, job, deptno, sal
from emp
where empno = &var_empno;
```

TIP

You'll get the most out of your preparation time for OCP if you teach yourself by example. Therefore, spend the extra time coding in these scripts by hand to test them on your system. The more experience you have with Oracle, the better you will do on your OCP exam. Also, if you don't want to use the set define *command to use the question mark to identify substitution variables, just replace every instance of ? previously with &.*

When you use the @ command to run this script in SQL*Plus, the following output is produced:

```
SQL> @c:\windows\empinfo
old   3: where empno = &var_empno
new   3: where empno = 7844
ENAME       JOB         DEPTNO      SAL
----------  ---------   ---------   ---------
TURNER      SALESMAN         30       1500
old   3: where empno = &var_empno
new   3: where empno = 7839
ENAME       JOB         DEPTNO      SAL
----------  ---------   ---------   ---------
KING        PRESIDENT        10       5000
```

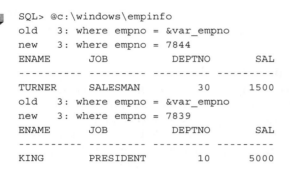

TIP
*The @@ command can also be used to execute scripts in SQL*Plus when the contents of one script call for execution of another script. When used, @@ tells SQL*Plus to look for the script in the same path where it found the currently executing script.*

The time spent actually keying in values for the variables named in the SQL `select` statement is eliminated with the `define` statement. Notice, however, that in between each execution of the SQL statement is a special statement using a command called `undefine`. In Oracle, the data that is defined with the `define` statement will remain defined for the variable for the entire session, unless the variable is undefined. By *undefining* a variable, you allow another `define` statement to reuse the variable in another execution of the same or a different statement.

TIP
You can also use the `define` command if you want to reuse substitution variables over different SQL statements, allowing you to pass a value from one statement to another.

`accept`: Another Way to Define Variables

You may have noticed that Oracle's method for identifying input, though not exactly cryptic, is fairly nonexpressive. You need not stick with Oracle's default messaging to identify the need for input. Instead, you can define a more expressive message that Oracle will use to prompt for input data. The name of the command that provides this functionality is the `accept` command. Check out the following code block, where it shows a slight modification to `empinfo.sql` that uses the `accept` command:

```
------------------------
--  empinfo2.sql -
--  This script selects information
--  from EMP and returns it to
--  the user
------------------------
accept var_empno prompt 'Enter EMPNO now => '
select ename, job, deptno, sal
from emp
where empno = &var_empno;
```

TIP
You'll get the most out of your preparation time for OCP if you teach yourself by example. Therefore, spend the extra time coding in these scripts by hand to test them on your system. The more experience you have with Oracle, the better you will do on your OCP exam. Also, notice the use of two dashes next to each other in the first few lines of this code block. That usage indicates a comment.

We can then run the script, as follows:

```
SQL> @c:\windows\empinfo2
Enter EMPNO now => 7844
old   3: where empno = &var_empno
new   3: where empno = 7844
ENAME      JOB          DEPTNO      SAL
---------- ---------- ---------- ---------
TURNER     SALESMAN          30       1500
```

Using the `accept` command can be preferable to Oracle's default output message in situations where you want to define a more accurate or specific prompt or when you want more output to display as the values are defined.

TIP
*By default, the datatype for a variable defined with
the* accept *command is CHAR. Fortunately,
Oracle can execute implicit type conversions from
CHAR to the datatype required for the input
variable, so usually, you won't have a problem. You
can also explicitly specify the datatype in the*
accept *command.*

For Review

1. Know the special character used to specify a lexical substitution variable (it's the ampersand).

2. Understand how to use the accept command and the benefits offered by the accept command.

3. Be sure you can tell how variables are defined within the SQL*Plus session using the define and undefine commands.

4. Know that two dashes next to each other (--) in a script indicates to SQL*Plus that everything else on that line is a comment.

Exercises

1. **Your sales database consists of one table, PROFITS, which lists profits for every product type the company sells, listed by quarter and by sales region. You need to develop a report that users can run interactively to show them the profits on toys for a given quarter. You have concerns about the users of this report because they have frequently complained about the readability and usability of your reports. Which of the following choices shows the contents of the script you should use for your report?**

   A.
   ```
   select profit from profits
   where prod_type = 'TOYS'
   and time_period = '&v_period';
   ```

   B.
   ```
   define v_period
   select profit from profits
   where prod_type = 'TOYS'
   and time_period = '&v_period';
   ```

    C. accept v_period prompt 'Enter the time period => '
       select profit from profits
       where prod_type = 'TOYS'
       and time_period = '&v_period';

    D. accept v_period
       select profit from profits
       where prod_type = 'TOYS'
       and time_period = '&v_period';

2. **Review the following code block containing the contents of a script called**
`dates.sql`:

```
accept v_hiredate prompt 'enter hire date => '
select empno, ename, job
from emp
where trunc(hiredate) = trunc('&v_hiredate');
```

Which of the following aspects of the script must be changed in order for
the script to function properly?

    A. Variable v_hiredate must be changed to accept DATE information.

    B. The trunc( ) function in the query should be eliminated.

    C. The prompt clause in the accept command is unnecessary.

    D. Nothing, the script will work fine as is.

3. **This is the string that must prefix lexical substitution variables if you want**
the value saved between statement executions: _____

Answer Key
1. C. Remember, part of your goal is pleasing the users. **2.** A. **3.** &&

Customizing SQL*Plus Environments

You can customize your SQL*Plus operating environment with the set
system_variable value command, where *system_variable* is the name of
a system variable you can set in SQL*Plus, and *value* is the value you would like
to set that system variable to. We'll cover some common system variables and their
acceptable values in this discussion. Each of the headers for the following subtopics

contains the full name of the system variable, followed by its abbreviation in brackets ([ ]), followed by its valid values in curly braces ({ }).

NOTE
This section is provided primarily for reference purposes and for your OCP study. No examples are provided, but it is assumed that you will practice using each of these commands on your own. Recognizing that this list of SQL*Plus commands is extensive, you may want to focus mainly on ARRAYSIZE, COLSEP, FEEDBACK, HEADING, LINESIZE, LONG, PAGESIZE, PAUSE, *and* TERMOUT *for OCP and use the rest of this information as a reference.*

ARRAYSIZE [ARRAY] {15|n} This command sets the number of rows that SQL*Plus fetches from the database at one time. Valid values are 1 to 5,000. A large value increases the efficiency of queries and subqueries that fetch many rows, but it requires more memory.

AUTOCOMMIT [AUTO] {OFF|ON|IMMEDIATE|n} This controls when Oracle commits pending changes to the database. ON commits pending changes to the database after Oracle executes each successful data change command or PL/SQL block. OFF suppresses automatic committing so that you must commit changes manually. IMMEDIATE functions in the same manner as the ON option. The value n commits pending changes to the database after Oracle executes n successful data change commands or PL/SQL blocks, where n cannot be less than zero or greater than 2,000,000,000.

AUTOTRACE [AUTOT] {OFF|ON|TRACEONLY|EXPLAIN|STATISTICS} This command displays a report on the execution of successful SQL statements. The report can include execution statistics and the query execution path. OFF does not display a trace report. ON displays a trace report. TRACEONLY displays a trace report but does not print query data, if any. Before using autotrace, you must run the plustrce.sql script found in the sqlplus/admin directory under your Oracle software home directory. The EXPLAIN and STATISTICS options can be used for performance tuning as well by displaying SQL statement execution plans and statistics from the cost-based optimizer, respectively.

CMDSEP [CMDS] {;|c|OFF|ON} This sets the nonalphanumeric character used to separate multiple SQL*Plus commands entered on one line to c. ON or OFF controls whether you can enter multiple commands on a line; ON automatically sets the command separator character to a semicolon (;).

COLSEP [COLSEP] { |text}   This command sets the text to be printed between selected columns. If the colsep variable contains blanks or punctuation characters, you must enclose it with single quotes. The default value for text is a single space. In multiline rows, the column separator does not print between columns that begin on different lines.

COMPATIBILITY [COM] {V7|V8|NATIVE}   This specifies the version of Oracle to which you are currently connected. Set compatibility to V7 for Oracle7 or V8 for Oracle8 and Oracle8i. Set compatibility to NATIVE if you want the database to determine the setting (for example, if you're connected to Oracle8 or Oracle8i, compatibility would default to V8). The compatibility variable must be correctly set for the version of Oracle to which you are connected; otherwise, you will be unable to run any SQL commands. However, you can set compatibility to V7 when connected to Oracle8i. This enables you to run Oracle7 SQL against Oracle8i.

CONCAT [CON] {.|c|OFF|ON}   This sets the character you can use to terminate a substitution variable reference if you want to immediately follow the variable with a character that SQL*Plus would otherwise interpret as a part of the substitution variable name. SQL*Plus resets the value of concat to a period when you switch concat on.

COPYCOMMIT [COPYC] {0|n}   This command controls the number of batches after which the copy command commits changes to the database. copy commits rows to the destination database each time it copies n row batches. Valid values are 0 to 5,000. You can set the size of a batch with the arraysize variable. If you set copycommit to 0, copy performs a commit operation only at the end of a copy operation.

COPYTYPECHECK [COPYTYPECHECK] {OFF|ON}   This sets the suppression of the comparison of datatypes while inserting or appending to tables with the copy command. This is to facilitate copying to DB2, which requires that a CHAR be copied to a DB2 DATE.

DESCRIBE [DESCRIBE] DEPTH {1|n|ALL} LINENUM {ON|OFF} INDENT {ON|OFF}   This command sets the depth of the level to which you can recursively describe an object. The valid range of the depth clause is from 1 to 50. If you issue the set describe depth ALL command, the depth will be set to 50, which is the maximum level allowed. You can also display the line number and indentation of the attribute or column name when an object contains multiple object types. Use the set linesize command to control the width of the data displayed.

ECHO [ECHO] {OFF|ON}   This controls whether the start command lists each command in a command file as the command is executed. ON lists the commands; OFF suppresses the listing.

EDITFILE [EDITF] {file_name[.ext]}   This command sets the default filename for the edit command. You can include a path and/or file extension. For information on changing the default extension, see the suffix variable of this command. The default filename and maximum filename length are operating system specific.

EMBEDDED [EMB] {OFF|ON}   This controls where on a page each report begins. OFF forces each report to start at the top of a new page. ON enables a report to begin anywhere on a page. Set embedded to ON when you want a report to begin printing immediately following the end of the previously run report.

ESCAPE [ESC] {\|c|OFF|ON}   This command defines the character you enter as the escape character. OFF undefines the escape character. ON enables the escape character. ON also changes the value of c back to the default (\). You can use the escape character before the substitution character (set through set define) to indicate that SQL*Plus should treat the substitution character as an ordinary character rather than as a request for variable substitution.

FEEDBACK [FEED] {6|n|OFF|ON}   This displays the number of records returned by a query when a query selects at least n records. ON or OFF turns this display on or off. Turning feedback ON sets n to 1. Setting feedback to 0 is equivalent to turning it OFF.

FLAGGER [FLAGGER] {OFF|ENTRY |INTERMEDIATE|FULL}   This command checks to make sure that SQL statements conform to the ANSI/ISO SQL92 standard. If any nonstandard constructs are found, the Oracle server flags them as errors and displays the violating syntax. This is the equivalent of the SQL language alter session set flagger command. You may execute set flagger even if you are not connected to a database. Flagging will remain in effect across SQL*Plus sessions until a set flagger OFF (or alter session set flagger = OFF) command is successful or you exit SQL*Plus.

FLUSH [FLU] {OFF|ON}   This controls when output is sent to the user's display device. OFF enables the host operating system to buffer output. ON disables buffering. Use OFF only when you run a command file noninteractively. The use of flush OFF may improve performance by reducing the amount of program I/O.

HEADING [HEA] {OFF|ON}   This command controls the printing of column headings in reports. ON prints column headings in reports; OFF suppresses column headings. The set heading OFF command will not affect the column width displayed; it only suppresses the printing of the column header itself.

HEADSEP [HEADS] {||c|OFF|ON}   This defines the character you enter as the heading separator character. The heading separator character cannot be alphanumeric or whitespace. ON or OFF turns heading separation on or off. When heading separation is OFF, SQL*Plus prints a heading separator character like any other character. ON changes the value of c back to the default (|).

INSTANCE [instance_path|LOCAL]   This command changes the default instance for your session to the specified instance path. Using this command does not connect you to the database. The default instance is used for commands when no instance is specified. Any commands preceding the first use of this command cause SQL*Plus to communicate with the default instance.

LINESIZE [LIN] {80|n}   This sets the total number of characters that SQL*Plus displays on one line before beginning a new line. You can define linesize as a value from 1 to a system-dependent maximum.

LOBOFFSET [LOBOF] {n|1}   This command sets the starting position from which large object (LOB) data is retrieved and displayed.

LONG [LONG] {80|n}   This sets the maximum width (in bytes) for displaying LONG, CLOB, and NCLOB values as well as for copying LONG values. The maximum value of n is 2GB.

LONGCHUNKSIZE [LONGC] {80|n}   This command sets the size (in bytes) of the increments in which SQL*Plus retrieves a LONG, CLOB, or NCLOB value.

NEWPAGE [NEWP] {1|n|NONE}   This sets the number of blank lines to be printed from the top of each page to the top title. A value of 0 places a form feed at the beginning of each page (including the first page) and clears the screen on most terminals. If you set newpage to NONE, SQL*Plus does not print a blank line or formfeed between the report pages.

NULL [NULL] {text}   This command sets the text that represents a NULL value in the result of a select command.

NUMFORMAT [NUMF] {format}   This sets the default format for displaying numbers. Enter a number format for `format`.

NUMWIDTH [NUM] {10|n}   This command sets the default width for displaying numbers.

TIP
More information about formatting numbers as output in SQL*Plus is offered in the next discussion.

PAGESIZE [PAGES] {24|n}   This sets the number of lines in each page. You can set `pagesize` to 0 to suppress all headings, page breaks, titles, the initial blank line, and other formatting information.

PAUSE [PAU] {OFF|ON|text}   This command enables you to control scrolling of your terminal when running reports. ON causes SQL*Plus to pause at the beginning of each page of report output. You must press ENTER after each pause. The text you enter specifies the text to be displayed each time SQL*Plus pauses. If you enter multiple words, you must enclose the text in single quotes. You can embed terminal-dependent escape sequences in the `pause` command. These sequences enable you to create inverse video messages or other effects on terminals that support such characteristics.

RECSEP [RECSEP] {WRAPPED|EACH|OFF}   This tells SQL*Plus where to make the record separation. For example, if you set `recsep` to WRAPPED, SQL*Plus prints a record separator only after wrapped lines. If you set `recsep` to EACH, SQL*Plus prints a record separator following every row. If you set `recsep` to OFF, SQL*Plus does not print a record separator.

RECSEPCHAR [RECSEPCHAR] { |c}   This command displays or prints record separators. A record separator consists of a single line of the record-separating character (`recsepchar`) repeated `linesize` times. The `recsepchar` command defines the record-separating character. A single space is the default.

SERVEROUTPUT [SERVEROUT] {OFF|ON} SIZE {N}   This controls whether to display the output from DBMS_OUTPUT.put_line( ) calls in PL/SQL blocks in SQL*Plus. OFF suppresses the output of DBMS_OUTPUT.put_line( ); ON displays the output. The `size` clause sets the number of bytes of the output that can be buffered within Oracle8i. The default for n is 2,000, and it cannot be less than 2,000 or greater than 1,000,000. This command can handle other values like WRAPPED, TRUNCATED, and FORMAT, but this functionality probably won't appear in the OCP exam.

SHIFTINOUT [SHIFT] {VISIBLE]|INVISIBLE]} This command enables correct alignment for terminals that display shift characters. The set shiftinout command is useful for terminals that display shift characters together with data (for example, IBM 3270 terminals). You can only use this command with shift-sensitive character sets (for example, JA16DBCS). Use VISIBLE for terminals that display shift characters as a visible character (for example, a space or a colon). INVISIBLE is the opposite and does not display any shift characters.

SHOWMODE [SHOW] {OFF|ON} This controls whether SQL*Plus lists the old and new settings of a SQL*Plus system variable when you change the setting with set. ON lists the settings; OFF suppresses the listing.

SQLBLANKLINES [SQLBL] {ON|OFF} This command controls whether SQL*Plus enables blank lines within a SQL command. ON interprets blank lines and new lines as part of a SQL command. OFF, the default value, does not enable blank lines or new lines in a SQL command. SQL*Plus returns to the default behavior when a SQL statement terminator or PL/SQL block terminator is encountered.

SQLCASE [SQLC] {MIXED|LOWER|UPPER} This converts the case of SQL commands and PL/SQL blocks just prior to execution. SQL*Plus converts all text within the command, including quoted literals and identifiers, as follows:

- Uppercase if sqlcase equals UPPER

- Lowercase if sqlcase equals LOWER

- Unchanged if sqlcase equals MIXED

TIP

The sqlcase keyword does not change the SQL buffer itself.

SQLCONTINUE [SQLCO] {>|text} This command sets the character sequence SQL*Plus displays as a prompt after you continue a SQL*Plus command on an additional line using a hyphen (-).

SQLNUMBER [SQLN] {OFF|ON} This sets the prompt for the second and subsequent lines of a SQL command or PL/SQL block. ON sets the prompt to be the line number. OFF sets the prompt to the value of sqlprompt.

SQLPREFIX [SQLPRE] {#|c} This command sets the SQL*Plus prefix character. While you are entering a SQL command or PL/SQL block, you can enter a SQL*Plus command on a separate line, prefixed by the SQL*Plus prefix character. SQL*Plus will execute this command immediately without affecting the SQL command or PL/SQL block that you are entering. The prefix character must be a nonalphanumeric character.

SQLPROMPT [SQLP] {SQL>|text}   This sets the SQL*Plus command prompt.

SQLTERMINATOR [SQLT] {;|c|OFF|ON}   This command sets the character used to end and execute SQL commands to *c*. OFF means that SQL*Plus recognizes no command terminator; you terminate a SQL command by entering an empty line. ON resets the terminator to the default—a semicolon (;).

SUFFIX [SUF] {SQL|text}   This sets the default file extension that SQL*Plus uses in commands that refer to command files. The value for suffix does not control extensions for spool files.

TAB [TAB] {OFF|ON}   This command determines how SQL*Plus formats whitespace in terminal output. OFF uses spaces to format whitespace in the output. ON uses the tab character. The tab character creates a space setting of eight blank characters. The default value for tab is system dependent.

TERMOUT [TERM] {OFF|ON}   This controls the display of output generated by commands executed from a command file. OFF suppresses the display so that you can spool output from a command file without seeing the output on the screen. ON displays the output. Setting termout OFF does not affect output from commands you enter interactively.

TIME [TI] {OFF|ON}   This command controls the display of the current time. ON displays the current time before each command prompt. OFF suppresses the time display.

TIMING [TIMI] {OFF|ON}   This controls the display of timing statistics. ON displays timing statistics on each SQL command or PL/SQL block run. OFF suppresses timing of each command.

TRIMOUT [TRIM] {OFF|ON}   This command determines whether SQL*Plus enables trailing blanks at the end of each displayed line. ON removes blanks at the end of each line, thus improving performance, especially when you access SQL*Plus from a slow communications device. OFF enables SQL*Plus to display trailing blanks. Setting trimout ON does not affect spooled output.

TRIMSPOOL [TRIMS] {ON|OFF}   This determines whether SQL*Plus enables trailing blanks at the end of each spooled line. ON removes blanks at the end of each line. OFF enables SQL*Plus to include trailing blanks. Using `trimspool ON` does not affect terminal output.

VERIFY [VER] {OFF|ON}   This command controls whether SQL*Plus lists the text of a SQL statement or PL/SQL command before and after SQL*Plus replaces substitution variables with values. ON lists the text; OFF suppresses the listing.

TIP
In most cases, if you want to see the value set for a particular SQL*Plus attribute, you can precede that attribute with the `show` command. For example, to see the value set for `linesize`, use the `show linesize` command.

For Review
Be sure you know how to customize the SQL*Plus running environment using the `set` command, including the use of common system variables such as `pagesize`, `linesize`, `termout`, `feedback`, `sqlprompt`, and `echo`.

Exercises
1. This SQL*Plus command is useful for determining whether the "N rows selected" message will appear: _____

2. This SQL*Plus command is useful for determining what extension SQL*Plus expects for files containing SQL commands:

   _____

3. Use of this command requires that you first run the `plustrce.sql` script: _____ .

Answer Key
1. feedback 2. suffix 3. autotrace

Producing Readable Output
Certain commands are also available to improve the look of your SQL*Plus output. These commands are explained in the following subtopics. If an abbreviation is available for the command, the abbreviation will be given inside brackets ([ ]). The valid values for this command will be given inside curly braces ({ }).

COLUMN {col} FORMAT {fmt} HEADING {string}   The most commonly used command for injecting readability into your SQL*Plus output by controlling column output format is the column *col* command, where *col* is the name of your column in the SQL query. You can turn formatting on and off by specifying column *col* on or column *col* off, respectively. You can also clear any setting by issuing column *col* clear. You can change the heading used for a column by using the heading '*string*' clause. You can also refine the format of output appearing in that column using the format *fmt* clause. For alphanumeric information appearing in a column, *fmt* is specified in the form a*num*, where *num* is a number representing how many characters wide the column should be. For numbers, *fmt* can be specified as a series of 9s representing the number of digits you want to see, optionally with currency symbols (L for local currency), commas, and/or periods. For example, column sal format $9,999.99 would display all numbers in the salary column of a query as follows:

```
SQL> column sal format $9,999.99
SQL> select sal from emp;
       SAL
----------
   $800.00
 $1,600.00
 $1,250.00
 $2,975.00
 $1,250.00
 $2,850.00
 $2,450.00
 $3,000.00
 $5,000.00
 $1,500.00
 $1,100.00
   $950.00
 $3,000.00
 $1,300.00
```

UNDERLINE [UND] {-|c|ON|OFF}   This command sets the character used to underline column headings in SQL*Plus reports to *c*. Note, *c* cannot be an alphanumeric character or a whitespace character. ON or OFF turns underlining on or off. ON changes the value of *c* back to the default (-). For example, you can use asterisks to underline column headings in the following way:

```
SQL> column empno format 99999
SQL> column ename format a12
SQL> set underline *
SQL> select empno, ename, sal
```

```
  2  from emp;
EMPNO ENAME              SAL
****** ************ **********
 7369 SMITH            $800.00
 7499 ALLEN          $1,600.00
 7521 WARD           $1,250.00
 7566 JONES          $2,975.00
 7654 MARTIN         $1,250.00
 7698 BLAKE          $2,850.00
 7782 CLARK          $2,450.00
 7788 SCOTT          $3,000.00
 7839 KING           $5,000.00
 7844 TURNER         $1,500.00
 7876 ADAMS          $1,100.00
 7900 JAMES            $950.00
 7902 FORD           $3,000.00
 7934 MILLER         $1,300.00
```

WRAP [WRA] {OFF|ON} The heading string specified for `column` can also contain a pipe character (|). For example, `column dname heading 'd|name'` denotes that you would like to split the heading into two separate lines. In some cases when you format column output in this way, the value for the column may not fit in the space allotted. The `wrap` variable controls whether SQL*Plus truncates the display of a `selected` row if it is too long for the current line width. `OFF` truncates the `selected` row; `ON` enables the `selected` row to wrap to the next line. If you want, you can also specify `recsep` and `recsepchar` to print separators between word-wrapped lines to make output clearer. Here's an example:

```
SQL> column dname heading d|name format a4
SQL> set recsep wrapped
SQL> set recsepchar '-'
SQL> select * from dept;
          d
   DEPTNO name LOC
--------- ---- -------------
       10 ACCO NEW YORK
          UNTI
          NG
-------------------------------------------------
       20 RESE DALLAS
          ARCH
-------------------------------------------------
       30 SALE CHICAGO
          S
-------------------------------------------------
```

```
        40 OPER BOSTON
           ATIO
           NS
------------------------------------------------
```

BREAK   Sometimes when the information returned by your SQL query is ordered on a column, you may have multiple rows of data, each with the same value in the ordered column. The output can be changed so that only the first in a series of rows, where the ordered column value is the same, will show the column value. Observe how this is accomplished in the following code block using the `break` command:

```
SQL> break on deptno
SQL> select deptno, ename from emp
  2  order by deptno;
   DEPTNO ENAME
--------- ----------
       10 CLARK
          KING
          MILLER
       20 SMITH
          ADAMS
          FORD
          SCOTT
          JONES
       30 ALLEN
          BLAKE
          MARTIN
          JAMES
          TURNER
          WARD
```

TIP
You can also use the `skip` n *or* `skip page`
clauses in the `break` *command to insert* n *blank*
lines or page breaks, respectively.

COMPUTE   You can also generate simple reports in SQL*Plus using the `compute` command in conjunction with the `break` command. The `compute` command performs one of several grouping functions on the column you are breaking on, including `sum`, `minimum`, `maximum`, `avg` (average), `std` (standard deviation), `variance`, `count`, and `number` (number of rows in the column). The following block illustrates a couple of uses for this command, in conjunction with `break`:

```
SQL> -- example 1
SQL> break on deptno skip 1
SQL> compute sum of sal on deptno
SQL> select deptno, ename, sal
  2  from emp order by deptno;
    DEPTNO ENAME           SAL
--------- ---------- ---------
       10 CLARK          2450
          KING           5000
          MILLER         1300
********* ---------- ---------
sum                      8750


       20 SMITH           800
          ADAMS          1100
          FORD           3000
          SCOTT          3000
          JONES          2975
********* ---------- ---------
sum                     10875


       30 ALLEN          1600
          BLAKE          2850
          MARTIN         1250
          JAMES           950
          TURNER         1500
          WARD           1250
********* ---------- ---------
sum                      9400
SQL> -- example 2
SQL> clear breaks
breaks cleared
SQL> clear computes
computes cleared
SQL> break on report
SQL> compute sum of sal on report
SQL> /
    DEPTNO ENAME           SAL
--------- ---------- ---------
       10 CLARK          2450
       10 KING           5000
       10 MILLER         1300
       20 SMITH           800
       20 ADAMS          1100
       20 FORD           3000
       20 SCOTT          3000
```

```
20 JONES            2975
30 ALLEN            1600
30 BLAKE            2850
30 MARTIN           1250
30 JAMES             950
30 TURNER           1500
                 ---------
sum                29025
```

TTITLE and BTITLE   The use of break and compute segues into a larger discussion of using SQL*Plus to write reports. If you want a top or bottom title to appear on each page of a report, you can place one through the use of the ttitle and btitle commands, respectively. The syntax is [btitle|ttitle] *position* 'title_text', where *position* can be LEFT, CENTER, RIGHT, or COL *n* to indicate a fixed number of characters from the left to start the title line.

TIP
Using linesize and pagesize to determine page width and how many lines of text appear on a page will also determine where btitle and ttitle place your top and bottom title lines, respectively.

For Review
Practice writing SQL*Plus reports using the commands covered in this and the previous discussion.

Exercises

1. This SQL*Plus command can be used for calculating sums of data on columns in the same way as a group function: _____

2. This SQL*Plus command can be used to enhance report readability by reducing the number of times a duplicate value appears in a sorted column: _____

3. This SQL*Plus command can be used for placing a footer title on the bottom of a report page: _____

Answer Key
1. compute 2. break 3. btitle

Creating and Executing Scripts

Each time you execute a SQL statement in SQL*Plus, that statement gets saved to a buffer used by SQL*Plus for repeat execution. One thing you might want to do when you have SQL statements you execute routinely in SQL*Plus is to save those statements as scripts. You can do this in a few different ways, one of which is to simply open up a text editor available on your operating system, enter the statements you want to execute routinely, and save the script to your host machine as a plain-text file. Another method available to you within SQL*Plus is to use the save command with a .sql extension, as follows:

```
SQL> select empno, ename, sal, deptno, hiredate
  2  from emp;
    EMPNO ENAME           SAL    DEPTNO HIREDATE
--------- ---------- --------- --------- ---------
     7369 SMITH          800        20 17-DEC-80
     7499 ALLEN         1600        30 20-FEB-81
     7521 WARD          1250        30 22-FEB-81
     7566 JONES         2975        20 02-APR-81
     7654 MARTIN        1250        30 28-SEP-81
     7698 BLAKE         2850        30 01-MAY-81
     7782 CLARK         2450        10 09-JUN-81
     7788 SCOTT         3000        20 19-APR-87
     7839 KING          5000        10 17-NOV-81
     7844 TURNER        1500        30 08-SEP-81
     7876 ADAMS         1100        20 23-MAY-87
     7900 JAMES          950        30 03-DEC-81
     7902 FORD          3000        20 03-DEC-81
     7934 MILLER        1300        10 23-JAN-82
SQL> save employee.sql
Created file employee.sql
```

You have already seen that, when you want to execute the script again, you can use the @ command within SQL*Plus. Let's take one more look for review:

```
SQL> @employee.sql
SQL> @employee.sql
    EMPNO ENAME           SAL    DEPTNO HIREDATE
--------- ---------- --------- --------- ---------
     7369 SMITH          800        20 17-DEC-80
     7499 ALLEN         1600        30 20-FEB-81
     7521 WARD          1250        30 22-FEB-81
     7566 JONES         2975        20 02-APR-81
     7654 MARTIN        1250        30 28-SEP-81
     7698 BLAKE         2850        30 01-MAY-81
```

```
7782  CLARK          2450     10  09-JUN-81
7788  SCOTT          3000     20  19-APR-87
7839  KING           5000     10  17-NOV-81
7844  TURNER         1500     30  08-SEP-81
7876  ADAMS          1100     20  23-MAY-87
7900  JAMES           950     30  03-DEC-81
7902  FORD           3000     20  03-DEC-81
7934  MILLER         1300     10  23-JAN-82
```

For Review

Be sure you understand which commands to use for saving and executing your scripts in SQL*Plus.

Exercises

1. This is the command for storing the contents of your SQL*Plus buffer as a command file: _____

2. This is a command for loading a SQL command file into the operating buffer and executing it: _____

Answer Key
1. save 2. @

Saving Customizations

To save customizations to a file, you should use the `store` command, which accepts the `set` keyword along with a filename to save the environment settings to. The following code block illustrates this principle:

```
SQL> set termout on
SQL> set pagesize 132
SQL> store set myfile.out
Created file myfile.out
SQL>
```

Once your settings are saved, you can look at them in the file SQL*Plus created. To restore your settings, you must execute the contents the file in SQL*Plus. Both of these points are demonstrated in the following code block:

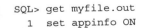
```
SQL> get myfile.out
   1  set appinfo ON
```

```
 2  set appinfo "SQL*Plus"
 3  set arraysize 15
 4  set autocommit OFF
 5  set autoprint OFF
 6  set autotrace OFF
 7  set shiftinout invisible
 8  set blockterminator "."
 9  set cmdsep OFF
10  set colsep " "
11  set compatibility NATIVE
12  set concat "."
13  set copycommit 0
14  set copytypecheck ON
15  set define "&"
16  set echo OFF
17  set editfile "afiedt.buf"
18  set embedded OFF
19  set escape OFF
20  set feedback 6
21  set flagger OFF
22  set flush ON
23  set heading ON
24  set headsep "|"
25  set linesize 100
26  set long 80
27  set longchunksize 80
28  set newpage 1
29  set null ""
30  set numformat ""
31  set numwidth 9
32  set pagesize 132
33  set pause OFF
34  set recsep WRAP
35  set recsepchar " "
36  set serveroutput OFF
37  set showmode OFF
38  set sqlcase MIXED
39  set sqlcontinue "> "
40  set sqlnumber ON
41  set sqlprefix "#"
42  set sqlprompt "SQL> "
43  set sqlterminator ";"
44  set suffix "sql"
45  set tab ON
46  set termout ON
47  set time OFF
```

```
48  set timing OFF
49  set trimout ON
50  set trimspool OFF
51  set underline "-"
52  set verify ON
53* set wrap ON
SQL> @myfile.out
SQL>
```

NOTE
Your settings for column, break, compute, *btitle, and* ttitle *will not be included in the output file.*

Alternately, if your environment file is stored in a file called login.sql, SQL*Plus can automatically execute the contents of the file so that the next time you log into SQL*Plus, your environment will be exactly the way you want it. This file must be stored either in the local directory from where you start SQL*Plus or on an operating system–specific path.

For Review

Be sure you understand how to store your environment settings and what the use of the login.sql file is.

Exercises

1. This is the command for writing all SQL*Plus environment data to a script for executing later: _____

2. This is the name of the script that will run whenever you start SQL*Plus to configure your environment settings: _____

Answer Key
1. store 2. login.sql

Chapter Summary

This chapter covered a lot of territory. You learned a great deal about advanced selection of data in SQL*Plus, including how to structure single-row, multiple-row, and correlated subqueries, as well as how to identify all those different types of queries. You also learned that subqueries ignore NULL results—a crucial fact to remember for OCP. After that, we discussed the many commands in SQL*Plus for formatting output for reports, how to write scripts, and how to enter variables into SQL queries for ease of use.

Two-Minute Drill

- The data used to determine the `having` clause can either be specified at runtime by the query or by a special embedded query, called a *subquery*, which obtains unknown search criteria based on known search methods.

- Subqueries can be used in other parts of the `select` statement to determine unknown search criteria, as well. Subqueries are generally included in this fashion in the `where` clause.

- Subqueries can use columns in comparison operations that are local to the table specified in the subquery, or they can use columns that are specified in tables named in any parent query to the subquery. This use is based on the principles of variable scope, as presented in this chapter.

- Various types of subqueries you might encounter when using Oracle include the following:

  - **Single-row subqueries** The main query expects the subquery to return only one value.

  - **Multiple-row subqueries** The main query can handle situations where the subquery returns more than one value.

  - **Inline views** A subquery in a `from` clause used for defining an intermediate result set to query from.

  - **Multiple-column subqueries** A subquery that contains more than one column of return data in addition to however many rows are given in the output.

- Be sure you understand how to set up and use a correlated subquery in Oracle to retrieve data.

- Recall that most subqueries (even those returning multiple rows) generally only return one column of output per row. However, you can construct subqueries that return multiple columns. Review the chapter to refresh your understanding of the syntax and semantics involved.

- Subqueries that contain `group by` expressions will ignore rows if the `group by` column contains NULL values for those rows. Be sure you understand how to rewrite such queries, if necessary, to obtain those NULL values.

- A subquery found in a `from` clause of the parent SQL query is called an *inline view*. Be sure you recall the syntax and semantics involved in using inline views, especially if you want to refer directly to columns in an inline view. Recall the use of inline views for top-N queries as well.

- Review the SQL*Plus environment characteristics that can be configured using the `set` command.

- In addition, be sure you understand completely how to use the following SQL*Plus commands for enhancing output readability:

  - `format`

  - `btitle`

  - `ttitle`

  - `break`

  - `compute`

- Variables can be set in a `select` statement at runtime with use of runtime variables. A runtime variable is designated with the ampersand character (&) preceding the variable name.

- The special character that designates a runtime variable can be changed using the `set define` command.

- The `define` command can identify a runtime variable value to be picked up by the `select` statement automatically.

- Once defined, the variable remains defined for the rest of the session or until it is undefined by the user or process with the `undefine` command.

- You can modify the message that prompts the user to input a variable value. This activity is performed with the `accept` command.

Fill-in-the-Blank Questions

1. In order to generate reports that display sums of information by report, you might use this SQL*Plus command: _____

2. After assigning a value to a variable in a SQL*Plus command, you can reassign that variable a value using this SQL*Plus command:

   _____

3. This SQL*Plus keyword is used for defining formats for how SQL*Plus displays column information: _____

4. This phrase describes a query that feeds one row of results to a parent query for the purpose of selection when the exact `where` clause criteria is not known: _____

Chapter Questions

1. **Once a variable is defined, how long will it remain defined in SQL*Plus?**

   A. Until the database is shut down

   B. Until the instance is shut down

   C. Until the statement completes

   D. Until the session completes

2. **You want to change the prompt Oracle uses to obtain input from a user. Which of the following choices are used for this purpose? (Choose two.)**

   A. Change the prompt in the `config.ora` file.

   B. Alter the `prompt` clause of the `accept` command.

   C. Enter a new prompt in the `login.sql` file.

   D. There is no way to change a prompt in Oracle.

3. **What is the default character for specifying substitution variables in `select` statements?**

   A. Ampersand

   B. Ellipses

   C. Quotation marks

   D. Asterisk

4. **The default character that identifies runtime variables is changed by which of the following?**

   A. Modifying the init*sid*.ora file

   B. Modifying the login.sql file

   C. Issuing the define *variablename* command

   D. Issuing the set define command

5. **You are developing a multiple-row query to handle a complex and dynamic comparison operation for the Olympics. Two tables are involved. CONTESTANT lists all contestants from every country, and MEDALS lists every country and the number of gold, silver, and bronze medals they have. If a country has not received one of the three types of medals, a zero appears in the column. Therefore, a query will always return data, even for countries that haven't won a medal. Which of the following queries shows only the contestants from countries with more than ten medallists of any type?**

   A. SELECT NAME FROM CONTESTANT C, MEDALS M WHERE
      C.COUNTRY = M.COUNTRY;

   B. SELECT NAME FROM CONTESTANT WHERE COUNTRY C IN
      (SELECT COUNTRY FROM MEDALS M WHERE C.COUNTRY =
      M.COUNTY)

   C. SELECT NAME FROM CONTESTANT WHERE COUNTRY C =
      (SELECT COUNTRY FROM MEDALS M WHERE C.COUNTRY =
      M.COUNTY)

   D. SELECT NAME FROM CONTESTANT WHERE COUNTRY IN
      (SELECT COUNTRY FROM MEDALS WHERE NUM_GOLD +
      NUM_SILVER + NUM_BRONZE > 10)

6. **You issue the following query in a SQL*Plus session:**

   ```
   SELECT NAME, AGE, COUNTRY FROM CONTESTANT
   WHERE (COUNTRY, AGE) IN ( SELECT COUNTRY, MIN(AGE)
   FROM CONTESTANT GROUP BY COUNTRY);
   ```

   Which of the following choices identifies both the type of query and the expected result from the Oracle database?

   A. Single-row subquery, the youngest contestant from one country.

   B. Multiple-row subquery, the youngest contestant from all countries.

C. Multiple-column subquery, the youngest contestant from all countries.

D. Multiple-column subquery; Oracle will return an error because = should replace IN.

7. **The contents of the CONTESTANT table are listed as follows:**

```
NAME                          AGE COUNTRY
------------      ---------------  ---------------
BERTRAND                       24 FRANCE
GONZALEZ                       29 SPAIN
HEINRICH                       22 GERMANY
TAN                            39 CHINA
SVENSKY                        30 RUSSIA
SOO                            21
```

You issue the following query against this table:

```
SELECT NAME FROM CONTESTANT
WHERE (COUNTRY, AGE) IN ( SELECT COUNTRY, MIN(AGE)
FROM CONTESTANT GROUP BY COUNTRY);
```

Which of the following contestants will not appear in the output from this query?

A. SOO

B. HEINRICH

C. BERTRAND

D. GONZALEZ

8. **User JANKO would like to insert a row into the EMPLOYEE table. The table has three columns: EMPID, LASTNAME, and SALARY. This user would like to enter data for EMPID 59694, LASTNAME Harris, but no salary. Which statement would work best?**

A. `insert into EMPLOYEE values (59694,'HARRIS', NULL);`

B. `insert into EMPLOYEE values (59694,'HARRIS');`

C. `insert into EMPLOYEE (EMPID, LASTNAME, SALARY) values (59694,'HARRIS');`

D. `insert into EMPLOYEE (select 59694 from 'HARRIS');`

9. **Omitting the `where` clause from a `delete` statement has which of the following effects?**

   A. The `delete` statement will fail because there are no records to delete.

   B. The `delete` statement will prompt the user to enter criteria for the deletion.

   C. The `delete` statement will fail because of a syntax error.

   D. The `delete` statement will remove all records from the table.

Fill-in-the-Blank Answers

1. compute

2. undefine

3. Set

4. Single-row subquery

Answers to Chapter Questions

1. D. Until the session completes

Explanation   A variable defined by the user during a session with SQL*Plus will remain defined until the session ends or until the user explicitly undefines the variable. Refer to the discussion of defining variables earlier in the chapter.

2. B and C. Alter the prompt clause of the accept command *and* enter a new prompt in the login.sql file.

Explanation   Choice D should be eliminated immediately, leaving choices A, B, and C. Choice A is incorrect because config.ora is a feature associated with Oracle's client/server network communications product. Choice C is correct because you can use the set sqlprompt command within your login.sql file. This is a special file Oracle users can incorporate into their use of Oracle that will automatically configure aspects of the SQL*Plus session, such as the default text editor, column and NLS data formats, and other items.

3. A. Ampersand

Explanation   The ampersand (&) character is used by default to define runtime variables in SQL*Plus. Review the discussion of the definition of runtime variables and the set define command.

4. D. Issuing the set define command

Explanation   Choice A is incorrect because a change to the initsid.ora file will alter the parameters Oracle uses to start the database instance. Use of this feature will be covered in the next unit. Choice B is incorrect because, although the login.sql file can define many properties in a SQL*Plus session, the character that denotes runtime variables is not one of them. Choice C is incorrect because the define command is used to define variables used in a session, not an individual statement. Review the discussion of defining runtime variables in select statements.

5. D. SELECT NAME FROM CONTESTANT WHERE COUNTRY IN (SELECT COUNTRY FROM MEDALS WHERE NUM_GOLD + NUM_SILVER + NUM_BRONZE > 10)

Explanation The SELECT NAME FROM CONTESTANT WHERE COUNTRY IN (SELECT COUNTRY FROM MEDALS WHERE NUM_GOLD + NUM_SILVER + NUM_BRONZE > 10) query is correct because it contains the subquery that correctly returns a subset of countries that have contestants who won ten or more medals of any type. Choice A is incorrect because it contains a join operation, not a subquery. Choice B is simply a rewrite of choice A to use a multiple-row subquery; however, it does not go far enough to restrict return data and is therefore incorrect. Choice C is a single-row subquery that does essentially the same thing as choice B and is therefore incorrect.

6. C. Multiple-column subquery, the youngest contestant from all countries.

Explanation Because the main query compares against the results of two columns returned in the subquery, this is a multiple-column subquery that will return the youngest contestant from all countries in the table. This multiple-column subquery is also a multiple-row subquery, but because the defining factor is the fact that two columns are present, you should focus more on that fact than on the rows being returned. This fact eliminates choices A and B. The subquery does return multiple rows, however. You should also be sensitive to the fact that the main query must use an IN clause, not the equals sign (=), thus making choice D incorrect as well.

7. A. SOO

Explanation If you guessed SOO, great job! The correct answer is SOO because the subquery operation specified by the IN clause ignores NULL values implicitly. Therefore, because SOO has no country defined, that row is not selected as part of the subquery. As a result, the output lists each of the youngest contestants from the named countries, so choices B, C, and D will all appear in the result set.

8. A. insert into EMPLOYEE values (59694,'HARRIS', NULL);

Explanation This choice is acceptable because the positional criteria for not specifying column order is met by the data in the values clause. When you would like to specify that no data be inserted into a particular column, one method of doing so is to insert a NULL. Choice B is incorrect because not all columns in the table have values identified. When you're using positional references to populate column data, values must be present for every column in the table. Otherwise, the columns that will be populated should be named explicitly. Choice C is incorrect because when a column is named for data insert in the insert into clause, a value must definitely be specified in the `values` clause. Choice D is incorrect because using the multiple-row `insert` option with a `select` statement is not appropriate in this situation. Refer to the discussion of `insert` statements for more information.

9. D. The `delete` statement will remove all records from the table.

Explanation   There is only one effect produced by leaving off the `where` clause from any statement that enables one—the requested operation is performed on all records in the table.

CHAPTER
5

Creating Oracle
Database Objects

n this chapter, you will learn about and demonstrate knowledge in the following topics:

- Creating the tables of an Oracle database
- Including constraints

The topics covered in this chapter include creating tables and including constraints. With mastery of these topics, your experience with Oracle moves from the level of casual user to the world of application development. Application developers usually create database objects and determine how casual users will access those objects in production environments. The database administrator (DBA) is the person who is responsible for migrating developed objects into production and then managing the needs of production systems. This chapter will lay the foundation for discussion of Oracle database object and constraint creation, which is important for both developers and DBAs, so pay close attention to this material. The OCP Exam 1 test questions in this subject area are worth 15 percent of the final score.

Creating the Tables of an Oracle Database

This section covers the following topics related to creating tables:

- Describing tables
- Creating tables
- Datatypes and column definitions
- Altering table definitions
- Dropping, renaming, and truncating tables

This section will explain the basic syntax required of developers and DBAs in order to produce the logical database objects in Oracle known as *tables*. You will learn the syntax and semantics of creating tables and related database objects. You will also learn how to identify characteristics of tables already created. The section will cover how to change the definition of existing tables and other advanced types of table manipulation in the database as well. Finally, you will see a fast, neat way for deleting records from tables while leaving the definition of the table intact.

Describing Tables

The best way to think of a table for most Oracle beginners is to envision a spreadsheet containing several records of data. Across the top, try to see a horizontal list of column names that label the values in these columns. Each record listed across the table is called a *row*. In SQL*Plus, the command `describe` enables you to obtain a basic listing of characteristics about the table. We've already seen this command earlier in the book, but let's take another look at it using our trusty standby demo table, EMP, owned by SCOTT:

```
SQL> describe scott.emp
 Name                     Null?    Type
 ---------------------    -------- --------------
 EMPNO                    NOT NULL NUMBER(4)
 ENAME                             VARCHAR2(10)
 JOB                               VARCHAR2(9)
 MGR                               NUMBER(4)
 HIREDATE                          DATE
 SAL                               NUMBER(7,2)
 COMM                              NUMBER(7,2)
 DEPTNO                            NUMBER(2)
```

TIP
The `describe` *command can be abbreviated as* `desc` *to obtain the same result with fewer keystrokes. This is not to be confused with the* `desc` *keyword used in conjunction with* `order by` *clauses to list output in descending order!*

Note some interesting characteristics about the output in the preceding code block. First, the `describe` command lists the columns in the EMP table by name. Sometimes, columns in a table are also referred to as *fields*. We prefixed table EMP with its schema owner, SCOTT. If we didn't, Oracle would assume we wanted to see a description of the EMP table in our own schema, if one existed. Second, notice the column with the heading *Null?* This information indicates whether the column listed allows NULL information. A listing of not NULL for the table column usually (although not always) indicates that the table column is the primary key for identifying unique rows in the table. Finally, notice that the output shows detailed information about the datatype for that table column.

TIP
You've progressed quite a bit in your knowledge of Oracle. Therefore, the demo tables we used in prior chapters are of less and less use to you. From here on out in the book, we're going to work with our own database objects, creating them first, then populating them, and then selecting information from them if necessary. You'll probably want to continue using the SCOTT user ID, however, because it has the privileges you need to execute these examples!

For Review

Know how to use the `describe` command and what its abbreviation is. Understand what three pieces of information are listed in the output for this command as well as what that information means.

Exercises

1. **You issue the following command in SQL*Plus: `describe PROFITS`. Which of the following choices identifies information that will not be shown in the results listed by this command?**

   A. Columns in the table

   B. Foreign keys from this table to other tables

   C. Datatypes of columns in the table

   D. The primary key of the table

2. **You issue the following command in SQL*Plus: `describe PROFITS`. Potential primary key information given in the output of the `describe` command will be listed under which of the following headings in the output?**

   A. NAME

   B. NULL?

   C. TYPE

   D. None of the above

3. **This is the keyword you can enter as an abbreviation for the** `describe`
   command: _____

Answer Key
1. B. **2.** B. **3.** `desc`

Creating Tables

To create a table in Oracle, you use the `create table` command. This statement
is one of many database object creation statements known in Oracle as the data
definition language (DDL). For our purposes in the next several examples, we're
going to create our own table of employees in a company of our own making. The
following code block provides the basic `create table` statement that will create
our new EMPLOYEE table:

```
SQL>  create table employee
  2  (empid varchar2(5),
  3   firstname varchar2(10),
  4   lastname varchar2(10),
  5   salary number(7));
Table created.
```

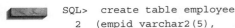

TIP
In order to create tables in the Oracle database, you
need the `create table` *privilege. User SCOTT*
has this privilege. You can find information for
granting the needed privileges to other users in
Chapter 8. Alternatively, you can ask your DBA at
work to grant the `create table` *privilege to the*
user ID you intend to use for working through the
examples in this chapter.

Notice the important aspects of this basic `create table` statement. We
define the table's name and then define all the columns we want in our table inside
parentheses and separated by commas. The absolute maximum number of columns
that a table may have is 1,000. Each column has an associated datatype that the
information stored in that column must conform to. We make sure to close off the
parentheses properly, and then Oracle creates our table for us. If a table called

EMPLOYEE already existed in our user schema, Oracle would give the following error and no table would be created:

```
SQL> create table employee
  2  (empid varchar2(5));
create table employee
              *
ERROR at line 1:
ORA-00955: name is already used by an existing object
```

> **TIP**
> *In the case where a table name you select is in use by an existing object in your schema, you can create the object in a different user schema, rename the object you want to create, rename the object that already exists, or remove the object that already exists.*

Creating Temporary Tables

Most of the time, when you create a table in Oracle, the records that eventually populate that table will live inside your database forever (or at least until someone removes them). However, there might be situations where you want records in a table to live inside the database only for a short while. In this case, you can create temporary tables in Oracle, where the data placed into the tables persists for only the duration of the user session, or for the length of your current transaction. A *transaction* is a span of time during which all data changes made are treated as one logical unit of work. You'll learn more about transactions later in Chapter 6.

A temporary table is created using the `create global temporary table` command. Why does a temporary table have to be global? So that the temporary table's definition can be made available to every user on the system. However, the contents of a temporary table are visible only to the user session that added information to the temporary table, even though everyone can see the definition. Temporary tables are a relatively new feature in Oracle, and Oracle hasn't had enough time yet to implement "local" temporary tables (that is, temporary tables that are only available to the user who owns them). Look for this functionality in later database releases. The appropriate `create global temporary table` command is shown in the following code block:

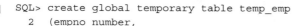

```
SQL> create global temporary table temp_emp
  2  (empno number,
```

```
   3   ename varchar2(10));
Table created.
```

So, to summarize quickly, let's review the following bullets with respect to temporary tables:

- The `create global temporary table` statement creates a temporary table that can be transaction-specific or session-specific.

- For transaction-specific temporary tables, data inserted into the temporary table persists for the life of the transaction.

- For session-specific temporary tables, data inserted into the temporary table persists for the life of the session.

- Data in a temporary table is private to the session, meaning that each session can see and modify only its own data in the temporary table.

Creating One Table with Data from Another

In most cases, when a developer creates a table in Oracle, the table is empty—it has no data in it. Once the table is created, the users or developers are then free to populate it as long as proper access has been granted. However, in some cases, the developer can create a table that already has data in it. The general statement used to create tables with data built in is the `create table as select` statement, as shown here:

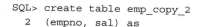

```
SQL> create table emp_copy
  2  as select * from emp
  3  where deptno = 10;
Table created.
```

Two things are worthy of note about the `create table as select` statement. First, notice we didn't have to define any column names in table EMP_COPY. This is because we used a wildcard in the column clause to obtain data from the EMP table, telling Oracle to create the columns in EMP_COPY just as they appear in EMP—same names, same datatype definitions. The second thing is that any `select` statement you can issue from SQL*Plus can also be included in the `create table as select` statement. Oracle then automatically obtains whatever data you selected from EMP and populates EMP_COPY with that data. However, if the `select` statement includes a specific list of columns named in the column clause, your `create table` clause must list the columns you want the table to include, enclosed in parentheses. Here's an example of what I mean:

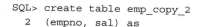

```
SQL> create table emp_copy_2
  2  (empno, sal) as
```

```
  3  select empno, sal from emp
  4  where deptno = 10;
Table created.
SQL> describe emp_copy_2
 Name                                Null?     Type
 ---------------------------------   --------  ----------------
 EMPNO                               NOT NULL  NUMBER(4)
 SAL                                           NUMBER(7,2)
SQL> select * from emp_copy_2;
    EMPNO       SAL
 ---------  ---------
      7782      2450
      7839      5000
      7934      1300
```

Table-Naming Conventions

Many philosophies about the naming of variables, tables, columns, and other items in software come from the early days of computing. Available memory and disk space was limited on those early machines, so the names of tables and columns in those environments were often small and cryptic. In systems today, however, developers are not faced with that restriction. The names of columns and tables need not be bound by the naming rules of yesteryear. However, standards for naming tables and columns still have value, if only for the sake of readability. There are also some hard-and-fast rules about table and column names in Oracle. For our purposes, we'll divide our rules into two categories: hard-n-fast and soft-n-stylish.

Keep Names Short and Descriptive   Your table- and column-naming conventions in your Oracle database may be compact, but someone viewing the tables and columns in your database for the first time should also have some idea of what the tables and columns represent.

- **Hard-n-fast** Oracle database object names must begin with a letter and can usually be between 1 and 30 characters long, except for databases (which have a maximum of eight characters) and database links (with a maximum of 128 characters). Names are not case-sensitive.

- **Soft-n-stylish** Calling a table EMP_LN_FN_SAL might not be as easily understood as simply calling the table EMPLOYEE, or even EMP.

Relate Names for Child Tables to Their Parent   In certain situations, the developers of an application may find themselves creating multiple tables to define a logical entity representing a parent-child relationship. Consider an example where an employee expense application contains two tables—one called EXPENSE, listing information such as total invoiced amount and employee name, and the other called EXPENSE_DETAIL, containing individual entries for airfare, car rental, hotel, and so on. Both are descriptive names, and it is obvious from those names that there is some relationship between the tables.

■ **Hard-n-fast**   A user cannot own or refer to two objects with the same name, so if both you and SCOTT own a table called EMPLOYEE, you must prefix references to EMPLOYEE with the schema owner.

■ **Soft-n-stylish**   Tables related by foreign key (that is, parent/child relationships) should share part of the same table name.

Foreign-Key Columns Should Have the Same Name in Both Tables   If you are creating foreign-key relationships between columns in two different tables, it also helps if the column appearing in both tables has the same name in both places, implying the potential existence of a foreign key a bit more obviously. Remember, you can use table aliases in your join statements when you reference columns that have the same name in both tables in order to avoid ambiguity.

■ **Hard-n-fast**   Don't name a table DUAL, because, as you know, Oracle already has a table called DUAL that is accessible by everyone.

■ **Soft-n-stylish**   Give columns shared in multiple tables for parent-child relationships the same name.

Names of Associated Objects Should Relate to the Table   Sometimes other objects exist in conjunction with tables in Oracle. These objects include integrity constraints, triggers, and indexes. You'll learn what all these objects are later. For now, just know that they exist, and that it is useful to give these objects meaningful names that relate back to the table.

■ **Soft-n-stylish**   Give objects that are associated with tables meaningful names that relate back to the table: for example, PK_EMP_01 (primary key for EMP table), IDX_EMP_01 (index on EMP table), and TRIG_EMP_01 (trigger on EMP table).

Avoid Quotes, Keywords, and Nonalphanumeric Characters   You can't use quotes in the name of a table or column, nor can you use most nonalphanumeric characters, with three exceptions: the dollar sign ($), the underscore (_), and the hash mark (#), sometimes also called the *pound sign*. The dollar sign is most notable in naming dynamic performance views, whereas the hash mark is used in some data dictionary tables owned by a privileged user called SYS in Oracle. In general, you should steer clear of using $ or #. The underscore is useful for separating two words or abbreviations.

■ **Hard-n-fast** Don't use table names beginning with SYS.

■ **Hard-n-fast** You can only use the following three special characters in table and column names: #, $, and _.

■ **Hard-n-fast** Don't use special characters from European or Asian character sets in a database name, global database name, or database link names.

■ **Hard-n-fast** An object name cannot be an Oracle reserved word, such as `select` or `from`; a datatype, such as NUMBER; or a built-in function, such as `decode ( )`. Oracle may not complain when you create the object, but it may give you an unpleasant surprise when you refer to the object in your SQL statement.

■ **Hard-n-fast** Depending on the product you plan to use to access a database object (for example, WebDB, JDeveloper, or Developer), names might be further restricted by other reserved words. For a list of a product's reserved words, see the manual for that specific product.

For Review

1. Know how to use the statements for creating tables, temporary tables, and tables with data already populated in them. Know that the maximum number of columns a table may have is 1,000.

2. Be sure you can identify some table-naming conventions for descriptiveness, syntactic and semantic correctness, and relatedness to other objects.

Exercises

1. **You are defining database tables in Oracle. Which of the following choices identifies a table name that is not valid for use?**

   A. TEST_NUMBER

   B. P$$#_LOC

   C. 1_COPY_OF_EMP

   D. FLOP_TEST_#3

2. **You are creating tables in the Oracle database. Which of the following statements identifies a table-creation statement that is not valid?**

   A. `create table cats (c_name varchar2(10), c_weight number, c_owner varchar2(10));`

B. `create table my_cats as select * from cats where owner = 'ME';`

C. `create global temporary table temp_cats (c_name varchar2(10), c_weight number, c_owner varchar2(10));`

D. `create table cats_over_5_lbs as select c_name, c_weight from cats where c_weight > 5;`

3. **Your attempt to create a table in Oracle results in the following error: `ORA-00955-name is already used by existing object`. Which of the following choices does not identify an appropriate correction for this situation?**

   A. Create the object as a different user.

   B. Drop the existing object with the same name.

   C. Change the column names in the object being created.

   D. Rename the existing object.

4. **In Oracle, all temporary tables are available to all users, implying the need for this keyword: _____**

Answer Key
1. C. 2. D. 3. C. 4. `global`

Datatypes and Column Definitions

The need for and use of datatypes when identifying the type of data columns in a table can hold has already been mentioned in Chapter 1. When we initially discussed it, we limited our discussion to only the datatypes used in the EMP table (VARCHAR2, DATE, and NUMBER) so that we could get busy learning how to develop queries. However, it is now necessary for us to discuss all the available datatypes in the Oracle database so that you know about all the datatypes available in order to pass the OCP exam. Here is a list of all the datatypes in Oracle, along with their descriptions:

Datatype	Description
VARCHAR2(*n*)	Contains variable-length text strings of length *n* bytes, where *n* can be of up to 4,000 bytes.
NVARCHAR2(*n*)	Contains single-byte or multibyte variable-length text strings of *n* bytes, where *n* can be up to 4,000 bytes in Oracle.
CHAR(*n*)	Contains fixed text strings of *n* bytes, where *n* can be up to 2,000 bytes in Oracle.
NCHAR(*n*)	Contains single-byte or multibyte fixed-length text strings of *n* bytes, where *n* can be up to 2,000 bytes in Oracle. Considered a unicode datatype because it stores unicode character data.
NUMBER(*n*[,*m*])	Contains numeric data up to *n* digits in length, where *n* can be up to 38 digits in Oracle. A NUMBER can also have an optional *m* number of digits to the right of the decimal point. This collection of digits is called a *mantissa*. The mantissa can have up to 38 digits as well. If no value is specified for *n*, Oracle defaults to 38.
DATE	Contains date information. DATE columns are seven bytes in length.
RAW	Contains binary data of up to 2,000 bytes in Oracle. This is a variable length datatype like VARCHAR2 in Oracle.
LONG	Contains text data of up to 2GB.
LONG RAW	Contains binary data of up to 2GB.
ROWID	Contains the address for rows in your table. These could be physical ROWIDs or logical ROWIDs.
BLOB	Stores large unstructured binary object data (available in Oracle8 and later versions only) of up to 4GB.
CLOB	Stores large database character set data (available in Oracle8 and later versions only) of up to 4GB.
NCLOB	Stores large single-byte or multibyte character-based unicode character set data (available in Oracle8 and later versions only) of up to 4GB.
BFILE	Stores pointers to large unstructured operating system files outside the Oracle database (available in Oracle8 and later versions only).

Text Datatypes Explained

There are two text datatypes that can contain alphanumeric information—CHAR and VARCHAR2. Although both CHAR and VARCHAR2 hold character strings, some subtle differences exist. First, the CHAR datatype only supports character strings up to a length of 2,000 bytes for Oracle, whereas the VARCHAR2 datatype supports character strings up to a length of 4,000 bytes for Oracle. The more important difference is demonstrated in the following code block:

```
SQL> create table tester
  2  (col1 char(10),
  3   col2 varchar2(10));
Table created.
SQL> insert into tester values ('BRADY','BRADY');
1 row created.
SQL> select vsize(col1), vsize(col2) from tester;
VSIZE(COL1) VSIZE(COL2)
----------- -----------
         10           5
```

TIP

We'll discuss data manipulation statements such as `insert` *in Chapter 6. For now, simply understand that* `insert` *is used for adding rows to a table in Oracle. Otherwise, nothing issued in this code block should be unfamiliar to you. If you don't remember what the* `vsize( )` *function tells us, review its explanation in Chapter 2.*

Notice that in our TESTER table, the value BRADY that we stored in COL1 takes up ten bytes. This is because Oracle pads the value stored in CHAR columns with blanks up to the declared length of the column. In contrast, Oracle does not store padded blank spaces if the same value is stored in a column defined as datatype VARCHAR2.

TIP

VARCHAR2 has the 2 on the end of its name because there was once a VARCHAR datatype defined in early releases of Oracle. Although VARCHAR and VARCHAR2 are currently synonymous, they may not be in the future, so Oracle recommends using VARCHAR2. VARCHAR is a valid datatype complying with the ANSI standard and Oracle includes that datatype so they can say they are ANSI-compliant.

The NUMBER Datatype

The NUMBER datatype stores number data and can be specified to store integers or real numbers. In order to understand how to define NUMBER columns, let's say you were defining a column as shown in the following code block:

```
SQL> create table tester2
  2  (col1 number(15,2));
Table created.
```

The overall number of digits that this NUMBER column will store is 15 in this case. Thirteen digits can appear in front of the decimal point, whereas two digits are reserved for the mantissa. Therefore, 1234567891011 can be stored in this column as shown below:

```
SQL> insert into tester2 values (1234567891011);
1 row created.
```

However, 12345678910111 cannot fit into this column, as you see here:

```
SQL> insert into tester2 values (12345678910111);
insert into tester2 values (12345678910111)
                            *
ERROR at line 1:
ORA-01438: value larger than specified precision allows
 for this column
```

Interesting things happen when we try to insert values in this column that exceed the mantissa's specified length of two digits, as you see here:

```
SQL> insert into tester2 values (1234567891011.121)
1 row created.
```

Wait a minute, you say. When we tried to add a number to this column that was more than 13 digits to the left of the decimal point, Oracle gave us an error. Yet, when we add a value with more than 15 digits, where the overflow digits appear after the decimal point, Oracle accepts the value. Well, that's only partially true. To better understand what happened, let's take a look at the contents of TESTER2:

```
SQL> column col1 format 9999999999999.99
SQL> select * from tester2;
          COL1
-----------------
 1234567891011.00
 1234567891011.12
```

The first command in the code block formats the output from COL1 so that we can read it more easily. Had we omitted that formatting command, Oracle would have returned the data in scientific notation. Second, notice in the second row of values from COL1 that Oracle changed our inserted value 1234567891011.121 to 1234567891011.12! Therefore, we can extrapolate two simple rules:

- Oracle always rounds off when you try to insert values that exceed the number of digits allowed, so long as those extra digits appear after the decimal point.

- If the extra digits appear in front of the decimal point, Oracle returns an error.

Other Datatypes in Oracle

Let's briefly cover the remaining datatypes in Oracle. We've seen the DATE datatype in action, which stores date values in a special Oracle format represented as the number of days since December 31, 4713 B.C.E. This datatype offers a great deal of flexibility when you want to perform date-manipulation operations, such as adding 30 days to a given date. Recall also that there are many functions that handle complex date operations. Another nice feature of Oracle's method for date storage is that it is inherently millennium-compliant.

Beyond the DATE datatype, there is an entire set of important type declaration options dedicated to the storage of small and large amounts of text and unformatted binary data. These datatypes include LONG, RAW, and LONG RAW. RAW datatypes in Oracle store data in binary format up to 2,000 bytes. It is useful to store graphics and sound files, used in conjunction with LONG, to form the LONG RAW datatype, which can accommodate up to 2GB of data. You can also declare columns as type LONG, which stores up to 2GB of alphanumeric text data. However, because data in a LONG or LONG RAW column is stored contiguously or *inline* with the rest of the table data, there can be only one column declared to be of type LONG in a table.

Storing large blocks of data has been enhanced significantly in Oracle8 and Oracle with the introduction of the BLOB, CLOB, and NCLOB datatypes. These four types can each contain up to 4GB of binary, single-byte, and multibyte character-based data, respectively. Data in a BLOB, CLOB, or NCLOB column is stored in the following way. If the value is less than 4KB, the information can also be stored contiguously (inline) with the rest of table data. Otherwise, a pointer to where Oracle has stored this data outside of the table is stored inline with the rest of the table. This is in contrast to earlier versions of Oracle, where the actual LONG or LONG RAW data must *always* be stored inline with the rest of the table information. As a result of this new way for storing large blocks of data, Oracle allows more than one BLOB, CLOB, or NCLOB column per table.

TIP
*Storing data "inline" means that the data in a LONG
datatype column is stored literally "in line" with the
rest of the data in the row, as opposed to Oracle
storing a pointer inline with row data, pointing to
LONG column data stored somewhere else.*

Finally, the ROWID datatype stores information related to the disk location of
table rows. Generally, no column should be created to store data using type
ROWID, but this datatype supports the ROWID pseudocolumn associated with
every table. A *pseudocolumn* can be thought of as a virtual column in a table. Every
table has several pseudocolumns, including one called ROWID. ROWIDs are
critical to your ability to store information in tables because they identify how
Oracle can locate the rows. They also uniquely identify the rows in your table. Every
table contains a ROWID pseudocolumn that contains the ROWID for the rows of
the table. The following code block illustrates that we can query data in the ROWID
column of a table, just as if it were any other column:

```
SQL> select rowid from emp;
ROWID
------------------
AAACwdAABAAAJGdAAA
AAACwdAABAAAJGdAAB
AAACwdAABAAAJGdAAC
AAACwdAABAAAJGdAAD
AAACwdAABAAAJGdAAE
AAACwdAABAAAJGdAAF
AAACwdAABAAAJGdAAG
AAACwdAABAAAJGdAAH
AAACwdAABAAAJGdAAI
AAACwdAABAAAJGdAAJ
AAACwdAABAAAJGdAAK
AAACwdAABAAAJGdAAL
AAACwdAABAAAJGdAAM
AAACwdAABAAAJGdAAN
```

TIP
*Although ROWIDs are essential for Oracle database
processing, you don't need to know too much about
how they work. ROWIDs are tested more
extensively on the OCP DBA Fundamentals I exam.*

Column Default Values

You can define tables to populate columns with default values as well using the
`default` clause in a `create table` command. This clause is included as part of
the column definition to tell Oracle what the default value for that column should
be. When a row is added to the table and no value is defined for the column in the
row being added, Oracle populates the column value for that row using the default
value for the column. The following code block illustrates this point:

```
SQL> create table display
  2   (col1 varchar2(10),
  3    col2 number default 0);
Table created.
SQL> insert into display (col1) values ('MYCOL');
1 row created.
SQL> select * from display;
COL1              COL2
----------   ---------
MYCOL                 0
```

For Review

1. Be sure you can name all the datatypes available in Oracle. Know the format
   of data stored in the DATE datatype and what the ROWID datatype is.

2. Know how to define NUMBER columns and know the significance of the
   value specified both for overall length and for the mantissa. Know what may
   happen when the value added to a NUMBER column exceeds the specified
   length both before and after the mantissa.

3. Understand the difference between the LONG and CLOB datatypes with
   respect to where data is stored in relation to the overall table.

4. Be able to describe the differences between the CHAR and the VARCHAR2
   datatypes—particularly with respect to CHAR's use of additional padding
   when storing text strings.

5. Know how to use the `default` clause within the `create table`
   command.

Exercises

1. **The PROFITS column inside the SALES table is declared as NUMBER(10,2).**
   Which of the following values cannot be stored in that column?

   A. 5392845.324

   B. 871039453.1

   C. 75439289.34

   D. 60079829.25

2. Employee KING was hired on November 17, 1981. You issue the following query on your Oracle database: `select vsize(hiredate) from emp where ename = 'KING;`. Which of the following choices identifies the value returned?

   A. 4

   B. 7

   C. 9

   D. 17

3. You define the PRODUCT_NAME column in your SALES table to be CHAR(40). Later, you add one row to this table with the value "CAT_TOYS" for PRODUCT_NAME. You then issue the following command: `select vsize(product_name) from sales`. Which of the following choices best identifies the value returned?

   A. 8

   B. 12

   C. 40

   D. 4,000

4. Data in LONG RAW columns over 4KB in size is stored _____ with respect to the rest of the data in the table.

5. The JOB table contains three columns: JOB_NAME, JOB_DESC, and JOB_WAGE. You insert a new row into the JOB_DESC table using the following command:

```
SQL> insert into job (job_name, job_desc)
  2  values ('LACKEY','MAKES COFFEE');
```

Later, you query the table, and receive the following result:

```
SQL> select * from job where job_name = 'LACKEY';
JOB_NAME   JOB_DESC      JOB_WAGE
---------  ------------  --------
LACKEY     MAKES COFFEE       35
```

Which of the following choices identify how JOB_WAGE was populated with data?

A. The row for LACKEY in the JOB table already existed with JOB_WAGE set to 35.

B. A `default` clause on the JOB_WAGE column defined when the table was created specified the value when the row was inserted.

C. The `values` clause in the `insert` statement contained a hidden value that was added when the row was added.

D. The only possible explanation is that a later `update` statement issued against the JOB table added the JOB_WAGE value.

Answer Key

1. B. **2.** B. **3.** C. **4.** inline. **5.** B. Choice D is not correct because either an `update` statement or the `default` clause explain the output given in the question.

Altering Table Definitions

Suppose that, after you create a table in Oracle, you discover there is some fact that the table needs to store that you forgot to include. Is this a problem? Absolutely not! You can modify existing Oracle tables with ease using the `alter table` statement. There are several basic changes you might want to make using this statement, as listed below:

- You can add more columns to a table.

- You can modify the size of existing columns in a table.

- You can remove columns from a table (but only in Oracle8i, Oracle9i, and later versions).

- You can add or modify constraints on columns in the table. Constraints in Oracle prevent users from entering invalid data into tables. We'll defer most of the discussion of this topic until later in the chapter.

TIP
A third type of change you can make with the `alter table` statement has to do with the way tables are stored inside the Oracle database. This is a big topic on OCP Exam 2 in the DBA track. You don't need to worry about this type of modification for OCP Exam 1.

Adding New Columns to a Table

You can use the `alter table` statement to add new columns to a table in Oracle. However, there are some restrictions on doing so. First, no two columns can have the same name in an Oracle table. Second, only one column of the LONG or LONG RAW datatype can appear in a table in Oracle. Third, the maximum number of columns a table may have is 1,000. The following code block shows an example of the `alter table` statement:

```
SQL> alter table employee add (hire_date date);
Table altered.
```

As mentioned, only one column in the table may be of type LONG within a table. That restriction includes the LONG RAW datatype. However, many columns of datatype BLOB, CLOB, NCLOB, and BFILE can appear in one table, in Oracle8 and later versions. It is sometimes useful to emulate Oracle in Oracle7 databases as well, by having a special table that contains the LONG column and a foreign key to the table that would have contained the column; this reduces the amount of data migration and row chaining on the database.

TIP
Row chaining *and* row migration *occurs when the Oracle RDBMS has to move row data around or break it up and save it in pieces inside the files on disk that comprise an Oracle database. This activity is a concern to DBAs because it hurts database performance.*

Modifying Column Datatypes

Another important aspect of table columns that can be modified using the `alter table` statement is the configuration of the column's datatype. Suppose that our newly formed company using our new EMPLOYEE table has just hired a woman named Martha Paravasini-Clark. Recall at the beginning of the chapter that we created our EMPLOYEE table with a LASTNAME column of type VARCHAR2(10). Unfortunately, Ms. Paravasini-Clark's last name has 16 characters, so we need to change the LASTNAME column to accept larger text strings. To resolve the issue, you can issue the following statement, making the LASTNAME column length longer:

```
SQL> alter table products modify (lastname varchar2(25));
Table altered.
```

When you're modifying existing columns' datatypes, the general rule of thumb is that increases are generally okay, but decreases are usually a little trickier. Here are some examples of operations that are generally acceptable:

- Increasing the size of a VARCHAR2 or CHAR column

- Increasing the size of a NUMBER column

However, decreasing the size of column datatypes usually requires special steps. Take a look at the following code block, where we reduce the size of COL2 from our TESTER table:

```
SQL> desc tester
 Name                          Null?    Type
 ----------------------        -------- -----------
 COL1                                   CHAR(10)
 COL2                                   VARCHAR2(10)
SQL> alter table tester modify (col2 varchar2(5));
alter table tester modify (col2 varchar2(5))
                            *
ERROR at line 1:
ORA-01441: column to be modified must be empty to decrease length
SQL> create table tester_col2
  2  (col2) as select col2 from tester;
Table created.
SQL> update tester set col2 = null;
1 row updated.
SQL> alter table tester modify (col2 varchar2(5));
Table altered.
SQL> update tester set col2 = (select col2 from tester_col2);
1 row updated.
```

> **TIP**
> *You've already seen examples of every statement used in the code block, and you know what a subquery is, so there shouldn't be anything confusing going on here. You'll learn more about the* update *statement later in Chapter 6.*

Let's walk through the statements in the preceding code block. First, we described the TESTER table to see how large COL2 was. Then, we attempted to reduce it from ten to five bytes. Oracle didn't like that, because COL2 contained data. Therefore, we had to copy all the data in COL2 to a temporary location using the create table as select command. We then changed the column values to NULL on the column we want to reduce the size of, and we made the actual change to the datatype size. Finally, we added the data back into the TESTER table using an `update` statement containing a subquery. Here are some other allowable operations that follow this principle:

- Reducing the size of a NUMBER column (empty column for all rows only)
- Reducing the length of a VARCHAR2 or CHAR column (empty column for all rows only)
- Changing the datatype of a column (empty column for all rows only)

Dropping Columns in Oracle

You can also drop columns in Oracle using the `alter table` statement. There are two ways to do so. The first is to instruct Oracle to ignore the column by using the `set unused column` clause. In this situation, no information is removed from the table column. Oracle simply pretends the column isn't there. Later, we can remove the column using the `drop unused columns` clause. Both steps are shown in the following block:

```
SQL> alter table employee set unused column salary;
Table altered.
SQL> alter table employee drop unused columns;
Table altered.
```

The second option is to remove the column and all contents entirely from the table immediately. This statement is shown in the following block:

```
SQL> alter table employee drop column salary;
Table altered.
```

TIP
If you're following along in your Oracle database, make sure you add the SALARY column back to the EMPLOYEE table when you're done practicing both methods for dropping columns. We refer back to the EMPLOYEE table quite often later.

For Review

1. Be sure you know how to add columns using the `alter table` statement with the `add` clause.

2. Know how to modify column datatype definitions using the `alter table` statement with the `modify` clause.

3. Understand both uses of the `alter table` command for dropping columns—one using the `set unused column` and `drop unused columns` syntax, and the other with the `drop column` syntax.

Exercises

1. **You want to reduce the size of a non-NULL NUMBER(10) column to NUMBER(6). Which of the following steps must be completed after the appropriate `alter table` command is issued?**

   A. Copy column records to a temporary storage location.

   B. Set the NUMBER column to NULL for all rows.

   C. Create a temporary location for NUMBER data.

   D. Copy column records from the temporary location back to the main table.

2. **You just issued the following statement: `alter table sales drop column profit;`. Which of the following choices identifies when the column will actually be removed from Oracle?**

   A. Immediately following statement execution

   B. After the `alter table drop unused columns` command is issued

   C. After the `alter table set unused column` command is issued

   D. After the `alter table modify` command is issued

3. **You want to increase the size of a non-NULL VARCHAR2(5) column to VARCHAR2(10). Which of the following steps must be accomplished after executing the appropriate `alter table` command?**

   A. Set the VARCHAR2 column to NULL for all rows.

   B. Create a temporary location for VARCHAR2 data.

   C. Copy the column records from the temporary location back to the main table.

   D. Nothing. The statement is executed automatically.

4. **You want to increase the size of the PRODUCT_TYPE column, declared as a VARCHAR(5) column, to VARCHAR2(10) in the SALES table. Which of the following commands is useful for this purpose?**

   A. `alter table sales add (product_type varchar2(10));`

   B. `alter table sales modify product_type varchar2(10));`

   C. `alter table sales set unused column product_type varchar2(10));`

   D. `alter table sales drop column product_type;`

Answer Key
1. D. 2. A. 3. D. 4. B.

Dropping, Renaming, and Truncating Tables

Some additional operations are available for the modification of tables; they are designed for handling various situations, such as removing a table, changing the name of a table, and removing all the data from a table while still leaving the definition of the table intact. Let's talk about each of these operations in detail.

Dropping Tables

First, let's talk about how to eliminate a table. In order for a table to be deleted from the database, the `drop table` command must be executed:

```
SQL> drop table emp_copy_2;
Table dropped.
```

As mentioned earlier, sometimes objects are associated with a table that exists in a database along with the table. These objects may include indexes, constraints, and triggers. If the table is dropped, Oracle automatically drops any index, trigger, or constraint associated with the table as well. Here are two other factors to be aware of with respect to dropping tables:

■ You cannot roll back a `drop table` command.

■ To drop a table, the table must be part of your own schema, or you must have the `drop any table` privilege granted to you.

Truncating Tables

Let's move on to discuss how you can remove all data from a table quickly using a special option available in Oracle. In this situation, the DBA or developer may use the `truncate table` statement. This statement is a part of the data definition language (DDL) of Oracle, much like the `create table` statement and completely unlike the `delete` statement. Truncating a table removes all row data from a table quickly, while leaving the definition of the table intact, including the definition of constraints and any associated database objects such as indexes, constraints, and triggers on the table. The `truncate` statement is a high-speed data-deletion statement that bypasses the transaction controls available in Oracle for recoverability in data changes. Truncating a table is almost always faster than executing the `delete` statement without a `where` clause, but once this operation has been completed, the data cannot be recovered unless you have a backed-up copy of the data. Here's an example:

```
SQL> truncate table tester;
Table truncated.
```

TIP

Truncating tables affects a characteristic about them that Oracle calls the high-water mark. This characteristic is a value Oracle uses to keep track of the largest size the table has ever grown to. When you truncate the table, Oracle resets the high-water mark to zero.

Renaming Tables

You can rename a table in Oracle by using either the `rename` command or the `alter table rename` command. These commands allow you to change the name of a table without actually moving any data physically within the database. The following code block demonstrates the use of these commands:

```
SQL> rename tester to tester2;
Table renamed.
SQL> alter table tester3 rename to tester;
Table altered.
```

Commenting Objects

You can also add comments to a table or column using the `comment` command. This is useful especially for large databases where you want others to understand some specific bits of information about a table, such as the type of information stored in the table. An example of using this command to add comments to a table appears in the following block:

```
SQL> comment on table employee is
  2  'This is a table containing employees';
Comment created.
```

You can see how to use the comment command for adding comments on table columns in the following code block:

```
SQL> comment on column employee.empid is
  2  'unique text identifier for employees';
Comment created.
```

TIP
Comment information on tables is stored in an object called USER_TAB_COMMENTS, whereas comment information for columns is stored in a different database object, called USER_COL_COMMENTS. These objects are part of the Oracle data dictionary. You'll find out more about the Oracle data dictionary later in the book.

For Review

1. Understand how to remove a table from your database. Be sure you can describe what happens to any objects associated with the dropped table, such as indexes, constraints, and triggers.

2. Be sure you know how to rename and truncate tables. Understand what is meant by a table's *high-water mark* and how it is affected by the truncate command. Know how to add comments to a table as well.

3. Make sure you understand the difference between dropping and truncating a table. Dropping the table removes the table and all its data completely from the Oracle database. Truncating the table removes the table data but preserves the table definition for data added later.

Exercises

1. **You want to change the name of an existing database table. Which of the following choices does not identify a practical method for doing so?**

    A. Use the `create table as select` statement; then drop the original table.

    B. Use the `rename` command.

    C. Drop the table; then re-create it with its new name.

    D. Use the `alter table rename` command.

2. **This is the name of the database object containing all comment information on tables:** _____

3. **BONUS QUESTION: You drop a table in an Oracle database that is the parent table in a parent-child data relationship. Which of the following objects will not be dropped when you drop the parent table?**

    A. Associated constraints

    B. The child column

    C. Associated triggers

    D. Associated indexes

Answer Key
1. C. 2. USER_TAB_COMMENTS 3. B. In fact, you will have trouble dropping the parent table if there is a child table due to Oracle's enforcement of existing foreign key constraints. You'll learn more about constraints in the next section.

Including Constraints

This section covers the following topics related to including constraints in your database:

- Describing constraints
- Creating and maintaining constraints

    Constraints have already been mentioned in some earlier discussions. This section will expand your understanding of constraints—those rules you can define in your Oracle tables that restrict the type of data you can place in the tables. In this section, you will learn more about the different types of constraints available in an Oracle system. You will also learn how to create and maintain the constraints you define in your Oracle database. This section also covers the different things you can do to modify, redefine, and manipulate your constraints. A note of caution: Constraints are one of the hardest areas to understand if you haven't used Oracle before. Proceed at your own pace.

Describing Constraints

Constraints accomplish three goals in an Oracle database. First, they create real and tangible relationships between the many tables that comprise the typical database application. We've already seen this to be the case in parent-child table relationships. Second, constraints prevent "unwanted" data from making its way into the database against your wishes. I put "unwanted" in quotes because ultimately, the definition of what constitutes unwanted data is entirely arbitrary and up to you as the developer of your system. But the point should be clear: *Constraints hold your database together and keep the bad data out.* Constraints perform an important third function as well—they also prevent the deletion of data if dependencies exist between tables.

Types of Constraints

Five basic types of constraints are available in Oracle, and they are listed in Table 5-1. The types of constraints are described in the following subsections.

Constraint	Description
Primary Key	Stipulates that values in the constrained column(s) must be unique and not NULL. If the primary key applies to multiple columns, then the combination of values in the columns must be unique and not NULL.
Foreign Key	Enforces that only values in the primary key of a parent table may be included as values in the constrained column of the child table.
Unique	Enforces uniqueness on values in the constrained column.
Check	Enforces that values added to the constrained column must be present in a static list of values permitted for the column.
Not Null	Enforces that a value must be defined for this column such that the column may not be NULL for any row.

TABLE 5-1. *Constraints in Oracle*

Primary Key   A constraint of this type identifies the column or columns whose singular or combined values identify uniqueness in the rows of your Oracle table. Every row in the table must have a value specified for the primary key column(s). Recall the EMP table used in earlier chapters. In it, EMPNO is a unique identifier for every row in the table. EMPNO, then, is the primary key because no two employees have the same number assigned to them in the EMPNO column. In relational database parlance, other columns in the EMP table are said to be *functionally dependent* on the primary key, EMPNO. This simply means that every other column describes a potentially non-unique attribute of this unique row. In other words, many employees could be named SMITH, but only one can be the employee named SMITH who has an EMPNO of 7369. Figure 5-1 diagrams this relationship in more detail.

Foreign Key   A constraint of this type signifies a parent-child relationship between two tables based on a shared column. The foreign key constraint is enforced on the shared column in the child table, whereas the shared column in the parent table must be enforced by a primary key constraint. When a foreign key

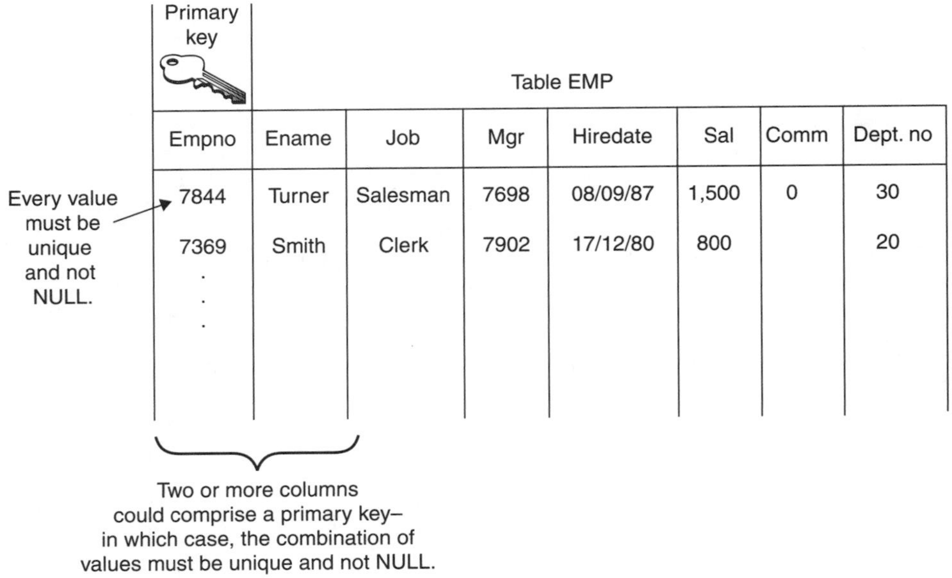

FIGURE 5-1.   *Primary key constraints in Oracle*

constraint exists on a shared column in the child table, Oracle checks to make sure that there is a corresponding value in the shared column of the parent table for every value placed in the shared column of the child table. Note that potentially many values in the parent table may not appear in the child table, but every value in the child table must have an associated value in the parent. Figure 5-2 diagrams this relationship in more detail.

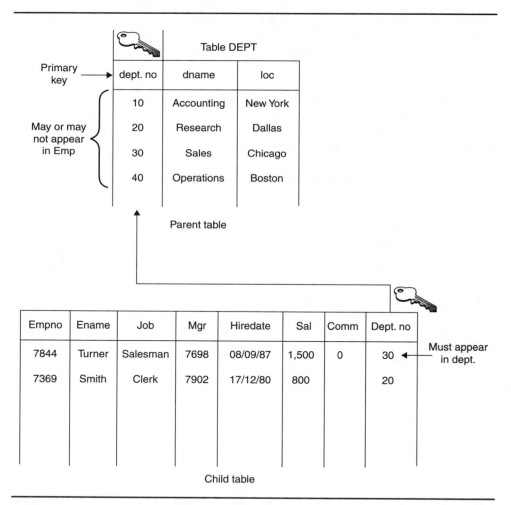

FIGURE 5-2. *Foreign key relationships in Oracle*

Unique Constraint A constraint of this type enforces uniqueness on the values placed in this column. A good example of data requiring a unique constraint would be social security or government ID number. Every employee needs a unique one for tax purposes, so we want to store it in a table of employee information. However, it isn't an appropriate number to use as the primary key for that table of employee information, because many people want to keep their government ID number private. Therefore, you might store social security or government ID numbers, but apply a unique constraint to prevent duplicated entries rather than use them as a primary key.

Check Constraint A constraint of this type enforces that values placed in this column meet specified static criteria. For example, a company may use check constraints to make sure that the salary entry for employees does not list an employee's salary as being over $250,000 per year. This is a static value that can easily be measured against an entered column value. Notice the repeated emphasis on *static* criteria. In the next discussion, you'll see what I mean by this.

TIP
Unique constraints, foreign keys, and check constraints usually allow NULL values to be placed in the column.

Not NULL Constraint A constraint of this type enforces that values placed in the column will not be NULL. This is actually a specific type of check constraint that only checks to see whether the value being entered into the column is NULL.

For Review
Be sure you can identify the five types of constraints in Oracle. With respect to primary key constraints, be sure you can identify what is meant by functional dependency between columns in a table and the primary key as well.

Exercises

1. **This type of constraint enforces uniqueness on column values and prevents NULL data from being entered for the column:**

   _____

2. **This type of constraint indicates a parent-child relationship between this child table and another table:** _____

3. **This type of constraint enforces that values entered for the column meet some predefined static criteria:** _____

Answer Key
1. Primary key. Remember, the constraint enforces uniqueness *and* does not allow NULL values to be entered. **2.** Foreign key. **3.** Check.

Creating and Maintaining Constraints

So much for the easy part, now let's get down to the tough stuff. Two methods exist for defining constraints: the *table constraint method* and the *column constraint method*. How can you tell the difference between the two? Well, here's how. The constraint is defined as a table constraint if the `constraint` clause syntax appears after the column and datatype definitions. The constraint is defined as a column constraint if the constraint definition syntax appears as part of an individual column's definition. All constraints can be defined either as table constraints or as column constraints, with two exceptions:

- Not NULL constraints can only be defined as column constraints.

- Primary keys consisting of two or more columns (known also as *composite primary keys*) can only be defined as table constraints. However, single-column primary keys can be defined either as column or table constraints.

Creating Primary Key Constraints

Enough with the definitions, already. Let's start by taking a look at some examples for defining primary key constraints. Take a look at the following code listing, which displays a `create table` statement for creating our own EMPLOYEE table using constraints defined as table constraints (note that the `constraint` clause appears in bold):

```
SQL>  create table employee
  2   (empid varchar2(5),
  3    lastname varchar2(25),
  4    firstname varchar2(25),
  5    salary number(10,4),
  6    constraint pk_employee_01
  7    primary key (empid));
Table created.
```

TIP
If we wanted to create a composite primary key consisting of two or more columns, we would include the names of two (or more) columns

inside the parentheses appearing after keywords
`primary key.`

Only one primary key is permitted per table. Now, take a look at a `create table` statement for generating the same EMPLOYEE table. This time, the code listing shows the definition of the primary key as a column constraint. The `constraint` clause appears in bold in the following example:

```
SQL> create table employee
  2   (empid varchar2(5)
  3     constraint pk_employee_01 primary key,
  4     lastname varchar2(25),
  5     firstname varchar2(25),
  6     salary number(10,4));
Table created.
```

TIP
Both constraint declaration methods allow you to define your own names for your constraints. Remember that this feature is useful because constraints are database objects associated with tables, and from our earlier discussion, you know it's helpful to give associated database objects similar names.

Notice in the previous examples that each primary key constraint was given a meaningful name when defined. Oracle strongly recommends that you give your constraints meaningful names in this way so that you can easily identify the constraint later. With so many similarities between table and column constraint declarations, you may ask, are there any differences between constraints declared as table constraints and those declared as column constraints? Absolutely! Remember, *you can declare composite primary keys only by using the table constraint syntax, and you can declare not NULL constraints only using the column constraint syntax.* Another difference is that you can simplify the constraint declaration by merely indicating to Oracle that you want a constraint on the column (shown in bold), as you can see in the following block:

```
SQL> create table department
  2   (department_num number(5) primary key,
  3     department_name varchar2(25),
  4     location varchar2(25));
Table created.
```

TIP
*When you simplify your column constraint
definition in this way, Oracle names the constraint
for you. When Oracle names the constraint for you,
the naming convention is SYS_Cnnnnn.*

Composite Primary Keys

So that you understand the nature of composite primary keys in Oracle for OCP, the
following code block shows how to define a composite primary key:

```
SQL> create table names
  2  (firstname varchar2(10),
  3   lastname  varchar2(10),
  4   constraint pk_names_01
  5   primary key (firstname, lastname));
Table created.
```

Uniqueness in a composite primary key is determined by combining the values
in all columns of the composite primary key. If the combination is unique, then the
key is unique. Check out the following code block to see some examples:

```
SQL> insert into names values ('JASON','COUCHMAN');
1 row created.
SQL> insert into names values ('JASON','LEE');
1 row created.
SQL> insert into names values ('COUCHMAN','JASON');
1 row created.
SQL> insert into names values ('JASON','COUCHMAN');
insert into names values ('JASON','COUCHMAN')
            *
ERROR at line 1:
ORA-00001: unique constraint (SCOTT.PK_NAMES_01) violated
```

In the second statement above, we add JASON LEE to the NAMES table. This is
OK, even though we already have a record where FIRSTNAME is JASON because
Oracle enforces uniqueness on the combination of values in FIRSTNAME and
LASTNAME. Thus, we can even reverse the values as we did in the third statement
above. However, the fourth statement causes an error because it is an exact
duplicate of the first.

Defining Foreign Key Constraints

To help you understand how to define foreign key constraints, let's think in terms of an example. Let's say we have our own table called DEPARTMENT, which we just created in the last code block. It lists the department number, name, and location for all departments in our own little company. Let's also say that we want to create our EMPLOYEE table with another column, called DEPARTMENT_NUM. Because there is an implied parent-child relationship between these two tables with the shared column, let's make that relationship official by using a foreign key constraint, shown in bold in the following block:

```
SQL>   create table employee
  2    (empid varchar2(5) primary key,
  3     lastname varchar2(25),
  4     firstname varchar2(25),
  5     salary number(10,4),
  6     department_num number(5)
  7     references department (department_num)
  8     on delete set null);
Table created.
```

For a foreign-key constraint to be valid, the same column appearing in both tables must have exactly the same datatype. You needn't give the columns the same names, but it's a good idea to do so. The foreign key constraint prevents the DEPARTMENT_NUM column in the EMP table from ever storing a value that can't also be found in the DEPT table. The final clause, `on delete set null`, is an option relating to the deletion of data from the parent table. If someone attempts to remove a row from the parent table that contains a referenced value from the child table, Oracle sets all corresponding values in the child to NULL. The other option is `on delete cascade`, where Oracle allows remove all corresponding records from the child table when a referenced record from the parent table is removed.

Let's also test your eyes for distinguishing table and column constraints. Is the foreign key in the previous example a table or column constraint? At first, it might seem like a table constraint because the constraint definition appears after all the columns. However, close examination yields two important features. For one, there is no `constraint` clause. Table constraints must have a `constraint` clause; otherwise, Oracle returns an error. For another, there is no comma separating the constraint definition from the rest of the columns defined. If you flip back to our other constraint definition examples and look again carefully, you'll realize that this example shows the foreign key defined as a column constraint, not a table constraint.

TIP
A foreign key constraint cannot be created on the child table until the parent table is created and the primary key is defined on that parent table.

Defining Unique Key Constraints

Let's say we also want our employee table to store social security or government ID information. The definition of a UNIQUE constraint on the GOVT_ID column prevents anyone from defining a duplicate government ID for any two employees in the table. Take a look at the following example, where the unique constraint definition is shown in bold:

```
SQL>  create table employee
   2  (empid varchar2(5) primary key,
   3  lastname varchar2(25),
   4  firstname varchar2(25),
   5  salary number(10,4),
   6  department_num number(5)
   7    references department (department_num),
   8  govt_id number(10) unique);
Table created.
```

TIP
Unlike primary keys, which require that the column value not be NULL in addition to enforcing uniqueness, a unique constraint permits NULL values to be added to the column. Only non-NULL column values must be unique when unique constraints are present on the column.

Defining Other Types of Constraints

The last two types of constraints are not NULL and CHECK constraints. By default, Oracle allows columns to contain NULL values. The not NULL constraint prevents the data value defined by any row for the column from being NULL. By default, primary keys are defined to be not NULL. All other columns can contain NULL data, unless you explicitly define the column to be not NULL. CHECK constraints allow Oracle to verify the validity of data being entered on a table against static criteria. For example, you could specify that the SALARY column cannot contain values over $250,000. If someone tries to create an employee row with a salary of

$1,000,000 per year, Oracle would return an error message saying that the record data defined for the SALARY column has violated the CHECK constraint for that column. Let's look at a code example where both not NULL and check constraints are defined in bold:

```
SQL> create table employee
  2  (empid varchar2(5) primary key,
  3   lastname varchar2(25) not null,
  4   firstname varchar2(25),
  5   salary number(10,4) check (salary <=250000),
  6   department_num number(5)
  7     references department (department_num),
  8   govt_id number(10) unique);
Table created.
```

TIP
Here's what is meant by static criteria for CHECK constraints: CHECK constraints can only compare data in that column to a specific set of constant values or operations on those values. A CHECK constraint cannot refer to any other column or row in this or any other table. It also cannot refer to special keywords, such as user, sysdate, currval, nextval, level, uid, userenv, rownum, *and* rowid.

Indexes Created by Constraints

Indexes are created automatically by Oracle to support integrity constraints that enforce uniqueness. The two types of integrity constraints that enforce uniqueness are PRIMARY KEY and UNIQUE constraints. When the primary key or UNIQUE constraint is declared, a unique index to support the column's uniqueness is also created, and all values in all columns that were defined as part of the primary key or UNIQUE constraint are placed into the index.

The name of the unique index created automatically to support unique and primary key constraints is the same name as the one given to the constraint. Therefore, if you were to explicitly name the primary key on your EMP table PK_EMPLOYEE_01, Oracle calls the unique index PK_EMPLOYEE_01 as well. If, however, you choose not to name your unique or primary key constraint, Oracle generates the name of your constraint for you. In this case, Oracle also gives the unique index the same name it gives the constraint.

TIP
*When a primary key or unique constraint is created,
a unique index corresponding to that constraint of
the table is created to enforce uniqueness.*

Adding Integrity Constraints to Existing Tables

Another constraint-related activity that you may need to do involves adding new
constraints to an existing table. This can be easy if there is no data in the table
already, but it can be a nightmare if data already exists in the table that doesn't
conform to the constraint criteria. The simplest scenario for adding the constraint is
to add it to the database before data is inserted. Take a look at the following code
block:

```
SQL> create table employee
  2  (empid varchar2(5),
  3   lastname varchar2(25),
  4   firstname varchar2(25),
  5   salary number(10,4),
  6   department_num number(5),
  7   govt_id number(10));
Table created.
SQL> alter table employee add constraint
  2  pk_employee_01 primary key (empid);
Table altered.
SQL> alter table employee add constraint
  2  fk_employee_01 foreign key (department_num)
  3  references department (department_num);
Table altered.
SQL> alter table employee add constraint
  2  ck_employee_01 check (salary <=250000);
Table altered.
SQL> alter table employee add constraint
  2  uk_employee_01 unique (govt_id);
Table altered.
SQL> alter table employee modify
  2  (lastname not null);
Table altered.
```

Notice that all the examples follow a general pattern of `alter table`
`table_name` add constraint `constraint_name type (definition)`,
except for not NULL constraints, which use the `alter table modify` statement

we saw in earlier discussions. The column on which the constraint is added must already exist in the database table; no constraint can be created for a column that does not exist in the table. Some of the other restrictions on creating constraints when data already exists in the table are listed here:

- **Primary keys**   Columns cannot contain NULL values, and all values must be unique.

- **Foreign keys**   Referenced columns in the other table must contain all values found in this one; otherwise, this column's value must be NULL.

- **UNIQUE constraints**   Columns must contain all unique values or NULL values, or a combination of the two.

- **CHECK constraints**   The new constraint will only be applied to data added or modified after the constraint is created.

- **Not NULL**   Columns cannot contain NULL values. If you want to add a column with a not NULL constraint to a table, you should use a `default` clause to identify a value Oracle can populate in this column for existing rows. If you want to define a not NULL constraint on an existing column, the table must be empty or else the column must already have no NULL values defined for any rows.

Disabling Constraints

A constraint can be turned on and off. When the constraint is disabled, it will no longer do its job of enforcing rules on the data entered into the table. The following code block demonstrates some sample statements for disabling constraints:

```
SQL> alter table employee disable primary key;
Table altered.
SQL> alter table employee disable constraint uk_employee_01;
Table altered.
```

You may experience a problem if you attempt to disable a primary key when existing foreign keys depend on that primary key. This problem is shown in the following situation:

```
SQL> alter table department disable primary key;
alter table department disable primary key
*
ERROR at line 1:
ORA-02297: cannot disable constraint (SCOTT.SYS_C001913) -
dependencies exist
```

If you try to drop a primary key when there are foreign keys depending on it, the `cascade` option is required as part of `alter table disable constraint`, as shown in the following code block:

```
SQL> alter table department disable primary key cascade;
Table altered.
```

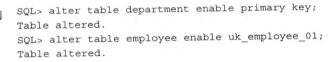

TIP
Disabling a constraint leaves the table vulnerable to inappropriate data being entered! Care should be taken to ensure that the data loaded during the period the constraint is disabled will not interfere with your ability to enable the constraint later. The cascade clause disables dependent integrity constraints. Disabling a primary or unique key removes the associated index from Oracle.

Enabling a Disabled Constraint

When the constraint is later enabled, the rules defined for the constraint are once again enforced, rendering the constraint as effective as it was when it was first added to the table. You can enable a disabled constraint as follows:

```
SQL> alter table department enable primary key;
Table altered.
SQL> alter table employee enable uk_employee_01;
Table altered.
```

TIP
Only constraints that have been successfully defined and are currently disabled can be enabled by this code. A constraint that fails on creation will not exist in the disabled state, waiting for you to correct the problem and reenable it. Enabling a unique or primary key constraint automatically rebuilds the index for that constraint.

When Existing Data in a Column Violates a Disabled Constraint

This topic is a bit advanced, so be forewarned. There are situations where you may want to disable a constraint for some general purpose, such as disabling a primary key in order to speed up a large number of `insert` statements. *Be careful when using this approach*! If you disable a constraint and then load data into the table column that violates the integrity constraint while the constraint is disabled, your attempt to enable the constraint later with the `alter table enable constraint` statement will fail. You will need to use a special table called EXCEPTIONS (created by running the `utlexcpt.sql` script in `rdbms/admin` under the Oracle software home directory) to identify and correct the offending records. The following example involving a primary-key constraint should give you an idea of how this works:

```
SQL> @@C:\ORACLE\ORA81\RDBMS\ADMIN\UTLEXCPT
Table created.
SQL> create table example_1 (col1 number);
Table created.
SQL> insert into example_1 values (10);
1 row created.
SQL> insert into example_1 values (1);
1 row created.
SQL> alter table example_1 add (constraint pk_01 primary key (col1));
Table altered.
SQL> select * from example_1;
COL1
---------
       10
        1
SQL> alter table example_1 disable constraint pk_01;
Table altered.
SQL> insert into example_1 values (1);
1 row created.
SQL> alter table example_1 enable constraint pk_01
  2   exceptions into exceptions;
alter table example_1 enable constraint pk_01
*
ERROR at line 1:
ORA-02437: cannot enable (SCOTT.PK_01) - primary key violated
SQL> desc exceptions
 Name                            Null?     Type
 ------------------------------- --------  ----
 ROW_ID                                    ROWID
 OWNER                                     VARCHAR2(30)
 TABLE_NAME                                VARCHAR2(30)
 CONSTRAINT                                VARCHAR2(30)
SQL> select e.row_id, a.col1
  2   from exceptions e, example_1 a
  3   where e.row_id = a.rowid;
ROW_ID                  COL1
```

```
------------------  --------
AAAAvGAAGAAAAPWAAB         1
AAAAvGAAGAAAAPWAAD         1
```

At this point, you have identified the ROWIDs of the offending rows in EXAMPLE_1 that break the rules of the primary key, which you can use either to modify the value of one of these rows or to remove one of the rows so the primary key can be unique. In the future, to ensure that enabling the constraint will be a smooth process, try not to load any data into columns with disabled constraints that would violate the constraint rules.

Removing Constraints

Usually, there is little about a constraint that will interfere with your ability to remove it, so long as you either own the table or have been granted appropriate privileges to do so. When a constraint is dropped, any index associated with that constraint (if there is one) is also dropped. Here is an example:

```
SQL> alter table employee drop unique (govt_id);
Table altered.
SQL> alter table employee drop primary key cascade;
Table altered.
SQL> alter table employee drop constraint ck_employee_01;
Table altered.
```

An anomaly can be found when disabling or dropping not NULL constraints. You cannot disable a not NULL constraint, per se—a column either accepts NULL values or it doesn't. Therefore, you must use the alter table modify clause in all situations where the not NULL constraints on a table must be added or removed. Here's an example:

```
SQL> alter table employee modify (lastname null);
Table altered.
SQL> alter table employee modify (lastname not null);
Table altered.
```

Dropping Parent Tables with Foreign Key Constraint References

In the same way that disabling a primary key constraint can be a problem when the primary key is referenced by a foreign key in a child table, dropping parent tables can also pose a problem when a child table is involved. If we wanted to drop the parent table DEPARTMENT in our parent-child relationship, the foreign key in the child table EMPLOYEE may interfere with our doing so. Let's take a look at what happens:

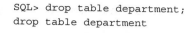

```
SQL> drop table department;
drop table department
         *
ERROR at line 1:
ORA-02449: unique/primary keys in table referenced by foreign keys
```

When there are constraints on other tables that reference the table to be dropped, you can use the `cascade constraints` clause in your `drop table` statement. The constraints in other tables that refer to the table being dropped are also dropped with `cascade constraints`:

```
SQL> drop table department cascade constraints;
Table dropped.
```

> **TIP**
> *Alternately, you can disable or drop the foreign key*
> *in the child table before dropping the parent table*
> *by using the `alter table drop constraint`*
> *statement from earlier in the chapter.*

Constraint Deferability in Oracle

When records are added to a database table, Oracle immediately validates the incoming records against any constraints that may exist on the columns in the table. If the data doesn't conform to the constraint criteria, Oracle returns an error immediately. However, you can modify this default behavior so that Oracle does not return an error immediately. Instead, you can force Oracle not to return an error until you are ready to end your transaction. Remember from an earlier discussion that a *transaction* is a series of data-change statements issued in a user session that comprise a logical unit of work. You will learn more about transaction processing later in Chapter 6. The concept of forcing Oracle not to return constraint violation errors until the end of your transaction is called *constraint deferability*.

In order for constraint deferability to work, you must define your constraint to be deferrable using the `deferrable initially deferred` syntax. For primary keys and unique constraints, this means that Oracle uses a nonunique index to store primary key values rather than a unique index. The nonunique index allows temporary storage of data in the primary key column until the transaction is completed and constraint violation errors can be reported. If you use the other deferability option, `deferrable initially immediate`, Oracle still creates a nonunique index to support the primary key, but it enforces the primary key when data is entered, not when the transaction ends. If you omit either of these clauses entirely, Oracle also enforces the constraint when data is entered, not when the transaction ends. Finally, remember that the keyword `deferrable` contains two Rs, not one.

The options you have for enabling or disabling deferrable constraints include `enable validate` and `enable novalidate`. If you try to enable your constraint without specifying one of these options, Oracle uses `enable validate` by default. Using the `enable validate` option when you're enabling constraints forces Oracle to validate all the data in the constrained column to ensure that it meets the constraint criteria. This is the default behavior unless otherwise specified. The `enable validate` command is the same as simply using the `enable` keyword—`validate` is the default behavior of Oracle. However, Oracle also allows you to use the `enable novalidate` option when you want to enforce the constraint for new data entering the table but don't care about data that already exists in the table.

Let's look at an example. Assume that a table called PRODUCTS is used for storing products our company sells. The following code block illustrates how to create, disable, and enable a deferrable primary key constraint using appropriate syntax, which is shown in bold:

```
SQL> create table products
  2  (product# number,
  3   product_name varchar2(15),
  4   quantity number,
  5   color varchar2(10),
  6   prod_size varchar2(10));
Table created.
SQL> insert into products values
  2  (1, 'FLIBBER', 34, 'GREEN', 'XXL');
1 row created.
SQL> insert into products values
  2  (2, 'blobber', 4, 'GREEN', 'P');
1 row created.
SQL> select * from products;
PRODUCT# PRODUCT_NAME    QUANTITY COLOR      PROD_SIZE
-------- ------------- --------- ---------- ----------
       1 FLIBBER              34 GREEN      XXL
       2 blobber               4 GREEN      P
SQL> alter table products add
  2  (constraint pk_products_01 primary key (product#)
  3  deferrable initially deferred);
Table altered.
SQL> alter table products disable primary key;
Table altered.
SQL> update products set product# = 1
  2  where product_name = 'blobber';
1 row updated.
SQL> commit;
```

```
Commit complete.
SQL> alter table products enable validate primary key;
alter table products enable validate primary key
                                     *
ERROR at line 1:
ORA-02437: cannot enable (SCOTT.PK_PRODUCTS_01) - primary
key violated
SQL> alter table products enable novalidate primary key;
Table altered.
SQL> select * from products;
PRODUCT# PRODUCT_NAME    QUANTITY COLOR      PROD_SIZE
-------- -------------- --------- ---------- ----------
       1 FLIBBER              34 GREEN      XXL
       1 blobber               4 GREEN      P
SQL> insert into products
  2  (product#, product_name, quantity, color, prod_size)
  3  values (1,'FLOBBER',23,'GREEN','L')
insert into products
            *
ERROR at line 1:
ORA-00001: unique constraint (SCOTT.PK_PRODUCTS_01) violated
```

TIP
*disable novalidate is the same as disable;
however, new in Oracle is disable validate,
which disables the constraints, drops the index, and
disallows any modification on the constrained
columns. The enable keyword implies validate
option unless novalidate is specified. The
disable keyword implies novalidate unless the
validate option is specified.*

For Review

1. Be sure you can identify some differences between defining constraints as
table constraints and as column constraints. Know how to define all five
constraints on existing tables and as part of new table definitions. Know
why defining a not NULL constraint is not like defining other types of
constraints.

2. Know how to enable a disabled constraint. Be sure you know the
restrictions on enabling constraints and how to create and use the
EXCEPTIONS table for enabling constraints when data that violates these
constraints exists in the table.

3. Be sure you can explain the concept of constraint deferability and the use of appropriate syntax for defining, enabling, and disabling deferrable constraints.

4. Understand that Oracle creates unique indexes in support of unique and primary key constraints. Know what determines the name given to an index created automatically.

Exercises

1. **The PROFITS table in your database has a primary key on the PRODUCT_NAME and SALE_PERIOD columns. Which of the following statements could *not* have been used to define this primary key?**

   A. `create table profits ( product_name varchar2(10), sale_period varchar2(10), profit number, constraint pk_profits_01 primary key (product_name, sale_period));`

   B. `alter table profits add constraint pk_profits_01 primary key (product_name, sale_period) deferrable initially immediate;`

   C. `alter table profits add (constraint pk_profits_01 primary key (product_name, sale_period));`

   D. `create table profits ( product_name varchar2(10) primary key, sale_period varchar2(10) primary key, profit number);`

2. **You are defining check constraints on your SALES table, which contains two columns, PRODUCT_TYPE and UNIT_SALES. Which of the following choices identify a properly defined check constraint? (Choose two.)**

   A. `alter table sales add constraint ck_sales_01 check (product_type in ('TOYS', 'HOT DOGS', 'PALM PILOTS'));`

   B. `alter table sales add constraint ck_sales_01 check (product_type in (select product_type from valid_products));`

   C. `alter table sales modify (product_type varchar2(30) check (product_type in ('TOYS', 'HOT DOGS', 'PALM PILOTS')));`

   D. `alter table sales add (product_name varchar2(30) check (product_name <> 'AK-47'));`

3. **Use the following code block to answer the question:**

```
SQL> create table prices
  2  ( product_name varchar2(30),
  3     price number(10,4));
Table created.
SQL> alter table prices add constraint pk_prices_01
  2  primary key (product_name);
Table altered.
SQL> insert into prices values ('DOGGY', 499.99);
1 row created.
SQL> alter table prices disable constraint pk_prices_01;
Table altered.
SQL> insert into prices values ('DOGGY', 449.99);
1 row created.
SQL> alter table prices enable novalidate pk_prices_01;
```

What happens next?

A. Existing entries are checked for violations, PK_PRICES_01 is enabled, and Oracle checks subsequent entries for violations immediately.

B. Existing entries are checked for violations, PK_PRICES_01 is not enabled, and Oracle does not check subsequent entries for violations immediately.

C. Existing entries are not checked for violations, PK_PRICES_01 is enabled, and Oracle checks subsequent entries for violations immediately.

D. Existing entries are checked for violations, PK_PRICES_01 is not enabled, Oracle checks subsequent entries for violations immediately.

4. **Your attempt to disable a constraint yields the following error:** `ORA-02297: cannot disable constraint - dependencies exist.` **Which of the following types of constraints is likely causing interference with your disablement of this one?**

A. Check constraint

B. Not NULL constraint

C. Foreign key constraint

D. Unique constraint

5. **You are disabling a not NULL constraint on the UNIT_PRICE column in the SALES table. Which of the following choices identifies the correct statement for performing this action?**

   A. `alter table sales modify (unit_prices null);`

   B. `alter table sales modify (unit_prices not null);`

   C. `alter table sales add (unit_prices null);`

   D. `alter table sales add (unit_prices not null);`

Answer Key

1. D. **2.** A and D. Nothing in the question said you can't add a new column. **3.** B. Remember, when a constraint cannot be enabled, it does not perform its job. **4.** C. **5.** A.

Chapter Summary

We covered a great deal of ground in this chapter. At the beginning, we discussed how to create tables in the Oracle database. We talked about how to alter our table definitions as well. After covering how to define and change the definition of tables with respect to columns, we spent a great deal of time discussing database constraints. You learned about the five different types of database constraints as well as how to create them when initially defining the table. You also learned how to create constraints after the fact using the `alter table` command. We then moved on to discuss indexes that can be created with constraints. We covered constraint deferability and how to correct problems where the data in a table column might violate the constraint on that column—two complex topics to know for OCP.

Two-Minute Drill

- The basic types of data relationships in Oracle include primary keys and functional dependency within a table as well as foreign key constraints from one table to another.

- A relational database is composed of objects that store data, objects that manage access to data, and objects that improve performance when accessing data.

- A table can be created with five different types of integrity constraints: PRIMARY KEY, FOREIGN KEY, UNIQUE, not NULL, and CHECK.

■   Referential integrity often creates a parent/child relationship between two tables—the parent being the referenced table and the child being the referring table. Often, a naming convention that requires child objects to adopt and extend the name of the parent table is useful in identifying these relationships.

■   The datatypes available for creating columns in tables are CHAR, VARCHAR2, NUMBER, DATE, RAW, LONG, LONG RAW, ROWID, BLOB, CLOB, NCLOB, and BFILE.

■   A table column can be added or modified with the `alter table` statement.

■   Columns can be added with little difficulty if they are nullable, using the `alter table add (`*`column_name datatype`*`)` statement. If a `not NULL` constraint is desired, add the column, populate the column with data, and then add the `not NULL` constraint separately.

■   Column datatype size can be increased with no difficulty by using the `alter table modify (`*`column_name datatype`*`)` statement. Column size can be decreased, or the datatype can be changed, only if the column contains NULL for all rows.

■   Constraints can be added to a column only if the column already contains values that will not violate the added constraint.

■   `PRIMARY KEY` constraints can be added with a table constraint definition by using the `alter table add (constraint` *`constraint_name`* `primary key (`*`column_name`*`))` statement or with a column constraint definition by using the `alter table modify (`*`column_name`* `constraint` *`constraint_name`* `primary key)` statement.

■   `UNIQUE` constraints can be added with a table constraint definition by using the `alter table add (constraint` *`constraint_name`* `unique (`*`column_name`*`))` statement or with a column constraint definition by using the `alter table modify (`*`column_name`* `constraint` *`constraint_name`* `unique)` statement.

■   `FOREIGN KEY` constraints can be added with a table constraint definition by using the `alter table add (constraint` *`constraint_name`* `foreign key (`*`column_name`*`) references` *`OWNER.TABLE`* `(`*`column_name`*`) [on delete cascade])` statement or with a column constraint definition by using the `alter table modify (`*`column_name`* `constraint` *`constraint_name`* `references` *`OWNER.TABLE`* `(`*`column_name`*`) [on delete cascade])` statement.

■ CHECK constraints can be added with a table constraint definition by using the alter table add (constraint *constraint_name* check (*check_condition*)) statement or with a column constraint definition by using the alter table modify (*column_name* constraint *constraint_name* check (*check_condition*)) statement.

■ The check condition cannot contain subqueries, references to certain keywords (such as user, sysdate, and rowid), or any pseudocolumns.

■ Not NULL constraints can be added with a column constraint definition by using the alter table modify (*column_name* NOT NULL) statement.

■ A named PRIMARY KEY, UNIQUE, CHECK, or FOREIGN KEY constraint can be dropped with the alter table drop constraint *constraint_name* statement. A not NULL constraint is dropped using the alter table modify (*column_name* NULL) statement.

■ If a constraint that created an index automatically (such as a primary key or UNIQUE constraint) is dropped, the corresponding index is also dropped.

■ If the table is dropped, all constraints, triggers, and indexes created for the table are also dropped.

■ Removing all data from a table is best accomplished with the truncate command rather than the delete from table_name statement because truncate resets the table's high-water mark and deallocates all the table's storage quickly, thus improving performance on select count ( ) statements issued after the truncation.

■ An object name can be changed with the rename statement or with the use of synonyms.

■ Indexes are created automatically in conjunction with primary key and UNIQUE constraints. These indexes are named after the constraint name given to the constraint in the definition of the table.

■ Tables are created without any data in them, except for tables created with the create table as select statement. These tables are created and prepopulated with data from another table.

Fill-in-the-Blank Questions

1. This constraint is useful for verifying data entered for a column against a static list of values identified as part of the table definition:

_____

2. This datatype is used for identifying each row uniquely in the table:

_____

3. The definition of the object can be made available to every user on the system. However, its contents are visible only to the user session that added the information to this object: _____

4. This keyword for constraint enablement specifies that Oracle not check to see whether the data conforms to the constraint until the user commits the transaction: _____

5. This database object in Oracle, created when the primary key is defined, is dropped when the table is dropped: _____

Chapter Questions

1. **Which of the following integrity constraints automatically create an index when defined? (Choose two.)**

A. Foreign keys

B. Unique constraints

C. Not NULL constraints

D. Primary keys

2. **Developer ANJU executes the following statement: `create table ANIMALS as select * from MASTER.ANIMALS;`. What is the effect of this statement?**

A. A table named ANIMALS will be created in the MASTER schema with the same data as the ANIMALS table owned by ANJU.

B. A table named ANJU will be created in the ANIMALS schema with the same data as the ANIMALS table owned by MASTER.

    C. A table named ANIMALS will be created in the ANJU schema with the same data as the ANIMALS table owned by MASTER.

    D. A table named MASTER will be created in the ANIMALS schema with the same data as the ANJU table owned by ANIMALS.

3. **No relationship officially exists between two tables. Which of the following choices is the strongest indicator that a parent/child relationship exists between these tables?**

    A. The two tables in the database are named VOUCHER and VOUCHER_ITEM, respectively.

    B. The two tables in the database are named EMPLOYEE and PRODUCTS, respectively.

    C. The two tables in the database were created on the same day.

    D. The two tables in the database contain none of the same columns.

4. **Which of the following are valid database datatypes in Oracle? (Choose three.)**

    A. CHAR

    B. VARCHAR2

    C. BOOLEAN

    D. NUMBER

    E. NUMERIC

    F. ROWNUM

5. **Which line of the following statements produces an error?**

    A. `create table GOODS`

    B. `(GOODNO number,`

    C. `GOOD_NAME varchar2(20) check(GOOD_NAME in (select NAME from AVAIL_GOODS)),`

    D. `constraint PK_GOODS_01`

    E. `primary key (GOODNO));`

    F. There are no errors in this statement.

6. **You are adding columns to a table in Oracle. Which of the following choices indicates what you would do to increase the number of columns accepting NULL values in a table?**

   A. Use the `alter table` statement.

   B. Ensure that all column values are NULL for all rows.

   C. First, increase the size of adjacent column datatypes and then add the column.

   D. Add the column, populate the column, and then add the not NULL constraint.

7. **A user issues the statement `select count(*) from employee`. The query takes an inordinately long time and returns a count of zero. What is the most cost-effective solution to this problem?**

   A. Upgrade the hardware.

   B. Truncate the table.

   C. Upgrade the version of Oracle.

   D. Delete the high-water mark.

8. **You are creating some tables in your database as part of the logical data model. Which of the following constraints has an index associated with it that is generated automatically by Oracle?**

   A. Unique

   B. Foreign key

   C. CHECK

   D. Not NULL

9. **Each of the following statements is true about referential integrity, except one. Which is it?**

   A. The referencing column in the child table must correspond with a primary key in the parent.

   B. All values in the referenced column in the parent table must be present in the referencing column in the child.

    C. The datatype of the referenced column in the parent table must be identical to the referencing column in the child.

    D. All values in the referencing column in the child table must be in present in the referenced column in the parent.

10. **You are managing constraints on a table in Oracle. Which of the following choices correctly identifies the limitations on check constraints?**

    A. Values must be obtained from a lookup table.

    B. Values must be part of a fixed set defined by `create` or `alter table`.

    C. Values must include reserved words, such as SYSDATE and USER.

    D. The column cannot contain a NULL value.

Fill-in-the-Blank Answers

1. Check

2. ROWID

3. Global temporary table

4. `novalidate`

5. Index

Answers to Chapter Questions

1. B and D. Unique constraints and primary keys

Explanation   Every constraint that enforces uniqueness creates an index to assist in the process. The two integrity constraints that enforce uniqueness are unique constraints and primary keys. Other types of integrity constraints like check, not NULL, and foreign keys, do not use indexes in any capacity for enforcing data integrity.

2. C. A table named ANIMALS will be created in the ANJU schema with the same data as the ANIMALS table owned by MASTER.

Explanation   This question requires you to look carefully at the `create table` statement in the question and to know some things about table creation. First, a table is always created in the schema of the user who created it. Second, because the `create table as select` clause was used, choices B and D are both incorrect because they identify the table being created as something other than ANIMALS, among other things. Choice A identifies the schema into which the ANIMALS table will be created as MASTER, which is incorrect for the reasons just stated. Refer to the discussion of creating tables for more information.

3. A. The two tables in the database are named VOUCHER and VOUCHER_ITEM, respectively.

Explanation   This choice implies the use of a naming convention similar to the one we discussed in this chapter, where tables with foreign key relationships have similar names. Although there is no guarantee that these two tables are related, the possibility is strongest in this case. Choice B implies the same naming convention, but because the two tables' names are dissimilar, there is little likelihood that the two tables are related in any way. Choice C is incorrect because the date a table is created has absolutely no bearing on what function the table serves in the database.

Choice D is incorrect because two tables *cannot* be related if there are no common columns between them. Refer to the discussion of creating tables using integrity constraints, naming conventions, and data modeling.

4. A, B, and D. CHAR, VARCHAR2, and NUMBER

Explanation BOOLEAN is the only invalid datatype in this listing. Although BOOLEAN is a valid datatype in PL/SQL, it is not a datatype available on the Oracle database, meaning that you cannot create a column in a table that uses the BOOLEAN datatype. Review the discussion of allowed datatypes in column definitions.

5. C. `GOOD_NAME varchar2(20) check(GOOD_NAME in (select NAME from AVAIL_GOODS)),`

Explanation A check constraint cannot contain a reference to another table, nor can it reference a virtual column, such as ROWID or SYSDATE. The other lines of the `create table` statement contain the correct syntax.

6. A. Use the `alter table` statement.

Explanation The `alter table` statement is the only choice offered that allows you to increase the number of columns per table. Choice B is incorrect because setting a column to all NULL values for all rows does simply that. Choice C is incorrect because increasing the adjacent column sizes simply increases the sizes of the columns, and choice D is incorrect because the listed steps outline how to add a column with a not NULL constraint—something not specified by the question.

7. B. Truncate the table.

Explanation Choices A and C may work, but an upgrade of hardware and software will cost far more than truncating the table. Choice D is partly correct, because there will be some change required to the high-water mark. However, the change will reset the high-water mark, not eliminate it entirely, and the method used is to issue the `truncate table` command.

8. A. Unique

Explanation Only unique and primary-key constraints require Oracle to generate an index that supports or enforces the uniqueness of the column values. Foreign keys, CHECK constraints, and not NULL constraints do not require indexes. Therefore, choices B, C, and D are incorrect.

9. B. All values in the referenced column in the parent table must be present in the referencing column in the child.

Explanation   Referential integrity is from child to parent, not vice versa. The parent table can have many values that are not present in child records, but the child record must correspond to something in the parent. Therefore, the correct answer is in this case is choice B.

10. B. Values must be part of a fixed set defined by `create table` or `alter table`.

Explanation   A check constraint may only use fixed expressions defined when you create or alter the table with the constraint definition. Reserved words such as SYSDATE and USER and values from a lookup table are not permitted, thus making choices A and C incorrect. Finally, NULL values in a column are constrained by not NULL constraints, a relatively unsophisticated form of check constraints. Therefore, choice D is incorrect.

CHAPTER
6

Manipulating
Oracle Data

his chapter covers the following topics related to manipulating Oracle data:

- Adding new rows to a table

- Making changes to existing row data

- Deleting data from the Oracle database

- Merging data in an Oracle table

- The importance of transaction control

I've shown some data-manipulation operations from time to time in the previous several chapters. Every time I've done so, I've promised to explain what these statements meant later. Well, now is my chance. This section will introduce you to all forms of data-change manipulation. The three types of data-change manipulation in the Oracle database are updating, deleting, and inserting data. These statements are collectively known as the *data-manipulation language* of Oracle, or DML for short. A collection of DML statements that form a logical unit of work is called a transaction. We'll also look at *transaction processing,* which is a mechanism that the Oracle database provides in order to facilitate the act of changing data. Without transaction-processing mechanisms, Oracle cannot guarantee that users won't overwrite one another's changes in midprocess or select data that is in the process of being changed by another user.

Adding New Rows to a Table

The first data-change manipulation operation that will be discussed is the act of inserting new rows into a table. Once a table is created, no data is in the table, unless the table is created and populated by rows selected from another table. Even in this case, the data must come from somewhere. This "somewhere" is from users who enter data into the table via `insert` statements. An `insert` statement has a different syntax from a `select` statement. The general syntax for an `insert` statement is `insert into` *tablename* `(`*column_list*`) values` `(`*values_list*`)`, where *tablename* is the name of the table you want to insert data into, *column_list* is the list of columns for which you will define values on the record being added, and *values_list* is the list of those values you will define. The datatype of the data you add as values in the values list must correspond to the datatype for the column identified in that same position in the column list. We can see the columns in the EMPLOYEE table we defined in Chapter 5 listed in the following code block:

```
SQL> desc employee
 Name                              Null?    Type
```

```
-------------------------------  --------  -------------
EMPID                            NOT NULL VARCHAR2(5)
LASTNAME                         NOT NULL VARCHAR2(25)
FIRSTNAME                                 VARCHAR2(25)
SALARY                                    NUMBER(10,4)
HIRE_DATE                                 DATE
DEPT                                      VARCHAR2(10)
```

TIP

We're dealing with our own EMPLOYEE table that we created in Chapter 5 in this example, so as not to disturb the contents of the EMP table shipped with every Oracle database.

The following code block shows three examples of how to use the `insert` command to add new values to this table:

```
SQL>  insert into employee (empid, lastname, firstname,
  2     salary, dept, hire_date)
  3   values ('39334','SMITH','GINA',75000, null, '15-MAR-97');
1 row created.
SQL> insert into employee (empid, lastname, firstname, salary,
  2  dept, hire_date)
  3   values ('49539','LEE','QIAN',90000, '504A', '25-MAY-99');
1 row created.
SQL> insert into employee (empid, lastname, firstname, salary,
  2  dept, hire_date)
  3   values ('60403','HARPER','ROD',45000, '504A', '30-APR-79');
1 row created.
```

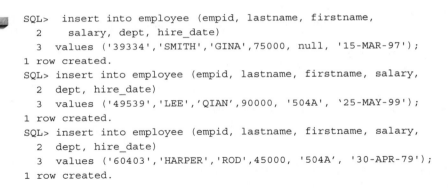

TIP

If you want to follow along on your Oracle database, remember that we've created several different versions of EMPLOYEE in the earlier discussion about constraints. Therefore, you need to ensure that your version of the EMPLOYEE table contains all the columns listed in the preceding `describe` *statement, using the appropriate* `alter table` *statements, before inserting data into your table.*

The preceding `insert` statements each have two parts. In the first part, the table to receive the inserted row is defined, along with the columns of the table that will have the column values inserted into them. The second portion of the statement defines the actual data values for the row to be added. This latter portion of the statement is denoted by the `values` keyword. Notice how each value in the values list matches up positionally to a column defined in the column list. If you look back at the description information for the table, you'll also notice that the datatype for each value matches the datatype Oracle expects for that column. Also, make sure you enclose character and date values in single quotation marks.

A Variation on a Theme

Oracle is capable of handling several variations on the `insert` statement. For example, you may not necessarily need to define explicit columns of the table. You only need to do that when you don't plan to populate every column in the record you are inserting with a value. Let's look at an example where we don't identify explicit columns because we intend to define values for every column listed in the EMPLOYEE table:

```
SQL> insert into employee values
  2  ('02039','WALLA','RAJENDRA',60000,'01-JAN-96','604B');
1 row created.
SQL> insert into employee values
  2  ('49392','SPANKY','STACY',100000,null,'604B');
1 row created.
SQL> insert into employee values
  2  ('49394','SMITH','BOB',50000,sysdate,'604B');
1 row created.
```

TIP
Notice how we used the NULL to insert a NULL value for HIRE_DATE in the row entry for user SPANKY. We had to do this because Oracle expects us to define explicitly a value for every column in the table.

Position, Position, Position

How does Oracle know which column to populate with what data? The answer is position. Position can matter in tables on the Oracle database; the position of the data in the `insert` statement must correspond to the position of the columns in the table. The user can determine the position of each column in a table by using the `describe` command or the output from the USER_TAB_COLUMNS dictionary view using COLUMN_ID to indicate position as part of the `order by` clause. The order in which the columns are listed in the output from the describe command is the same order in which values should be placed to insert data into the table without explicitly naming the columns of the table. Take a look for yourself:

```
SQL> select column_name, column_id
  2  from user_tab_columns
  3  where table_name = 'EMPLOYEE'
  4  order by column_id;
COLUMN_NAME          COLUMN_ID
------------------  -----------
EMPID                        1
LASTNAME                     2
FIRSTNAME                    3
SALARY                       4
HIRE_DATE                    5
DEPT                         6
SQL> describe employee
 Name                            Null?      Type
 ---------------------------    --------   ------------
  EMPID                         NOT NULL  VARCHAR2(5)
  LASTNAME                      NOT NULL  VARCHAR2(25)
  FIRSTNAME                               VARCHAR2(25)
  SALARY                                  NUMBER(10,4)
  HIRE_DATE                               DATE
  DEPT                                    VARCHAR2(10)
```

I cannot stress enough the fact that inserting data of the correct datatype into the correct column by matching the position of the value in the value listing to the position of the column in the column listing is not as easy as it sounds. If the datatype of data you add to a column does not match the datatype defined for the table, Oracle returns an error. Let's look at an example where we try to add text information to a NUMBER column:

```
SQL> insert into emp (empno, ename, sal)
  2  values ('SMITHERS',7444,900);
values ('SMITHERS',7444,900)
        *
ERROR at line 2:
ORA-01722: invalid number
```

Luckily, Oracle notified us of the mismatched datatypes so that we could then make the correction. You won't always be so luckily, especially if the datatype of the value added matches the datatype Oracle expects for the column, but the data is otherwise incorrect for the column. Let's look at another example where we accidentally add a new record to EMP with the job information incorrectly placed in the ENAME column:

```
SQL> insert into emp (empno, ename, job, sal)
  2  values (7444,'LACKEY','SMITHERS',900);
1 row created.
```

We know that LACKEY isn't this employee's name, nor is his or her job accurately described as SMITHERS. However, Oracle didn't produce an error, so if you're not careful, you could wind up adding a lot of junk data to your tables. So, the moral of the story is this: be careful to insert new records to a table so as to avoid errors, but be even more careful to avoid problems where you add data that doesn't cause an error but is contextually incorrect.

Another Variation

Another variation on the `insert` theme is the option to populate a table using data obtained from other tables using a `select` statement. This method of populating table data is similar to the method used by the `create table as select` statement. In this case, the `values` clause can be omitted entirely. However, the rules regarding column position of the inserted data still apply in this situation, meaning that if you can select data for all columns of the table having data inserted into it, you need not name the columns in the `insert into` clause. The following is an example:

```
SQL> insert into scott.employee (select * from master.employee);
```

> **TIP**
> In order to put data into a table, a special privilege must be granted from the table owner to the user who needs to perform the `insert` operation. A more complete discussion of object privileges appears in Chapter 8.

Can I Insert Into More Than One Table at a Time?

Sometimes, newcomers to Oracle think that because you can insert more than one row of data at a time into a single table with the `insert` command, you should also be able to insert data into more than one table at a time with a single issuance of the `insert` command. However, this would be too confusing both for Oracle and for us. You would need to tell Oracle explicitly what data to put in which table.

If you have to specify which data goes into what table, you'd be better off issuing two separate `insert` statements anyway. Thus, you can use the `insert` command to add data to only one table at a time. You can insert into one table using data from another table, however, and we've already seen how to accomplish this task.

Inserting Data and Integrity Constraints

No data can be inserted into a table when a column value for that new record being added violates an integrity constraint on the table. For example, if you used the `utlsampl.sql` script to build the EMP table we used in previous discussions, Oracle built a primary key constraint on the EMPNO column, designed to enfoce uniqueness on that column. The following code block shows how Oracle would react if you tried to insert a new row into EMP for an employee named SMITHERS using the EMPNO value defined for SMITH:

```
SQL> insert into emp (empno, ename, job)
  2  values (7369,'SMITHERS','LACKEY');
insert into emp (empno, ename, job)
*
ERROR at line 1:
ORA-00001: unique constraint (SCOTT.PK_EMP) violated
```

When you attempt to add new data to a table that violates an integrity constraint on that table, Oracle returns an error as we see in the previous example. However, you should also know that Oracle does not add the record to the table. See for yourself in the following code block that SMITHERS was not added to the table or overwrite SMITH's record in any way:

```
SQL> select empno, ename, job
  2  from emp
  3  where empno = 7369;
    EMPNO ENAME      JOB
---------- ---------- ---------
     7369 SMITH      CLERK
```

TIP
For inserting records into tables with foreign key constraints, you must first insert the new row into the parent table, and then insert new rows into the child(ren) table(s).

Specifying Explicit Default Values

Oracle**9*i*** and higher · Recall from Chapter 5 that we can define our table columns to carry default values. If no value is specified for a particular column by an `insert` statement adding new rows to the table, Oracle can populate that column anyway using the default value. To refresh your memory, consider the following code block where we define a table with a default column value, populate that table without specifying a value for the column, and then look at the result:

```
SQL> create table sample
  2  (col1 number,
  3   col2 varchar2(30) default 'YOU FORGOT ME');
Table created.
SQL> insert into sample (col1) values (1);
1 row created.
SQL> select * from sample;
     COL1 COL2
--------- ------------------------------
        1 YOU FORGOT ME
```

We can see in the previous code block that Oracle populated the column we forgot to specify data for anyway. We can invoke this feature explicitly as well by using the `default` keyword in our `insert` statement. Check out the following code block to understand how:

```
SQL> insert into sample (col1, col2) values (2, default);
1 row created.
SQL> select * from sample;
     COL1 COL2
--------- ------------------------------
        1 YOU FORGOT ME
        2 YOU FORGOT ME
```

For Review

Know the statement used to place new data into an Oracle table. Know how to code several derivatives of this statement as well.

Exercises

1. **You are adding data to the PRODUCTS table in an Oracle database. This table contains three columns: PRODUCT_NAME, PRODUCT_TYPE, and PRICE. Which of the following choices does not identify a well-formed `insert` statement on this table?**

   A. `insert into products (product_name, product_type, price) ('BARNEY DOLL','TOYS',49.99);`

B. `insert into products (product_name, product_type,`
`price) values ('BARNEY DOLL','TOYS',49.99);`

C. `insert into products values ('BARNEY`
`DOLL','TOYS',49.99);`

D. `insert into products (select product_name,`
`product_type, price from master_products);`

2. **Examine the following statement:**

`insert into SALES values ('BARNEY DOLL','31-MAR-93',29483854.39);`

Which of the following choices identifies a statement you cannot use to verify whether the correct information is placed into the correct columns?

A. `select * from sales;`

B. `select column_name, column_id from all_tab_columns`
`where table_name = 'SALES';`

C. `describe sales`

D. `select column_name, column_position from`
`all_ind_columns where table_name = 'SALES';`

3. **The absence of a `values` clause in an `insert` statement indicates that the `insert` statement contains a _____.**

4. **This keyword enables us to tell Oracle explicitly to populate a column with its default value: _____.**

Answer Key
1. A. 2. D. 3. subquery. 4. default

Making Changes to Existing Row Data

Data manipulation on Oracle tables does not end after you add new records to your tables. Often, the rows in a table will need to be changed. In order to make those changes, the `update` statement can be used. Updates can be made to any row in a database except in two cases. One case is where you don't have enough access privileges to update the data. You will learn more about access privileges in Chapter 8. The other case is where some other user on the database is making changes to the row you want to change. You will learn more about transaction control at the end of this section in the discussion titled "The Importance of Transaction Control."

Otherwise, you can change data by issuing an `update` statement, as shown in the following example:

```
SQL> update employee set salary = 99000
  2  where lastname = 'SPANKY';
1 row updated.
```

The typical `update` statement has three clauses:

- An `update` clause, where the table that will be updated is named.

- A `set` clause, where all columns whose values will be changed are named and the new values assigned.

- The `where` clause (optional), which lists one or more comparison operations to determine which rows Oracle will update. Omitting the `where` clause in an `update` statement has the effect of applying the data change to every row that presently exists in the table. Specific rows are modified whenever you specify the `where` clause.

Advanced Data Changes in Oracle

You can modify the values in more than one column using a single `update` statement, and you can also use subqueries in `update` statements. The following code block illustrates examples of both these statements:

```
SQL> update employee
  2  set firstname = 'ATHENA', lastname = 'BAMBINA'
  3  where empid = '49392';
1 row updated.
SQL> update employee
  2   set lastname = (select ename from emp where empno = 7844)
  3  where empid = '49392';
1 row updated.
```

Can I Update Data in More Than One Table at a Time?

Like the `insert` command, the `update` command permits you to make changes to records in only one table at a time, for largely the same reasons. You would have to indicate which columns to change in what tables, and this additional layer of granularity would make the `update` statement too burdensome and complex.

Data Changes and Integrity Constraints

Your data changes cannot violate the integrity constraints defined for the table. For example, you can't change the value set for EMPNO in the EMP table if it would cause a duplicate value to exist in that column. If you try to issue this kind of change, Oracle will return an error and will not make the change. However, be sensitive to issues related to context that we saw in the previous discussion on the insert statement. Also, if you try to update a record in a parent table where a corresponding record exists in the child table, Oracle will return an error if your change would create orphan records in the child table and disallow your change. You should first modify the records in the child table, and then modify the records in the parent.

Using the default Keyword

You can use the default keyword to set a column value to its specified default value in update statements as well. To do so, you simply set the column whose default value you want to use using the default keyword. For the next example, we'll use the SAMPLE table I defined in the earlier discussion about the use of the default keyword in insert commands. Observe the following code block:

```
SQL> insert into sample (col1, col2) values (3,'NO I DID NOT');
1 row created.
SQL> select * from sample;
     COL1 COL2
--------- ----------------------------
        1 YOU FORGOT ME
        2 YOU FORGOT ME
        3 NO I DID NOT
SQL> update sample set col2 = default where col1 = 3;
1 row updated.
SQL> select * from sample;
     COL1 COL2
--------- ----------------------------
        1 YOU FORGOT ME
        2 YOU FORGOT ME
        3 YOU FORGOT ME
```

For Review

Know how to use update statements to change data in an Oracle table. Understand the two mandatory clauses, update and set, and the optional clause, where. Also, understand the use of the default keyword in update statements to populate columns with their default values explicitly.

Exercises

1. You are updating data in an Oracle table. Which of the following statements best describes how you may use the `where` clause in an `update` statement?

   A. You may use whatever expressions are appropriate, except for single-row functions.

   B. You may use whatever expressions are appropriate, except for subqueries.

   C. You may use whatever expressions are appropriate, except for `in` expressions.

   D. You may use whatever expressions are appropriate with no limitations.

2. You are updating data in an Oracle table. Which of the following choices identifies the keyword that indicates the columns you would like to update the values of?

   A. `update`

   B. `set`

   C. `where`

   D. `order by`

Answer Key
1. D. 2. B.

Deleting Data from the Oracle Database

The removal of data from a database is as much a fact of life as putting the data there in the first place. The `delete` statement in SQL*Plus is used to remove database rows from tables. The syntax for the `delete` statement is detailed in the following code block. Note that in this example, you cannot delete data from selected columns in a row in the table; this act is accomplished with the `update` statement, with the columns that are to be deleted being set to NULL by the `update` statement:

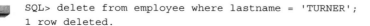

```
SQL> delete from employee where lastname = 'TURNER';
1 row deleted.
```

As in the case with database updates, `delete` statements use the `where` clause to help determine which rows are meant to be removed. Like an `update` or `select` statement, the `where` clause in a `delete` statement can contain any type of comparison operation, range operation, subquery, or any other operation acceptable for a `where` clause. Like an `update` statement, if the `where` clause is left off the `delete` statement, the deletion will be applied to all rows in the table.

TIP

Data deletion should be undertaken with care. It can be costly to replace data that has been inappropriately deleted from the database, which is why the privilege of deleting information should only be given out to those users who really should be able to delete records from a table.

Don't Forget the `where` Clause!

I cannot overemphasize the importance of using a `where` clause in your `delete` commands. If you don't use a `where` clause, you'll delete every row from your table. Only specific rows from the table that conform to the criteria noted in your `where` clause are removed when you include a `where` clause in your `delete` command. Let's take a look at an example of a `delete` command where we use the `where` clause to limit removal of data to a few particular records:

```
SQL> delete from emp where deptno = 20;
5 rows deleted.
SQL> select empno, ename, job from emp;
    EMPNO ENAME      JOB
--------- ---------- ---------
     7499 ALLEN      SALESMAN
     7521 WARD       SALESMAN
     7654 MARTIN     SALESMAN
     7698 BLAKE      MANAGER
     7782 CLARK      MANAGER
     7839 KING       PRESIDENT
     7844 TURNER     SALESMAN
     7900 JAMES      CLERK
     7934 MILLER     CLERK
9 rows selected.
```

Now, take a look at what would have happened if we omitted the `where` clause from the `delete` command in the previous example:

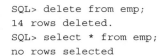

```
SQL> delete from emp;
14 rows deleted.
SQL> select * from emp;
no rows selected
```

Can I Delete Data from More Than One Table at a Time?

In general, removing data from a database with the `delete` command can be dangerous because once eliminated, it is tough to get the data back again without requiring some database downtime. Oracle does not let you remove data from more than one table at a time with the `delete` command for both this reason and for the rationale already presented for limiting the application of an `insert` or `update` command to only one table at a time.

Deleting Data and Integrity Constraints

You can remove data from a table without regard for integrity constraints on that table, except for one small detail. You must be careful when deleting records from a parent table with foreign key constraints on it. If your removal of a record from the parent table would produce orphan records in the child table, then Oracle returns an error and prevents you from making the deletion. You should first remove the records in the child table, and then remove the records from the parent table.

For Review

Be sure you understand how to use `delete` statements to remove data from an Oracle table. Also, understand how to use the mandatory clause, `delete from`, and the optional clause `where`.

Exercises

1. This is the clause in a `delete` statement that identifies which rows to remove: _____

2. You would like to delete data in the PROFITS column of the SALES table for all rows where PRODUCT_TYPE is set to 'TOYS'. Which of the following choices identifies how to accomplish this task?

   A. `delete from sales where product_type = 'TOYS';`

   B. `delete profits from sales where product_type = 'TOYS';`

C. update sales set profits = NULL where product_type = 'TOYS';

D. delete from sales;

Answer Key
1. where 2. C.

Merging Data in Oracle Tables

Oracle **9i** and higher   Consider the following scenario. Say you manage a movie theater that is part of a national chain. Everyday, the corporate headquarters sends out a data feed that you put into your digital billboard over the ticket sales office, listing out all the movies being played at that theater, along with showtimes. The showtime information changes daily for existing movies in the feed. Let's create the example using the following code block:

```
SQL> create table movies
  2  (movie_name varchar2(30),
  3   showtime varchar2(30),
  4   constraint pk_movies primary key (movie_name));
Table created.
SQL> insert into movies ('GONE WITH THE WIND','6:00 PM');
1 row created.
SQL> select * from movies;
MOVIE_NAME          SHOWTIME
------------------- ------------------------
GONE WITH THE WIND  6:00 PM
```

Every week, new movies are added to the lineup and existing movies have their showtimes changed. Past versions of Oracle SQL were not able to handle this situation. For example, if we tried first to `insert` a new record for movies being added and then tried to `update` existing records with new movie times in our MOVIES table, Oracle would give us an error on either the `insert` (for existing movies) or the `update` (for new movies). Take a look at the following example, where we try to add a new record for the movie *Gone With The Wind*, even though that record already exists in our table:

```
SQL> insert into movies ('GONE WITH THE WIND','7:30 PM');
insert into movies ('GONE WITH THE WIND','7:30 PM');
*
```

```
ERROR at line 1:
ORA-00001: unique constraint (SCOTT.PK_EMP) violated
```

If we wanted to avoid errors, we would have to program a PL/SQL routine. This routine would need to use an `if-then` statement to test for the presence of a row when the showtime for an existing movie needed to be changed, or else add a new row if that movie isn't currently being shown.

The `merge` Command: Concept

In Oracle9i, however, we can use the `merge` command to handle the work for us. The merge command syntax is `merge into table1 using table2 on (join_condition) when matched update set col1 = value when not matched insert (column_list) values (column_values)`. The statement components work in the following way:

1. In the `merge into table1` clause, you identify a table into which you would like to update data in an existing row or add new data if the row doesn't already exist as `table1`.

2. In the using `table2` clause, you identify a second table from which rows will be drawn in order to determine if the data already exists as `table2`. This can be a different table or the same table as `table1`. However, if `table2` is the same table as `table1`, or if the two tables have similar columns, then you must use table aliases to preface all column references with the correct copy of the table. Otherwise, Oracle will return an error stating that your column references are ambiguously defined.

3. In the on (`join_condition`) clause, you define the join condition to link the two tables together. This join condition follows the same requirements as table joins in Chapter 3, meaning that you should include both an equality comparison to avoid any Cartesian products and any filter conditions required to eliminate unneeded data. If `table2` in the using clause is the same table as `table1` in the `merge into` clause, or if the two tables have similar columns, then you must use table aliases or the `table.column` syntax when referencing columns in the join or filter conditions. Otherwise, Oracle will return an error stating that your column references are ambiguously defined.

4. In the `when matched then update set col1 = value` clause, you define the column(s) Oracle should `update` in the first table if a match in the second table is found. If `table2` in the using clause is the same table as `table1` in the `merge into` clause, or if the two tables have similar columns, then you must use table aliases or the `table.column` syntax

when referencing columns in the update operation. Otherwise, Oracle will return an error stating that your column references are ambiguously defined.

5. In the when not matched then insert (*column_list*) values (*value_list*) clause, you define what Oracle should insert into the first table if a match in the second table is not found. If *table2* in the using clause is the same table as *table1* in the merge into clause, or if the two tables have similar columns, then you must use table aliases or the table.column syntax to preface all column references in *column_list*. Otherwise, Oracle will return an error stating that your column references are ambiguously defined.

TIP
Implicit in the use of the merge command is the concept that you are merging the contents of one table into another based on whether values exist in the second table, extending the table join principles you learned about in Chapter 3. For this discussion, we'll work with only one table using the self-join concept you learned in that chapter as well.

The merge Command: Implementation

At first glance, this command can seem to be a tricky solution to a seemingly easy problem. Let's take a look at an example of how we would implement the addition of data to an existing row in our MOVIES table using the merge statement shown in the following code block:

```
SQL> merge into movies M1
  2   using movies M2 on (M2.movie_name = M1.movie_name
  3                       and M1.movie_name = 'GONE WITH THE WIND')
  4   when matched then update set M1.showtime = '7:30 PM'
  5   when not matched then insert (M1.movie_name, M1.showtime)
  6   values ('GONE WITH THE WIND','7:30 PM');
1 row merged.
SQL> select * from movies;
MOVIE_NAME           SHOWTIME
-------------------  -------------------------
GONE WITH THE WIND   7:30 PM
```

Let's examine the code block in more detail. The first line instructs Oracle to merge rows in the MOVIES table. The second line tells Oracle how to match the data using a copy of the MOVIES table. Essentially, we're telling Oracle to use the contents of a second copy of the MOVIES table in order to determine whether a record for *Gone With The Wind* already exists in the table. If so, I want Oracle to change the showtime to 7:30 P.M. If not, I want Oracle to add a new record for that movie with the correct showtime. Notice also that I've used table aliases everywhere to eliminate ambiguity. Now, let's look at what happens when we want to merge data into our MOVIES table for a movie not currently present in that table:

```
SQL> merge into movies M1
  2  using movies M2 on (M2.movie_name = M1.movie_name
  3                      and M2.movie_name = 'LAWRENCE OF ARABIA')
  4  when matched then update set M1.showtime = '9:00 PM'
  5  when not matched then insert (M1.movie_name, M1.showtime)
  6  values ('LAWRENCE OF ARABIA','9:00 PM');
1 row merged.
SQL> select * from movies;
MOVIE_NAME           SHOWTIME
-------------------- ------------------------
GONE WITH THE WIND   7:30 PM
LAWRENCE OF ARABIA   9:00 PM
```

Everything is the same in this code block as it was in the previous, except that I want Oracle to check for a record for the movie *Lawrence of Arabia* instead. Because no record exists for that movie, Oracle used the `insert` operation I specified in my `when not matched` clause to add a new record to the MOVIES table.

TIP
It would be nice if the `merge` command enabled the `using` clause to be optional so that we could simplify our command for situations where we want to operate only on one table. Perhaps Oracle will include this feature in a future edition of the database. Until then, be sure you are familiar with the multitabular nature of this command.

Watch Out for Errors in Your Join and Filter Conditions!

As with table joins, the merge command is fraught with peril especially if you don't formulate your join and filter conditions properly in the on clause. Let's consider what happens if I do not specify my join condition to include a filter condition to identify which movie Oracle should look for. Take a look at the following code block:

```
SQL> merge into movies M1
  2   using movies M2 on (M2.movie_name = M1.movie_name )
  3   when matched then update set M1.showtime = '9:30 PM'
  4   when not matched then insert (M1.movie_name, M1.showtime)
  5   values ('THE MUMMY','9:30 PM');
2 row merged.
SQL> select * from movies;
MOVIE_NAME             SHOWTIME
------------------- -------------------------

GONE WITH THE WIND  9:30 PM
LAWRENCE OF ARABIA  9:30 PM
```

In this situation, I correctly defined my join condition to avoid a Cartesian product in my self-join. However, I forgot to include a filter condition telling Oracle to verify whether a record for the movie *The Mummy* exists in my MOVIES table. Thus, Oracle simply went ahead and changed every row in the table according to the value set in my when matched clause. Now, watch what happens if I forget about the join condition and include only a filter condition instead:

```
SQL> merge into movies m1
  2   using movies m2 on (m2.movie_name = 'THE MUMMY')
  3   when matched then update set m1.showtime = '12:00 AM'
  4   when not matched then insert (m1.movie_name, m1.showtime)
  5   values ('THE MUMMY','12:00 AM');
merge into movies m1
*
ERROR at line 1:
ORA-00001: unique constraint (SCOTT.PK_MOVIES) violated
```

At first glance, it might seem strange that Oracle returns a constraint violation. After all, the row we're trying to add for the movie *The Mummy* does not violate the primary key constraint on the MOVIE_NAME column. Actually, the reason you receive this error relates back to the fact that we forgot our join condition between the two copies of the MOVIES table. Behind the scenes, Oracle formed a Cartesian product, which generated duplicate rows for the movie *The Mummy*. The error was produced when Oracle tried to insert a duplicate row for *The Mummy* into the MOVIES table. Take another look at what happens when we disable the primary key on the MOVIES table:

```
SQL> alter table movies disable constraint pk_movies;
Table altered.
SQL> merge into movies m1
  2   using movies m2 on (m2.movie_name = 'THE MUMMY')
  3   when matched then update set m1.showtime = '12:00 AM'
  4   when not matched then insert (m1.movie_name, m1.showtime)
```

```
  5  values ('THE MUMMY','12:00 AM');
2 rows merged.
SQL> select * from movies;
MOVIE_NAME          SHOWTIME
------------------- ------------------------
GONE WITH THE WIND  9:30 PM
LAWRENCE OF ARABIA  9:30 PM
THE MUMMY           12:00 AM
THE MUMMY           12:00 AM
```

For Review

1. Know the business problem the `merge` command is intended to solve.

2. Understand the complex syntax for the `merge` command, including the clauses for joining the tables and determining what to do if a match does or does not occur between the records.

3. Be sure you can employ a `merge` command properly. Know how to correct the errors caused by incorrect join and/or filter conditions on the joining tables.

Exercises

1. **Review the following code block:**

```
SQL> merge into emp e1
  2  using emp e2 on (e2.ename = 'SMITHERS')
  3  when matched then update set e1.sal = e1.sal *1.1
  4  when not matched then insert (e1.empno, e1.ename, e1.sal)
  5  values (7999,'SMITHERS',800);
```

   Which of the following choices identify a line in the preceding merge command that will cause Oracle to return an error?

   A. `merge into emp e1`

   B. `using emp e2 on (e2.ename = 'SMITHERS')`

   C. `when matched then update set e1.sal = e1.sal * 1.1`

   D. `when not matched then insert (e1.empno, e1.ename, e1.sal)`

   E. `values (7999,'SMITHERS',800);`

2. **You want to use the `merge` command in Oracle. Which of the following statements are *not* true concerning merge commands?**

A. A `merge` command can operate effectively on as few as one table.

B. A `merge` command must include reference to at least two distinct tables.

C. A `merge` command must contain properly defined join conditions or else a Cartesian product is formed.

D. A `merge` command must contain filter conditions in order to determine if the row is or is not present in the table.

Answer Key
1. B. **2.** B. Remember, you can use two copies of the same table and then conduct a self-join.

The Importance of Transaction Control

We've made a great deal of changes to our Oracle database over the last several chapters. Some might say we've even made quite a mess of our data. *However, not a single one of those changes was actually saved to the database, and none are visible to any other user on your database besides you.* How can that be, you ask? It's because of the magic of Oracle transaction control! One of the great benefits Oracle provides you is the ability to make changes and then decide later whether we want to save or discard them. Oracle enables you to execute a series of data-change statements together as one logical unit of work, called a *transaction*, that's terminated when you decide to save or discard the work. A transaction begins with your first executable SQL statement. Some advantages for offering transaction processing in Oracle include the following:

■ Transactions enable you to ensure read-consistency to the point in time a transaction began for all users in the Oracle database.

■ Transactions enable you to preview changes before making them permanent in Oracle.

■ Transactions enable you to group logically related SQL statements into one logical unit of work.

Underlying Transaction Controls
Transaction processing consists of a set of controls that enable a user issuing an `insert`, `update`, or `delete` statement to declare a beginning to the series of data-change statements he or she will issue. When the user has finished making the

changes to the database, the user can save the data to the database by explicitly ending the transaction. Alternatively, if a mistake is made at any point during the transaction, the user can have the database discard the changes made to the database in favor of the way the data existed before the transaction.

Transactions are created with the use of two different elements in the Oracle database. The first element is the set of commands that define the beginning, breakpoint, and end of a transaction. The second element is the special locking mechanisms designed to prevent more than one user at a time from making a change to row information in a database. Locks will be discussed after the transaction control commands are defined. The commands that define transactions are as follows:

- **set transaction**   Initiates the beginning of a transaction and sets key features. This command is optional. A transaction will be started automatically when you start SQL*Plus, commit the previous transaction, or roll back the previous transaction.

- **commit**   Ends the current transaction by saving database changes and starts a new transaction.

- **rollback**   Ends the current transaction by discarding database changes and starts a new transaction.

- **savepoint**   Defines breakpoints for the transaction to enable partial rollbacks.

set transaction

This command can be used to define the beginning of a transaction. If any change is made to the database after the `set transaction` command is issued but before the transaction is ended, all changes made will be considered part of that transaction. The `set transaction` statement is not required, because a transaction begins under the following circumstances:

- As soon as you log onto Oracle via SQL*Plus and execute the first command

- Immediately after issuing a `rollback` or `commit` statement to end a transaction

- When the user exits SQL*Plus

- When the system crashes

- When a data control language command such as `alter database` is issued

By default, a transaction will provide both read and write access unless you override this default by issuing set transaction read only. You can set the transaction isolation level with set transaction as well. The set transaction isolation level serializable command specifies serializable transaction isolation mode as defined in SQL92. If a serializable transaction contains data manipulation language (DML) that attempts to update any resource that may have been updated in a transaction uncommitted at the start of the serializable transaction, the DML statement fails. The set transaction isolation level read committed command is the default Oracle transaction behavior. If the transaction contains DML that requires row locks held by another transaction, the DML statement waits until the row locks are released. The following is an example:

```
SQL> SET TRANSACTION READ ONLY;
Transaction set.
SQL> rollback;
Rollback complete.
SQL> SET TRANSACTION READ WRITE;
Transaction set.
SQL> rollback;
Rollback complete.
SQL> SET TRANSACTION ISOLATION LEVEL SERIALIZABLE;
Transaction set.
SQL> rollback;
Rollback complete.
SQL> SET TRANSACTION ISOLATION LEVEL READ COMMITTED;
Transaction set.
SQL> rollback;
Rollback complete.
```

TIP

A set transaction command can appear only as the first statement in the beginning of a transaction. Therefore, we must explicitly end each transaction with the rollback command before starting another with the set transaction command.

commit

The commit statement in transaction processing represents the point in time where the user has made all the changes he or she wants to have logically grouped together, and because no mistakes have been made, the user is ready to save the work. The `work` keyword is an extraneous word in the `commit` syntax that is designed for readability. Issuing a `commit` statement also implicitly begins a new transaction on the database because it closes the current transaction and starts a new one. By issuing a `commit`, data changes are made permanent in the database. The previous state of the data is lost. All users can view the data, and all savepoints are erased. It is important also to understand that an implicit `commit` occurs on the database when a user exits SQL*Plus or issues a data-definition language (DDL) command such as a `create table` statement, used to create a database object, or an `alter table` statement, used to alter a database object. The following is an example:

```
SQL> COMMIT;
Commit complete.
SQL> COMMIT WORK;
Commit complete.
```

rollback

If you have at any point issued a data-change statement you don't want, you can discard the changes made to the database with the use of the `rollback` statement. The previous state of the data is restored. Locks on the affected rows are released. After the `rollback` command is issued, a new transaction is started implicitly by the database session. In addition to rollbacks executed when the `rollback` statement is issued, implicit `rollback` statements are conducted when a statement fails for any reason or if the user cancels a statement with the CTRL-C cancel command. The following is an example:

```
SQL> ROLLBACK;
Rollback complete.
SQL> ROLLBACK WORK;
Rollback complete.
```

Once you issue a commit in Oracle, you cannot rollback the change. You can see this in the following example:

```
SQL> update emp set sal = 20000 where ename = 'KING';
1 row updated.
SQL> select sal from emp where ename = 'KING';
     SAL
--------
   20000
SQL> commit;
Commit complete.
SQL> rollback;
```

```
Rollback complete.
SQL> select sal from emp where ename = 'KING';
     SAL
--------
   20000
```

savepoint

In some cases involving long transactions or transactions that involve many data changes, you may not want to scrap all your changes simply because the last statement issued contains unwanted changes. Savepoints are special operations that enable you to divide the work of a transaction into different segments. You can execute rollbacks to the savepoint only, leaving prior changes intact. Savepoints are great for situations where part of the transaction needs to be recovered in an uncommitted transaction. At the point the `rollback to savepoint` `so_far_so_good` statement completes in the following code block, only changes made before the savepoint was defined are kept when the `commit` statement is issued:

```
SQL> UPDATE products
  2   SET quantity = 55
  3   WHERE product# = 59495;
1 row updated.
SQL> SAVEPOINT so_far_so_good;
Savepoint created.
SQL> UPDATE spanky.products
  2   SET quantity = 504;
1 row updated.
SQL> ROLLBACK TO SAVEPOINT so_far_so_good;
Rollback complete.
SQL> COMMIT;
Commit complete.
SQL> select quantity from spanky.products
  2   where product# = 59495;
QUANTITY
--------
      55
```

A Word about Read-Consistency

Read-consistency is a feature of crucial importance in Oracle, especially because the database permits multiple users to access the database at the same time. Consider the importance of read-consistency by point of example. Let's say two users are on the Oracle database. User A is reading the contents of the EMP table to making changes elsewhere in the database, while User B is changing the records A is reading within the EMP table. If User A had access to User B's changes before

User B was ready to make them permanent in the database by issuing the commit command, User A could wind up making changes elsewhere in the database based on faulty information. Thus, all users must have a read-consistent view of data for the duration of their Oracle transaction. Oracle provides this functionality, and it is crucial for preventing conflicting data changes in the Oracle database.

Locks

The final aspect of the Oracle database that enables the user to employ transaction processing is the lock, the mechanism by which Oracle prevents data from being changed by more than one user at a time. Several different types of locks are available, each with its own level of scope. Locks available on a database are categorized into table-level locks and row-level locks.

A table-level lock enables only the user holding the lock to change any piece of row data in the table, during which time no other users can make changes anywhere on the table. A table lock can be held in any of several modes: row share (RS), row exclusive (RX), share (S), share row exclusive (SRX), and exclusive (X). The restrictiveness of a table lock's mode determines the modes in which other table locks on the same table can be obtained and held.

A row-level lock gives the user the exclusive ability to change data in one or more rows of the table. However, any row in the table that is not held by the row-level lock can be changed by another user.

TIP
An update statement acquires a special row-level lock called a row-exclusive lock, which means that for the period of time the update statement is executing, no other user in the database can view or change the data in the row. The same goes for delete or insert operations. Another update statement—the select for update statement— acquires a more lenient lock called the share row lock. This lock means that for the period of time the update statement is changing the data in the rows of the table, no other user may change that row, but users may look at the data in the row as it changes.

For Review

1. Be sure you can identify what a transaction is. Know when a transaction begins and when it ends. Be able to use the set transaction, savepoint, commit, and rollback keywords with respect to transaction processing.

2. Know how locks support transactions by preventing other users from seeing the data in your table.

Exercises

1. You are done with your transaction and would like to issue another. Which of the following statements can only appear at the very beginning of the transaction and sets up many characteristics about the transaction?

   A. `set transaction`

   B. `rollback`

   C. `savepoint`

   D. `commit`

2. You are engaged in transaction processing on your Oracle database. Which command can you use to define logical breakpoints within the transaction?

   A. `set transaction`

   B. `rollback`

   C. `savepoint`

   D. `commit`

3. This is the database component that prevents other users from changing data that you are in the process of changing: _____

Answer Key

1. A. 2. C. 3. Lock.

Chapter Summary

In this chapter, we covered how to manipulate data with `insert`, `update`, and `delete` statements as well as how to engage in Oracle transaction processing. This information comprises just one topic objective for the OCP exam on SQL. However, just because we covered only one topic in this chapter does not mean we didn't review important material. A full 10 percent of the OCP exam deals exclusively with the topic of adding, changing, and removing user data via the `update`, `insert`, and `delete` commands, as well as the use of transaction control.

Two-Minute Drill

- New rows are put into a table with the `insert` statement. The user issuing the `insert` statement can insert one row at a time with one statement or can perform a mass `insert` operation with `insert into table_name (select . . .)`.

- Existing rows in a database table can be modified using the `update` statement. The `update` statement contains a `where` clause similar in function to the `where` clause of `select` statements.

- Existing rows in a table can be deleted using the `delete` statement. The `delete` statement also contains a `where` clause similar in function to the `where` clause in `update` and `select` statements.

- Transaction processing controls the change of data in an Oracle database.

- Transaction controls include commands that identify the beginning, breakpoint, and end of a transaction as well as the locking mechanisms that prevent more than one user at a time from making changes in the database.

Fill-in-the-Blank Questions

1. This transaction-processing command identifies a logical break within the transaction, not an end to the current transaction:

   _____

2. This five-word command specifies that the transaction should execute every DML statement serially and in isolation, as defined in SQL92:

   _____

Chapter Questions

1. **User JANKO would like to insert a row into the EMPLOYEE table. The table has three columns: EMPID, LASTNAME, and SALARY. This user would like to enter data for EMPID 59694, LASTNAME Harris, but no salary. Which statement would work best?**

   A. `insert into EMPLOYEE values (59694,'HARRIS', NULL);`

   B. `insert into EMPLOYEE values (59694,'HARRIS');`

   C. `insert into EMPLOYEE (EMPID, LASTNAME, SALARY) values (59694,'HARRIS');`

   D. `insert into EMPLOYEE (select 59694 from 'HARRIS');`

2. **Omitting the `where` clause from a `delete` statement has which of the following effects?**

   A. The `delete` statement will fail because there are no records to delete.

   B. The `delete` statement will prompt the user to enter criteria for the deletion.

   C. The `delete` statement will fail because of a syntax error.

   D. The `delete` statement will remove all records from the table.

3. **The transaction control that prevents more than one user from updating data in a table is which of the following?**

   A. `lock`

   B. `commit`

   C. `rollback`

   D. `savepoint`

4. **Two tables exist, EXPENSES and EXPENSE_ITEMS, for handling employee expense disbursements. Rows for expense #2701 for employee SMITHERS, which had 5 expense items, were added to the EXPENSES and EXPENSE_ITEMS tables a week ago. SMITHERS received reimbursement for #2701 yesterday. The expense disbursements manager now wants to get rid of the data. An excerpt from his SQL*Plus session appears in the following block:**

```
SQL> delete from expenses where expense_id = 2701;
```

What happens next?

A. Oracle returns an error and does not remove the record.

B. Oracle returns an error but removes the record from the EXPENSES table anyway.

C. Oracle returns a warning but removes the record anyway.

D. Oracle removes the record from EXPENSES without warning or error.

5. **You are adding new records to the PROFITS table. The excerpt from your SQL*Plus session can be found in the following code block:**

```
SQL> describe profits
 Name                    Null?    Type
 ------------------- -------- --------------
 PRODUCT_NAME            NOT NULL VARCHAR2(10)
 PRODUCT_ID                       NUMBER(10)
 QTR_END_DATE                     DATE
 SALESPERSON                      VARCHAR2(10)
 PROFIT                           NUMBER
SQL> insert into profits
  2  values ('TURNER',12345,'1-MAR-01','BARNEY TOY',54938);
```

What happens next?

A. Oracle returns a datatype mismatch error and does not add the record.

B. Oracle returns an invalid number error and does not add the record.

C. Oracle returns a warning but adds the record anyway.

D. Oracle adds the record to the table without warnings or errors.

Fill-in-the-Blank Answers

1. `savepoint`

2. `set transaction isolation level serializable`

Answers to Chapter Questions

1. A. `insert into EMPLOYEE values (59694,'HARRIS', NULL);`

Explanation This choice is acceptable because the positional criteria for not specifying column order is met by the data in the `values` clause. When you would like to specify that no data be inserted into a particular column, one method of doing so is to insert a NULL. Choice B is incorrect because not all columns in the table have values identified. When you're using positional references to populate column data, values must be present for every column in the table. Otherwise, the columns that will be populated should be named explicitly. Choice C is incorrect because when a column is named for data insert in the `insert into` clause, a value must definitely be specified in the `values` clause. Choice D is incorrect because using the multiple-row `insert` option with a `select` statement is not appropriate in this situation. Refer to the discussion of `insert` statements for more information.

2. D. The `delete` statement will remove all records from the table.

Explanation One effect is produced by leaving off the `where` clause from any statement that enables one—the requested operation is performed on all records in the table.

3. A. Lock

Explanation A *lock* is the mechanism that prevents more than one user at a time from making changes to a database. All other options refer to the commands that are issued to mark the beginning, middle, and end of a transaction. Review the discussion of transaction controls.

4. A. Oracle returns an error and does not remove the record.

Explanation When you try to remove a record from a table that has a foreign key constraint with child records, Oracle will not let you do so if removal would produce orphan records. Thus, choices B and C are incorrect. Choice D is incorrect because Oracle will return an error indicating that a child record exists.

5. D. Oracle adds the record to the table without warnings or errors.

Explanation Even though the data being added will cause the record to have some problems with context, Oracle will not return an error or prevent the record from being added to the table. Thus, choices A, B, and C are incorrect, because the dataypes technically have no errors or the like in this record being added.

CHAPTER
7

Creating Other
Database Objects
in Oracle

In this chapter, you will learn about and demonstrate knowledge in the following areas:

- Creating views
- Other database objects

At this point, you should already know how to select data from tables, design database tables, create relationships between those tables, restrict data from entering the tables, and populate tables with data. These functions represent important cornerstones of functionality that Oracle can provide. However, the design of a database does not stop there. The Oracle architecture has features that can make certain data available to some users but not to others, speed access to data, and generate sequential numbers for primary keys or other purposes. These are advanced database features of Oracle tested in the OCP Exam 1. The material in this chapter comprises 11 percent of the material covered on the exam.

Creating Views

This section covers the following topics concerning views:

- Creating simple views
- Creating views that enforce constraints
- Creating complex views
- Modifying and removing views

It has been said that the eyes are the windows to the soul. Although this may or may not be true, it is true that your eyes can be used to look at data in a table. In order to make sure the right eyes see the right data, however, some special "windows" on the data in a table can be created. These special windows are called *views*. Views are queries stored in Oracle that dynamically assemble data into a virtual table. You can treat this virtual table as though it were a real one, which is exactly what we did on the Oracle data dictionary views of the last chapter. To the person using the view, manipulating the data from the view is just like manipulating the data from a table. In some cases, it is even possible for the user to change data in a view as though the view *were* a table. Let's now explore the topic of creating, using, and managing views in more detail.

TIP
We are deviating somewhat from the Oracle DBA
OCP Candidate Guide with respect to titles for the

topic areas. Although the titles and organization of this content are different from the Candidate Guide, the content covers all the information you need to know for OCP. You covered the information you need to know for inline views and Top-N analysis techniques back in Chapter 4 in the discussion of subqueries in from *clauses.*

Creating Simple Views

Views act like tables by enabling you to query them like tables. However, views are logical representations of data, whereas tables physically store data. Views do not actually store any data. The data in a view comes from a table that the view queries to obtain its own contents. Views can be used to restrict access to data in tables. This is because views use queries to obtain and display selective information. That said, let's start by looking at the simplest example of a create view statement—the statement used for creating views in the Oracle database—and perform some simple table-like actions on the view we create. The create view statement is shown in bold in the following example:

```
SQL> create view emp_view as
  2  (select * from emp
  3   where job = 'ANALYST');
View created.
SQL> describe emp_view
 Name                          Null?     Type
 ----------------------------- --------- ------------
 EMPNO                         NOT NULL  NUMBER(4)
 ENAME                                   VARCHAR2(10)
 JOB                                     VARCHAR2(9)
 MGR                                     NUMBER(4)
 HIREDATE                                DATE
 SAL                                     NUMBER(7,2)
 COMM                                    NUMBER(7,2)
 DEPTNO                                  NUMBER(2)
SQL> select empno, ename from emp_view;
    EMPNO ENAME
 --------- ----------
     7788 SCOTT
     7902 FORD
```

TIP
A view will not be created if the base table you specify does not exist. However, you can overcome this restriction by using the force *keyword in the* create view *command. This keyword forces Oracle to create the view anyway. However, the view will be invalid because no underlying table data is available to draw from.*

Notice the two components of our basic create view statement. In the first part, we identify the name of the view we want Oracle to create. In the second part, we define in parentheses the query Oracle should use for obtaining data to populate our virtual table. The underlying table whose information is used as the basis for data in the view is sometimes called the *base table*. You can create views based on the contents of other views as well. Once the view is created, we can do anything with it that we might have done with the underlying table. Everything in our view, EMP_VIEW, looks just like the underlying EMP table, except for one small detail: EMP_VIEW only contains employee data for the analysts! Therefore, *a view can add extra security to data by enabling you to restrict data shown to users looking at the view instead of at the real table.* For example, let's say you have a table containing data across an entire corporation and you want to allow employees in particular departments to access data in the table pertaining only to their department. A view would be useful in this context because you could define the view to contain data only for a specific department, and then have the employees of that department query the view instead of the underlying table.

TIP
Once a view is created, you can list the columns of the view using the describe *command, just as you would for a table.*

Appropriately enough, the type of view we just created is known as a *simple view*. Oracle considers this a simple view because it uses data from only one table. Because views contain select statements, you should know some things about what sorts of select statements are accepted in simple views:

■ Most any select statement on a single table you can issue from SQL*Plus can be used for creating a simple view. Basic queries on single tables in Oracle containing single-row operations such as decode ( ), nvl ( ), and so on are permitted.

- Query operations containing `order` by clauses are also permitted, so long as the `order` by clause appears outside the parentheses. The following is an example of what I mean: `create view my_view as (select * from emp) order by empno`.

- Oracle also permits view queries to contain `group` by clauses, `connect` by clauses, and group functions such as `count ( )`, so long as each function has an alias.

- Oracle permits views containing the `distinct` keyword, using syntax similar to `create view my_view as (select distinct(job) as my_jobs from emp`.

- Although references to more than one table are permitted in the queries used in `create view` commands, the view created is not a simple view. It is a complex view (sometimes called a *join view*). We'll talk more about those views in the next discussion.

TIP
Information about views in your database are stored in the data dictionary in a view titled USER_VIEWS. Also, you cannot create a view containing a `for update` clause.

Hierarchical Queries: A Brief Digression

A word of warning: Read this section only if my point about views not accepting queries containing `connect` by clauses has piqued your interest about the type of query known in Oracle as a *hierarchical query*. This topic usually isn't tested on OCP. The hierarchical query can link together the table's rows into a hierarchy. Like most companies, the one whose employees are listed in EMP is a hierarchical one, where every employee reports to another employee all the way up to KING, the president of the company. It is possible to obtain a listing of all employees in that hierarchy using a hierarchical query such as this one:

```
SQL>  select empno, ename, job
  2  from emp
  3  connect by prior empno = mgr;
```

TIP
Like Shakespeare's Polonius, I believe "brevity is the soul of wit." Therefore, I won't show the output of this query because we are digressing from the heart

*of our topic—views and the OCP exam. However, if
you find that you like hierarchical queries and want
to play with them on your own time, the Oracle
documentation has some interesting things to say
about them. Good luck!*

And Now, Back to Simple Views

Related to the idea that views can help you secure your data against prying eyes,
let's explore the use of certain keywords to ensure data security as well. For
example, consider our trusty EMP table. It contains data about employee salaries—
something that most organizations typically don't like to publish widely. To batten
down the hatches on SAL and COMM data in the EMP table from SCOTT's prying
eyes (which are disgruntled by being underpaid), consider the following code block:

```
SQL> create or replace view emp_view as
  2  ( select empno, ename, job, mgr, hiredate,
  3            decode(ename, user, sal, 'KING', sal, 0) as sal,
  4            decode(ename, user, comm, 'KING', sal, 0) as comm,
  5            deptno from emp);
View created.
SQL> select ename, sal from emp_view
  2  where job = 'ANALYST';
ENAME          SAL
---------- ---------
SCOTT          3000
FORD              0
```

Notice a few things about the bold code in the preceding example. We used the
`decode( )` function to determine what to return for SAL and COMM information,
which we know is allowed. Also notice that we used the keyword `user`, which is a
function that identifies the name of the user logged into the system, in order to
figure out whose salary and commission information we'll show and to whom.
Next, notice that we also built in some functionality so that KING can see
everyone's salary (he is the president of the company, after all). After that, notice that
we had to create an alias for that column so Oracle would know what to call the
column in our virtual table. Besides being required to create the view, column
aliases, as you'll recall, simplify the otherwise confusing column name Oracle
would generate based on our use of the single-row function.

Finally, observe our use of the `create or replace view EMP_VIEW`
syntax in this example. Before, we simply said `create view EMP_VIEW`, but in
this case our view creation would have failed because EMP_VIEW already exists, if

we hadn't included the or replace keywords. These keywords are useful when you want to redefine an existing view based on new needs or criteria. Why not simply use the alter view command, you ask? Because the only job alter view can perform is recompiling an invalid view. We'll discuss alter view in more detail later in the section.

Changing Underlying Table Data Through Simple Views

Now, let's try doing something completely different. Say securing the salary data about other employees from the prying eyes of SCOTT wasn't enough to persuade him not to begrudge the company for his lousy pay. Now SCOTT is irritated enough to take matters into his own hands by changing his pay against company rules. Assuming SCOTT doesn't know about the underlying EMP table, let's see if he can change information in that table, anyway, via EMP_VIEW:

```
SQL> update emp_view set sal = 6000
  2  where ename = 'SCOTT';
update emp_view set sal = 6000
                    *
ERROR at line 1:
ORA-01733: virtual column not allowed here
```

Apparently, he can't. Remember, we didn't use simple column references for SAL and COMM in our view. Instead, we referred to them by way of the decode( ) function, which effectively created virtual columns in EMP_VIEW containing salary and commission information that can't be updated. You might think that this security measure is more of a technicality than a way to enhance security, and in truth, you're probably right. Nevertheless, we thwarted SCOTT's attempt to defraud the company. However, let's say that now SCOTT is fighting mad and is willing to do anything to get even with the company, even if it means calling the president a fool in front of everyone, as shown in the following code block:

```
SQL> update emp_view set ename = 'FOOL! '
  2  where job = 'PRESIDENT';
1 row updated.
SQL> select ename from emp
  2  where job = 'PRESIDENT';
ENAME
----------
FOOL!
```

Sure enough, SCOTT can call the president of the company a fool by modifying the EMP table via an update on EMP_VIEW, although no doubt SCOTT will pay the consequences when KING discovers SCOTT's destructive act.

Changing Data in Underlying Tables
Through Simple Views: Restrictions

Now let's extrapolate a general rule. *You can insert, update, or delete information on an underlying table via simple views,* subject to the following restrictions:

- In general, all constraint restrictions defined on the underlying table also apply to modifying data via the view. For example, you can't add data to an underlying table via a view that violates the table's primary key constraint.

- If the underlying table has not NULL constraints on columns not appearing in your view, you will likely have trouble when you try to insert data into a view. This problem can be solved by using default values for the not NULL column(s) in the table definition.

- Generally speaking, you can delete records from underlying tables using the view, even when the view doesn't contain all the columns or all the rows the underlying table contains.

- You cannot update data in a column of an underlying table via a simple view if the column was defined using a single-row function or function-based keywords such as `user` or `sysdate`. You *can* update a column of an underlying table if the simple view did *not* use a single-row function to define the column.

- You may not insert, update, or delete data on the table underlying the simple view if the `select` statement creating the view contains a `group by` clause, group function, or `distinct` clause.

- You cannot modify data in a view if the pseudocolumn ROWNUM keyword is used or if the columns are defined by expressions.

TIP
If you yearn for some adventure as you follow along in your own database, try creating simple views that don't violate these restrictions but otherwise do odd things. Then see if you can add, change, or remove rows from the underlying table. The following is an example. Try to insert a row into the EMP table via a view created as follows: `create view my_view as (select rowid as row_id, empno from emp)`. *If you find any restrictions in your adventures that I may have missed in the bulleted list, send an e-mail to jcouchman@mindspring.com and I'll acknowledge you by name in my next book.*

For Review

1. Understand what a view is and what it is not. A view is a `select` statement that generates the contents of a virtual table dynamically. Although views behave like tables, they do not actually contain table data.

2. Know the basic syntax for creating a view in Oracle. Understand the kinds of queries you can use to create a view. Basically, just about anything goes.

3. Be able to identify situations where it is possible to add data to a table via a view and when it is not possible to add data to a table via a view.

Exercises

1. **SCOTT creates a view on the EMP table using the following code block:**

```
SQL> create or replace view emp_view as
  2  ( select empno, ename, job, mgr, hiredate,
  3          decode(ename, user, sal, 'KING', sal, 0) as sal,
  4          decode(ename, user, comm, 'KING', sal, 0) as comm,
  5          deptno from emp);
View created.
```

   Which of the following DML statements will successfully make a change to data in the EMP table?

   A. `insert into emp_view values (2345, 'SMITHERS','MANAGER', 7839, 4500, 0, 10);`

   B. `update emp_view set job = 'CLERK', comm = 0 where ename = 'TURNER';`

   C. `delete from emp_view where ename = 'SMITH';`

   D. `update emp_view set comm = comm*1.3 where ename = 'TURNER';`

2. **Use the view shown in the preceding code block to answer this question. User SCOTT logs into Oracle and issues the following query:**

```
SQL> select ename, sal from emp_view
  2  where job = 'ANALYST';
ENAME          SAL
---------- ---------
SCOTT         3000
FORD             0
```

   Later, TURNER logs into Oracle and issues the same query. What will be the result listed for SCOTT in TURNER's output?

A. 0

B. 1500

C. 3000

D. 6000

3. **User SCOTT creates a view using the statement in the following code block:**

```
SQL> create or replace view my_view as
  2   (select user as orcl_user, rowid as row_id, empno
  3    from emp
  4    where ename = user)
  5    order by empno;
View created.
```

Then SCOTT issues the following DML statement: `insert into my_view values ('JASON','weraqwetrqwer',3421);`. Which of the following choices correctly identifies how Oracle will respond and why?

A. Oracle will return an error because you cannot perform DML on views created with an `order by` clause.

B. Oracle will return an error because no data can be added on a column defined using `user`.

C. Oracle will return an error because no data can be added on a column defined using the ROWID pseudocolumn.

D. Oracle will insert the new row into the underlying table because the statement contains no errors.

4. **Use the code defined for creating MY_VIEW in the previous question to answer this question. You issue the following statement in Oracle: `delete from my_view where orcl_user = 'SCOTT';`. How many rows are removed from the EMP table?**

A. 0

B. 1

C. 2

D. 14

Answer Key
1. C. 2. A. 3. B. 4. B.

Creating Views That Enforce Constraints

Tables that underlie views often have constraints that limit the data that can be
added to those tables. As I said earlier, views cannot add data to the underlying
table that would violate the table's constraints. However, you can also define a view
to restrict the user's ability to change underlying table data even further, effectively
placing a special constraint for data manipulation through the view. This additional
constraint says that `insert` or `update` statements issued against the view are
cannot create rows that the view cannot subsequently select. In other words, if after
the change is made, the view will not be able to select the row you changed, the
view will not let you make the change. This viewability constraint is configured
when the view is defined by adding the `with check option` to the `create`
`view` statement. Let's look at an example to clarify my point:

```
SQL> create or replace view emp_view as
  2  (select empno, ename, job, deptno
  3   from emp
  4   where deptno = 10)
  5  with check option constraint emp_view_constraint;
View created.
SQL> update emp_view set deptno = 20
  2  where ename = 'KING';
update emp_view set deptno = 20
         *
ERROR at line 1:
ORA-01402: view WITH CHECK OPTION where-clause violation
```

TIP
*On some systems, you may not get the ORA-01402
error in this context. Instead, Oracle may simply
state that zero rows were updated by your change.*

Notice, first, the code in bold in the preceding block where the viewability
constraint is defined. We've effectively said that no user can make a change to the
EMP table via this view that would prevent the view from selecting a row. After that,
we test this constraint by attempting to update the DEPTNO column for KING from

10 to 20, thus causing the view not to be able to pick up that row later. Oracle prevents this data change with an ORA-01402 error, as you can see. Finally, take a look again at the constraint clause in the line in bold. This optional clause lets us define a name for our view constraint. If we omitted the clause, Oracle would generate its own name for the constraint. By naming it ourselves, we can easily identify the constraint later in dictionary views containing data about constraints, such as USER_CONSTRAINTS. Output for USER_CONSTRAINTS listing our viewability constraint is shown in the following example:

```
SQL> select constraint_name, constraint_type
  2  from user_constraints;
CONSTRAINT_NAME                 C
------------------------------- -
SYS_C00905                      P
SYS_C00903                      C
PK_EMPLOYEE_01                  P
SYS_C00921                      C
CK_EMPLOYEE_01                  C
EMP_VIEW_CONSTRAINT             V
PK_01                           P
PK_PRICES_01                    P
```

TIP
The CONSTRAINT_TYPE column in USER_CONSTRAINTS and ALL_CONSTRAINTS will list the first character of the first word that best describes each type of constraint in Oracle: primary key, foreign key, check, not NULL, unique key, or viewability.

Creating Simple Views That Can't Change Underlying Table Data

In some cases, you may find that you want to create views that don't let your users change data in the underlying table. In this case, you can use the with read only clause. This clause will prevent any user of the view from making changes to the base table. Let's say that after reprimanding SCOTT severely for calling him a fool, KING wants to prevent all employees from ever changing data in EMP via the EMP_VIEW again. The following shows how he would do it:

```
SQL> create or replace view emp_view
  2  as (select * from emp)
  3  with read only;
```

The next time SCOTT tries to call KING a fool, the following happens:

```
SQL> update emp_view set ename = 'FOOL!'
  2  where ename = 'KING';
where ename = 'KING'
      *
ERROR at line 2:
ORA-01733: virtual column not allowed here
```

For Review

1. Be sure you can explain how viewability constraints placed on views work and how to use the `with check option` and `constraint` clause in `create view` statements in order to create this type of constraint.

2. Understand how to use the `with read only` clause in order to prevent users from making changes to underlying base tables via a view on those tables.

Exercises

1. **Use the code in the following block to answer this question:**

```
SQL> create or replace view emp_view as
  2  (select empno, ename, job, deptno
  3   from emp
  4   where job = 'MANAGER')
  5   with check option;
View created.
SQL> select * from emp_view;
    EMPNO ENAME      JOB        DEPTNO
--------- ---------- --------- ---------
     7566 JONES      MANAGER        20
     7698 BLAKE      MANAGER        30
     7782 CLARK      MANAGER        10
```

Which of the following data changes will *not* be accepted by Oracle on this view?

A. `update emp set job = 'ANALYST' where job = 'MANAGER' and empno = 7566;`

B. `update emp set ename = 'BARNEY' where job = 'MANAGER' and ename = 'JONES';`

C. `update emp set empno = 7999 where job = 'MANAGER' and deptno = 10;`

D. `update emp set deptno = 30 where job = 'MANAGER' and empno = 7782;`

2. **Use the contents of the following code block to answer this question:**

```
SQL> create or replace view emp_view as
  2  (select empno, ename, job, deptno
  3   from emp
  4   where job = 'MANAGER')
  5   with check option;
View created.
SQL> select constraint_name, constraint_type
  2  from user_constraints;
CONSTRAINT_NAME                 C
------------------------------- -
SYS_C00905                      P
SYS_C00903                      C
SYS_C00921                      C
SYS_C00929                      V
```

Which of the following constraints is the viewability constraint created in support of EMP_VIEW?

A. SYS_C00905

B. SYS_C00903

C. SYS_C00929

D. SYS_C00921

3. **Use the following code block to answer this question:**

```
SQL> create or replace view emp_view as
  2  (select empno, ename, job, deptno
  3   from emp
  4   where job = 'MANAGER')
  5   with read only;
View created.
```

Which of the following data-change statements will Oracle accept to make changes to the underlying table?

A. `insert into emp_view values (2134, 'SMITHERS','MANAGER',10);`

B. `update emp_view set ename = 'JOHNSON' where empno = 7844;`

C. `delete from emp_view where ename = 'KING';`

D. None of the above

Answer Key
1. A. 2. C. 3. D.

Creating Complex Views

I mentioned earlier that you can create views that join data from more than one table. These are called *complex views*. Complex views provide complicated data models where many base tables are drawn together into one virtual table. Let's take a look at your basic complex view where we join the contents of the EMP and DEPT tables together to form one virtual table:

```
SQL> create view emp_dept_view as
  2  (select empno, ename, job, dname, loc
  3   from emp e, dept d
  4   where e.deptno = d.deptno
  5   and job in ('ANALYST','CLERK','MANAGER'));
View created.
```

The contents of this view are listed as follows:

```
SQL> select * from emp_dept_view;
    EMPNO ENAME       JOB        DNAME           LOC
--------- ----------- ---------- --------------- -------------
     7782 CLARK       MANAGER    ACCOUNTING      NEW YORK
     7934 MILLER      CLERK      ACCOUNTING      NEW YORK
     7369 SMITH       CLERK      RESEARCH        DALLAS
     7566 JONES       MANAGER    RESEARCH        DALLAS
     7876 ADAMS       CLERK      RESEARCH        DALLAS
     7902 FORD        ANALYST    RESEARCH        DALLAS
     7788 SCOTT       ANALYST    RESEARCH        DALLAS
     7698 BLAKE       MANAGER    SALES           CHICAGO
     7900 JAMES       CLERK      SALES           CHICAGO
```

TIP

The same sort of `select` statements permitted for defining simple views are generally accepted on complex views as well. You may want to refer back to the list of `select` statements that are accepted in simple views for a refresher on complex views. You can even define complex views using the outer join (+) operator as well!

Updating Base Tables of a Complex View

For the most part, complex views will not enable you to change data in any of the base tables if you haven't properly defined foreign key and primary key relationships between the joined tables using appropriate Oracle integrity constraints. Let's take a look at what I mean by this statement. The dictionary view USER_UPDATABLE_ COLUMNS can tell you whether the columns in a complex view can be modified. Let's take a look:

```
SQL> create or replace view emp_dept_view as
  2  (select empno, ename, job, loc
  3  from emp e, dept d
  4  where e.deptno = d.deptno);
View created.
SQL> select column_name, updatable
  2  from user_updatable_columns
  3  where table_name = 'EMP_DEPT_VIEW';
COLUMN_NAME                     UPD
------------------------------- ---
EMPNO                           NO
ENAME                           NO
JOB                             NO
LOC                             NO
```

However, after I properly define my foreign key and primary key relationships between the EMP and DEPT tables, I can create a complex view that will enable partial modification of data in the base tables via the view. Let's look at an example of such a view, which is called an *updatable join view* or *modifiable join view*. A *join view* is simply another name for a complex view, which makes sense, considering that complex views contain join operations. Let's look at the code:

```
SQL> alter table emp add constraint pk_emp_01
  2  primary key (empno);
Table altered.
SQL> alter table dept add constraint pk_dept_01
  2  primary key (deptno);
Table altered.
SQL> alter table emp add constraint fk_emp_01
  2  foreign key (deptno) references dept (deptno);
Table altered.
SQL> create or replace view emp_dept_view as
  2  (select empno, ename, job, loc
  3  from emp e, dept d
  4  where e.deptno = d.deptno);
View created.
SQL> select column_name, updatable
```

```
    2  from user_updatable_columns
    3  where table_name = 'EMP_DEPT_VIEW';
COLUMN_NAME                          UPD
-----------------------------        ---
EMPNO                                YES
ENAME                                YES
JOB                                  YES
LOC                                  NO
```

TIP
Views containing outer joins generally won't contain key-preserved tables unless the outer join generates no NULL values. Even in such a case, the updatability is dependent on your data, so for all intents and purposes, you should just assume that outer join views are not updatable.

That's more like it. Now, when we issue an `update` statement on EMP_DEPT_VIEW that modifies the EMPNO, ENAME, or JOB column, Oracle will let us make the change. Yet, notice that we still cannot update one column. To understand why, we have to talk about the concept of a key-preserved table. A key-preserved table is a table in a complex view whose primary key column is present in the view *and whose values are all unique and not NULL in the view.* In a sense, the key-preserved table's primary key can also be thought of as the primary key for the data in the view. In some cases, many tables in the complex view may be key-preserved if the primary key for the view is the primary key in several of the joined tables. Only columns from the key-preserved table can be modified via the complex view. Columns from the non-key-preserved table (the LOC column in DEPT, in this case) cannot be modified via the complex view. In conclusion, you can execute data-change statements on a complex view only when all the following conditions are met:

- The statement must affect only one of the tables in the join.

- For `update` statements, all columns changed must be extracted from a key-preserved table. In addition, if the view is created using the `with check option` clause, join columns and columns taken from tables that are referenced more than once in the view cannot be part of the `update`.

- For `delete` statements, the join may only have one key-preserved table. This table may be present more than once in the join, unless the view has been created using the `with check option` clause.

■ For insert statements, all columns in which values are inserted must come from a key-preserved table, and the view must not have been created using the with check option clause.

■ The complex view does not contain group functions, group by expressions, set operations, the distinct keyword, start with or connect by clauses, or the ROWNUM pseudocolumn. Pseudocolumns are virtual columns in a table that you cannot add data to or change data on.

TIP
Set operations include the UNION, UNION ALL, INTERSECT, and MINUS keywords, which are used for joining the output of one select statement with the output of another. For example, select empno from emp UNION select sal from emp is a set operation. Set operations are typically not tested on the OCP exam and therefore will not be covered in this book in any great detail.

For Review

1. Be able to define the meaning of a complex or join view. Know how a complex view differs from a simple view. Be sure you can identify the types of select statements permitted in defining a complex view.

2. Know the factors that limit your ability to make changes to underlying base tables in a complex view. In particular, understand the importance of constraints in the underlying tables to solidify the relationship between the two tables, and the concept of key-preserved tables.

3. Be sure you can list the items a complex view cannot contain if you want the ability to modify the underlying tables.

Exercises

1. **Your database of sales information consists of four tables: PROFITS lists the profit amount for every product sold by the company, listed by product name, type, sales region, and quarter; PRODUCT_TYPES lists all valid product types that are sold by your company; PRICES lists the name of every product, along with the associated price; and UNIT_SALES lists**

every product sold by the company and units sold of the product by quarter. You create a view on this database using the following block:

```
SQL> create or replace view profits_view as
  2  (select a.product_name, a.product_type, b.product_desc,
  3  c.product_price,
  4  d.unit_sale, a.quarter
  5  from profits a, product_types b, prices c, unit_sales d
  6  where a.product_type = b.product_type
  7  and a.product_name = c.product_name
  8  and a.product_name = d.product_name
  9  and a.quarter = d.quarter);
View created.
```

Assuming all the proper integrity constraints are in place, which of the following tables in this view is not a key-preserved table?

A. PROFITS

B. PRODUCT_TYPES

C. PRICES

D. UNIT_SALES

2. You are developing complex views in Oracle. Which of the following choices identifies an item that may not be included in the query defining the view if you intend to allow users to update key-preserved tables joined in the view?

A. avg( )

B. decode( )

C. nvl( )

D. to_char( )

3. Key-preserved tables share this in common with the output of complex views they underlie: _____

Answer Key
1. B. 2. A. 3. Primary key.

Modifying and Removing Views

Notice that on several occasions, we have altered the definition of views that already existed in the database. However, we didn't follow the same precedent with views that we used for other objects, such as tables, when we wanted to modify them. That's because views don't follow the syntax conventions of other database objects. Although an `alter view` statement appears in the Oracle SQL language, it is used for recompiling or revalidating the view *as it exists already*. The following is an example:

```
SQL> alter view emp_dept_view compile;
View altered.
```

When we wanted to alter the underlying data used in the definition of a view, we used the `create or replace view` statement. When a `create or replace view` statement is issued, Oracle will disregard the error that arises when it encounters the view that already exists with that name, and it will overwrite the definition for the old view with the definition for the new one. The following code block illustrates the use of the `create or replace view` statement from the first exercise in the previous discussion:

```
SQL> create or replace view profits_view as
  2  (select a.product_name, a.product_type, b.product_desc,
  3  c.product_price,
  4  d.unit_sale, a.quarter
  5  from profits a, product_types b, prices c, unit_sales d
  6  where a.product_type = b.product_type
  7  and a.product_name = c.product_name
  8  and a.product_name = d.product_name
  9  and a.quarter = d.quarter);
View created.
```

TIP
You'll have to create your own versions of each of these four tables in order to follow along in your Oracle database, using what you know about. When doing so, make sure the datatypes for the shared PRODUCT_NAME, PRODUCT_TYPE, and QUARTER columns match in each of the tables those columns appear in. Also, make sure you define the appropriate primary and foreign key integrity constraints between the tables. No script is available for creating these tables automatically—I

*believe it's very important that you get hands-on
practice developing complex views for OCP!*

We see from the last line in the block that Oracle created the view with no
errors. If we wanted to verify the status of the view, we could look in the
USER_OBJECTS view, as shown in the following example:

```
SQL> column object_name format a20
SQL> select object_name, status
  2  from user_objects
  3  where object_name = 'PROFITS_VIEW';
OBJECT_NAME          STATUS
-------------------- -------
PROFITS_VIEW         VALID
```

TIP
The USER_VIEWS view does not *contain the validity
status of your view. Be sure you memorize that the
status of all your database objects is found in
USER_OBJECTS or ALL_OBJECTS for OCP.*

Let's now drop the PRICES table, which is a base table for PROFITS_VIEW, as
you'll recall from the question. Notice what happens to PROFITS_VIEW:

```
SQL> drop table prices;
Table dropped.
SQL> select object_name, status
  2  from user_objects
  3  where object_name = 'PROFITS_VIEW';
OBJECT_NAME          STATUS
-------------------- -------
PROFITS_VIEW         INVALID
```

So you see, Oracle doesn't remove views from the database if a base table is
destroyed. Instead, Oracle simply marks PROFITS_VIEW as invalid to indicate that
the object dependency that PROFITS_VIEW had on PRICES is now fractured. This is
what happens when you try to obtain data from PROFITS_VIEW:

```
SQL> select * from profits_view;
select * from profits_view
              *
ERROR at line 1:
ORA-04063: view "SCOTT.PROFITS_VIEW" has errors
```

The way to solve this problem is to re-create the PRICES table and recompile PROFITS_VIEW, as shown in the following block. When the view recompiles successfully, you will be able to select data from the view again:

```
SQL> create table prices
  2  (product_name varchar2(10) primary key,
  3   product_price number(10,4));
Table created.
SQL> alter view profits_view compile;
View altered.
```

TIP
Alternately, to fix a view that has become invalid due to the redefinition or deletion of a table that underlies it, you can modify the view with the `create or replace view` *statement.*

Removing Views

A time may come when you need to remove a view. The command for executing this function is the `drop view` statement. No cascading scenarios exist that the person dropping a view must be aware of, except in situations where the view being dropped acts as a base table for another view. In this case, the view that's left will be marked invalid. The `drop view` statement removes the view definition from the database. Dropping views has no effect on the tables on which the view was based. The following statement illustrates the use of `drop view` for deleting views from the database:

```
SQL> drop view profits_view;
View dropped.
```

For Review

1. Know how to use the `alter view` statement for recompiling views and the `create or replace view` statement for redefining the view query.

2. Know that object dependency is when a database object depends on another database object for information. Views have object dependencies on their base tables. Know what happens to the status of a view when its base table gets dropped as well as how to repair the problem.

Exercises

1. You have just replaced a base table for a view that was dropped inadvertently. Which two of the following statements can be used to update the status of the view in one step? (Choose two.)

   A. create view

   B. create or replace view

   C. alter view

   D. drop view

2. What is the term that describes the relationship between a view and its base table (two words)? _____

3. You would like to identify the status of views in your database. Which of the following dictionary views would you use?

   A. USER_VIEWS

   B. USER_TAB_COLUMNS

   C. USER_OBJECTS

   D. USER_TABLES

Answer Key
1. B and C. 2. Object dependency. 3. C.

Other Database Objects

This section covers the following topics related to other database objects in Oracle:

- Overview of other database objects
- Using sequences
- Using indexes
- Using public and private synonyms

So far, you've gotten some exposure to a few of the types of objects available for use in an Oracle database. This section will change that. In this section, you get an overview of many other important objects available in Oracle. You will also get some hands-on exposure to the creation and use of sequences in the Oracle database. After that, you will gain exposure to indexes, Oracle's performance-giving objects in the database. Finally, you will learn about the use of both public and private synonyms on an Oracle database.

Overview of Other Database Objects

Some of the objects that are part of the relational database produced by Oracle and that are used in the functions just mentioned are as follows:

- **Tables, views, and synonyms** Used to store and access data. Tables are the basic unit of storage in Oracle. Views logically represent subsets of data from one or more tables. Synonyms provide alternate names for database objects.

- **Indexes and the Oracle RDBMS** Used to speed access to data.

- **Sequences** Used for generating numbers for various purposes.

- **Triggers and integrity constraints** Used to maintain the validity of data entered.

- **Privileges, roles, and profiles** Used to manage database access and usage.

- **Packages, procedures, and functions** Application PL/SQL code used in the database.

TIP
This is only a partial listing of all the different types of objects available in Oracle. In reality, dozens of different types of objects are available that aren't covered in this book. But, you do not need to know how to create or use the database object types not listed here in order to pass OCP Exam 1. You should know what the objects listed previously are, however, because we either have discussed or will discuss these objects at some point during this book.

For Review

Be sure you can identify the different basic types of objects found in Oracle databases that are listed in this brief discussion. They are discussed in this book.

Other database objects exist in Oracle; however, they are not covered on the OCP exam.

Exercises

1. This is the database object comprised of PL/SQL code stored in the database that performs some programmatic task:

   _____

2. This is the database object designed to enforce validity rules on data added to the database that does not use PL/SQL code:

   _____

3. This is a database object that generates numbers in order:

   _____

Answer Key

1. Package. (*Procedure* or *function* is also acceptable.) **2.** Constraint. **3.** Sequence.

Using Sequences

A *sequence* is a database object that generates integers according to rules specified at the time the sequence is created. A sequence automatically generates unique numbers and is sharable between different users in Oracle. Sequences have many purposes in database systems—the most common of which is to generate primary keys automatically. However, nothing binds a sequence to a table's primary key, so in a sense it's also a sharable object. This task is common in situations where the primary key is not generally used for accessing data in a table. The common use of sequences to create primary keys has one main drawback. Because it is simply a sequential number, the primary key itself and the index it creates are somewhat meaningless. However, if you only need the key to guarantee uniqueness and don't care that you're creating a nonsense key, it is perfectly all right to do so. Sequences are created with the `create sequence` statement. The following explains each clause in the statement:

- **start with** *n* Enables the creator of the sequence to specify the first value generated by the sequence. Once created, the sequence will generate the value specified by `start with` the first time the sequence's NEXTVAL virtual column is referenced. If no `start with` value is specified, Oracle defaults to a start value of 1.

- **increment by** *n*   Defines the number by which to increment the sequence every time the NEXTVAL virtual column is referenced. The default for this clause is 1 if it is not explicitly specified. You can set *n* to be positive for incrementing sequences or negative for decrementing or countdown sequences.

- **minvalue** *n*   Defines the minimum value that can be produced by the sequence. If no minimum value is specified, Oracle will assume the default, `nominvalue`.

- **maxvalue** *n*   Defines the maximum value that can be produced by the sequence. If no maximum value is desired or specified, Oracle will assume the default, `nomaxvalue`.

- **cycle**   Enables the sequence to recycle values produced when `maxvalue` or `minvalue` is reached. If cycling is not desired or not explicitly specified, Oracle will assume the default, `nocycle`. You cannot specify `cycle` in conjunction with `nomaxvalue` or `nominvalue`. If you want your sequence to cycle, you must specify `maxvalue` for incrementing sequences or `minvalue` for decrementing or countdown sequences.

- **cache** *n*   Enables the sequence to cache a specified number of values to improve performance. If caching is not desired or not explicitly specified, Oracle will assume the default, which is to cache 20 values.

- **order**   Enables the sequence to assign values in the order in which requests are received by the sequence. If order is not desired or not explicitly specified, Oracle will assume the default, `noorder`.

Consider now an example for defining sequences. The integers that can be specified for sequences can be negative as well as positive. The following example uses a decrementing sequence. The `start with` integer in this example is positive, but the `increment by` integer is negative, which effectively tells the sequence to decrement instead of increment. When zero is reached, the sequence will start again from the top. This sequence can be useful in programs that require a countdown before an event will occur. The following shows an example:

```
SQL> CREATE SEQUENCE countdown_20
  2   START WITH 20
  3   INCREMENT BY -1
  4   MAXVALUE 20
  5   MINVALUE 0
  6   CYCLE
  7   ORDER
  8   CACHE 2;
Sequence created.
```

TIP
Some real-world uses for sequences include automatic generation of tracking numbers, invoice numbers, or other numerical information.

   Once the sequence is created, it is referenced using the CURRVAL and NEXTVAL pseudocolumns. The users of the database can view the current value of the sequence by using a `select` statement. Similarly, the next value in the sequence can be generated with a `select` statement. Because sequences are not tables—they are only objects that generate integers via the use of virtual columns—the DUAL table acts as the "virtual" table from which the virtual column data is pulled. As stated earlier, values cannot be placed into the sequence; instead, they can only be selected from the sequence.
   The following example demonstrates how COUNTDOWN_20 cycles when `minvalue` is reached:

```
SQL> select countdown_20.nextval from dual;
  NEXTVAL
---------
       20
SQL> /
  NEXTVAL
---------
       19

...

SQL> /
NEXTVAL
---------
        1
SQL> /
NEXTVAL
---------
        0
SQL> /
NEXTVAL
---------
       20
```

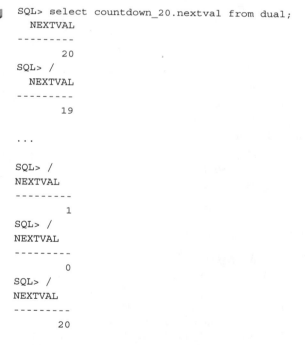

TIP
References to sequences cannot be used in subqueries of `select` statements (including those with `having`), views, `select` statements using set

operations (such as union and minus), or any select statement that requires a sort to be performed.

Once the NEXTVAL column is referenced, the value in CURRVAL is updated to match the value in NEXTVAL, and the prior value in CURRVAL is lost. The next code block illustrates this point:

```
SQL> select countdown_20.currval from dual;
   CURRVAL
---------
        20
SQL> select countdown_20.nextval from dual;
   NEXTVAL
---------
        19
SQL> select countdown_20.currval from dual;
   CURRVAL
---------
        19
```

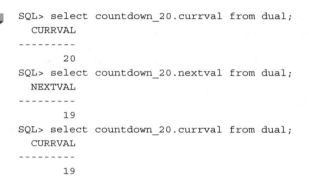

TIP
CURRVAL is set to the start with value until NEXTVAL is referenced for the first time after sequence creation. After that, CURRVAL is set to the value for NEXTVAL. Every time NEXTVAL is referenced, CURRVAL changes. Interestingly, the first time you reference NEXTVAL, it gets set to the start with value also, so effectively that the value for CURRVAL doesn't change!

Referencing Sequences in Data Changes

Sequence-value generation can be incorporated directly into data changes made by insert and update statements. This direct use of sequences in insert and update statements is the most common use for sequences in a database. In the situation where the sequence generates a primary key for all new rows entering the database table, the sequence would likely be referenced directly from the insert statement. Note, however, that this approach sometimes fails when the sequence is referenced by triggers. Therefore, it is best to reference sequences within the user interface or within stored procedures. The following statements illustrate the use of sequences directly in changes made to tables:

```
SQL> INSERT INTO expense(expense_no, empid, amt, submit_date)
  2  VALUES(countdown_20.nextval, 59495, 456.34, '21-NOV-99');
1 row inserted.
SQL> UPDATE product
  2  SET product_num = countdown_20.currval
  3  WHERE serial_num = 34938583945;
1 row updated.
```

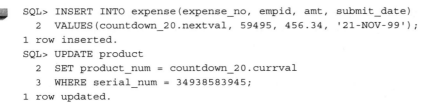

TIP
*These trivial code block examples are for tables that
we may or may not have referred to in earlier
discussions. You can formulate your own sequences
for similar use on tables we have already worked on
or tables of your own design.*

Modifying Sequence Definitions

The time may come when the sequence of a database will need its rules altered in
some way. For example, you may want COUNTDOWN_20 to decrement by a
different number. Any parameter of a sequence can be modified by issuing the
`alter sequence` statement. The following is an example:

```
SQL> select countdown_20.nextval from dual;
NEXTVAL
-------
     16
SQL> alter sequence countdown_20
  2  increment by -4;
Sequence altered.
SQL> select countdown_20.nextval from dual
  2  ;
  NEXTVAL
---------
       12
SQL> /
  NEXTVAL
---------
        8
```

The effect is immediate. In this example, the statement will change
COUNTDOWN_20 to decrement each NEXTVAL by 4 instead of 1.

Any parameter of a sequence that is not specified by the `alter sequence`
statement will remain unchanged. Therefore, by altering the sequence to use

nocycle instead of cycle, we cause the COUNTDOWN_20 sequence in the following listing to run through one countdown from 20 to 0 only. After the sequence hits 0, no further references to COUNTDOWN_20.NEXTVAL will be allowed:

```
SQL> alter sequence countdown_20
  2  nocycle;
Sequence altered.
SQL> select countdown_20.nextval from dual;
  NEXTVAL
---------
        4
SQL> /
  NEXTVAL
---------
        0
SQL> /
select countdown_20.nextval from dual
*
ERROR at line 1:
ORA-08004: sequence COUNTDOWN_20.NEXTVAL goes below MINVALUE
and cannot be instantiated
```

Beware of Effects of Modifying Sequences

Modifying sequences is a simple process. However, the impact of the changes can be complex, depending on how an application uses these sequences. The main concern with changing sequences is monitoring the effect on tables or other processes that use the values generated by the sequences.

For example, resetting the value returned by a sequence from 1,150 to 0 is not difficult to execute. However, if the sequence was being used to generate primary keys for a table, for which several values between 0 and 1,150 had already been generated, you will encounter problems when the sequence begins generating values for insert statements that depend on the sequence to create primary keys. This problem won't show up when the sequence is altered, but later insert operations will have primary key constraint violations on the table. The only way to solve the problem (other than deleting the records already existing in the table) is to alter the sequence again. Gaps can arise in the values of the primary key from this same premise as well.

Dropping Sequences

When a sequence is no longer needed, it can be removed. To do so, the DBA or owner of the sequence can issue the drop sequence statement. Dropping the sequence renders its virtual columns, CURRVAL and NEXTVAL, unusable. However, if the sequence was being used to generate primary key values, the values generated by the sequence will continue to exist in the database. No cascading effect occurs on the values generated by a sequence when the sequence is removed. The following shows an example:

```
SQL> DROP SEQUENCE countdown_20;
Sequence dropped.
SQL> select countdown_20.currval from dual;
select countdown_20.currval from dual
       *
ERROR at line 1:
ORA-02289: sequence does not exist
```

TIP
You can find information about your sequences and the sequences available to you in the USER_SEQUENCES and ALL_SEQUENCES dictionary views, respectively. Also, sequences are not tied to a table. Generally, you should name the sequence after its intended use; however, the sequence can be used anywhere, regardless of its name.

Gaps in Sequence

Although sequence generators issue sequential numbers without gaps, this action occurs independent of a `commit` or `rollback`. Therefore, if you roll back a statement containing a sequence, the number is lost. Also, another event that can cause gaps in the sequence is a system crash. If the sequence caches values in the memory, then those values are lost if the system crashes. Finally, because sequences are not tied directly to tables, the same sequence can be used for multiple tables. If you do so, each table can contain gaps in the sequential numbers.

For Review

1. Be sure you know that a sequence is an object that generates numbers in a sequence you define. Sequences can be used for many purposes, but they are most commonly used for generating unique numbers for primary key columns.

2. Know how to use the `create sequence`, `alter sequence`, and `drop sequence` statements. Also, be sure you can identify the information

contained in the CURRVAL and NEXTVAL pseudocolumns of a sequence as well as what happens to CURRVAL when NEXTVAL is selected.

3. Understand the different ways to refer to a sequence with `select`, `update`, and `insert` statements. Know how to use sequences in conjunction with the DUAL table as well.

Exercises

1. This sequence pseudocolumn contains the most recently generated value the sequence has derived: _____

2. This sequence pseudocolumn contains the last value the sequence has derived: _____

Answer Key
1. NEXTVAL. 2. CURRVAL.

Using Indexes

Indexes are objects in the database that provide a mapping of all the values in a table column, along with the ROWID(s) for all rows in the table that contain that value for the column. A ROWID is a unique identifier for a row in an Oracle database table. Indexes have multiple uses on the Oracle database. Indexes can be used to ensure uniqueness on a database, and they can also boost performance when you're searching for records in a table. Indexes are used by the Oracle Server to speed up the retrieval of rows by using a pointer. The improvement in performance is gained when the search criteria for data in a table include a reference to the indexed column or columns. In Oracle, indexes can be created on any column in a table except for columns of the LONG datatype. Especially on large tables, indexes make the difference between an application that drags its heels and an application that runs with efficiency. However, many performance considerations must be weighed before you make the decision to create an index. Performance is not improved simply by throwing a few indexes on the table haphazardly. Indexes can reduce disk I/O by using a rapid path access method to locate data quickly. Indexes are used and maintained automatically by the Oracle server. Indexes can be created either manually or automatically.

B-tree Index Structure

The traditional index in the Oracle database is based on a highly advanced algorithm for sorting data called a *B-tree*. A B-tree contains data placed in layered, branching order, from top to bottom, resembling an upside-down tree. The midpoint of the entire list is placed at the top of the "tree" and is called the *root node*. The midpoints of each half of the remaining two lists are placed at the next level, and so on, as illustrated in Figure 7-1.

By using a divide-and-conquer method for structuring and searching for data, the values of a column are only a few hops away on the tree, rather than several thousand sequential reads through the list away. However, traditional indexes work best when many distinct values are in the column or when the column is unique.

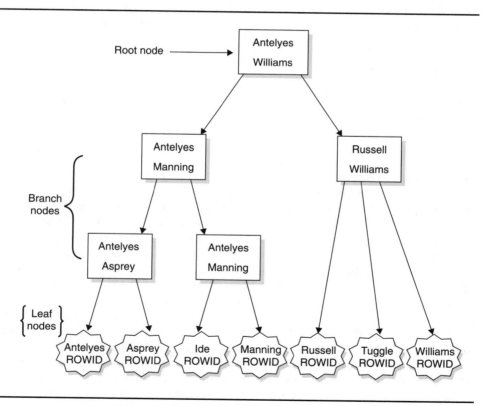

FIGURE 7-1.   *A B-tree index, displayed pictorially*

The algorithm works as follows:

1. Compare the given value to the value in the halfway point of the list. If the value at hand is greater, discard the lower half of the list. If the value at hand is less, discard the upper half of the list.

2. Repeat step 1 for the remaining part of the list until a value is found or the list exhausted.

Along with the data values of a column, each individual node of an index also stores a piece of information about the column value's row location on disk. This crucial piece of lookup data is called a ROWID. The ROWID for the column value points Oracle directly to the disk location of the table row corresponding to the column value. A ROWID identifies the location of a row in a data block in the datafile on disk. With this information, Oracle can then find all the data associated with the row in the table.

TIP
The ROWID for a table is an address for the row on disk. With the ROWID, Oracle can find the data on disk rapidly.

Bitmap Index Structure

This topic is pretty advanced, so consider yourself forewarned. The other type of index available in Oracle is the *bitmap index*. Try to conceptualize a bitmap index as being a sophisticated lookup table, having rows that correspond to all unique data values in the column being indexed. Therefore, if the indexed column contains only three distinct values, the bitmap index can be visualized as containing three rows. Each row in a bitmap index contains four columns. The first column contains the unique value for the column being indexed. The next column contains the start ROWID for all rows in the table. The third column in the bitmap index contains the end ROWID for all rows in the table. The last column contains a bitmap pattern, in which every row in the table will have one bit. Therefore, if the table being indexed contains 1,000 rows, this last column of the bitmap index will have 1,000 corresponding bits in this last column of the bitmap index. Each bit in the bitmap index will be set to 0 (off) or 1 (on), depending on whether the corresponding row in the table has that distinct value for the column. In other words, if the value in the indexed column for that row matches this unique value, the bit is set to 1; otherwise, the bit is set to 0. Figure 7-2 displays a pictorial representation of a bitmap index containing three distinct values.

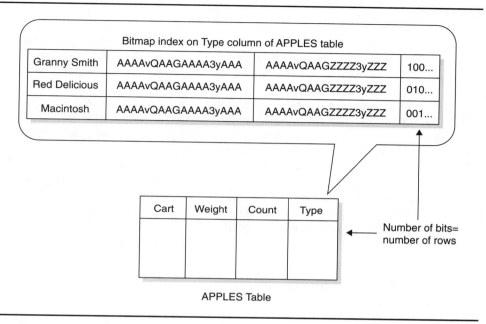

FIGURE 7-2. *A bitmap index, displayed pictorially*

Each row in the table being indexed adds only a bit to the size of the bitmap pattern column for the bitmap index, so growth of the table won't affect the size of the bitmap index too much. However, each distinct value adds another row to the bitmap index, which adds another entire bitmap pattern with one bit for each row in the table. Be careful about adding distinct values to a column with a bitmap index, because these indexes work better when few distinct values are allowed for a column. The classic example of using a bitmap index is where you want to query a table containing employees based on a GENDER column, indicating whether the employee is male or female. This information rarely changes about a person, and only two distinct possibilities, so a traditional B-tree index is not useful in this case. However, this is exactly the condition where a bitmap index would aid performance. Therefore, the bitmap index improves performance in situations where traditional indexes are not useful, and vice versa.

TIP

Up to 32 columns from one table can be included in a single B-tree index on that table, whereas a bitmap index can include a maximum of 30 columns from the table.

Creating Indexes

You can create a unique B-tree index on a column manually by using the `create index` *name* on *table* (*column*) statement containing the `unique` keyword. This process is the manual equivalent of creating a unique or primary key constraint on a table. (Remember, unique indexes are created automatically in support of those constraints.)

You can index a column that contains NULL or repeated values, as well, simply by eliminating the `unique` keyword. Creating a composite index with more columns named is possible as well. You can also create a *reverse-key index*, where the contents of the index correspond to a reversed set of data from the indexed column. For example, if you are indexing the LASTNAME column of the EMPLOYEE table, a row containing "COUCHMAN" in that column would have a corresponding value in the reverse-key index of "NAMHCOUC." Reverse-key indexes are often found in Oracle Parallel Server environments to improve parallel query performance. Finally, you can create a bitmap index by substituting the `bitmap` keyword for the `unique` keyword. The following shows an example:

```
SQL> -- unique indexes
  2   CREATE UNIQUE INDEX emp_empno_01
  3   ON emp (empno);
Index created.
SQL> -- nonunique indexes
  2   CREATE INDEX emp_sal_01
  3   ON emp (sal);
Index created.
SQL> -- composite indexes
  2   CREATE UNIQUE INDEX employee_empno_ename_indx_01
  3   ON emp (empno, ename);
Index created.
SQL> -- reverse key indexes
  2   CREATE INDEX emp_ename_reverse_indx
  3   ON emp (ename) REVERSE;
Index created.
SQL> -- bitmap indexes
  2   CREATE BITMAP INDEX emp_deptno_indx_01
  3   ON emp (deptno);
Index created.
```

TIP
You can create all these indexes on the EMP table we've been using throughout the book. Alternatively, you can use these code blocks as templates for creating these types of indexes on tables of your own design.

To create an index in your schema, you must have the CREATE TABLE privilege. To create an index in any schema, you need the CREATE ANY INDEX privilege or the CREATE TABLE privilege on the table on which you are creating the index.

In order to replace the definition of the index, the entire index must be dropped and re-created. However, information about the index can be found in several different ways. The ALL_INDEXES dictionary view displays storage information about the index, along with the name of the table with which the index is associated. The ALL_OBJECTS dictionary view displays object information about the index, including the index status. The ALL_IND_COLUMNS view displays information about the columns that are indexed on the database. This last view is especially useful for determining the order of columns in a composite index.

Creating Function-Based Indexes

To create a function-based index in your own schema on your own table, you must have the CREATE INDEX and QUERY REWRITE system privileges. To create the index in another schema or on another schema's table, you must have the CREATE ANY INDEX and GLOBAL QUERY REWRITE privileges. The table owner must also have the EXECUTE object privilege on the functions used in the function-based index.

The function-based index is a new type of index in Oracle that is designed to improve query performance by making it possible to define an index that works when your where clause contains operations on columns. Traditional B-tree indexes won't be used when your where clause contains columns that participate in functions or operations. For example, suppose you have table EMP with four columns: EMPID, LASTNAME, FIRSTNAME, and SALARY. The SALARY column has a B-tree index on it. However, if you issue the select * from EMP where (SALARY*1.08) > 63000 statement, the RDBMS will ignore the index, performing a full table scan instead. Function-based indexes are designed to be used in situations like this one, where your SQL statements contain such operations in their where clauses. The following code block shows a function-based index defined:

```
SQL> CREATE INDEX ixd_emp_01
  2  ON emp(SAL*1.08);
Index created.
```

By using function-based indexes like this one, you can optimize the performance of queries containing function operations on columns in the where clause, like the query shown previously. As long as the function you specify is repeatable, you can create a function-based index around it. A *repeatable function* is one whose result will never change for the same set of input data. For example,

2 + 2 will always equal 4. In other words, it will never change one day so that it equals 5. Therefore, the addition operation is repeatable. To enable the use of function-based indexes, you must issue two `alter session` statements, as follows:

```
SQL> alter session set query_rewrite_enabled = true;
Session altered.
SQL> alter session set query_rewrite_integrity=trusted;
Session altered.
```

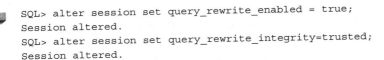

TIP
Bitmap indexes can also be function-based indexes, and function-based indexes can also be partitioned.

Removing Indexes

When an index is no longer needed in the database, the developer can remove it with the `drop index` command. Once an index is dropped, it will no longer improve performance on searches using the column or columns contained in the index. No mention of that index will appear in the data dictionary any more either. You cannot drop the index that is used for a primary key.

The syntax for the `drop index` statement is the same, regardless of the type of index being dropped (unique, bitmap, or B-tree). If you want to rework the index in any way, you must first drop the old index and then create the new one. The following is an example:

```
SQL> DROP INDEX employee_last_first_indx_01;
Index dropped.
```

Guidelines for Creating Indexes

Although the best performance improvement can be seen when a column containing all unique values has an index created on it, similar performance improvements can be made on columns containing some duplicate values or NULL values. Therefore, data in a column need not be unique in order for you to create an index on the column. Some guidelines are available for ensuring that the traditional index produces the performance improvements desired. The guidelines for evaluating performance improvements given by traditional indexes and some consideration of the performance and storage trade-offs involved in creating these indexes will be presented later in this section of the chapter.

Using indexes for searching tables for information can provide incredible performance gains over searching tables using columns that are not indexed.

However, care must be taken to choose the right index. Although a completely unique column is preferable for indexing with a B-tree index, a non-unique column will work almost as well if only about 10 percent of its rows, or even less, have the same values. Switch or flag columns, such as ones for storing the sex of a person, are not appropriate for B-tree indexes. Neither are columns used to store a few valid values, or columns that store a token value representing valid or invalid, active or inactive, yes or no, or any such types of values. Bitmap indexes are more appropriate for these types of columns. Finally, you will typically use reverse-key indexes in situations where Oracle Parallel Server is installed and running and you want to maximize parallelism in the database. Table 4-1 summarizes some handy rules of thumb on the topic of when to create and when not to create indexes.

TIP

The uniqueness of the values in a column is referred to as cardinality. *Unique columns or columns that contain many distinct values have* high cardinality, *whereas columns with few distinct values have* low cardinality. *Use B-tree indexes for columns with high cardinality and bitmap indexes for columns with low cardinality. Also, the USER_INDEXES data dictionary view contains the name of the index and its uniqueness. The USER_IND_COLUMNS view contains the index name, the table name, and the column name.*

When to Create an Index	When Not to Create an Index
When you have a large table	When you have a small table
When the table is used mainly for queries	When users make DML changes to the table frequently
When you generally query the table for one or a few distinct values	When your query results contain substantial portions of the data the table actually stores
When a large number of NULLs are in the column	When the table is updated frequently

TABLE 7-1.   *When to Create and When Not to Create an Index*

For Review

1. Know what an index is and how to create one. Understand the difference between a unique index and a nonunique index. Also, be sure you can create B-tree, bitmap, function-based, reverse-key, and composite indexes.

2. Be sure you understand that, on unique indexes containing more than one column, uniqueness for the row is determined by unique combinations of all columns in the index.

3. Understand what is meant by cardinality. Know when you might use a B-tree index to improve performance and when you might you might use a bitmap index to improve performance instead. Know also that you can look in USER_INDEXES and USER_IND_COLUMNS for information about indexes.

Exercises

1. You want to create an index that will improve performance on salary reviews. The query needs to determine what an employee's salary would be if the employee were given a 12 percent raise. Which of the following `create index` commands would handle this situation?

   A. `create index my_idx_1 on employee (salary * 1.12);`

   B. `create unique index my_idx_1 on employee (salary);`

   C. `create bitmap index my_idx_1 on employee (salary);`

   D. `create index my_idx_1 on employee (salary) reverse;`

2. Your table, which contains name and telephone number information for the states of California, New York, and Texas, needs an index on the LASTNAME column. In order to improve performance, which of the following indexes would be most appropriate?

   A. `create unique index my_idx_1 on people_phone (lastname);`

   B. `create index my_idx_1 on people_phone (lastname);`

   C. `create bitmap index my_idx_1 on people_phone (lastname);`

   D. `create index my_idx_1 on people_phone (lastname) reverse;`

3. **You are creating an index for the US_GOVT_SS table in the U.S. Government Social Security application on the SS_NUM column. Which of the following choices best identifies the statement you will use on this column?**

    A. `create index my_idx_1 on US_govt_SS (ss_num);`

    B. `create bitmap index my_idx_1 on US_govt_SS (ss_num);`

    C. `create unique index my_idx_1 on US_govt_SS (ss_num);`

    D. `create index my_idx_1 on US_govt_SS (ss_num) reverse;`

4. **This word describes the uniqueness of values in an indexed column:**

    _____

Answer Key
1. A. 2. B. 3. C. 4. Cardinality.

Using Public and Private Synonyms

The objects in Oracle you create are available only in your schema unless you grant access to the objects explicitly to other users. We'll discuss privileges and user access in the next section. However, even when you grant permission to other users for using an object, the boundary created by schema ownership will force other users to prefix the object name with your schema name in order to access your object. For example, SCOTT owns the EMP table. If TURNER wants to access SCOTT's EMP table, he must refer to EMP as SCOTT.EMP. If TURNER doesn't, the following happens:

```
SQL> connect turner/ike
Connected.
SQL> SELECT * FROM emp
  2  WHERE empno = 7844;
SELECT * FROM emp
              *
ORA-00942: table or view does not exist.
```

TIP
*We'll cover the issue of creating TURNER's user ID
and the privileges associated with accessing a table
in the next section. For now, focus on the issue of
schema ownership.*

So, TURNER can't even see his own employee data—in fact, Oracle tells him
that the EMP table doesn't even exist (pretty sneaky, eh?). Yet, as soon as TURNER
prefixes the EMP table with its schema owner, SCOTT, a whole world of data opens
up for TURNER, as you can see in the following code block:

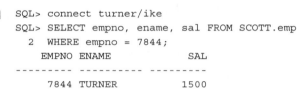

```
SQL> connect turner/ike
SQL> SELECT empno, ename, sal FROM SCOTT.emp
  2  WHERE empno = 7844;
   EMPNO ENAME             SAL
-------- ---------- ---------
    7844 TURNER           1500
```

How Synonyms Can Help

If remembering which user owns which table seems unnecessarily complicated,
synonyms can be used on the database for schema transparency. *Synonyms* are
alternative names that can be created as database objects in Oracle to refer to a
table or view. You can refer to a table owned by another user using synonyms.
Creating a synonym eliminates the need to qualify the object name with the schema
and provides you with an alternative name for a table, view, sequence, procedure,
or other objects. Synonyms are also used to shorten lengthy object names. Two types
of synonyms exist in Oracle: private synonyms and public synonyms. You can use a
private synonym within your own schema to refer to a table or view by an
alternative name. Private synonyms are exactly that—they are private to your
schema and therefore usable only by you. A private synonym name must be distinct
from all other objects owned by the same user.

Think of private synonyms as giving you the ability to develop "pet names" for
database objects in Oracle. You can use public synonyms to enable all users in
Oracle to access database objects you own without having to prefix the object
names with your schema name. This concept of referencing database objects
without worrying about the schema the objects are part of is known as *schema
transparency*. Public synonyms are publicly available to all users of Oracle;
however, you need special privileges to create public synonyms. We'll talk more
about the privilege required for creating public synonyms in the next section. For
now, the following code block demonstrates how to create private and public
synonyms, respectively:

```
SQL> create synonym all_my_emps for emp;
Synonym created.
SQL> create public synonym emp for scott.emp;
Synonym created.
```

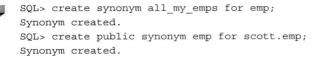

TIP
*Neither public nor private synonyms alter the details
of the table's or view's definition. They just simply
act as alternative names for the table or view.*

Now that SCOTT has his own private synonym for the EMP table, he can start
referring to EMP by his pet name right away:

```
SQL> connect scott/tiger
Connected.
SQL> select empno, ename, sal
  2  from all_my_emps
  3  where empno = 7369;
   EMPNO ENAME             SAL
--------- ---------- ---------
    7369 SMITH             800
```

Meanwhile, TURNER no longer needs to refer to EMP using SCOTT's schema
prefixed to the table name. He can simply call it EMP, as he does in the following
example:

```
SQL> connect turner/ike
Connected.
SQL> select empno, ename, sal
  2  from emp
  3  where empno = 7844;
   EMPNO ENAME             SAL
--------- ---------- ---------
    7844 TURNER           1500
```

Note another interesting thing about private synonyms. If no public synonym
existed for TURNER to use for referencing the EMP table without prefixing SCOTT's
schema, TURNER could create his own private synonym for the object, as shown in
the following:

```
SQL> connect turner/ike
Connected.
SQL> create synonym emp for scott.emp;
Synonym created.
```

```
SQL> select empno, ename, sal
  2  from emp
  3  where empno = 7844;
    EMPNO ENAME            SAL
--------- ---------- ---------
     7844 TURNER          1500
```

TIP

*Synonyms do not give you access to data in a table
that you do not already have access to. Only
privileges can do that. Synonyms simply enable you
to refer to a table without prefixing the schema
name to the table reference. When resolving a
database table name, Oracle looks first to see
whether the table exists in your schema. If Oracle
doesn't find the table, Oracle searches for a private
synonym. If none is found, Oracle looks for a public
synonym.*

Dropping Synonyms

Synonyms are dropped using the `drop synonym` command, as shown in the
following code block:

```
SQL> connect turner/ike
Connected.
SQL> drop synonym emp;
Synonym dropped.
SQL> connect scott/tiger
Connected.
SQL> drop public synonym emp;
Synonym dropped.
SQL> drop synonym all_my_emps;
Synonym dropped.
```

For Review

1. Understand how synonyms are used to facilitate schema transparency.

2. Know the difference between public synonyms and private synonyms.
   Know that private synonyms can be referenced only by the user who
   created them, whereas public synonyms can be referenced by every user in
   Oracle.

Exercises

1. **User DAVIS would like to access table PROFITS, which is owned by user WATTERSON, without prefixing the schema owner. Assuming the privilege issue is worked out, which of the following choices do *not* resolve the schema transparency issue? (Choose two.)**

   A. `create synonym profits for watterson.profits;`
   `(issued by WATTERSON)`

   B. `create public synonym for watterson.profits;`
   `(issued by WATTERSON);`

   C. `create synonym profits for watterson.profits;`
   `(issued by DAVIS)`

   D. `create synonym profits for profits; (issued by DAVIS)`

2. **This type of synonym is accessible by every user in the Oracle database (two words):** _____

3. **This type of synonym is accessible only by the user in the Oracle database who created the synonym (two words):** _____

Answer Key
1. A and D. 2. Public synonym. 3. Private synonym.

Chapter Summary

This chapter has covered a great deal of information you need to know about objects other than tables in the Oracle database. We started the chapter with a lengthy discussion on how to define both simple and complex views. You learned about how to modify data in base tables using a view as well as when this is not possible in certain circumstances using complex views. We then moved on to cover how to use indexes in the Oracle database. You learned about the different types of indexes available to Oracle as well as the different uses for those types of indexes. The chapter then covered the use of sequences for generating numbers for various purposes in Oracle. Finally, the chapter covered the use of synonyms for creating schema transparency in your database.

Two-Minute Drill

- A view is a virtual table defined by a `select` statement.

- Views can distill data from tables that may be inappropriate for some users, and they can hide the complexity of data joined from several tables. You can also mask the complexity that arises when you perform many single-row or group operations on the data returned by the view's query.

- The two types of views are simple and complex.

- Simple views are those that have only one underlying table.

- Complex views are those with two or more underlying tables that have been joined together.

- Data may be inserted into simple views, except in the following cases:

  - If the `with check option` clause is used, the user may not insert, delete, or update data on the table underlying the simple view if the view itself is not able to select that data for the user.

  - The user may not insert, delete, or update data on the table underlying the simple view if the `select` statement creating the view contains `group by`, `order by`, or a single-row operation.

  - No data may be inserted in simple views that contain references to any virtual columns, such as ROWID, CURRVAL, NEXTVAL, and ROWNUM.

  - No data may be inserted into simple views that are created with the `read only` option.

- Data may be inserted into complex views when all the following conditions are true:

  - The statement affects only one of the tables in the join.

  - For `update` statements, all columns changed are extracted from a key-preserved table. In addition, if the view is created with the `with check option` clause, join columns and columns taken from tables that are referenced more than once in the view are not part of the update.

  - For `delete` statements, the join has only one key-preserved table. This table may be present more than once in the join, unless the view has been created with the `with check option` clause.

■ For `insert` statements, all columns where values are inserted must come from a key-preserved table, and the view must not have been created with the `with check option` clause.

■ The `with check option` clause, upon creating a view, enables this simple view to limit the data that can be inserted or otherwise changed on the underlying table by requiring that the data change be selectable by the view.

■ Modifying the data selected by a view requires re-creating the view with the `create or replace view` statement or dropping the view first and issuing the `create view` statement.

■ An existing view can be recompiled by executing the `alter view` statement if for some reason it becomes invalid due to object dependency.

■ A view is dropped with the `drop view` statement.

■ A sequence generates integers based on rules that are defined by sequence creation.

■ Options that can be defined for sequences include the first number generated, how the sequence increments, the maximum value, the minimum value, whether the sequence can recycle numbers, and whether numbers will be cached for improved performance.

■ Sequences are used by selecting from the CURRVAL and NEXTVAL virtual columns.

■ The CURRVAL column contains the current value of the sequence.

■ Selecting from NEXTVAL increments the sequence and changes the value of CURRVAL to whatever is produced by NEXTVAL.

■ The rules that a sequence uses to generate values can be modified using the `alter sequence` statement.

■ A sequence can be deleted with the `drop sequence` statement.

■ Some indexes in a database are created automatically, such as those supporting the primary key and the unique constraints on a table.

■ Other indexes are created manually to support database performance improvements.

■ Indexes created manually are often on non-unique columns.

■ B-tree indexes work best on columns that have high cardinality—that is, columns that contain a large number of distinct values and few duplicates.

- B-tree indexes improve performance by storing data in a binary search tree and then searching for values in the tree using a divide-and-conquer methodology, as outlined in this chapter.

- Bitmap indexes improve performance on columns with low cardinality—that is, columns that contain few distinct values and many duplicates.

- Columns stored in an index can be changed only by dropping and recreating the index.

- Indexes can be deleted by issuing the `drop index` statement.

- The Oracle database security model consists of two parts: limiting user access with password authentication and controlling object use with privileges.

- Available privileges in Oracle include system privileges, for maintaining database objects, and object privileges, for accessing and manipulating data in database objects.

- Changing a password can be performed by a user with the `alter user identified by` statement.

- Granting system and object privileges is accomplished with the `grant` command.

- Taking away system and object privileges is accomplished with the `revoke` command.

- Creating a synonym is accomplished with the `create public synonym` command.

Fill-in-the-Blank Questions

1. Schema transparency can be created in an Oracle database through the use of this type of database object: _____

2. Obtaining a sequence's value without actually changing that value is done by referencing this Oracle pseudocolumn: _____

3. A view containing data from two or more tables where the user can actually modify values in the underlying tables is called what?

   _____

4. This type of database index is used for applying a repeatable programmatic operation to all values in a column: _____

5. This type of constraint automatically creates an underlying index in your database: _____

6. This clause enables a view to enforce the rule that if the view itself cannot see the data change, the data change is not allowed:

   _____

7. Obtaining a new value from a sequence is accomplished by querying this Oracle pseudocolumn: _____

Chapter Questions

1. **Dropping a table has which of the following effects on a non-unique index created for the table?**

   A. No effect.

   B. The index will be dropped.

   C. The index will be rendered invalid.

   D. The index will contain NULL values.

2. **Which of the following statements about indexes is true?**

   A. Columns with low cardinality are handled well by B-tree indexes.

   B. Columns with low cardinality are handled poorly by bitmap indexes.

   C. Columns with high cardinality are handled well by B-tree indexes.

3. **Which of the following choices represents the step you would take to add the number of columns selected by a view?**

   A. Add more columns to the underlying table.

   B. Issue the `alter view` statement.

   C. Use a correlated subquery in conjunction with the view.

   D. Drop and re-create the view with references to select more columns.

4. **You are creating a sequence on the Oracle database. Which of the following choices is a valid parameter for sequence creation?**

   A. `identified by`

   B. `using temporary tablespace`

   C. `maxvalue`

   D. `on delete cascade`

5. **The following statement is issued against the Oracle database:**

   ```
   create view EMP_VIEW_01
   as select E.EMPID, E.LASTNAME, E.FIRSTNAME, A.ADDRESS
   from EMPLOYEE E, EMPL_ADDRESS A
   where E.EMPID = A.EMPID
   with check option;
   ```

   Which line will produce an error?

   A. `create view EMP_VIEW_01`

   B. `as select E.EMPID, E.LASTNAME, E.FIRSTNAME, A.ADDRESS`

   C. `from EMPLOYEE E, EMPL_ADDRESS A`

   D. `where E.EMPID = A.EMPID`

   E. `with check option;`

   F. This statement contains no errors.

6. **You are working with sequences in Oracle. After referencing NEXTVAL, the value in CURRVAL is changed to which in the following ways or to which of the following values?**

   A. Is incremented by one

   B. Is now in PREVVAL

    C. Is equal to NEXTVAL

    D. Is unchanged

7. The EMP_SALARY table has two columns: EMP_USER and SALARY. EMP_USER is set to be the same as the Oracle username. To support user MARTHA, the salary administrator, you create a view with the following statement:

```
CREATE VIEW EMP_SAL_VW
AS SELECT EMP_USER, SALARY
FROM EMP_SALARY
WHERE EMP_USER <> 'MARTHA';
```

MARTHA is supposed to be able to view and update anyone's salary in the company except her own through this view. Which of the following clauses do you need to add to your view-creation statement in order to implement this functionality?

    A. `with admin option`

    B. `with grant option`

    C. `with security option`

    D. `with check option`

8. The INVENTORY table has three columns: UPC_CODE, UNITS, and DELIV_DATE. The primary key is UPC_CODE. New records are added daily through a view. The view was created using the following code:

```
CREATE VIEW DAY_INVENTORY_VW
AS SELECT UPC_CODE, UNITS, DELIV_DATE
FROM INVENTORY
WHERE DELIV_DATE = SYSDATE
WITH CHECK OPTION;
```

What happens when you try to insert a record with duplicate UPC_CODE?

    A. The statement fails due to the `with check option` clause.

    B. The statement will succeed.

    C. The statement fails due to the primary key constraint.

    D. The statement will insert everything except the date.

9. **You are cleaning information out of an Oracle database. Which of the following statements will get rid of all views that use a table at the same time you eliminate the table from the database?**

   A. `drop view`

   B. `alter table`

   C. `drop index`

   D. `alter table drop` constraint

10. **You create a view with the following statement:**

    ```
    CREATE VIEW BASEBALL_TEAM_VW
    AS SELECT B.JERSEY_NUM, B.POSITION, B.NAME
    FROM BASEBALL_TEAM B
    WHERE B.NAME = USER;
    ```

    What will happen when user JONES attempts to select a listing for user SMITH?

    A. The `select` statement will receive an error.

    B. The `select` statement will succeed.

    C. The `select` statement will receive the NO ROWS SELECTED message from Oracle.

    D. The `select` statement will add data only to BASEBALL_TEAM.

Fill-in-the-Blank Answers

1. Synonym

2. CURRVAL

3. Updatable join view

4. Function-based index

5. Primary key (unique constraint also acceptable)

6. `with check option`

7. NEXTVAL

Answers to Chapter Questions

1. B. The index will be dropped.

Explanation   Like automatically generated indexes associated with a table's primary key, the indexes created manually on a table to improve performance will be dropped if the table is dropped. Choices A, C, and D are therefore invalid because the effects listed in those choices do not take place in this context.

2. C. Columns with high cardinality are handled well by B-tree indexes.

Explanation   Columns with low cardinality are the bane of B-tree indexes, thus eliminating choice A. Furthermore, bitmap indexes are primarily used for performance gains on columns with low cardinality, thus eliminating choice B. The correct answer is choice C. Review the discussion of how B-tree indexes work for more information.

3. D. Drop and re-create the view with references to select more columns.

Explanation   Choice A is incorrect because adding columns to the underlying table will not add columns to the view; instead, it will likely invalidate the view. Choice B is incorrect because the `alter view` statement simply recompiles an existing view definition, whereas the real solution in this example is to change the existing view definition by dropping and recreating the view. Choice C is incorrect because a correlated subquery will likely worsen performance. This underscores the real problem—a column must be added to the view. Review the discussion of altering the definition of a view.

4. C. `maxvalue`

Explanation The `maxvalue` option is a valid option for sequence creation. Choices A and B are both part of the `create user` statement, whereas choice D is a part of a constraint declaration in an `alter table` or `create table` statement. Review the discussion on creating sequences.

5. F. This statement contains no errors.

Explanation Even though the reference to `with check option` is inappropriate, considering that `insert` operations into complex views are not possible, the statement will not actually produce an error when compiled. Therefore, no errors occur in the view. This is not something that can be learned. It requires hands-on experience with Oracle.

6. C. Is equal to NEXTVAL

Explanation Once NEXTVAL is referenced, the sequence increments the integer and changes the value of CURRVAL to be equal to NEXTVAL. Refer to the discussion of sequences for more information.

7. D. `with check option`

Explanation The appropriate clause is `with check option`. You can add this clause to a `create view` statement so that the view will not let you add rows to the underlying table that cannot then be selected in the view. The `with {admin| grant}` option clauses are used to assign administrative ability to users, along with granting them privileges. Therefore, choices A and B are incorrect. The `with security` option is fictitious—it does not exist in Oracle. Therefore, choice C is incorrect.

8. C. The statement fails due to the primary key constraint.

Explanation It should be obvious that the statement fails—the real question here is why. The reason is because of the primary key constraint on UPC_CODE. As soon as you try to add a duplicate record, the table will reject the addition. Although the view has `with check option` specified, this is not the reason the addition fails. It would be the reason an `insert` fails if you attempt to add a record for a day other than today, however.

9. A. `drop view`

Explanation When a table is dropped, Oracle eliminates all related database objects, such as triggers, constraints, and indexes—except for views. Views are actually considered separate objects, and although the view will not function properly after you drop the underlying table, Oracle will keep the view around after the table is dropped.

> **10.** C. The `select` statement will receive the NO ROWS SELECTED message from Oracle

Explanation   Although the query will succeed (translation: you won't receive an error), you must beware of the distracter in choice B. In reality, choice C is the better answer because it more accurately identifies what really will occur when you issue this statement. Oracle will behave as it would for any `select` statement you issue when you list criteria in the `where` clause that no data satisfies—by returning the NO ROWS SELECTED message. This is not an error condition, but you wouldn't call it a successful search for data either, making choices A and B incorrect. Finally, `select` statements never add data to a table. Therefore, choice D is incorrect.

CHAPTER
8

User Access
Control in Oracle

n this chapter, you will learn about and demonstrate knowledge in the following areas of user access and privileges in the Oracle database:

- Creating users
- Granting and revoking object privileges
- Using roles to manage database access

The most secure database is one with no users, but take away the users of a database and the whole point of having a database is lost. In order to address the issues of security within Oracle, a careful balance must be maintained between providing access to necessary data and functions and preventing unnecessary access. Oracle provides a means of doing this with its security model, which consists of several options for limiting connect access to the database and for controlling what a user can and cannot see once a connection is established. Database security includes system security and data security. System security specifies using the database at the system level (includes username, password, and diskspace allocated to users). Database security specifies the use of database objects and the actions that the users can perform on the database objects. This section will focus on security on the Oracle database—from creating users, to administering passwords, to administering security on individual objects in the database. This chapter covers 7 percent of the material tested on OCP Exam 1.

Creating Users

The basic Oracle database security model consists of two parts. The first part consists of password authentication for all users of the Oracle database. Password authentication is available either directly from the Oracle server or from the operating system supporting the Oracle database. When Oracle's own authentication system is used, password information is stored in Oracle in an encrypted format. For the purposes of OCP Exam 1, we'll focus exclusively on Oracle's own authentication mechanism. The second part of the Oracle security model consists of controlling which database objects a user may access, the level of access a user may have to these objects, and whether a user has the authority to place new objects into the Oracle database. At a high level, these controls are referred to as *privileges*. We'll talk about privileges and database access later in this section.

TIP
In Oracle, the Oracle security model has additional components, including such features as fine-grained access control, certificate-based authentication, and advanced password-management functions such as

*password rotation expiry and complexity
verification. These features are tested extensively in
OCP Exam 2, but not on OCP Exam 1. Oracle9i
promises to offer even more security features, such
as Oracle Label Security.*

How to Create Users

Let's start our discussion of creating users with an example. We referred to user
TURNER in an earlier example. He's a divorced salesman working for our company
who used to have ties to Hollywood. Only privileged users such as the DBA can
create other users in Oracle. For now, we'll pretend that user SCOTT is the DBA.
SCOTT creates TURNER's user ID in Oracle with the `create user` command. You
must have CREATE USER system privilege to be able to create users. The most basic
version of the command for creating users defines only the user we want to create,
along with a password, as seen in the following example:

```
SQL> connect scott/tiger
Connected.
SQL> create user turner identified by ike;
User created.
```

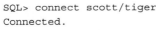

TIP
*The user does not have privileges at this point. The
DBA can then grant privileges to the user. The
privileges determine the actions that the user can do
with the objects in the database. Also, usernames
can be up to 30 characters in length and can
contain alphanumeric characters as well as the $, #,
and _ characters.*

Creating a User Authenticated by the Host

Host authentication isn't used by Oracle databases too often, but it can be. Host
authentication means that you create a user in Oracle whose password is validated
by the underlying host system. When the user logs onto the host with a correct
password, Oracle then trusts the host's authentication and gives the user access to
Oracle without providing another password. The username identifying the user in
Oracle must match that used on the host system, prefixed by OPS$, as shown in the
following example:

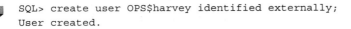

```
SQL> create user OPS$harvey identified externally;
User created.
```

Later, when HARVEY wants to connect to Oracle from a host system command prompt, he can specify the following to do so and does not need to provide a password:

```
C:\windows> c:\oracle\ora81\bin\sqlplus /
```

TIP
You must first be connected directly to the host system (via Telnet on UNIX or at a DOS prompt) in order for host authentication to work.

Finding Information about Users

Once users are created in Oracle, you can look in the dictionary view ALL_USERS to gain some basic information about them, including the username and the day each user was created. Take a look at the following code block:

```
SQL> select * from all_users;
USERNAME                        USER_ID CREATED
------------------------------ --------- ---------
SYS                                   0 23-JUN-99
SYSTEM                                5 23-JUN-99
OUTLN                                11 23-JUN-99
DBSNMP                               18 23-JUN-99
PO8                                  26 17-JUL-00
AURORA$ORB$UNAUTHENTICATED            23 23-JUN-99
JASON                                27 18-JUL-00
STUDENT2                             46 30-OCT-00
STUDENT1                             45 30-OCT-00
SPANKY                               43 30-OCT-00
JASON2                               48 31-OCT-00
SCOTT                                52 19-MAR-01
JASON3                               49 16-NOV-00
JASON10                              50 18-NOV-00
GIANT                                51 08-DEC-00
TURNER                               53 21-MAR-01
```

TIP
The USER_USERS dictionary view also gives important information about your own user ID, related to the advanced password-management features available in Oracle (not tested on OCP

*Exam 1). Take a look at this view and try to figure
out what it contains before moving onto the
exercises at the end of this discussion.*

Getting Users Started with System Privileges

Now that SCOTT has created user TURNER, let's have SCOTT help TURNER get
started by having SCOTT grant TURNER some privileges. Remember, privileges are
the second part of the basic Oracle security model. Privileges are the right to
execute particular SQL statements. The database administrator is a high-level user
with the ability to grant users access to the database and its objects.
Everything you can possibly do in an Oracle database is regulated by privileges. Two
types of privileges exist in Oracle: object privileges and system privileges. *Object
privileges* regulate access to database objects in Oracle, such as querying or
changing data in tables and views, creating foreign key constraints and indexes on
tables, executing PL/SQL programs, and a handful of other activities. Fewer than ten
object privileges can be granted in Oracle, so they are easy to memorize. You'll
learn more about object privileges in the next discussion. *System privileges* govern
every other type of activity in Oracle, such as connecting to the database, creating
tables, creating sequences, creating views, and much, much more.

TIP

*All told, more than 100 separate privileges can be
granted in Oracle, the vast majority of which are
system privileges. We'll focus our discussion only
on those system and object privileges tested on
OCP Exam 1.*

Privileges are given to users with the grant command, and they are taken away
with the revoke command. The ability to grant privileges to other users in the
database rests on users who can administer the privileges. The owner of a database
object can administer object privileges related to that object, whereas the DBA
administers system privileges. We'll keep pretending that SCOTT is the DBA for our
system as we take a look at some grant commands that give TURNER various
system privileges to work on the database:

```
SQL> connect scott/tiger
Connected.
SQL> grant create session to turner;
Grant succeeded.
SQL> grant create table to turner;
Grant succeeded.
```

```
SQL> grant create sequence to turner;
Grant succeeded.
SQL> grant create procedure to turner;
Grant succeeded.
```

Now, when TURNER attempts to connect to Oracle and do some work, he'll be able to

```
SQL> connect turner/ike
Connected.
SQL> create table my_table
  2  (my_column number);
Table created.
```

> **TIP**
> *You can grant multiple privileges at the same time with the* grant *command, such as* grant
> select, update on emp to *ELMO or* grant
> create session, create table to *ELMO.*

Taking Away System Privileges

Now, let's say that management has decided that TURNER is all washed up with our company. KING hands TURNER a pink slip, and TURNER returns to his cubicle to clean out his desk. SCOTT now has to keep TURNER out of Oracle, but let's say he's too busy to do all the work today. SCOTT can simply revoke TURNER's ability to create sessions by using the following command:

```
SQL> connect scott/tiger
Connected.
SQL> revoke create session from turner;
Revoke succeeded.
```

TURNER is quite steamed about being fired, as you might imagine. He has been with the company for a long time and is going through some serious personal issues. While cleaning out his desk, TURNER decides to get even with his employer by sabotaging the data in Oracle. However, because SCOTT has revoked his ability to create database sessions, the following happens to TURNER:

```
SQL> connect turner/ike
ERROR:
ORA-01045: user TURNER lacks CREATE SESSION privilege; logon denied
```

TIP
Even though TURNER can no longer log into
Oracle, he still has all the other privileges that have
been granted to him.

System Privileges to Know for OCP

Several categories of system privileges relate to each object. Those categories
determine the scope of ability that the privilege grantee will have. The classes or
categories of system privileges are listed in this section. Note that in the following
subtopics, the privilege itself gives the ability to perform the action against your own
database objects, and the `any` keyword refers to the ability to perform the action
against any database object of that type in Oracle.

Database Access   These privileges control who accesses the database, when he
or she can access it, and what he or she can do regarding management of his or her
own session. Privileges include `create session`, `alter session`, and
`restricted session`.

Users   These privileges are used to manage users on the Oracle database.
Typically, these privileges are reserved for DBAs or security administrators. Privileges
include `create user`, `become user`, `alter user`, and `drop user`.

Tables   You already know that tables store data in the Oracle database. These
privileges govern which users can create and maintain tables. The privileges include
`create table`, `create any table`, `alter any table`, `backup any`
`table`, `drop any table`, `lock any table`, `comment any table`, `select`
`any table`, `insert any table`, `update any table`, and `delete any`
`table`. The `create table` or `create any table` privilege also enables you to
drop the table. The `create table` privilege also bestows the ability to create
indexes on the table and to run the `analyze` command on the table. To be able to
truncate a table, you must have the `drop any table` privilege granted to you.

Indexes   You already know that indexes are used to improve SQL statement
performance on tables containing lots of row data. The privileges include `create`
`any index`, `alter any index`, and `drop any index`. You should note that
no `create index` system privilege exists. The `create table` privilege also
enables you to alter and drop indexes that you own and that are associated with the
table.

Synonyms   A synonym is a database object that enables you to reference another
object by a different name. A public synonym means that the synonym is available

to every user in the database for the same purpose. The privileges include `create synonym`, `create any synonym`, `drop any synonym`, `create public synonym`, and `drop public synonym`. The `create synonym` privilege also enables you to alter and drop synonyms that you own.

Views   You already know that a view is an object containing a SQL statement that behaves like a table in Oracle, except that it stores no data. The privileges include `create view`, `create any view`, and `drop any view`. The `create view` privilege also enables you to alter and drop views that you own.

Sequences   You already know that a sequence is an object in Oracle that generates numbers according to rules you can define. Privileges include `create sequence`, `create any sequence`, `alter any sequence`, `drop any sequence`, and `select any sequence`. The `create sequence` privilege also enables you to drop sequences that you own.

Roles   Roles are objects that can be used for simplified privilege management. You create a role, grant privileges to it, and then grant the role to users. Privileges include `create role`, `drop any role`, `grant any role`, and `alter any role`.

TIP
We'll talk more about roles later in this chapter.

Transactions   These privileges are for resolving in-doubt distributed transactions being processed on the Oracle database. Privileges include `force transaction` and `force any transaction`.

PL/SQL   There are many different types of PL/SQL blocks in Oracle. These privileges enable you to create, run, and manage those different types of blocks. Privileges include `create procedure`, `create any procedure`, `alter any procedure`, `drop any procedure`, and `execute any procedure`. The `create procedure` privilege also enables you to alter and drop PL/SQL blocks that you own.

Triggers   A trigger is a PL/SQL block in Oracle that executes when a specified DML activity occurs on the table to which the trigger is associated. Privileges include `create trigger`, `create any trigger`, `alter any trigger`, and `drop any trigger`. The `create trigger` privilege also enables you to alter and drop triggers that you own.

Using Dictionary Views to Display Privileges

To display privileges associated with users and roles, you can use the following views:

- ■ **USER_SYS_PRIVS**   Shows all system privileges associated with this user
- ■ **SESSION_PRIVS**   Shows all privileges available in this session

Changing Passwords

Security in the database is a serious matter, so users have to keep their passwords a secret. Most small organizations let the DBA handle database security, but larger ones use a security administrator. However, depending on the environment, developers, DBAs, or even end users may need to understand the options available in the Oracle security model for the version of Oracle the organization uses.

Toward that end of tighter security, SCOTT's new responsibilities as DBA require that he change his password to something less obvious. SCOTT must do this because he's worried that TURNER may try to log into Oracle using the SCOTT user ID and password. Like tables, passwords can contain alphanumeric characters (including $, #, and _). Let's look at what SCOTT must do with the `alter user` command in order to change his password:

```
SQL> connect scott/tiger
Connected.
SQL> alter user scott identified by 1#secure_pw;
User altered.
```

TIP
Several other options are available in both the `create user` *and* `alter user` *commands. However, basic user creation and password definition is all that's tested in OCP. If password management piques your interest, you can check out the Oracle documentation to see what other options are available. More advanced user management is tested on OCP Exam 2 in the DBA track.*

For Review

1. Be sure you can identify the two basic components of the Oracle security model: password authentication and privilege administration.

2. Know how to create a user along with his or her password using the `create user` command. Also, be sure you know how to change a password using the `alter user` command.

3. Understand where to look in the data dictionary for information about users.

4. Be sure you know what system and object privileges are and how to use `grant` and `revoke` to give out and take away privileges.

Exercises

1. User IMADBA wants to give user DAVIS, a brand-new employee who started today, the ability to create tables in the Oracle database. Which of the following choices identifies a step that doesn't need to take place before DAVIS can start creating tables?

   A. `create user davis identified by new_employee;`

   B. `grant create session to davis;`

   C. `grant create table to davis;`

   D. `grant create public synonym to davis;`

2. This is the privilege required for connecting to the Oracle database:

   _____

3. This is the privilege required for creating some public synonyms:

   _____

4. This is the clause used in the `alter user` statement for changing a password: _____

Answer Key
1. D. 2. `create session` 3. `create public synonym` 3. `identified by`

Granting and Revoking Object Privileges

As mentioned before, every possible activity in Oracle is governed by privileges. We already covered system privileges, so let's talk now about object privileges. All granting of object privileges is managed with the `grant` command. In order to grant an object privilege, the grantor must either have been granted the privilege with the `with grant option` privilege or must own the object. To grant an object privilege, the grantor of the privilege must determine the level of access a user requires on the object. Then, the privilege must be granted. An *object privilege* is a privilege or right to perform a particular action on a specific table, view, sequence, or procedure. Each object has a particular set of grantable privileges.

Available Object Privileges

The object privileges for any database object belong to the user who created that object. Object privileges can be granted to other users for the purpose of enabling them to access and manipulate the object. Object privileges include the following:

- **select**   Permits the grantee of this object privilege to access the data in a table, sequence, view, or snapshot.

- **insert**   Permits the grantee of this object privilege to insert data into a table or, in some cases, a view. You can also restrict this privilege to specified columns of a table.

- **update**   Permits the grantee of this object privilege to update data in a table or view. You can also restrict this privilege to specified columns of a table.

- **delete**   Permits the grantee of this object privilege to delete data from a table or view. You can also restrict this privilege to specified columns of a table.

- **alter**   Permits the grantee of this object privilege to alter the definition of a table or sequence *only*; the `alter` privileges on all other database objects are considered system privileges.

- **index**   Permits the grantee of this object privilege to create an index on a table already defined.

- **references**   Permits the grantee of this object privilege to create or alter a table in order to create a foreign key constraint against data in the referenced table.

- **execute**   Permits the grantee of this object privilege to run a stored procedure or function.

TIP
Oracle has less than ten object privileges. In contrast, it has dozens of system privileges. If you want an easy way to distinguish the two, try

memorizing the object privileges. Then, you can simply assume that any privilege you encounter on the OCP exam that is not an object privilege is a system privilege.

Granting Object Privileges in Oracle

The administrative abilities over an object privilege include the ability to grant the privilege or revoke it from anyone as well as the ability to grant the object privilege to another user with administrative ability over the privilege. For these examples, let's say that KING has reconsidered his haste in firing TURNER and has allowed TURNER back on a probationary basis. Now, SCOTT has to set up TURNER with access to the EMP table, as follows:

```
SQL> GRANT select, update, insert ON emp TO turner;
Grant succeeded.
SQL> GRANT references ON emp.empno TO turner;
Grant succeeded.
SQL> GRANT select, update, insert ON emp TO turner;
Grant succeeded.
```

Open to the Public

Another aspect of privileges and access to the database involves a special user on the database. This user is called PUBLIC. If a system privilege or object privilege is granted to the PUBLIC user, then every user in the database has that privilege. Typically, it is not advised that the DBA should grant many privileges or roles to PUBLIC, because if a privilege or role ever needs to be revoked, then every stored package, procedure, or function will need to be recompiled. Let's take a look:

```
SQL> GRANT select, update, insert ON emp TO public;
Grant succeeded.
```

TIP
Roles can be granted to the PUBLIC user as well. We'll talk more about roles in the next discussion.

Granting Object Privileges All at Once

The keyword `all` can be use as a consolidated method for granting object privileges related to a table. Note that `all` in this context is not a privilege; it is merely a specification for all object privileges for a database object. The following code block shows how `all` is used:

```
SQL> GRANT ALL ON emp TO turner;
Grant succeeded.
```

Giving Administrative Ability along with Privileges

When another user grants you a privilege, you then have the ability to perform whatever task the privilege enables you to do. However, you usually can't grant the privilege to others, nor can you relinquish the privilege without help of the user who granted the privilege to you. If you want some additional power to administer the privilege granted to you, the user who gave you the privilege must also give you administrative control over that privilege. For example, let's say KING now completely trusts TURNER to manage the creation of tables (a system privilege) and wants to give him access to the EMP table (an object privilege). Therefore, KING tells SCOTT to give TURNER administrative control over both these privileges, as follows:

```
SQL> GRANT CREATE TABLE TO turner WITH ADMIN OPTION;
Grant succeeded.
SQL> GRANT SELECT, UPDATE ON turner TO SPANKY WITH GRANT OPTION;
Grant succeeded.
```

TIP
The GRANT OPTION is not valid when granting an object privilege to a role. You'll learn more about roles later in this chapter.

A system privilege or role can be granted with the ADMIN OPTION. A grantee with this option has several expanded capabilities. The grantee can grant or revoke the system privilege or role to or from any user or other role in the database. However, a user cannot revoke a role from himself. The grantee can further grant the system privilege or role with the ADMIN OPTION. The grantee of a role can alter or drop the role.

The `with admin option` clause gives TURNER the ability to give or take away the `create table` *system* privilege to others. The `with grant option` clause gives TURNER that same ability for the `select` and `update` *object* privileges on table EMP. TURNER can make other users administrators of those privileges as well.

TIP
Finally, if a role is granted using the with admin
option *clause, the grantee can alter the role or
even remove it. You'll learn more about roles in the
next discussion.*

You can grant INSERT, UPDATE, or REFERENCES privileges on individual
columns in a table.

Revoking Object Privileges in Oracle

Let's say that, once again, KING changed his mind and has fired TURNER. Revoking
object privileges is handled with the revoke command. If you want to revoke
system or object privileges granted with the with admin option clause or an
object privilege granted with the with grant option clause, no additional
syntax is required for doing so. Simply revoke the privilege, and the ability to
administer that privilege gets revoked, too. You can see some examples of using this
command for object privileges in the following code block:

```
SQL> revoke select, update, insert ON emp from turner;
Revoke succeeded.
SQL> revoke references ON emp.empno from turner;
Revoke succeeded.
SQL> revoke select, update, insert on emp from turner;
Revoke succeeded.
```

TIP
*When the CASCADE CONSTRAINTS option is
specified, any foreign key constraints currently
defined that use the revoked REFERENCES privilege
are dropped.*

Cascading Effects of Revoking System Privileges

Consider the following situation related to the cascading effects of system privileges.
User SCOTT gives TURNER the ability to create tables with administrative ability,
and TURNER turns around and gives the same privilege to FORD, an aging auto
factory worker who switched into computer programming:

```
SQL> connect scott/tiger
Connected.
SQL> grant create table to turner with admin option;
```

```
Grant succeeded.
SQL> connect turner/ike
Connected.
SQL> create table my_table
  2  (my_column number);
Table created.
SQL> grant create table to ford;
Grant succeeded.
SQL> connect ford/henry
Connected.
SQL> create table my_table
  2  (my_column number);
Table created.
```

SCOTT finds out that TURNER gave the `create table` privilege to FORD, who is only supposed to be able to create PL/SQL programs. SCOTT gets mad at TURNER and revokes the `create table` privilege from TURNER, along with the administrative ability, as follows:

```
SQL> connect scott/tiger
Connected.
SQL> revoke create table from turner;
Revoke succeeded.
```

Will FORD continue to be able to create tables? Let's see:

```
SQL> connect ford/henry
Connected.
SQL> create table my_table_2
  2  (my_column number);
Table created.
```

As you can see, FORD still has the ability to create tables, even though TURNER (the guy who gave FORD the privilege) does not. This means that no cascading effects of revoking system privileges from users occur. FORD keeps his ability to create tables, and TURNER's table, called MY_TABLE, doesn't get dropped. If you want to take away a system privilege from a user, you have to explicitly revoke that privilege directly from the user as well as drop whatever objects that user has created while having the privilege.

Cascading Effects of Revoking Object Privileges
Now let's consider the same situation, only this time, the privilege in question is an object privilege. SCOTT grants `select` access on EMP to TURNER with

administrative ability, who turns around and gives it to FORD. Check it out in the following block:

```
SQL> connect scott/tiger
Connected.
SQL> grant select on emp to turner with grant option;
Grant succeeded.
SQL> connect turner/ike
Connected.
SQL> select ename, job from scott.emp
  2  where empno =7844;
ENAME      JOB
---------- ---------
TURNER     SALESMAN
SQL> grant select on scott.emp to ford;
Grant succeeded.
SQL> connect ford/henry
Connected.
SQL> select ename, job from scott.emp
  2  where empno = 7369;
ENAME      JOB
---------- ---------
SMITH      CLERK
```

SCOTT then finds out what TURNER did and revokes the privilege from TURNER:

```
SQL> connect scott/tiger
Connected.
SQL> revoke select on emp from turner;
Revoke succeeded.
```

Will FORD still be able to access table EMP? Take a look a the following:

```
SQL> connect ford/henry
Connected.
SQL> select ename, job
  2  from scott.emp
  3  where empno = 7360;
from scott.emp
          *
ERROR at line 2:
ORA-00942: table or view does not exist
```

So, when an object privilege is revoked from a grantor of that privilege, all grantees receiving the privilege from the grantor also lose the privilege. However, in cases where the object privilege involves `update`, `insert`, or `delete`, if subsequent grantees have made changes to data using the privilege, the rows already changed don't get magically transformed back the way they were before.

Facts to Remember about Granting and Revoking Object Privileges

You should try to remember the following facts about granting and revoking object privileges before taking OCP:

■ If a privilege has been granted on two individual columns, the privilege cannot be revoked on only one column—the privilege must be revoked entirely and then regranted on the individual column.

■ If the user has been given the `references` privilege and has used it to create a foreign key constraint to another table, you must use the `cascade constraints` clause to revoke the `references` privilege (otherwise, the revoke will fail), as follows:

```
REVOKE REFERENCES ON emp FROM spanky CASCADE CONSTRAINTS.
```

■ The `insert`, `update`, and `references` privileges can be granted on columns within the database object. However, if a user has the `insert` privilege on several columns in a table but not all columns, the privilege administrator must ensure that no columns in the table that do not have the `insert` privilege granted are not NULL columns.

■ If a user has the ability to execute a stored procedure owned by another user, and the procedure accesses some tables, the object privileges required to access those tables must be granted to the *owner* of the procedure, not the user to whom `execute` privileges were granted. What's more, the privileges must be granted directly to the user, not through a role.

■ Depending upon what is granted or revoked, a grant or revoke takes effect at different times. All grants/revokes of privileges (system and schema object) to users, roles, or PUBLIC are immediately observed. All grants/revokes of roles to users, other roles, or PUBLIC are observed only when a current user session issues a SET ROLE statement to reenable the role after the grant/revoke, or when a new user session is created after the grant/revoke.

For Review

1. Be sure you can identify all the object privileges and use the `grant` and `revoke` commands to give the privileges to users and take them away.

2. Know what happens when you grant object privileges to the PUBLIC user. Know when and how to use the `all` keyword when granting object privileges on a table to a user.

3. Understand how to grant administrative abilities over a privilege to other users along with the privilege itself. Memorize the syntax difference between granting system privileges with the `with admin option` clause and granting object privileges with the `with grant option` clause.

4. Be sure you know the differences between system and object privileges with respect to cascading effects of revoking those privileges.

5. Make sure you understand all the points I made about special conditions with respect to granting and revoking object privileges.

Exercises

1. You want to grant user TIMOTHY the ability to update data in the EMP table as well as the ability to administer that access for others. Which of the following commands would you issue?

   A. `grant update to timothy;`

   B. `grant update on emp to timothy;`

   C. `grant update on emp to timothy with grant option;`

   D. `grant update on emp to timothy with admin option;`

2. User REED can administer the `create session` privilege. User REED grants the same `create session` privilege to MANN using the `with admin option` clause. MANN then grants the privilege to SNOW. REED discovers MANN issued the privilege to SNOW and revokes the privilege from MANN. Who can connect to Oracle?

   A. REED only

   B. SNOW and MANN only

   C. REED, MANN, and SNOW

   D. REED and SNOW only

3. User SNOW owns table SALES, and she grants `delete` privileges to user REED using the `with grant option` clause. REED then grants `delete` privileges on SALES to MANN. SNOW discovers MANN has the privilege and revokes it from REED. Which of the following users can delete data from the SALES table?

   A. MANN only

   B. SNOW only

   C. SNOW and MANN only

   D. REED and MANN only

4. When this user has the privilege, everyone has the privilege:

   _____

5. When revoking the references privilege after a user has built a foreign key constraint using that privilege, you must include this clause (two words):

   _____

Answer Key
1. C. 2. D. 3. B. 4. Public. 5. `cascade constraints`

Using Roles to Manage Database Access

When your databases has lots of tables, object privileges can become unwieldy and hard to manage. You can simplify the management of privileges with the use of a database object called a *role*. A role acts in two capacities in the database. First, the role can act as a focal point for grouping the privileges to execute certain tasks. Second, the role can act as a "virtual user" of a database, to which all the object privileges required to execute a certain job function can be granted, such as data entry, manager review, batch processing, and so on. Figure 8-1 illustrates how to manage privileges with roles. In order to use roles, your privilege-management process must consist of four steps:

1. You must logically group certain types of users together according to the privileges they need to do their jobs.

2. You must define a role (or roles) for each user type.

3. You must grant the appropriate privileges to each of the roles.

4. You can then grant the roles to specific users of each type.

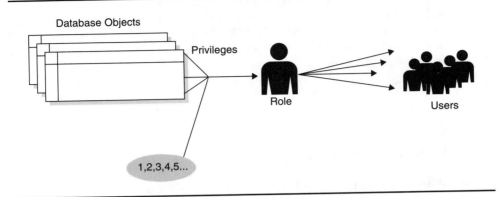

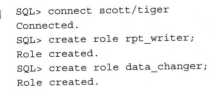

FIGURE 8-1. *Managing privileges with roles*

Creating Roles to Correspond to User Types

Step 1 is a process that can happen outside the database. A role mechanism can be used to provide authorization. A single person or a group of people can be granted a role or a group of roles. One role can be granted in turn to other roles. By defining different types of roles, administrators can manage access privileges much more easily. You simply sit down and think to yourself, how many different purposes will users be accessing this application for? Once this step is complete, you can create the different roles required to manage the privileges needed for each job function. Let's say people using the EMP table have two different job roles: those who can query the table and those who can add records to the table. The next step is to create roles that correspond to each activity. This architecture of using roles as a middle layer for granting privileges greatly simplifies administration of user privileges. Let's take a look at how to create the appropriate roles:

```
SQL> connect scott/tiger
Connected.
SQL> create role rpt_writer;
Role created.
SQL> create role data_changer;
Role created.
```

TIP
You must have the CREATE ROLE system privilege to create a role.

Modifying Roles

Let's say that after we create our roles, we realize that changing records in the EMP table is serious business. To create an added safeguard against someone making a change to the EMP table in error, the DATA_CHANGER role can be altered to require a password by using the `alter role identified by` statement. Anyone wanting to modify data in EMP with the privileges given via the DATA_CHANGER role must first supply a password. Code for altering the role is shown in the following example:

```
SQL> alter role data_changer
  2  identified by highly#secure;
Role altered.
```

Granting Privileges to Roles

The next step is to grant object privileges to roles. You can accomplish this task using the same command as you would use to grant privileges directly to users—the `grant` command. The following code block demonstrates how to grant privileges to both our roles:

```
SQL> grant select on emp to rpt_writer;
Grant succeeded.
SQL> grant update, delete, insert on emp to data_changer;
Grant succeeded.
```

TIP
Revoking privileges from roles works the same way as it does for users. System privileges are granted and revoked with roles in the exact same way they are with users as well.

Granting Roles to Users

Once a role is created and privileges are granted to it, the role can then be granted to users. This step is accomplished with the `grant` command. Let's see an example of how this is done:

```
SQL> grant rpt_writer to turner;
Grant succeeded.
SQL> grant data_changer to ford;
Grant succeeded.
```

TIP
If a role already granted to a user is later granted another privilege, that additional privilege is available to the user immediately. The same statement can be made for privileges revoked from roles already granted to users, too.

Defining User Default Roles

Now user TURNER can execute all the privileges given to him via the RPT_WRITER role, and user FORD can do the same with the privileges given from DATA_CHANGER. Or can he? Recall that we specified that DATA_CHANGER requires a password in order for the grantee to utilize its privileges. Let's make a little change to FORD's user ID so that this status will take effect:

```
SQL> alter user ford default role none;
User altered.
```

TIP
You can use the following keywords in the `alter user default role` *command to define default roles for users:* `all, all except rolename,` *and* `none`*. Note that users usually cannot issue* `alter user default role` *themselves to change their default roles—only a privileged user such as the DBA can do it for them.*

By default, when a role is granted to a user, that role becomes a default role for the user. We changed FORD's default role with the preceding code so that FORD has no role. Let's see how this factor affects things when FORD tries to modify the contents of the EMP table:

```
SQL> connect ford/henry
Connected.
SQL> insert into scott.emp (empno, ename, job)
  2  values (1234, 'SMITHERS','MANAGER');
insert into scott.emp (empno, ename, job)
            *
ERROR at line 1:
ORA-00942: table or view does not exist
```

TIP
Roles can be granted to other roles!

Enabling the Current Role

FORD knows he is supposed to be able to accomplish this task because he has the DATA_CHANGER role. Then he remembers that this role has a password on it. FORD can use the set role command to enable the DATA_CHANGER role in the following way:

```
SQL> set role data_changer identified by highly#secure;
Role set.
```

Now FORD can make the change he needs to make:

```
SQL> insert into scott.emp (empno, ename, job)
  2  values (1234, 'SMITHERS','MANAGER');
1 row created.
```

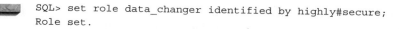

TIP
You must already have been granted the roles that you name in the SET ROLE statement. Also, you can disable all roles with the SET ROLE NONE statement.

Revoking and Dropping Roles

Finally, a role can be revoked by the role's owner or by a privileged administrative user using the revoke statement, much like revoking privileges:

```
SQL> connect scott/tiger
Connected.
SQL> revoke rpt_writer from turner;
Revoke succeeded.
SQL> revoke data_changer from ford;
Revoke succeeded.
```

Roles can be deleted from the database using the `drop role` statement. When a role is dropped, the associated privileges are revoked from the users granted the role. The following code block shows how to eliminate roles from Oracle:

```
SQL> connect scott/tiger
Connected.
SQL> drop role rpt_writer;
Role dropped.
SQL> drop role data_changer;
Role dropped.
```

Some Predefined Roles Available in Oracle

Some special roles are available to the users of a database. The roles available at database creation from Oracle7 onward include the CONNECT, RESOURCE, DBA, EXP_FULL_DATABASE, and IMP_FULL_DATABASE roles. Additionally, Oracle adds the roles DELETE_CATALOG_ROLE, EXECUTE_CATALOG_ROLE, and SELECT_CATALOG_ROLE to the mix, and much more. The predefined roles you might need to know about for OCP Exam 1 include the following:

- **CONNECT**   Enables the user extensive development ability within his or her own user schema, including the ability to perform `create table`, `create cluster`, `create session`, `create view`, `create sequence`, and more. The privileges associated with this role are platform specific; therefore, the role can contain a different number of privileges, but typically the role never enables the creation of stored procedures.

- **RESOURCE**   Enables the user moderate development ability within his or her own user schema, such as the ability to execute `create table`, `create cluster`, `create trigger`, and `create procedure`. The privileges associated with this role are platform specific; therefore, the role can contain a different number of privileges.

- **DBA**   Enables the user to administer and use all system privileges.

Dictionary Views for Roles

The following views are available in the Oracle data dictionary pertaining to role information:

- **USER_ROLE_PRIVS**   Identifies the roles granted to you
- **ROLE_ROLE_PRIVS**   Identifies the roles granted to other roles in the database
- **ROLE_TAB_PRIVS**   Identifies object privileges granted to roles

- **ROLE_SYS_PRIVS** Identifies system privileges granted to roles
- **SESSION_ROLES** Identifies roles available to the current session

For Review

1. Know what a role is and how it can assist you in managing privileges in Oracle. Understand the four steps required for managing privileges when you want to do so with roles.

2. Know how to use the `create role`, `alter role identified by`, `alter user default role`, `set role`, and `drop role` commands. Also, understand how to use the `grant` and `revoke` commands with respect to roles.

3. When a role has an associated password, you shouldn't grant it to users as a default role. By granting a role to a user as a non-default role, you force the grantee to enable the role using the `set role identified by` command. This extra step enforces a higher level of security on that user when the user wants to employ the privileges granted by the role.

4. Know the available dictionary views that contain information about roles.

Exercises

1. **User THOMAS has been granted the role SALES_ANALYZER, which gives her to access the SALES table for writing reports. However, when she tries to do so, she gets the following error:**

   ```
   ORA-00942: table or view does not exist.
   ```

   Which of the following statements can she issue in order to resolve the problem?

   A. `alter user thomas default role sales_analyzer;`

   B. `set role sales_analyzer;`

   C. `grant select on sales to sales_analyzer;`

   D. `grant sales_analyzer to thomas;`

2. **User FRANKLIN owns the PROFITS table and the SALES_ANALYZER role, which has already been granted to DAVIS. FRANKLIN grants `select` privileges on PROFITS to the SALES_ANALYZER role. At what point will that privilege be made available to DAVIS?**

   A. The next time DAVIS logs into Oracle

   B. The next time FRANKLIN grants the SALES_ANALYZER role to DAVIS

    C. The next time FRANKLIN grants the privilege to SALES_ANALYZER

    D. Immediately after the privilege is granted to SALES_ANALYZER

3. **You are defining default roles for a user. Under which of the following circumstances should a role not be made a default role for a user?**

    A. When the role has object privileges granted to it

    B. When the role has system privileges granted to it

    C. When the role has a password assigned to it

    D. When the role has other roles assigned to it

4. **This dictionary view can identify the roles available to you in your current connection to Oracle:** _____

Answer Key
1. B. 2. D. 3. C. 4. SESSION_ROLES.

Chapter Summary

This chapter has covered a great deal of information you need to know about user access control in the Oracle database. We started the chapter by covering how to create users in Oracle. We then discussed privileges, covering what they are and how to use them to control access to information in the Oracle database. You learned that access to everything in the database is controlled by a privilege. We also discussed how to use roles to manage privileges more efficiently.

Two-Minute Drill

- The Oracle database security model consists of two parts: limiting user access with password authentication and controlling object use with privileges.

- Available privileges in Oracle include system privileges, for maintaining database objects, and object privileges, for accessing and manipulating data in database objects.

■ Changing a password can be performed by a user with the `alter user identified by` statement.

■ Granting system and object privileges is accomplished with the `grant` command.

■ Taking away system and object privileges is accomplished with the `revoke` command.

■ Creating a synonym is accomplished with the `create public synonym` command.

Fill-in-the-Blank Questions

1. This type of database object can act as an intermediary for consolidating privileges granted to users around job functions:

   _____

2. This command is used for enabling a default role in Oracle:

   _____

3. This clause is used for defining a password for a user:

   _____

4. This command is used for giving privileges to users:

   _____

5. This command is used for taking privileges away from users:

   _____

Chapter Questions

1. **You are granting privileges on your table to another user. Which object privilege enables the user to create his or her own table with a foreign key on a column in your table?**

   A. `references`

   B. `index`

   C. `select`

   D. `delete`

2. **Which of the following statements are true about roles? (Choose three.)**

   A. Roles can be granted to other roles.

   B. Privileges can be granted to roles.

   C. Roles can be granted to users.

   D. Roles can be granted to synonyms.

3. **You want to connect to the Oracle database. Which of the following choices identifies a method that will *not* be required in order for you to connect?**

   A. Granting `create session` privilege

   B. Granting the CONNECT role

   C. Issuing the `create user` statement

   D. Granting the `create table` privilege

4. **A user named JACOB is configured in Oracle so that he can create some tables. Then user ESAU is configured to insert some data into JACOB's tables with administrative ability. JACOB then revokes all insert privileges from ESAU. Which of the following choices identifies an event that will happen when the DBA revokes ESAU's `insert` privilege?**

   A. ESAU will be able to insert data into JACOB's tables.

   B. ESAU's records added to JACOB's tables will be removed

   C. Any users ESAU granted insert access to JACOB's tables will no longer have those privileges.

   D. Any users ESAU granted insert access to JACOB's tables will continue to have those privileges.

5. **You are attempting to grant the `create table` privilege to user TABLEMAKER with administrative ability. Which of the following choices identifies the proper `with` clause you will use for this purpose?**

   A. `with admin option`

   B. `with grant option`

   C. `with check option`

   D. `with summary as`

Fill-in-the-Blank Answers

1. Role

2. set role

3. identified by

4. grant

5. revoke

Answers to Chapter Questions

1. A. references

Explanation The references privilege gives the user the ability to refer back to your table in order to link to it via a foreign key from his or her table to yours. Choice B is incorrect because the index privilege enables the user to create an index on a table, whereas choice C is incorrect because the select privilege enables the user to query data in your table. Finally, choice D is incorrect because the insert privilege is only required for enabling the user to insert data into your table.

2. A, B, and C.

Explanation Choice D is the only option not available to managing roles. Roles cannot be granted to synonyms. Refer to the discussion of roles and privileges in this chapter.

3. D. Granting the create table privilege

Explanation You do not need the create table privilege in order to connect to the Oracle database. Choice A is incorrect because the create session privilege is required for connecting to Oracle. Choice B is incorrect because the CONNECT role has the create session privilege granted to it to enable users to connect to Oracle. Choice C is incorrect because you have to create the user first before that user can connect to Oracle.

4. C. Any users ESAU granted insert access to JACOB's tables will no longer have those privileges.

Explanation Cascading effects for revoking object privileges occur in Oracle. If a user who was granted administrative abilities over an object privilege grants that privileges to others, and that user then has the object privilege revoked, then all users to whom that user granted the object privilege will also lose the privilege. Choice A is incorrect because ESAU will no longer have insert access to JACOB's tables. Choice B is incorrect because any records ESAU added to JACOB's tables will be removed. Choice D is incorrect because it is the logical opposite of the correct answer, choice C.

5. A. with admin option

Explanation   The with admin option clause is used for granting system privileges like create table with administrative ability. The with grant option clause is used for granting object privileges like insert with administrative ability, making choice B incorrect. Choice C is incorrect because the with check option is used for enforcing heightened security on changing data in tables via views on those tables. Finally, choice D is incorrect because the with summary as clause is used for eliminating redundancy in subqueries.

PART
II

OCA Oracle9i SQL
Practice Exams

CHAPTER
9

OCA Exam 1:
Introduction to SQL

CP Exam 1 in the Oracle DBA track covers concepts and practices involving the use of SQL commands. To pass this exam, you need to demonstrate an understanding of the basic SQL constructs available in Oracle, including built-in functions. You should also understand the basic concepts of an Oracle relational database management system (RDBMS). In more recent editions of OCP Exam 1, the focus has shifted to a complete understanding of use of the SQL programming language. In addition, new features introduced in Oracle9*i* are tested, so you should also be sure you understand these new features.

Practice Exam I

1. You are formulating a SQL statement to retrieve data from Oracle. Which of the following SQL statements is invalid?

   A. `select NAME, JERSEY_NO where Jersey_No = 6;`

   B. `select NAME, JERSEY_NO from PLAYERS;`

   C. `select * from PLAYERS where JERSEY_NO = 6;`

   D. `select JERSEY_NO from PLAYERS;`

2. You are processing some data changes in your SQL*Plus session as part of one transaction. Which of the following choices does not typically indicate the end of a transaction?

   A. Issuing an `update` statement

   B. Issuing a `commit` statement

   C. Issuing a `rollback` statement

   D. Ending your session

3. You have just removed 1,700 rows from a table. In order to save the changes you've made to the database, which of the following statements is used?

   A. `savepoint`

   B. `commit`

   C. `rollback`

   D. `set transaction`

4. To identify the columns that are indexed exclusively as the result of their inclusion in a constraint, which of the following dictionary views is appropriate?

    A.   USER_INDEXES

    B.   USER_TAB_COLUMNS

    C.   USER_COLUMNS

    D.   USER_CONS_COLUMNS

5. You are creating some tables in your database as part of the logical data model. Which of the following constraints can only be created as a column constraint (that is, not as a table constraint) either when you create or alter the table?

    A.   Unique

    B.   Foreign key

    C.   Check

    D.   Not NULL

6. You have a table with three associated indexes, two triggers, two references to that table from other tables, and a view. You issue the `drop table cascade constraints` statement. Which of the following objects will still remain after the statement is issued?

    A.   The triggers

    B.   The indexes

    C.   The foreign keys in the other tables

    D.   The view

7. You are using SQL operations in Oracle. All of the following DATE functions return a DATE datatype except one. Which one is it?

    A.   NEW_TIME

    B.   LAST_DAY

    C.   ADD_MONTHS

    D.   MONTHS_BETWEEN

8. You issue a `select` statement on the BANK_ACCT table containing the `order by` clause. Which of the following uses of the `order by` clause would produce an error?

   A. `order by acctno DESC;`

   B. `order by 1;`

   C. `order by sqrt(1);`

   D. `order by acctno ASC;`

9. You execute the query `select 5 + 4 from DUAL`. You have never inserted data into the DUAL table before. Which of the following statements best describes the DUAL table?

   A. Dictionary view containing two schema names

   B. Table with one column and one row used in various operations

   C. Dictionary view containing two index names

   D. Table with two columns and no rows used in various operations

10. You issue the following statement:

    ```
    SELECT DECODE(ACCTNO, 123456, 'CLOSED', 654321, 'SEIZED',
    590395, 'TRANSFER','ACTIVE') FROM BANK_ACCT;
    ```

    If the value for ACCTNO is 503952, what information will this statement display?

    A. ACTIVE

    B. TRANSFER

    C. SEIZED

    D. CLOSED

11. You are entering several dozen rows of data into the BANK_ACCT table. Which of the following statements enables you to execute the same statement again and again, entering different values for variables at statement runtime?

    A. `insert into BANK_ACCT (ACCTNO, NAME) VALUES (123456,'SMITH');`

    B. `insert into BANK_ACCT (ACCTNO, NAME) VALUES (VAR1, VAR2);`

   C. `insert into BANK_ACCT (ACCTNO, NAME) VALUES (&VAR1, '&VAR2');`

   D. `insert into BANK_ACCT (select ACCTNO, NAME from EMP_BANK_ACCTS);`

12. You execute the following SQL statement: `select ADD_MONTHS ('28-APR-97',120) from DUAL`. What will Oracle return?

   A. 28-APR-03

   B. 28-APR-07

   C. 28-APR-13

   D. 28-APR-17

13. On Monday, June 26, 2037, at 10:30 P.M., you issue the following statement against an Oracle database:

```
ALTER SESSION SET NLS_DATE_FORMAT =
'DAY MONTH DD, YYYY: HH:MIAM';
```

Then you issue the following statement:

```
SELECT SYSDATE FROM DUAL;
```

What will Oracle return?

   A. 26-JUN-37

   B. June 26, 2037, 22:30

   C. 26-JUN-2037

   D. MONDAY JUNE 26, 2037: 10:30PM

14. You want to join the data from two tables, A and B, into one result set and display that set in your session. Tables A and B have a common column, called C in both tables. Which of the following choices correctly displays the `where` clause you should use if you want to see the data in table A where the value in column C equals 5, even when no corresponding value appears in table B?

   A. `where A.C = 5 AND A.C = B.C;`

   B. `where A.C = 5 AND A.C = B.C (+);`

   C. `where A.C = 5 AND A.C (+) = B.C(+);`

   D. `where A.C = 5;`

15. Each of the following statements is true about associated columns and datatypes except one. Which of the following statements is not true?

   A. A column designed to hold data in a table must be declared with a datatype large enough to hold values for that column.

   B. When creating composite primary keys, the datatypes in all columns within the primary key must be the same datatype.

   C. When creating referential integrity constraints between two tables, the datatype of the referenced column in the parent table must be identical to the referencing column in the child.

   D. When creating record variables designed to hold a row's worth of data, each element's datatype in the record must be large enough to hold the associated column from the table.

16. You have a group of values from a column in a table, and you would like to perform a group operation on them. Each of the following functions operates on data from all rows as a group except for which of the following choices?

   A. avg ( )

   B. sqrt ( )

   C. count ( )

   D. stddev ( )

17. You have a situation where you need to use the nvl ( ) function. All the following statements about the nvl ( ) function are true except one. Which is it?

   A. nvl ( ) returns the second value passed if the first value is NULL.

   B. nvl ( ) handles values of many different datatypes.

   C. nvl ( ) returns NULL if the first value is not equal to the second.

   D. Both the values passed for nvl ( ) must be the same datatype.

18. You create a sequence with the following statement:

```
CREATE SEQUENCE MY_SEQ
START WITH 394
INCREMENT BY 12
NOMINVALUE
NOMAXVALUE
NOCACHE
NOCYCLE;
```

A user issues SQL statements to obtain NEXTVAL three times, and then issues SQL statements to obtain CURRVAL four times. What is the current value of the sequence?

A. 406

B. 418

C. 430

D. 442

19. Table EMP has 17,394,430 rows in it. You issue a delete from EMP statement, followed by a commit. Then you issue a select count (*) to find out how many rows are in the table. Several minutes later, Oracle returns zero. Why did it take so long for Oracle to obtain this information?

    A. The table was not empty.

    B. The high-water mark was not reset.

    C. Oracle always performs slowly after a commit is issued.

    D. The table data did not exist to be counted anymore.

20. After creating a view, you realize that several columns were left out. Which of the following statements should you issue in order to add some columns to your view?

    A. alter view

    B. create or replace view

    C. insert into view

    D. create view

21. You are testing several SQL statements for accuracy and usefulness. A SQL statement will result in a Cartesian product as the result of which of the following items?

    A. A join statement without a where clause

    B. The result of the sum ( ) operation

    C. select * from DUAL

    D. The result of the avg ( ) operation

22. **In order to set your SQL*Plus session so that your NLS_DATE_FORMAT information is altered in a specific way every time you log into Oracle, what method should you use?**

    A. Setting preferences in the appropriate menu option

    B. Creating an appropriate `login.sql` file

    C. Issuing the `alter user` statement

    D. Issuing the `alter table` statement

23. **The EMP_SALARY table has two columns: EMP_USER and SALARY. EMP_USER is set to be the same as the Oracle username. To allow user MARTHA, the salary administrator, to see her own salary only, you create a view with the following statement:**

    ```
    CREATE VIEW EMP_SAL_VW
    AS SELECT EMP_USER, SALARY
    FROM EMP_SALARY
    WHERE EMP_USER = 'MARTHA';
    ```

    Later, you decide to deploy this view to other users. Which of the following choices identifies a revision of this view that would prevent users from seeing any salary information other than their own?

    A. `create or replace view emp_sal_vw as select emp_user,_salary from emp_salary where emp_user <> user;`

    B. `create or replace view emp_sal_vw as select emp_user,_salary from emp_salary where emp_user = user;`

    C. `create or replace view emp_sal_vw as select emp_user,_salary from emp_salary where emp_user <> 'MARTHA';`

    D. `create or replace view emp_sal_vw as select emp_user,_salary from emp_salary where emp_user in (select emp_user from emp_salary where emp_user <> 'MARTHA');`

24. **You are trying to store data in an Oracle table. All of the following scalar datatypes can be stored in an Oracle database except one. Which is it?**

    A. CHAR

    B. RAW

    C. DATE

    D. INTEGER

25. **You are performing some conversion operations in your SQL*Plus session. To convert a date value into a text string, you should use which of the following conversion functions?**

    A. CONVERT

    B. TO_CHAR

    C. TO_NUMBER

    D. TO_DATE

26. **Your attempt to read the trigger code stored in the Oracle data dictionary view ALL_TRIGGERS has encountered a problem. The contents of the TRIGGER_BODY column appear to be getting cut off at the end. In order to resolve this problem, which of the following measures is appropriate?**

    A. Grant appropriate `select` privileges on ALL_TRIGGERS to yourself.

    B. Increase your memory allocation limit with the `alter user` statement.

    C. Use the `set` command to allow for larger LONG column values.

    D. Drop and recreate the ALL_TRIGGERS view.

27. **You issue the following `update` statement against the Oracle database:**

```
UPDATE BANK_ACCT SET NAME = 'SHAW';
```

    Which records will be updated in that table?

    A. The first record only

    B. All records

    C. The last record only

    D. None of the records

28. **You create a table but then subsequently realize you need a few new columns. To add those columns later, you should issue which of the following statements?**

    A. `create or replace table`

    B. `alter table`

    C. `create table`

    D. `truncate table`

29. You are busy creating your tables based on a logical data model. Which of the following constraints requires the `references` privilege in order to be created?

    A. `unique`

    B. `foreign key`

    C. `check`

    D. `not NULL`

30. The INVENTORY table has three columns: UPC_CODE, UNITS, and DELIV_DATE. The primary key is UPC_CODE. You want to add new records daily through a view. The view will be created using the following code:

    ```
    CREATE VIEW DAY_INVENTORY_VW
    AS SELECT UPC_CODE, UNITS, DELIV_DATE
    FROM INVENTORY
    WHERE DELIV_DATE = SYSDATE
    ORDER BY UPC_CODE;
    ```

    What happens when you try to create the previous view?

    A. Oracle returns an error stating that the `order by` clause is not permitted on views.

    B. Oracle returns an error stating that the `with check option` clause is required for creating this view.

    C. Oracle returns an error stating that the `select` statement must be enclosed in parentheses.

    D. Oracle creates the view successfully.

31. You need to search for text data in a column, but you only remember part of the string. Which of the following SQL operations enables the use of wildcard comparisons?

    A. `in`

    B. `exists`

    C. `between`

    D. `like`

32. You have a script you plan to run using SQL*Plus that contains one SQL statement that inserts data into one table. Which of the following options is the easiest way for this script to enable you to specify values for

variables once in the script in a way where no user interaction is required at the SQL*Plus prompt?

A. Use `define` to capture values.

B. Use `accept` to capture values for each run.

C. Use `&` to specify values at runtime for the statement.

D. Use hard-coded values in the statement.

33. You join data from two tables, EXPNS and EMP, into one result set and display that set in your session. The tables have a common column called EMPID. Which of the following choices correctly displays the `where` clause you would use if you wanted to see the data in table EMP where the value in column EMPID equals 39284, but only when a corresponding value appears in table EXPNS?

A. `where EMP.EMPID = 39284 AND EMP.EMPID = EXPNS.EMPID;`

B. `where EMP.EMPID = 39284 (+) AND EMP.EMPID = EXPNS.EMPID;`

C. `where EMP.EMPID = EXPNS.EMPID;`

D. `where EMP.EMPID = 39284 AND EMP.EMPID = EXPNS.EMPID (+);`

34. Review the following transcript of a SQL*Plus session:

```
INSERT INTO INVENTORY (UPC_CODE, PRODUCT )
VALUES (503949353,'HAZELNUT COFFEE');
INSERT INTO INVENTORY (UPC_CODE, PRODUCT)
VALUES (593923506,'SKIM MILK');
INSERT INTO INVENTORY (UPC_CODE, PRODUCT)
VALUES (402392340,'CANDY BAR');
SAVEPOINT INV1;
UPDATE INVENTORY SET UPC_CODE = 50393950
WHERE UPC_CODE = 402392340;
UPDATE INVENTORY SET UPC_CODE = 4104930504
WHERE UPC_CODE = 402392340;
COMMIT;
UPDATE INVENTORY SET PRODUCT = (
SELECT PRODUCT FROM INVENTORY
WHERE UPC_CODE = 50393950)
WHERE UPC_CODE = 593923506;
ROLLBACK;
```

Which of the following UPC codes will not have records in the INVENTORY table as a result of this series of operations?

A. 593923506

B. 503949353

C. 4104930504

D. 50393950

35. You are removing a table from the Oracle database. When you issue the `drop table` command to remove the table, what happens to any of the views that may have an object dependency on that table?

   A. The views are dropped automatically along with the table.

   B. Views in the same schema as the table are dropped automatically, but views outside that schema are not dropped.

   C. Views in the same database as the table are dropped automatically, but views that access the table via database link are not dropped.

   D. Views with object dependencies on the table being dropped are rendered invalid automatically, but are not dropped.

36. You want to join data from four tables into one result set and display that set in your session. Table A has a column in common with table B, table B with table C, and table C with table D. You want to further restrict data returned from the tables by only returning data where values in the common column shared by A and B equal 5. How many conditions should you have in the `where` clause of your `select` statement?

   A. Two

   B. Three

   C. Four

   D. Five

37. You are attempting to explain the Oracle security model for an Oracle database to the new security administrator. What are two components of the Oracle database security model?

   A. Password authentication and granting privileges

   B. Password authentication and creating database objects

   C. Creating database objects and creating users

   D. Creating users and password authentication

38. You have a script you plan to run using SQL*Plus that contains several SQL statements that manage milk inventory in several different tables based on various bits of information. You want the output to go into a file for review later. Which command should you use?

A. `prompt`

B. `echo`

C. `spool`

D. `define`

39. You have a table called TEST_SCORE that stores test results by student personal ID number, test location, and date the test was taken. Tests given in various locations throughout the country are stored in this table. A student is not allowed to take a test for 30 days after failing it the first time, and a check in the application prevents the student from taking a test twice in 30 days at the same location. Recently, it has come to everyone's attention that students are able to circumvent the 30-day rule by taking a test in a different location. Which of the following SQL statements would be useful for identifying the students who have done so?

A.
```
select A.STUDENT_ID, A.LOCATION, B.LOCATION from
TEST_SCORE A, TEST_SCORE B where A.STUDENT_ID =
B.STUDENT_ID AND A.LOCATION = B.LOCATION AND
trunc(A.TEST_DATE)+30 <= trunc(B.TEST_DATE) AND
trunc(A.TEST_DATE)-30 >= trunc(B.TEST_DATE);
```

B.
```
select A.STUDENT_ID, A.LOCATION, B.LOCATION from
TEST_SCORE A, TEST_SCORE B where A.STUDENT_ID =
B.STUDENT_ID AND A.LOCATION <> B.LOCATION AND
trunc(A.TEST_DATE)+30 >= trunc(B.TEST_DATE) AND
trunc(A.TEST_DATE)-30 <= trunc(B.TEST_DATE);
```

C.
```
select A.STUDENT_ID, A.LOCATION, B.LOCATION from
TEST_SCORE A, TEST_SCORE B where A.STUDENT_ID =
B.STUDENT_ID AND A.LOCATION = B.LOCATION AND
trunc(A.TEST_DATE)+30 >= trunc(B.TEST_DATE) AND
trunc(A.TEST_DATE)-30 <= trunc(B.TEST_DATE);
```

D.
```
select A.STUDENT_ID, A.LOCATION, B.LOCATION from
TEST_SCORE A, TEST_SCORE B where A.STUDENT_ID =
B.STUDENT_ID AND A.LOCATION <> B.LOCATION AND
trunc(A.TEST_DATE)+30 <= trunc(B.TEST_DATE) AND
trunc(A.TEST_DATE)-30 >= trunc(B.TEST_DATE);
```

40. In an expense application, you are searching for employee information in the EMPLOYEE table corresponding to an invoice number you have. The INVOICE table contains EMPID, the primary key for EMPLOYEE. Which of the following options is appropriate for obtaining data from EMPLOYEE using your invoice number?

    A. `select * from EMPLOYEE where empid = &empid;`

    B. `select * from EMPLOYEE where empid = 69494;`

    C. `select * from EMPLOYEE where empid = (select empid from invoice where invoice_no = 4399485);`

    D. `select * from EMPLOYEE;`

41. Which of the following uses does not describe an appropriate use of the `having` clause?

    A. To put returned data into sorted order

    B. To exclude certain data groups based on known criteria

    C. To include certain data groups based on unknown criteria

    D. To include certain data groups based on known criteria

42. You are managing data access for an application with 163 tables and 10,000 users. Which of the following objects would assist in managing access in this application by grouping privileges into an object that can be granted to users at once?

    A. Sequences

    B. Tables

    C. Indexes

    D. Roles

43. After logging onto Oracle the first time to access table EMP, user SNOW is told to change his password. Which of the following statements enables him to do so?

    A. `alter user`

    B. `alter table`

    C. `alter role`

    D. `alter index`

44. User SNOW executes the following statement: `select * from EMP`. This statement executes successfully, and SNOW can see the output. User REED owns table EMP. What object is required in order for this scenario to happen?

A. User SNOW needs the role to view table EMP.

B. User SNOW needs the privileges to view table EMP.

C. User SNOW needs a synonym for table EMP.

D. User SNOW needs the password for table EMP.

45. You issue the following statement in Oracle:

```
SELECT * FROM EMP WHERE DEPT IN
(SELECT DEPT FROM VALID_DEPTS
WHERE DEPT_HEAD = 'SALLY'
ORDER BY DEPT);
```

Which of the following choices best indicates how Oracle will respond to this SQL statement?

A. Oracle returns the data selected.

B. Oracle returns data from EMP but not VALID_DEPTS.

C. Oracle returns data from VALID_DEPTS but not EMP.

D. Oracle returns an error.

46. You are coding SQL statements in SQL*Plus. Which of the following is a valid SQL statement?

A. `select nvl(sqrt(59483)) from dual;`

B. `select to_char(nvl(sqrt(59483), 0)) from dual;`

C. `select to_char(nvl(sqrt(59483), 'VALID')) from dual;`

D. `select (to_char(nvl(sqrt(59483), '0')) from dual;`

47. The following output is from a SQL*Plus session:

```
select PLAY_NAME||', ' || AUTHOR play_table from PLAYS;
My Plays and Authors
-------------------------------------
Midsummer Night's Dream, SHAKESPEARE
Waiting For Godot, BECKETT
The Glass Menagerie, WILLIAMS
```

Which of the following SQL*Plus commands produced it?

A. `column PLAY_TABLE alias "My Plays and Authors"`

B. `column PLAY_TABLE format a12`

C. `column PLAY_TABLE heading "My Plays and Authors"`

D. `column PLAY_TABLE as "My Plays and Authors"`

48. **You create a view with the following statement:**

```
CREATE VIEW BASEBALL_TEAM_VW
AS SELECT B.JERSEY_NUM, B.POSITION, B.NAME
FROM BASEBALL_TEAM B
WHERE B.NAME = (SELECT UNAME FROM MY_USERS);
```

The contents of the MY_USERS table are listed as follows:

```
UNAME
-----
JONES
SMITH
FRANK
JENNY
```

Which of the following players will not be listed when user JONES attempts to query the view?

A. JONES

B. SMITH

C. BABS

D. JENNY

49. **Your attempt to read the view-creation code stored in the Oracle data dictionary has encountered a problem. The view code appears to be getting cut off at the end. In order to resolve this problem, which of the following measures is appropriate?**

A. Increase the size of the dictionary view.

B. Increase your user view allotment with the `alter user` statement.

C. Use the `set long` statement.

D. Use the `set NLS_DATE_FORMAT` statement.

50. **Inspect the following SQL statement:**

```
SELECT FARM_NAME, COW_NAME,
COUNT(CARTON) AS NUMBER_OF_CARTONS
FROM COW_MILK
GROUP BY COW_NAME;
```

Which of the following choices contains the line with the error?

A. `select FARM_NAME, COW_NAME,`

B. `count(CARTON) as NUMBER_OF_CARTONS`

C. `from COW_MILK`

D. `group by COW_NAME;`

E. This statement has no errors.

51. **Inspect the following SQL statement:**

```
SELECT COW_NAME,
  MOD(CARTON, FILL_STATUS)
FROM COW_MILK
GROUP BY COW_NAME;
```

Which of the following lines contains an error?

A. `select COW_NAME,`

B. `mod(CARTON, FILL_STATUS)`

C. `from COW_MILK`

D. `group by COW_NAME;`

E. This statement has no errors.

52. **You are writing queries against an Oracle database. Which of the following queries takes advantage of an inline view?**

A. `select * from EMP_VW where EMPID = (select EMPID`
`from INVOICE where INV_NUM = 5506934);`

B. `select A.LASTNAME, B.DEPT_NO from EMP A, (select`
`EMPID, DEPT_NO from DEPT) B where A.EMPID =`
`B.EMPID;`

C. `select * from EMP where EMPID IN (select EMPID from`
`INVOICE where INV_NUM > 23);`

D. `select 'select * from EMP_VW where EMPID is not`
`NULL;' from USER_TABLES;`

53. You have several indexes on a table that you want to remove. You want to avoid removing the indexes associated with constraints, however. Each of the following statements will remove the index associated with a constraint except one. Which choice will not remove the index associated with a constraint?

 A. `drop index`

 B. `alter table drop primary key cascade`

 C. `alter table drop constraint`

 D. `drop table`

54. You are managing constraints on a table in Oracle. Which of the following choices correctly identifies the limitations on primary key constraints?

 A. Every primary key column value must be unique.

 B. No primary key column value can be NULL.

 C. Every primary key column value must be unique and none can be NULL.

 D. Every primary key column must be the same datatype as other columns in the table.

55. Review the following statement:

```
CREATE TABLE FOOBAR
( MOO VARCHAR2(3),
  BOO NUMBER);
```

This table contains 60,000,000 rows. You issue the following statement:

```
SELECT MOO, BOO FROM FOOBAR WHERE MOO = 'ABC'
```

This value is unique in column MOO, yet the query takes several minutes to resolve. Which of the following explanations is the best reason why?

 A. Oracle didn't use the existing primary key index.

 B. `select` statements that do not use views take longer to resolve.

 C. Table FOOBAR has no primary key, and therefore has no index on MOO.

 D. The table had been dropped and recreated.

56. You have created a table called EMP with a primary key called EMP_PK_01. In order to identify any objects that may be associated with that table and primary key, what dictionary views and characteristics would you look for?

A. USER_SEQUENCES, sequences created at the same time

B. USER_TABLES, tables with the same number of columns

C. USER_IND_COLUMNS, constraints with the same name as the table

D. USER_INDEXES, indexes with the same name as the constraint

57. You are designing your database and attempting to determine the best method for indexing your tables. Which of the following is a main advantage of using bitmap indexes on a database?

A. To improve performance on columns with many unique values

B. To improve performance on columns with few unique values

C. To improve performance on columns with all unique values

D. To improve performance on sequences with all unique values

58. User HARRIS would like to change a row into the EMPLOYEE table that has three columns: EMPID, LASTNAME, and SALARY. The user would like to update salary data for employee number 59694. Which statement would work best?

A. `update employee set salary = 5000 where empid = 59694;`

B. `update employee set empid = 45939 where empid = 59694;`

C. `update employee set lastname = 'HARRIS' where empid = 59694;`

D. `update employee set salary = 5000 where lastname = 'HARRIS';`

59. You want to grant user TIMOTHY the ability to update data in the EMP table as well as the ability to administer that access for others. Which of the following commands would you issue?

A. `grant update to timothy;`

B. `grant update on emp to timothy;`

C. `grant update on emp to timothy with grant option;`

D. `grant update on emp to timothy with admin option;`

60. User REED can administer the `create session` privilege. User REED grants the same `create session` privilege to MANN using the appropriate clause. MANN then grants the privilege to SNOW. REED discovers MANN issued the privilege to SNOW and revokes the privilege from MANN. Who can connect to Oracle?

   A. REED only

   B. SNOW and MANN only

   C. REED, MANN, and SNOW

   D. REED and SNOW only

Practice Exam 2

1. You join data from two tables, COW_MILK (C) and CARTON_CRATE (C1), into one result set and display that set in your session. The tables have a common column, called CARTON_NUM in both tables. You want to see the data in table COW_MILK for BESS the cow and all corresponding information in CARTON_CRATE, but if no data is in CARTON_NUM, you don't want to see the data in COW_MILK. Which of the following choices correctly displays the `where` clause you should use?

   A. `where C.COW_NAME <> 'BESS' AND C.CARTON_NUM = C1.CARTON_NUM;`

   B. `where C.CARTON_NUM = C1.CARTON_NUM;`

   C. `where C.COW_NAME = 'BESS';`

   D. `where C.COW_NAME = 'BESS' AND C.CARTON_NUM = C1.CARTON_NUM;`

   E. `where C.COW_NAME = 'BESS' AND C.CARTON_NUM = C1.CARTON_NUM (+);`

2. You create a table with a primary key that is populated on `insert` with a value from a sequence, and then you add several hundred rows to the table. You then drop and recreate the sequence with the original sequence code. Suddenly, your users are getting constraint violations. Which of the following explanations is most likely the cause?

   A. Dropping a sequence also removes any associated primary keys.

   B. Any cached sequence values before the sequence was dropped are unusable.

   C. The table is read-only.

   D. The `insert` statements contain duplicate data due to the reset sequence.

3. You are developing SQL statements for the application. Which of the following SQL operations requires the use of a subquery?

   A. `in`

   B. `exists`

   C. `between`

   D. `like`

4. **Review the following transcript from a SQL*Plus session:**

```
SELECT CEIL(4093.505) FROM DUAL;
CEIL(4093.505)
-------------------
          4094
```

Which single-row function could not be used to produce 4093 from the number passed to the ceil( ) function?

A. round( )

B. trunc( )

C. floor( )

D. abs( )

5. **You have a script you plan to run using SQL*Plus that contains several SQL statements that update banking information for one person in several different tables based on name. Because the script only changes information for one person, you want the ability to enter the name only once and have that information reused throughout the script. Which of the following options is the best way to accomplish this goal in such a way that you don't need to modify the script each time you want to run it?**

A. Use define to capture the name value for each run.

B. Use accept to capture the name value for each run.

C. Use the & character to specify lexical substitution for names at runtime.

D. Hard-code names in all SQL statements, and change the value for each run.

6. **You need to undo some data changes. Which of the following data changes cannot be undone using the rollback command?**

A. update

B. truncate

C. delete

D. insert

7. **You are developing some code to handle transaction processing. Each of the following items signifies the beginning of a new transaction except one. Which is it?**

A. savepoint

B. set transaction

C. Opening a new session

D. commit

8. The following SQL statement is invalid:

```
SELECT   PRODUCT, BRAND
WHERE UPC_CODE = '650-35365656-34453453454-45';
```

Which of the following choices indicates an area of change that would make this statement valid?

A. A select clause

B. A from clause

C. A where clause

D. An order by clause

9. You are at the beginning of your current transaction and want to prevent your transaction from being able to change data in the database. To prevent any statements in the current transaction from altering database tables, which statement is used?

A. set transaction

B. rollback

C. commit

D. savepoint

10. Your application searches for data in the EMP table on the database on a nullable column indicating whether a person is male or female. To improve performance, you decide to index the table. The table contains more than 2,000,000 rows, and the column contains few NULL values. Which of the following indexes would be most appropriate?

A. Nonunique B-tree index

B. Unique B-tree index

C. Bitmap index

D. Primary key index

11. Your employee expense application stores information for invoices in one table. Each invoice can have several items, which are stored in another table. Each invoice may have one or more items, or none at all, but every item must correspond to one invoice. The relationship between the INVOICE table and INVOICE_ITEM table is best described as which of the following?

    A. Parent to child

    B. Detail to master

    C. Primary key to foreign key

    D. Foreign key to primary key

12. **You issue the following statement:**

```
SELECT DECODE(UPC_CODE, 40390, 'DISCONTINUED', 65421, 'STALE',
90395, 'BROKEN', 'ACTIVE') FROM INVENTORY;
```

    If the value for UPC_CODE is 20395, what information will this statement display?

    A. DISCONTINUED

    B. STALE

    C. BROKEN

    D. ACTIVE

13. **You are developing advanced queries for an Oracle database. Which of the following where clauses makes use of Oracle's capability to logically test values against a set of results returned without explicitly knowing what the set is before executing the query?**

    A. where COL_A = 6

    B. where COL_A in (6,7,8,9,10)

    C. where COL_A between 6 AND 10

    D. where COL_A in (select NUM from TAB_OF_NUMS)

14. **You are developing a multiple-row query to handle a complex and dynamic comparison operation in the Olympics. Two tables are involved. CONTESTANT lists all contestants from every country, and MEDALS lists every country and the number of gold, silver, and bronze medals they have. If a country has not received one of the three types of medals, a zero appears in the column. Thus, a query will always return data, even for countries that haven't won a medal. Which of the following queries shows only the contestants from countries with more than ten medalists of any type?**

    A. select NAME from CONTESTANT C, MEDALS M where
        C.COUNTRY = M.COUNTRY;

B. select NAME from CONTESTANT where COUNTRY C in
(select COUNTRY from MEDALS M where C.COUNTRY =
M.COUNTY)

C. select NAME from CONTESTANT where COUNTRY C =
(select COUNTRY from MEDALS M where C.COUNTRY =
M.COUNTY)

D. select NAME from CONTESTANT where COUNTRY in
(select COUNTRY from MEDALS where NUM_GOLD +
NUM_SILVER + NUM_BRONZE > 10)

15. **You issue the following query in a SQL*Plus session:**

```
SELECT NAME, AGE, COUNTRY FROM CONTESTANT
WHERE (COUNTRY, AGE) IN ( SELECT COUNTRY, MIN(AGE)
FROM CONTESTANT GROUP BY COUNTRY);
```

Which of the following choices identifies both the type of query and the expected result from the Oracle database?

A. Single-row subquery, the youngest contestant from one country

B. Multiple-row subquery, the youngest contestant from all countries

C. Multiple-column subquery, the youngest contestant from all countries

D. Multiple-column subquery; Oracle will return an error because = should replace in

16. **The contents of the CONTESTANTS table are listed as follows:**

```
NAME                             AGE COUNTRY
----------------  --------------- ----------------
BERTRAND               24 FRANCE
GONZALEZ               29 SPAIN
HEINRICH               22 GERMANY
TAN                    39 CHINA
SVENSKY                30 RUSSIA
SOO                    21
```

You issue the following query against this table:

```
SELECT NAME FROM CONTESTANT
WHERE (COUNTRY, AGE) IN ( SELECT COUNTRY, MIN(AGE)
FROM CONTESTANT GROUP BY COUNTRY);
```

Which of the following contestants will not be listed among the output?

A. SOO

B. HEINRICH

C. BERTRAND

D. GONZALEZ

17. An object in Oracle contains many columns that are functionally dependent on the key column for that object. The object requires segments to be stored in areas of the database other than the data dictionary. The object in question is correctly referred to as which of the following objects?

A. Synonym

B. Table

C. Sequence

D. View

18. You need to compute an *N*-dimensional cross-tabulation in your SQL statement output for reporting purposes. Which of the following clauses can be used for this purpose?

A. having

B. cube

C. rollup

D. trim( )

19. You are indexing Oracle data in an application. The index will be on a column containing sequential numbers with at least seven significant digits. Most, if not all, entries will start with the digit 1. Which of the following indexes is best suited for the task?

A. B-tree indexes

B. Reverse-key indexes

C. Bitmap indexes

D. Descending indexes

20. You need to store a large block of text data in Oracle. These text blocks will be around 3,500 characters in length. Which datatype should you use for storing these large objects?

A. VARCHAR2

B. CLOB

C. BLOB

D. BFILE

21. **Dropping a table has which of the following effects on a non-unique index created for the table?**

   A. It has no effect.

   B. The index is dropped.

   C. The index is rendered invalid.

   D. The index contains NULL values.

22. **Which of the following statements about indexes is true?**

   A. Columns with low cardinality are handled well by B-tree indexes.

   B. Columns with low cardinality are handled poorly by bitmap indexes.

   C. Columns with high cardinality are handled well by B-tree indexes.

23. **Which of the following methods should you use to add to the number of columns selected by a view?**

   A. Add more columns to the underlying table.

   B. Issue the `alter view` statement.

   C. Use a correlated subquery in conjunction with the view.

   D. Drop and recreate the view with references to select more columns.

24. **Which of the following choices is a valid parameter for sequence creation?**

   A. `identified by`

   B. `using temporary tablespace`

   C. `maxvalue`

   D. `on delete cascade`

25. **The following options each show a line in a statement issued against the Oracle database. Which line will produce an error?**

   A. `create view EMP_VIEW_01`

   B. `as select E.EMPID, E.LASTNAME, E.FIRSTNAME, A.ADDRESS`

   C. `from EMPLOYEE E, EMPL_ADDRESS A`

   D. `where E.EMPID = A.EMPID`

   E. `with check option;`

   F. This statement contains no errors.

26. You are granting privileges on your table to another user. Which object privilege enables the user to create his or her own table with a foreign key on a column in your table?

    A. references

    B. index

    C. select

    D. delete

27. Which of the following statements about roles are true? (Choose three.)

    A. Roles can be granted to other roles.

    B. Privileges can be granted to roles.

    C. Roles can be granted to users.

    D. Roles can be granted to synonyms.

28. After referencing NEXTVAL, what happens to the value in CURRVAL?

    A. It is incremented by one.

    B. It is now in PREVVAL.

    C. It is equal to NEXTVAL.

    D. It is unchanged.

29. The EMP_SALARY table has two columns: EMP_USER and SALARY. EMP_USER is set to be the same as the Oracle username. To support user MARTHA, the salary administrator, you create a view with the following statement:

```
CREATE VIEW EMP_SAL_VW
AS SELECT EMP_USER, SALARY
FROM EMP_SALARY
WHERE EMP_USER <> 'MARTHA';
```

    MARTHA is supposed to be able to view and update anyone's salary in the company except her own through this view. Which of the following clauses do you need to add to your view-creation statement in order to implement this functionality?

    A. with admin option

    B. with grant option

   C. with security option

   D. with check option

30. **The INVENTORY table has three columns: UPC_CODE, UNITS, and DELIV_DATE. The primary key is UPC_CODE. New records are added daily through a view. The view was created using the following code:**

```
CREATE VIEW DAY_INVENTORY_VW
AS SELECT UPC_CODE, UNITS, DELIV_DATE
FROM INVENTORY
WHERE DELIV_DATE = SYSDATE
WITH check OPTION;
```

   What happens when a user tries to insert a record with duplicate UPC_CODE?

   A. The statement fails due to the with check option clause.

   B. The statement succeeds.

   C. The statement fails due to the primary key constraint.

   D. The statement inserts everything except the date.

31. **You are cleaning information out of the Oracle database. Which of the following statements gets rid of all views that use a table at the same time you eliminate the table from the database?**

   A. drop view

   B. alter table

   C. drop index

   D. alter table drop constraint

32. **You create a view with the following statement:**

```
CREATE VIEW BASEBALL_TEAM_VW
AS SELECT B.JERSEY_NUM, B.POSITION, B.NAME
FROM BASEBALL_TEAM B
WHERE B.NAME = USER;
```

   What will happen when user JONES attempts to select a listing for user SMITH?

   A. The select receives an error.

   B. The select succeeds.

   C. The select receives NO ROWS SELECTED.

   D. The select adds data only to BASEBALL_TEAM.

33. **Which of the following integrity constraints automatically create an index when defined? (Choose two.)**

    A. Foreign keys

    B. `unique` constraints

    C. `not NULL` constraints

    D. Primary keys

34. **Which of the following dictionary views gives information about the position of a column in a primary key?**

    A. ALL_PRIMARY_KEYS

    B. USER_CONSTRAINTS

    C. ALL_IND_COLUMNS

    D. ALL_TABLES

35. **Developer ANJU executes the following statement: `create table ANIMALS as select * from MASTER.ANIMALS;`. What is the effect of this statement?**

    A. A table named ANIMALS is created in the MASTER schema with the same data as the ANIMALS table owned by ANJU.

    B. A table named ANJU is created in the ANIMALS schema with the same data as the ANIMALS table owned by MASTER.

    C. A table named ANIMALS is created in the ANJU schema with the same data as the ANIMALS table owned by MASTER.

    D. A table named MASTER is created in the ANIMALS schema with the same data as the ANJU table owned by ANIMALS.

36. **User JANKO would like to insert a row into the EMPLOYEE table that has three columns: EMPID, LASTNAME, and SALARY. The user would like to enter data for EMPID 59694 and LASTNAME Harris, but no salary. Which statement would work best?**

    A. `insert into EMPLOYEE values (59694,'HARRIS', NULL);`

    B. `insert into EMPLOYEE values (59694,'HARRIS');`

    C. `insert into EMPLOYEE (EMPID, LASTNAME, SALARY) values (59694,'HARRIS');`

    D. `insert into EMPLOYEE (select 59694 from 'HARRIS');`

37. **No relationship officially exists between two tables. Which of the following choices is the strongest indicator of a parent-child relationship?**

    A. Two tables in the database are named VOUCHER and VOUCHER_ITEM, respectively.

    B. Two tables in the database are named EMPLOYEE and PRODUCTS, respectively.

    C. Two tables in the database were created on the same day.

    D. Two tables in the database contain none of the same columns.

38. **Which of the following are valid database table datatypes in Oracle? (Choose three.)**

    A. CHAR

    B. VARCHAR2

    C. BOOLEAN

    D. NUMBER

39. **Omitting the `where` clause from a `delete` statement has which of the following effects?**

    A. The `delete` statement fails because no records are present to delete.

    B. The `delete` statement prompts the user to enter criteria for the deletion.

    C. The `delete` statement fails because of syntax error.

    D. The `delete` statement removes all records from the table.

40. **The following options each show a line in a statement. Which line will produce an error?**

    A. `create table GOODS`

    B. `(GOODNO NUMBER,`

    C. `GOOD_NAME VARCHAR2(20) check(GOOD_NAME in (select NAME from AVAIL_GOODS)),`

    D. `constraint PK_GOODS_01`

    E. `primary key (GOODNO));`

    F. This statement has no errors.

41. Which of the following is the transaction control that prevents more than one user from updating data in a table?

   A. Locks

   B. Commits

   C. Rollbacks

   D. Savepoints

42. Which of the following methods should you use to increase the number of nullable columns for a table?

   A. Use the `alter table` statement.

   B. Ensure that all column values are NULL for all rows.

   C. First, increase the size of adjacent column datatypes, and then add the column.

   D. Add the column, populate the column, and then add the `not NULL` constraint.

43. A user issues the statement `select count(*) from EMPLOYEE`. The query takes an inordinately long time and returns a count of zero. Which of the following is the most cost-effective solution?

   A. Upgrade the hardware.

   B. Truncate the table.

   C. Upgrade the version of Oracle.

   D. Delete the high-water mark.

44. You are creating some tables in your database as part of the logical data model. Which of the following constraints have an index associated with them that is generated automatically by Oracle?

   A. `unique`

   B. `foreign key`

   C. `check`

   D. `not NULL`

45. Each of the following statements is true about referential integrity except one. Which is it?

   A. The referencing column in the child table must correspond with a primary key in the parent.

B. All values in the referenced column in the parent table must be present in the referencing column in the child.

C. The datatype of the referenced column in the parent table must be identical to the referencing column in the child.

D. All values in the referencing column in the child table must be in present in the referenced column in the parent.

46. **You are managing constraints on a table in Oracle. Which of the following choices correctly identifies the limitations on `check` constraints?**

A. Values must be obtained from a lookup table.

B. Values must be part of a fixed set defined by `create` or `alter table`.

C. Values must include reserved words like `sysdate` and `user`.

D. Column cannot contain a NULL value.

47. **Which of the following is not a group function?**

A. `avg ( )`

B. `sqrt ( )`

C. `sum ( )`

D. `max ( )`

48. **In order to perform an inner join, which criteria must be true?**

A. The common columns in the join do not need to have shared values.

B. The tables in the join need to have common columns.

C. The common columns in the join may or may not have shared values.

D. The common columns in the join must have shared values.

49. **Once defined, how long will a variable remain defined in SQL*Plus?**

A. Until the database is shut down

B. Until the instance is shut down

C. Until the statement completes

D. Until the session completes

50. You want to change the prompt Oracle uses to obtain input from a user. Which of the following choices are used for this purpose? (Choose two.)

A. Change the prompt in the `config.ora` file.

B. Alter the `prompt` clause of the `accept` command.

C. Enter a new prompt in the `login.sql` file.

D. A prompt in Oracle cannot be changed.

51. No search criteria for the EMPLOYEE table are known. Which of the following options is appropriate for use when search criteria are unknown for comparison operations in a `select` statement? (Choose two.)

A. `select * from EMPLOYEE where EMPID = &empid;`

B. `select * from EMPLOYEE where EMPID = 69494;`

C. `select * from EMPLOYEE where EMPID = (select empid from invoice where INVOICE_NO = 4399485);`

D. `select * from EMPLOYEE;`

52. Which of the following is the default character for specifying substitution variables in `select` statements?

A. Ampersand

B. Ellipses

C. Quotation marks

D. Asterisk

53. A user is setting up a join operation between tables EMPLOYEE and DEPT. The user wants the query to return some of the employees in the EMPLOYEE table, but the employees are not assigned to department heads yet. Which `select` statement is most appropriate for this user?

A. `select e.empid, d.head from EMPLOYEE e, dept d;`

B. `select e.empid, d.head from EMPLOYEE e, dept d`
`where e.dept# = d.dept#;`

C. `select e.empid, d.head from EMPLOYEE e, dept d`
`where e.dept# = d.dept# (+);`

D. `select e.empid, d.head from EMPLOYEE e, dept d`
`where e.dept# (+) = d.dept#;`

54. **Which of the following uses of the `having` clause are appropriate? (Choose three.)**

    A. To put returned data into sorted order

    B. To exclude certain data groups based on known criteria

    C. To include certain data groups based on unknown criteria

    D. To include certain data groups based on known criteria

55. **Which of the following best describes a Cartesian product?**

    A. A group function

    B. Produced as a result of a join `select` statement with no `where` clause

    C. The result of fuzzy logic

    D. A special feature of Oracle server

56. **Which of the following methods is used to change the default character that identifies runtime variables?**

    A. Modifying the `init.ora` file

    B. Modifying the `login.sql` file

    C. Issuing the `define` *variablename* command

    D. Issuing the `set define` command

57. **User THOMAS has been granted the role SALES_ANALYZER, which gives her access the SALES table for writing reports. However, when she tries to do so, she gets this error: `ORA-00942: table or view does not exist`. Which of the following statements can she issue in order to resolve the problem?**

    A. `alter user thomas default role sales_analyzer;`

    B. `set role sales_analyzer;`

    C. `grant select on sales to sales_analyzer;`

    D. `grant sales_analyzer to thomas;`

58. **User FRANKLIN owns the PROFITS table and the SALES_ANALYZER role, which has already been granted to DAVIS. FRANKLIN grants `select` privileges on PROFITS to the SALES_ANALYZER role. At what point will that privilege be made available to DAVIS?**

    A. The next time DAVIS logs into Oracle

    B. The next time FRANKLIN grants the SALES_ANALYZER role to DAVIS

C. The next time FRANKLIN grants the privilege to SALES ANALYZER

D. Immediately after the privilege is granted to SALES_ANALYZER

59. User IMADBA wants to give user DAVIS, a brand-new employee who started today, the ability to create tables in the Oracle database. Which of the following choices identifies a step that doesn't need to take place before DAVIS can start creating tables?

A. `create user davis identified by new_employee;`

B. `grant create session to davis;`

C. `grant create table to davis;`

D. `grant create public synonym to davis;`

60. You are granting privileges on the Oracle database. Which of the following choices identifies a system privilege enabling you to connect to the database?

A. CONNECT

B. RESOURCE

C. `create session`

D. `references`

Practice Exam 3

1. You issue the following `select` statement in Oracle:

```
SQL> select e.empno, e.ename, d.loc
from emp e, dept d
  3   where e.deptno = d.deptno
  4   and substr(e.ename,1,1) = 'S';
```

   Which of the following statements identifies an ANSI-compliant equivalent statement usable on the Oracle database?

   A. `select empno, ename, loc from emp join dept on emp.deptno = dept.deptno where substr(emp.ename,1,1) = 'S';`

   B. `select empno, ename, loc from emp, dept on emp.deptno = dept.deptno where substr(emp.ename,1,1) = 'S';`

   C. `select empno, ename, loc from emp join dept where emp.deptno = dept.deptno and substr(emp.ename,1,1) = 'S';`

   D. `select empno, ename, loc from emp join dept on emp.deptno = dept.deptno and substr(emp.ename,1,1) = 'S';`

2. You are trying to manipulate data on the Oracle database. Which of the following choices identifies a capacity of `select` statements in Oracle and does not require the use of a subquery?

   A. You can change data in Oracle using `select` statements.

   B. You can remove data from Oracle using `select` statements.

   C. You can create a table with the contents of another using `select` statements.

   D. You can truncate tables using `select` statements.

3. You issue a query in the Oracle database. Which of the following choices does not identify a component of your query if you want the query to execute a mathematical operation on user-defined static expressions?

   A. Column clause

   B. Table clause

   C. The DUAL table

   D. The where clause

4. **You are manipulating data in Oracle. Which of the following is not a SQL command?**

   A. `select * from dual;`

   B. `set define ?`

   C. `update emp set empno = 6543 where ename = 'SMITHERS';`

   D. `create table employees (empid varchar2(10) primary key);`

5. **You are defining SQL queries in Oracle. Which of the following database objects cannot be referenced directly from a `select` statement?**

   A. Tables

   B. Sequences

   C. Indexes

   D. Views

6. **You need to filter return data from your query on the PROFITS table according to the PRODUCT_NAME column. Which of the following clauses in your SQL query will contain reference to the appropriate filter criteria?**

   A. `select`

   B. `from`

   C. `where`

   D. `having`

7. **A partial listing of output from the PROFITS table is shown in the following code block:**

```
PRODUCT_NAME PRODUCT_TYPE QTR_END_DATE      PROFIT
------------ ------------ ------------ -------------
BARNEY DOLL  TOY          31-MAR-2001     6575430.30
GAS GRILL    APPLIANCE    31-MAR-2001     1234023.88
PENCIL       OFFICE       30-JUN-2001       34039.99
```

   Which of the following choices identifies the proper setup of a where clause for a query that calculates the total profits for all appliances sold in the six-month period from January 1 to June 30, 2001?

   A. `where product_name = 'GAS GRILL' and qtr_end_date between '01-JAN-2001' and '01-JUL-2001';`

B. where product_type = 'APPLIANCE' and product_name = 'GAS GRILL' and qtr_end_date = '31-JAN-2001' or '30-JUN-2001';

C. where product_type = 'APPLIANCE' and qtr_end_date between '01-JAN-2001' and '01-JUL-2001';

D. where product_name = 'GAS GRILL' and qtr_end_date = '01-JAN-2001' or '30-JUN-2001';

Use the contents of the EMP table shown in the following code block to answer the next eight questions:

```
EMPNO ENAME     JOB          MGR HIREDATE    SAL COMM DEPTNO
--------- -------- --------- ----- --------- ---- ---- ------
     7369 SMITH    CLERK      7902 17-DEC-80  800            20
     7499 ALLEN    SALESMAN   7698 20-FEB-81 1600  300       30
     7521 WARD     SALESMAN   7698 22-FEB-81 1250  500       30
     7566 JONES    MANAGER    7839 02-APR-81 2975            20
     7654 MARTIN   SALESMAN   7698 28-SEP-81 1250 1400       30
     7698 BLAKE    MANAGER    7839 01-MAY-81 2850            30
     7782 CLARK    MANAGER    7839 09-JUN-81 2450            10
     7788 SCOTT    ANALYST    7566 09-DEC-82 3000            20
     7839 KING     PRESIDENT       17-NOV-81 5000            10
     7844 TURNER   SALESMAN   7698 08-SEP-81 1500    0       30
     7876 ADAMS    CLERK      7788 12-JAN-82 1100            20
     7900 JAMES    CLERK      7698 03-DEC-81  950            30
     7902 FORD     ANALYST    7566 03-DEC-81 3000            20
     7934 MILLER   CLERK      7782 23-JAN-82 1300            10
```

8. Which of the following choices identifies the value that would be returned from the following query: `select sum(sal) + sum(comm) from emp where job = 'ANALYST' or ename like 'J%'`?

   A. 6000

   B. 9925

   C. 9975

   D. NULL

9. Which of the following choices identifies the value that would be returned from the following query: `select count(mgr) from emp where deptno = 10`?

   A. One

   B. Two

    C. Three

    D. NULL

10. Which of the following choices identifies the value returned if you issued the following query: `select count(*) from emp where mgr = 7700-2`?

    A. Five

    B. Six

    C. Seven

    D. NULL

11. Which of the following choices identifies the third employee listed from the top of the output from the following SQL command: `select ename, sal from emp where job = 'SALESMAN' order by empno desc`?

    A. ALLEN

    B. MARTIN

    C. TURNER

    D. WARD

12. Which of the following choices identifies the third employee listed from the top in the output generated from the following SQL command: `select ename, job from emp where job = 'SALESMAN' order by 1 desc`?

    A. ALLEN

    B. MARTIN

    C. TURNER

    D. WARD

13. Which of the following choices identifies the value returned by Oracle when you issue the following query: `select substr(job, 1,3) from emp where ename like upper('_ _ar%')`?

    A. ANA

    B. CLE

    C. MAN

    D. SAL

14. Which of the following choices identifies the value returned by Oracle when you issue: `select trunc(months_between(min(hiredate), max(hiredate))) from emp`?

    A. 24

    B. 25

    C. –24

    D. –25

15. Which of the following choices identify the value returned by Oracle when you issue the following query: `select * from emp where hiredate > '23-JAN-82'`? (Choose two.)

    A. ADAMS

    B. MILLER

    C. SCOTT

    D. SMITH

16. A table called TEST contains two columns: TESTCOL, defined as a NUMBER(10) datatype; and TESTCOL_2, defined as a VARCHAR2(10) datatype. You issue the following statement on Oracle: `insert into test (testcol, testcol_2) values (null, 'FRANCIS')`. You then issue the following query against that table: `select nvl(testcol,'EMPTY') as testcol from test where testcol_2 = 'FRANCIS'`. Which of the following choices correctly identifies the result?

    A. Oracle returns zero as the result.

    B. Oracle returns EMPTY as the result.

    C. Oracle returns NULL as the result.

    D. Oracle returns an error as the result.

17. You want to obtain data from the ORDERS table, which contains three columns: CUSTOMER, ORDER_DATE, and ORDER_AMT. Which of the following choices identifies how you would formulate the `where` clause in a query against the ORDERS table when you want to see orders for customer LESLIE that exceed 2700?

    A. `where customer = 'LESLIE';`

    B. `where customer = 'LESLIE' and order_amt < 2700;`

C. `where customer = 'LESLIE' or order_amt > 2700;`

D. `where customer = 'LESLIE' and order_amt > 2700;`

18. Use the following output to answer the question (assume that the information shown comes from the EMP table we've been using in the chapter):

```
ENAME
----------
SMITH-dog-
ALLEN-dog-
WARD-dog-d
JONES-dog-
MARTIN-dog
BLAKE-dog-
CLARK-dog-
SCOTT-dog-
KING-dog-d
TURNER-dog
ADAMS-dog-
JAMES-dog-
FORD-dog-d
MILLER-dog
```

Which of the following choices identifies the SQL statement that produced this output?

A. `select trim(trailing '-dog' from ename) as ename from emp;`

B. `select rpad(ename, 10, '-dog') as ename from emp;`

C. `select substr(ename, 1, 10) as ename from emp;`

D. `select lpad(ename, 10, '-dog') as ename from emp;`

19. Use the following code block to answer the question:

```
SQL> select _____ (-45) as output from dual;
OUTPUT
------
   -45
```

Which of the following choices identifies a single-row function that could not have produced this output?

A. `abs( )`

B. `ceil( )`

C. floor( )

D. round( )

20. **For a certain row in a table, a VARCHAR2 column contains the value SMITHY, padded to the right with seven spaces by the application. When the** length( ) **function processes that column value, what will be the value returned?**

   A. 6

   B. 13

   C. 30

   D. 60

21. **You issue the following statement in SQL*Plus:**

```
SQL> select ceil(-97.342),
  2  floor(-97.342),
  3  round(-97.342,0),
  4  trunc(-97.342)
  5  from dual;
```

   Which of the following choices identifies the function that will not return –97 as the result?

   A. ceil( )

   B. floor( )

   C. round( )

   D. trunc( )

22. **You issue the following statement in SQL*Plus:**

```
SQL> select ceil(256.342),
  2  floor(256.342),
  3  round(256.342,0),
  4  trunc(256.342)
  5  from dual;
```

   Which of the following choices identifies the function that will not return 256 as the result?

   A. ceil( )

   B. floor( )

   C. round( )

   D. trunc( )

23. **You issue the following query in Oracle:**

```
SQL> select months_between('15-MAR-83', '15-MAR-97') from dual;
```

What will Oracle return?

A. 14

B. −14

C. 168

D. −168

24. **You want to use a format mask for date information in Oracle. In which of the following situations is this format mask not appropriate?**

A. `to_date( )`

B. `to_char( )`

C. `alter session set nls_date_format`

D. `to_number( )`

25. **Two tables, PRODUCT and STORAGE_BOX, exist in a database. Individual products are listed in the table by unique ID number, product name, and the box a particular product is stored in. Individual storage boxes (identified by number) listed in the other table can contain many products, but each box can be found in only one location. Which of the following statements will correctly display the product ID, name, and box location of all widgets in this database?**

A. `select p.prod_id, p.prod_name, b.box_loc from product p, storage_box b where p.prod_id = b.prod_id and prod_name = 'WIDGET';`

B. `select p.prod_id, p.prod_name, b.box_loc from product p, storage_box b where prod_name = 'WIDGET';`

C. `select p.prod_id, p.prod_name, b.box_loc from product p, storage_box b where p.stor_box_num = b.stor_box_num and p.prod_name = 'WIDGET';`

D. `select prod_id, prod_name, box_loc from product, storage_box where stor_box_num = stor_box_num and prod_name = 'WIDGET';`

26. **You want to join information from three tables as part of developing a report. The tables are EMP, DEPT, and SALGRADE. Only records**

corresponding to employee, department location, and salary range are required for employees in grades ten and higher for the organization. How many comparison operations are required for this query?

A. Two

B. Three

C. Four

D. Five

27. You want to join the contents of two tables, PRODUCT and STORAGE, to list the location of all boxes containing widgets. PRODUCT has three columns: ID, NAME, and BOX#. STORAGE has two columns: BOX# and LOC. Which of the following choices will not give the desired result?

A. `select product.id, product.name, storage.loc from product, storage where product.box# = storage.box#;`

B. `select product.id, product.name, storage.loc from product join storage on product.box# = storage.box#;`

C. `select product.id, product.name, storage.loc from product natural join storage on product.box# = storage.box#;`

D. `select product.id, product.name, storage.loc from product natural join storage;`

28. You are defining an outer join statement. Which of the following choices is true concerning outer join statements?

A. Because outer join operations permit NULL values from one of the tables, you do not have to specify equality comparisons to join those tables.

B. In outer join statements on tables A and B, you specify the right outer join when you want all of table A's rows, even when no corresponding record exists in table B.

C. In outer join statements on tables A and B, you specify the left outer join when you want all of table B's rows, even when no corresponding record exists in table A.

D. Even though outer join operations permit NULL values from one of the tables, you still need to specify equality comparisons to join those tables.

29. Two tables, PRODUCT and STORAGE_BOX, exist in a database. Individual products are listed in the table by unique ID number, product name, and the box a particular product is stored in. Individual storage boxes (identified by number) listed in the other table can contain many products, but the box can be found in only one location. Which of the following statements will correctly display the product ID, name, and box location of all widgets in this database that have or have not been assigned to a storage box?

   A. ```
   select p.prod_id, p.prod_name, b.box_loc from
   product p left outer join storage_box b on
   p.stor_box_num = b.stor_box_num where p.prod_name =
   'WIDGET' (+);
   ```

   B. ```
   select p.prod_id, p.prod_name, b.box_loc from
   product p left outer join storage_box b on
   p.stor_box_num = b.stor_box_num where p.prod_name =
   'WIDGET';
   ```

   C. ```
   select p.prod_id, p.prod_name, b.box_loc from
   product p right outer join storage_box b where
   b.stor_box_num = p.stor_box_num (+) and p.prod_name
   = 'WIDGET';
   ```

   D. ```
   select p.prod_id, p.prod_name, b.box_loc from
   product p full outer join storage_box b on
   p.stor_box_num = b.stor_box_num where
   b.stor_box_num is NULL;
   ```

30. You issue the following command in Oracle:

   ```
   SQL> select e.ename, a.street_address, a.city, a.state, a.post_code
   from emp e, addr a
     3  where e.empno = a.empno (+)
     4  and a.state = 'TEXAS';
   ```

   Which of the following choices shows the ANSI/ISO equivalent statement?

   A. ```
   select e.ename, a.street_address, a.city, a.state,
   a.post_code from emp e outer join addr a on e.empno
   = a.empno where a.state = 'TEXAS';
   ```

   B. ```
   select e.ename, a.street_address, a.city, a.state,
   a.post_code from emp e left outer join addr a on
   e.empno = a.empno where a.state = 'TEXAS';
   ```

   C. ```
   select e.ename, a.street_address, a.city, a.state,
   a.post_code from emp e right outer join addr a on
   e.empno = a.empno where a.state = 'TEXAS';
   ```
   ```

D. `select e.ename, a.street_address, a.city, a.state,`
`a.post_code from emp e right outer join addr a`
`where e.empno = a.empno (+) and a.state = 'TEXAS';`

31. **Examine the following output from SQL*Plus:**

```
PRODUCT.ID PRODUCT.NAME BOX.LOCATION
---------- ------------- ------------
578-X      WIDGET        IDAHO
                         TENNESSEE
456-Y      WIDGET
```

Which of the following choices identifies the type of query that likely produced this result?

A. Full outer join

B. Left outer join

C. Right outer join

D. Equijoin

32. **You are developing a query on the PROFITS table, which stores profit information by company region, product type, and quarterly time period. Which of the following SQL statements will display a cross-tabulation of output showing profits by region, product type, and time period?**

A. `select region, prod_type, time, sum(profit) from`
`profits group by region, prod_type, time;`

B. `select region, prod_type, time from profits group`
`by rollup (region, prod_type, time);`

C. `select region, prod_type, time from profits group`
`by cube (region, prod_type, time);`

D. `select region, prod_type, time, sum(profit) from`
`profits group by cube (region, prod_type, time);`

33. **Which of the following choices identifies a `group by` query that will not result in an error from Oracle when run against the database?**

A. `select deptno, job, sum(sal) from emp group by job,`
`deptno;`

B. `select sum(sal), deptno, job from emp group by job,`
`deptno;`

C. `select deptno, job, sum(sal) from emp;`

D. `select deptno, sum(sal), job from emp group by job,`
`deptno;`

34. **Review the following SQL statement:**

```
SQL> select a.deptno, a.job, b.loc, sum(a.sal)
  2  from emp a, dept b
  3  where a.deptno = b.deptno
  4  group by a.deptno, a.job, b.loc
  5  order by sum(a.sal);
```

Which of the following choices identifies the column upon which the order of output from this query will be returned?

A. A.DEPTNO

B. A.JOB

C. B.LOC

D. sum(A.SAL)

35. **You are developing a query on the PROFITS table, which stores profit information by company region, product type, and quarterly time period. Which of the following choices identifies a query that will obtain the average profits greater than $100,000 by product type, region, and time period?**

A. select region, prod_type, period, avg(profit) from profits where avg(profit) > 100000 group by region, prod_type, period;

B. select region, prod_type, period, avg(profit) from profits where avg(profit) > 100000 order by region, prod_type, period;

C. select region, prod_type, period, avg(profit) from profits group by region, prod_type, period having avg(profit) > 100000;

D. select region, prod_type, period, avg(profit) from profits group by region, prod_type, period having avg(profit) < 100000;

36. **The company has an employee expense application with two tables. One table, called EMP, contains all employee data. The other, called EXPENSE, contains expense vouchers submitted by every employee in the company. Which of the following queries will obtain the employee ID and name for those employees who have submitted expenses whose total value exceeds their salary?**

A. select e.empno, e.ename from emp e where e.sal < (select sum(x.vouch_amt) from expense x) and x.empno = e.empno;

B. `select e.empno, e.ename from emp e where e.sal <`
   `(select x.vouch_amt from expense x where x.empno =`
   `e.empno);`

C. `select e.empno, e.ename from emp e where sal <`
   `(select sum(x.vouch_amt) from expense x where`
   `x.empno = e.empno);`

D. `select e.empno, e.ename from emp e where exists`
   `(select sum(x.vouch_amt) from expense x where`
   `x.empno = e.empno);`

37. **Take a look at the following statement:**

```
SQL>   select ename
 2     from emp
 3     where empno in
 4       ( select empno
 5         from expense
 6         where vouch_amt > 10000 );
```

Which of the following choices identifies a SQL statement that will produce the same output as the preceding statement, rewritten to use the `exists` operator?

A. `select e.ename from emp e where exists (select`
   `x.empno from expense x where x.vouch_amt > 10000)`
   `and x.empno = e.empno;`

B. `select e.ename from emp e where exists (select`
   `x.empno from expense x where x.vouch_amt > 10000`
   `and x.empno = e.empno);`

C. `select e.ename from emp e where x.empno = e.empno`
   `and exists (select x.empno from expense x where`
   `x.vouch_amt > 10000);`

D. `select e.ename from emp e, expense x where x.empno`
   `= e.empno and x.vouch_amt > 10000 and exists`
   `(select x.empno from expense x where x.vouch_amt >`
   `10000);`

38. **Use the following code block to answer the question:**

```
SQL> select deptno, job, avg(sal)
 2   from emp
 3   group by deptno, job
 4   having avg(sal) >
```

```
5      ( select sal
6        from emp
7        where ename = 'MARTIN');
```

Which of the following choices identifies the type of subquery used in the preceding statement?

A. A single-row subquery

B. A multirow subquery

C. A from clause subquery

D. A multicolumn subquery

39. **The company's sales database has two tables. The first, PROFITS, stores the amount of profit made on products sold by the different corporate regions in different quarters. The second, REGIONS, stores the name of each departmental region, the headquarter location for that region, and the name of the region's vice president. Which of the following queries will obtain total profits on toys for regions headed by SMITHERS, FUJIMORI, and LAKKARAJU?**

A. select sum(profit) from profits where region in (
select region from regions where reg_head in
('SMITHERS', 'FUJIMORI', 'LAKKARAJU')) and product
= 'TOYS';

B. select sum(profit) from profits where region in (
select region from regions where reg_head in
('SMITHERS', 'FUJIMORI', 'LAKKARAJU') and product =
'TOYS');

C. select sum(profit) from profits where region = (
select region from regions where reg_head in
('SMITHERS', 'FUJIMORI', 'LAKKARAJU')) and product
= 'TOYS';

D. select sum(profit) from profits where region in (
select region from regions where reg_head in
('SMITHERS', 'FUJIMORI', 'LAKKARAJU') and product =
'TOYS';

40. **The following code block shows a query containing a subquery:**

```
SQL> select dname, avg(sal) as dept_avg
  2  from emp, dept
  3  where emp.deptno = dept.deptno
  4  group by dname having avg(sal) >
```

```
5   (select avg(sal) * 1/4
6    from emp, dept
7    where emp.deptno = dept.deptno)
8   order by avg(sal);
```

Which of the following choices identifies a clause you might use to redefine this query to remove redundancy of group function execution in the subquery and in the main query?

A. group by

B. order by

C. with

D. having

41. **Use the output in the code block to answer the following question:**

```
SQL> select e.deptno, e.ename, e.job, e.sal
  2  from emp e
  3  where e.sal =
  4  (select max(e2.sal)
  5   from emp e2
  6* where nvl(e.deptno,99) = nvl(e2.deptno,99));
   DEPTNO ENAME      JOB           SAL
--------- ---------- --------- ---------
       30 BLAKE      MANAGER       2850
       10 CLARK      MANAGER       2450
       20 SCOTT      ANALYST       3000
          KING       PRESIDENT     5000
       20 FORD       ANALYST       3000
```

In order to display a value of 99 in the DEPTNO column in the preceding return set, which of the following SQL statements might be appropriate?

A. select nvl(e.deptno,99), e.ename, e.job, e.sal from emp e where (e.deptno, e.sal) =(select max(e2.sal) from emp e2 where nvl(e.deptno,99) = nvl(e2.deptno,99));

B. select nvl(e.deptno,99), e.ename, e.job, e.sal from emp e where e.sal =(select max(e2.sal) from emp e2 where nvl(e.deptno,99) = nvl(e2.deptno,99));

C. select nvl(e.deptno,99), e.ename, e.job, e.sal from emp e where (e.deptno, e.sal) =(select e2.deptno, max(e2.sal) from emp e2 where nvl(e.deptno,99) = nvl(e2.deptno,99));

D. select nvl(e.deptno,99), e.ename, e.job, e.sal from
emp e where (e.deptno, e.sal) =(select e2.deptno,
max(e2.sal) from emp e2 where nvl(e.deptno,99) =
nvl(e2.deptno,99) group by e2.deptno);

42. **Your company's sales database contains one table, PROFITS, which stores profits listed by product name, sales region, and quarterly time period. If you wanted to obtain a listing of the five best-selling products in company history, which of the following SQL statements would you use?**

    A. select p.prod_name, p.profit from (select
    prod_name, profit from profits order by profit
    desc) where rownum <= 5;

    B. select p.prod_name, p.profit from (select
    prod_name, sum(profit) from profits group by
    prod_name order by sum(profit) desc) subq where
    p.prod_name = subq.prod_name;

    C. select prod_name, profit from (select prod_name,
    sum(profit) from profits group by prod_name order
    by sum(profit) desc) where rownum <=5;

    D. select prod_name, profit from (select prod_name,
    sum(profit) from profits order by sum(profit) desc)
    where rownum <=5;

43. **Your sales database consists of one table, PROFITS, which lists profits for every product type the company sells listed by quarter and by sales region. You need to develop a report that users can run interactively to show them the profits on toys for a given quarter. You have concerns about the users of this report because they have frequently complained about the readability and usability of your reports. Which of the following choices shows the contents of the script you should use for your report?**

    A. select profit from profits where prod_type = 'TOYS'
    and time_period = '&v_period';

    B. define v_periodselect profit from profits where
    prod_type = 'TOYS' and time_period = '&v_period';

    C. accept v_period prompt 'Enter the time period =>
    'select profit from profits where prod_type =
    'TOYS' and time_period = '&v_period';

    D. accept v_periodselect profit from profits where
    prod_type = 'TOYS' and time_period = '&v_period';

44. Review the following code block containing the contents of a script called `dates.sql`:

```
accept v_hiredate prompt 'enter hire date => '
select empno, ename, job
from emp
where trunc(hiredate) = trunc('&v_hiredate');
```

Which of the following aspects of the script must be changed in order for the script to function properly?

A. Variable `v_hiredate` must be changed to accept DATE information.

B. The `trunc( )` function in the query should be eliminated.

C. The `prompt` clause in the `accept` command is unnecessary.

D. Nothing; the script will work fine as is.

45. You are creating tables in the Oracle database. Which of the following statements identifies a table-creation statement that is not valid?

A. `create table cats (c_name varchar2(10), c_weight number, c_owner varchar2(10));`

B. `create table my_cats as select * from cats where owner = 'ME';`

C. `create global temporary table temp_cats (c_name varchar2(10), c_weight number, c_owner varchar2(10));`

D. `create table cats-over-5-lbs as select c_name, c_weight from cats where c_weight > 5;`

46. Your attempt to create a table in Oracle results in the following error: `ORA-00955 - name is already used by existing object.` Which of the following choices does not identify an appropriate correction for this situation?

A. Create the object as a different user.

B. Drop the existing object with the same name.

C. Change the column names in the object being created.

D. Rename the existing object.

47. The PROFITS column inside the SALES table is declared as NUMBER(10,2). Which of the following values cannot be stored in that column?

A. 5392845.324

B. 871039453.1

C. 75439289.34

D. 60079829.25

48. Employee KING was hired on November 17, 1981. You issue the following query on your Oracle database: `select vsize(hiredate) from emp where ename = 'KING;`. Which of the following choices identifies the value returned?

    A. 4

    B. 7

    C. 9

    D. 17

49. You define the PRODUCT_NAME column in your SALES table to be CHAR(40). Later, you add one row to this table with the value CAT_TOYS for PRODUCT_NAME. You then issue the following command: `select vsize(product_name) from sales`. Which of the following choices best identifies the value returned?

    A. 8

    B. 12

    C. 40

    D. 4000

50. The JOB table contains three columns: JOB_NAME, JOB_DESC, and JOB_WAGE. You insert a new row into the JOB_DESC table using the following command:

```
SQL> insert into job (job_name, job_desc)
  2   values ('LACKEY','MAKES COFFEE');
```

    Later, you query the table, and receive the following result:

```
SQL> select * from job where job_name = 'LACKEY';
JOB_NAME   JOB_DESC      JOB_WAGE
---------  ------------  --------
LACKEY     MAKES COFFEE        35
```

    Which of the following choices identifies how JOB_WAGE was populated with data?

   A. The row for LACKEY in the JOB table already existed with JOB_WAGE set to 35.

   B. A `default` clause on the JOB_WAGE column defined when the table was created specified the value when the row was inserted.

   C. The `values` clause in the `insert` statement contained a hidden value that was added when the row was added.

   D. The only possible explanation is that a later `update` statement issued against the JOB table added the JOB_WAGE value.

51. You want to reduce the size of a non-NULL NUMBER(10) column to NUMBER(6). Which of the following steps must be completed after the appropriate `alter table` command is issued?

   A. Copy column records to a temporary storage location.

   B. Set the NUMBER column to NULL for all rows.

   C. Create a temporary location for NUMBER data.

   D. Copy column records from the temporary location back to the main table.

52. You just issued the following statement: `alter table sales drop column profit;`. Which of the following choices identifies when the column will actually be removed from Oracle?

   A. Immediately following statement execution

   B. After the `alter table drop unused columns` command is issued

   C. After the `alter table set unused column` command is issued

   D. After the `alter table modify` command is issued

53. You want to increase the size of a non-NULL VARCHAR2(5) column to VARCHAR2(10). Which of the following steps must be accomplished after executing the appropriate `alter table` command?

   A. Set the VARCHAR2 column to NULL for all rows.

   B. Create a temporary location for VARCHAR2 data.

   C. Copy the column records from the temporary location back to the main table.

   D. Nothing; the statement is executed automatically.

54. You want to increase the size of the PRODUCT_TYPE column, declared as a VARCHAR(5) column, to VARCHAR2(10) in the SALES table. Which of the following commands is useful for this purpose?

   A. `alter table sales add (product_type varchar2(10));`

   B. `alter table sales modify product_type varchar2(10));`

   C. `alter table sales set unused column product_type varchar2(10));`

   D. `alter table sales drop column product_type;`

55. You drop a table in an Oracle database that is the parent table in a parent-child data relationship. Which of the following objects will not be dropped when you drop the parent table?

   A. Associated constraints

   B. The child column

   C. Associated triggers

   D. Associated indexes

56. The PROFITS table in your database has a primary key on the PRODUCT_NAME and SALE_PERIOD columns. Which of the following statements could *not* have been used to define this primary key?

   A. `create table profits ( product_name varchar2(10), sale_period varchar2(10), profit number, constraint pk_profits_01 primary key (product_name, sale_period));`

   B. `alter table profits add constraint pk_profits_01 primary key (product_name, sale_period) deferrable initially immediate;`

   C. `alter table profits add (constraint pk_profits_01 primary key (product_name, sale_period));`

   D. `create table profits ( product_name varchar2(10) primary key, sale_period varchar2(10) primary key, profit number);`

57. You are defining check constraints on your SALES table, which contains two columns: PRODUCT_TYPE and UNIT_SALES. Which of the following choices identify a properly defined check constraint? (Choose two.)

A. `alter table sales add constraint ck_sales_01 check (product_type in ('TOYS', 'HOT DOGS', 'PALM PILOTS'));`

B. `alter table sales add constraint ck_sales_01 check (product_type in (select product_type from valid_products));`

C. `alter table sales modify (product_type varchar2(30) check (product_type in ('TOYS', 'HOT DOGS', 'PALM PILOTS')));`

D. `alter table sales add (product_name varchar2(30) check (product_name <> 'AK-47'));`

58. Use the following code block to answer the question:

```
SQL> create table prices
  2  ( product_name varchar2(30),
  3      price number(10,4));
Table created.
SQL> alter table prices add constraint pk_prices_01
  2  primary key (product_name);
Table altered.
SQL> insert into prices values ('DOGGY', 499.99);
1 row created.
SQL> alter table prices disable constraint pk_prices_01;
Table altered.
SQL> insert into prices values ('DOGGY', 449.99);
1 row created.
SQL> alter table prices enable novalidate constraint pk_prices_01;
```

What happens next?

A. Existing entries are checked for violations, PK_PRICES_01 is enabled, and Oracle checks subsequent entries for violations immediately.

B. Existing entries are checked for violations, PK_PRICES_01 is not enabled, and Oracle does not check subsequent entries for violations immediately.

C. Existing entries are not checked for violations, PK_PRICES_01 is enabled, and Oracle checks subsequent entries for violations immediately.

D. Existing entries are checked for violations, PK_PRICES_01 is not enabled, Oracle checks subsequent entries for violations immediately.

59. Your attempt to disable a constraint yields the following error: `ORA-02297: cannot disable constraint-dependencies exist.` Which of the following types of constraints is likely causing interference with your disablement of this one?

    A. Check constraint

    B. Not NULL constraint

    C. Foreign key constraint

    D. Unique constraint

60. You are disabling a not NULL constraint on the UNIT_PRICE column in the SALES table. Which of the following choices identifies the correct statement for performing this action?

    A. `alter table sales modify (unit_prices null);`

    B. `alter table sales modify (unit_prices not null);`

    C. `alter table sales add (unit_prices null);`

    D. `alter table sales add (unit_prices not null);`

Answers to Practice Exam 1

1. A. `select NAME, JERSEY_NO where JERSEY_NO = 6;`

Explanation   SQL statements in Oracle must have a `from` clause. A SQL statement can lack a `where` clause, in which case, all of the data in the table will be returned. However, if the statement does not have a `from` clause, Oracle will not know what table to retrieve data from. Recall that a special table called DUAL assists in situations where you don't want to retrieve data from a table, but instead only want to manipulate expressions. **(Topic 2.1)**

2. A. Issuing an `update` statement

Explanation   The only choice that does not end a transaction is the one that continues the transaction, namely issuing another `update` statement. A `commit` tells Oracle to save your data changes and end the transaction. A `rollback` tells Oracle to discard your data changes and end the transaction. Closing SQL*Plus or otherwise ending the session is usually treated as an implicit `commit` and ends your transaction as well. **(Topic 8.3)**

3. B. `commit`

Explanation   In order to save any change you make in Oracle, you use the `commit` command. The `savepoint` command merely identifies a logical breakpoint in your transaction that you can use to break up complex units of work. The `rollback` command discards every change you made since the last `commit`. Finally, the `set transaction` command sets up the transaction to be read-only against the Oracle database. **(Topic 8.6)**

4. D. USER_CONS_COLUMNS

Explanation   The USER_CONS_COLUMNS dictionary view shows you all of the columns in tables belonging to that user that are part of indexes used to enforce constraints. USER_INDEXES is incorrect because that view only displays information about the index itself, not the columns in the index. USER_TAB_COLUMNS displays all the columns in all tables owned by the user. Finally, USER_COLUMNS is not an actual view in the Oracle database. **(Topic 12.2)**

5. D. Not NULL

Explanation   Not NULL integrity constraints can only be declared as column constraints, meaning that the actual syntax for defining the constraint will appear next to the constrained column, as opposed to at the end of the column listing. Choices A, B, and C all identify constraints that can be defined as table constraints or as column constraints. **(Topic 10.2)**

6. D. The view

Explanation When you drop a table with the `cascade constraints` option, Oracle removes from other tables all associated indexes, triggers, and constraints that reference that table. Oracle does not remove the views that use that table, however. You must remove a view manually with the `drop view` statement. **(Topic 11.2)**

7. D. MONTHS_BETWEEN

Explanation Each of the choices accepts a DATE datatype as input and returns a DATE datatype, with one exception. The MONTHS_BETWEEN function returns a number indicating how many months there are between the two dates you give it. This number will be displayed with numbers to the right of the decimal point, which you can round off if you like. **(Topic 3.2)**

8. C. `order by sqrt(1);`

Explanation The `order by` clause in the `select` clause of the `select` statement enables you to refer to the column you want the table order determined by, either by the column name or by the number representing the column order. However, you cannot perform any sort of numeric function on that column-order number. Both the `asc` and `desc` keywords are valid for the `order by` clause, indicating ascending order (default) and descending order, respectively. **(Topic 2.2)**

9. B. Table with one column and one row used in various operations

Explanation The DUAL table is a special table in Oracle used to satisfy the requirement of a `from` clause in your SQL statements. It contains one column and one row of data. It is not a dictionary view; rather, it is an actual table. You could use the DUAL table in arithmetic expressions and not actually pull real data from the database. You should never insert data into the DUAL table under any circumstances. **(Topic 3.2)**

10. A. ACTIVE

Explanation The `decode ( )` function is used as a case statement, where Oracle will review the value in the column identified in the first parameter (in this case, ACCTNO). If that value equals the second parameter, the third parameter is returned. If that value equals the fourth parameter, the fifth parameter is returned, and so on. If the value equals no parameter, the default value provided in the last parameter (in this case, ACTIVE) is returned. TRANSFER would be returned if ACCTNO equaled 590395, SEIZED would be returned if ACCTNO equaled 654321, and CLOSED would be returned if ACCTNO equaled 123456. **(Topic 3.2)**

11. C. insert into BANK_ACCT (ACCTNO, NAME) VALUES (&VAR1, '&VAR2');

Explanation In order to have statement reusability where you can enter a value on-the-fly, you must use lexical references as runtime variables. These references are preceded with an ampersand (&) character, as in the correct answer. Although you can use nested subqueries in your insert statements, this has the effect of inserting multiple rows at once without requiring input from the user. **(Topic 7.1)**

12. B. 28-APR-07

Explanation For this question, you really need to put on your thinking cap. ADD_MONTHS adds a specified number of months, indicated by the second parameter to the value in the first parameter. The parameter 120 months is ten years, so if you add ten to the year in the date given, you should come up with 28-APR-07, which is the correct answer. When you are taking the exam, beware of having too much of your time sucked up by this sort of brainteaser question. **(Topic 3.2)**

13. D. MONDAY JUNE 26, 2037: 10:30PM

Explanation The first statement in this question alters the date format shown in your SQL*Plus session. The second statement returns the current date and time in that specific format. In this case, your format is the day of the week, followed by the month of the year, the date, the year, and the time in A.M./P.M. format. This being the case, the correct answer is MONDAY JUNE 26, 2037: 10:30PM. **(Topic 3.2)**

14. B. where A.C = 5 AND A.C = B.C (+);

Explanation The correct choice illustrates the use of Oracle's outer join function. The question indicates that you want to see data in table A, whether or not corresponding data exists in table B. Thus, you place the outer join operation (it looks like a (+)) next to the reference to the C column in table B. If the outer join operation is removed, Oracle will only return data from table A for which corresponding data exists in table B. If the outer join operator is used for both tables, you will get a syntax error. If you omit the join operator comparing values from table A to table B, Oracle will return a Cartesian product of the data you requested from A with all the data from table B. **(Topic 4.2)**

15. B. When creating composite primary keys, the datatypes in all columns within the primary key must be the same datatype.

Explanation No restriction exists on column datatypes for composite primary keys requiring that all columns in the primary key have the same datatype. Choice A is incorrect because you must ensure that the variables designed to hold data from table columns are large enough for the values in those columns. Choice D is incorrect for largely the same reason. Finally, choice C is incorrect because Oracle forces you to declare the column in a child table with the exact same datatype as it has in the parent table. **(Topic 10.2)**

16. B. sqrt ( )

Explanation All the choices indicate group by functions except for the sqrt ( ) function. sqrt ( ) is a single-row function acting on each value in each column row, one at a time or individually. avg ( ) processes data from multiple rows in a column and produces one result: the average value for all of them. count ( ) processes all values in a column or columns and counts the number of row values in that column or columns. The stddev ( ) function takes all values in a column of rows and determines the standard deviation for that set of values. **(Topic 5.1)**

17. C. nvl ( ) returns NULL if the first value is not equal to the second.

Explanation The only statement that is not true is nvl ( ) returns NULL if the first value is not equal to the second. nvl ( ) is specifically designed to avoid returning NULL for a column by substituting another value that you pass as the second parameter. nvl ( ) handles many different datatypes, and both values passed must be the same datatype. **(Topic 3.3)**

18. B. 418

Explanation Regardless of what you think you know about Oracle, the only true way to know what Oracle does is to experience it. Three requests for NEXTVAL from MY_SEQ does not mean that each request increments the sequence because the first request for NEXTVAL returns the initial value. Take a look:

```
SQL> create sequence my_seq
  2    start with 394
  3    increment by 12
  4    nominvalue
  5    nomaxvalue
  6    nocycle
  7    nocache;
Sequence created.
SQL> select my_seq.nextval from dual;
  NEXTVAL
---------
      394
SQL> /
  NEXTVAL
---------
      406
```

```
SQL> /
   NEXTVAL
---------
       418
SQL> select my_seq.currval from dual;
   CURRVAL
---------
       418
SQL> /
   CURRVAL
---------
       418
SQL> /
   CURRVAL
---------
       418
SQL> /
   CURRVAL

-------
       418
```

Thus, the sequence has only been incremented twice, so the answer is 418. **(Topic 12.1)**

19. B. The high-water mark was not reset.

Explanation   The `select count(*)` statement takes a long time because Oracle needed to inspect the table in its entirety in order to derive the row count, even though the table was empty. To avoid this situation on large tables, use the `truncate` statement rather than `delete`. `truncate` resets the high-water mark on your table, thus reducing the time it takes Oracle to perform `select count(*)` operations. **(Topic 9.5)**

20. B. `create or replace view`

Explanation   The column definitions for a view can be changed only by recreating the view with the `create or replace view` statement. The `alter view` command is used only to recompile a view. `insert into view` is not a valid SQL statement. Although `create view` will technically work, you must first drop the view you want to recreate, which requires two statements, not one. `create or replace view` is the most accurate choice offered. **(Topic 11.2)**

21. A. A `join` statement without a `where` clause

Explanation   Cartesian products are the result of `select` statements that contain malformed `where` clauses. `sum( )` and `avg( )` operations are group functions and do not produce Cartesian products. Selecting data from the DUAL table will not produce a Cartesian product because only one table is involved—and a table with only one row at that! **(Topic 4.1)**

22. B. Creating an appropriate `login.sql` file

Explanation   SQL*Plus shows its roots in UNIX systems through the `login.sql` file. This file is used to specify settings used in your session. `login.sql` runs automatically after you log into Oracle. SQL*Plus in Windows environments does not have a Preferences menu, eliminating that choice. You shouldn't attempt to use the `alter table` or `alter user` statements for this purpose either. **(Topic 7.3)**

23. B. `create or replace view emp_sal_vw as select`
`emp_user, salary from emp_salary where emp_user =`
`user;`

Explanation   The command in choice B is correctly defined for creating a view that will only enable users to see their own salary information from the underlying table. Choice A is incorrect because the view defined will show all salary information except for salary data for the user issuing the query. Choices C and D are incorrect because the view will show only salary data for users other than MARTHA. **(Topic 11.2)**

24. D. INTEGER

Explanation   Although you can declare variables in PL/SQL blocks using the INTEGER datatype, you cannot store INTEGER datatype data in Oracle tables. All other datatypes shown—CHAR, RAW, and DATE—can be stored in the Oracle database. **(Topic 9.3)**

25. B. TO_CHAR

Explanation   TO_CHAR is used to convert DATE values, numbers, and other things into text strings. The CONVERT operation is used to convert a text string from one character set to another. The TO_NUMBER operation converts numeric text to true numbers. The TO_DATE function is used to convert a properly formatted text string into a DATE value. **(Topic 3.3)**

26. C. Use the `set` command to allow for larger LONG column values.

Explanation   The TRIGGER_BODY column in the ALL_TRIGGERS view is declared as a LONG datatype column, and SQL*Plus is most likely cutting off data from the output. Choice A is incorrect because the question says you are able to see some of the data in the view, just not all the data. Choice B is incorrect because memory allocation has nothing to do with the problem identified in the question. Finally, choice D is incorrect because nothing is wrong with the ALL_TRIGGERS view. The problem lies instead with how SQL*Plus is currently configured to display LONG column data. **(Topic 7.2)**

27. B. All records

Explanation   Because the `update` statement does not contain a `where` clause, the change will be made to every record in the table. It is not possible to accurately update only the first or last record in the table. None of the records will be updated only if something is wrong with the `update` statement, such as a column being referenced incorrectly. **(Topic 8.3)**

28. B. `alter table`

Explanation   The `alter table` statement enables you to easily add columns after the table is created, with minimal impact to your system. Unlike when you want to change views, you do not use the `or replace` keyword for this effort, thus creating a powerful distraction for the user who is more familiar with views than with underlying tables. The `create table` statement could be used for the task, but you would first need to issue the `drop table` statement to get rid of the initial table. **(Topic 9.4)**

29. B. foreign key

Explanation   Foreign key relationships require that you grant `references` privileges on a table to the user who is creating the foreign key relationship from his or her table to yours. No particular special privilege must be granted to create `unique`, `check`, or `not NULL` constraints other than `create table`. **(Topic 10.2)**

30. D. Oracle creates the view successfully.

Explanation   When you issue the `create view` command shown in the question, Oracle creates the view successfully. A view can be created with the `order by` clause, making choice A incorrect. You do not need to enclose the `select` statement in your `create view` command in parentheses, as choice C suggests. Finally, Choice B is incorrect because you do not need to use the `with check option` clause for creating a view. **(Topic 11.2)**

31. D. `like`

Explanation   In the situation where you want to use wildcards, Oracle offers the `like` comparison operator. This operator enables you to search for text strings like the one you're looking for. The in operator specifies a set of values to which the comparison value can be equal to one of. exists enables you to use a subquery as a lookup validity test for some piece of information. between specifies a range comparison, such as between 1 AND 5. **(Topic 2.1)**

32. A. Use define to capture values.

Explanation   The define command can be used to identify a variable and assign it a value for use throughout a script running in SQL*Plus. This is useful when you are executing a number of SQL statements in batch. Although the accept command can perform the same function, the key factor that makes this the wrong answer is the mention of no user interaction in the question. Hard-coded values will work, but they make the script almost completely not reusable. Finally, although lexical references using an ampersand (&) followed by a label will provide statement reusability, your users will need to keep entering values every time a statement containing the lexical reference is processed. **(Topic 7.1)**

33. A. where EMP.EMPID = 39284 AND EMP.EMPID = EXPNS.EMPID;

Explanation   Because you only want data from each table where a match appears in the other, you are performing a regular join or equijoin operation. In Oracle, you would not use the outer join (+) operator for this purpose. This eliminates both of the answer choices that contain an outer join operator. **(Topic 4.1)**

34. C. 4104930504

Explanation   The only record that will not be present from the choices given is 4104930504, because UPC code 402392340 does not exist at the time this statement is issued. It was already changed to 50393950, and thus the 4104930504 update statement fails when you issue it. In order to get the answer correct, you need to read the question for a long time, and that wastes time when you're taking the OCP exams. Be aware that this question can take up an enormous amount of time if you're not careful. **(Topic 8.2)**

35. D. Views with object dependencies on the table being dropped will be rendered invalid automatically, but will not be dropped.

Explanation   Oracle does not remove views when you drop underlying tables. Instead, Oracle merely marks the view as invalid. Thus, because choices A, B, and C all indicate in various different ways that the view will be dropped, all those choices are incorrect. **(Topic 11.3)**

36. C. Four

Explanation   The general rule of thumb here is that if you have *n* tables you want to join—four in this case—you will generally need *n* - 1 comparison operations in your `where` clause joined together by `AND`—three in this case. In addition, the question states that you want to further restrict return data based on values in the first table. Thus, your `where` clause would have four conditions, and may look something like the following block:

```
WHERE
A.COLUMN1 = 5          AND
A.COLUMN1 = B.COLUMN1  AND
B.COLUMN2 = C.COLUMN2  AND
C.COLUMN3 = D.COLUMN3
```

(Topic 4.1)

37. A. Password authentication and granting privileges

Explanation Although in order to get database access you need to create user privileges, the two real components of the Oracle security model are password authentication and granting privileges. When users are created, they will still not be able to connect to Oracle unless they are granted a privilege (`create session`), and even when they connect, they still cannot see anything unless someone gives them permission via the `grant` command. **(Topic 13.1)**

38. C. `spool`

Explanation The `spool` command makes SQL*Plus write an output file containing all information transacted in the session, from the time you turn spooling on and identify the output file to the time you either turn spooling off or end the session. `prompt` causes SQL*Plus to prompt you to enter data using a custom request message. `echo` causes an error because it is not a valid command in SQL*Plus. Finally, the `define` command is used for variable definition and variable assignment in SQL*Plus scripts. **(Topic 1.3)**

39. B. `select A.STUDENT_ID, A.LOCATION, B.LOCATION from TEST_SCORE A, TEST_SCORE B where A.STUDENT_ID = B.STUDENT_ID AND A.LOCATION <> B.LOCATION AND trunc(A.TEST_DATE)+30 >= trunc(B.TEST_DATE) AND trunc(A.TEST_DATE)-30 <= trunc(B.TEST_DATE);`

Explanation Because it ensures that the student is the same, that the date the test was taken violated the 30-day rule, and that the test location is not the same, choice B is the correct answer. This question is probably the hardest on the exam. Even if you have a bit of SQL experience, this question will take you a while. When taking the OCP exam, the last thing you need is time-waster questions to throw you off. A good technique to avoid having questions like this one consume all your time is to skip it if you cannot answer it within 30 seconds. You'll most likely have some time at the end of the exam to review the questions you skipped. **(Topic 4.3)**

40. C. `select * from EMPLOYEE where empid = (select empid from invoice where invoice_no = 4399485);`

Explanation   If you can use a subquery, you should do so. Only one choice displays a subquery, so that one must be the correct answer. All the other choices depend on the EMPID being provided, not using the invoice number. **(Topic 6.2)**

41. A. To put returned data into sorted order

Explanation   The `having` clause is best used to include or exclude certain data groups, not to return data in sort order. The `order by` clause handles that task. **(Topic 2.2)**

42. D. Roles

Explanation   Roles enable you to group privileges together into one object and grant the privileges to the user at one time. No privileges are related to indexes other than the privilege to access the associated table. Tables and sequences both require privileges to be granted to a user or role; they do not simplify the act of privilege management in any way. **(Topic 13.2)**

43. A. `alter user`

Explanation   The `alter user` statement with the `identified by` clause is used to change a user's password. `alter role` is used for modifying the actual role object, and affects users insofar as the user has been granted the role. Of the remaining choices, although user SNOW may be able to execute those statements depending on what privileges he is granted, none of these privileges will handle what the question requires. **(Topic 13.1)**

44. C. User SNOW needs a synonym for table EMP.

Explanation   User SNOW needs a synonym in order to refer to a table he doesn't own without prefixing that reference with a schema owner. Without privileges, SNOW would not see the data, but even with the appropriate privileges granted, SNOW still needs to prefix the table name with the schema information if no synonym exists for the table in that schema. If no synonym exists, SNOW still must prefix references to EMP with REED, as in REED.EMP. Tables don't have passwords like databases do, so that choice is patently incorrect. **(Topic 12.3)**

45. D. Oracle returns an error.

Explanation   In this situation, you cannot use the `order by` clause in a subquery. Oracle will return an error. Thus, no data will be returned from any table, so all of the other choices are wrong. **(Topic 6.4)**

46. B. `select to_char(nvl(sqrt(59483), 0)) from dual;`

Explanation   The `select to_char(nvl(sqrt(59483), 0)) from dual;` statement is a valid statement. The `select nvl(sqrt(59483)) from dual;` statement does not pass enough parameters to the `nvl( )` function. The `select TO_CHAR(nvl(sqrt(59483), 'VALID')) from dual;` statement breaks the rule in `nvl( )` that states that both parameters passed into the function must be the same datatype. The `select (to_char(nvl(sqrt(59483), '0')) from dual;` statement is missing a matching closing parenthesis after `'0'`. **(Topic 1.2)**

47. C. `column PLAY_TABLE heading "My Plays and Authors"`

Explanation   The `heading` clause to the `column` command in SQL*Plus acts in the same way as a `column` alias does in SQL—it modifies the output of the query to use a heading of your design. Despite its similarity, however, the `heading` clause is not the same as an alias in SQL. Thus, both the choice identifying the `alias` clause and the choice using the `as` keyword are incorrect. The choice containing the `format` clause should be easy to eliminate. **(Topic 1.3)**

48.   C. BABS

Explanation   Because BABS is not listed in the contents of the MY_USERS table, JONES will not see BABS when he queries the view. Choices A, B, and D all identify users who are listed in the MY_USERS view, and thus will be seen by JONES when he queries BASEBALL_TEAM_VW. **(Topic 11.3)**

49.   C. Use the `set long` command

Explanation   The `set long` command is used for adjusting the SQL*Plus output produced from data dictionary views with long columns. The view containing view creation code contains a long column, so adjusting how SQL*Plus displays that information will solve the issue. Choice A is incorrect because you cannot change the size of a dictionary view. Choice D is incorrect because the `alter user` statement does not somehow adjust view alottments. Finally, the NLS_DATE_FORMAT controls date formatting, not long columns. **(Topic 1.3)**

50.   D. `group by COW_NAME;`

Explanation   When the column clause contains a mix of group and non-group expressions, all non-group expressions must be listed to the left of the group expression, and all non-group expressions listed in the column clause must also be listed in the `group by` clause. Otherwise, Oracle returns an error indicating a problem with the `group by` expression, making choice D the correct answer. **(Topic 5.3)**

51. D. `group by COW_NAME;`

Explanation The `mod( )` function is not a group function, so no `group by` clause is necessary in this query. Thus, choice D is the correct answer. **(Topic 5.3)**

52. B. `select A.LASTNAME, B.DEPT_NO from EMP A, (select EMPID, DEPT_NO from DEPT) B where A.EMPID = B.EMPID;`

Explanation An inline view is a subquery appearing in the table clause of your SQL query. Thus, because choice B is the only query showing a subquery in the `from` clause, it is the only query that uses an inline view and therefore is the correct answer. Choices A and C are incorrect because the subqueries are used in the `where` clause. Choice D is incorrect because the subquery in the column clause is really a static text string that will be listed once for as many rows as there are in the USER_TABLES view. **(Topic 11.5)**

53. A. `drop index`

Explanation An index associated with a constraint cannot be dropped using the `drop index` command, making choice A the correct answer. The other statements all indicate methods that can be used for removing indexes associated with constraints. Constraints will be removed when the table is removed or whenever you drop the constraint. **(Topic 12.2)**

54. C. Every primary key column value must be unique and none can be NULL.

Explanation Choice C is the only answer that encapsulates all the restrictions on data in primary key columns, so it is therefore the correct answer. Although choices A and B each identify some of the restrictions on primary key constraints, neither choice alone is the correct answer. Choice D does not identify a restriction on data in primary key columns so you can discard that choice immediately. **(Topic 10.1)**

55. C. Table FOOBAR has no primary key, and therefore no index on MOO.

Explanation Because no primary key was defined when you created the FOOBAR table, the later query on that table cannot use any unique index on the MOO column to speed access to data in your FOOBAR table. Thus, choice C is the correct answer. Choice A is incorrect because you have no information indicating a primary key index is present, whereas choice B is incorrect because nothing states that a query takes longer to resolve when operating on a table rather than a view—if anything, the opposite is true. Finally, choice D is incorrect because again, you have no information indicating that the table was dropped and recreated. **(Topic 10.1)**

56. D. USER_INDEXES, indexes with the same name as the constraint

Explanation   The object associated with the table and the primary key is an index, and the USER_INDEXES dictionary view contains a listing of all indexes owned by the current user. You can query this dictionary view to find indexes with the same name as the constraint identified in the question text, making choice D the correct answer. Choice A is incorrect because USER_SEQUENCES contains information about sequences, which wasn't a topic for the question. USER_TABLES contains information about tables, which also wasn't a topic for the question, making choice B incorrect as well. Finally, USER_IND_COLUMNS contains information about indexed columns, which aren't objects separate from the table or constraint, making choice C incorrect as well. Oracle has been de-emphasizing dictionary view questions on this exam of late, so consider it a bonus if you knew the correct answer. **(Topic 12.2)**

57. B. To improve performance on columns with few unique values

Explanation   Bitmap indexes are designed to improve performance on columns with few unique values. Traditional or B-tree indexes are designed for indexes with many or all unique values, making choices A and C incorrect. Sequences do not need an index, making choice D incorrect. A question about bitmap indexes may or may not be on the OCP exam, so consider it a bonus if you knew the correct answer. **(Topic 12.2)**

58. A. `update employee set salary = 5000 where empid = 59694;`

Explanation   Choice A correctly identifies a statement that will correspond to the requirements of the statement, whereby the salary information for employee 59694 is changed. Choice B is incorrect because the `update` statement changes EMPID column information, not SALARY. Choice C is incorrect because the statement changes LASTNAME column information, not SALARY. Finally, choice D is incorrect because although SALARY information is being changed, it is being done based on LASTNAME information, not EMPID information. **(Topic 8.3)**

59. C. `grant update on emp to timothy with grant option;`

Explanation   The statement offered by choice C is used for giving object privileges to other users along with the ability to grant that privilege to others. Choice D is incorrect because `with admin option` is used for giving administrative ability over system privileges with respect to other users. Choice A is not a properly formulated grant command for object privileges, making it an incorrect answer. Choice B is incorrect because although the privilege itself was given to TIMOTHY, administrative ability was not. **(Topic 13.3)**

60. D. REED and SNOW only

Explanation   SNOW does not lose the ability to create sessions with Oracle just because REED revoked the privilege from MANN because Oracle does not cascade revocation of system privileges. Thus, REED still has the privilege because no one revoked it from her, and SNOW still has the privilege because Oracle didn't cascade the revocation. **(Topic 13.1)**

Answers to Practice Exam 2

1. D. where C.COW_NAME = 'BESS' AND C.CARTON_NUM = C1.CARTON_NUM;

Explanation   Two components are required in your where clause—you need a join clause and something that only pulls records from COW_MILK for BESS. The right answer is where C.COW_NAME = 'BESS' AND C.CARTON_NUM = C1.CARTON_NUM;. Another choice is similar to this one, but because it uses the not equal (<>) clause for getting information only for BESS, it is not the choice you want. The other two choices are incomplete, and therefore wrong. **(Topic 2.1)**

2. D. The insert statements contain duplicate data due to the reset sequence.

Explanation   The correct answer is that the insert statements contain duplicate data due to the reset sequence. When you drop and re-create the sequence from its original code, you reset the start value for that sequence. Subsequent insert statements will then attempt to add rows where the value in the primary key is duplicated information. The question has no information about read-only status, so you should assume that the answer concerning the table being read-only is not correct. Dropping a sequence does nothing to a table's primary key—no relationship exists between the two. Finally, although it is true that any cached sequence values that existed when the sequence was dropped are now unusable, this point has little relevance to the question at hand. **(Topic 12.1)**

3. B. exists

Explanation   Only when using the exists statement must you use a correlated subquery. Although you can use a subquery with your use of in, you are not required to do so because you can specify a set of values instead. The between keyword indicates a range of values and does not permit the use of a subquery. The like keyword is used for wildcard comparisons and also does not permit the use of a subquery. **(Topic 2.1)**

4. D. abs ( )

Explanation   All of the functions except for abs ( ) will give you a result of 4093 when you pass them 4093.505. abs ( ) returns the absolute value of the number you pass into the function. round ( ) can give you a result of 4093 if you also pass in a second parameter defining the precision to which you want to round the function, whereas trunc ( ) will give you a result of 4093 with only 4093.505 as input. floor ( ) gives you a result of 4093, because it is the logical opposite of the ceil ( ) function. **(Topic 3.2)**

5. B. Use accept to capture the name value for each run.

Explanation   The accept command is the best way to handle the situation. Although you could use define to assign a value to a variable used throughout the script, only accept enables you to dynamically enter a value for that variable. Lexical substitutions identified with the & character will only work for the current statement, meaning that the same value assigned in one statement will not be used in the next statement unless you reenter it. **(Topic 7.3)**

6. B. truncate

Explanation   Once a truncate operation is complete, that's it—the change is made and saved. This is because truncate is not a DML operation that can be performed as part of a transaction. The truncate command is a DDL operation, and as such, it has an implied commit at the end of its execution. If you want to get the data back after truncating, you need to recover it. For the other operations listed as choices in this question—insert, update, and delete statements—Oracle enables you to discard the changes using the rollback command. **(Topic 9.5)**

7. A. savepoint

Explanation   savepoint operations simply act as logical breakpoints in a transaction. They do not cause Oracle to save or discard data, but merely act as a breakpoint with which you can perform partial transaction rollbacks later. The set transaction and commit commands indicate the beginning of a new transaction. Creating a new session with Oracle implicitly begins a transaction as well. **(Topic 8.6)**

8. B. A from clause

Explanation   No SQL statement can survive without a from clause. For this reason, Oracle provides you with the DUAL table, so that you can perform arithmetic operations on expressions and not on table data while still satisfying this syntactic construct. Because this statement already has a select clause, you don't need to add another. The `where` clause is optional, but because the statement already has one, you don't need to add another. Finally, your SQL statement does not require an `order by` clause. **(Topic 1.2)**

9. A. `set transaction`

Explanation The `set transaction` command is used to define the transaction state to be read-only. `rollback` and `commit` statements are used to end the transaction. The `savepoint` command denotes logical breakpoints for the transaction. **(Topic 8.6)**

10. C. Bitmap index

Explanation Bitmap indexes work well in situations where the data in the column is static. In this case, the column contains gender information, which rarely changes. The number of distinct possible values is limited to only two as well. Thus, this column is a bad candidate for B-tree indexes of any sort, but perfect for bitmap indexes. Remember that B-tree indexes work well for columns with high cardinality or number of distinct values corresponding to the overall number of entries in the column. **(Topic 12.2)**

11. A. Parent to child

Explanation This question describes the relationship between the INVOICE and INVOICE_ITEM table, and the appropriate answer is parent to child. This is because the relationship described between invoices and invoice items is optional, given that invoices may have no invoice items, but that all invoice items must have a corresponding invoice. **(Topic 10.2)**

12. D. `ACTIVE`

Explanation The `decode( )` function acts as a case statement. The first parameter indicates the column whose values you want decoded. If the value in the column equals parameter 2, then `decode( )` returns parameter 3. If the value in the column equals parameter 4, `decode( )` returns parameter 5, and so on. If the value in the column doesn't equal any of the other parameters specified, then `decode( )` returns the default value specified as the last parameter. Thus, because the column value is not specified for any of the parameters, the returned value is the default, `ACTIVE`. **(Topic 3.2)**

13. D. `where COL_A in (select NUM from TAB_OF_NUMS)`

Explanation The `where` clause in choice D is an excellent example of the definition of a subquery, which is the example being asked for in the question. Choice A is not a comparison operation between a column and a set of values, because only one value is being compared. Choice B is a comparison of a column to a set of values, but the set is static and defined at the time the query is issued. Choice C is a range-comparison operation, a variant on choice B, and therefore also wrong. Only choice D enables Oracle to dynamically generate the list of values to which COL_A will be compared. **(Topic 6.2)**

14. D. `select NAME from CONTESTANT where COUNTRY in (select COUNTRY from MEDALS where NUM_GOLD + NUM_SILVER + NUM_BRONZE > 10)`

Explanation   The query in choice D is correct because it contains the subquery that correctly returns a subset of countries that have contestants who won ten or more medals of any type. Choice A is incorrect because it contains a join operation, not a subquery. Choice B is simply a rewrite of choice A to use a multiple-row subquery, but does not go far enough to restrict return data. Choice C is a single-row subquery that does essentially the same thing as choice B. **(Topic 6.4)**

15. C. Multiple-column subquery, the youngest contestant from all countries

Explanation   Because the main query compares against the results of two columns returned in the subquery, this is a multiple-column subquery that will return the youngest contestant from every country in the table. This multiple-column subquery is also a multiple-row subquery, but because the defining factor is that two columns are present, you should focus more on that fact than on the rows being returned. This fact eliminates choices A and B. The subquery does return multiple rows, however. You should also be sensitive to the fact that the main query must use an `in` clause, not the equal sign (=), making choice D incorrect as well. **(Topic 6.3)**

16. A. SOO

Explanation   The correct answer is SOO because the subquery operation specified by the `in` clause ignores NULL values implicitly. Thus, because SOO has no country defined, that row is not selected as part of the subquery. As a result, SOO won't show up as having the youngest age in the results of this query. **(Topic 6.4)**

17. B. Table

Explanation   The object being referred to is a table. A table has many columns, each of which is functionally dependent on the key column. Choice A is incorrect because a synonym is simply another name you can use to reference a table, not an actual table itself. A sequence is a number generator in Oracle that, again, does not require storage in a segment other than a dictionary segment, making choice C incorrect. Finally, a view is similar to a table in that it contains many columns, each of which is functionally dependent on the key. However, views contain no data needing to be stored in a segment, so choice D is wrong as well. **(Topic 9.1)**

18. B. cube

Explanation   The cube keyword included in a group by clause of a SQL statement in Oracle8i enables you to perform *N*-dimensional cross-tabulations within the Oracle database, returning the result set directly to the client. This keyword is useful in queries within data warehouses. Choice C is incorrect because even though the rollup keyword was also added to SQL queries in Oracle8i, this keyword supports subtotal and grand total calculations of grouped data. Although the having expression is also available in group operations, choice A is incorrect because you do not need to define a having clause in order to use either cube or rollup. Finally, choice D is incorrect because the trim( ) function combines the capabilities of ltrim( ) and rtrim( ). **(Topic 5.3)**

19. B. Reverse-key indexes

Explanation   A reverse-key index is one where the contents of the indexed column are reversed. This gives a higher amount of lead-in selectivity than a straight B-tree index would, because the cardinality of the root node in the B-tree would be low. This is based on the fact that most records would begin with the digit 1 (recall the question content if you don't understand why), whereas the reverse of that key would have greater cardinality. Be careful of choice A because although cardinality is high, choice B gives a better option for performance. Choice C is incorrect because bitmap indexes are designed for low-cardinality records like status or gender. Finally, choice D indicates an index type that wouldn't suit this situation. **(Topic 12.2)**

20. A. VARCHAR2

Explanation   Because the text blocks are within the size limits imposed in Oracle8i for the VARCHAR2 datatype, it is best to use the scalar type rather than a large object for simplicity sake. If the block were larger than 4,000 bytes, you would most likely use a CLOB, but because the size requirement is less than 4,000 bytes, choice C is incorrect. You would use a BLOB to store binary large objects, making choice B incorrect. Finally, the text block is not stored as an external file (you would not use the BFILE type), making choice D incorrect. **(Topic 9.3)**

21. B. The index is dropped.

Explanation   Like automatically generated indexes associated with a table's primary key, the indexes created manually on a table to improve performance will be dropped if the table is dropped. Choices A, C, and D are therefore invalid. **(Topic 12.2)**

22. C. Columns with high cardinality are handled well by B-tree indexes.

Explanation Columns with low cardinality are the bane of B-tree indexes, eliminating choice A. Furthermore, bitmap indexes are primarily used for performance gains on columns with low cardinality, eliminating choice B. **(Topic 12.2)**

23. D. Drop and recreate the view with references to select more columns.

Explanation Choice A is incorrect because adding columns to the underlying table will not add columns to the view, but will likely invalidate the view. Choice B is incorrect because the alter view statement simply recompiles an existing view definition, whereas the real solution here is to change the existing view definition by dropping and recreating the view. Choice C is incorrect because a correlated subquery will likely worsen performance, and underscores the real problem—a column must be added to the view. **(Topic 11.2)**

24. C. maxvalue

Explanation The maxvalue option is a valid option for sequence creation. Choices A and B are both part of the create user statement, whereas choice D is a part of a constraint declaration in an alter table or create table statement. **(Topic 12.1)**

25. F. This statement contains no errors.

Explanation Even though the reference to with check option is inappropriate, considering that inserts into complex views are not possible, the statement will not actually produce an error when compiled. Therefore, the view has no errors. This is not something that can be learned. It requires hands-on experience with Oracle. **(Topic 11.4)**

26. A. references

Explanation The references privilege gives the user the ability to refer back to your table in order to link to it via a foreign key from his or her table to yours. Choice B is incorrect because the index privilege enables the user to create an index on a table, whereas choice C is incorrect because the select privilege enables users to query data in your table. Finally, choice D is incorrect because the delete privilege is only required for enabling the other user to delete data into your table. **(Topic 13.3)**

27. A, B, and C. Roles can be granted to other roles, privileges can be granted to roles, and roles can be granted to users.

Explanation Choice D is the only option not available to managing roles. Roles cannot be granted to synonyms. **(Topic 13.2)**

28. C. It is equal to NEXTVAL.

Explanation Once NEXTVAL is referenced, the sequence increments the integer and changes the value of CURRVAL to be equal to NEXTVAL. **(Topic 12.1)**

29. D. with check option

Explanation The appropriate clause is with check option. You can add this clause to a create view statement so that the view will not let you to add rows to the underlying table that cannot then be selected in the view. The with admin option and with grant option clauses are used to assign administrative ability to users along with granting them a privilege. The with security option is a work of fiction—it does not exist in Oracle. **(Topic 11.4)**

30. C. The statement fails due to the primary key constraint.

Explanation It should be obvious that the statement fails—the real question here is why. The reason is because of the primary key constraint on UPC_CODE. As soon as you try to add a duplicate record, the table will reject the addition. Although the view has with check option specified, this is not the reason the addition fails. It would be the reason an insert fails if you attempt to add a record for a day other than today, however. **(Topic 10.2)**

31. A. drop view

Explanation When a table is dropped, Oracle eliminates all related database objects, such as triggers, constraints, and indexes. However, Oracle does not remove views. Views are actually considered separate objects, and although the view will not function properly after you drop the underlying table, Oracle will keep the view around after the table is dropped. **(Topic 11.2)**

32. C. The select receives NO ROWS SELECTED.

Explanation Although the query will succeed (translation: you won't receive an error), you must beware of the distracter in choice B. In reality, choice C is the better answer because it more accurately identifies what really will occur when you issue this statement. This view will behave as any select statement would when you list criteria in the where clause that no data satisfies—by returning NO ROWS SELECTED. This is not an error condition, but you wouldn't call it a successful search for data either, making both those choices incorrect. Finally, `select` statements never add data to a table. **(Topic 1.2)**

33.   B and D. `unique` constraints and primary keys

Explanation   Every constraint that enforces uniqueness creates an index to assist in the process. The two integrity constraints that enforce uniqueness are unique constraints and primary keys. **(Topic 10.2)**

34.   C. ALL_IND_COLUMNS

Explanation   This view is the only one listed that provides column positions in an index. Because primary keys create an index, the index created by the primary key will be listed with all the other indexed data. Choice A is incorrect because no view exists in Oracle called ALL_PRIMARY_KEYS. Choice B is incorrect because, although USER_CONSTRAINTS lists information about the constraints in a database, it does not contain information about the index created by the primary key. Choice D is incorrect because ALL_TABLES contains no information related to the position of a column in an index. **(Topic 12.2)**

35.   C. A table named ANIMALS is created in the ANJU schema with the same data as the ANIMALS table owned by MASTER.

Explanation   This question requires you to look carefully at the `create table` statement in the question and to know some things about table creation. First, a table is always created in the schema of the user who created it. Second, because the `create table as select` clause was used, choices B and D are both incorrect because they identify the table being created as something other than ANIMALS, among other things. Choice A identifies the schema into which the ANIMALS table will be created as MASTER, which is incorrect for the reasons just stated. **(Topic 9.2)**

36.   A. `insert into EMPLOYEE values (59694,'HARRIS', NULL);`

Explanation   This choice is acceptable because the positional criteria for not specifying column order are met by the data in the `values` clause. When you would like to specify that no data be inserted into a particular column, one method of doing so is to insert a NULL. Choice B is incorrect because not all columns in the table have values identified. When using positional references to populate column data, values must be present for every column in the table. Otherwise, the columns that will be populated should be named explicitly. Choice C is incorrect because when a column is named for data insert in the `insert into` clause, a value must definitely be specified in the `values` clause. Choice D is incorrect because using the multiple row `insert` option with a `select` statement is not appropriate in this situation. **(Topic 8.2)**

37. A. Two tables in the database are named VOUCHER and VOUCHER_ITEM, respectively.

Explanation This choice implies the use of a naming convention similar to the one we discussed earlier, where the two tables with a foreign key relationship are given similar names. Although it is not guaranteed that these two tables are related, the possibility is strongest in this case. Choice B implies the same naming convention, and because the two tables' names are dissimilar, it is unlikely that the tables are related in any way. Choice C is incorrect because the date a table is created has absolutely no bearing on what function the table serves in the database. Choice D is incorrect because two tables *cannot* be related if no common columns exist between them. **(Topic 10.1)**

38. A, B, and D. CHAR, VARCHAR2, and NUMBER

Explanation BOOLEAN is the only invalid datatype in this listing. Although BOOLEAN is a valid datatype in PL/SQL, it is not a datatype available in the Oracle database, meaning that you cannot create a column in a table that uses the BOOLEAN datatype. **(Topic 9.3)**

39. D. The `delete` statement removes all records from the table.

Explanation Only one effect is produced by leaving off the `where` clause from any statement that permits one: The requested operation is performed on all records in the table. **(Topic 8.4)**

40. C. `GOOD_NAME VARCHAR2(20) check(GOOD_NAME in (select NAME from AVAIL_GOODS)),`

Explanation A `check` constraint cannot contain a reference to another table, nor can it reference a virtual column, such as ROWID or SYSDATE. The other lines of the `create table` statement contain correct syntax. **(Topic 10.2)**

41. A. Locks

Explanation Locks are the mechanisms that prevent more than one user at a time from making changes to the database. All other options refer to the commands that are issued to mark the beginning, middle, and end of a transaction. Remember, the `commit` and `rollback` keywords end the current transaction and begin a new one, whereas the `savepoint` keyword marks a logical breakpoint within the transaction. **(Topic 8.6)**

42. A. Use the `alter table` statement.

Explanation The `alter table` statement is the only choice offered that enables the developer to increase the number of columns per table. Choice B is incorrect because setting a column to all NULL values for all rows does simply that. Choice C is incorrect because increasing the adjacent column sizes simply increases the sizes of the columns. Choice D is incorrect because the listed steps outline how to add a column with a `not NULL` constraint, something not specified by the question. **(Topic 9.4)**

43. B. Truncate the table.

Explanation   Choices A and C may work, but an upgrade of hardware and software will cost far more than truncating the table (choice B). Choice D is partly correct, as some change will be required to the high-water mark, but the change is to reset, not eliminate entirely. **(Topic 9.5)**

44. A. `unique`

Explanation   Only `unique` and `primary key` constraints require Oracle to generate an index that supports or enforces the uniqueness of the column values. `foreign key`, `check`, and `not NULL` constraints do not require an index. **(Topic 10.1)**

45. B. All values in the referenced column in the parent table must be present in the referencing column in the child.

Explanation   Referential integrity is from child to parent, not vice versa. The parent table can have many values that are not present in child records, but the child record must correspond to something in the parent. Thus, the correct answer is all values in the referenced column in the parent table must be present in the referencing column in the child. **(Topic 10.1)**

46. B. Values must be part of a fixed set defined by `create` or `alter table`.

Explanation   A `check` constraint may only use fixed expressions defined when you create or alter the table with the constraint definition. The reserved words like `sysdate` and `user`, or values from a lookup table, are not permitted, making those answers incorrect. Finally, NULL values in a column are constrained by `not NULL` constraints, a relatively unsophisticated form of check constraints. **(Topic 10.1)**

47. B. `sqrt ( )`

Explanation   Square root operations are performed on one column value. **(Topic 3.2)**

48. B. The tables in the join need to have common columns.

Explanation   It is possible that a join operation will produce no return data, just as it is possible for any `select` statement not to return any data. Choices A, C, and D represent the spectrum of possibilities for shared values that may or may not be present in common columns. However, joins themselves are not possible without two tables having common columns. **(Topic 4.1)**

49. D. Until the session completes

Explanation A variable defined by the user during a session with SQL*Plus will remain defined until the session ends or until the user explicitly undefines the variable. **(Topic 1.3)**

50. B and C. Alter the `prompt` clause of the `accept` command and enter a new prompt in the `login.sql` file.

Explanation Choice D should be eliminated immediately, leaving the user to select between choices A, B, and C. Choice A is incorrect because `config.ora` is a feature associated with Oracle's client/server network communications product. Choice C is correct because you can use the `set sqlprompt` command within your `login.sql` file. This is a special Oracle file that will automatically configure aspects of the SQL*Plus session, such as the default text editor, column and NLS data formats, and other items. **(Topic 7.1)**

51. A and C. `select * from EMPLOYEE where EMPID = &empid;` and `select * from EMPLOYEE where EMPID = (select empid from invoice where INVOICE_NO = 4399485);`

Explanation Choice A details the use of a runtime variable that can be used to have the user input appropriate search criteria after the statement has begun processing. Choice C details the use of a subquery that enables the user to select unknown search criteria from the database using known methods for obtaining the data. Choice B is incorrect because the statement simply provides a known search criterion; choice D is incorrect because it provides no search criteria at all. **(Topic 7.1)**

52. A. Ampersand

Explanation The ampersand (`&`) character is used by default to define runtime variables in SQL*Plus. **(Topic 7.1)**

53. C. `select e.empid, d.head from EMPLOYEE e, dept d where e.dept# = d.dept# (+);`

Explanation Choice C details the outer join operation most appropriate to this user's needs. The outer table in this join is the DEPT table, as identified by the `(+)` marker next to the DEPT# column in the comparison operation that defines the join. **(Topic 4.2)**

54. B, C, and D. To exclude certain data groups based on known criteria, to include certain data groups based on unknown criteria, and to include certain data groups based on known criteria

Explanation   All exclusion or inclusion of grouped rows is handled by the `having` clause of a `select` statement. Choice A is not an appropriate answer because sort order is given in a `select` statement by the `order by` clause. **(Topic 5.4)**

55. B. Produced as a result of a join `select` statement with no `where` clause

Explanation   A Cartesian product is the result dataset from a `select` statement where all data from both tables is returned. A potential cause of a Cartesian product is not specifying a `where` clause for the join `select` statement. **(Topic 4.1)**

56. D. Issuing the `set define` command

Explanation   Choice A is incorrect because a change to the `init.ora` file alters the parameters Oracle uses to start the database instance. Choice B is incorrect because, although the `login.sql` file can define many properties in a SQL*Plus session, the character that denotes runtime variables is not one of them. Choice C is incorrect because the `define` command is used to define variables used in a session, not an individual statement. **(Topic 1.3)**

57. B. `set role sales_analyzer;`

Explanation   The problem likely occurs because SALES_ANALYZER was not the default role assigned to THOMAS. She can enable this role using the `set role` command, making choice B the correct answer. Because the appropriate privileges are already granted to THOMAS via the role, the `grant` command needn't be issued, making choices C and D incorrect. Finally, choice A is incorrect because a user cannot alter his or her own user settings using the `alter user` statement to change role information; he or she can only use the `alter user` statement to change his or her own password. **(Topic 13.2)**

58. D. Immediately after the privilege is granted to SALES_ANALYZER

Explanation   Access to objects granted by giving the appropriate privilege to the appropriate role takes effect immediately. DAVIS does not need to log into Oracle again, making choice A incorrect. Choice B is incorrect because the SALES_ANALYZER role needn't be granted to DAVIS again. Finally, choice C is incorrect because the privilege needn't be granted to SALES_ANALYZER again. **(Topic 13.3)**

59. D. `grant create public synonym to davis;`

Explanation DAVIS doesn't need the ability to create public synonyms in order to create tables. Thus, choice D is correct. However, DAVIS will need a user ID setup on Oracle by IMADBA, making choice A incorrect. DAVIS will also need the ability to log into Oracle using the privilege identified in choice B and the ability to create tables given by the privilege in choice C. Thus, those other answers are incorrect. **(Topic 12.3)**

60. C. `create session`

Explanation The `create session` privilege enables you to connect to the Oracle database, making C the correct answer. Choices A and B both identify Oracle-created roles that already have the appropriate privileges for logging into Oracle granted to them, but remember—these are roles, not privileges themselves. Finally, choice D is incorrect because the `references` privilege is an object privilege that does not give you the ability to connect to Oracle. **(Topic 13.3)**

Answers to Practice Exam 3

1. A. `select empno, ename, loc from emp join dept on emp.deptno = dept.deptno where substr(emp.ename,1,1) = 'S';`

Explanation Choice A identifies the correct ANSI-compliant syntax for setup of table joins in Oracle9i. Choice B is incorrect because the `on` keyword is used only in the presence of the `join` keyword, which is not present in the syntax of that choice. Choice C is incorrect because the join condition must be identified as part of the `on` clause when the `join` keyword is present. Finally, choice D is incorrect because determining whether the first character in the ENAME column is S is not a join condition—it is a filtering condition. Thus, that condition should not be included in the `on` clause, but rather in a `where` clause. **(Topic 4.1)**

2. C. You can create a table with the CONTENTS of another using `select` statements.

Explanation Choice C is correct because the `create table as select` command involves a `select` statement that is not used as a subquery. Choices A and B are incorrect because the `update` and `delete` commands must include a subquery in order for you to change or remove data with the use of a `select` command. Finally, it is not possible to include a subquery in a `truncate` command. **(Topic 6.1)**

3. D. The `where` clause

Explanation If you are using a `select` statement to perform a mathematical operation on static expressions, you do not need to use the `where` clause. Choice A is incorrect because your query must include the static expressions and the math operation in the column clause. Choice B is incorrect because all SQL statements need to include a `from` clause. Finally, choice C is incorrect because your `from` clause in this scenario will reference the DUAL table. **(Topic 2.1)**

4. B. `set define ?`

Explanation The `set` command is not a SQL command in Oracle. Rather, it is an Oracle tool command that operates in a tool-specific way. For SQL*Plus, the `set` command enables you to define aspects of your SQL operating environment. Choices A and C are incorrect because the `select` and `update` commands are part of SQL data manipulation language. Choice D is incorrect because the `create table` command is part of SQL data definition language. **(Topic 1.3)**

5. C. Indexes

Explanation You cannot reference an index directly from a SQL command, but Oracle may use one behind the scenes to improve performance under certain conditions. Choice A is incorrect because the `select` command enables you to query Oracle for the contents of a table. You can also reference sequences directly in `select` commands, making choice B incorrect as well. Finally, choice D is incorrect because you can also reference views directly using SQL `select` commands. **(Topic 12.2)**

6. C. `where`

Explanation Filter conditions are always properly placed in the `where` clause of your SQL query. Choice A is incorrect because the columns you want to see in the output are listed in the `select` clause. Choice B is incorrect because the tables you want to query are listed in the `from` clause. Finally, choice D is incorrect because the `having` clause acts as an additional filter usually when you want to see only the output that conforms to filter conditions when a `group by` clause is used. **(Topic 2.1)**

7. C. `where product_type = 'APPLIANCE' and qtr_end_date between '01-JAN-2001' and '01-JUL-2001';`

Explanation Because you want to get the total profits for all appliances for the first six months of 2001, choice C is your best answer because it filters based on that criteria in the columns PRODUCT_TYPE and QTR_END_DATE. Choice A is incorrect because that `where` clause filters on the PRODUCT_NAME column, and although gas grills are certainly appliances, other appliances could be listed in the PROFITS table that are not gas grills that we would want to include in the total profits calculation. Choice B is incorrect because again, not all appliances are gas grills. Furthermore, the filter condition on the QTR_END_DATE column is malformed. Finally, choice D is incorrect because no filter condition appears on the PRODUCT_TYPE column and the filter condition on the QTR_END_DATE column is malformed. **(Topic 2.1)**

8. D. NULL

Explanation   This is a difficult question that tests your knowledge of how group functions react when NULL information is given. Take another look at the contents of the COMM column in the EMP table. Many rows in that table contain NULL values for the COMM column. When NULL data is fed into group functions, the result is always NULL. Thus, although the sum of salaries and commissions for analysts or employees whose names begin with the letter J is 9925, Oracle returns NULL as the answer. **(Topic 5.2)**

9. B. Two

Explanation   Again, this difficult question tests your knowledge on how group functions react when NULL information is given. Although three employees have a value of ten in the DEPTNO column, Oracle does not count KING's record because the MGR column for KING's record contains a NULL value. Thus, choice C is incorrect. **(Topic 5.2)**

10. A. Five

Explanation   7700 minus 2 equals 7698. Five employees have a value in the MGR column of 7698, so the answer is choice A. All other choices are incorrect. Be sure you understand that you can include math operations on static expressions in the filter comparisons of your SQL queries. **(Topic 1.3)**

11. D. WARD

Explanation   Take a moment to reread the question text, and attempt to rephrase what the question is asking for in your own words. First, this question asks you to identify the employees who are salesmen. Second, it asks you to list the output in descending order based on EMPNO, meaning that the employee with the highest value for EMPNO gets listed first, followed by the second highest, and so on. The listed output will be TURNER, MARTIN, WARD, and ALLEN, in that order. Finally, the question asks you to identify the employee listed third from the top of that list. Thus, choice D is the correct answer. **(Topic 2.2)**

12. B. MARTIN

Explanation   Take a moment to reread the question text, and try to rephrase the question in your own words. First, this question asks you to figure out which employees are salesmen. Second, the question asks you to list the output in descending order based on the values in the first column in the output: the ENAME column. The listed output will be WARD, TURNER, MARTIN, and ALLEN, in that order. Finally, the question asks you to identify the employee listed third from the top of that list. Thus, choice B is the correct answer. **(Topic 2.2)**

13. C. MAN

Explanation   Recall that when the `like` keyword is used, Oracle will use the wildcard characters _ and % to identify data via pattern matching. The _ character indicates that this single letter in the text string can be anything, whereas the % character indicates that the prior or subsequent text in the string can be anything. In this case, we are looking for the row whose value for ENAME can contain any letter for the first two characters, followed by AR, followed by anything. Only one name in the list matches this criteria—CLARK. The value in the JOB column for CLARK is MANAGER, and the first three characters of that text string are MAN. Thus, choice C is correct. **(Topic 3.2)**

14. C. –24

Explanation   The result Oracle produces when the query in this question is issued is –24, so choice C is correct. The result will be negative because Oracle subtracts the greater, or more recent hire date from the lesser, more distant hire date. Thus, choices A and B are incorrect. Choice D is incorrect because the `trunc( )` function truncates the value to the right of the decimal point and returns the value –24, not –25. **(Topic 3.2)**

15. A and C. ADAMS and SCOTT

Explanation   Oracle will only return rows where the value in the HIREDATE column is greater or more recent than January 23, 1982. Only two rows contain values meeting this criterion. They are shown in choices A and C. Choices B and D are both incorrect because the hire dates shown in the HIREDATE column for those two rows are both less recent than January 23, 1982. **(Topic 1.2)**

16. D. Oracle returns an error as the result.

Explanation   Any substitution value specified using the `nvl( )` function must be the same datatype as the column specified in the call to that function. Thus, because the TESTCOL column is of NUMBER datatype and 'EMPTY' is a text string, Oracle returns an error. Had we specified the TESTCOL_2 column instead of TESTCOL in our call to `nvl( )`, then choice B would have been the correct answer. **(Topic 3.2)**

17. D. `where customer = 'LESLIE' and order_amt > 2700;`

Explanation   To see order information for LESLIE where the total order exceeds $2,700, you must use the `where` clause identified in choice D. Choice A is incorrect because Oracle will indiscriminately return every order LESLIE has placed. Choice B is incorrect because Oracle will return orders LESLIE placed whose total is less than $2,700. Finally, choice C is incorrect because Oracle will return all orders that LESLIE placed and all orders for more than $2,700, even if LESLIE didn't place the order—this is too much information. **(Topic 2.1)**

18. B. `select rpad(ename, 10, '-dog') as ename from emp;`

Explanation   Each employee name is padded to the right with the text -dog repeated over and over to fill up to ten places. Thus, we have to use the `rpad( )` function. Choice A is incorrect because the `trim( )` function removes text specified from the string you pass to the function. Choice C is incorrect because the `substr( )` function returns a subset of text from a string you pass to the function. Finally, choice D is incorrect because the `lpad( )` function pads to the left with the text you specify in order to fill up to a specific number of spaces. **(Topic 3.2)**

19. A. `abs( )`

Explanation   The `abs( )` function returns the absolute value of a number, defined as the distance from zero of that number. Absolute values are always positive, so this function could not have produced the output identified in the question. Choices B, C, and D are all incorrect because the `ceil( )`, `floor( )`, and `round( )` functions all could have produced the amount given. **(Topic 3.2)**

20. B. 13

Explanation   Blank spaces are still counted as part of the overall length of a text string. Because SMITHY has six characters and seven blank spaces, the `length( )` function returns 13 for the length of this string. Choice A is incorrect because the value given doesn't take into account the blank spaces padded into the value stored in the column. Choice D would have been correct if the column had been declared as a CHAR(60) column rather than a VARCHAR2(60) column. Finally, you have no logical basis for arriving at 30 as the answer, so choice C can be eliminated immediately. **(Topic 3.2)**

21. B. `floor( )`

Explanation   The `floor( )` function always rounds to the lower integer value when given a decimal to work with, and because –98 is smaller than –97.342, that is the result `floor( )` returns. Choices A, C, and D are all incorrect because `ceil( )`, `round( )`, and `trunc( )` all return –97 as the result of this query. **(Topic 3.2)**

22. A. `ceil( )`

Explanation   The `ceil( )` function always rounds up to the next highest integer value when presented with a decimal, and because 257 is the next highest integer, that is what `ceil( )` returns. Choices B, C, and D are all incorrect because those functions round down to the next lowest integer when given the decimal value in this question. **(Topic 3.2)**

23. D. –168

Explanation   Oracle returns –168 as the result of this query because 168 months are between March 15, 1983, and March 15, 1997. The result is negative because 1983 is a lesser value than 1997, and because Oracle subtracts the second value from the first, the result is negative. Had the dates passed into `months_between ( )` been reversed, choice C would have been the correct answer. Choices A and B are obviously incorrect. **(Topic 3.2)**

24. D. `to_number( )`

Explanation   Although date information is stored internally within Oracle as a number, you cannot use the `to_number( )` function to convert the date to an actual number, thus making it unnecessary and wrong to use a date format mask with the `to_number( )` function. Choices A, B, and C all indicate functions or situations where it is appropriate to use a date format mask. **(Topic 3.3)**

25. C. `select p.prod_d, p.prod_name, b.box_loc from product p, storage_box b where p.stor_box_num = b.stor_box_num and p.prod_name = 'WIDGET';`

Explanation   The join and filter conditions required for this query are represented correctly in choice C because the common column in both tables is joined and the filtering condition on PROD_NAME for all widgets is represented correctly. Choice A is incorrect because the PRODUCT and STORAGE_BOX tables do not share the PROD_ID column in common—they share the STOR_BOX_NUM column in common. Choice B is incorrect because no joining condition exists between the two tables, which will cause the output to form a Cartesian product. Finally, choice D is incorrect because the join condition refers to the STOR_BOX_NUM columns ambiguously in both tables. **(Topic 4.1)**

26. B. Three

Explanation You will need *n* - 1 join conditions, where *n* is the number of tables, plus a filter comparison, to obtain the result requested in this question. Because three tables are present, you will need two join conditions, plus the filter condition, for a total of three comparison operations. **(Topic 4.1)**

27. C. `select product.id, product.name, storage.loc from product natural join storage on product.box# = storage.box#;`

Explanation Natural joins do not require you to identify a join condition because Oracle assumes the join will be executed on the common columns in both tables. Thus, the on clause in choice C is unnecessary, and will result in an error. Choice A identifies the traditional way to define a join in Oracle, whereas choice B identifies the ANSI/ISO-compliant way to define a join in Oracle. Finally, choice D is incorrect because it properly defines how to specify a natural join in Oracle. **(Topic 4.1)**

28. D. Even though outer join operations permit NULL values from one of the tables, you still need to specify equality comparisons to join those tables.

Explanation Choice D is the logical opposite of choice A, and therefore is the correct answer. For this reason, choice A is also incorrect. Choice B is incorrect because you specify a left join in order to see all of table A's rows, even when no corresponding record exists in table B. Finally, choice C is incorrect because you specify a right join in order to see all of table B's rows, even when no corresponding record exists in table A. **(Topic 4.2)**

29. B. `select p.prod_id, p.prod_name, b.box_loc from product p left outer jon storage_box b on p.stor_box_num = b.stor_box_num where p.prod_name = 'WIDGET';`

Explanation Choice B is the only statement that properly defines an outer join meeting the criteria specified by the question. Choices A and C are easy targets to eliminate because they combine the ANSI/ISO outer join syntax with the traditional Oracle syntax—this is not permitted in the Oracle database, and Oracle will return an error if you attempt to do so. Choice D is incorrect because it specifies a full outer join of all rows in both tables that would otherwise not have been returned if an equijoin was executed. **(Topic 4.2)**

30. C. `select e.ename, a.street_address, a.city, a.state, a.post_code from emp e right outer join addr a on e.empno = a.empno where a.state = 'TEXAS';`

Explanation   Choice C is correct because the Oracle outer join operator is on the right side of the join comparison operation. This signifies that you must execute a right outer join using the ANSI/ISO syntax. Choice A is incorrect because the left or right keyword is missing from the statement. Choice B is incorrect because a left outer join will return records from EMP even where no corresponding record exists in ADDR. Choice D is incorrect because the traditional Oracle syntax for outer joins is incorrectly used in the same statement as the ANSI/ISO syntax. **(Topic 4.2)**

> **31.** A. Full outer join

Explanation   The output in this question clearly shows a situation where records from both PRODUCT and BOX are returned even when no corresponding record exists in either table. This is precisely the functionality provided by full outer joins. Choices B and C are incorrect because full outer joins return both the records from left and right outer joins. Finally, choice D is incorrect because an equijoin operation would not have returned the second or the third records listed in the output of the query. **(Topic 4.2)**

> **32.** D. `select region, prod_type, time, sum(profit) from profits group by cube (region, prod_type, time);`

Explanation   When you see a question indicating that the output of a query should produce a cross-tabulation of information, you should automatically know that the result requested is produced by the `cube` keyword. Choice A identifies a properly formed column clause containing a group function needed by the `group by` clause, but does not contain the needed `cube` keyword, so it is therefore incorrect. Choice B is incorrect because the column clause contains no group function. Choice C is incorrect for the same reason. **(Topic 5.2)**

> **33.** A. `select deptno, job, sum(sal) from emp group by job, deptno;`

Explanation   The statement in choice A is correct because it contains reference to a group function. The `group by` clause is correct even though the columns referenced are in a different order than they appear in the column clause of the query, which is acceptable so long as all non-group columns are listed before the group expression. Choice B is incorrect because the group expression is listed before the non-group expressions, which results in an error. Choice C is incorrect because no `group by` clause appears in the query, resulting in an error. Finally, choice D is incorrect for the same reason that choice B is incorrect—the group expression is listed to the left of a non-group expression, resulting in an error. **(Topic 5.2)**

34. D. sum(A.SAL)

Explanation When an order by clause is present, then Oracle lists output of the query according to the expression included in the order by clause. Otherwise, Oracle sorts the output by columns listed in the group by clause. Thus, choices A, B, and C are all incorrect. **(Topic 5.1)**

35. C. select region, prod_type, period, avg(profit) from profits group by region, prod_type, period having avg(profit) > 100000;

Explanation Choice C contains a well-formed column clause and group by clause, and uses the having clause to filter the results according to the criteria identified in the question. A careful read of choice D enables you to discard it, because the having clause in that choice filters results where average profits are less than $100,000, not greater than that amount. Choices A and B inappropriately attempt to use the where clause in order to filter unwanted data. **(Topic 5.4)**

36. C. select e.empno, e.ename from emp e where sal < (select sum(x.vouch_amt) from expense x where x.empno = e.empno);

Explanation To obtain the correct result, you will need to have Oracle calculate the total amount for all vouchers submitted by each employee listed in the EMP table, and only choice C correctly shows the correlated subquery required for the task. Choice A shows the sum of all vouchers in the EXPENSE table, an amount that will surely be greater than everyone's salary. Choice B is incorrect because it likely results in an error where a single-row subquery expected by the parent query returns more than one row. Choice D is incorrect because the exists operator is an inappropriate comparison between parent and subquery, given the need for a listing of employees whose expense vouchers total more than the employee's salary. **(Topic 6.4)**

37. B. select e.ename from emp e where exists (select x.empno from expense x where x.vouch_amt > 10000 and x.empno = e.empno);

Explanation The statement in choice B is correct because it properly uses the exists operator and forms the correlated subquery required to obtain the same result as the query shown in the question. Choice A is incorrect because the reference to the EXPENSE table in the parent query is out of scope. Choice C is incorrect for the same reason. Finally, the where clause forming a join and using the exists operation in choice D is redundant and therefore incorrect. **(Topic 6.2)**

38. A. A single-row subquery

Explanation   The way to determine what kind of subquery is shown in this question is to determine how much output is produced by the query. Because only one record in the EMP table contains the value 'MARTIN' for ENAME, this subquery returns only one row and is therefore a single-row subquery. Choice B is incorrect for this reason. Choice C is incorrect because a `from` clause subquery is the same as an inline view, and no subquery is shown in the `from` clause of the query in this question. Finally, choice D is incorrect because the subquery does not contain reference to multiple columns. **(Topic 6.3)**

39. A. `select sum(profit) from profits where region in`
`(select region from regions where reg_head in`
`('SMITHERS', 'FUJIMORI', 'LAKKARAJU')) and product =`
`'TOYS';`

Explanation   To obtain the correct result, you need a multiple-row subquery listing the regions headed by the region heads identified in the question. You also want a filtering condition on the PRODUCT column so only toys are returned. Choice A gives you all these things. Choice B is incorrect because the subquery incorrectly includes filter conditions operating on the REGIONS table that are meant to operate on the PROFITS table. Choice C is incorrect because the equality comparison between the REGION column and the values returned from the subquery will result in an error because the single-row subquery the parent query expects will in fact return more than one row. Finally, choice D is incorrect for the same reason as choice B, and because of a missing parenthesis at the end of the query. **(Topic 6.1)**

40. C. `with`

Explanation   The `with` clause can be used to define a summary dataset to avoid redundancy in both the parent query and the subquery in Oracle. You would not use the `group by` clause for this purpose, eliminating choice A, nor would you use the `order by` clause for this purpose, eliminating choice B. Finally, you would not use the `having` clause for this purpose, eliminating choice D. **(Topic 6.1)**

41. B. `select nvl(e.deptno,99), e.ename, e.job, e.sal from`
`emp e where e.sal = (select max(e2.sal) from emp e2`
`where nvl(e.deptno,99) = nvl(e2.deptno, 99));`

Explanation   Even SQL experts should find this question challenging. You are asked to determine which of these statements will return 99 in the DEPTNO column where the DEPTNO column is currently NULL in the dataset shown in the question. The most obvious answer is to find the query where the column clause contains a `nvl( )` function on the DEPTNO column in the column clause. The problem is that all the choices contain references to the `nvl( )` function in the column clause. Thus, you have to look beyond that factor for other clues, and your best bet is to try to find reasons to eliminate wrong answers rather than clues to find the right answer. Your first clue comes in choice A, where the parent query `where` clause tips you off that the multiple-column subquery is expected by the parent query but not provided, making that choice incorrect. Second, you should notice that in choice C, the group expression in the subquery necessitates a `group by` clause that is not provided in the subquery, making that choice incorrect as well. If you noticed these important clues, you've narrowed down your odds of guessing the right answer to 50/50. If you recall that 99 is not a value actually stored in the DEPTNO column and that group by clauses ignore NULL values by default, you should be able to eliminate choice D therefore leaving you with the correct answer, choice B. **(Topic 6.1)**

42. C. `select prod_name, profit from (select prod_name, sum(profit) from profits group by prod_name order by sum(profit) desc) where rownum <=5;`

Explanation   Choice C correctly indicates the query containing an inline view that will produce a listing of the five best-selling products in the company's history. Choice A is incorrect because profits are not grouped by product name over the entire company's history in the inline view, but rather broken out by quarter, which will produce the wrong result. Choice B is incorrect because you do not need to join the contents of the PROFITS table with the inline view. Moreover, choice B does nothing to filter out the five top-selling products in company history. Finally, the inline view in choice D does not contain a `group by` clause, which will result in an error due to the presence of the group function in the inline view's column clause, making that choice incorrect. **(Topic 6.3)**

43. C. `accept v_period prompt 'Enter the time period => 'select profit from profits where prod_type = 'TOYS' and time_period = '&v_period';`

Explanation   Because the users have complained about readability and interaction according to the text of the question, you should base your answer on the choice that provides interactive definition of the time period and does so with a readable prompt. Choice C provides for these conditions. Choice D is close but does not provide for a readable prompt, so that choice is incorrect. Choice A is incorrect because the prompt Oracle will use does not address the readability requirement. Choice B is incorrect because the use of the `define` command limits interaction between SQL*Plus and the user. **(Topic 7.1)**

44. A. Variable `v_hiredate` must be changed to accept DATE information.

Explanation   When variables are defined using the `accept` command in SQL*Plus, Oracle implicitly defines the datatype as CHAR. You must therefore specify the datatype when the variable is meant to accept non-CHAR information. Thus, choice A is the answer. Choice B is incorrect because the `trunc( )` function is acceptable in this query. Choice C is incorrect because you needn't eliminate the `prompt` clause. Finally, the script does not work fine as is, so choice D is incorrect. **(Topic 7.1)**

45. D. `create table cats-over-5-lbs as select c_name, c_weight from cats where c_weight > 5;`

Explanation   You cannot include hyphens or dashes as part of the name of any table in Oracle, thus making choice D the correct answer. Choice A is incorrect because that choice identifies a proper `create table` command. Choice B is incorrect because that choice identifies a proper `create table as select` command. Choice C is incorrect because that choice identifies a proper `create global temporary table` command. **(Topic 9.2)**

46. C. Change the column names in the object being created.

Explanation   Changing the column names in a table when an object with that table's name already exists in Oracle will not prevent the same error from happening again. Instead, you should create the table as a different user, drop the existing object with the same name, or rename the existing object. Thus, choice C is correct, and all other choices are incorrect. **(Topic 9.4)**

47. B. 871039453.1

Explanation   Because the column was defined as datatype NUMBER(10,2), Oracle only permits numbers with up to eight places to the left of the decimal point to be placed into the column on this table. Thus, choice B is correct because that number has nine digits to the left of the decimal point. Choices C and D both identify proper numbers for this column. The number in choice A can also be stored in this column, but Oracle implicitly rounds off to the hundredths place to the right of the decimal point. **(Topic 9.3)**

48. B. 7

Explanation   The `vsize( )` function returns a value of 7 for all columns of DATE datatype, no matter what the actual date appears to be. The information about KING's specific value for HIREDATE is only there to distract you. **(Topic 3.3)**

49. C. 40

Explanation   The vsize( ) function always returns a value equivalent to the size of the CHAR column regardless of the actual value stored in that column. This is because Oracle pads whatever value you specify for storage in a CHAR column with blanks up to the width of the CHAR column. Had the column been defined as a VARCHAR2 column, choice A would have been correct. All other choices should be easy to eliminate once you understand Oracle datatypes. **(Topic 3.3)**

50. B. A default clause on the JOB_WAGE column defined when the table was created specified the value when the row was inserted.

Explanation   The purpose of a default clause is to specify a default value for a column whenever users don't explicitly identify the value to populate in the column for a row being added to the table. Choice A is incorrect because an insert statement will not populate column values for existing rows in the table. Choice C is incorrect because you cannot hide values in a values clause of an insert statement. Finally, choice D is incorrect because changing the JOB_WAGE column via a later update statement isn't the only way this value could have been added to the table. **(Topic 9.3)**

51. D. Copy column records from the temporary location back to the main table.

Explanation   If you review all choices carefully before selecting an answer, you should notice that several steps of the process required to perform the task identified by the question are listed as choices. Its up to you to put those steps in order. The correct order is: C, A, B, D. The question then states that you have just completed the step identified in choice B. Thus, the only step left to perform is the one identified in choice D, the correct answer. **(Topic 9.4)**

52. A. Immediately following statement execution

Explanation   Oracle drops the PROFIT column as soon as the statement identified in the answer choice is executed. Choices B and C identify the other way to remove columns from Oracle using the set unused column and drop unused columns clauses. However, we didn't see that option being used in the question, so those choices are incorrect. Finally, you cannot remove a column using the alter table modify command. **(Topic 9.4)**

53. D. Nothing; the statement is executed automatically.

Explanation   Once you've issued the appropriate alter table statement to increase the size of a column, you are done with this task. Oracle will then automatically increase the size of the column. Choices A, B, and C identify steps appropriate for either decreasing the size of a column or altering that column's datatype, and therefore are incorrect. **(Topic 9.4)**

54. B. `alter table sales modify product_type varchar2(10);`

Explanation   To increase the size of a column, you use the `alter table modify` command shown in choice B. Choice A is incorrect because that choice adds an extra column to the table unnecessarily. Choices C and D are incorrect because they identify steps in a process for removing a column from the table, which is not required by the question. **(Topic 9.4)**

55. B. The child column

Explanation   Dropping a parent table will not remove the common column from the child table, making choice B the correct answer. Choice A is incorrect because associated constraints on the parent table are most certainly removed when you drop the parent table. Triggers and indexes on the parent table are dropped when the parent table is dropped as well, making choices C and D incorrect. **(Topic 9.5)**

56. D. `create table profits (product_name varchar2(10) primary key, sale_period varchar2(10) primary key, profit number);`

Explanation   The primary key clause used for defining a primary key as a column constraint for both the PRODUCT_NAME and SALE_PERIOD columns as shown in choice D is not permitted in the Oracle database. Other choices show composite primary keys defined properly. **(Topic 10.2)**

57. B. `alter table sales add constraint ck_sales_01 check (product_type in (select product_type from valid_products));`

Explanation   You cannot use subqueries when defining valid values for check constraints—all values must be static. Choices A, C, and D all identify check constraints defined with static valid values and are permitted within the Oracle database. **(Topic 10.2)**

58. B. Existing entries are checked for violations, PK_PRICES_01 is not enabled, and Oracle does not check subsequent entries for violations immediately.

Explanation   Oracle ignores the `novalidate` keyword because the constraint wasn't defined as deferrable in the question. Oracle thus checks existing entries for violations, and finds violations. PK_PRICES_01 will not be enabled, and Oracle does not check for future violations because the constraint isn't enabled. Choices A, C, and D are all incorrect for this reason. **(Topic 10.2)**

59. C. Foreign key constraint

Explanation Foreign key constraints in child tables create dependencies that later make it difficult to disable primary key constraints on parent tables. Choice A is incorrect because check constraints cannot create relationships between tables. Choice B is incorrect for the same reason. Finally, unique constraints also cannot create relationships between tables and is incorrect as well. **(Topic 10.1)**

60. A. `alter table sales modify (unit_prices null);`

Explanation The syntax for removing a not NULL constraint from a table is shown correctly in choice A. Choice B is incorrect because it defines a not NULL constraint. Choices C and D identify improper syntax for defining nullabililty in Oracle columns. **(Topic 10.2)**

PART
III

Preparing for OCA Database Administration Fundamentals I Exam

The following list shows the topic and subtopic objectives covered on the OCP Oracle9i Database Administration Fundamentals I exam:

1. Oracle Architectural Components
    1.1. Describe the Oracle architecture and its main components.
    1.2. List the structures involved in connecting a user to an Oracle instance.

2. Getting Started with Oracle Server
    2.1. Identify the common database administrative tools available to a DBA.
    2.2. Identify the features of Oracle Universal Installer (OUI).
    2.3. Explain the benefits of Optimal Flexible Architecture (OFA).
    2.4. Set up password file authentication.
    2.5. List the main components of the Oracle Enterprise Manager (OEM) and their uses.

3. Managing an Oracle Instance
    3.1. Create and manage initialization parameter files.
    3.2. Configure an Oracle-Managed File (OMF).
    3.3. Start up and shut down an instance.
    3.4. Monitor the use of diagnostic files.

4. Creating a Database
    4.1. Describe the prerequisites necessary for database creation.
    4.2. Create a database using Oracle Database Configuration Assistant.
    4.3. Create a database manually.

5. Data Dictionary Content and Usage
    5.1. Identify key data dictionary components.
    5.2. Identify the contents and uses of the data dictionary.
    5.3. Query the data dictionary.

6. Maintaining the Control File
    6.1. Explain the uses of the control file.
    6.2. List the contents of the control file.
    6.3. Multiplex and manage the control file.
    6.4. Manage the control file with OMF.
    6.5. Obtain control file information.

7. Maintaining Redo Log Files
    7.1. Explain the purpose of online redo log files.
    7.2. Describe the structure of online redo log files.

7.3. Control log switches and checkpoints.

7.4. Multiplex and maintain online redo log files.

7.5. Manage online redo log files with OMF.

8. Managing Tablespaces and Datafiles

8.1. Describe the logical structure of the database.

8.2. Create tablespaces.

8.3. Change the size of tablespaces.

8.4. Allocate space for temporary segments.

8.5. Change the status of tablespaces.

8.6. Change the storage settings tablespaces.

8.7. Implement OMF.

9. Storage Structure and Relationships

9.1. Describe the logical structure of the database.

9.2. List the segment types and their uses.

9.3. List the keywords that control block space usage.

9.4. Obtain information about storage structures from the data dictionary.

9.5. List criteria for separating segments.

10. Managing Undo Data

10.1. Describe the purpose of undo data.

10.2. Implement automatic undo management.

10.3. Create and configure undo segments.

10.4. Obtain undo segment information from the data dictionary.

11. Managing Tables

11.1. Identify the various methods of storing data.

11.2. Describe Oracle datatypes.

11.3. Distinguish between extended and restricted ROWIDs.

11.4. Describe the structure of a row.

11.5. Create regular and temporary tables.

11.6. Manage storage structures within a table.

11.7. Reorganize, truncate, and drop a table.

12. Managing Indexes

12.1. List the different types of indexes and their uses.

12.2. Create various types of indexes.

12.3. Reorganize indexes.

12.4. Drop indexes.

12.5. Get index information from the data dictionary.

12.6. Monitor the usage of an index.

13. Maintaining Data Integrity
    13.1. Implement data integrity constraints.
    13.2. Maintain integrity constraints.
    13.3. Obtain constraint information from the data dictionary.

14. Managing Password Security and Resources
    14.1. Manage passwords using profiles.
    14.2. Administer profiles.
    14.3. Control use of resources using profiles.
    14.4. Obtain information about profiles, password management, and resources.

15. Managing Users
    15.1. Create new database users.
    15.2. Alter and drop existing database users.
    15.3. Monitor information about existing users.

16. Managing Privileges
    16.1. Identify system and object privileges.
    16.2. Grant and revoke privileges.
    16.3. Identify auditing capabilities.

17. Managing Roles
    17.1. Create and modify roles.
    17.2. Control availability of roles.
    17.3. Remove roles.
    17.4. Use predefined roles.
    17.5. Display role information from the data dictionary.

18. Using Globalization Support
    18.1. Choose database character set and national character set for a database.
    18.2. Specify the language-dependent behavior using initialization parameters, environment variables, and the `alter session` command.
    18.3. Use the different types of National Language Support (NLS) parameters.
    18.4. Explain the influence on language-dependent application behavior.
    18.5. Obtain information about globalization support.

CHAPTER
10

Basics of the Oracle
Database Architecture

n this chapter, you will learn about and demonstrate knowledge in the following areas:

- Oracle architectural components
- Getting started with the Oracle server
- Managing an Oracle instance
- Creating an Oracle database

To be a successful Oracle database administrator (DBA) and to pass OCP DBA Fundamental I, you must understand the Oracle database architecture. An Oracle database in action consists of several elements, including memory structures, special processes that make things run faster, and recovery mechanisms that enable the DBA to restore systems after seemingly unrecoverable problems. Whatever the Oracle feature, it's all here. Review this chapter carefully because these concepts form the foundation for material covered in the rest of the unit and book, the OCP exam, and your work as a DBA. This is an important chapter covering approximately 20 percent of the material tested on the OCP DBA Fundamentals I exam.

Oracle Architectural Components

In this section, you will cover the following topics related to the Oracle architecture:

- Oracle server architecture
- Structures that connect users to Oracle servers
- Stages in processing queries, changes, and commits

The Oracle database server consists of many different components. Some of these components are memory structures, whereas others are background processes that execute certain tasks behind the scenes. There are also disk resources that store the data that applications use to track data for an entire organization, and special resources designed to help recover data from problems ranging from incorrect entry to disk failure. The memory structures and the background processes constitute an Oracle *instance*, whereas the Oracle instance with the remaining structures constitutes an Oracle *database*. This section explains each component of the Oracle database as well as what Oracle is doing when users issue queries, data-change statements, or data manipulation language (DML) statements, and save their work to Oracle by issuing commit commands.

Oracle Server Architecture

Figure 10-1 demonstrates the various disk, memory, and process components of the Oracle instance. Every Oracle database, from the smallest Oracle application running on a hand-held device to terabyte data warehouses that run on mainframes and supercomputers, has these features working together to manage data. They allow for applications, ranging from online transaction processing (OLTP) apps to *N*-tier apps to data marts to data warehouses, to process their data efficiently and effectively.

The System Global Area (SGA): Oracle's Primary Memory Component

Focus first on the memory components of the Oracle instance. There are two basic memory structures in Oracle. The first and most important is the System Global Area (SGA). When DBAs talk about most things related to memory, they usually mean the SGA. The SGA consists of several different items: the buffer cache, the shared pool, and the redo log buffer, as well as a few other items that will be discussed later in the unit. The following subtopics explain the primary components of the Oracle SGA.

TIP
Although they are not emphasized to a great extent on the OCP exam, you should also be aware that the Java pool and large pool are also part of the Oracle SGA.

Buffer Cache   This memory structure consists of buffers, each the size of a database block, that store data needed by Structured Query Language (SQL) statements issued by user processes. You can imagine the buffer cache as a beehive with each unit in it as a buffer and all buffers being of equal size. That is why the size of a buffer cache is indicated in a parameter file as the number of buffers and not in bytes. A database block is the most granular unit of information storage in Oracle in which Oracle can place several rows of table data. The buffer cache has two purposes: to improve performance for subsequent repeated `select` statements on the same data and to enable Oracle users to make data changes quickly in memory. Oracle writes those data changes to disk later.

Shared Pool   The Oracle shared pool has two mandatory structures and one optional structure. The first required component is the *library cache*, which is used for storing parsed SQL statement text and the statement's execution plan for reuse. The second is the *dictionary cache*, which is sometimes referred to as the *row*

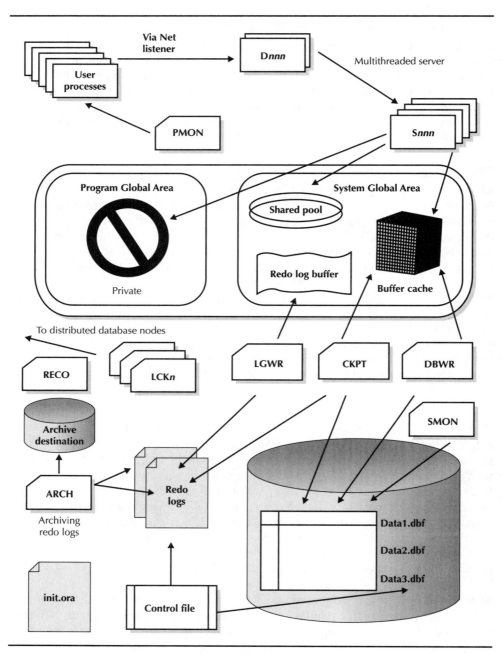

FIGURE 10-1. *The Oracle database architecture*

cache, which is used for storing recently accessed information from the Oracle data dictionary, such as table and column definitions, usernames, passwords, and privileges. (If you don't know what the data dictionary is, you'll find out more about it in the section "More Introductions: SYS, SYSTEM, and the Data Dictionary" later in this chapter.) These two components are designed to improve overall Oracle performance in multiuser environments. The optional shared pool structure contains session information about user processes connected to Oracle. When will Oracle include this optional component in the SGA? You'll find out shortly.

Redo Log Buffer   This SGA component temporarily stores in memory the redo entry information generated by DML statements run in user sessions until Oracle writes the information to disk. DML statements include update, delete, and insert statements run by users. What is a redo entry? It is a small amount of information produced and saved by Oracle to reconstruct, or redo, changes made to the database by insert, update, delete, create, alter, and drop statements. If some sort of failure occurred, the DBA can use redo information to recover the Oracle database to the point of database failure.

The Program Global Area (PGA): The Oracle User's Memory Area

The other memory structure in the Oracle instance is the Program Global Area (PGA). The PGA helps user processes execute by storing information like bind variable values, sort areas, and other aspects of cursor handling. Why do users need their own area to execute? Even though the parse information for SQL or Procedural Language/Structured Query Language (PL/SQL) may already be available in the library cache of the shared pool, the values upon which the user wants to execute the select or update statement cannot be shared. The PGA is used to store real values in place of bind variables for executing SQL statements.

Reading Data from Disk for Users: The Server Process

Let's move on to quickly cover Oracle background processes. Several types of processes are running all the time in Oracle. These types are *background*, *server*, and *network* processes. The most important one from a user perspective is the server process. This process acts on the user's behalf to pull Oracle data from disk into the buffer cache, where the user can manipulate it. There are two ways DBAs can set up Oracle to run server processes: shared servers and dedicated servers. The following subtopics identify the primary differences between these two configurations.

TIP
Think of the Oracle server process as a genie—the magical being from the story of Aladdin—because your wish for Oracle data is the server process' command!

Dedicated Servers: One Genie, One Master   In this setup, every single user connecting to Oracle will have a personal genie handling data retrieval from disk into the buffer cache. If there are 150 users connected to Oracle, there will also be 150 genies out there grabbing data from disk and putting it in the buffer cache for those users. This architectural setup means that every user gets his or her data retrieval requests acted upon immediately. It also means there will be additional memory and central processing unit (CPU) overhead on the machine running the Oracle database, and each dedicated server process will, depending on the workload and the access method, sit idle most of the time. Still, this is the setup chosen by many DBAs for overall performance reasons when hardware resources are readily available.

Shared Servers: One Genie, Many Masters   In this setup, there is a small pool of server processes running in Oracle that support data retrieval requests for a large number of users. Several users are served by one server process. Oracle manages this utilization by means of a network process called the *dispatcher*. User processes are assigned to a dispatcher, the dispatcher puts the user requests for data into one queue, and the shared server processes fulfill all the requests one at a time. This does not mean that there will be only one dispatcher process for the entire database. You will be able to configure the database to have many dispatchers and many server processes. This configuration can reduce memory and CPU burden on the machine that hosts Oracle, as well as limit server process idle time. On the contrary, in dedicated server mode, the user process has to take time to create a dedicated server process for each connection that comes through, whereas in shared server mode, they save time by being served by an existing dispatcher process and server process. That is why a *multithreaded server* (MTS) is preferred in cases where there are a large number of users in the database as well as when a large number of users connect and disconnect from the database (Internet databases).

TIP
In addition to server processes, Oracle uses background processes for a multitude of operations. These processes include database writer (DBW0), log writer (LGWR), checkpoint (CKPT), system monitor (SMON), process monitor (PMON), and a host of others. We will discuss the functionality of

*these background processes as they relate to other
components of the database and as they are tested
on the OCP exam.*

Locating User Session Info: Shared Pool or PGA?

Let's return to the point raised earlier about the optional component of the shared
pool, where user session information is stored in Oracle. Oracle will store session
information in the shared pool only if the DBA configures Oracle to use shared
servers to handle user data retrieval requests. This option is known as the MTS
architecture. Otherwise, if dedicated servers are used, user session information is
housed in the PGA.

For Review

1. Be sure you understand the difference between an Oracle instance and the
   Oracle database.

2. Know the main memory structure in Oracle. Be sure you can list its
   components for OCP. Also, understand the components of the PGA.

3. Understand the purpose of background processes in the Oracle database. At
   this point, you should be able to name at least two and describe their
   function. LGWR writes redo information to disk in the background, whereas
   DBW0 writes data blocks from the buffer cache to disk periodically.

Exercises

1. **You are managing an Oracle database. Which of the following choices
   correctly describes the difference between an Oracle instance and an
   Oracle database?**

   A. An Oracle instance is a saved version of Oracle on disk, whereas a
   database is a running version of the Oracle server.

   B. An Oracle instance is the background processes of the Oracle server,
   whereas a database is the memory allocated to the server.

   C. An Oracle instance is the memory and background processes of a
   running Oracle server, whereas a database consists of an instance and
   files on disk.

   D. The term "Oracle instance" is synonymous with the term "Oracle
   database."

2. You are managing an Oracle database. Which of the following is not a component of Oracle server's shared memory allocation when dedicated servers are being used?

   A. Buffer cache

   B. Shared pool

   C. Redo buffer

   D. PGA

3. You are managing an Oracle database. Which of the following choices identifies the background process that handles writing data blocks to disk on a periodic basis?

   A. LGWR

   B. CKPT

   C. DBW0

   D. S000

4. You are configuring the Oracle database for user activity. Which of the following choices identifies where user session information will be stored when MTSs are being used?

   A. Shared pool

   B. PGA

   C. Buffer cache

   D. Log buffer

Answer Key
1. C. 2. D. 3. C. 4. A.

Structures That Connect Users to Oracle Servers

Let's spend another quick moment covering a few other important Oracle network processes. The first is called the *listener process*. The Oracle listener process does just that—it listens for users trying to connect to the Oracle database via the network. When a user connects to the machine hosting the Oracle database, the listener process does one of two things. If dedicated server processes are being used, the listener tells Oracle to generate a new dedicated server and then assigns the user process to that dedicated server. If MTS is being used, the listener sends the user process to another process called the *dispatcher process*, which has already been mentioned. Once the listener hands over the user connection to either a dedicated server or a dispatcher, it is no longer involved in that connection. It will return to servicing new incoming connections.

The term "request from a user" is actually more precise than it sounds. It is a single program-interface call that is part of the user's SQL statement. When the database is operating in MTS mode, when a user makes a call, the dispatcher servicing the user process places the request in the *request queue*, where it is picked up by the next available shared server process. The request queue is in the SGA and is shared by all dispatcher processes of an instance. The shared server processes check the common request queue for new requests, picking up new requests on a first-in-first-out basis. One shared server process picks up one request in the queue and makes all the necessary calls to the database to complete that request. When the server completes the request, it places the response on the calling dispatcher's response queue. Each dispatcher has its own response queue in the SGA. The dispatcher then returns the completed request to the appropriate user process. That is the magic of how queries are processed in an Oracle server running in MTS mode.

TIP

Here's a quick summary of server, background, and network processes. The server process handles user requests for data. Background processes are Oracle processes that handle certain aspects of database operation behind the scenes. Network processes are used for network connectivity between user processes running on other machines to server processes running on the machine hosting the Oracle database.

For Review

1. Be sure you can distinguish between background, server, and network processes that operate in conjunction with the Oracle database.

2. Be sure you understand the different procedures Oracle undertakes to connect users to servers when the dedicated server or MTS architecture is being used.

3. Know the performance implications for using shared versus dedicated servers. Understand the circumstances where it is appropriate to use MTS versus dedicated servers.

4. Understand that the loss of a listener process does not affect existing connections to the database, but that it does prevent new users from connecting until the listener is restarted.

Exercises

1. **You are configuring the use of servers in your Oracle database. Which of the following statements describes what happens after the listener process detects a user attempting to connect to Oracle when dedicated servers are being used?**

   A. The listener spawns a new server process.

   B. The listener passes the request to a dispatcher.

   C. The listener passes the request to LGWR.

   D. The listener passes the request to DBW0.

2. **You are configuring the MTS on your Oracle database. Which of the following statements describes what happens after the listener process detects a user attempting to connect to Oracle when MTS is being used?**

   A. The listener spawns a new server process.

   B. The listener passes the request to a dispatcher.

   C. The listener passes the request to LGWR.

   D. The listener passes the request to DBW0.

3. **Finish the following sentence: When a listener process fails, _____(A) _____ users will not be able to _____(B)_____ to the Oracle database, whereas _____(C)_____ users remain unaffected by the listener process failure.**

4. **You are configuring the server architecture of your Oracle database. Which of the following choices identifies a situation where the MTS architecture is designed to handle more effectively than the dedicated server architecture?**

   A. Small workgroup database configurations

   B. Internet database configurations

   C. Single-user configurations

   D. Configurations on systems with plenty of available memory

Answer Key

1. A. **2.** B. **3.** (A) new; (B) connect; (C) existing (connected is also okay). **4.** B.

Stages in Processing Queries, Changes, and `commits`

Now that you know how Oracle connects a user process with a server process, it's time for you to learn how Oracle behaves when the user wants to do something with the server, such as selecting Oracle data. You already know most of the main players, including the server process, user process, buffer cache, and library cache of the shared pool. You know all players, that is, except one—the Oracle relational database management system (RDBMS). SQL is a functional programming language, as opposed to a procedural language like COBOL or C. You write your code in terms of your desired outcome, not the process by which Oracle should get there. The RDBMS translates the outcome defined in your SQL statement into a process by which Oracle will obtain it.

Stages in Processing Queries

With all components established in the world of processing Oracle queries, let's look now at how Oracle processes queries. There are several ways to process an Oracle `select` statement. The operations involved in executing both `select` and DML statements fall into a general pattern, which is shown in Figure 10-2. The specific flow of operation in processing a `select` statement is as follows:

1. *Search shared pool.* The RDBMS will first attempt to determine if a copy of this parsed SQL statement exists in the library cache.

2. *Validate statement.* The RDBMS accomplishes this step by checking SQL statement syntax.

3. *Validate data sources.* The RDBMS ensures that all columns and tables referenced in this statement exist.

4. *Acquire locks.* The RDBMS acquires parse locks on objects referenced in this statement so that their definitions don't change while the statement is parsed.

5. *Check privileges.* The RDBMS ensures that the user attempting to execute this SQL statement has enough privileges in the database to do so.

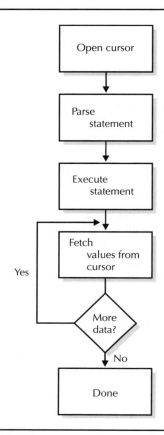

FIGURE 10-2. *Steps in Oracle SQL statement processing*

6. *Parse statement.* The RDBMS creates a *parse tree*, or *execution plan*, for the statement and places it in the library cache based on what Oracle believes is the optimal method for executing the SQL statement. This is a list of operations the RDBMS uses to obtain data. If a parse tree already exists for this statement, the RDBMS can omit this step.

7. *Execute statement.* The RDBMS performs all processing to execute the `select` statement. At this point, the server process will retrieve data from disk into the buffer cache.

8. *Fetch values from cursor.* Once the `select` statement has been executed, all data returned from Oracle is stored in the cursor. That data is then placed into bind variables, row by row, and returned to the user process.

When complete, both the statement execution plan and the data in blocks retrieved from the disk stick around in the library cache and buffer cache, respectively, for a variable length of time, just in case that user or another user wants to execute the same `select` statement. In multiuser application environments, a performance gain is achieved every time user processes execute the same `select` statement because the RDBMS spends less time parsing the statement and the server process spends less time retrieving data.

Stages in Processing DML Statements

At this point, meet yet another behind-the-scenes player in Oracle transaction processing—the *undo segment*. The undo segment is a database object in Oracle that stores old versions of data being changed by DML statements issued by the user process. Undo segments only store the old values, not the new values—the new values are stored in the object itself.

With this in mind, return to the processing of DML statements. There are several differences between how Oracle processes `select` statements and how it processes DML statements such as `update`, `insert`, and `delete`. Although the operations involved in executing DML statements fall into the same general pattern as those for `select` statements (shown in Figure 10-2), the specific flow of operation in processing DML statements is as follows:

1. *Parse statement.* The RDBMS creates a parse tree, or execution plan, for the statement and places it in the library cache. This is a list of operations the RDBMS uses to process the data change. If a parse tree already exists for this statement, the RDBMS can omit this step.

2. *Execute statement.* The RDBMS performs all processing to execute the DML statement. For `update` or `delete` statements, the server process will retrieve the data from disk into the buffer cache, implicitly acquire a lock on the data to be changed, and then make the specified data change in the buffer cache. A *lock* is an Oracle internal resource that one user process acquires before updating or deleting existing data to prevent other users from doing the same thing. For `insert` statements, the server process retrieves a block from a disk that has enough space available to house the new row of data and places that new row into the block. Also, part of executing the DML statement is writing the old and new versions of the data to the undo segment acquired for that transaction. A lock must be acquired on the undo segment to write changes to an undo segment as well.

3. *Generate redo information.* Recall from the prior lesson that the redo log buffer stores redo or data-change information produced as the result of DML operations running in user sessions. After issuing DML statements, the user process must write a redo entry to the redo log buffer. In this way,

Oracle can recover a data change if damage is later done to the disk files containing Oracle data.

TIP
Acquiring a lock is how one Oracle user says to the other users, "Hey! Hands off this data! I'm changing it now, so that means you can't have it until I let go of my lock!" Locks can be acquired at the row level implicitly as part of update *or* delete *statements, or at the table level through explicit methods described later in the book.*

Moving Data Changes from Memory to Disk

Once the DML statement has been executed, there is no need to fetch values as there was for select statements. However, as with select statements, the execution plan for the DML statement sticks around in the library cache for a variable period of time in case another user tries to execute the same statement. The changed blocks in the buffer cache are now considered "dirty" because the versions in the buffer cache and on disk are no longer identical. Those dirty buffers stick around in the buffer cache as well, but they will need to be copied to disk eventually in order to prevent Oracle from losing the data changes made. Also, new information appears in the redo log buffer as a result of the data changes made by the DML statement. By making all the data changes in memory, Oracle is able to achieve superior response to DML statements. This is achieved because it is faster to change and manipulate data in memory rather than on the disk. Secondly, the user does not have to wait for the changed data to be written back to the disk. Oracle does this by running two background processes, DBW0 and LGWR, that write the data changes from buffer cache and redo log buffer to disk; these processes are asynchronous, meaning that they occur sometime after the user actually made the change. The following subtopics explain the role of each background process.

The Role of DBW0   Called the *database writer* process, the DBW0 background process writes dirty data blocks from buffer cache to disk. Historically, this process is also called DBWR, but in more recent versions of Oracle, this term has become somewhat obsolete because Oracle now supports the use of more than one DBW0 process. The writes are done for any of the following reasons:

- When the server process needs to make room in the buffer cache to read more data for user processes

- When DBW0 is told to write data to disk by the LGWR process

- Every three seconds due to a timeout

- When the number of dirty buffers reaches a threshold value

The event that causes LGWR to tell DBW0 to write to disk is called a *checkpoint*. You will learn more about checkpoints in Chapter 11. Because Oracle enables multiple DBW0s to run on the host machine, the database writer process is referred to as DBW0, where 0 can be any digit between zero and nine, because there can be one of several DBW0 processes running in Oracle. Oracle accepts a maximum of ten DBW0 processes for a single instance.

The Role of LGWR   Called the *log writer* process, the LGWR background process writes redo log entries from the redo log buffer in memory to online redo log files on disk. LGWR has some other specialized functions related to the management of redo information that you will learn about in Chapter 11. LGWR also tells DBW0 to write dirty buffers to disk at checkpoints, as mentioned earlier. The redo log buffer writes to the redo log file under the following situations:

- When a transaction commits

- When the redo log buffer is one-third full

- When there is more than a megabyte of changes recorded in the redo log buffer

- Before DBW0 writes modified blocks in the database buffer cache to the datafiles

Stages in Processing commits

Issuing a `commit` statement ends the current transaction by making any data change the user process may have issued to the Oracle database permanent. A `rollback` statement discards the data change in favor of how the data appeared before the change was made. The undo segment is how Oracle manages to offer this functionality. By keeping a copy of the old data in the undo segment for the duration of the transaction, Oracle can discard any change made by the transaction until the `commit` statement is issued.

Before proceeding any further, make sure you understand the following important point—issuing `commit` does not imply that the data modified by the user process is safely written into the disk by the DBW0 process. Only a checkpoint, a timeout, or a need for room in the buffer cache for blocks requested by users will make DBW0 write dirty blocks to disk. With that point in mind, what exactly does processing a `commit` statement consist of? The following list tells all:

- *Release table/row locks acquired by transaction.* The `commit` statement releases all row locks (or even table locks, if any were acquired) held by the user transaction issuing the `commit` statement. Other users can then modify the rows (or tables) previously locked by this user.

■ *Release undo segment locks acquired by transaction.* Changes to undo segments are subject to the same locking mechanisms as other objects. Once the change is committed, the space to hold both old and new versions of data for that transaction in the undo segment is available for another user's transaction. However, Oracle is lazy in that it does not actually discard or remove any information from the undo segment. Instead, Oracle merely overwrites the undo segment's contents when the space is needed by another transaction.

■ *Generate redo for committed transaction.* Once the commit takes place, a redo entry is generated by the user process stating that all the changes associated with that transaction have now been committed by the user. A commit also results in flushing the content of the redo log buffer into redo log files—committed as well as uncommitted statements.

An interesting question remains: How does Oracle know which DML statement redo entries to associate with each transaction? The answer is the system change numbers (SCNs). An SCN is an ID that Oracle generates for each and every transaction that a user process engages. Every redo entry for every data change lists the change that was made and the SCN that the change is associated with. The redo entry for the commit also identifies the SCN and simply notes that this SCN has been committed. Thus, Oracle can easily keep track of the status of every transaction via the SCN.

For Review

1. Be sure you understand that SQL lets users obtain their data via desired characteristics of that data rather than via the procedure Oracle should use to obtain the data. Oracle has its own underlying mechanisms for data retrieval—you should be sure you understand these mechanisms for OCP.

2. Know the point at which Oracle server processes actually retrieve data from the buffer cache.

3. Be sure you can describe the function and purpose of undo segments, locks, and SCNs in Oracle.

4. Be sure you can describe the process that Oracle server executes in order to support DML changes to data, including how changes in actual data and redo entries are moved from memory to disk.

Exercises

1. A user issues a `select` command against the Oracle database. Which of the following choices describes a step that Oracle will execute in support of this statement?

   A. Acquire locks on table queried.

   B. Generate redo for statement.

   C. Fetch data from disk into memory.

   D. Write changes to disk.

2. A user issues an `insert` statement against the Oracle database. Which of the following choices describes a step that Oracle will execute in support of this statement?

   A. Make changes to data block in memory.

   B. Parse statement if parse tree already exists in shared pool.

   C. Write changed records to undo segment.

   D. Write redo for transaction to datafile.

3. A user issues a `commit` statement on the Oracle database. Which of the following choices indicates what Oracle must do next?

   A. Save changes made to data in datafile.

   B. Wait for feedback from the user to write redo to disk.

   C. Eliminate the data block from buffer cache to make room for new changes.

   D. Write redo to indicate that a transaction has been committed.

Answer Key
1. C. 2. A. 3. D.

Getting Started with the Oracle Server

In this section, you will cover the following topics related to getting started with the Oracle server:

- Common database administrative tools

- The Oracle Universal Installer (OUI)

- Optimal Flexible Architecture (OFA) and its benefits

- Setting up password file authentication

- Using Oracle Enterprise Manager (OEM) components

In the past few years, there has been an explosion in the use of administrative tools for Oracle databases. These tools are designed to simplify many aspects of Oracle database administration, including tablespace, instance, storage, object, and backup and recovery management. However, OCP certification on Oracle7 did not focus on using administrative tools. Instead, it focused on the importance of understanding server internals, such as V$ views and issuing commands from the command line. Although the importance of these Oracle components can hardly be diminished, administrative tools such as OEM matured and expanded their functionality, and these areas have risen to take similar levels of importance in the repertoire of every DBA. Plus, they make your job a heck of a lot easier. Therefore, be prepared to see some questions on administrative tools on the Oracle 9i OCP DBA Fundamentals I exam.

Common Database Administrative Tools

The most common database administrative tools that you would use as the DBA of an Oracle9i database would be the various configuration assistants. These assistants are used to create databases, configuring Oracle networking and migrating databases from previous versions to Oracle9i. As you will see in subsequent chapters, the Database Configuration Assistant is used to create the databases and/or database templates. Templates are definitions of databases that you could create and store and later use in order to create similar databases. This tool has been enhanced to practically define anything to create a database.

The Network Configuration Assistant is another tool that you would use to configure and administer your Oracle networking. This tool helps you to create `listener.ora` or `tnsnames.ora` files. The Oracle Migration Assistant can be used to migrate databases from lower releases to Oracle9i. Where appropriate, we'll discuss the use of these tools in addition to covering the command-line options you may need to execute in order to accomplish administrative tasks.

The final tools to be used by DBAs in order to manage the Oracle database include OEM, Oracle DBA Studio, and SQL*Plus. These tools are used for common administrative tasks. In addition, SQL*Plus can be used by end users for accessing and manipulating data in the Oracle database. For the most part, we'll emphasize how to execute common administrative tasks from within SQL*Plus using command-line interface (CLI) statements rather than graphical user interface (GUI) processes.

For Review

1. Be sure you can identify the administrative tools used by Oracle DBAs in order to administer the Oracle database.

2. Understand that the primary administrative tools for handling common DBA tasks are OEM (GUI) and SQL*Plus (CLI).

Exercises

1. **You are administering the Oracle database. Which of the following tools would you use if you wanted to administer the database via statements issued on a command line?**

   A. Database Configuration Assistant

   B. SQL*Plus

   C. Network Configuration Assistant

   D. Enterprise Manager

2. **This is the name of the database management tool that enables you to create a new database via a template: _____.**

3. **This is the name of a file that can be managed via the Oracle Network Configuration Assistant: _____.**

Answer Key

1. B. 2. Database Configuration Assistant. 3. `listener.ora` or `tnsnames.ora` or `sqlnet.ora`.

The OUI

The OUI is a very versatile tool that Oracle provides in order to make the installation of Oracle software simple, interactive, and wizard driven. The OUI interface is the same in all operating system platforms because it uses a Java run-time environment, enabling it to be used on multiple platforms.

The first thing you will undoubtedly notice when installing your Oracle database is that many versions of Oracle for various host systems now come with the OUI. Figure 10-3 shows the OUI running in Windows environments. However, it is important to note that the same version of Oracle Universal Installer and Packager used in Windows environments also looks and works the same on other operating system platforms.

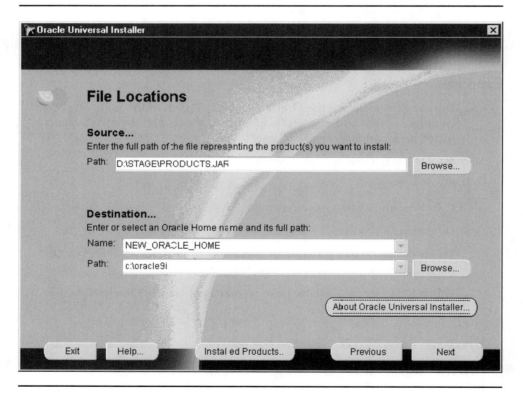

FIGURE 10-3. *Installing Oracle with Oracle Universal Installer and Packager*

TIP
There won't likely be too many questions about
OUI on the OCP DBA Fundamentals I exam, but
you should understand its capabilities nevertheless.

OUI Features

The following bullets list some of the features of OUI:

- The look and feel of the Oracle Universal Installer and Packager is nice, and you can obtain help with installing your Oracle software at any step of the way. Some of the new features of this interface include the capability to install Oracle database software, client software, and management and integration software unattended.

- OUI not only installs the database software, but it also provides you with an option to create different types of databases using configuration assistants. Details follow in later sections.

- It accepts automated software installation if you define a response file for noninteractive installation of Oracle products on a machine. The response file contains information and variable settings that the OUI needs in order to complete an Oracle software installation.

- It tracks its own activities with a log file, showing the activities of the Oracle Universal Installer and Packager.

Installation of Oracle9i Software

You should be aware of a few issues regarding software installation. Oracle9i is a large application that comes on three CDs, and it requires well over 1GB of space on your hard drive just for the application software. In addition, on UNIX systems you will be required to `mount` and `umount` your CD-ROM drive repeatedly as Oracle switches from one CD for installation to another. The booklet that comes with your Oracle9i software distribution CDs has an explanation of how this process is executed. For example, the following code block shows the command used for several operating systems:

```
# HP-UX
nohup /usr/sbin/pfs_mountd &
nohup /usr/sbin/pfsd &
/usr/sbin/pfs_mount -t rrip -x unix /def/dsk/c5t2d0/SD_CDROM

# IBM AIX
```

```
mount -r -v cdrfs /dev/cd0 /cdrom

# SuSE Linux
mount -t iso9660 /dev/cdrom /cdrom

# SPARC/Solaris
mount -r -F hsfs /dev/dsk/c0t6d0s2 /cdrom
```

Additionally, you should be aware of the following steps to unmount the CD-ROM drive in order to eject the current disk and replace it with the next one Oracle requires:

1. In your `telnet` or `xterm` window, press RETURN to return to the shell prompt.

2. Type `cd /` to return to the root directory.

3. Type `su` and press RETURN. This will give you the `root` privileges you need to unmount the CD-ROM before ejecting. You'll need the password for `root` in order to become the superuser. Involve your system administrator if you don't already have this privilege in your organization.

4. Type `unmount/cdrom` to unmount the CD-ROM drive. If you try to do this while logged in as `oracle`, you'll likely get errors indicating the device is busy. If so, return to step 3.

5. Eject the current CD from the CD-ROM drive and replace it with the disk OUI requested.

6. Enter the `mount` command appropriate for your system from the previous code block.

7. Return to OUI and click OK to continue.

Windows users of Oracle won't need to worry as changing CDs for installation is more common in those environments. As with all Oracle databases, you should try to have at least three separate disk devices available to dedicate to Oracle resources. For large enterprise installations, you will definitely want at least 6 or 7, or perhaps as many as 20 to 30, depending on what sort of operation you plan to use your Oracle database for.

For smaller machines, you may find Oracle9i Enterprise Edition difficult to install due to memory constraints, even if you follow Oracle's recommendation of having 128MB of random access memory (RAM) at a minimum. In reality, you should have 256 to 512MB of RAM available on the host machine, and even then the installation process will run slowly because OUI runs completely within a Java Virtual Machine environment. However, you can tailor your Oracle configuration later to minimize the amount of memory the database will require.

We can offer a couple of additional suggestions for the installation of Oracle9i on smaller machines to reduce problems. You can choose the Minimal Installation radio button on the wizard screen for defining the type of Oracle9i installation you want to perform, which requires less memory for the installation. This is a good option for installing Oracle9i on machines with 256 to 384MB of RAM. Otherwise, if you want to run the typical installation, you should increase the available real memory on the machine hosting the Oracle database to 512MB of RAM or more. On starting the OUI, the following occurs:

- You will be prompted whether you want to install the Enterprise or Standard Edition of the software or custom install the software.

- You will then be prompted whether you want to install just the software or whether you want to have a general installation (install software and preconfigured database) or an installation with a specific type of database. The databases are created during the installation by using the Configuration Assistant tool.

- You will be asked questions related to the software installation location, and if you choose to create a database, you will be prompted for the database name and the location for the database files.

- If you have chosen the Custom Installation option, you will be prompted to select the components you want to install. Make sure you include OUI in your selection.

- The Database Configuration Assistant will be invoked to assist in creating the database. Then the Oracle Network Configuration Assistant will be invoked to create the necessary network configuration files and start the listener process. If you are installing in a UNIX environment, you will be prompted to run `root.sh` file to handle.

Installation Log

OUI creates the `oraInventory` directory the first time it is run to keep an inventory of the products that it installs. OUI creates a file in this directory called `installActions.log` that stores the log of the recent installation. In UNIX, the location of this directory is stored in a file called `oraInst.loc`.

Noninteractive Installation

You may perform a noninteractive installation of the Oracle9i software by supplying OUI with a *response file*. OUI uses the information provided in the response file to provide answers to the Installer prompts and complete the installation. For further details, refer to Oracle installation documents provided with your distribution software.

TIP
Operating-system-specific information for installing Oracle is not tested on the OCP exam. Nevertheless, you should attempt to install Oracle9i at least once before taking the OCP DBA Fundamentals I exam to give yourself the hands-on experience necessary to practice for database administration.

For Review

1. Understand the purpose of OUI and how it differs from versions of Oracle Installer that you may have used in Oracle8i or earlier editions of the Oracle database.

2. Be sure you understand the host system requirements that Oracle9i imposes on your organization before upgrading to Oracle9i.

3. Understand the basic OUI components required for noninteractive installation and where to look for information Oracle logged during installation.

Exercises

1. This is the name of the directory OUI uses to store a log of all installation activities: _____.

2. Complete the following statement: OUI runs within the _____ (three words).

3. This is the name of the file you would use if you wanted OUI to run in unattended installation mode: _____ (two words).

Answer Key
1. `oraInventory`. 2. Java Virtual Machine. 3. Response file.

Benefits of Optimal Flexible Architecture (OFA)

As we discussed earlier in the chapter, Oracle databases consist of many different files residing within a host system. Some of these files pertain to the application software, whereas others are used for storing actual data in your database. Still others are used for administering your database. As Oracle evolved into a complex and powerful software product, DBAs faced numerous challenges in determining the best way to lay out the Oracle software, database, and administrative files on their host systems in order to effectively manage the task of administering Oracle databases. In response to this task, the Oracle Corporation published a specification identifying a standard filesystem configuration that DBAs could use in order to lay out the files of a working Oracle database system. The underlying idea was that if DBAs followed this standard for every database used in the organization, it would be much easier for others to find where the filesystem components were located rather than forcing them to dig around for each component. The result was an Oracle standard called the Optimal Flexible Architecture (OFA). Let's now explore OFA in more detail.

What Is OFA?

OFA is an industry standard that defines how to set up Oracle software and databases. OFA provides maximum flexibility in supporting multiple versions of Oracle software and a single listener process to support Oracle instances that may be running under different versions of Oracle software. This brings us to a concept known as ORACLE_HOME. ORACLE_HOME corresponds to the environment in which Oracle products run. The environment could be the location of the installed products files (/u01/app/oracle/product/9.0.1 for UNIX or C:\oracle\ora90 in Windows) or the PATH variable pointing to the location of the binary files, and, in the case of Windows NT, the registry entries, service names, and program groups. Figure 10-4 gives you an example of directories on a filesystem laid out in accordance with OFA.

Some Benefits of Using OFA

OFA has been a boon to many DBAs looking to minimize support headaches. Let's now explore why we might want to use OFA rather than just simply come up with our own organizational standards for database layout:

- OFA is designed to organize large amounts of database datafiles and Oracle software on disks to improve the performance of the database and minimize input/output (I/O) contention among many disks that house the databases.

- OFA is designed to be flexible enough to facilitate the growth of the databases.

- OFA encourages consistent database file-naming conventions. This enables the DBA to clearly distinguish the datafiles, control files, and other files that belong to one database from the other. OFA also helps in associating datafiles to their corresponding tablespaces.

```
/u02/
    oradata/
        db01/
            system01.dbf
            control01.ctl
            redo0101.rdo
        db02/
            system01.dbf
            control01.ctl
            redo0101.rdo

    ...

/u03/
    oradata/
        db01/
            users01.dbf
            control02.ctl
            redo0102.rdo
        db02/
            tools01.dbf
            control02.ctl
            redo0102.rdo
```

FIGURE 10-4. *OFA*

- By keeping the contents of the tablespace separate, OFA minimizes fragmentation and I/O contention. Take for example the separation of tables and indexes in different tablespaces. This gives the flexibility to move the tablespaces to different disk drives in the event that I/O contention goes up.

- OFA supports multiple ORACLE_HOME locations. This enables you to execute multiple releases of Oracle concurrently. For example, you could have a database instance running on 8.1.7 while at the same time have another database instance running on 9.0.1 without causing any disruption to each other.

- OFA enables you to have one listener spawning connections to databases of multiple Oracle software home directories.

- OFA keeps the administration information of each database separate.

For Review

1. Be sure you can define what OFA is and why it is beneficial to you as the DBA and to your organization.

2. Know what ORACLE_HOME means with respect to environments running the Oracle database.

Exercises

1. **You are implementing Oracle in your organization. Which of the following identifies a feature of OFA?**

   A. OFA lumps software, database, and administrative files into one area so they are easy for DBAs to locate.

   B. The use of OFA enables DBAs to define their own filesystem layouts using proprietary naming conventions in order to facilitate the management of Oracle databases.

   C. The use of OFA reduces support headaches by standardizing filesystem layouts for all Oracle installations.

   D. OFA lumps all database objects like tables and indexes into one tablespace so they are easy for DBAs to manage.

2. **Finish the following sentence: The use of OFA is _____ when creating, configuring, and managing Oracle databases.**

3. **Finish the following sentence: When configuring an Oracle database on your host system, OFA minimizes _____(A)_____ contention because different _____(B)_____ can be placed on different _____(C)_____.**

Answer Key
1. C. 2. Optional. 3. (A) I/O; (B) tablespaces; (C) disks.

Setting Up Password File Authentication

How you plan to support the Oracle database you create determines to a large extent how you will set up Oracle to handle *administrative authentication*. Authentication requires the DBA to provide a password in order to gain entry for administrative tasks onto the machine hosting the Oracle database, the database itself, or both. There are two methods of providing administrative authentication: operating system and password file authentication. If you plan to connect to the machine hosting the Oracle database via `telnet`, `xterm`, or a Windows client such as Citrix Metaframe in order to administer the database, operating system authentication might be acceptable. But realistically, if you plan to manage the site from software running on your desktop computer, such as the Enterprise Manager, then you should set up password file authentication.

Another nice feature about a password file is that it enables many DBAs to manage databases, each with varying levels of control. For example, the organization might want the junior DBA to handle backups and user creation, but not the startup and shutdown of the instance. Password files work well to support organizations wanting a team of DBAs to have a range of capabilities on the machine.

More Introductions: SYS, SYSTEM, and the Data Dictionary

Another round of introductions is in order. *SYS* and *SYSTEM* are two users Oracle creates when you install your database. Each has its own default password. The default password for SYS is `change_on_install`, and for SYSTEM it is `manager`. Be careful to protect the passwords for both these users by changing them after installing Oracle. These two privileged users have the power to administer most features of the Oracle database. SYS is more important than SYSTEM because SYS will wind up owning all Oracle system tables from which the data dictionary is derived.

The Oracle data dictionary is the system resource you will turn to in order to find out just about anything about your database, from which users own what objects to the initialization parameter settings, to performance monitoring, and more. There are two basic categories for Oracle database views: those that show information about database objects and those that show dynamic performance. The views showing information about objects are data dictionary views. The views showing information about performance are dynamic performance views. You'll learn more about setting up and using the data dictionary in Chapter 11.

Using Operating System Authentication

Operating system authentication offers the comfort of a familiar face to old-school UNIX folks in the same way that the vi text editor and Korn shell do. Because of this, the discussion of operating system authentication will focus primarily on its implementation in UNIX. However, operating system authentication has few real advantages and many disadvantages compared to the password file method of authentication. The main benefit operating system authentication offers is easy login to Oracle via the slash (/) character, as shown in the following:

```
UNIX(r) SYSTEM V TTYP01 (23.45.67.98)
Login: bobcat
Password:
User connected. Today is 12/17/99 14:15:34
[companyx] /home/bobcat/> sqlplus /
```

```
SQL*PLUS Version 8.1.7.0.0
(c) 2001 Oracle Corporation(c) All rights reserved.
Connected to Oracle9i Enterprise Edition 9.0.1 - Production
With the Java option.
SQL>
```

Operating system authentication has many disadvantages. For one thing, you must have a machine login to use Oracle. When might this pose a problem? For example, you may not want to make the host machine's command prompt accessible to your 10,000+ user base for a production system. For development and test environments, however, operating system authentication may be fine.

To use operating system authentication, a special group called dba must be created on the operating system before you even install your Oracle software. Later, when Oracle is installed and configured, you can log into the operating system via Telnet as a user belonging to the dba group (such as the Oracle software owner). From there, you run SQL*Plus in line mode and perform startup and shutdown operations after issuing the connect name as sysdba command and then providing the appropriate password. The sysdba keyword denotes a collection of privileges that are used for the administration of Oracle databases, including the capability to start and stop the database. The following block illustrates its simple usage:

```
SQL> connect sys as sysdba
Password:
Connected.
```

TIP
Those old-school Oracle DBAs who are familiar with the connect internal *command should know that* connect internal *is no longer supported in Oracle9. Use* connect sys as sysdba *instead.*

Oracle creates certain operating system roles during its UNIX installation. They are osoper and osdba. These should be granted to those operating system users who are database operators (OSOPER) or database administrators (OSDBA). These operating system roles are not granted from the database. However there are two equivalent Oracle privileges that provide the same functionality. They are sysoper and sysdba. These are granted from Oracle database.

There are some small differences between the osoper and sysoper, and osdba and sysdba, that you may use to your advantage for breaking out DBA roles and responsibilities. The osoper role and sysoper privilege enable you to start and stop the instance, mount or open the database, back up the database, initiate archiving redo logs, initiate database recovery, and change database access to restricted session mode. The `sysoper` and `sysdba` roles offer the same privileges as `osoper` and `sysoper`, and add the capability to execute and administer all Oracle system privileges, the `create database` privilege, and all privileges required for time-based incomplete database recovery. Obviously, `osoper` or `sysoper` is given to the DBA to ultimately be responsible for the operation of the database.

TIP
The implementation of operating system authentication in Oracle depends heavily on the operating system you use. Because operating-system-specific issues are not part of the OCP DBA Fundamentals I exam, they will not be covered here. If you need more information on operating system authentication, consult the appropriate operating-system-specific Oracle administrative manual.

Some Initialization Parameters to Remember for Operating System Authentication
You need to set the REMOTE_LOGIN_PASSWORDFILE = NONE when your database is initially created in order to configure operating system authentication. This ensures that you can only start and stop your database from a terminal session on the actual machine hosting the Oracle database or from the console for that machine. In Oracle9i, the default value for this parameter is NONE.

Special Notes for Windows Users
When setting up operating system authentication on Windows, you must execute the following additional steps:

1. Create a new local Windows NT users' group called ORA_*SID*_DBA and ORA_*SID*_OPER that is specific to an instance or ORA_DBA and ORA_OPER that is not specific to an instance.

2. Add a Windows NT operating system user to that group. Once you access this domain, you are automatically validated as an authorized DBA.

3. Ensure that you have the following line in your `sqlnet.ora` file: SQLNET.AUTHENTICATION_SERVICES = (NTS).

4. Set the REMOTE_LOGIN_PASSWORDFILE parameter to NONE in your `init.ora` file.

5. Connect to the database with the privilege `sysdba` or `sysoper`:

```
SQL> CONNECT JASON AS SYSDBA
Password:
Connected.
```

Authentication with the Password File

Oracle's other method of authenticating DBAs is the password file. It is far more important that you understand this option than operating system authentication for the OCP DBA Fundamentals I exam. The DBA creates the password file, and passwords for all others permitted to administer Oracle are stored in the file. The password file is created with the ORAPWD utility. The name of this executable varies by operating system. For example, it is `orapwd` on both UNIX and on Windows.

When executing ORAPWD, you will pass three parameters: FILE, PASSWORD, and ENTRIES. To determine what to specify for FILE, you usually place the password file in $ORACLE_HOME/dbs and name it `orapwsid.pwd`, substituting the name of your database for *sid*. For PASSWORD, be aware that as you define the password for your password file, you are also simultaneously assigning the password for logging into Oracle as SYS. Later, if the DBA connects as SYS and issues the `alter user` *name* `identified by` *password* command, the password for SYS and the password file are all changed. The final parameter is ENTRIES, specifying the number of user entries allowed for the password file. Be careful, because you can't add more later without deleting and re-creating the password file, which is risky. The actual execution of ORAPWD in Windows may look something like this from the command line:

```
D:\oracle\bin\>orapwd FILE=D:\oracle\dbs\orapworgdb01.pwd
PASSWORD=jason ENTRIES=5
```

In UNIX, it may look something like this:

```
/home/oracle> orapwd \
FILE=/u01/app/oracle/product/9.0.1/dbs/orapwdorgdb01.pwd \
 PASSWORD=jason ENTRIES=5
```

After creating the password file, you must do a few other things to provide administrative access to the database. First, set the value for the REMOTE_LOGIN_PASSWORDFILE parameter in the `initsid.ora` parameter file. This parameter accepts `none`, `shared`, and `exclusive` as its values. The `none` setting means the database won't allow privileged sessions over nonsecure connections. When operating system authentication is used, the REMOTE_LOGIN_PASSWORDFILE is set to none to disallow remote database administration. Setting REMOTE_LOGIN_PASSWORDFILE to shared means that only SYS can log into Oracle to perform administrative functions remotely. Finally, setting REMOTE_LOGIN_PASSWORDFILE to exclusive means that a password file exists and any user/password combination in the password file can log into Oracle remotely and administer that instance. If this setting is used, the DBA may use the create user command in Oracle to create the users who are added to the password file and grant sysoper and/or sysdba system privileges to those users. After that, users can log into the database as themselves with all administrator privileges. In addition, EXCLUSIVE indicates that only one instance can use the password file and that the password file contains names other than SYS. SHARED indicates that more than one instance can use the password file. The only user recognized by the password file is SYS.

After creating the password file with the ORAPWD utility and setting the REMOTE_LOGIN_PASSWORDFILE parameter to exclusive in order to administer a database remotely, the DBA can then connect to the database as a user with sysdba privileges, as shown in the following:

```
SQL>  CONNECT sys AS SYSDBA;
Password:
Connected.
```

TIP
Remember two important points about password files. First, to find out which users are in the database password file, use the V$PWFILE_USERS dynamic performance view. (More information on the data dictionary will be presented in Chapter 11.) Second, any object created by anyone logging in as sysdba *or* sysoper *will be owned by SYS.*

Password File Default Locations

Password file default locations depend on the operating system hosting the Oracle database. On UNIX, the password files are usually located in the $ORACLE_HOME/dbs directory. On Windows, the password file is usually located in the %ORACLE_HOME%\DATABASE directory. You can specify a nondefault location of the password file in the Windows registry with the key ORA_SID_PWFILE. You can set the password during installation by using the Custom Installation option.

For Review

1. Understand that there are two methods for administrative authentication in Oracle: operating system and password file. In general, you should understand how to set up and use password file authentication.

2. Know that the OCP DBA Fundamentals I exam focuses on the use of password file authentication.

3. Remember that the REMOTE_LOGIN_PASSWORDFILE init.ora parameter is used for configuring password file authentication, whereas the ORAPWD utility is used for actually creating the password file.

4. Understand the SYS and SYSTEM users and their purpose in the Oracle database architecture.

Exercises

1. You are configuring password file usage for administering the Oracle database. You want to set it such that DBAs listed in the password file will be able to administer a single database. Which of the following choices identifies the appropriate REMOTE_LOGIN_PASSWORDFILE setting in the init.ora file?

   A. NONE

   B. SHARED

   C. EXCLUSIVE

   D. ORAPWD

2. You are creating a password file in Oracle. Which of the following choices identifies how you will specify this command if you want your password file named orapwdORCL.pwd, located in the /u01/app/oracle/database directory, to allow up to 100 other DBAs to connect and administer the database?

   A. orapwd directory=/u01/app/oracle/database
   file=orapwdORCL.pwd

   B. orapwd file=/u01/app/oracle/database/orapwdORCL.pwd
   password=oracle entries=100

   C. orapwd file=/u01/app/oracle/database/orapwdORCL.pwd
   entries=100

   D. orapwd file=orapwdORCL.pwd password=oracle
   entries=100

3. **You execute the ORAPWD utility to generate your password file in Oracle, specifying `password=fritz26`. Which of the following users will have his or her password set to `fritz26`?**

   A. OUTLN

   B. SYS

   C. SYSTEM

   D. None, the PASSWORD parameter is used for authentication of the user running ORAPWD to create the password file.

Answer Key
1. C. 2. B. 3. B.

Using OEM Components

OEM is a suite of applications that enables you to manage your Oracle database in a GUI. Almost anything you can do from SQL*Plus, you can do from OEM, provided you have set up a password file for remote database administration. More information about how to do this appears in the next section. If you do not have a password file set up for administering your Oracle database remotely, then you cannot start up and shut down the Oracle database using OEM, but you can do most anything else.

There is no such thing as easy database administration, but using the administrative tools available in OEM can simplify many areas of managing your database. OEM is usually run from your desktop. Assuming you use Windows, the location of OEM components under the Start button can vary. One way you can identify the tools at your disposal as part of OEM is by looking under Start | Programs | Oracle | Enterprise Manager. Figure 10-5 illustrates the OEM Console with the Applications button bar, which can be used to access any of the administrative applications available in OEM. The following list identifies the applications available for OEM, along with a brief description of their use:

- **Database Wizards**   Used for backup management, data management, analysis, and so on.

- **Change Management Pack**   This contains the tools for change management.

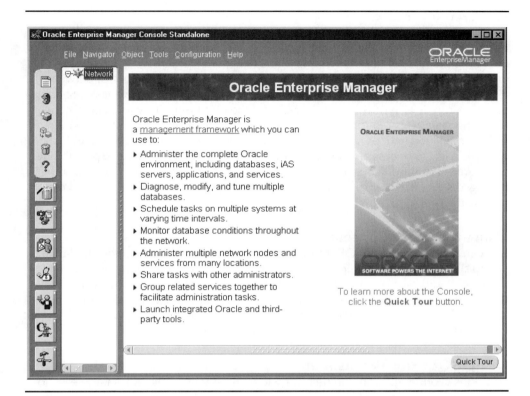

FIGURE 10-5.   *OEM Console*

- **Database Applications Pack**   This pack contains tools to maintain database applications—the most important of which is SQL*Plus Worksheet, which is graphical version of the popular SQL*Plus tool.

- **Diagnostic Pack**   This pack contains tools to diagnose problems such monitoring locks, top sessions, top SQL, and so on.

- **Service Management Pack**   This contains the Net Manager, which is the Oracle networking tool to create network configuration files.

- **Standard Management Pack**   This pack contains the Change Manager and Performance Manager tools.

- **Tuning Pack**   This pack contains the tools for tuning the databases.

OEM Architecture

OEM is a three-tier model. The first tier consists of a Java-based console and integrated applications that can be installed or run from a Web browser. The second-tier component of OEM is the Oracle Management Server (OMS). The main function of the OMS is to provide centralized intelligence and distributed control between clients and managed nodes, which process and administer all system tasks. Sharing the repository is also possible. The OMS uses the OEM repository as its persistent back-end store. This repository maintains system data, application data, and the state of managed entities distributed throughout the environment. OEM enables multiple users to access and share repository data for systems where responsibilities are shared. The third tier is composed of targets, such as databases, nodes, or other managed services. The Intelligent Agent functions as the executor of jobs and events sent by the OMS.

Using the OEM Console

You can choose to run the OEM Console first. This program has methods that enable you to start and use the other components mentioned. The first time you run OEM Console, it will ask you to set up your management server and repository. You will then be prompted to add a database(s) into the *database tree*, which is a tree structure listing multiple databases that can be administered from the OEM Console. Figure 10-6 displays how to add a database to the tree.

Using SQL*Plus Worksheet

SQL*Plus Worksheet is one of the most widely used tools. This tool is fairly easy to use, and you can start it either from the Start button in Windows or from within the OEM Console. Once you've started the tool and logged into Oracle, you should see two windows. The top window is where you enter your SQL statements as you would in SQL*Plus. The bottom window is where you see the output generated by Oracle in response to your SQL query. On Windows NT, you should experiment to determine whether you can access the SQL*Plus Worksheet from the OEM Console under Database Applications. The regular SQL*Plus is available on the Start | Programs | Oracle | Application Development.

Using OEM

You could practically administer every aspect of an Oracle database using OEM. With Oracle9i, the look and feel of OEM has been modified, but the general functionality remains the same. In Oracle9i OEM, you will see that all database tools or managers are available in a tree fashion like in Windows Explorer. The Instance Manager enables you to administer the instance such as starting and shutting the database, editing initialization parameters, monitoring long transactions, and so on. Figure 10-7 gives a view of the Instance Manager. The

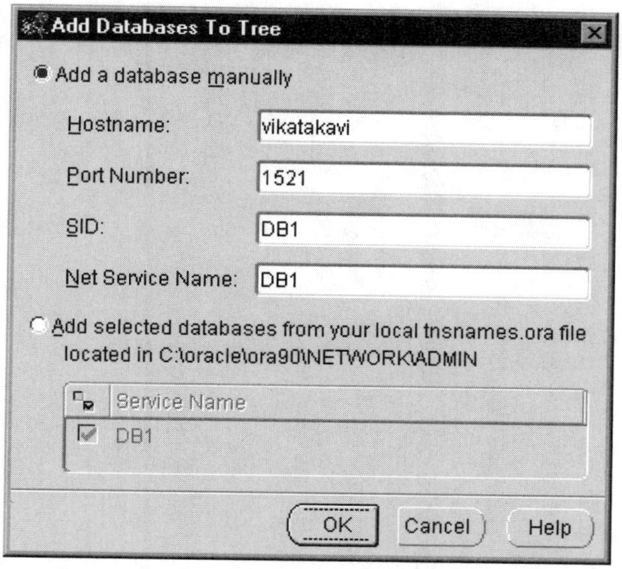

FIGURE 10-6. *Adding a database to the tree*

Schema Manager enables you to administer database objects such as tables and indexes. You can create, drop, and alter objects under this tool. The Security Manager enables you administer the users, roles, and profiles. You can grant privileges and roles, and create, alter, and drop users, roles, and profiles. The Storage Manager enables you to administer objects such as tablespaces, rollback segments, datafiles, and redo logs. You also have other tools such as the Replication Manager, Java Virtual Machine, and Workspace.

For Review

1. Be sure you understand the basic purpose of OEM, namely to assist DBAs in support of Oracle databases by providing a GUI interface for handling most administrative tasks.

2. Know the different categories of tools OEM provides. It is not important to know how to use them for OCP, but you should be able to identify the existence of tools identified in this discussion.

3. Be able to describe the role that an OMS plays within OEM.

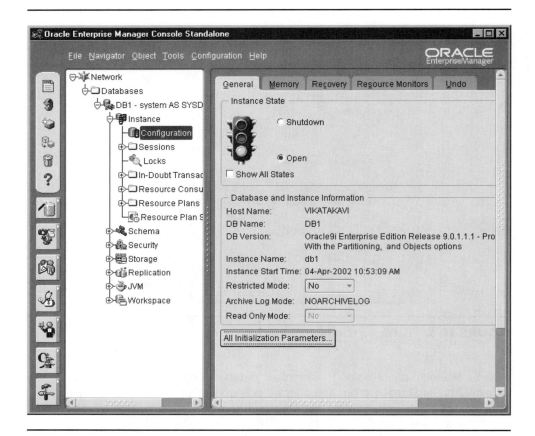

FIGURE 10-7. *Instance Manager*

Exercises

1. The _____ Manager tool helps you to start and stop a running Oracle server.

2. The _____ Manager tool lets you create database objects like tables and indexes.

3. The _____ (two words) tool is used for obtaining an overall view of all Oracle databases in an organization.

Answer Key

1. Instance. **2.** Schema. **3.** OEM Console.

Managing an Oracle Instance

In this section, you will cover the following topics related to starting and stopping the instance:

- Creating and managing your parameter file
- Configuring Oracle-Managed Files (OMF)
- Stating and shutting down your database
- Monitoring the log and diagnostic files of the database

After installing the Oracle software, the DBA should master the management of an Oracle instance. Several important things should be done to manage the Oracle instance before you even think about setting up the Oracle database. Important questions about authentication must be answered, and the parameter file must be developed and managed. This parameter file is generically referred to as `initsid.ora` by many DBAs. Starting up and shutting down the instance and opening and closing the database are key areas both before and after the database is created. Finally, the management of sessions and the places to look for information about the Oracle instance in action are covered in this section.

Creating and Managing Initialization Parameter File

How well or poor your database performs is determined to a great extent by how you configure your Oracle instance. You configure your instance dynamically when you start it by using a parameter file. This parameter file is commonly referred to by DBAs as the `initsid.ora` file. The real name of the parameter file for your database is arbitrary and completely up to you; however, when you install Oracle and create your first database, Oracle will generate a parameter file for you named after the database if you use the Oracle Database Configuration Assistant to create your Oracle database. Thus, if your database is named ORGDB01, your default name for the `initsid.ora` file will be `initORGDB01.ora`. Throughout the discussions in this book, this file will be referred to as the `init.ora` or `initsid.ora` file.

You can create your parameter file from scratch, but why bother when Oracle creates one for you? The parameter file Oracle creates for you will contain several different options for the most essential initialization parameters you need to include when creating a new database. However, Oracle has hundreds of initialization parameters, documented and undocumented. The following code block shows a sample parameter file in use on a small Oracle database running under UNIX. It was created automatically when the Oracle Database Configuration Assistant created the database and was then later modified manually. The pound sign (#) is used to denote comments in the parameter file.

```
#########################################################
# Copyright (c) 1991, 2001 by Oracle Corporation
#########################################################
#########################################################

# Cache and I/O
#########################################################
db_block_size = 8192
db_cache_size = 20971520

#########################################################
# Cursors and Library Cache
#########################################################
open_cursors = 300

#########################################################
# Diagnostics and Statistics
#########################################################
background_dump_dest=/u01/app/oracle/product/9.0.1/admin/oracle/bdump
user_dump_dest=/u01/app/oracle/product/9.0.1/admin/oracle/udump
core_dump_dest=/u01/app/oracle/product/9.0.1/admin/oracle/core
# timed_statistics = TRUE

#########################################################
# Distributed, Replication, and Snapshot
#########################################################
db_domain = ""
remote_login_passwordfile = EXCLUSIVE

#########################################################
# File Configuration
#########################################################
control_files = ("/u01/oradata/oracle/control01.ctl",
                 "/u02/oradata/oracle/control02.ctl",
                 "/u03/oradata/oracle/control03.ctl")
```

```
##########################################################
# MTS
##########################################################
dispatchers="(PROTOCOL=TCP)(SER=MODOSE)", "(PROTOCOL=TCP)
(PRE=oracle.aurora.server.GiopServer)", "(PROTOCOL=TCP)
(PRE=oracle.aurora.server.SgiopServer)"


##########################################################
# Miscellaneous
##########################################################
compatible = 9.0.0
db_name = oracle


##########################################################
# Network Registration
##########################################################
instance_name = ORCL


##########################################################
# Pools
##########################################################
java_pool_size = 10485760
large_pool_size = 1048576
shared_pool_size = 31457280


##########################################################
# Processes and Sessions
##########################################################
processes = 15


##########################################################
# Redo Log and Recovery
##########################################################
fast_start_mttr_target = 300


##########################################################
# Resource Manager
##########################################################
resource_manager_plan = SYSTEM_PLAN


##########################################################
# Sort, Hash Joins, Bitmap Indexes
##########################################################
sort_area_size = 524288
```

```
#########################################################
# System Managed Undo and Rollback Segments
#########################################################
undo_management = AUTO
undo_tablespace=UNDOTBS


#########################################################
# Other Database Parameters
#########################################################
utl_file_dir = /u01/oradata/oracle/misc
```

In general, when working with parameter files, it is best not to start from scratch. Use the Oracle default or borrow one from another DBA. However, be sure that you alter the parameters in the file to reflect your own database, including DB_NAME, DB_BLOCK_SIZE, CONTROL_FILES, and others. You should remember where you store your parameter files on the machine hosting the Oracle database. Do not leave multiple copies in different directories; this could lead you to make a change to one but not the other and then start your instance with the old parameter file later, which would cause problems. However, it can be useful to have a few different copies of a parameter file for various administrative purposes, such as one for production environments and one for running the database in restricted mode for DBA maintenance operations.

By default, a pointer to the `init.ora` file in your OFA-compliant `admin/SID/pfile` administrative directory (where *SID* is replaced with the name of your Oracle database) is located in the `$ORACLE_HOME/dbs` directory on a UNIX machine. In Windows, the actual `init.ora` file is located in the `%ORACLE_HOME%\database` directory. If the `init.ora` is not in the default location, it has to be explicitly specified while bringing up the database. If you don't, Oracle will complain.

Once your instance is started, you can obtain the values set for the instance on initialization through several different ways. The first and least effective way to view parameter values in your database is to look at the `initsid.ora` file. This choice does not give you all parameters, and, what's more, the parameters in your parameter file may have changed since the last time you started Oracle. A much better way to obtain parameter values is to select them from a special view in Oracle called V$PARAMETER. Still another effective way for obtaining parameter values in Oracle is to use SQL*Plus. The `show parameter` command will list all parameters for the instance. Finally, you can use the OEM Instance Manager to display instance parameters, as shown in Figure 10-8. Can you guess where the Instance Manager and SQL*Plus draw their initialization parameter information from? If you said V$PARAMETER, you were right!

Parameter Name	Value	Default	Dynamic	Category
O7_DICTIONARY_ACCESSIBILITY	FALSE	✔		Security and Auditing
active_instance_count		✔		Cluster Database
aq_tm_processes	0	✔	✔	Miscellaneous
archive_lag_target	0	✔	✔	Miscellaneous
audit_trail	NONE	✔		Security and Auditing
background_core_dump	partial	✔		Diagnostics and Statistics
background_dump_dest	E:\oracle\admi...		✔	Diagnostics and Statistics
backup_tape_io_slaves	FALSE	✔	✔	Backup and Restore
bitmap_merge_area_size	1048576	✔		Sort, Hash Joins, Bitmap Indexes
blank_trimming	FALSE	✔		ANSI Compliance
buffer_pool_keep		✔		Cache and I/O
buffer_pool_recycle		✔		Cache and I/O
circuits	170	✔		MTS
cluster_database	FALSE	✔		Miscellaneous
cluster_database_instances	1	✔		Miscellaneous
cluster_interconnects		✔		Miscellaneous

Edit Database : Configuration - system@DB1

All Parameters

OK   Save As...   Description   Cancel   Help

FIGURE 10-8. *Instance parameters in Instance Manager*

TIP
*Some other important V$ views available in the
Oracle9i database to be aware of include
V$FIXED_TABLE, V$SGA, V$PARAMETER,
V$OPTION, V$PROCESS, V$SESSION,
V$VERSION, V$INSTANCE, V$THREAD,
V$CONTROLFILE, V$DATABASE, V$DATAFILE,
V$DATAFILE_HEADER, and V$LOGFILE.*

Setting parameters is done in one of two ways. By far, the most effective way to
set a database parameter is to add the name of the parameter and the value to the
init*sid*.ora file for your instance. After that, shut down and start up your
instance using the init*sid*.ora file. Unfortunately, in the world of multiuser

database environments, DBAs do not always have the luxury of bouncing the database whenever they want. You can always try to schedule this sort of thing, or if the need is not critical, wait until the weekend. Another method for setting parameters is with the `alter system`, `alter session`, or `alter system deferred` commands. These used to not be effective methods for changing parameters because not all initialization parameters could be changed using these commands, but Oracle9*i* has changed this fact along with the introduction of server parameter files, which will be discussed shortly.

TIP
Query the V$PARAMETER or V$SYSTEM_PARAMETER view to list information about the modified parameter. Pay particular attention to the Boolean values in the ISMODIFIED, ISDEFAULT, ISADJUSTED, ISSYS_MODIFIABLE, and ISSES_MODIFIABLE columns. They can be used to identify whether the default value for that parameter is modified or adjusted and whether the value is modifiable with the `alter system` *or* `alter session` *commands, respectively.*

For Review

1. Be sure you understand the purpose of an `init.ora` file in Oracle and that you know some ways for obtaining the values set for parameters on a running database.

2. Understand the use of the `alter system`, `alter session`, and `alter system deferred` commands in order to change values set for parameters once the instance is up and running.

3. Be sure you know where to find actual copies of `init.ora` files and where links to actual copies of `init.ora` files exist in your Oracle database.

Exercises

1. **You are configuring initialization parameters in your Oracle database. Which of the following choices identifies a file where parameter values can be specified?**

    A. `init.ora`

    B. Instance Manager

    C. SQL*Plus

    D. `control01.ctl`

2. **You are managing the Oracle database. Which of the following choices correctly identifies when Oracle reads the contents of the `init.ora` file?**

    A. When the instance is started

    B. When the database is mounted

    C. When the database is opened

    D. When the database is closed

3. **You are managing an Oracle database. Which of the following choices indicates a V$ view where the values set in the `init.ora` file can be viewed for the currently active Oracle instance?**

    A. V$SESSION

    B. V$PARAMETER

    C. V$DATABASE

    D. V$VERSION

Answer Key
1. A. 2. A. 3. B.

Configuring OMF

In the past, Oracle DBAs have always faced a conundrum when working with database administrative tasks. Not only does database administration require a thorough knowledge of how Oracle works, but it also requires a strong understanding of how the underlying operating system works. Why would this be the case? Because often DBAs have to perform administrative cleanup tasks following important database management activities.

    Nowhere is this more apparent than in the creation and removal of datafiles related to tablespace management. You'll learn more about creating tablespaces in Chapter 11, but for now try to understand that tablespaces are logical areas where Oracle stores the contents of database objects like tables and indexes. Underlying the logical concept of tablespaces is the physical datafile or datafiles where the bits and bytes are actually stored. As the last statement implies, a tablespace can be comprised of one or more datafiles in Oracle. In past versions of Oracle, when a

DBA removed a tablespace from Oracle using the appropriate command (which, incidentally, is `drop tablespace`, but we're getting ahead of ourselves here), all the DBA really did was remove the reference to the datafiles comprising that tablespace from the Oracle data dictionary. The actual datafiles still existed on the host system, which required the DBA to find the datafiles and remove them manually using whatever operating-system-specific command was appropriate for the job. If the DBA forgot to remove those datafiles, it was possible that the disk might fill up with datafiles Oracle wasn't using, which could cause unexpected administrative problems.

OMF is a new feature introduced in Oracle9i to simplify database administration with respect to database files. In previous versions of Oracle, when you created new tablespaces using the appropriate command (`create tablespace`, but again, we're getting ahead of ourselves), Oracle expected you to specify the filesystem location and filename for all datafiles to be used in conjunction with storing information in this tablespace. In Oracle9i with OMF enabled, you would specify two simple components instead:

■ A location of your OMF file directory in your `init.ora` file using a parameter

■ The name of the datafile to be created and its size

From there, Oracle takes care of creating the datafile in its appropriate location with the name you specify. By using this feature, DBAs relieve themselves of the obligation to delete the datafiles later when the tablespace is dropped. Instead, Oracle9i will remove them for you.

Implementing OMF—Initialization Parameters

As we indicated earlier, you implement OMF in two steps. First, you specify the location of OMF directories by setting the appropriate parameters in your `init.ora` file. You can specify directory locations by using two parameters. The first is DB_CREATE_FILE_DEST, and it is used to identify the filesystem location Oracle will use for automatically creating datafiles. If no filesystem directory is specified in any command that Oracle must create a file to complete, this directory will be used. The directory you specify must exist before you assign it as a value for this parameter. If the directory does not exist, Oracle will not create it for you. An example of how to set DB_CREATE_FILE_DEST is shown in the following code block:

```
DB_CREATE_FILE_DEST = /u01/oradata/oracle
```

The second parameter to set is DB_CREATE_ONLINE_LOG_DEST_*N*, where *N* is set to some numeric value. This parameter is used for setting default online redo log directory locations for all your online redo logs. For greater fault tolerance and improved performance, Oracle recommends that you set at least two locations. An example for doing so in a UNIX environment is shown in the following code block:

```
DB_CREATE_ONLINE_LOG_1 = /u02/oradata/oracle
DB_CREATE_ONLINE_LOG_2 = /u03/oradata/oracle
```

TIP
In both cases, the directory specified for either of these OMF parameters must be set so that the user on your host system who owns all Oracle software has read and write permissions for that directory.

OMF in Action

Now that the appropriate parameters are set, you can omit the specification of filesystem locations in commands that would ordinarily require you to specify a filesystem location, such as `create tablespace`. We will see some examples of how to use OMF in action when we cover the creation and removal of tablespaces and datafiles in Chapter 11.

TIP
When online redo log locations are specified using the appropriate parameter, Oracle automatically handles the setup of online log multiplexing for you. For more information on multiplexing, see Chapter 11.

For Review

1. Understand what is meant by Oracle-Managed Files (OMF). Your understanding should include the functionality OMF provides.

2. Be sure you know which `init.ora` parameters to set as part of OMF, including those for datafiles and for online redo logs.

Exercises

1. You issue the following command in Oracle: `create tablespace BOB_TBS datafile <\#34>bob01.dbf<\#34> size 2M;`. Later queries against the database reveal that the tablespace is located in the /u01/oradata/oracle directory. Which of the following choices identifies how Oracle likely determined what directory to place `bob01.dbf` in?

   A. DB_CREATE_FILE_DEST

   B. DB_CREATE_ONLINE_LOG_1

   C. DB_CREATE_ONLINE_LOG_2

   D. The directory is an operating-system-specific default value in Oracle that can neither be specified manually nor changed.

2. You have configured OMF on your Oracle database system. After careful analysis, you determine that a tablespace must be removed from the database. Which of the following choices identifies how OMF can assist you in this task?

   A. OMF will automatically update the data dictionary to remove reference to the tablespace datafiles.

   B. OMF will automatically remove the underlying datafiles from the host environment.

   C. OMF will tell Oracle to automatically stop using the datafiles associated with the tablespace.

   D. None of the previous choices identifies the functionality provided by OMF.

3. Choose the appropriate choice to complete the following statement: If you want to use OMF to handle specifying the location of your online redo logs, then you must specify at least _____ destinations for Oracle to use through the definition of OMF-related `init.ora` parameters.

   A. One

   B. Two

   C. Three

   D. Four

Answer Key
1. A. 2. B. 3. B.

Starting an Instance

Recall that we made an important distinction earlier between an Oracle instance and an Oracle database. To refresh your memory, the Oracle database is a set of tables, indexes, procedures, and other objects used for storing data. More precisely, an Oracle database, identified by the database name (DB_NAME), represents the physical structures and is composed of operating system files. Although it is possible to use a database name that is different from the name of the instance, you should use the same name for ease of administration. The Oracle instance, on the other hand, is the memory structures, background processes, and disk resources, which all work together to fulfill user data requests and changes.

With that distinction in mind, let's consider starting the Oracle instance. You must do this before creating a new database or before allowing access to an existing database. To start the instance, follow these steps:

1. From the command line on the host machine, start SQL*Plus and log in as `sysdba`:

```
[ oracle : orgdbux01 ] > sqlplus
Oracle SQL*Plus Release 8.1.7.0.0 - Production
(c)Copyright 2000, Oracle Corporation. All Rights Reserved.
Enter user-name: sys as sysdba
Enter password:
Connected to an idle instance.
SQL>
```

TIP
The password for user `sys` *when logging in as* `sysdba` *is usually set to* `oracle` *by default. Obviously, you'll want to change the password from its default in order to avoid security problems from knowledgeable DBAs!*

2. From within SQL*Plus, use the `startup` *start_option* `[`*dbname*`]` command to start the instance. Several options exist for *start_option*, including `nomount`, `mount`, `open`, and `open force`. If Oracle cannot find the `init.ora` file where it expects to find it ($ORACLE_HOME/dbs in

UNIX and X:\%ORACLE_HOME%\admin\SID\pfile on Windows), the PFILE parameter should be used to identify the exact init*sid*.ora file you want to use. An example of `startup nomount` is shown in the following code block:

```
SQL> startup nomount
ORACLE instance started.
Total System Global Area            227174560 bytes
Fixed Size                              42764 bytes
Variable Size                        93999104 bytes
Database Buffers                     81920000 bytes
Redo Buffers                         51208192 bytes
SQL>
```

Options for Starting Oracle

You can also start a database with OEM Instance Manager. All the options discussed for SQL*Plus are available via Instance Manager, except through a GUI. You may also want to note that starting Oracle databases in Windows is not necessarily handled with SQL*Plus or even OEM, but instead may be handled as a *service*. A service in Windows is similar to a *daemon* in UNIX. Both of these operating system functions let Oracle start automatically when the machine boots. (We're getting a little off the topic here, but if you're interested in more information, consult the *Oracle9i Installation Guide for Windows NT*, which comes with that distribution of Oracle.) There are several different options for starting Oracle instances, with or without opening the database.

startup nomount   This option starts the instance without mounting the database. That means all the memory structures and background processes are in place, but no database is attached to the instance. You will use this option later for creating the Oracle database. You can specify this option with or without specifying an init*sid*.ora file for the PFILE parameter. If you do not specify PFILE, Oracle has some default places it will check in order to find the initialization file. For UNIX, Oracle looks in the $ORACLE_HOME/dbs directory. For Windows, Oracle looks in the X:\%ORACLE_HOME%\admin\SID\pfile directory. If Oracle doesn't find an initialization file and you don't supply an explicit value for PFILE, Oracle will not start your database. In summary, starting an instance without mounting the database includes the following tasks:

- Reading the parameter file `init.ora`
- Allocating the SGA
- Starting the background processes
- Opening the ALERT log file and the trace files

Note that neither the control files nor the database datafiles are opened in this mode.

startup mount   This option starts the instance, reads the control file, and attaches the database, but it does not open it. You can't mount a database you haven't created yet. This option is useful in situations where you have to move physical database files around on the machine hosting the Oracle database or when database recovery is required. You can specify this option with or without specifying an init*sid*.ora file for the PFILE parameter. If you do not specify PFILE, Oracle has some default places it will check in order to find the initialization file. For UNIX, Oracle looks in the $ORACLE_HOME/dbs directory. For Windows, Oracle looks in the X:\%ORACLE_HOME%\admin\SID\pfile directory. If Oracle doesn't find an initialization file and you don't supply an explicit value for PFILE, Oracle will not start your database. If the instance is already started but the database is not mounted, use `alter database mount` instead. In summary, mounting the database includes the following tasks:

- Associating a database with a previously started instance

- Locating and opening the control files specified in the parameter file

- Reading the control files to obtain the names and status of the datafiles and redo log files

startup open   This option starts your instance, attaches the database, and opens it. This is the default option for starting Oracle. It is used when you want to make your database available to users. You can't open a database you haven't created yet. You can specify this option with or without specifying an init*sid*.ora file for the PFILE parameter. If you do not specify PFILE, Oracle has some default places it will check in order to find the initialization file. For UNIX, Oracle looks in the $ORACLE_HOME/dbs directory. For Windows, Oracle looks in the X:\%ORACLE_HOME%\admin\SID\pfile directory. If Oracle doesn't find an initialization file and you don't supply an explicit value for PFILE, Oracle will not start your database. If the instance is started and the database is mounted, use `alter database open` instead. If you omit the `open` keyword when issuing the `startup` command, `startup open` is assumed. Opening the database includes the following tasks:

- Opening the online datafiles

- Opening the online redo log files

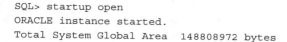

```
SQL> startup open
ORACLE instance started.
Total System Global Area   148808972 bytes
```

```
Fixed Size                     70924 bytes
Variable Size               40566784 bytes
Database Buffers           108093440 bytes
Redo Buffers                   77824 bytes
Database mounted.
Database opened.
```

startup force   This option forces the instance to start and the database to open. It is used in situations where other `startup` options are met with errors from Oracle, and no `shutdown` options seem to work either. This is an option of last resort, and there is no reason to use it generally unless you cannot start the database with any other option. You can specify this option with or without specifying an `initsid.ora` file for the PFILE parameter. If you do not specify PFILE, Oracle has some default places it will check in order to find the initialization file. For UNIX, Oracle looks in the $ORACLE_HOME/dbs directory. For Windows, Oracle looks in the X:\%ORACLE_HOME%\admin\SID\pfile directory. If Oracle doesn't find an initialization file and you don't supply an explicit value for PFILE, Oracle will not start your database.

Two other cases for database startup include `startup recover` for handling database recovery and `startup restrict` for opening the database while simultaneously preventing all users but the DBA from accessing database objects.

TIP
Oracle9i introduces a new mode of operation called quiescing. When a database is placed in quiesced state, only DBA transactions, queries, or PL/SQL statements are allowed to execute. This is achieved by the statement `alter system quiesce restricted`.

The OEM Console or Instance Manager enables the DBA to change and view the initialization parameters. They can be stored either in a local parameter file or in the OEM repository by using stored configurations. If using stored configurations, the DBA must be connected by the way of an OMS to get access to a repository. In earlier versions of OEM (1.*x*), the initialization parameters were stored locally in the Windows NT registry.

Other Modes of Database Operations

Oracle9i has introduced at least two other modes of database operations. The database can be brought in a quiescing state where only DBA transactions, queries, or PL/SQL statements are allowed to execute. This is achieved by the statement `alter system quiesced restricted`. This state is best suited for DBAs for their maintenance work. Oracle9i also can suspend and resume the databases. Suspending a database will halt all input and output to datafiles and control files, but all preexisting I/O operations are allowed to complete. New database accesses are placed in a queued state. The `alter system suspend` statement suspends the database and the `alter system resume` statement resumes the database operation.

TIP

If you suspend database operation from a SQL*Plus prompt while logged in as `sysdba`, *the only statement you can issue following* `alter system suspend` *is* `alter system resume`. *Issuing any other statement will cause your session to hang.*

Starting the Database Automatically

Most DBAs want their database to start automatically whenever the host machine is rebooted. In Windows environments, the database can be opened by starting the OracleServiceSID service. This service is created for the database instance SID when you install Oracle on Windows environments. To start the database automatically, you will have to make sure that the parameter `ORA_SID_AUTOSTART` is set to TRUE in the Windows registry. For more information, refer to the Oracle software installation guide specific for the Windows operating system. On UNIX, automating database startup and shutdown can be controlled by the entries in the `oratab` file in the /var/opt/oracle directory. For more information, refer to the Oracle software installation guide for a UNIX operating system, such as Solaris.

Read-Only Database Features

Any database can be opened as read-only, as long as it is not already open in read/write mode. The feature is especially useful for a standby database to offload query processing from the production database. If a query needs to use a temporary tablespace—for example, to do disk sorts—the current user must have a locally managed tablespace assigned as the default temporary tablespace; otherwise, the query will fail. For the user SYS, a locally managed tablespace is required.

For Review

1. Be sure you understand the difference between starting an Oracle instance and opening an Oracle database for use. Know the commands for each.

2. Understand why Oracle has so many different modes for starting an instance and opening the database rather than just simply having one command to do the job.

Exercises

1. You are administering the Oracle instance for startup. Which of the following choices indicates the names of tools that can be used for starting Oracle instances and databases?

   A. Schema Manager

   B. Server Manager

   C. SQL*Plus

   D. Network Configuration Assistant

2. You are administering an instance of your Oracle database. Which of the following choices identifies a command that can be used to tell Oracle to temporarily cease database operations?

   A. `startup nomount`

   B. `alter database open read only`

   C. `alter system suspend`

   D. `alter system resume`

3. Complete the following statement: When you issue the `startup nomount` command, the Oracle instance is _____(A)_____ and the database is _____(B)_____ opened.

Answer Key
1. C. 2. C. 3. (A) started; (B) not.

Shutting Down an Instance

Shutting down the Oracle instance works in much the same way as starting the instance. You must be logged onto Oracle as a user with `sysdba` privileges. The task can be accomplished from SQL*Plus or OEM Instance Manager, or as a Windows service. The steps for shutting down an Oracle database from SQL*Plus are as follows:

1. From the command line on the host machine, start SQL*Plus and log in as sysdba:

   ```
   [ oracle : orgdbux01 ] > sqlplus
   Oracle SQL*Plus Release 8.1.7.0.0 - Production
   ```

```
(c)Copyright 2000, Oracle Corporation. All Rights Reserved.
Enter user-name: sys as sysdba
Password:
Connected to an idle instance.
```

2. From within SQL*Plus, use the shutdown *shutdown_option* command to shut down the instance. Several options exist for *shutdown_option*, including immediate, normal, or abort. An example of shutdown immediate is shown in the following code block:

```
SQL> shutdown immediate
ORA-01507: database not mounted
ORACLE instance shut down.
```

Options for Stopping Oracle

There are four priorities that can be specified by the DBA for shutting down the database. They include shutdown normal, shutdown immediate, shutdown abort, and shutdown transactional. The next four subtopics will explain each of these options and give cases where their use might be appropriate.

shutdown normal   This is the lowest-priority shutdown. When shutdown normal is issued, Oracle will wait for users to log out before actually shutting down the instance and closing the database. Oracle follows three rules during shutdown normal. First, Oracle will not let new users access the database. Second, Oracle will not force users already logged onto the system to log off in order to complete the shutdown. Third, this is the most graceful shutdown of all. Therefore, when a database is shut down this way, Oracle will not need to do an instance recovery when the instance is brought up again.

```
SQL> shutdown normal
Database closed.
Database dismounted.
ORACLE instance shut down.
```

shutdown immediate   This is a higher-priority shutdown that the DBA can use when shutdown normal would take too long. The shutdown immediate command shuts down a database as follows. No new users will be able to connect to the database once the shutdown immediate command is issued. Oracle will not wait for a user to log off as it does for shutdown normal; instead, it terminates user connections immediately and rolls back uncommitted transactions. Immediate database shutdown, although more drastic than shutdown normal, does not require any instance recovery. The output of the shutdown immediate command is shown in the beginning of this discussion.

shutdown abort   This is the highest priority database shutdown command. In all cases where this priority is used, the database will shut down immediately. All users are immediately disconnected, no transactions are rolled back, and media recovery will be required when the database starts up again. You use this option only when media or disk failure has taken place on the machine hosting your Oracle database.

```
SQL> shutdown abort
ORACLE instance shut down.
```

shutdown transactional   A transactional shutdown prevents clients from losing work. A transactional database shutdown proceeds with the following conditions: No client can start a new transaction on this particular instance, a client is disconnected when the client ends the transaction that is in progress, and a `shutdown immediate` occurs when all transactions have finished. The next startup will not require an instance recovery.

```
SQL> shutdown transactional
Database closed.
Database dismounted.
ORACLE instance shut down.
```

For Review

Understand the command used for shutting down an Oracle instance and closing the database. Be sure you can name the four different priorities for database shutdown.

Exercises

1. You need to shut down the Oracle database on short notice. Which of the following choices indicates the command you would use if you were prepared to let Oracle execute instance recovery the next time the database was opened?

   A. `shutdown abort`

   B. `shutdown transactional`

   C. `shutdown normal`

   D. `shutdown immediate`

2. You are shutting down the Oracle database. If you use the shutdown command for this purpose with no priority identified, what priority would Oracle shut down your database with?

A. abort

B. transactional

C. normal

D. immediate

Answer Key
1. A. **2.** C.

Monitoring the Use of Diagnostic Files

There are many situations where you as the DBA might want to find out more information about what Oracle is doing behind the scenes in order to address issues related to its operation. Two ways exist for doing so—you can either guess or use diagnostic files. For the record, Oracle recommends that you use diagnostic files. There are two types of diagnostic files in a typical Oracle configuration that Oracle will utilize while your database is up and running. These two types of files are *log files* and *trace files*. Let's look at each in more detail.

Trace Files

Background processes generate trace files whenever something goes wrong with the background process' operation. Network processes generate trace files as well whenever they malfunction. Additionally, network processes enable you to specify that you want trace files generated upon request for troubleshooting purposes.

The name of a background process trace file typically contains the name of the background process concatenated with the value specified by INSTANCE_NAME in the `init.ora` file. Any trace file generated by Oracle will have the filename extension `.trc`. Trace files generated by background processes are stored in the directory specified by the parameter BACKGROUND_DUMP_DEST in the parameter file. If you want, review the discussion on `init.ora` files presented earlier in the chapter to see an example of an `init.ora` file—there you'll find an example of BACKGROUND_DUMP_DEST with a directory value set. The name of the trace file also indicates which background process has generated it. They contain detailed information about what caused the background process to malfunction. It is a good procedure to check these trace files when the database behaves or crashes abnormally. They mostly contain information that only Oracle support could decipher. Many times you will be requested by Oracle support to provide these trace files for them to pinpoint the source of the problems.

Other processes such as the listener process may also generate trace files from time to time. These trace files are stored in locations specified in their corresponding configuration files. For example, the listener process configuration file is listener.ora. The details of the trace information in these trace files can be regulated. They are extremely useful in troubleshooting Oracle networking problems. However, make sure that you turn them off when they are not needed as they could grow very fast and fill the disk.

TIP
Server processes managing data on behalf of Oracle users may also generate trace files if you request them to. These trace files can be found in the directory specified by USER_DUMP_DEST. Oracle typically names user session trace files after the process ID number generated in the background for the server process acting on behalf of the user. You usually have to dig through user session trace files or else look at the date and time the file was created in order to figure out which is which.

Log Files

The second type of diagnostic files that Oracle generates are the log files. The most important log file that you should be aware of and monitor often is the *ALERT log file*. The ALERT log file is created automatically by Oracle as soon as you create an instance. It is also stored in the location specified by the parameter BACKGROUND_DUMP_DEST in the init.ora file. The name of this file is alert_*SID*.log or *SID*ALRT.log, where *SID* is the name specified by the parameter INSTANCE_NAME in init.ora.

The ALERT log file stores information that is extremely useful in order to know the health of the database. It records the starting and stopping of the databases, the creation of new redo log file (which happens every time a log switch occurs), the creation of tablespaces, the addition of new datafiles to the tablespaces, and most importantly the errors that are generated by Oracle. This is the most often requested file by Oracle support. It tends to grow big with the passage of time. Parts of the file need to be removed or archived on a regular basis.

One of the best practices as a DBA is to scan this file periodically for any error reports (they usually start with ORA-). A much better approach is to have an automated script that scans this file at regular intervals and pages the DBA if it comes across any ORA- occurrences in the file. Other processes such the Oracle network processes also generate log files. These log files give enough information to gauge the health of Oracle and its network processes. The main difference between log files and trace files is that the log files are needed all the time by DBAs as only important information is reported in them. The trace files are needed for troubleshooting. Oracle reports much more information in trace files than via l og files.

TIP
If you start getting really weird errors in your database and your ALERT log contains ORA-00600 *errors, you should call Oracle Support and start looking in the USER_DUMP_DEST and BACKGROUND_DUMP_DEST directories ASAP!*

For Review

1. Be sure you understand the difference between trace and log files. Know the types of files as well as the processes that might generate those files that are stored in the directory identified by the BACKGROUND_DUMP_DEST and USER_DUMP_DEST parameters.

2. Understand when background processes generate trace files. Also, know what is stored in the ALERT log file. Know that this is the first place you look if your database crashes abnormally.

Exercises

1. The following excerpt of a trace file was taken from an Oracle database:

```
Tue Jul 18 17:04:33 2000
alter database dismount
Completed: alter database dismount
archiving is disabled
Dump file c:\Oracle\admin\orcl\bdump\orclALRT.LOG
Tue Jul 18 17:05:00 2000
ORACLE V9.0.1.0.0 - Production vsnsta=0
vsnsql=d vsnxtr=3
Windows NT V4.10, OS V192.0, CPU type 586
Starting up ORACLE RDBMS Version: 9.0.1.0.0.
System parameters with non-default values:
  processes               = 59
  shared_pool_size        = 15728640
  java_pool_size          = 20971520
  disk_asynch_io          = FALSE
  control_files           = c:\Oracle\ORADATA\orcl\control01.ctl,
c:\Oracle\ORADATA\orcl\control02.ctl
```

```
db_block_buffers          = 200
db_block_size             = 2048
compatible                = 9.0.1.0.0
log_buffer                = 8192
log_checkpoint_interval   = 10000
log_checkpoint_timeout    = 0
```

Which of the following choices identify the most likely name for that trace file?

A. orclDBW0.trc

B. orclLGWR.trc

C. orclALRT.trc

D. orcl13095.trc

2. **You are trying to identify the location of a trace file generated by the listener process. Where would you look for that information?**

A. init.ora

B. BACKGROUND_DUMP_DEST

C. listener.ora

D. USER_DUMP_DEST

3. **You are exploring background process trace files for your LGWR process. Under which of the following scenarios would you find a trace file generated for this process?**

A. When specifically requested by the user

B. When the database is closed

C. When the database crashes

D. When Oracle cannot write to the ALERT log

Answer Key
1. C. 2. C. 3. C.

Creating an Oracle Database

In this section, you will cover the following topics related to creating an Oracle database:

- Prerequisites necessary for creating a database
- Creating databases using Oracle Database Configuration Assistant
- Creating the database manually

The act of creating a database is nothing but the creation of a *physical* database. Before a physical database is created, the database designers design the *logical* database using an entity-relationship diagram (ERD). The ERD shows the relationship between the tables, the columns they contain, the constraint, and other information. A DBA translates this logical design into a physical design by mapping where the tables need to be created, what tablespaces they should reside in, how large they have to be, and so on. Just as with installing the Oracle software, a DBA has to do many tasks before and after the creation of the database. The focus of the OCP DBA Fundamentals I exam is on the tasks required to create the physical database. In this section, we'll cover how to perform preinstallation tasks, creating a database using Oracle's wizard-driven Database Configuration Assistant and then creating a database manually.

Prerequisites for Database Creation

There are a few things you should do at the operating system level before creating your database. Because every operating system is different, you'll be introduced to the general concepts here for the purpose of preparing for OCP. If you have further questions, refer to the operating-system-specific Oracle installation guide that came with your software distribution. Some of these steps are things you should be aware of at the time you install the Oracle software on your host machine, whereas others can wait until the time you are ready to issue the `create database` statement. In general, you should make sure your machine has the capacity to handle Oracle. At a minimum, make sure you have at least three separately controlled disk resources. Configuring certain environment settings is an important task executed at this point as well. If you are installing Oracle on a machine that currently hosts another Oracle database, make sure you shut down and back up the other Oracle databases running on the host. Finally, if it's appropriate, make sure that operating system patches recommended by Oracle are installed on the machine. More details about each of these items follow:

- *Make sure your machine has the capacity to handle Oracle.* Almost any machine made these days has the capacity to install Oracle successfully.

However, not every machine has the guts to run a full-scale Oracle Enterprise database application. Before creating an Oracle environment, be sure to assess whether your host machine has the CPU power, memory, and disk space it takes to run an Oracle database in a multiuser environment.

■ *Ensure that you have at least three separately controlled disk resources.* A running Oracle database has many moving parts. Often, these parts are also moving at the same time. Putting every Oracle resource on the same hard drive is a recipe for slow performance on all but the smallest single-user database setups. Oracle recommends three separately controlled disk resources. An enterprise production installation of Oracle can require 20 or more. Again, think before you create.

■ *Configure certain environment settings.* You may need to configure a few environment variables before creating your database, such as ORACLE_BASE, ORACLE_HOME, ORACLE_SID, ORA_NLS33, LD_LIBRARY_PATH, and others. These are items that you will set up in your machine configuration files or user configuration files. Where possible, you should try to follow the OFA. This is Oracle's recommended guideline for filesystem directory paths, and following it will help Oracle Support find files for you when you call in the inevitable emergency production-support issue.

■ *Shut down and back up other Oracle databases running on the host.* Unless you like long hours spent in a computer room handling recovery, don't care about your data, or both, you should never install an Oracle database on a machine already hosting Oracle without shutting down and backing up that other database first. The `reuse` keyword in the `create database` command as well as the CONTROL_FILES parameter in your `init`*sid*`.ora` file make it possible for one Oracle database to overwrite the files of another database on the same machine. Avoid problems by taking the extra time to back up your data and put different Oracle database files in different directories.

■ *Install Oracle-recommended operating system patches on the machine.* This final point is as much an Oracle software installation issue as it is a database creation issue. Because the exact operating system version and required patches vary from operating system to operating system, you should consult the Oracle installation guide that came with your software for specifics, while being mindful that operating system patches may need to be applied for Oracle to work properly.

■ *Perform UNIX specific tasks.* Specifically for UNIX, edit the `oratab` file to include the name of the database being created, its ORACLE_HOME, and whether it has to automatically shut down in the event of a system start or shutdown. This task is not mandatory for working of Oracle, but is essential for many of the administration tasks.

Using OFA

Implementing the OFA standard may be the most important thing you have to do in order keep your administration simple and prevent accidents from happening. We have already discussed the details of OFA in previous sections in this chapter. Make sure to create the administration directory under ORACLE_BASE (you configure a directory for ORACLE_BASE such as the Oracle software owner's home directory as part of configuring environment settings) to store the database administration and diagnostic files. If the datafiles of the database being created are stored in their own directories as recommended in OFA, then make sure to create the directories. In UNIX, these datafiles will not be created unless the directories exist.

Preparing the Parameter File

You've already learned about the parameter file so now focus on the values that must be set in order to create a new Oracle database. As mentioned, Oracle provides a generic copy of that parameter file, `initsid.ora`, in the software distribution used to install Oracle server on the machine hosting the Oracle database. Generally, the DBA will take this generic parameter file and alter certain parameters according to his or her needs. Several parameters must be changed as part of setting up a new database. The following subtopics identify and describe the parameters you need to change.

DB_NAME   This is the local name of the database on the machine hosting the Oracle database and one component of a database's unique name within the network. If the value for this parameter is the same as another Oracle database running on the host, permanent damage may result in the event that a database is created. Try to limit this name to approximately eight characters. Do not leave the name as DEFAULT. There is a name for the database and a name for the instance, and they should be the same. DB_NAME is required for the creation of the database, and it should be unique among all Oracle databases running in your organization.

DB_DOMAIN   This identifies the domain location of the database name within a network. It is the second component of a database's unique name within the network. This is usually set either to WORLD or to the domain name appearing in your e-mail address at your organization, such as EXAMPILOT.COM.

DB_BLOCK_SIZE   This is the size in bytes of data blocks within the system. This is also called standard block size in Oracle9i. Data blocks are unit components of datafiles into which Oracle places the row data from indexes and tables. This is one parameter that cannot be changed once the database is created. Oracle9i supports multiple block sizes. The *standard block size* is defined by the parameter DB_BLOCK_SIZE and it supports additional four nonstandard block sizes. The standard block size is used for SYSTEM tablespace, whereas nonstandard block size may be specified when creating tablespaces.

CONTROL_FILES   This is a name or list of names for the control files of the database. The control files document the location of all disk files used by the Oracle. If the name(s) specified for this parameter does not match filenames that currently exist, then Oracle will create a new control file for the database at startup only when you create a new database. Otherwise, Oracle simply tells you it won't start because it can't find the control files it needs to open your existing database. Only during the creation of a new database will Oracle overwrite the contents of a file of the same name as the control file you specified in init*sid*.ora with the physical layout of the database being created. Beware of this feature, as it can cause a control file on an existing database to be overwritten if you are creating a second database to run on the same machine.

DB_CACHE_SIZE   DB_BLOCK_BUFFERS continues to exist in Oracle9i, but is used for backward compatibility. Unlike DB_BLOCK_BUFFERS, which specifies the number of data block-sized buffers that can be stored in SGA, Oracle9i introduces a new parameter, DB_CACHE_SIZE, which can be used to specify the size of the buffer cache in the Oracle SGA. It specifies the size of the default buffer pool for buffers with the standard block size (as defined in DB_BLOCK_SIZE parameter). Unlike DB_BLOCK_BUFFERS, which is specified in number of buffers, this new parameter is defined in bytes.

LOG_BUFFER   This is the size of the redo log buffer in bytes. As stated earlier, the redo log buffer stores redo log entries in memory until LGWR can write the entries to online redo logs on disk. There will be more information about this in Chapter 11.

UNDO_MANAGEMENT   This parameter is set to AUTO to indicate that Oracle9i will handle undo segment management automatically for you. An undo segment is the same thing as a rollback segment. As of Oracle9i, you no longer have to create rollback segments manually.

UNDO_TABLESPACE   This parameter is set to the name of the tablespace you want to use to house undo segments generated and managed automatically by Oracle. Make sure you specify and use a tablespace that houses nothing other than undo segments for this purpose.

PROCESSES This is the number of processes that can connect to Oracle at any given time. This value includes background processes (of which there are at least five) and server processes. This value should be set high in order to avoid errors that prevent users from connecting.

The Server Parameter File Feature in Oracle9i

The server parameter file is a new feature in Oracle9i. It enables you to relieve yourself of the burden of constantly updating your `init.ora` file yourself whenever you decide you need to change an initialization parameter. This is a nice touch, considering that Oracle9i also makes it possible to change most every initialization parameter you would ever care to change dynamically while the database is online and available for users. Oracle can also provide a large degree of self-tuning due to its capability to control its initialization parameter settings dynamically. Additionally, the server parameter file feature enables Oracle9i to remember settings for initialization parameters that were changed dynamically across sessions.

Server parameter files are created from standard `init.ora` files. They are housed inside your Oracle database, so obviously they won't be available until the database is created. You can create a server parameter file in the following way:

1. You define the settings you want in your initial Oracle9i database configuration before the database is actually created, using the guidelines we've already discussed so far, by creating an `init.ora` file. You can use one you already have so long as you make the changes we've already discussed.

2. You then create the database.

3. Once the database exists, you issue the `create spfile` command to create your server parameter file in the following way:

```
SQL> create spfile from
  2  pfile = '/u01/app/oracle/admin/oracle/pfile/init.ora';
```

From there, Oracle9i will create a server parameter file on the machine hosting the Oracle database. Oracle9i will be able to update that file every time you use the `alter system set init_parm = value` command to change a parameter's setting dynamically. Oracle9i will also read that file every time the instance starts in addition to your `init.ora` file, in order to determine what settings to use initially when the instance starts. A new clause exists on the `alter system` command called `scope` as well, in order to help you specify whether you want Oracle to update its server parameter file with the new setting or not. The `scope` clause has three possible settings: SPFILE, MEMORY, or BOTH. If you define the scope of the dynamic parameter change to be SPFILE or MEMORY, then Oracle9i changes the parameter setting in the server parameter file or existing instance memory configuration only, respectively. If you use BOTH, then Oracle9i sets the new parameter value in both the server parameter file and makes the change to the current instance. The following code block contains the proper syntax for all three settings:

```
alter system set shared_pool_size = 10485760 scope = spfile;
alter system set shared_pool_size = 10485760 scope = memory;
alter system set shared_pool_size = 10485760 scope = both;
```

TIP
You can also export the contents of your server parameter file to a traditional init.ora *file using the* create pfile from spfile *command.*

For Review

1. Know that there are certain init.ora parameters that must be changed in order to create a new database, such as CONTROL_FILES, DB_NAME, and DB_BLOCK_SIZE, especially if you've copied the init.ora file from another database location. If these parameters are not set to a value appropriate for the new database and you have existing databases on the host, you could damage those existing databases.

2. Understand the new SPFILE feature available in Oracle9i for dynamic instance parameter configuration, management, and tuning.

Exercises

1. **You are preparing to create an Oracle database. Which of the following parameters must be changed in your** init.ora **file in order to create a new database that will not interfere with any existing databases on the machine hosting the Oracle database when you've copied the** init.ora **file from one of those other databases for use in this one?**

   A. CONTROL_FILES

   B. DB_BLOCK_SIZE

   C. DB_DOMAIN

   D. SHARED_POOL_SIZE

2. **You are configuring your Oracle** init.ora **file to create a new database. Which of the following parameters is the newer version of the DB_BLOCK_BUFFERS parameter?**

      A. DB_CACHE_SIZE

      B. SHARED_POOL_SIZE

      C. LARGE_POOL_SIZE

      D. JAVA_POOL_SIZE

3. **This is the name of the feature that enables Oracle to dynamically manage its own `init.ora` settings (three words):** _____.

Answer Key

1. A. **2.** A. **3.** Server parameter files.

Creating Databases Using the Database Configuration Assistant

The Oracle Database Configuration Assistant is one of the many GUI tools that Oracle provides in support of your Oracle database. The Database Configuration Assistant is used to create databases, and it handles a lot of the tricky work behind the scenes so you don't have to. With the Database Configuration Assistant, you can perform the following tasks with ease:

- You can create a database from scratch by specifying all the information needed to create one. You can either specify the tool to create the database after you specify information or generate the scripts necessary to create the database manually or store the information in a template to be used later to create other databases. It is the last feature that makes this tool very useful to DBAs. You will learn more about it in the following sections.

- You can delete an existing database.

- You can clone an existing database with and without the data. You can reverse-engineer a template of an existing database as well.

TIP

The Database Configuration Assistant uses OFA standards, so database files, administrative files, and parameter files follow OFA naming standards and placement practices.

What Are Database Configuration Assistant Templates?

The concept of a template started with Oracle9i. A template is a definition of a database. Oracle provides a set of predefined templates and Database Configuration Assistant enables you to custom create templates for your own needs. When creating a template, it lets you specify everything possible from the location of control files, redo log file, database datafiles, the size of your SGA, the location of administrative files, the parameters in `init.ora` file, and many other things. The Database Configuration Assistant was made even easier by letting us define variables commonly defined as part of configuring your Oracle operating environment. For example, if you are familiar with UNIX, these environment settings are what you would find in a file such as `.profile`. These variables, such as ORACLE_BASE, SID, and others can be used in the filenames and such places to replace them with information specific to the instance you are creating.

TIP
Even though the Oracle8i version of the Database Configuration Assistant provided us with a basic way to create databases, the tool was limited to only creating databases in a few simple ways. The Database Configuration Assistant is now a complete product with the capability to define practically any aspect of your databases used for various purposes, including transaction processing databases, decision support systems, data warehouses, and databases for hybrid purposes.

To create a database, you may choose an existing template that Oracle provides or you may create one built to suit your needs. Once you have a database template that looks close to what you are building, you use that template, change a few things, and use it to create your database. This is a time-saving tool for the DBAs.

Creating a Database Using the Database Configuration Assistant

The Database Configuration Assistant can create a database from either predefined templates provided by Oracle or custom-created templates created by you or just create a database without using any of the templates. The Database Configuration Assistant wizard goes through the same displays as the one used in template creation and gathers the necessary information to create the database. As a final step, you could just create a database, create a database and save the database creation scripts, or just save the scripts. You may choose the last option to take a look at the scripts and execute them manually to create the database.

For Review

1. Understand the basic use of the Oracle Database Configuration Assistant, and be sure you can describe the advantages of using this tool versus manually creating an Oracle database.

2. Understand the concept of a database template. Be sure you can describe the benefits offered by database templates.

3. Know that any database created by the Database Configuration Assistant will be OFA-compliant in terms of its directory and file layout.

Exercises

1. **You are creating Oracle databases in your host system. Which of the following choices identifies a benefit for using the Database Configuration Assistant for this purpose rather than creating a database manually?**

   A. The Database Configuration Assistant simplifies many of the behind-the-scenes tasks you would otherwise have to handle.

   B. You have more control over the placement of certain datafiles with the Database Configuration Assistant.

   C. The Database Configuration Assistant interface is wizard-driven and therefore complex.

   D. The Database Configuration Assistant simplifies the creation of Oracle databases by creating databases suited for only one purpose.

2. **You are using the Database Configuration Assistant to configure your Oracle database. Which of the following terms pertains to the creation of an object from which the creation of other databases can be based?**

   A. Clone

   B. Copy

   C. Template

   D. Terminal

Answer Key

1. A. **2.** C.

Creating a Database Manually

Of course, you also have the option to create a database yourself manually. Moreover, there are some compelling reasons to do so. First, you retain a great deal of control over the nuances of how your database will be created. Using scripts for database creation also gives you a template of sorts from which you can base the creation of other databases. Scripts may be necessary in situations where you want to create a database on a remote machine as well and do not have access to the graphical desktop of that remote machine in order to run the Database Configuration Assistant on it. The creation of the Oracle database is accomplished with the `create database` statement. The following steps are executed before creating the database:

1. Make sure that the `init.ora` file exists and the entries in it refer to the correct database name. You can execute a global search-and-replace operation to identify and correct discrepancies within any text editor, but be sure you comb through each situation manually so that you don't make a mistake accidentally. Now is also the time to verify one last time that the location of control files in this file is accurate.

2. Make sure the directories specified for BACKGROUND_DUMP_DEST, USER_DUMP_DEST, CORE_DUMP_DEST, UTL_FILE_DIR, and any other administrative directories used by Oracle actually exist on your filesystem. If those directories do not exist, the creation process for your new database may fail when you try to start the instance.

3. Start SQL*Plus and connect to the database as sys as sysdba.

4. Start up the instance in `nomount` mode so that no existing database is mounted to the instance.

5. Execute the `create database` statement to create the database by either typing it into SQL*Plus or by running a script with contents similar to the code block containing the `create database` command, as shown in the following:

```
CONNECT SYS AS SYSDBA

CREATE DATABASE orgdb01
CONTROLFILE REUSE
LOGFILE
   GROUP 1 ('/u01/oradata/oracle/redo1a.log',
            '/u02/oradata/oracle/redo1b.log') SIZE 5M,
   GROUP 2 ('/u02/oradata/oracle/redo2a.log',
            '/u01/oradata/oracle/redo2b.log') SIZE 5M
MAXLOGFILES 40
DATAFILE '/u03/oradata/oracle/sys01.dbf'
```

```
       SIZE 50M AUTOEXTEND ON NEXT 30M MAXSIZE 150M
  MAXDATAFILES 240
  CHARACTERSET WE8IS08859P1;
  EXIT;
```

6. If your database creation process is successful, you can then mount the
database you just created using the `alter database mount` command
and then open it using the `alter database open` command. Your
database now contains one tablespace, called SYSTEM, with one or more
datafiles.

7. Then you create the tablespaces for undo segments, users, temp, and other
data. We'll see some examples of create tablespace commands in
Chapter 11.

8. In versions of Oracle prior to Oracle9i, you would then create the undo
segments and bring them online. In Oracle9i, however, all you need to do
is create the undo tablespace—Oracle creates its own undo segments.

9. Finally, you run the scripts provided by Oracle to create the data dictionary
(also called Catalog) and other database objects necessary for database
administration.

What Happens When You Execute
the `create database` Command?

When the database is brought up in `nomount` mode, Oracle reads the `init.ora`
file, which it uses to figure out where to create the control files. Oracle also uses the
settings for parameters in this file to specify the size of the SGA, where to place to
log and trace files, and other important information. With this information, it creates
the SGA in memory and the background processes.

■ When the `create database` command is executed, it creates the control
files as specified in `init.ora` file, and the redo log files and the SYSTEM
tablespace datafile as specified in the command itself.

■ SYS and SYSTEM accounts are created. A single undo segment is created in
the SYSTEM tablespace.

The Datafiles of the SYSTEM Tablespace

The files created as part of the `datafile` clause of the `create database`
command are SYSTEM tablespace datafiles. A *tablespace* is a logical collection of
disk files collectively used to store data. The SYSTEM tablespace can be compared
to the root directory of a machine's filesystem. The SYSTEM tablespace houses the
tables comprising the basis for the Oracle data dictionary as well as the system undo
segments. The tables of the data dictionary and system undo segment will all be

owned by user SYS. Oracle creates one system undo segment in the SYSTEM tablespace at database creation for Oracle to acquire at database startup. Without this system undo segment, the database won't start. In the interest of preserving the integrity of the Oracle database, the DBA should ensure that only the data dictionary and system undo segments are placed in the SYSTEM tablespace. No data objects owned by any user other than SYS should be placed in the SYSTEM tablespace. Instead, you will create other tablespaces to store those database objects. You will learn more about tablespaces and datafiles in Chapter 11.

Minimum Two Online Redo Log Groups

Redo logs are created with the `logfile` clause. Redo logs are entries for data changes made to the database. You must create at least two redo log groups for your new database, each with at least one member. In the database created with the preceding code block, redo log group 1 consists of two members, called `log1a.dbf` and `log1b.dbf`, respectively. If any file specified in the `create database` statement currently exists on the system and the `reuse` keyword is used, Oracle will overwrite the file. Be careful when reusing files to prevent accidentally overwriting the files in your existing database on the host machine. You will learn more about redo logs in Chapter 11.

Other Items in `create database` Statements

Other options set when the database is created include `maxdatafiles` and `maxlogfiles`. The `maxdatafiles` option is used to specify the maximum number of datafiles that can be open while the database is open. The setting of this number dictates the size set aside in the control file to store datafile information. For example, if you set this option to 100 but you create only ten datafiles, Oracle creates a control file that will accommodate storing information for 100 datafiles. The initialization parameter DB_FILES also dictates the maximum number of datafiles that are accessible to the database. If an attempt is made to add files greater than those specified in `maxdatafiles` but less than DB_FILES initialization parameter, then Oracle will expand the control file automatically to accommodate the growth of the files.

The `maxlogfiles` option defines the maximum number of redo log file groups and the `maxlogmembers` option defines the maximum number of members for a redo log file group that can be created in the database. These settings define the amount of space set aside in control file to store the information about redo log groups and members.

You can use the `autoextend` option when defining datafiles. When `autoextend` is used, the datafiles will automatically allocate more space when the datafile fills, up to a total size specified by the `maxsize` keyword. However, you'll want to take care to ensure that Oracle does not try to extend the datafile to more space than the filesystem has available.

The final item in the `create database` statement was `characterset`, which is used to identify the character set used in the Oracle database for information storage. Another option you can use in `create database` commands is `archivelog`. When `archivelog` is used, Oracle archives the redo logs generated. Finally, the `create database` command uses several initialization parameters set in the `init`*sid*`.ora` file in database creation. These include DB_BLOCK_SIZE and certain National Language Support (NLS) environment settings.

For Review

1. Understand the process for manually creating a database using the `create database` command. Be sure you can identify the various clauses used as part of issuing that command.

2. Be sure you understand that any datafiles created as part of the `create database` command will belong to the SYSTEM tablespace. Also, know that you must create at least two online redo logs as part of this process.

3. When manually creating an Oracle database, know that your instance must be started but that you cannot have any other database already mounted to that instance.

Exercises

1. **You are about to create a database manually in Oracle. Which of the following `startup` commands would be appropriate for the instance in this context?**

   A. `startup nomount`

   B. `startup mount`

   C. `startup open`

   D. `startup force`

2. **You have just created an Oracle database using the `create database` command. To which of the following tablespaces will any datafile identified as part of the `datafile` clause for the `create database` command belong?**

   A. DATA

   B. INDEX

   C. UNDO_TBS

   D. SYSTEM

Answer Key

1. A. **2.** D.

Chapter Summary

This chapter covered several important topics that got you started in your preparation for the OCP DBA Fundamentals I exam. The first topic we discussed was the theoretical underpinnings of the Oracle database architecture. You learned about the memory structures, disk files, and background processes used in conjunction with Oracle, and explored each of these areas in some detail. We also looked at how Oracle connects users to the database for data access and manipulation. Next, we discussed how to get started as the DBA of an Oracle system. You learned about installation of Oracle using the Oracle Universal Installer (OUI) and listed the administrative components of Oracle that are shipped with the database. We also provided an overview of the Oracle Enterprise Manager (OEM), Oracle's graphical tool for handling many common administrative tasks. We described how to create password files as well. After that, we focused our attention on how to manage an Oracle instance. A few times in the chapter, we pointed out the difference between an Oracle instance and a database. You learned about how to start up and shut down a running instance, and the various methods for opening and closing a database. We talked a lot about initialization parameters and parameter files as well. You explored the use of log and trace files related to Oracle database administration, an important concept tested on the OCP DBA Fundamentals I exam. The new Oracle9i Oracle-Managed Files (OMF) feature was also covered in some depth. Finally, we turned our attention to understanding the process by which databases are created, both with the wizard-driven Database Configuration Assistant and manually using scripts and the `create database` command. This is an important chapter covering approximately 20 percent of the material tested on the OCP DBA Fundamentals I exam.

Two-Minute Drill

- Several structures are used to connect users to an Oracle server. They include memory structures like the System Global Area (SGA) and Program Global Area (PGA), network processes like listeners and dispatchers, shared or dedicated server processes, and background processes like database writer (DBW0) and log writer (LGWR).

- The SGA consists of the buffer cache for storing recently accessed data blocks, the redo log buffer for storing redo entries until they can be written to disk, and the shared pool for storing parsed information about recently executed SQL for code sharing.

■ The fundamental unit of storage in Oracle is the data block.

■ SQL `select` statements are processed in the following way: A cursor or address in memory is opened, the statement is parsed, bind variables are created, the statement is executed, and values are fetched.

■ SQL DML statements such as `update`, `delete`, and `insert` are processed in the following way: A cursor or address in memory is opened, the statement is parsed, and the statement is executed.

■ Several background processes manage Oracle's capability to write data from the buffer cache and redo log buffer to appropriate areas on disk. They are DBW0 for writing data between the disk and buffer cache, and LGWR for writing redo log entries between the redo log buffer and the online redo log on disk.

■ DBW0 writes data to disk in three cases. They are every three seconds (when a timeout occurs), when LGWR tells it to (during a checkpoint), or when the buffer cache is full or a server process needs to make room for buffers required by user processes.

■ Server processes are like genies from the story of Aladdin because they retrieve data from disk into the buffer cache according to the user's command.

■ There are two configurations for server processes: shared servers and dedicated servers. In dedicated servers, a listener process listens for users connecting to Oracle. When a listener hears a user, the listener tells Oracle to spawn a dedicated server. Each user process has its own server process available for retrieving data from disk.

■ In shared server configurations (also called multithreaded server [MTS] configurations), a user process attempts to connect to Oracle. The listener hears the connection and passes the user process to a dispatcher process. A limited number of server processes, each handling multiple user requests, are monitored by a dispatcher, which assigns user processes to a shared server based on which has the lightest load at the time of user connection.

■ The `commit` statement may trigger Oracle to write changed data in the buffer cache to disk, but not necessarily. It only makes a redo log buffer entry that says all data changes associated with a particular transaction are now committed.

■ The Oracle Universal Installer (OUI) is the software installer for Oracle products. It is written in Java and runs on multiple platforms.

- OUI permits automated, noninteractive software installation through the use of a response file.

- When installing Oracle9i on certain platforms, you need to make sure that you install the software to a separate home directory. This is a requirement of the new version of OUI.

- You can have OUI install a preconfigured database for you with minimal user interaction. In this case, all scripts, such as `catalog.sql` and `catproc.sql`, are run automatically, and a few basic tablespaces, such as DATA, INDEX, and UNDOTBS, are created with the following information:

  - SID is `ORC0` or `ORCL`.

  - `SYS` password is `change_on_install`.

  - `SYS as SYSDBA` password is `oracle`.

  - SYSTEM password is `manager`.

- Oracle9i lets you change most instance parameters dynamically while the database is available for use. For example, SGA parameters can be altered such that Oracle9i's shared memory is changeable while the database is online.

- The server parameter file feature in Oracle9i enables you to create a server parameter file that Oracle9i can dynamically modify in support of changes to the configuration of your instance.

- Server parameter files are created using the `create spfile from 'filename'` command.

- When you use the `alter system` command in Oracle9i to change the settings for instance parameters, you can specify a new clause, `scope`, to determine where Oracle should make the instance parameter change:

  - **SPFILE** Oracle9i changes the parameter setting in the server parameter file only.

  - **MEMORY** Oracle9i changes the parameter setting for the current instance only.

  - **BOTH** Oracle9i changes the parameter setting for both server parameter file and current instance.

- Two user authentication methods exist in Oracle: operating system authentication and Oracle authentication.

- DBAs require two privileges to perform their function on the database. In Oracle authentication environments, they are called `sysdba` and `sysoper`.

- To use Oracle authentication, the DBA must create a password file using the ORAPWD utility.

- To start and stop a database, the DBA must connect as `internal` or `sysdba`.

- The tool used to start and stop the database in Oracle9i is SQL*Plus.

- Another tool for managing database administration activity is Oracle Enterprise Manager (OEM). OEM has many administrative tools available, including the Daemon Manager, Instance Manager, Replication Manager, Schema Manager, Security Manager, SQL Worksheet, Storage Manager, Net8 Assistant, and Software Manager.

- There are several options for starting a database:

  - **startup nomount** Starts the instance and does not mount a database

  - **startup mount** Starts the instance and mounts, but does not open the database

  - **startup open** Starts the instance and mounts and opens the database

  - **startup restrict** Starts the instance, mounts and opens the database, but restricts access to those users with the `restricted session` privilege granted to them

  - **startup recover** Starts the instance, leaves the database closed, and begins recovery for a disk failure scenario

  - **startup force** Makes an instance start that is having problems either starting or stopping

- When a database is open, any user with a username and password and the `create session` privilege can log into the Oracle database.

- Closing or shutting down a database must be done by the DBA while running SQL*Plus and while the DBA is connected to the database as `sysdba`.

- There are four options for closing a database:

  - **shutdown normal** No new existing connections are allowed, but existing sessions may take as long as they want to wrap up.

  - **shutdown immediate** No new connections are allowed, existing sessions are terminated, and their transactions are rolled back.

- ■ **shutdown transactional** No new connections are allowed, existing sessions are allowed to complete current transaction, and then disconnected.

- ■ **shutdown abort** No new connections are allowed, existing sessions are terminated, and transactions are not rolled back.

■ Instance recovery is required after shutdown abort is used.

■ You can obtain values for initialization parameters from several sources:

- ■ V$PARAMETER dynamic performance view

- ■ show parameter command in SQL*Plus

- ■ OEM Instance Manager administrative tool

■ Several important run-time logging files exist on the machine hosting the Oracle database. Each background process, such as LGWR and DBW0, will have a trace file if some error occurs in their execution, and the instance has a special trace file called the ALERT log. Trace files are written whenever the background process has a problem executing. The ALERT log is written whenever the instance is started or stopped, whenever the database structure is altered, or whenever an error occurs in database.

■ Trace files and ALERT logs are found in the directory identified by the BACKGROUND_DUMP_DEST parameter in the init*sid*.ora file.

■ Before creating the database, assess several things on the operating system level:

- ■ Are there enough individual disk resources to run Oracle without I/O bottlenecks?

- ■ Is there enough CPU, memory, and disk space for Oracle processing?

- ■ Are disk resources for different Oracle databases on the same host in separate directories?

- ■ Are environment settings correct for the database creation?

■ The first step in creating a database is to back up any existing databases already on the host machine.

■ The second step in creating a database is for the DBA to create a parameter file with unique values for several parameters, including the following:

- ■ **DB_NAME** The local name for the database

- ■ **DB_DOMAIN** The networkwide location for the database

- ■ **DB_BLOCK_SIZE** The size of each block in the database

- ■ **DB_CACHE_SIZE** The size of DB buffer cache

- ■ **PROCESSES** The maximum number of processes available on the database

- ■ **UNDO_MANAGEMENT and UNDO_TABLESPACE** Defines how Oracle should handle configuration and management of undo segments

■ After creating the parameter file, the DBA executes the `create database` command, which creates the datafiles for the SYSTEM tablespace, an initial undo segment, SYS and SYSTEM users, and redo log files. On conclusion of the `create database` statement, the database is created and open.

■ The default password for SYS is `change_on_install`.

■ The default password for SYSTEM is `manager`.

■ The number of datafiles and redo log files created for the life of the database can be limited with the `maxdatafiles` and `maxlogfiles` options of the `create database` statement.

■ The size of a datafile is fixed at its creation, unless the `autoextend` option is used.

■ The size of a control file is directly related to the number of datafiles and redo logs for the database.

Fill-in-the-Blank Questions

1. The initialization parameter used for defining the name of your Oracle database is _____.

2. In order to increase the size of a datafile, these keywords can be used so that Oracle can automatically add more space when necessary: _____.

3. Once the database is created, the frequency with which you can alter the database's block size is _____.

4. Of the database shutdown options, this one requires instance recovery the next time the database is started: _____.

5. The utility that supports password file authentication by creating the password file is _____.

Chapter Questions

1. The user is trying to execute a `select` statement. Which of the following background processes will obtain data from a disk for the user?

   A. DBW0

   B. LGWR

   C. SERVER

   D. USER

   E. DISPATCHER

2. In order to perform administrative tasks on the database using Oracle password authentication, the DBA should have the following two privileges granted to them:

   A. `sysdba` or `sysoper`

   B. CONNECT or RESOURCE

   C. `restricted session` or `create session`

3. Which component of the SGA stores parsed SQL statements is used for process sharing?

   A. Buffer cache

   B. Private SQL area

   C. Redo log buffer

   D. Library cache

   E. Row cache

4. Which of the following choices does not identify an aspect of shared server processing architecture?

   A. Each user gets his or her own server process for data retrieval.

   B. A dispatcher process is involved.

   C. A listener process is involved.

   D. The server process sits idle infrequently.

5. Which of the following is the `init`*sid*`.ora` parameter that indicates the size of each buffer in the buffer cache?

   A. DB_BLOCK_BUFFERS

   B. BUFFER_SIZE

   C. DB_BLOCK_SIZE

   D. ROLLBACK_SEGMENTS

6. The datafiles named in a `create database` statement are used as storage for which of the following database components?

   A. SYSTEM tablespace

   B. `init`*sid*`.ora` file

   C. Redo log member

   D. ALERT log

7. Changing the password used to manage the password file changes the password for which of the following?

   A. SYSTEM

   B. RPT_BATCH

   C. CONNECT

   D. SYS

8. Which is the default password for the SYS user?

   A. `change_on_install`

   B. NO_PASSWORD

   C. `manager`

   D. ORACLE

   E. NULL

9. DBAs who are planning to administer a database remotely should use all of the following choices except which of the following?

   A. ORAPWD

   B. REMOTE_LOGIN_PASSWORDFILE set to `shared`

   C. OS_AUTHENT_PREFIX set to `OPS$`

   D. A password file

10. **Power will disconnect on the machine running Oracle in two minutes, but user JASON has left for the day while still connected to Oracle. His workstation is locked, so he cannot be logged out from his desktop. How should the DBA shut down the instance?**

    A. `shutdown normal`

    B. `shutdown immediate`

    C. `shutdown abort`

    D. `shutdown force`

    E. `shutdown recover`

11. **Which of the following administrative tools in OEM can be used to view the initialization parameter settings for Oracle?**

    A. Schema Manager

    B. Instance Manager

    C. Security Manager

    D. Data Manager

    E. Software Manager

12. **Which two of the following items are required for killing a user session?**

    A. Username

    B. SID

    C. Serial number

    D. Password

13. **You are using the Universal Installer and Packager to install Oracle8i on a server that already hosts an Oracle7 database. Which of the following should not be performed when installing Oracle8i or Oracle9i on a machine already hosting earlier editions of the Oracle database?**

    A. Shut down the network listener.

    B. Shut down the database.

    C. Make a backup of existing databases.

    D. Install Oracle8i software to the same directory used for Oracle7 software.

Fill-in-the-Blank Answers

1. DB_NAME

2. AUTOEXTEND ON

3. NEVER

4. ABORT

5. ORAPWD

Answers to Chapter Questions

1. C.   SERVER

Explanation   The server process handles data access and retrieval from disk for all user processes connected to Oracle. Choice A, DBW0, moves data blocks between disk and the buffer cache, and therefore is not correct. Choice B, LGWR, copies redo entries from the redo log buffer to online redo logs on disk and therefore is not correct. Choice D, USER, is the process for which the server process acts in support of. Choice E, DISPATCHER, is used in the Oracle MTS architecture and routes user processes to a server, but does not handle reading data from disk on behalf of the user process.

2. A.   `sysdba or sysoper`

Explanation   Choices B and C are incorrect. Each privilege listed has some bearing on access, but none of them give any administrative capability. Refer to the discussion of choosing an authentication method.

3. D.   Library cache

Explanation   Choice A is incorrect because the buffer cache is where data blocks are stored for recently executed queries. Choice B is incorrect because the private SQL area is in the PGA where the actual values returned from a query are stored, not the parse information for the query. Choice C is incorrect because the redo log buffer stores redo entries temporarily until LGWR can write them to disk. Choice E is incorrect because the row cache stores data dictionary row information for fast access by users and Oracle. Refer to the discussion of Oracle architecture.

4. A.   Each user gets his or her own server process for data retrieval.

Explanation   The shared server or MTS architecture uses several elements that correspond to the choices. A dispatcher process assigns users to a shared server, while the listener process routes user processes either directly to a server in the case of dedicated server processing or to a dispatcher in MTS. The final choice, D, indicates a benefit of the MTS architecture. Because many users utilize the same server process, that server process will sit idle less frequently than in the dedicated server architecture. Choice A indicates the dedicated server architecture only and is the correct answer to the question.

5. C.   DB_BLOCK_SIZE

Explanation   Because each buffer in the buffer cache is designed to fit one data block, the size of buffers in the database block buffer cache will be the same size as the blocks they store. The size of blocks in the database is determined by DB_BLOCK_BUFFERS. Refer to the discussion of initialization parameters to be changed during database creation.

6. A.   SYSTEM tablespace

Explanation   Because datafiles can only be a part of tablespaces (more on this in Chapter 11), all other choices must be eliminated immediately. Another reason to eliminate at least choices B and D is that neither the init*sid*.ora file nor the ALERT log are created in the create database statement. So, as long as you know that redo logs are composed of online redo log members, and tablespaces like SYSTEM are composed of datafiles, you should have no problem getting a question like this one right.

7. D.   SYS

Explanation   Choice A is incorrect because the SYSTEM password has no affiliation with the password for the password file. SYS does. Choice B is incorrect because RPT_BATCH is not a password created by Oracle in a create database statement. Choice C is incorrect because CONNECT is a role, not a user.

8. A.   change_on_install

Explanation   This is a classic piece of Oracle trivia. Memorize it, along with the SYSTEM password, which incidentally is manager. This is all fine for OCP, but beware of others who may also have memorized these facts. Don't let a hacker use this information against you. Make sure you change the default passwords for SYS and SYSTEM after creating your database.

9. C.   OS_AUTHENT_PREFIX set to OPS$

Explanation   A DBA should use password file authentication when planning to administer a database remotely. This action consists of a password file, the ORAPWD utility, and setting the REMOTE_LOGIN_PASSWORDFILE parameter to be shared. The OS_AUTHENT_PREFIX parameter is used to alter the prefix Oracle requires on Oracle users when operating system authentication is being used. This one, obviously, is not required for Oracle password authentication.

10. B. `shutdown immediate`

Explanation A power outage can cause damage to an Oracle instance if it is running when the power goes out. However, choice C is just too drastic, given that you are basically treating the situation as if it required media recovery. After all, you know that JASON is not executing a transaction, so no additional time to finish the `rollback` will be required before shutdown. Choice A will not do it either, though, because `shutdown normal` will wait all night for JASON to come in and log off. Choice B is the logical choice. Choices D and E are not valid options for shutting down a database instance.

11. B. Instance Manager

Explanation The Instance Manager tool handles all instance-related tasks, including display and modification of initialization parameters set in the `initsid.ora` file. The Schema Manager handles tasks involving database object creation and modification, eliminating choice A. The Security Manager handles user privilege and role management, which eliminates choice C. The Data Manager handles the loading and unloading of data from EXPORT binary or flat file format, eliminating choice D. Finally, the Software Manager handles enterprise deployment of Oracle software, eliminating choice E.

12. B and C. SID *and* serial number

Explanation To disconnect a database user with the `alter system kill session` statement, you must have the SID and serial number. Both these pieces of information for the session you want to kill can be found in the V$SESSION dictionary view. You only need username and password information to establish the connection, not eliminate it, which in turn eliminates choices A and D.

13. D. Install Oracle8i or Oracle9i software to the same directory used for Oracle7 software.

Explanation Using Universal Installer and Packager, you cannot install Oracle8i or Oracle9i to the same directory that contains a prior release of Oracle installed with an earlier release of Oracle Installer. You should shut down any existing databases and listeners and make a backup of the existing database before installing a new version of Oracle on a machine already hosting an Oracle database.

CHAPTER
11

Managing the Physical
Database Structure

n this chapter, you will understand and demonstrate knowledge in the following areas:

- Data dictionary views and standard packages
- Managing the control file
- Maintaining redo log files

In this chapter, you will examine Oracle's physical disk resources in detail. Oracle disk resources are broken into two categories: physical and logical. Oracle physical disk resources include control files, datafiles, and redo log files. Logical disk resources, which include tablespaces, segments, extents, and Oracle blocks, will be discussed in the next chapter. After reading this chapter you will get a good understanding of the how the control files, redo log files, and the datafiles work with the background processes to make a working database. With these foundational concepts, you will have a better understanding of the rest of the topics in this book. In addition, you will be introduced to important information that is stored in the SYSTEM tablespace—data dictionary.

Data Dictionary Content and Usage

In this section, you will cover the following points about dictionary views and standard packages:

- Key components of the data dictionary
- Contents of the data dictionary and how they are used
- How to query the data dictionary views

The data dictionary is the first set of database objects the DBA should create after issuing the `create database` command. Every object in the database is tracked in some fashion by the Oracle data dictionary. Oracle generally creates the data dictionary without any intervention from the DBA at database creation time with the use of the `catalog.sql` and `catproc.sql` scripts. If you are using Database Configuration Assistant to create the database, the tool takes care to run these scripts. If you are manually creating the database, make sure to run these scripts soon after the database is created. This section will explain how Oracle creates the data dictionary using these different scripts the components of the data dictionary and how to use the data dictionary.

Constructing the Data Dictionary Views

The first script, `catalog.sql`, is used to create the objects that comprise the data dictionary. The data dictionary supports virtually every aspect of Oracle database operation, from finding information about objects to performance tuning, and everything in between.

To create a data dictionary, you run the `catalog.sql` script from within SQL*Plus while connected as the administrative privilege `sysdba`. This script performs a laundry list of `create view` statements, as well as executing a series of other scripts in order to create other data dictionary views in special areas and special public synonyms for those views. Within the `catalog.sql` script, there are calls to several other scripts, which are listed in the following:

- **`cataudit.sql`** Creates the SYS.AUD$ dictionary table, which tracks all audit trail information generated by Oracle when the auditing feature of the database is used.

- **`catldr.sql`** Creates views that are used for the SQL*Loader tool, which is used to process large-volume data loads from one system to another.

- **`catexp.sql`** Creates views that are used by the IMPORT/EXPORT utilities.

- **`catpart.sql`** Creates views that support Oracle9i's partitioning option.

- **`catadt.sql`** Creates views that support user-defined types and object components of Oracle9i's object features.

- **`standard.sql`** Creates the STANDARD package, which stores all Oracle scalar or simple datatypes like VARCHAR2 and BLOB; STANDARD also contains built-in SQL functions like `decode( )` and others.

It is important to remember that `catalog.sql` calls these other scripts automatically. All the scripts can be found in the `rdbms/admin` directory under the Oracle software home directory. The following code block demonstrates the commands necessary to run the `catalog.sql` file on UNIX:

```
# cd $ORACLE_HOME/rdbms/admin
# sqlplus
Oracle SQL*Plus Release 9.0.1.0.0 - Production
(c)Copyright 2001, Oracle Corporation. All Rights Reserved.
Enter user-name: sys as sysdba
Enter password:
Connected to:
Oracle9i Enterprise Edition Release 9.0.1.0.0 - Production
With the Partitioning and Objects options
SQL> @catalog
```

The second script, `catproc.sql`, creates procedural options and utilities for PL/SQL. There are two different types of scripts that are run by `catproc.sql`. If you look in the script, you will see references to other scripts in the `rdbms/admin` directory, such as `dbmsutil.sql` and `dbmssql.sql`. These scripts ending in `.sql` are package specifications for the various Oracle server packages. Package specification contains the procedure, function, type, and constant definitions that are available in the package, but not actual code. The other type of script is a `.plb` script, such as `prvtutil.plb` and `prvtpipe.plb`. This extension denotes PL/SQL code that has been encrypted using a wrapper program to prevent you from seeing the application code logic.

It is important to remember that `catproc.sql` calls these other scripts automatically. All the scripts can be found in the `rdbms/admin` directory under the Oracle software home directory. The following code block demonstrates the commands necessary to run the `catproc.sql` file on UNIX:

```
/home/oracle/app/oracle/product/9.0.1> cd rdbms/admin
/home/oracle/app/oracle/product/9.0.1/rdbms/admin> sqlplus
Oracle SQL*Plus Release 8.1.7.0.0 - Production
(c)Copyright 2000, Oracle Corporation. All Rights Reserved.
Enter user-name: sys as sysdba
Enter password:
Connected to:
Oracle9i Enterprise Edition Release 9.0.1.0.0 - Production
With the Partitioning and Objects options
SQL> @catproc
```

It is not possible to create the dictionary views unless you have created the database first already. Because you run the scripts while connected as user `sys as sysdba`, the SYS user winds up owning the database objects that comprise the data dictionary, and these objects are stored in the SYSTEM tablespace, neither of which will exist until you issue the `create database` statement. In addition to these two scripts mentioned, there are other scripts that can be executed to create different options. These other scripts will be described as they pertain to matters tested on the OCP exam. You can also refer to Oracle documentation for a complete list of the scripts.

For Review

1. Data dictionary keeps track of every aspect of the database from tables being created to performance information of the database.

2. Executing the `catalog.sql` and `catproc.sql` scripts soon after creation of the database creates the data dictionary.

3. The data dictionary is owned by SYS and created in the SYSTEM tablespace.

Exercises

1. **You are determining when to create your Oracle data dictionary. Which of the following choices indicates the most appropriate time to do so?**

   A. Before the database has been created

   B. Before creating Oracle-supplied packages

   C. Before creating the SYSTEM tablespace

   D. Before giving users access to the database

2. **You are about to create your Oracle-supplied packages for use with the database. Which of the following scripts is most appropriate for doing so?**

   A. `catproc.sql`

   B. `catalog.sql`

   C. `catldr.sql`

   D. `catexp.sql`

3. **You are about to create your Oracle data dictionary for use with the database. Which of the following users would you connect to the database as for this purpose in Oracle9i and later releases?**

   A. SYSTEM

   B. OUTLN

   C. INTERNAL

   D. SYS

Answer Key

1. B. **2.** A. **3.** D. The INTERNAL user has been made obsolete for Oracle9i and later releases.

Key Data Dictionary Components and Contents

Oracle's data dictionary has two components—base tables and user-accessible views. The following discussion covers the differences between the two. You should always remember to use the user-accessible views in the Oracle data dictionary. Never access the base tables directly. Now, let's look at other aspects of the data dictionary components you need to understand for OCP.

Base Tables

Data in the data dictionary is stored in a set of tables that are created during the initial stages of database creation. These tables are called *base tables*. They are the X$ tables created in the SYSTEM tablespace, whose sole purpose is to store these data dictionary base tables. These tables are created during the execution of `catalog.sql` script. Only user SYS as the privileges necessary to access these tables directly. You should avoid logging into Oracle as SYS whenever possible to avoid damaging the dictionary base tables, and you should never grant direct access to base tables to others using the Oracle database.

User-Accessible Views

During the same time the base tables are created and populated, the `catalog.sql` script creates a set of user-friendly views that enables users to view the data dictionary data through these views. Hence, data dictionary that we normally refer to is a set of views and not tables. Oracle creates public synonyms on many data dictionary views so users can access them conveniently. For the rest of the discussion, we'll focus on the views available in the data dictionary rather than on the base tables. The use of the data dictionary is where OCP exams will test your knowledge.

Oracle software uses the data dictionary extensively. It is used from validating the user connections coming into the database to verifying the existence of the tables that are being queried to the looking for indexes of the tables to improve the performance of the transactions. Due to constant access of the data dictionary, it is cached in the *dictionary cache* of the System Global Area (SGA) to improve the access to it.

Available Dictionary Views

A wealth of information about objects and data in your database can be found in a relatively small number of tables owned by a special privileged user in Oracle called SYS. Although Oracle prevents you from looking at these tables directly, several views are available for you to access this information. These views comprise the feature in Oracle known as the *data dictionary*.

Data dictionary views help you avoid referring to the tables of the data dictionary directly. This safeguard is important for two reasons. First, it underscores the sensitivity of the SYS-owned tables that store dictionary data. If something happens to those tables, causing either data to be lost or a table to be removed, the effects could seriously damage your Oracle database—possibly even rendering it completely unusable! Second, the dictionary views distill the information in the data dictionary into highly understandable and useful formats.

What's in a Name?

Let's start by considering an example. Take a look at the following code block. In it, we can see the contents of a dictionary view called USER_TABLES:

```
SQL> select table_name from user_tables;
TABLE_NAME
-----------------------------
BONUS
DEPARTMENT
DEPT
DUMMY
EMP
EMPLOYEE
EXAMPLE_1
PRICES
SALGRADE
TESTER
```

I logged into Oracle as user SCOTT to obtain this output, so you can see that the output of this query displays the name of almost every table we've worked with. Look more carefully for a moment at the name of the view I used: USER_TABLES. Its very name implies two vitally important aspects of this (and indeed every) view in the data dictionary:

- The view's topic (in this case, tables)
- The view's scope (in this case, tables owned by the user SCOTT)

TIP
The scope and topic of the dictionary view are separated by an underscore.

Discerning a Dictionary View's Scope

Let's discuss the view's scope first. Dictionary views are divided into three general categories corresponding to how much of the related topic the database user querying the view is permitted to see. The categories are discussed in the following subsections.

USER   These views enable you to see relevant database objects owned by you. These views have the narrowest scope because they only display the database objects that are in your schema. Therefore, if SCOTT owns a table called EMP and I log into Oracle as user JASON to issue `select * from USER_TABLES`, I'm not going to see EMP listed among the output. Why? Because the table belongs to SCOTT.

ALL   These views enable you to see relevant database objects that you may or may not own but nevertheless are accessible to you. These views have a wider scope than the USER views because they include every relevant object that you can access, regardless of ownership. However, the scope is still limited to you, the user. In order to be able to access a database object, one of three conditions must be true:

- You created the object.

- You were granted access to the object by the object owner.

- The PUBLIC user was granted access privileges on the object by the owner.

TIP
The PUBLIC user in the database is a special user who represents the access privileges every user has. Therefore, when an object owner creates a table and grants access to the table to user PUBLIC, every user in the database has access privileges to the table created.

DBA   These powerful views enable you to see all relevant database objects in the entire database, whether or not they are owned by or accessible to you. These views are incredibly handy for DBAs (and sometimes also for developers) needing information about every database object.

NOTE
You can grant a special role to users called SELECT_CATALOG_ROLE in order to let them look at the DBA views.

Identifying a Dictionary View's Topic
The second part of any dictionary view's name identifies the topic of that view. Based on this fact, we know that the topic of the USER_TABLES view is tables, whereas the topic for the ALL_INDEXES view is all indexes. The views that correspond to areas that have been or will be discussed are listed in the following:

■ **USER_OBJECTS, ALL_OBJECTS, DBA_OBJECTS** Gives information about various database objects owned by the current user, available to the current user, or all objects in the database, respectively.

■ **USER_TABLES, ALL_TABLES, DBA_TABLES** Displays information about tables owned by or available to the current user, respectively, or all tables in the Oracle database.

■ **USER_INDEXES, ALL_INDEXES, DBA_INDEXES** Displays information about indexes owned by or available to the current user, respectively, or all indexes in the Oracle database.

■ **USER_VIEWS, ALL_VIEWS, DBA_VIEWS** Displays information about views owned by or available to the current user, respectively, or all views in the Oracle database (including dictionary views).

■ **USER_SEQUENCES, ALL_SEQUENCES, DBA_SEQUENCES** Displays information about sequences owned by or available to the current user, respectively, or all sequences in the Oracle database.

■ **USER_USERS, ALL_USERS, DBA_USERS** Displays information about the current user or about all users in Oracle, respectively.

■ **USER_CONSTRAINTS, ALL_CONSTRAINTS, DBA_CONSTRAINTS** Displays information about constraints owned by or available to the current user, respectively, or all constraints in the Oracle database.

■ **USER_CONS_COLUMNS, ALL_CONS_COLUMNS, DBA_CONS_COLUMNS** Displays information about table columns that have constraints owned by or available to the current user, respectively, or all table columns in Oracle that have constraints on them.

■ **USER_IND_COLUMNS, ALL_IND_COLUMNS, DBA_IND_COLUMNS** Displays information about table columns that have indexes owned by or available to the current user, respectively, or all columns in Oracle tables that have indexes on them.

■ **USER_TAB_COLUMNS, ALL_TAB_COLUMNS, DBA_TAB_COLUMNS** Displays information about columns in tables owned by or available to the current user, respectively, or all columns in all tables in Oracle.

■ **USER_ROLES, ALL_ROLES, DBA_ROLES** Displays information about roles owned by or available to the current user, respectively, or all roles in the Oracle database.

■ **USER_TAB_PRIVS, ALL_TAB_PRIVS, DBA_TAB_PRIVS** Displays information about object privileges on objects owned by the user or available to the current user, respectively, or all object privileges available to all users in Oracle.

- **USER_SYS_PRIVS, ALL_SYS_PRIVS, DBA_SYS_PRIVS** Displays information about object privileges on objects owned by the user or available to the current user, respectively, or all system privileges granted to all users in Oracle.

- **USER_SOURCE, ALL_SOURCE, DBA_SOURCE** Displays the source code for PL/SQL programs owned by the user or available to the current user, respectively, or all PL/SQL source code in the entire Oracle database.

- **USER_TRIGGERS, ALL_TRIGGERS, DBA_TRIGGERS** Displays information about triggers owned by the user or available to the current user, respectively, or all triggers in the Oracle database.

- **ROLE_TAB_PRIVS, ROLE_SYS_PRIVS, ROLE_ROLE_PRIVS** Displays information about object privileges, system privileges, or roles granted to roles in the database, respectively.

- **DBA_TABLESPACES, DBA_TS_QUOTAS** Displays information about all tablespaces in Oracle, as well as space quotas assigned to users in each tablespace.

- **DBA_DATAFILES, DBA_SEGMENTS, DBA_EXTENTS, DBA_FREE_SPACE** Displays information about datafiles in your Oracle database, as well as segments, extents, and free space in each datafile, respectively.

- **DBA_PROFILES** Displays information about user profiles in Oracle. Profiles are a way for you as the DBA to restrict the physical resources of the host system (such as process memory allocation, CPU cycles, and so on) that users may utilize in conjunction with Oracle processing.

TIP
These are just some of the views available in the Oracle data dictionary. We'll discuss others as they become relevant to topics tested on the OCP exam.

The Dynamic Performance Views

Another important classification of views in the Oracle database is the dynamic performance views. These are not part of the Oracle dictionary per se, but nevertheless are useful for managing your database. Dynamic performance views are updated constantly by Oracle with important data about database operation. Some examples of dynamic performance views include

- **V$DATABASE** General information about the database mounted to your instance is kept here.

■ **V$SYSSTAT**   Most information about the performance of your database is kept here.

■ **V$SESSION, V$SESSTAT**   Most information about performance for individual user sessions is stored here.

■ **VLOG, VLOGFILE**   Information about online redo logs can be found here.

■ **V$DATAFILE**   Information about Oracle datafiles can be found here.

■ **V$CONTROLFILE**   Information about Oracle control files can be found here.

A Look at the Views Themselves

As you know, views do not actually contain any data—they are merely `select` statements stored as objects in Oracle. Every time you refer to a view in your own queries, Oracle dynamically executes the view's underlying `select` statement to obtain the contents of that view. Dictionary view definitions can be quite complex. So that you can appreciate this hidden complexity, the following code block shows you the definition of the ALL_TABLES view in Oracle. Because this view contains a column called TEXT that is defined as the LONG datatype, we have to do a little extra formatting via the `set long 9999` command to ensure that we'll see the output appropriately:

```
SQL> SET LONG 9999;
SQL> SELECT text FROM all_views WHERE view_name = 'ALL_TABLES';
TEXT
-----------------------------------------
select u.name, o.name, ts.name, co.name,
t.pctfree$, t.pctused$,
t.initrans, t.maxtrans,
s.iniexts * ts.blocksize, s.extsize * ts.blocksize,
s.minexts, s.maxexts, s.extpct,
decode(s.lists, 0, 1, s.lists), decode(s.groups, 0, 1, s.groups),
decode(bitand(t.modified,1), 0, 'Y', 1, 'N', '?'),
t.rowcnt, t.blkcnt, t.empcnt, t.avgspc, t.chncnt, t.avgrln,
lpad(decode(t.spare1, 0, '1', 1, 'DEFAULT', to_char(t.spare1)), 10),
lpad(decode(mod(t.spare2, 65536), 0, '1', 1, 'DEFAULT',
to_char(mod(t.spare2, 65536))), 10),
lpad(decode(floor(t.spare2 / 65536), 0, 'N', 1, 'Y', '?'), 5),
decode(bitand(t.modified, 6), 0, 'ENABLED', 'DISABLED')
from sys.user$ u, sys.ts$ ts, sys.seg$ s,
 sys.obj$ co, sys.tab$ t, sys.obj$ o
where o.owner# = u.user#
and o.obj# = t.obj#
```

```
and t.clu# = co.obj# (+)
and t.ts# = ts.ts#
and t.file# = s.file# (+)
and t.block# = s.block# (+)
and (o.owner# = userenv('SCHEMAID')
or o.obj# in
(select oa.obj#
from sys.objauth$ oa
where grantee# in ( select kzsrorol from x$kzsro))
or /* user has system privileges */
exists (select null from v$enabledprivs
where priv_number in (-45 /* LOCK ANY TABLE */,
-47 /* SELECT ANY TABLE */,
-48 /* INSERT ANY TABLE */,
-49 /* UPDATE ANY TABLE */,
-50 /* DELETE ANY TABLE */)))
```

TIP

If you want to obtain a full listing of all data dictionary views available in Oracle, you can execute select * from DICTIONARY, *and Oracle will list all the dictionary views for you. Comments on the use of each dictionary view are offered in DICTIONARY as well. Some objects in Oracle that are synonymous with DICTIONARY are DICT, CATALOG, and CAT.*

For Review

1. Know what the data dictionary is. Be sure you can distinguish between dictionary views and the SYS-owned tables underlying those views.

2. Understand how to identify the topic and scope of a dictionary view based on the name of that view. Also, be sure you can identify all the views defined in this discussion.

3. Be sure you can identify the data dictionary views that will list all the dictionary views available in the Oracle database.

Exercises

1. **You want to list all the indexed columns for objects you own in the Oracle database. Which of the following views would you use?**

    A. USER_TAB_COLUMNS

    B. ALL_TAB_COLUMNS

    C. USER_IND_COLUMNS

    D. ALL_IND_COLUMNS

2. **You are identifying dictionary objects in the Oracle database. Which of the following is a view in the data dictionary?**

    A. V$DATABASE

    B. DBA_TABLES

    C. SYS.AUD$

    D. EMP

3. **This is the user who owns all the data dictionary objects in Oracle:**
    _____.

4. **This is an object you can query to obtain a listing of all data dictionary objects in Oracle:** _____.

5. **Which of the following choices identifies a dynamic performance view in the Oracle database?**

    A. DBA_DATA_FILES

    B. DBA_SEGMENTS

    C. V$DATAFILE

    D. DBA_EXTENTS

Answer Key
1. C. 2. B. 3. SYS. 4. CATALOG, CAT, DICTIONARY, or DICT. 5. C.

Querying the Data Dictionary

We'll now look at some examples of querying the dictionary so you can better understand how useful the data dictionary is in Oracle. (For the purposes of this section, the DBA_ views will be used, except where noted.) Recall that you can use the `describe` command on data dictionary views, just as if they were tables. The following code block shows what happens when you do so:

```
SQL> describe dba_source
 Name                            Null?    Type
 ------------------------------ -------- ----------------
 OWNER                          NOT NULL VARCHAR2(30)
 NAME                           NOT NULL VARCHAR2(30)
 TYPE                                    VARCHAR2(12)
 LINE                           NOT NULL NUMBER
 TEXT                                    VARCHAR2(4000)
```

The DBA_INDEXES view contains information about the indexes on tables that are available to the user. Some of the information listed in this view details the features of the index, such as whether all values in the indexed column are unique. Other information in the view identifies the storage parameters of the index and where the index is stored. The following shows an example:

```
SQL> column owner format a10
SQL> column index_name format a15
SQL> column table_name format a12
SQL> column uniqueness format a10
SQL> select owner, index_name, table_name, uniqueness
  2  from dba_indexes
  3  where owner = 'SCOTT';
OWNER       INDEX_NAME      TABLE_NAME   UNIQUENESS
----------  --------------- ------------ ----------
SCOTT       PK_01           EXAMPLE_1    UNIQUE
SCOTT       SYS_C00905      DEPARTMENT   UNIQUE
SCOTT       UK_EMPLOYEE_01  EMPLOYEE     UNIQUE
```

TIP
For those of you following along on your own database, I've shown some useful formatting commands for cleaning up the output from these queries.

The next view is the DBA_USERS view. This view is used to give the current user of the database more information about all users known to the Oracle database:

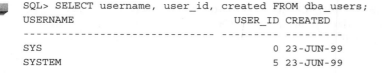

```
SQL> SELECT username, user_id, created FROM dba_users;
USERNAME                        USER_ID CREATED
------------------------------- --------- ---------
SYS                                   0 23-JUN-99
SYSTEM                                5 23-JUN-99
```

```
OUTLN                               11  23-JUN-99
DBSNMP                              18  23-JUN-99
AURORA$ORB$UNAUTHENTICATED         23  23-JUN-99
JASON                              27  18-JUL-00
STUDENT2                           46  30-OCT-00
STUDENT1                           45  30-OCT-00
SPANKY                             43  30-OCT-00
JASON2                             48  31-OCT-00
SCOTT                              52  19-MAR-01
JASON3                             49  16-NOV-00
JASON10                            50  18-NOV-00
GIANT                              51  08-DEC-00
```

Querying Dictionary Views for Constraints

Here's a trickier example. In keeping with our work on constraints in this chapter, the next few views are related to constraints. Let's look at combining the contents of two views: DBA_CONSTRAINTS and DBA_CONS_COLUMNS. The DBA_CONSTRAINTS view is used to display information about the constraints that have been defined in the database, while DBA_CONS_COLUMNS displays all columns in integrity constraints in Oracle. Consider the following situation. Say we can't remember whether we have followed the book's advice for naming shared columns in multiple tables the same name. Is this a problem? Not with the Oracle data dictionary on hand! We can still determine the referenced column using DBA_CONSTRAINTS and DBA_CONS_COLUMNS, as shown in the following block:

```
SQL> column table_name format a12
SQL> column column_name format a12
SQL> select a.table_name, b.column_name, c.table_name, c.column_name
  2  from DBA_constraints a, DBA_cons_columns b, DBA_cons_columns c
  3  where a.constraint_name = b.constraint_name
  4  and a.r_constraint_name = c.constraint_name;
TABLE_NAME    COLUMN_NAME        TABLE_NAME    COLUMN_NAME
------------  -----------------  ------------  --------------
EMPLOYEE      DEPARTMENT_NUM     DEPARTMENT    DEPARTMENT_NUM
```

Using Other Dictionary Views

Similar information to the contents of DBA_CONS_COLUMNS can be found in DBA_IND_COLUMNS. However, the dictionary view DBA_IND_COLUMNS will contain columns used in constraint-related indexes as well as columns used in other types of indexes. Check out the following code block:

```
SQL> create index ix_employee_01 on employee (lastname);
Index created.
SQL> select index_name, table_name, column_name, column_position
```

```
  2  from DBA_ind_columns
  3  where table_name = 'EMPLOYEE';
INDEX_NAME       TABLE_NAME    COLUMN_NAME        COLUMN_POSITION
---------------  ------------  -----------------  ---------------
PK_EMPLOYEE_01   EMPLOYEE      EMPID                            1
UK_EMPLOYEE_01   EMPLOYEE      GOVT_ID                          1
IX_EMPLOYEE_01   EMPLOYEE      LASTNAME                         1
```

For Review

Be sure you can develop queries against dictionary views.

Exercises

1. **Use the following code block to answer this question:**

   ```
   TEXT
   ----------------------------------------------
   declare
     x varchar2(10);
   begin
     x := 'hello world';
     dbms_output.put_line(x);
   end;
   ```

   Which of the following queries might have produced this output?

   A. DBA_ERRORS

   B. DBA_SOURCE

   C. DBA_VIEWS

   D. DBA_TRIGGERS

2. **Use the following code block to answer this question:**

   ```
   SQL> select text from DBA_views where view_name =
     2  'DBA_TABLES';
   TEXT
   --------------------------------------------------------------

   select u.name, o.name,
          decode(bitand(t.property, 4194400), 0, ts.name, null),
   ```

   Which of the following choices identifies a formatting command that can be used for displaying the rest of the output?

   A. `set long 9999`

   B. `column text format a9999`

    C. `set long 50`

    D. `column text format a50`

3. To identify some aspects about all users in the database, you would use this view: _____.

Answer Key
1. B. 2. A. 3. DBA_USERS.

Maintaining Control Files

In this section, you will cover the following points about managing control files:

- How control files are used
- Examining control file contents
- Managing control files with Oracle-Managed Files
- Obtaining information about control files
- Multiplexing control files

    Control files are to the physical structure of the Oracle database what the data dictionary is to the logical structure. The control files keep track of all the files' Oracle needs and where they are on the host machine. The control files also contain information about the redo log member filenames and where they are located in the filesystem. Without control files, the Oracle database server would be unable to find its physical components. The names of the control files are specified in the `init.ora` file for each Oracle instance. In this section, we will talk about how Oracle uses control files, what is stored in the control files, where to obtain information about your control files, and the importance of storing multiple copies of control files on separate disks.

How Control Files Are Used

When you enter SQL*Plus to bring the database online, Oracle looks in the control file to find all the components it needs in order to bring that database online. For example, if the control file on your database has three files associated with it and only two are available, Oracle will complain that the third file was missing, and it won't start your database. After database startup, control files will be modified or used by Oracle in the following situations:

- When new physical disk resources (such as tablespaces) are created

- When an existing disk resource is modified in some way (for example, when a datafile is added to a tablespace)

- When LGWR stops writing one online redo log and starts writing to another (log switch)

Using the CONTROL_FILES Parameter

The CONTROL_FILES parameter in the `init.ora` file defines the location of your control files on the database server and indicates where Oracle will look on instance startup to find its control files. When you start the instance before creating the database or when you are migrating from one version of Oracle to another, Oracle will create control files based on the filenames and locations you provide in the CONTROL_FILES `init.ora` parameter. In subsequent instance startups, if Oracle does not find the control files it expects to find based on the content of the CONTROL_FILES parameter, Oracle won't start. You will learn in subsequent sections that if you create Oracle-managed control files then there is no need for the CONTROL_FILES parameter and Oracle will look for default directory or directories for the control files.

By default in both Windows and UNIX environments, the Oracle Database Configuration Assistant (DBCA) will create three control files and put them in the oradata/*database_name* directory under the Oracle software home directory. DBCA gives them the name `controlnn.dbf` (although sometimes DBCA may also use the `.ctl` or `.ora` extensions), where *n* is a number between 01 and 03 (the number could be operating system specific). You can follow whatever naming convention you like when you define your own control files. You are also not restricted to placing the control files in the directory $ORACLE_HOME/dbs. You can put them wherever you want. For reasons we will explore shortly, Oracle recommends you use multiple control files placed on separate disks. Be sure to include the absolute pathname for the location of your control file when defining values for the CONTROL_FILES parameter.

For Review

1. Control files are used to keep track of all the physical components of the database such as location of the data files, redo logs, name of the database, and so on.

2. Normally, Oracle expects to see the control files at the location indicated by CONTROL_FILES parameter. Starting with Oracle9i, this is not true if

you are using Oracle-Managed Files (OMF). For our purposes, we'll assume you're not using OMF, but be mindful that some OCP questions may take OMFs into account.

Exercises

1. **You are attempting to locate your control files on an Oracle database called ORCL. In which of the following files might you look for this information?**

   A. `control01.ctl`

   B. `pwdORCL.ora`

   C. `catalog.sql`

   D. `init.ora`

2. **Your attempts to start the Oracle database have failed. After looking in the appropriate location, you ascertain the value for the CONTROL_FILES parameter to be set to /u01/oradata/orcl/control01.ctl. Which of the following choices identifies the next likely step you would take to troubleshoot the problem?**

   A. Verify the actual directory location of your control file.

   B. Check the hardware to see if the memory card is defective.

   C. Verify the actual directory location of your SYSTEM datafile.

   D. Check to see if you have created two redo logs.

3. **You are configuring your Oracle database. Under which of the following features in Oracle would you not have to configure the CONTROL_FILES parameter for an individual instance?**

   A. When Real Application Clusters are used

   B. When OMF is used

   C. When temporary tablespaces are used

   D. When transportable tablespaces are used

Answer Key

1. D. **2.** A. **3.** B.

Examining Control File Contents

Control files have several items contained in them. However, you can't just open a control file in your favorite text editor and see what it holds. This is because the control file is written in binary, and only the Oracle database can understand its contents. However, rest assured—we're going to tell you what the control file contains so that you know this information for OCP! The control file contains the following:

- Database name and identifier information that you supplied when you created the database.

- Database creation date and time information that you supplied when you created the database.

- Datafiles and redo log filesystem locations that you supplied when you created the database and when you added datafiles or redo logs.

- Tablespace names and the associations between tablespaces and datafiles that you supplied when you created the database or tablespaces, or when you added more datafiles to existing tablespaces later.

- History of when archive logs were taken. This information is typically generated automatically by Oracle.

- Information about when backups were taken. This information is generated when you take your backups.

- The current online redo log sequence number. This information is typically generated automatically by Oracle.

- Current checkpoint information. Again, this information is typically generated automatically by Oracle.

Re-creating a Control File

Sometimes control files must be re-created for various purposes. For example, you might like to rename the database because you're making a copy of it on the same machine hosting the original database (Oracle doesn't permit two databases to have the same name on the same host system). Or, you might need to change database settings such as maxlogfiles that you set when you created the database. You may have even lost the control file. Whatever the reason, your method is the same. Issue the `alter database backup controlfile to trace` statement. The `trace` keyword in this statement indicates that Oracle will generate a script containing a `create controlfile` command and store it in the trace directory identified in the `init.ora` file by the USER_DUMP_DEST parameter. A sample control file creation script generated by this command is displayed in the following code block:

```
# The following commands will create a new control file and use it
# to open the database.
# Data used by the recovery manager will be lost. Additional
# logs may be required for media recovery of offline data
# files. Use this only if the current version of all online
# logs are available.
STARTUP NOMOUNT
CREATE CONTROLFILE REUSE DATABASE "ORGDB01" NORESETLOGS
NOARCHIVELOG
    MAXLOGFILES 16
    MAXLOGMEMBERS 2
    MAXDATAFILES 240
    MAXINSTANCES 1
    MAXLOGHISTORY 113
LOGFILE
  GROUP 1 ('/oracle/disk_01/log1a.dbf',
'/oracle/disk_02/log1b.dbf') SIZE 30M,
  GROUP 2 ('/oracle/disk_03/log2a.dbf',
'/oracle/disk_04/log2b.dbf') SIZE 30M
DATAFILE
  '/oracle/disk_05/system01.dbf',
  '/oracle/disk_05/system02.dbf'
;
# Recovery is required if any of the datafiles are restored
# backups, or if the last shutdown was not normal or immediate.
RECOVER DATABASE
# Database can now be opened normally.
ALTER DATABASE OPEN;
```

From this script, you can guess what the correct syntax for a `create controlfile` statement would be—you have it right in front of you. For example, if you wanted to clone an existing database, you would follow this procedure:

1. From SQL*Plus, issue the `alter system backup controlfile to trace` command. Oracle generates a script containing the `create controlfile` command similar to the one shown in the previous code block.

2. Shut your existing database down from SQL*Plus using the `shutdown normal` or `shutdown immediate` commands. Do not use `shutdown abort`.

3. Copy all datafiles and redo logs to an alternate filesystem location (preferably using OFA conventions identified in Chapter 1) using operating system commands.

4. Modify the script generated in step 1 using your favorite text editor. You'll need to change the previous reuse database "name" clause to set database "newname". You'll also need to review and modify the filesystem location of every datafile listed in the `datafile` clause of the `create controlfile` command to reflect the new location of the files you copied. You'll need to do the same for online redo logs as well. Also, remove all commented lines beginning with the # character. Later in step 8, you won't necessarily encounter an error if some datafiles weren't copied properly or if Oracle did not find the datafiles where it expected to find them. Thus, it is very important that you verify the filesystem locations for all datafiles and redo logs in your script before proceeding to step 5. Also, remove the `recover database` and `alter database open` commands. You'll perform these steps manually in a later step.

5. Copy the `init.ora` file for the existing database to a new location. In your favorite text editor, change the value set for the CONTROL_FILES parameter in your `init.ora` file to a new filesystem location. In addition, you'll need to modify other `init.ora` settings like DB_NAME and so on, as if you were creating a new database, so refer back to Chapter 1 for further information. If you do not perform this step, then Oracle will not let you rename your new database and may even corrupt your old one!

6. From SQL*Plus, start the Oracle instance with the `startup nomount` command.

7. Run the script you modified in steps 4 and 5 using the `run` or `@` command in SQL*Plus. This step creates you new control file.

8. In SQL*Plus, mount the new database with the `alter table mount` command.

9. In SQL*Plus, open the new database with the `alter table open` command.

10. In SQL*Plus, open the old database with the `startup open` command.

TIP
This is a topic Oracle will most likely cover on the Oracle Database Administration Fundamentals II exam, but explaining it here serves an important purpose—namely, to introduce you to the contents of your control file and how to manipulate it.

For Review

1. Control files are the most important files of a database from a filesystem layout and management perspective. It contains information related to the physical location of every datafile and redo log file in your database.

2. Control files are created the first time you create your Oracle database. If no control file exists already in the location specified by the CONTROL_FILES parameter, then Oracle creates a new control file automatically when the `create database` command is issued. You can re-create a control file for an associated database later using the `create controlfile` command.

3. Control files are opened and read every time the database is opened. The contents of control files are modified every time the structure of the database is changed such as by adding a tablespace, datafile, or online redo log. The control file is also changed when you archive your redo logs, backup the database, and whenever a log switch happens.

Exercises

1. **You are about to create an Oracle database. Which of the following choices identifies a database component not created when the `create database` statement is issued?**

A. Password files

B. Control files

C. Redo log files

D. Datafiles

2. **You are attempting to rename your Oracle database using the `create controlfile` command. Which of the following choices identifies the step you would most likely take immediately after you shut down your original database to copy the original files to their new locations?**

A. Issue the `alter database backup controlfile to trace` command.

B. Modify the script containing your `create controlfile` command to reflect the new filesystem locations for files copied.

C. Modify appropriate parameters in a copy of the existing database's `init.ora` file.

D. Remove the control files on your existing database with operating system commands.

3. **BONUS: You are managing control files on an Oracle database. At which of the following points will the contents of your control file not be modified?**

   A. When you open the control file in a text editor

   B. When you issue the `alter tablespace` command

   C. When you issue the `alter database rename file` command

   D. When you issue the `alter database add logfile` command

Answer Key

1. A. **2.** B. Because the question refers to copying files to new locations, the most appropriate next step is to note the new filesystem locations in your script. **3.** A. Although you haven't learned about the commands listed in choices B, C, and D yet, this question should not be too tricky.

Managing Control Files with Oracle-Managed Files

Oracle**9i** and higher In Chapter 1, we introduced the concept of Oracle-Managed Files (OMF). This is a new feature in Oracle9i that is designed to minimize the amount of filesystem handling you must execute as an Oracle DBA in support of creating and managing the Oracle database. Let's continue this discussion with respect to the management of your control files. Recall that in order to set up OMF, you must configure appropriate values for the following `init.ora` parameters:

- **DB_CREATE_FILE_DEST** Defines the location of the default filesystem directory where Oracle will create the datafiles. The following code block shows an OFA-compliant example of how you might set this parameter for a database called DB1:

```
DB_CREATE_FILE_DEST = '/u01/oradata/db1'
```

- **DB_CREATE_ONLINE_LOG_DEST_*n*** Defines the location of the default filesystem directory for online redo log files and control file creation. The following code block shows an OFA-compliant example of how you might set this parameter for a database called DB1:

```
DB_CREATE_ONLINE_LOG_DEST_1 = '/u01/oradata/db1'
DB_CREATE_ONLINE_LOG_DEST_2 = '/u02/oradata/db1'
```

TIP
When the OMF parameters for defining multiple locations to place online redo logs are specified, then Oracle will place control files in those redo log directories. This multiplexes your control file. You'll learn more about control file multiplexing later in this section.

Changing OMF Settings Later

Values that you set for these two parameters can be dynamically changed using
`alter system set` *parameter* = *value* command, where *parameter* is the
parameter whose settings you want to change, and *value* is the directory you want
to change that OMF parameter to. The following code block shows an example:

```
SQL> alter system set DB_CREATE_ONLINE_LOG_DEST_2 = '/u03/oradata/db1';
System altered.
```

Oracle-Managed Control Files During Database Creation

The following are a few facts to keep in mind about OMFs for the OCP Database
Administration Fundamentals I exam. If you've specified the CONTROL_FILES
parameter in `init.ora` file, but didn't specify values for either OMF parameters,
then Oracle will create control files in the locations you defined with the
CONTROL_FILES parameter. These files will not be managed by the OMF feature,
although Oracle will write any changes in database structure to those control files
automatically, as we've already explained. Conversely, if you've chosen not to
specify a value for the CONTROL_FILES parameter but instead specified values
for OMF parameters, then Oracle creates an OMF-managed control file in the
destination you specified for the OMF parameters, subject to the following
conditions:

- If you specified a directory for DB_CREATE_FILE_DEST but not for the parameter DB_CREATE_ONLINE_LOG_DEST_*n*, the OMF-managed control file is placed in the directory assigned for DB_CREATE_FILE_DEST.

- If you specified a directory for DB_CREATE_ONLINE_LOG_DEST_*n* but not for DB_CREATE_FILE_DEST, then Oracle places an OMF-managed control file in each directory specified in the DB_CREATE_ONLINE_LOG_DEST_1 and DB_CREATE_ONLINE_LOG_DEST_2 parameters.

- If you specified directories for both parameter types, then Oracle places an OMF-managed control file in each directory specified in the DB_CREATE_ONLINE_LOG_DEST_1 and DB_CREATE_ONLINE_LOG_DEST_2 parameters.

OMF Control File-Naming Conventions

When you use OMF, you relinquish power to Oracle to name the files according to its own conventions. The Oracle-managed control file uses a default naming convention of `ora_%u.ctl`, where `%u` is a unique name generated by Oracle. This name will not necessarily correlate with the name of the database or with parameter settings in `init.ora` such as DB_NAME. The following is an example:
`ora_cmr3u45r.ctl`.

TIP
Most DBAs will likely not use OMF for production systems. This is because many files that should be placed on separate disks for performance purposes are all dumped onto the same disk when the OMF feature is used. However, OMFs are great for an organization just getting started with Oracle databases that needs to get up and running very quickly.

For Review

1. Oracle-Managed Files are created by specifying two `init.ora` parameters: DB_CREATE_FILE_DEST and DB_CREATE_ONLINE_LOG_DEST_*n*.

2. When one of these two types of parameters is specified but not the other, then Oracle-managed control files are generated in the filesystem location identified by the parameter that was specified.

3. If both parameters are specified then Oracle-managed control files are created in the locations specified by DB_CREATE_ONLINE_LOG_DEST_*n* parameter.

4. The values set for these parameters can be dynamically changed using `alter system` command.

Exercises

1. **Examine the following excerpt from an `init.ora` file:**

```
DB_CREATE_ONLINE_LOG_DEST_1 = /u01/oradata/db1
DB_CREATE_ONLINE_LOG_DEST_2 = /u02/oradata/db1
DB_CREATE_ONLINE_LOG_DEST_3 = /u03/oradata/db1
DB_CREATE_FILE_DEST = /u04/oradata/db1
```

Which of the following choices does *not* identify the location where Oracle will place your control file when the database gets created?

    A. /u01/oradata/db1

    B. /u02/oradata/db1

    C. /u03/oradata/db1

    D. /u04/oradata/db1

2. **You are using OMF in conjunction with the management of your Oracle database control file. Which of the following choices identifies an aspect of control file management that Oracle handles regardless of whether OMF is used or not?**

    A. Placement of the control file in the appropriate directory

    B. Multiplexing control files to multiple destinations

    C. Updates to the contents of the control file when new tablespaces are added

    D. Assigning values automatically to the CONTROL_FILES parameter

3. **Complete the following sentence: In order for Oracle to know where to store control files, a value *either* for the _____(A)_____ *or* the _____(B)_____ *and* _____(C)_____ must be specified.**

Answer Key

1. D. **2.** C. **3.** (A) CONTROL_FILES; (B) DB_CREATE_FILE_DEST; (C) DB_CREATE_ONLINE_LOG_DEST_*n*.

Obtaining Information about Control Files

From time to time, you might need to obtain information about the control files in your Oracle database. You can do so using some important dynamic performance and data dictionary views available to DBAs on an Oracle database. Let's take a look at these views in more detail.

Control Filename and Availability

The main view available in the Oracle data dictionary for control file use and management is the V$CONTROLFILE view. This view has only two columns: STATUS and NAME. Their contents are explained in the following:

■ **STATUS** Displays INVALID if the control filename cannot be determined; otherwise, it will be NULL.

■ **NAME** Gives the absolute path location of the file on your host machine as well as the control filename.

The information in the V$CONTROLFILE view corresponds to the values set for the initialization parameter CONTROL_FILES. The following code block shows the SQL statement used to obtain information from the V$CONTROLFILE view about the control files for Oracle on a Windows machine, as well as the output:

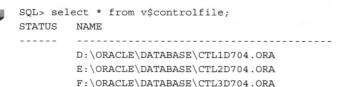

```
SQL> select * from v$controlfile;
STATUS    NAME
------    ----------------------------------------
          D:\ORACLE\DATABASE\CTL1D704.ORA
          E:\ORACLE\DATABASE\CTL2D704.ORA
          F:\ORACLE\DATABASE\CTL3D704.ORA
```

Finding Information about Important Control File Contents

You can find other information about your control files from the V$DATABASE view. This dynamic performance view gives information that Oracle normally also stored within the control file. You can see an example of using this view in the following code block, and you should also be aware that several columns in this view give information about your control file:

■ **CONTROLFILE_TYPE** The section type in the control file

■ **CONTROLFILE_CREATED** This indicates when the current control file was created

■ **CONTROLFILE_SEQUENCE#** The current sequence number for the database, which is recorded in the control file

■ **CONTROLFILE_CHANGE#** The current system change number for the database, which is recorded in the control file

■ **CONTROLFILE_TIME** The last time the control file was updated

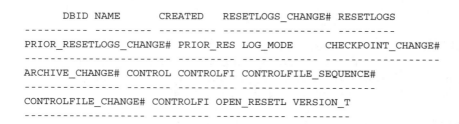

```
SQL> select * from v$database;

      DBID NAME      CREATED    RESETLOGS_CHANGE# RESETLOGS
---------- --------- ---------- ----------------- ---------
PRIOR_RESETLOGS_CHANGE# PRIOR_RES LOG_MODE    CHECKPOINT_CHANGE#
----------------------- --------- ----------- ------------------
ARCHIVE_CHANGE# CONTROL CONTROLFI CONTROLFILE_SEQUENCE#
--------------- ------- --------- ---------------------
CONTROLFILE_CHANGE# CONTROLFI OPEN_RESETL VERSION_T
------------------- --------- ----------- ---------
```

```
1674500680 ORGDB01    21-JAN-00              33409 21-JAN-00
                  1 06-OCT-98 NOARCHIVELOG                    736292
          716268 CURRENT 21-JAN-00                      4412
               736292            NOT ALLOWED 21-JAN-00
```

More Granular Info about Control File Contents

A final view available for displaying control file information is the
V$CONTROLFILE_RECORD_SECTION view. A working control file is divided
into several sections, each storing different information about the database in action.
For example, there is a section in the control file that keeps track of the sequence
number of the current online redo log, a section that contains information about
the physical disk file layout of the Oracle database, and so on. This view displays
information about each of those sections, such as the size of each record in the
control file for that section, the total number of records allocated to each section,
and so on. The following code block shows output from this view:

```
SQL> select * from v$controlfile_record_section where rownum < 6;
TYPE           RECORD_SIZE RECORDS_TOTAL RECORDS_USED FIRST_INDEX LAST_INDEX
------------- ----------- ------------- ------------ ----------- ----------
LAST_RECID
----------
DATABASE           316            1            1            0          0
        0
CKPT PROGRESS     2036            1            0            0          0
        0
REDO THREAD        228            1            1            0          0
        0
REDO LOG            72           30            5            0          0
        5
DATAFILE           428          400           18            0          0
       20
```

TIP
*You can also find the names of your control files by
issuing* select VALUE from V$PARAMETER
where NAME = 'control_files'. *Be sure that
the parameter name is in lowercase.*

For Review

1. Control file information can be found in several V$ performance views.

2. V$CONTROL_FILE provides the basic information about the status and
   location of the control files.

3. V$DATABASE view provides information such as when the control file is created, and the most recent sequence number and SCN number recorded in the control file.

4. V$CONTROLFILE_RECORD_SECTION shows information stored in different sections of the control file.

Exercises

1. **You want to find out the current sequence number stored in your control file for backup purposes. Which two of the following views would you query?**

   A. V$PARAMETER

   B. V$DATABASE

   C. V$CONTROLFILE

   D. V$CONTROLFILE_RECORD_SECTION

2. **You want to find out the names and locations of all control files in your database. Which two of the following performance views would you query?**

   A. V$PARAMETER

   B. V$DATABASE

   C. V$CONTROLFILE

   D. V$CONTROLFILE_RECORD_SECTION

3. **You want to find out when your control file was created. Which of the following views would you query for this information?**

   A. V$PARAMETER

   B. V$DATABASE

   C. V$CONTROLFILE

   D. V$CONTROLFILE_RECORD_SECTION

Answer Key
1. B and D. 2. A and C. 3. B.

Multiplexing Control Files

If you have multiple disk drives available for Oracle, you should store copies of the control files on different disks to minimize the risk of losing these important physical disk resources. If you stick with the default creation of control files, Oracle recommends that you move these control files to different disk resources and set the CONTROL_FILES parameter to let Oracle know that there are multiple copies of the control file to be maintained. This is called *multiplexing*, or *mirroring*, the control file. Multiplexing control files reduces Oracle's dependence on any one disk available on the host machine. In the event of a failure, the database is more recoverable because multiple copies of the control file have been maintained. In no case should you ever use only one control file for an Oracle database, because of the difficulty in recovering a database when the control file is lost. Having several copies of the control file and parameter file on different disks will minimize the possibility of one disk failure rendering your database inoperable.

Control File Multiplexing: Implementation

The actual process of making additional copies of your control file and moving them to different disk resources is something you handle outside of Oracle. You can create a duplicate copy of the control file by simply using the operating system copy command. In Windows, that command is `copy`, whereas in UNIX it is `cp`. However, that file will be unusable unless you follow these steps:

1. In SQL*Plus, execute the `shutdown normal`, `shutdown immediate`, or `shutdown transactional` command to shut down the instance and close the database.

2. Copy the control file to another disk using your operating system's file copy command.

3. Modify the CONTROL_FILES parameter in `init.ora` to include the additional control file.

4. Restart the instance in SQL*Plus with the `startup open` command. Oracle will now maintain an additional copy of the control file.

TIP
By specifying multiple control files in the `init.ora` *file before database creation, you will start your database administration on that database on the right foot, making the database easy to maintain.*

Backing Up the Control File

You've already seen how to backup your control file using the `alter database backup controlfile to trace` command. As you know, this command generates a script that can be used to re-create the control file later in the event of a problem. You can also use the `alter database backup controlfile` command to make a copy of the actual control file to some alternate location. Once backed up, however, Oracle will not maintain that control file when new datafiles or tablespaces or redo logs are added. Thus, you cannot simply make a backup copy of the control file if you want Oracle to maintain that copy with new information about the database's physical structure. The following code block shows an example of how to use the `alter database backup controlfile` command for making backups of actual control files:

```
SQL> alter database backup controlfile to '/u05/backup/db1/control01.ctl';
Database altered.
```

For Review

1. Oracle can maintain multiple copies of a control file for redundancy purposes. This is called multiplexing.

2. Make sure all your databases have multiplexed control files placed in different physical disks. Their location should be specified in the CONTROL_FILES parameter.

3. You can take regular backups either of the actual control file or of a script to re-create the control file using the `alter database backup controlfile` command.

Exercises

1. **You are implementing control file multiplexing. Which of the following choices identifies the method you can use in order to generate the control file copies that Oracle will maintain?**

   A. Issue `alter database backup controlfile to` *filename*.

   B. Make a copy of the control file with the database shut down.

   C. Issue `alter database backup controlfile to trace`.

   D. Make a copy of the control file with the database still running.

2. **You are implementing control file multiplexing. Which of the following choices identifies how Oracle knows the locations of the control files it is supposed to maintain?**

A. Values specified for CONTROL_FILES.

B. Values specified for BACKGROUND_DUMP_DEST.

C. Values specified in V$DATABASE.

D. None of the above; Oracle knows automatically where to look.

Answer Key
1. B. 2. A.

Maintaining Redo Log Files

In this section, you will cover the following points about maintaining redo log files:

- The purpose and structure of online redo logs

- Controlling log switches and checkpoints

- Multiplexing and maintaining redo log files

- Managing online redo log files with OMFs

Redo logs are disk resources that store data changes made by users on Oracle. In this section, we will look at how redo logs are used in Oracle and where you can look to find information about redo log status. The special role of the LGWR background process in maintaining redo logs, and its behavior, will be examined. You will learn more about the importance of maintaining two or more copies of each redo log on your machine, in the same way you do for control files. Finally, we will cover how to manage online redo log files using OMF.

The Purpose and Structure of Online Redo Logs

Oracle uses redo logs to track data changes users make to the database such as changes made to data segment blocks of the tables or indexes. Each user process that makes such a change generates a redo log entry, which identifies the change that was made. This redo log entry is placed in the area of the SGA called the redo log buffer, which you learned about in Chapter 1. The LGWR process writes those changes to files on disk called online redo log files. Oracle expects a minimum of two redo log files. Each of the redo log files is called a *redo log group*. Oracle also enables you to mirror each of the redo log files for sake of redundancy. Those mirrored files are called *members of the group*.

TIP
*This discussion covers two official exam objectives
listed on the candidate guide for the OCP Database
Fundamentals I exam.*

The operation of online redo logs occurs in this way. As the redo log buffer fills with redo entries from user processes or if an active transaction gives the `commit` command, then LGWR writes the content of the redo log buffer to each member of the group. This is sometimes referred to as *flushing* the redo buffer. The flushing of the entire redo log buffer happens even if a single active transaction commits. The group being written is considered the current group because LGWR is currently writing into it. LGWR writes redo log entries to the active group until the group is full, at which point LGWR switches to writing redo entries to the next redo log group. This is referred to as *log switch*. When the other group fills, LGWR will then switch to the next available group until it reaches the last redo log file. After filling the last log group, LGWR loops back to the first group and continues writing redo entries.

So, What Happens to the Contents of the First Group?
The answer to that question depends on the archiving mode your Oracle database is running in. A database could be running either in ARCHIVELOG or NOARCHIVELOG mode. When running in the NOARCHIVELOG mode, the LGWR writes into each of the log group and then loops back to the first group and overwrites what it contains. In the event of a failure, this type of mode cannot recover the database to the point of failure. In ARCHIVELOG mode, the redo entries written into the redo groups are copied to a different location by an archiver process (ARC*n*). To speed this archiving process you could activate more than one archiver processes. While running in this mode, the database could recover to the point of failure by applying these archived redo log entries to the restored backup.

Many DBAs with less experience managing Oracle systems at this point wonder the following—if Oracle let's you recover to the point of database failure when the database runs in ARCHIVELOG mode, why would anyone want to run his or her database in NOARCHIVELOG mode? The answer is simple. An Oracle database running in ARCHIVELOG mode runs slower than a database running in NOARCHIVELOG mode, although the performance difference is minimal when the database has been tuned properly. Also, not every Oracle database needs to have all its redo archived. For example, a read-only database used for data warehouse queries wouldn't need to run in ARCHIVELOG mode because once the data has been loaded, users won't be able to make changes anyway.

Another situation where you might not care about archiving user data changes is on development systems. Unlike production systems, wherever user change is important, development systems usually are only utilized by developers coding new programs or enhancing existing systems. The developer may only care that the database structure is the same in development as in production. The developer may populate the development tables with junk data for the purposes of testing. When testing is finished, the developer may want to blow away all the changes and start again from scratch. In this case, archiving all data changes made by the developer would be unnecessary and potentially even counterproductive. Thus, Oracle lets you decide whether or not to archive redo information based on the business needs of the system the database supports.

Switching Archive Modes

In order to switch between these two modes, you must follow these steps:

1. In SQL*Plus, shut down the database you want to change archiving mode on using the `shutdown normal` or `shutdown immediate` command.

2. Start the instance and mount but do not open the database. You can use the `startup mount` command to set up the database in the proper state.

3. Change the archiving status of the database using the `alter database archivelog` or `alter database noarchivelog` command. This command will modify the contents of the control file. If you restart the database using the startup open command, Oracle will bring up the database in the mode you specify here.

4. You should shut down the database at this point and take a complete offline backup. If you don't perform this step and later have to recover the database from datafiles backed up before you changed the archive mode, then the recovered database will not reflect the change in archiving mode. Additionally, if you switched from NOARCHIVELOG mode to ARCHIVELOG mode and didn't backup your database afterward, you will not be able to recover to the point of database failure. This is because the datafiles you use to recover will reflect the fact that Oracle was running in NOARCHIVELOG mode when you took the backup.

5. Reopen the database for normal use with the `alter database open` command.

For Review

1. Online redo log files are the physical files storing the information from the redo log buffers in SGA.

2. Changes made to the data blocks in the database are stored as redo entries in the redo log buffer in SGA.

3. When transactions are committed or this buffer gets full, the redo log entries are flushed into online redo log files.

4. The online redo log files could have mirrored files. Each set of files containing the same data is called a redo log group while the mirrored files in a group are called redo log members.

5. If the database is operating in ARCHIVELOG mode, then the data in online redo log files are archived in the archived redo log files as soon as it gets filled up. This could be done either manually or by using an automatic archiver processes.

6. If the database is operating in NOARCHIVELOG mode, then you do not have to worry about archiving the online redo logs.

Exercises

1. **You are analyzing the redo log structure of your Oracle database. Which of the following choices identifies the name of the background process that writes changes from online redo logs to archived copies in support of a database running in ARCHIVELOG mode?**

   A. LGWR

   B. CKPT

   C. DBW0

   D. ARC0

2. **You are switching your production system from NOARCHIVELOG mode to ARCHIVELOG mode. Which of the following choices identifies the next step to execute after you've issued the appropriate `alter database` statement to change archiving mode?**

   A. Restart the instance.

   B. Mount but do not open the database.

   C. Shut down the database and take a backup.

   D. Open the database and make it available to users.

3. **Finish the following sentence: When transactions get committed, Oracle _____ the contents of the redo buffer to disk.**

Answer Key
1. D. 2. C. 3. Flushes.

Controlling Log Switches and Checkpoints

Redo logs are written sequentially. As Oracle users make changes, the server process generates redo to re-create the changes made within the user's transaction. The redo gets written to the redo buffer. From there, LGWR writes the change to an online redo log. Redo logs are finite in size. When one fills, LGWR has to start writing to the next one in the sequence. A *log switch* occurs at the point at which LGWR completely fills the online redo log group and switches to start writing into the next group.

At every log switch, several events occur. Oracle generates a new sequence number for the online redo log LGWR is about to write. Oracle also performs a checkpoint. A checkpoint occurs every time a log switch occurs. Checkpoints can also occur more often than log switches. During a checkpoint, the checkpoint background process CKPT updates the headers of all datafiles and control files to reflect that it has completed successfully, and signals the DBW*n* to flush the dirty buffers into the data files. The number of buffers being written by DBW*n* is determined by the parameter FAST_START_IO_TARGET (or FAST_START_MTTR_TARGET), if specified. The frequency with which checkpoints occur affects the amount of time Oracle requires for instance recovery. If an instance experiences failure, the dirty blocks that haven't been written to disk must be recovered from redo logs. Even though this instance recovery is handled automatically by SMON, the amount of time it takes to recover depends on the time difference between the checkpoints.

The events that occur at a log switch are as follows. First, LGWR stops writing the redo log it filled. Second, CKPT signals the DBW*n* to flush the dirty buffers into the data files and finally CKPT updates the control files and the data file headers with the checkpoint information. With the checkpointing tasks completed, the LGWR will be allowed to start writing into the next redo log group with a new sequence number.

The DBA has only a small amount of control over log switches. Because users will always change data, there is little the DBA can do to stop redo information from being written. With that said, you can control how often a log switch will occur by changing the size of the online redo log members or manually by forcing a log switch with `alter system switch logfile` command. Larger member files make log switches less frequent, whereas smaller member files make log switches more frequent.

A checkpoint happens not just at the time of log switch, but it can also be configured to happen at the regular intervals by CKPT. You will learn how to do this in the following section. If you configure CKPT to checkpoint at regular intervals, then checkpoints will happen at regular intervals as well as during redo log switch.

Specifying Checkpoint Frequency

If your database redo logs are very large, you should set up the database so that checkpoints happen more often than just at log switches. You can specify more frequent checkpoints with LOG_CHECKPOINT_INTERVAL or LOG_CHECKPOINT_TIMEOUT in the init.ora file. These two parameters reflect two different principles on which checkpoint frequency can be based: volume-based intervals and time-based intervals.

LOG_CHECKPOINT_INTERVAL sets checkpoint intervals to occur on a volume basis. When LGWR writes as much information to the redo log as is specified by LOG_CHECKPOINT_INTERVAL, the checkpoint occurs. Periods of high transaction volume require flushing the dirty buffer write queue more often; conversely, periods of low transaction volume require fewer redo log entries to be written, and fewer checkpoints are needed. The effect of using LOG_CHECKPOINT_INTERVAL is much the same as using smaller redo logs, but it also eliminates the additional overhead of a log switch, such as the archiving of the redo log.

In versions of Oracle prior to Oracle8i, the value you set for LOG_CHECKPOINT_INTERVAL is the number of operating system blocks LGWR should write to the redo log (after a log switch) before a checkpoint should occur. However, this definition changed a little bit with Oracle8i and later. When LOG_CHECKPOINT_INTERVAL is specified, the target for the checkpoint position cannot lag the end of the log more than the number of redo log blocks specified by this parameter. This ensures that no more than a fixed number of redo blocks will need to be read during instance recovery.

The other way of specifying checkpoint frequency is to use a time-based interval. This is defined with the LOG_CHECKPOINT_TIMEOUT init.ora parameter. Time-based checkpoint intervals are far simpler to configure than volume-based ones, although they make checkpoints occur at uniform intervals regardless of the transaction volume on the system. When LOG_CHECKPOINT_TIMEOUT is specified, it sets the target for checkpoint position to a location in the log file where the end of the log was this many seconds ago. This ensures that no more than the specified number of seconds' worth of redo blocks needs to be read during recovery. However, there is no difference to Oracle8i except for the formulation. To disable time-based checkpoints, set the LOG_CHECKPOINT_TIMEOUT to zero. Also, recall the mention of the new parameter FAST_START_IO_TARGET. This parameter improves the performance of crash and instance recovery. The smaller the value of this parameter, the better the recovery performance, because fewer blocks need to be recovered. When the parameter is set, the DBWn writes dirty buffers out more aggressively.

One concern you may have when specifying checkpoints to occur at regular intervals is that a checkpoint may occur just before a log switch. In order to avoid log switches causing checkpoints to occur in rapid succession, determine the average time it takes the redo log to fill and specify a time interval that factors in the checkpoint that happens at log switches. To do so, review the trace file generated by LGWR in the directory specified by the BACKGROUND_DUMP_DEST parameter.

Finally, you can force checkpoints to occur either by forcing a log switch or by forcing a checkpoint. Both can be done with the alter system command. To force a log switch, issue the `alter system switch logfile` command. To force a checkpoint, issue the `alter system checkpoint` command. Checkpoints that occur without a corresponding log switch are called *fast checkpoints,* whereas checkpoints involving log switches are *full,* or *complete checkpoints.*

For Review

1. A checkpoint is a regular event in the database that signals the database writer to flush the dirty buffers to the data files and to update the control files and the file headers with checkpoint information. This checkpoint frequency is one of the factors that influence the time required for the database to recover from an unexpected failure.

2. Checkpoints occur at least as often as log switches. They can also occur by specifying more frequent intervals using `init.ora` parameters.

3. If the CKPT checkpoint interval exceeds the size of the redo log file, then checkpoints occur only during the redo log switch.

Exercises

1. **You are managing an Oracle database. Which of the following choices describes an event that takes place during a checkpoint?**

   A. DBW0 writes dirty buffers to disk.

   B. LGWR writes new log sequence information to datafile headers.

   C. ARC0 copies archived redo to an alternate location.

   D. CKPT writes redo information to disk.

2. **You would like to reduce the frequency of checkpoints. Which of the following is one way to do so that doesn't impact your `init.ora` file?**

   A. Increase the size of online redo logs.

   B. Adjust LOG_CHECKPOINT_INTERVAL.

   C. Adjust LOG_CHECKPOINT_TIMEOUT.

   D. Disable the ARC0 process.

Answer Key

1. A. 2. A.

Multiplexing and Maintaining Redo Log Files

There are several important details involved in configuring the redo log files of a database. The important detail is the importance of multiplexing your redo logs. In order to improve recoverability in the event of disk failure, the DBA should configure Oracle to multiplex or store each redo log member in a group on different disk resources. This means that Oracle will maintain two or more members for each redo log group. Figure 11-1 illustrates the concept of multiplexing redo log members.

By multiplexing redo log members, you keep multiple copies of the redo log available to LGWR. If LGWR has a problem with a disk that holds the redo log (for example, if the disk controller fails), the entire instance will continue running because another redo log member is available on a different disk. If the redo log group has only one member, or if multiple online redo log members are not multiplexed, and the same failure occurs, LGWR will not be able to write redo log entries and the Oracle instance will fail. This is because LGWR must write redo log entries to disk in order to clear space in the redo log buffer so that user processes can continue making changes to the database. If LGWR cannot clear the space in memory by writing the redo log entries to disk, no further user changes are allowed.

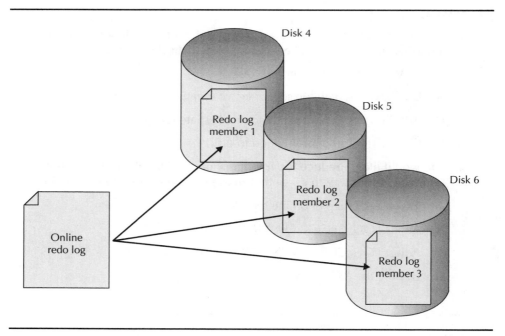

FIGURE 11-1. *Mirroring online redo logs*

Multiplexing redo logs on separate disks benefits the database in other ways, too. The archiver process (ARCn) handles the archiving of redo logs automatically when it is enabled. When the database is run in ARCHIVELOG mode, ARCn can be set up to run. When ARCn is running, it automatically moves archived redo logs to an archive destination specified by the LOG_ARCHIVE_DEST_*n* parameter in the init.ora file every time a log switch occurs. If redo log groups are on one disk, contention can arise at log switch time when ARCn tries to copy the filled redo log to the archive destination at the same time that LGWR tries to write to the next redo log group. If redo log members and the archive log destination are on different disks, there is little possibility for ARCn and LGWR to contend, because ARCn can work on one disk while LGWR continues on another.

Adding and Removing Redo Logs and Members

A redo log group must have at least one member. To add additional members, use the alter database add logfile member '*filename*' to group *grpnum*, where *filename* is the name of the file with the absolute path that the group will now have and *grpnum* is the number of the group to which you are adding the member. You can also add new online redo log groups with the alter database add logfile group *grpnum* '*filename*' statement. Finally, if you have more than two redo log groups, you can remove redo logs, provided at least two logs will remain and the one you want to remove is not currently being written by LGWR. The statement used to remove an online redo log from Oracle is alter database drop logfile group *grpnum*. Note that dropping the redo log group does not remove the actual file from your host machine. Those files do get automatically removed from the machine when the redo log group or members are dropped.

TIP
Group number and status information for online redo logs can be obtained from V$LOG, as described previously in this chapter.

Renaming Redo Log Files

You can rename redo log member files as well. This functionality can also be used to move an online redo log to another disk location on the machine hosting the Oracle database. In addition, be aware that by moving a redo log, you are also making changes to the control file. If you don't have a backup copy of your control file, it may be difficult to back out of this change to your database later. Thus, you should make a copy of your database (including the control file) before renaming a redo log file. Assuming you've made a backup, the following steps can be used to rename a redo log member file:

1. Issue the shutdown command. The database cannot be open while you rename a redo log file.

2. Copy the redo log files from their old location to the new location desired using operating system commands.

3. Start up the instance and mount but do not open the database.

4. Within SQL*Plus, issue the alter database rename file command to alert Oracle to the new location of your log file. After issuing this command, you can remove your copy of the redo log from its old (but not its new!) location.

5. Open the database.

6. Make a backup copy of your new control file.

TIP
If the database complains about corrupted redo log file, you can reinitialize the redo log without having to shut down the database. alter database clear logfile group *n will do the magic.*

For Review

1. Just like the control file, online redo log files are important for the functioning of database. To prevent accidental loss of them, Oracle enables mirroring of the redo log files. You should definitely mirror members of a redo log group in different disks.

2. If you are archiving the online redo logs, try to alternate the locations of the online redo groups between different disks so that LGWR and ARC*n* do not face disk contention.

3. There will be times when you need to add log groups or log members or drop log groups or log members or even rename log files. Oracle enables you to do all of these using alter database commands.

Exercises

1. **Your Oracle database is apparently hung. Users are waiting for their changes to be processed, and no new users can connect to the database. If you wanted to relieve the situation without restarting the Oracle database, which of the following choices identifies a method you might attempt?**

    A. Issue alter database backup controlfile to trace.

    B. Issue alter database archivelog.

     C. Issue `alter system switch logfile group`.

     D. Issue `alter system set nls_date_format = 'DD-MON-RRRR';`.

2. **You are considering multiplexing your online redo logs in Oracle. Which of the following choices identifies a reason you might consider doing so?**

     A. To reduce contention between the DBW0 and CKPT process

     B. To reduce the risk of database failure due to missing redo logs

     C. To eliminate contention between control file and datafile write activity

     D. To increase DBW0's pace in writing dirty buffers to disk

---

Answer Key
1. C. 2. B.

Managing Online Redo Log Files with OMF

Managing Oracle-managed redo log files is exactly the same as managing Oracle-managed control files. They both use the same `init.ora` parameters and behave in the same way. Refer to the previous section on "Managing Control Files with Oracle-Managed Files" for a full discussion on this topic. We will discuss only the salient points of this feature. Recall that your redo logs are created when you create the database. You can create new redo logs by issuing the `alter database add logfile group` command.

When the database is configured to use OMF by specifying either or both of the `init.ora` parameters for OMF (DB_CREATE_FILE_DEST and DB_CREATE_ONLINE_LOG_DEST_*n*), then there is no need to specify the location or names of the redo log files during the creation of the database. Oracle takes care to create them in a location specified in the OMF parameters and with a standard naming convention. The same is true while creating the redo log groups or members. The value *n* in parameter DB_CREATE_ONLINE_LOG_DEST_*n* specifies the location for a multiplexed copy of the online redo log or control file. You can specify up to five multiplexed copies.

If only DB_CREATE_FILE_DEST parameter is specified, then an Oracle-managed redo log file member is created in the directory specified in the parameter. If both DB_CREATE_FILE_DEST and DB_CREATE_ONLINE_LOG_DEST_*n* parameters are specified, then the later parameter takes the precedence. Whereas the rest of the tablespace Oracle-managed data files are created in the location specified by

DB_CREATE_FILE_DEST, an Oracle-managed log file member is created in each directory specified in the parameters (up to MAXLOGMEMBERS for the database).

The default size of Oracle-managed redo log file is 100MB. This value can be overridden by specifying the size of the redo log files in the `logfile` clause of the `create database` or `alter database` commands. The Oracle-managed redo log file will have the following name format: `ora_%g_%u.log`, where `%g` is the online redo log file group number and `%u` is a unique eight character string. For example, a redo log file could be `/u01/oradata/db1/ora_1_xyz12345.log`. As in the case of any Oracle-Managed Files, when an Oracle-managed online redo log file is dropped its corresponding OMFs on the host are removed automatically.

For Review

1. Online redo logs are created during the database creation and later can be created or dropped using the `alter database` command. In order to create them as Oracle-managed redo log files, two `init.ora` parameters, DB_CREATE_FILE_DEST and DB_CREATE_ONLINE_LOG_DEST_*n*, need to be specified.

2. If only DB_CREATE_FILE_DEST is specified, then all OMFs including redo log files will be created at the location specified by this parameter. Your online redo logs will not be multiplexed in this scenario.

3. When DB_CREATE_ONLINE_LOG_DEST_*n* is specified, regardless of whether DB_CREATE_FILE_DEST is specified or not, the Oracle-managed redo log files will be created in the location specified by the former parameter.

4. If multiple locations are specified by DB_CREATE_ONLINE_LOG_DEST_*n* parameter, then Oracle will create the mirror images of redo logs in each of these locations.

Exercises

1. **You have implemented OMF for redo log management. Which of the following choices reflects a log filename that might be employed when OMF is enabled?**

    A. `log01.log`

    B. `logORCL01.log`

    C. `1_2.log`

    D. `ora_1_asdf1234.log`

2. **Finish the following statement: When values are assigned to initialization parameters DB_CREATE_ONLINE_LOG_1 and DB_CREATE_ONLINE_LOG_2, then Oracle will** _____ **the redo logs it creates for you.**

Answer Key

1. D. 2. Multiplex.

Chapter Summary

In this chapter, you covered a number of concepts vital in the preparation for the OCP Database Fundamentals I exam. First, you learned about the Oracle data dictionary. You covered how to create the data dictionary using Oracle-supplied scripts. You also covered the difference between dictionary views and base tables, and learned why it is important to use the views and not the base tables. Some of the most important dictionary views in Oracle were also listed in the chapter, along with a description of the data you could find in those views. You learned how to distinguish between dictionary views and dynamic performance views as well. You also learned how to create the Oracle-supplied packages using Oracle-supplied scripts.

After that, we discussed the management of your control files in the Oracle database. You learned about the purpose control files serve in Oracle, as well as how to obtain information from them. You also learned about generating scripts that contain the `create controlfile` command. Last, you learned about managing online redo logs in Oracle. You covered the purpose served by online redo logs and about how to get data about your logs and control files from the data dictionary. Interspersed in these discussions was some coverage of Oracle-Managed Files (OMF), and how to use them pertaining to the creation and maintenance of control files and online redo logs.

Two-Minute Drill

- The Oracle data dictionary contains a host of views to be aware of, which contain information about the contents in and ongoing activities on the Oracle database.

- Some of the dictionary views to be aware of include those in the following list:

  - **USER_OBJECTS, ALL_OBJECTS, DBA_OBJECTS** Gives information about various database objects owned by the current user, available to the current user, or all objects in the database, respectively.

  - **USER_TABLES, ALL_TABLES, DBA_TABLES** Displays information about tables owned by or available to the current user, respectively, or all tables in the Oracle database.

  - **USER_INDEXES, ALL_INDEXES, DBA_INDEXES** Displays information about indexes owned by or available to the current user, respectively, or all indexes in the Oracle database.

  - **USER_VIEWS, ALL_VIEWS, DBA_VIEWS** Displays information about views owned by or available to the current user, respectively, or all views in the Oracle database (including dictionary views).

  - **USER_SEQUENCES, ALL_SEQUENCES, DBA_SEQUENCES** Displays information about sequences owned by or available to the current user, respectively, or all sequences in the Oracle database.

  - **USER_USERS, ALL_USERS, DBA_USERS** Displays information about the current user or about all users in Oracle, respectively.

  - **USER_CONSTRAINTS, ALL_CONSTRAINTS, DBA_CONSTRAINTS** Displays information about constraints owned by or available to the current user, respectively, or all constraints in the Oracle database.

  - **USER_CONS_COLUMNS, ALL_CONS_COLUMNS, DBA_CONS_COLUMNS** Displays information about table columns that have constraints owned by or available to the current user, respectively, or all table columns in Oracle that have constraints on them.

  - **USER_IND_COLUMNS, ALL_IND_COLUMNS, DBA_IND_COLUMNS** Displays information about table columns that have indexes owned by or available to the current user, respectively, or all columns in Oracle tables that have indexes on them.

  - **USER_TAB_COLUMNS, ALL_TAB_COLUMNS, DBA_TAB_COLUMNS** Displays information about columns in tables owned by or available to the current user, respectively, or all columns in all tables in Oracle.

  - **USER_ROLES, ALL_ROLES, DBA_ROLES** Displays information about roles owned by or available to the current user, respectively, or all roles in the Oracle database.

- **USER_TAB_PRIVS, ALL_TAB_PRIVS, DBA_TAB_PRIVS** Displays information about object privileges on objects owned by the user or available to the current user, respectively, or all object privileges available to all users in Oracle.

- **USER_SYS_PRIVS, ALL_SYS_PRIVS, DBA_SYS_PRIVS** Displays information about object privileges on objects owned by the user or available to the current user, respectively, or all system privileges granted to all users in Oracle.

- **USER_SOURCE, ALL_SOURCE, DBA_SOURCE** Displays the source code for PL/SQL programs owned by the user or available to the current user, respectively, or all PL/SQL source code in the entire Oracle database.

- **USER_TRIGGERS, ALL_TRIGGERS, DBA_TRIGGERS** Displays information about triggers owned by the user or available to the current user, respectively, or all triggers in the Oracle database.

- **ROLE_TAB_PRIVS, ROLE_SYS_PRIVS, ROLE_ROLE_PRIVS** Displays information about object privileges, system privileges, or roles granted to roles in the database, respectively.

- **DBA_TABLESPACES, DBA_TS_QUOTAS** Displays information about all tablespaces in Oracle, as well as space quotas assigned to users in each tablespace.

- **DBA_DATAFILES, DBA_SEGMENTS, DBA_EXTENTS DBA_FREE_SPACE** Displays information about datafiles in your Oracle database, as well as segments, extents, and free space in each datafile, respectively.

- **DBA_PROFILES** Displays information about user profiles in Oracle. Profiles are a way for you as the DBA to restrict the physical resources of the host system (such as process memory allocation, CPU cycles, and so on) that users may utilize in conjunction with Oracle processing.

- Additionally, there are a host of dynamic performance views that contain information about the ongoing performance of Oracle software. These views include those listed in the following:

  - **V$DATABASE** General information about the database mounted to your instance is kept here.

  - **V$SYSTEM, V$SYSSTAT** Most information about the performance of your database is kept here.

- **V$SESSION, V$SESSTAT**   Most information about performance for individual user sessions is stored here.

- **VLOG, VLOGFILE**   Information about online redo logs can be found here.

- **V$DATAFILE**   Information about Oracle datafiles can be found here.

- **V$CONTROLFILE**   Information about Oracle control files can be found here.

- The `catalog.sql` script creates the data dictionary. Run it after creating a database while connected to Oracle administratively through SQL*Plus.

- The `catproc.sql` script creates the Oracle-supplied packages used often in PL/SQL development. Run it after creating a database while connected to Oracle administratively through SQL*Plus.

- Understand all Oracle physical disk resources—they are control files, redo logs, and datafiles.

- Control files are used to tell the Oracle instance where to find the other files it needs for normal operation.

- The contents of a control file can be found in the script to create it, which Oracle generates with an `alter database backup controlfile to trace`. This file is then found in the directory specified by the USER_DUMP_DEST initialization parameter.

- You will find information about control files, such as where they are located on your host machine, in V$CONTROLFILE, V$CONTROLFILE_RECORD_SECTION, and V$DATABASE.

- It is important to multiplex control files in order to reduce dependency on any single disk resource in the host machine. This is done using the CONTROL_FILES parameter in `init.ora`.

- The Oracle redo log architecture consists of the following components: redo log buffer to store redo entries from user processes, LGWR to move redo entries from memory onto disk, and online redo logs on disk to store redo entries taken out of memory.

- Online redo logs are referred to as groups. The group has one or more files, called members, where LGWR writes the redo log entries from memory. There must be at least two online redo log groups for the Oracle instance to start.

■ Checkpoints are events in which LGWR tells DBWR to write all changed blocks to disk. They occur during log switches, which are when LGWR stops writing the filled log and starts writing a new one. At this point, LGWR will also write the redo log file sequence change to datafile headers and to the control file.

■ Understand the process LGWR uses to write redo data from one log to another and then back again, what happens when archiving is used, what the role of the ARCH process is, and how LGWR can contend with ARCH.

■ Understand how to multiplex redo logs using both the `create database` and `alter database` statements, and why it is important to do so.

■ The OMF feature in Oracle can be used to manage the placement of control files and redo logs on disk. Be sure you understand the use of the appropriate parameters for configuring OMF and the standard filename formats Oracle employs when OMF is used.

Chapter Questions

1. **Flushing dirty buffers out of the buffer cache is influenced to the greatest extent by which of the following processes?**

   A. LGWR

   B. SMON

   C. ARCH

   D. SERVER

2. **How can you decrease the number of checkpoints that occur on the database?**

   A. Set LOG_CHECKPOINT_INTERVAL to half the size of the online redo log.

   B. Set LOG_CHECKPOINT_INTERVAL to twice the size of the online redo log.

   C. Set LOG_CHECKPOINT_TIMEOUT to the number of bytes in the online redo log.

   D. Set LOG_CHECKPOINT_TIMEOUT to half the number of bytes in the online redo log.

3. **Which of the following strategies is recommended when customizing the redo log configuration?**

   A. Store redo log members on the same disk to reduce I/O contention.

   B. Run LGWR only at night.

   C. Store redo log members on different disks to reduce I/O contention.

   D. Run DBW0 only at night.

4. **By allowing user processes to write redo log entries to the redo log buffer, how does Oracle affect I/O contention for disks that contain redo log entries?**

   A. Increases because user processes have to wait for disk writes

   B. Decreases because user processes have to wait for disk writes

   C. Increases because user processes do not have to wait for disk writes

   D. Decreases because user processes do not have to wait for disk writes

5. Which of the following choices identifies a database component that will be used for multiplexing control files?

   A. `init.ora`

   B. V$CONTROLFILE

   C. V$DATABASE

   D. DBA_DATAFILES

6. By default, checkpoints happen at least as often as _____.

   A. Redo log switches.

   B. `update` statements are issued against the database.

   C. The SYSTEM tablespace is accessed.

   D. SMON coalesces free space in a tablespace.

7. If all redo log members become unavailable on the database, _____.

   A. The instance will fail.

   B. The instance will continue to run, but media recovery is needed.

   C. The database will continue to remain open, but instance recovery is needed.

   D. The system will continue to function as normal.

Answers to Chapter Questions

1. A.   LGWR

Explanation   At a checkpoint, LGWR signals DBW0 to write changed blocks stored in the dirty buffer write queue to their respective datafiles. Choice B is incorrect because SMON handles instance recovery at instance startup and periodically coalesces free space in tablespaces. Choice C is incorrect because ARCH handles automatic archiving at log switches, and even though checkpoints happen at log switches, the overall process is not driven by ARCH. Choice D is incorrect because the server process retrieves data from disk in support of user processes.

2. B.   Set LOG_CHECKPOINT_INTERVAL to twice the size of the online redo log.

Explanation   The other three choices are incorrect because each of them actually increases the number of checkpoints that will be performed by Oracle. In addition, choices C and D indicate that values set for LOG_CHECKPOINT_TIMEOUT depend on the size of the redo log in bytes, which is not true. LOG_CHECKPOINT_TIMEOUT is a numeric value that determines the timed intervals for checkpoints. Refer to the discussion on checkpoints.

3. C.   Store redo log members on different disks to reduce I/O contention.

Explanation   Choice A is incorrect because storing all redo log members on the same disk increases I/O contention when log switches occur. Choices B and D are incorrect because DBWR and LGWR should be running at all times on the database. Refer to the discussion on redo logs.

4. D.   Decreases because user processes do not have to wait for disk writes

Explanation   Allowing users to write redo entries to the redo memory buffer while LGWR handles the transfer of those entries to disk does reduce I/O dependency for user processes. This means that choice D is correct. Choices B and C are paradoxical statements—how can increased wait times lead to better throughput or vice versa? Choice A is the logical opposite of choice D, meaning that choice A is the wrong answer.

5. A.   `init.ora`

Explanation   Choice A is the `init.ora` file, which contains the CONTROL_FILES parameter. This parameter is where you would define whether you wanted to use multiple copies of the control file and where Oracle should look for them. All other choices are incorrect. They refer to places where you can look for data about your control file, but remember this—the data dictionary can only inform you of the database configuration, never modify it.

6. A.   Redo log switches.

Explanation   Choice A is the only choice given that relates to checkpoints. Refer to the discussion of checkpoints. Working with the SYSTEM tablespace and SMON's coalescing behavior have nothing whatsoever with the behavior of checkpoints. You might be able to make a small case for `update` statements, but even then you have little indication of whether the data change is frequent, infrequent, heavy, or light, and these are the things you'd need to know in order to determine checkpoint intervals. In addition, `update` activity still won't determine checkpoints if you are using LOG_CHECKPOINT_TIMEOUT. Oracle also ensures that the number of redo blocks between the checkpoint and the most recent redo record is less than 90 percent of the size of the smaller redo log. Oracle does this to ensure that the position of the checkpoint has advanced to the current log before that log completely fills.

7. A.   The instance will fail.

Explanation   If a disk becomes unavailable that contains all redo log members for the redo log currently being written, the instance will fail. All other choices are incorrect because they depend on the instance being fully available, which is not the case in this situation. Refer to the discussion of redo log components.

CHAPTER
12

Managing Tablespaces and Datafiles

n this chapter, you will understand and demonstrate knowledge in the following areas:

- Describing the logical structure of the database
- Creating tablespaces
- Changing tablespace size using various methods
- Allocating space for temporary segments
- Changing tablespace status
- Changing tablespace storage settings
- Implementing OMF for tablespaces

Oracle tablespace management is a fascinating concept because it involves mapping plain old files on a disk in your host system to a more abstract concept of space that your Oracle database can store information in. The physical and logical component being mapped together is the basis for understanding what we'll present in this chapter. In it, you will learn about what a tablespace is, how it is managed, and what you must do as an Oracle DBA to keep things flowing smoothly from a storage management perspective. Be sure to pay close attention, because the concepts presented in this chapter will constitute a full 9 percent of material tested on the OCP DBA Fundamentals I exam.

Describing the Logical Structure of the Database

Meet three players in the world of logical Oracle disk resources: tablespaces, segments, and extents. A *tablespace* is a logical database structure that is designed to store other logical database structures. Oracle sees a tablespace as a large area of space into which Oracle can place new objects. Space in tablespaces is allocated in segments. A *segment* is an allocation of space used to store the data of a table, index, undo segment, or temporary object. When the database object runs out of space in its segment and needs to add more data, Oracle lets it allocate more space in the form of an extent. An *extent* is similar to a segment in that the extent stores information corresponding to a table, index, undo segment, or temporary object. You will learn more about segments and extents in the next chapter on storage structures and relationships, so for now, we will focus on tablespaces. When you are logged into Oracle and manipulate storage factors, you are doing so with the logical perspective of tablespaces.

The other perspective you will have on your Oracle database is that provided by the operating system of the host machine. Underlying the logical storage in Oracle is the physical method your host system uses to store data, the cornerstone of which is the *block*. Segments and extents are composed of data blocks, and in turn, the blocks are taken together to comprise a *datafile*. Recall that you specified a value in bytes for an initialization parameter called DB_BLOCK_SIZE. This parameter determined the standard size of each Oracle block. Block size is typically specified as a multiple of operating system block size. Oracle blocks are usually 2KB, 4KB, 8KB, and sometimes 16KB.

Prior versions of Oracle released before Oracle9i required that the entire database use only one block size and that once the block size for the database was defined, you couldn't change it later. In Oracle9i, Oracle enables you to specify up to five nonstandard block sizes for your database, providing a great deal more flexibility in terms of using one database to fill multiple data management roles in your organization. More information about standard and nonstandard block sizes is discussed in the next chapter.

A tablespace may consist of one or many datafiles, and the objects in a tablespace can be stored by Oracle anywhere within the one or multiple datafiles comprising the tablespace. Although a tablespace may have many datafiles, each datafile can belong to only one tablespace. Figure 12-1 shows you the glasses through which you can view logical and physical disk storage in your Oracle database.

How Oracle Handles Space Management in Tablespaces

Free space management is an important task for Oracle because without it, Oracle would not know where to put things like tables or indexes when you wanted to create and modify them. Prior to Oracle8i, all tablespaces were created as *dictionary-managed* tablespaces. Dictionary-managed tablespaces rely on Oracle populating data dictionary tables housed in the SYSTEM tablespace to track free space utilization. With Oracle8i and later, there is a new type of tablespace called the *locally managed* tablespace. Locally managed tablespaces use bitmaps stored within the header of the datafiles comprising a tablespace to track the space utilization of the tablespaces. This bitmap represents every block in the datafile, and each bit in the map represents whether that block is free or not.

Within tablespaces, Oracle manages free space by coalescing it into contiguous segments. The system monitor, or SMON background process, in Oracle handles this coalescing activity automatically. When new database objects are created, Oracle will acquire the requested amount of contiguous storage space in the form of a segment for the new object. The amount of space SMON will use is based either on the object's own `storage` clause, the `default storage` clause for that tablespace, or on the uniform extent allocation configured for the tablespace. For OCP, remember that SMON is the process that handles this coalescing of free space

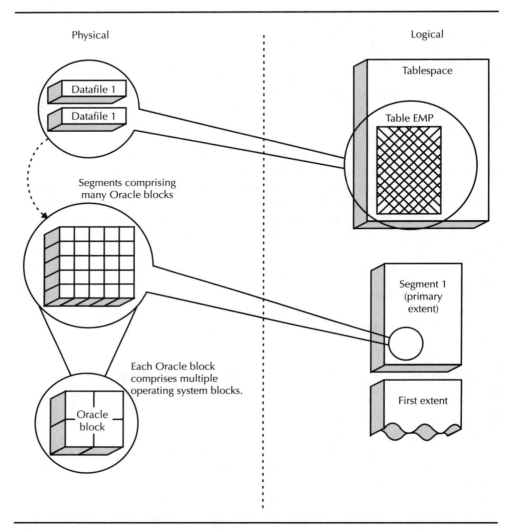

FIGURE 12-1. *The logical and physical views of a database*

into contiguous chunks on an ongoing basis while Oracle is running. As SMON coalesces free space, it either updates the dictionary tables in the SYSTEM tablespace to notify Oracle where the free space is in dictionary-managed tablespaces, or it maintains the bitmap in the datafiles of the tablespace when locally managed tablespaces are used.

TIP
The SYSTEM tablespace is always a dictionary-managed tablespace. Why? Because the dictionary files are in the SYSTEM tablespace anyway, so you don't really get much performance gain with locally managed SYSTEM tablespaces if the data dictionary is already local to the tablespace!

Why might we want to use locally managed tablespaces rather than dictionary-managed tablespaces? Locally managed tablespaces offer better performance because Oracle stores the storage information in file headers and bitmap blocks, eliminating the recursive operations that are required with dictionary-managed space allocation. Beginning in Oracle9i, the default space management for tablespaces other than the SYSTEM tablespace is locally managed. However, you can explicitly specify that you want to create a dictionary-managed tablespace.

TIP
We'll discuss the syntax of creating locally managed and dictionary-managed tablespaces in a later section.

Permanent Tablespaces versus Temporary Tablespaces

Regardless of how you configure Oracle to handle space management in your tablespace, the tablespace itself will generally be configured to store two types of segments: permanent and temporary. A permanent segment is one designed to store data for a table or other object that's going to house data for a long time in your database. For example, if you're using Oracle to manage employee information for a large corporation, chances are the employee data is going to stay in the database for many months or years. Thus, you would use permanent segments to house that data in your database. Along that same line of thinking, you would want to house your permanent segments inside a permanent tablespace. In fact, Oracle requires that permanent segments be housed in permanent tablespaces.

In contrast, some forms of data in Oracle are stored only temporarily for the duration of a particular database operation. An example of such an operation is a disk sort, when a user queries Oracle for a very large set of records that must be returned sorted in alphabetical order to the user. A sort operation can require a lot of memory temporarily. Sometimes the sort operation may require more memory than Oracle has available to use. To cope with the lack of memory, Oracle starts writing records to disk in a temporary segment. When Oracle is finished with the sort, Oracle no longer needs the data housed in the temporary segment, so Oracle deletes the temporary segment automatically behind the scenes from both the user and the DBA. You should understand that permanent tablespaces in Oracle are designed to house temporary segments for backward compatibility purposes. However, the space allocation and deallocation required to handle disk sorts take place within a matter of seconds and could be very disruptive to other permanent objects housed in a tablespace, so Oracle also offers a special type of tablespace called a *temporary tablespace*. The temporary tablespace is only used for housing temporary objects. No permanent database objects are allowed.

Default Temporary Tablespaces

Because it is possible for any user in Oracle to issue a long-running query to return data in sorted order, every user in Oracle must be assigned a tablespace where Oracle can write temporary segments in case Oracle must perform a disk sort on behalf of that user. Prior versions of Oracle handled this assignment when the user was created using the optional but highly recommended `temporary tablespace` *tablespacename* clause in the `create user` command. For now, understand that this approach has one tragic flaw. If you didn't specify a `temporary tablespace` clause in your `create user` command, Oracle assigned the user to the SYSTEM tablespace for temporary segment storage needs. This is very bad, because as you will certainly recall, temporary segment storage allocations can be very disruptive to permanent segments stored in the database. In Oracle9*i*, you can create a default temporary tablespace when creating a database by including the `default temporary tablespace` clause in your `create database` command. If you do not create one, then SYSTEM will become the default temporary storage location. However, you will be warned in the alert log about the missing default temporary tablespace. Let's take a quick look at the `create database` command we saw in Chapter 1; however, this time, we've revised it to include a default temporary tablespace:

```
CREATE DATABASE orgdb01
CONTROLFILE REUSE
LOGFILE
   GROUP 1 ('/u01/oradata/oracle/redo1a.log',
            '/u02/oradata/oracle/redo1b.log') SIZE 5M,
   GROUP 2 ('/u02/oradata/oracle/redo2a.log',
            '/u01/oradata/oracle/redo2b.log') SIZE 5M
MAXLOGFILES 40
DATAFILE '/u03/oradata/oracle/sys01.dbf'
   SIZE 50M AUTOEXTEND ON NEXT 30M MAXSIZE 150M
MAXDATAFILES 240
CHARACTERSET WE8IS08859P1
DEFAULT TEMPORARY TABLESPACE temp
TEMPFILE '/u04/oradata/oracle/temp01.dbf' SIZE 100M;
```

TIP
The default temporary tablespace can also be allocated after the database has been created using the `create default temporary tablespace` *command.*

For Review

1. Oracle supports three types of logical disk storage resources—tablespaces, segments, and extents. Underlying these logical structures are the physical structures on the host machine that make up the physical Oracle database: datafiles and Oracle blocks. Tablespaces can have many datafiles, but each datafile must be assigned to only one tablespace.

2. Oracle handles storage management of a tablespace either by storing records in the data dictionary or locally in the headers of each datafile in the tablespace. This difference produces two types of tablespaces: dictionary-managed and locally managed tablespaces, respectively. Starting with Oracle9i, Oracle creates non-SYSTEM tablespaces to be locally managed by default.

3. With the creation and dropping of database objects, tablespaces end up with noncontiguous chunks of free space that need coalescing periodically. SMON takes care of this task for us.

4. In Oracle9i, you can create a default temporary tablespace to prevent from making the SYSTEM tablespace the temporary tablespace. The default temporary tablespace is created when the database is created.

Exercises

1. **You are conceptualizing the logical to physical mapping of disk storage components of your Oracle database. Which of the following physical database components maps to the tablespace logical component of Oracle?**

   A. Datafile

   B. Segment

   C. Extent

   D. Block

2. You are configuring Oracle to handle space management tasks. Which of the following background processes coalesces free space in datafiles when locally managed tablespaces are in use?

   A. PMON

   B. SMON

   C. ARCH

   D. RECO

3. You haven't configured default temporary storage management on your Oracle database. You then issue the `create user smithers identified by associate`, along with the appropriate privileges. As his first act, SMITHERS issues `select * from emp order by ename` against the EMP table, which contains over 8 million rows. Which of the following choices identifies where temporary segments will be created?

   A. TEMP

   B. UNDO

   C. DATA

   D. SYSTEM

4. You are configuring space management on your Oracle database. Which of the following choices identifies the location where free space information can be found when locally managed tablespaces are in use?

   A. The SYSTEM tablespace

   B. Datafile headers in the SYSTEM tablespace

   C. The local tablespace

   D. Datafile headers in the local tablespace

5. You are configuring locally managed tablespaces for your Oracle database. Which of the following choices identifies the location where free space information can be found for the SYSTEM tablespace when locally managed tablespaces are in use?

   A. The SYSTEM tablespace

   B. Datafile headers in the SYSTEM tablespace

   C. The local tablespace

   D. Datafile headers in the local tablespace

Answer Key

1. A. 2. B. SMON handles coalescing free space regardless of how you configure tablespace free space management. 3. D. 4. D. 5. A.

Creating Tablespaces

Historically in Oracle, the SYSTEM tablespace was the only tablespace you could create during the creation of the database. This done by explicitly specifying the location of the SYSTEM tablespace datafile in the `create database` command. You can still do things this way, but starting with Oracle9i, you can also create two other types of tablespaces at the same time. We've already seen one example, where we created a default temporary tablespace in the `create database` command. The other example is the *undo segment tablespace*. For those of you approaching Oracle9i with experience as an Oracle DBA on prior versions, you should make a mental note that undo is the same as rollback. You can create your SYSTEM, temporary, and UNDOTBS tablespaces when you create the Oracle database in Oracle9i.

What Are Some Tablespaces You Might Want to Create?

On a typical database, you'll want to segregate different types of data into different tablespaces. At a minimum, you will typically want to create the following tablespaces:

- **SYSTEM**   Every database must have a SYSTEM tablespace. This tablespace is created when you create the database.

- **DATA**   A DATA tablespace is used to house table data.

- **INDEX**   An INDEX tablespace is used to house indexes separate from other types of objects.

- **UNDOTBS**   An UNDOTBS tablespace houses undo segments (called *rollback segments* in prior versions of Oracle). These need to be kept separate from other types of objects due to volatility in allocating extents.

- **TEMP**   A TEMP tablespace houses temporary segments. These also need to be kept separate from other types of objects due to volatility in allocating extents.

- **TOOLS**   A TOOLS tablespace houses objects that support administrative or other tools you might use in conjunction with your database, such as Oracle Enterprise Manager.

TIP
We'll focus on the creation of a tablespace to house object data for the rest of the chapter. Keep in mind that the principles you will learn also apply to the manual creation of these other types of tablespaces.

Creating Tablespaces to House Permanent Segments

All other tablespaces must be created using the `create tablespace` command after the database has been created. Let's look at an example, where we create a locally managed tablespace for a database hosted in a Windows environment that we will probably use to hold table data in our database. How do we know this tablespace will hold table data? Because of the nomenclature—notice that the name of the tablespace is DATA. This typically indicates that the tablespace will be used for housing table data. Let's now look at the actual command:

```
SQL> CREATE TABLESPACE DATA DATAFILE
  2    'E:\oradata\Oracle\data01.dat' SIZE 20M,
  3    'F:\oradata\Oracle\data02.dat' SIZE 30M
  4    AUTOEXTEND ON NEXT 10M MAXSIZE 50M
  5    MINIMUM EXTENT 150K
  6    EXTENT MANAGEMENT LOCAL
  7    PERMANENT ONLINE;
```

TIP
The creation of a tablespace can take a long time, depending on how large you specified your tablespace datafiles to be. This is because Oracle has to physically allocate itself a file of whatever size you specify on the host system. You should be patient during this operation, particularly if you've specified your tablespace to be quite large.

As you can see, there are several components to the `create tablespace` statement. First, you specify the datafiles your tablespace will own, using absolute pathnames. (If you are using an operating system like UNIX to host your Oracle database, be sure the pathnames you specify for your datafiles are ones Oracle has permission to write.) Notice that one of our datafiles has an `autoextend` clause defined for it. This feature enables the datafile to grow past its originally defined size automatically in order to accommodate data growth.

The next step is to specify the `default storage` clause to set options that will be applied to database object creation if the object created does not have storage parameters defined for it. If an object placed in this tablespace has its own `storage` clause defined, then the object's `storage` clause settings will override the tablespace's `default storage` clause settings, with one exception. There is one storage option that when defined in a tablespace cannot be overridden. That option is `minimum extent`, which ensures that every extent size used in the tablespace is a multiple of the specified integer value. The other details of the `default storage` parameters will be explained shortly.

TIP
Permanent tablespaces like the one created in the previous code block can house both permanent segments and temporary segments. This functionality is provided by Oracle for backward compatibility purposes. However, you should put temporary segments in temporary tablespaces.

After that, notice that we define this tablespace to be locally managed using the `extent management local` clause. This is the default space management setting for tablespaces in Oracle9i and later releases, so we didn't need to specify the clause in order to achieve local extent management. If we wanted to specify dictionary-managed tablespaces, we would have used the `extent management dictionary` clause instead. You can specify that the tablespace houses permanent database objects with the `permanent` keyword; however, Oracle assumes that the tablespace is a permanent tablespace if the `permanent` keyword is omitted. Finally, we instruct Oracle to bring the tablespace online after creating it using the `online` keyword. This is the default availability status of your tablespace after you create it: online. If you omit the `online` keyword from your `create tablespace` statement, it will still be online. You can also ensure that it is online later by issuing `alter tablespace` *name* `online`.

NOTE
If no specification is made in a `create tablespace` *command whether it is locally managed or dictionary-managed, Oracle9i will create it as a locally managed tablespace.*

Creating Tablespaces for Temporary Segments

Most of your tablespaces on the database will house permanent objects that will stick around in your database for a long time. However, remember that you will also want a special tablespace for housing temporary segments. If you have not created a default temporary tablespace during the database creation, then you can create a tablespace to store temporary objects. You should do so for two reasons. The first is to take advantage of Oracle's more efficient usage of sort segments compared to temporary segments. The second reason is to prevent anyone from creating a permanent database object, such as a table or index with data, in the tablespace used for temporary segments. There are some important keywords you should be aware of that are different for creating temporary tablespaces. Take a moment to review the following code block, paying special attention to the keywords in bold:

```
SQL> CREATE TEMPORARY TABLESPACE temp
  2  TEMPFILE '/u06/oradata/oracle/temp01.dbf' SIZE 300M
  3  extent management local;
Tablespace created.
```

Another way to create a temporary tablespace is to include the `temporary` keyword at the end of the `create tablespace` command. Note that we use the `datafile` keyword rather than `tempfile` when we create a temporary tablespace in this manner. The following code block illustrates:

```
SQL> CREATE TABLESPACE temp
  2  DATAFILE '/u06/oradata/oracle/temp01.dbf' SIZE 300M
  3  TEMPORARY;
Tablespace created.
```

Like permanent tablespaces, your temporary tablespace will be brought online automatically after Oracle creates it. You can view the status of your temporary tablespaces in the data dictionary view DBA_TEMP_FILES. You can also view whether a tablespace is temporary or not by viewing the CONTENTS column of the DBA_TABLESPACES data dictionary view.

NOTE
All tablespaces in the database will use the standard block size defined for the database. A standard block size is the size of the Oracle block that is defined by the parameter DB_BLOCK_SIZE. However, you may also create a tablespace with a nonstandard block size. This could be useful when transporting tablespaces between databases of different block sizes. To use nonstandard block sizes, you must configure subcaches within the buffer cache of System Global Area (SGA) for all the nonstandard block sizes that you intend to use. There are platform-specific restrictions and some platforms may not support it.

Default Storage Options Defined

The `default storage` clause defines storage options that will be applied to newly created database objects if the `create` statement does not have storage parameters defined for it. The initial and next options specify the size of the object's initial segment and next allocated extent, respectively. If `minimum extent` is defined for the tablespace you put your object in, and the value specified for `next` on your database object is less than `minimum extent`, Oracle rounds up to the next highest multiple for `minimum extent` and creates the initial or next extent as that size. This feature can reduce the amount of fragmentation in a tablespace.

TIP

This is really the old way of doing things. You'll want to use locally managed uniform extent allocation in order to take advantage of the new technology. However, you should be familiar with the old way to do this as well in case there's a question on the OCP exam.

The `minextents` and `maxextents` options specify the minimum and maximum number of extents the object can allocate in the tablespace. If you specify `minextents` greater than one and the tablespace has more than one datafile, Oracle will tend to spread extents over multiple datafiles, which can improve performance if those datafiles are also located on different disk resources.

Finally, `pctincrease` enables you to specify a percentage increase in the amount of space allocated for the next extent in the object. For example, if `next` is set to 200KB and `pctincrease` is 50, the second extent would be 200KB in size, the third extent would be 300KB (50 percent more than the second extent), the fourth extent would be 450KB (50 percent more than the third extent), and so on. The minimum value is 0, and the default value is 50. The calculated value is rounded up to the next data block, which is a multiple of five times DB_BLOCK_SIZE. To make all extents the same size, specify `pctincrease` to be zero.

For Review

1. Non-SYSTEM tablespaces in Oracle are created through the `create tablespace` command.

2. You can specify to autoextend the datafile as the data grows and you can specify the default storage parameters for objects that are created in it. The `default storage` parameters could be the sizes of initial and next extents, and the minimum and maximum number of extents for the object being created.

3. If an object is being created in this tablespace with no storage option, then Oracle takes the default storage parameters of the tablespace while creating the object.

4. Permanent tablespaces can store both permanent and temporary objects in them. Temporary tablespaces, in contrast, can house only temporary segments.

Exercises

1. You are preparing to create a temporary tablespace for housing a particular type of segment. Which of the following choices identifies the keyword that begins the clause where you will define the absolute path and filename of datafiles associated with this tablespace?

   A. `permanent`

   B. `temporary`

   C. `datafile`

   D. `tempfile`

2. You are managing tablespaces to house your data. Which of the following statements is true regarding tablespaces in an Oracle database?

   A. Permanent tablespaces can house permanent and temporary segments, whereas temporary tablespaces can house only temporary segments.

   B. Permanent tablespaces can house only permanent segments, whereas temporary tablespaces can house only temporary segments.

   C. Permanent tablespaces can house permanent and temporary segments, and temporary tablespaces can also house permanent and temporary segments.

   D. Permanent tablespaces can house temporary segments, and temporary tablespaces can house permanent segments.

3. You issue the following statement on the Oracle database:

```
create tablespace tbs_temp
datafile '/u05/oradata/oracle/tbs_temp01.dbf' size 600M
extent management dictionary online;
```

Which of the following choices correctly describes the tablespace you just created?

   A. You created a locally managed temporary tablespace.

   B. You created a dictionary-managed temporary tablespace.

    C. You created a locally managed permanent tablespace.

    D. You created a dictionary-managed permanent tablespace.

4. **You are creating tablespaces in Oracle. Which of the following keywords or clauses permits the datafiles of a tablespace to grow automatically in order to accommodate data growth?**

    A. `default storage`

    B. `extent management`

    C. `autoextend`

    D. `datafile`

5. **You are creating tablespaces in Oracle with the `create database` command. Which three of the following tablespaces can be created with this command in Oracle9i and later releases?**

    A. SYSTEM

    B. DATA

    C. UNDO

    D. TEMP

Answer Key

1. D. **2.** A. **3.** D. Although the name implies that it is temporary, the tablespace is actually permanent because you omitted the `temporary` and `tempfile` keywords. **4.** C.
5. A, C, and D.

Changing Tablespace Size

Once a tablespace is created, there are a few different ways to modify the size of a tablespace. The first is by adding new datafiles to the tablespace. This task is accomplished with the `alter tablespace add datafile` statement. You can add as many datafiles to your tablespace as you want, subject to two restrictions. First, you cannot add datafiles that will exceed the physical size of your disk resources (that restriction is pretty straightforward). Let's look at an example of increasing the size of your tablespace by adding datafiles:

```
SQL> ALTER TABLESPACE data ADD DATAFILE
  2  'G:\oradata\Oracle\data03.dat' SIZE 50M;
```

TIP
The length of time Oracle requires to complete this operation depends directly on the size of the datafile you want to add.

The other restriction relates to the following point about `maxdatafiles`. If you have added the maximum number of datafiles permitted for your database as specified by this parameter, and you still need more room, you can increase the size of existing datafiles in your tablespace with the `resize` keyword. Resizing a datafile upward is rarely met with difficulty, unless there is not enough space in the file system. Usually, you can also resize a datafile to be smaller, either through dropping datafiles with `alter database datafile` *filename* `offline drop` or by resizing a datafile to be smaller. This is not always safe, however, especially if the datafile contains segments or extents owned by database objects. Be careful when attempting this sort of activity. Resizing a datafile upward is an operation you perform on individual datafiles, not at the tablespace level. To do so, issue the following statement:

```
SQL> ALTER DATABASE DATAFILE
  2  'G:\oradata\Oracle\data03.dat'
  3  RESIZE 1088M;
```

A third way to expand the size of your existing datafiles is through the use of the `autoextend` feature in Oracle. We've already seen an example of how this is used. As with resizing datafiles, enabling the `autoextend` feature is an operation you perform on individual datafiles, not on the tablespace to which the datafile belongs. To enable automatic extension of your datafile, execute the following statement:

```
SQL> ALTER DATABASE DATAFILE
  2  'G:\oradata\Oracle\data03.dat'
  3  AUTOEXTEND ON NEXT 100M MAXSIZE 1988M;
```

Notice a few important features of the `autoextend` clause. First, you define the size of the next block of space Oracle will acquire for the datafile using the `next` clause. In this case, we tell Oracle to acquire another 100MB whenever it needs to extend the size of the datafile. Second, we tell Oracle the maximum size we want the datafile to be able to grow to using the `maxsize` clause. The value specified for this clause must be larger than the datafile's current size. In this case, we tell Oracle we want this datafile to grow to a size of just under 2GB.

For Review

1. You can grow a tablespace by enabling auto extension of the datafile. By doing so, that datafile will automatically grow when space is needed. You can specify how large it can grow and how big each growth can be.

2. Secondly, you can resize the tablespace to either grow or shrink.

3. Finally, you can grow a tablespace by adding more datafiles.

Exercises

1. **You are increasing the size of your tablespace. Which of the following choices does not identify a command that can be used for this purpose?**

   A. `alter datafile resize`

   B. `alter datafile autoextend`

   C. `alter database add datafile`

   D. `alter tablespace add datafile`

2. **You are resizing a datafile in your Oracle database. Which of the following choices represents an issue you may face when doing so to adjust the size of a datafile in the downward direction?**

   A. SMON may have trouble coalescing free space later.

   B. A segment assigned to a database object may restrict the operation.

   C. Adjusting a datafile size too often may cause Oracle to drop the datafile automatically.

   D. There are no restrictions about adjusting datafiles in the downward direction.

3. **You are increasing the size of your Oracle tablespace by adding more datafiles. Which of the following choices describes a restriction you may encounter in this process?**

   A. The maximum number of datafiles defined for the database could be exceeded.

   B. You might run out of space on disk if the datafile is sized too large.

   C. Choices A and B are both correct.

   D. None of the above

Answer Key
1. C. The add datafile clause is not valid for the alter database command.
2. B. **3.** C.

Allocating Space for Temporary Segments

Recall that temporary segments can be housed in both permanent tablespaces and temporary tablespaces. This functionality is provided for backward compatibility; however, you should always design your databases so that temporary segments are housed in temporary tablespaces and permanent segments are housed in permanent tablespaces. You cannot put a permanent database object (a table, for example) in a temporary tablespace. You can switch a tablespace between being permanent and temporary, provided the permanent tablespace does not contain permanent database objects when you try to switch it to a temporary tablespace. The following code block illustrates this:

```
SQL> create tablespace test01 datafile 'D:\ORACLE\test01.dat'
  2   size 1M default storage ( initial 10K
  3   next 10K pctincrease 0
  4   minextents 1 maxextents 5 ) temporary;
Tablespace created.
SQL> create table dummy3 (dummy varchar2(10)) tablespace test01;
create table dummy3 (dummy varchar2(10)) tablespace test01;
ERROR at line 1:
ORA-02195: Attempt to create PERMANENT object in a TEMPORARY
tablespace
SQL> alter tablespace test01 permanent;
Command completed successfully;
SQL> create table dummy3 (dummy varchar2(10)) tablespace test01;
Table created.
SQL> alter tablespace test01 temporary;
alter tablespace test01 temporary
ERROR at line 1:
ORA-01662: tablespace 'TEST01' is non-empty and cannot be made temporary
```

Temporary Segments in Permanent Tablespaces

A user may be assigned to either a permanent or temporary tablespace for sorting. Users create temporary segments in a tablespace when a disk sort is required to support their use of select statements containing the group by, order by, distinct, or union clauses, or the create index statement, as mentioned earlier. Users can be assigned to either permanent or temporary tablespaces for creating temporary segments. If the user is assigned to a permanent tablespace for creating temporary segments, the temporary segment will be created at the time the disk sort is required. When the disk sort is complete, the SMON process drops the temporary segment automatically to free the space for other users. Because this activity causes high fragmentation, it is advisable to create a separate temporary tablespace to store the temporary segments for all users.

Temporary Segments in Temporary Tablespaces

Temporary space is managed differently in temporary tablespaces. Instead of allocating temporary segments on-the-fly, only to have them be dropped later by SMON, the Oracle instance allocates one sort segment for the first statement requiring a disk sort. All subsequent users requiring disk sorts can share that segment. There is no limit to the number of extents that can be acquired by the sort segment either. The sort segment is released at instance shutdown. Management of temporary segments in this manner improves performance in two ways. First, Oracle saves time by assigning transactions to temporary segments that have been preallocated. Second, Oracle does not deallocate the primary temporary segment once the sorting operation is complete. Rather, Oracle simply eliminates the extents and keeps the primary segment available for the next transaction requiring a sort. All space management for the sort segment in a temporary tablespace is handled in a new area of the SGA called the *sort extent pool*. A process needing space for disk sorts can allocate extents based on information in this area.

Using Locally Managed Temporary Tablespaces

Your temporary tablespaces should be locally managed. This is because Oracle needs fast access to free space information when performing a disk sort, and because disk sorts are notoriously poor performers anyway, there's no sense in making your data dictionary yet another bottleneck in the process. The following is an example for how to create a locally managed temporary tablespace:

```
CREATE TEMPORARY TABLESPACE temp
TEMPFILE '/DISK2/temp_01.dbf' SIZE 500M
EXTENT MANAGEMENT LOCAL
UNIFORM SIZE 10M;
```

You've already seen the use of the `tempfile` and `temporary` keywords to define temporary tablespaces in this manner. However, the `uniform extent size` clause is new to you. Uniform extent sizing is a feature in the world of tablespace management designed to simplify how extents are allocated to objects. Rather than having every object define its own extent allocation via a `storage` clause, or having the tablespace assign objects a storage allocation via the `default storage` clause, `uniform extent management` simplifies the process by assigning every object in the tablespace the exact same extent management configuration. When an object is placed in a tablespace using `uniform extent management`, the tablespace's `uniform extent management` setting overrides any storage configuration included in the object's creation statement.

Space Allocation in Temporary Tablespaces

Temporary tablespaces offer improved performance for disk sorts and better multiuser space management. If you use the `default storage` clause to govern how temporary segments and extents are sized in this tablespace, there are some special rules you should know when defining values for these storage options. Because, by the definition of a disk sort, the data written to disk will equal SORT_AREA_SIZE, your extents must be at least that large. Size your initial sort segment according to the `formula num` × SORT_AREA_SIZE + DB_BLOCK_SIZE, where *num* is a small number of your choice used as a multiplier of SORT_AREA_SIZE. This sizing formula allows for header block storage as well as multiple sort data to be stored in each extent. Next, as with undo segments, sort segments should acquire extents that are all the same size, so set `initial` equal to `next`. Also, `pctincrease` should be zero. Finally, the `maxextents` storage option is not used in temporary tablespaces.

You can also create multiple temporary tablespaces to support different types of disk sorts required by your users. For example, you might have an extremely large temporary tablespace for long-running `select order by` statements in report batch processes or for the creation of an index on a large table that is periodically reorganized. In addition, you might include a smaller temporary tablespace for disk sorts as the by-product of ad hoc queries run by users. Each of these temporary tablespaces can then be assigned to users based on their anticipated sort needs.

Obtaining Temporary Segment Information from Oracle

There are several data dictionary views available for obtaining information about temporary segments. The views in the dictionary displaying this information base their content either on temporary segments that exist in the database or on dynamic performance information about temporary segments collected while the instance is running. The views you should remember for viewing temporary segment information include the following:

- **DBA_SEGMENTS** This gives information about the name, tablespace location, and owner of both types of temporary segments in Oracle. Note that you will only see information on temporary segments in permanent tablespaces while those segments are allocated, but you will see information about temporary segments in temporary tablespaces for the life of the instance.

- **V$SORT_SEGMENT** This gives information about the size of the temporary tablespaces, current number of extents allocated to sort segments, and sort segment high-water mark information.

- **V$SORT_USAGE** This gives information about sorts that are happening currently on the database. This view is often joined with V$SESSION, described earlier in the chapter.

You can obtain the name, segment type, and tablespace storing sort segments using the DBA_SEGMENTS view. Note that this segment will not exist until the first disk sort is executed after the instance starts. The following code block is an example:

```
SQL> select owner, segment_name, segment_type, tablespace_name
  2  from dba_segments;
OWNER SEGMENT_NAME SEGMENT_TYPE TABLESPACE_NAME
----- ------------ ------------ ----------------
SYS   13.2         TEMPORARY    TEST01
```

You can get the size of sort segments allocated in temporary tablespaces by issuing queries against V$SORT_SEGMENT, which you will find useful in defining the sizes for your temporary tablespaces on an ongoing basis. The following query illustrates how to obtain this sort segment high-water mark information from V$SORT_SEGMENT:

```
SQL> select tablespace_name, extent_size,
  2  total_extents, max_sort_blocks
  3  from v$sort_segment;
TABLESPACE_NAME EXTENT_SIZE TOTAL_EXTENTS MAX_SORT_SIZE
--------------- ----------- ------------- -------------
TEST01              3147776            14      44068864
```

Finally, you can see information about sorts currently taking place on the instance by joining data from the V$SESSION and V$SORT_USAGE views. The following code block displays an example:

```
SQL> select a.username, b.tablespace,
  2  b.contents, b.extents, b.blocks
  3  from v$session a, v$sort_usage b
  4  where a.saddr = b.session_addr;
USERNAME TABLESPACE  CONTENTS  EXTENTS BLOCKS
-------- ----------- --------- ------- ------
SPANKY   TEST01      TEMPORARY      14  21518
```

Dictionary Views for Temporary Tablespace Management

There are a couple of new dictionary views for managing temporary tablespaces:

- **DBA_TEMP_FILES**   This dictionary view gives you information about every datafile in your database that is associated with a temporary tablespace.

- **V$TEMPFILE**   Similar to DBA_TEMP_FILES, this performance view gives you information about every datafile in your database that is associated with a temporary tablespace.

For Review

1. For the performance of sorting, the extent size of the temporary tablespace should be properly sized. It should be equal to multiple of SORT_AREA_SIZE × DB_BLOCK_SIZE. This is because Oracle always sorts in sizes of SORT_AREA_SIZE.

2. Also, make sure that all extents in temporary tablespace are equal in size, the percentage increase is always zero, and are not coalesced. It is also advisable to have multiple temporary tablespaces for different kinds of sorting needs.

3. Oracle provides many data dictionary views to know about the temporary segments. DBA_SEGMENTS is one static view and V$SORT_SEGMENT and V$SORT_USAGE give dynamic information about the sort segments in existence and how they are being utilized.

4. To know about the temporary tablespaces, Oracle provides DBA_TEMP_FILES and V$TEMPFILE views.

Exercises

1. **You want to find out more information about the space usage allocations for temporary segments. Which of the following dictionary views would assist you in this task?**

    A. V$SORT_SEGMENT

    B. V$TEMPFILE

    C. DBA_TEMP_FILES

    D. DBA_SEGMENTS

2. **You want to convert a temporary tablespace into a permanent tablespace. Which of the following statements is true regarding this operation?**

A. Temporary tablespaces can be converted into permanent tablespaces when only temporary segments are stored in the tablespace.

B. Temporary tablespaces can be converted into permanent tablespaces when permanent segments are housed in the tablespace.

C. Temporary tablespaces can be converted into permanent tablespaces only when the tablespace is not in use.

D. Temporary tablespaces can be converted into permanent tablespaces with no restrictions.

3. **You want to configure space allocation in temporary tablespaces. Which of the following choices identifies a feature in Oracle that, when implemented, will force the tablespace segment allocations to all be the same size regardless of storage allocations defined on objects placed in the tablespace?**

A. `default storage`

B. `storage`

C. `uniform extent management`

D. `autoextend`

Answer Key
1. A. 2. C. 3. C.

Changing Tablespace Status

One of the `create tablespace` code blocks from a previous lesson describes how to create the tablespace so that it is online and available for use as soon as it's created. Recall also that the `alter tablespace name online` statement enables you to bring a tablespace online after creation. You can also take a tablespace offline using the `alter tablespace name offline` statement. You might do this if you were trying to prevent access to the data in that tablespace while simultaneously leaving the rest of the database online and available for use. Individual datafiles can be taken online and offline as well, using the `alter database datafile filename online` or `alter database datafile filename offline` statements.

A tablespace can be taken offline with one of several priorities, including `normal`, `temporary`, and `immediate`. Depending on the priority used to take the tablespace offline, media recovery on that tablespace may be required. A tablespace taken offline with normal priority will not require media recovery, but a tablespace taken offline with immediate priority will. A tablespace taken offline with temporary priority will not require media recovery if none of the datafiles were offline prior to taking the tablespace offline. However, if any of the datafiles were offline before the tablespace was taken offline temporarily due to read or write errors, then media recovery will be required to bring the tablespace back online. The following code block demonstrates taking a tablespace offline with each of the three possible priorities. Note that if you leave off a priority specification, normal priority is assumed.

```
ALTER TABLESPACE data OFFLINE;
ALTER TABLESPACE data OFFLINE NORMAL;
ALTER TABLESPACE data OFFLINE IMMEDIATE;
ALTER TABLESPACE data OFFLINE TEMPORARY;
```

On occasion, you may also have situations that make use of Oracle's capability to specify tablespaces to only be readable. The following code block demonstrates both the code required to make a tablespace readable but not writable, and then to change it back to being writable again:

```
ALTER TABLESPACE data READ ONLY;
ALTER TABLESPACE data READ WRITE;
```

Finally, if you want to eliminate a tablespace, use the `drop tablespace` command. This command has a few additional clauses, such as `including contents` for removing all database objects contained in the tablespace as well as the tablespace itself, and the `cascade constraints` keywords to remove any constraints that may depend on database objects stored in the tablespace being dropped. The following code block demonstrates a `drop tablespace` command:

```
DROP TABLESPACE data INCLUDING CONTENTS CASCADE CONSTRAINTS;
```

TIP
You can now use the same command and take the datafiles out of the operating system with statement `drop tablespace name including contents cascade constraints and datafiles.`

Making a Tablespace Read-Only Online

Recall that a tablespace is the logical view of disk storage and that it may be composed of multiple datafiles. Oracle uses relative datafile numbering conventions that make the datafile number unique to the tablespace, as opposed to earlier versions of Oracle prior to Oracle8, where datafile number is absolutely unique throughout the entire database. A read-only tablespace is one where no user can make a data change to any of the objects stored in that tablespace. There are a few exceptions to this rule. For example, you can drop items, such as tables and indexes, from a read-only tablespace, because these commands only affect the data dictionary, but you cannot create or alter items such as tables or index in read-only tablespaces. This is possible because the `drop` command only updates the data dictionary, not the physical files that make up the tablespace.

In order to make a tablespace read-only, certain conditions have to be met. The tablespace has to be online, the tablespace must not contain any active undo segments, and the tablespace must not be in online backup mode.

In versions of Oracle prior to Oracle8i, to make a tablespace read-only, you had to ensure that no user was currently making changes to any of the objects in that tablespace before issuing the `alter tablespace read only` statement. If any active transactions were processing data in the tablespace you wanted to make read-only, an error would occur when you attempted to issue the statement. In Oracle8i and later, this is no longer the case. Instead, you can issue the `alter tablespace read only` statement, and Oracle will wait until all active transactions complete, and then make the tablespace read-only. While Oracle waits for the transactions to complete, the tablespace is placed in a transitional read-only mode during which no further write transactions are allowed against the tablespace while the existing transactions are allowed to commit or rollback.

TIP

In Oracle8i and later releases, we do not have to wait for transactions to finish in order to make a tablespace read only. Also, a tablespace must be read-only before you transport it to another database.

For Review

1. Tablespaces could be in many states. They could be online or offline and read-only or read-write only. Under normal situations where tablespaces are actively used, they are in an online and read-write state. However, under certain conditions, you may want to bring a tablespace in an offline mode (to rename the datafiles) or read-only (to preserve the data in the tablespace).

2. There are many ways a tablespace can brought offline—normal, immediate, and temporary.

3. In order to make a tablespace read-only, certain conditions have to be met. The tablespace should be online and there should be no active undo segments in it. For this reason, the SYSTEM tablespace can never be made read-only as it contains system undo segment in it. Also, the tablespace should not be in online backup mode.

Exercises

1. **You want to make the tablespaces of your Oracle database read-only. Which of the following tablespaces cannot be taken offline due to active undo segments?**

   A. SYSTEM

   B. DATA

   C. INDEX

   D. TEMP

2. **You are about to drop a tablespace. Which of the following statements can be used for dropping tablespaces that contain parent tables in foreign key relationships?**

   A. alter database datafile offline drop

   B. alter tablespace offline immediate

   C. drop tablespace cascade constraints

   D. drop tablespace including contents

Answer Key
1. A. 2. C.

Changing Tablespace Storage Settings

Now, consider again the default storage parameters you set for a tablespace when you create it. They have no bearing on the tablespace itself, but rather are used as default settings when users issue create table, create index, or create undo segment statements that have no storage parameter settings explicitly defined. You can change the default settings for your tablespace by issuing the `alter tablespace` command, as shown in the following block:

```
SQL> ALTER TABLESPACE data DEFAULT STORAGE ( INITIAL 2M NEXT 1M );
```

You needn't specify all the `default storage` parameters available—only the ones for which you want to change values. However, keep in mind that changing the `default storage` settings has no effect on existing database objects in the tablespace. It only affects storage settings on new database objects and only when those new database objects do not specify their own storage settings explicitly.

Relocating Tablespace Datafiles

Depending on the type of tablespace, the database administrator can move datafiles using one of two methods: the `alter tablespace` command or the `alter database` command. Relocating datafiles underlying a tablespace in Oracle offers tremendous value, particularly when you were trying to eliminate hot spots in the database or distribute I/O load or disk use more evenly across the host machine. When relocating or renaming the datafiles within a single tablespace, use the `alter tablespace` command and when relocating the datafiles for many tablespaces, use the `alter database` command. In either case, executing these commands only modifies the pointers to the datafiles as recorded in the control file. They do not physically rename or move the files in the operating system. The actual renaming or relocation of the datafiles has to be done on the operating system level. The following discussion gives detailed steps how to do the relocation.

> **NOTE**
> *Even though you may rename the datafiles underlying the tablespaces, you cannot rename the tablespace names using Oracle commands. In order to rename a tablespace, you have to delete the tablespace and re-create it with the new name.*

Relocating Datafiles with `alter database`

To relocate datafiles with the `alter database` command, you execute the following steps:

1. Shut down the database.

2. Use an operating system command to move the files.

3. Mount the database.

4. Execute the `alter database rename file` command.

5. Open the database.

6. Back up the database and the control file.

The following code block illustrates these steps in Windows:

```
D:\ORACLE\DATABASE\> sqlplus
Oracle SQL*Plus Release 9.0.1.0.0 - Production
(c)1999, Oracle Corporation. All Rights Reserved.
Enter user-name: sys as sysdba
Enter password:
Connected to:
Oracle9i Enterprise Edition Release 9.0.1.0.0 - Production
With the Partitioning and Objects options
PL/SQL Release 9.0.1.0.0 - Production
SQL> shutdown immediate
Database closed.
Database dismounted.
ORACLE instance shut down.
SQL> host move tmp1jsc.ora temp1jsc.ora
        1 file(s) moved.
SQL> startup mount pfile=initjsc.ora
Total System Global Area            14442496 bytes
Fixed Size                             49152 bytes
Variable Size                       13193216 bytes
Database Buffers                     1126400 bytes
Redo Buffers                           73728 bytes
Database mounted.
SQL> alter database rename file
    2> 'D:\ORACLE\DATABASE\TMP1JSC.ORA'
    3> to
    4> 'D:\ORACLE\DATABASE\TEMP1JSC.ORA';
Statement Processed.
SQL> alter database open;
Statement processed.
```

Relocating Datafiles with `alter tablespace`

Use the following process to rename a datafile with the `alter tablespace` command:

1. Take the tablespace offline.

2. Use an operating system command to move or copy the files.

3. Execute the `alter tablespace rename datafile` command.

4. Bring the tablespace online.

5. Back up the database and the control file.

Limitations in Oracle9i

In general, you will experience the following limitations in Oracle9i with respect to tablespaces:

- The maximum number of tablespaces per database is 64,000.

- The operating system-specific limit on the maximum number of datafiles allowed in a tablespace is typically 1,023 files; however, this number varies by operating system.

For Review

1. When creating database objects such as tables and indexes, if no storage parameters are specified, Oracle takes the tablespace storage parameters as the defaults and uses them for creating these objects.

2. These default storage parameters of a tablespace can be modified after the tablespaces are created using `alter tablespace` command. The modified default storage parameters of a tablespace take effect only on the new objects that will be created but not the existing ones.

3. Very often you would need to rename or relocate the tablespace datafiles. Depending on how many datafiles you need to rename or relocate, you have the option to use two Oracle commands—`alter tablespace` and `alter database`.

4. When using the `alter database` command, you need to shut down the database, move the datafiles, mount the database, give the Oracle command, and then bring up the database.

5. When using the `alter tablespace` command, you can either shut down the database or bring the tablespace offline, move the datafiles, mount the database, give the Oracle command, and open the database.

6. After relocating or renaming the datafiles, it is highly advisable to back up the database and the control file.

Exercises

1. **You are moving a datafile from one location on disk to another. After copying the physical file to the new location, which of the following steps would be appropriate to continue the task?**

   A. Bring the tablespace online.

   B. Bring the database online.

   C. Issue the appropriate `alter database` command to inform Oracle of the move.

   D. Issue the appropriate `alter system` command to inform Oracle of the move.

2. **You alter a tablespace's `default storage` settings in the Oracle database to increase the size of initial extents. Which of the following choices identifies when the change will take effect for tables that already exist in that tablespace?**

   A. The change takes effect immediately.

   B. The change takes effect when data is added to the table.

   C. The change takes effect when data is removed from the table.

   D. The change will not take effect for existing tables.

Answer Key
1. C. 2. D.

Oracle-Managed Files (OMF)

By this time, you have been introduced to Oracle-Managed Files (OMF) at least three times: once as an introduction in the first chapter and twice to introduce Oracle-managed redo log files and Oracle-managed control files. We will not spend too much time in this section on the functionality of this feature except to introduce how they are used while creating or dropping tablespaces. OMF is not intended for production systems but more for development or test databases to simplify the datafile management while managing the tablespaces. To create Oracle-managed datafiles for tablespaces or tempfiles or UNDOTBS tablespaces, you need to define the parameter DB_CREATE_FILE_DEST in the `init.ora` file. This parameter should point to the default location where all Oracle-managed datafiles or tempfiles need to be created. The following is an example of defining this parameter in Windows:

```
DB_CREATE_FILE_DEST = 'C:\Oracle\oradata\DB1'
```

Creating OMF Datafiles for Tablespaces

OMF datafiles can be created for regular tablespaces and UNDOTBS tablespaces. (UNDOTBS tablespaces will be discussed further in Chapter 4.) When creating the tablespace, the `datafile` clause is optional. If you include the `datafile` clause, then the datafile name is optional. If the `datafile` clause is omitted entirely or does not include a filename, then your datafile is created in the location specified by the DB_CREATE_FILE_DEST parameter. The following code block contains an example of how OMF datafiles can be created or altered:

```
SQL> show parameter db_create_file_dest
NAME                      TYPE        VALUE
------------------------- ----------- --------------------
db_create_file_dest       string      C:\oracle\oradata\DB1
SQL> create tablespace data datafile size 25M;
Tablespace created.
SQL> select file_name, tablespace_name, bytes/1024/1024 as megs
  2  from dba_data_files
  3  where tablespace_name = 'DATA';
FILE_NAME                                        TABLESPACE MEGS
------------------------------------------------ ---------- ----
C:\ORACLE\ORADATA\DB1\ORA_DATA_ZVSRKH00.DBF      DATA         25
```

The previous code shows the creation of tablespace with no filename specification or the location it has to be created except for the size. When you query the location of the datafile for the tablespace created, you will find it created at the location specified by the parameter DB_CREATE_FILE_DEST. Note the name of the file and the size. When you drop a tablespace containing Oracle-managed datafiles, the datafiles are automatically removed from the underlying operating system.

Creating OMF Tempfiles for Temporary Tablespaces

When creating the temporary tablespace with OMF, the `tempfile` clause is optional. If you include the `tempfile` clause, then the filename is optional. If the `tempfile` clause or the filename is not specified, then the datafile will be created at the location specified by DB_CREATE_FILE_DEST parameter. The following code block contains an example of how OMF tempfiles can be created or altered.

```
SQL> create temporary tablespace temptbs;
Tablespace created.
```

```
SQL> select tablespace_name, contents from dba_tablespaces
  2  where tablespace_name = 'TEMPTBS';
TABLESPACE CONTENTS
---------- ---------
TEMPTBS    TEMPORARY
SQL> select file_name, tablespace_name
  2  from dba_temp_files;
FILE_NAME                                          TABLESPACE
-------------------------------------------------- ----------
C:\ORACLE\ORADATA\DB1\TEMP01.DBF                   TEMP
C:\ORACLE\ORADATA\DB1\ORA_TEMPTBS_ZVSRZ200.TMP     TEMPTBS
```

For Review

1. Oracle-Managed Files (OMF) is a new feature of Oracle9i that eases the administration of datafiles for tablespaces, control files, and redo log files. Defining the parameter DB_CREATE_FILE_DEST in `init.ora` file activates OMF for tablespaces. This parameter should point to a location on the machine where the OMF datafiles will be created by default.

2. With OMF active, you do not need to specify the `datafile` clause or even the datafile name while creating the tablespaces. The same holds true while creating the temporary tablespaces where you don't have to specify the `tempfile` clause. By skipping these clauses, Oracle creates the datafiles in the default location specified by the previous `init.ora` parameter. If no filename is specified, then Oracle uses a default naming convention that keeps the datafiles unique from each other.

Exercises

1. **You are creating a tablespace on a database where OMF is enabled. Which of the following choices identifies how Oracle determines what the name of the file will be?**

   A. Oracle must use the contents of the mandatory `datafile` clause to name the file.

   B. Oracle must use the contents of the mandatory `tempfile` clause to name the file.

   C. Oracle will name the file according to its own default settings in all cases.

   D. Oracle will name the file according to its own default settings if no `datafile` or `tempfile` clause is specified.

2. **You are implementing OMF on your Oracle database. When OMF is enabled, Oracle manages creation and removal of datafiles from the host system for which of the following tablespaces?**

   A.   SYSTEM tablespace only

   B.   UNDOTBS tablespaces only

   C.   TEMP tablespace only

   D.   All tablespaces in the database

Answer Key
1. D. 2. D.

Chapter Summary

In this chapter, you learned the core concepts of Oracle related to tablespaces and their management. We covered the physical mapping of datafiles and blocks to their logically associated counterparts: the tablespace, segment, and extent. We also covered how to create tablespaces. You learned about the different types of free space management that Oracle supports, including dictionary-managed tablespaces and locally managed tablespaces. You also learned about the differences between permanent tablespaces and temporary tablespaces with respect to the types of segments each can store. You learned how to change the size of tablespaces using various methods, such as adding more datafiles or increasing the size of datafiles. The use of the `autoextend` feature for datafiles was also discussed in some detail. We then discussed temporary tablespaces in some detail, including the different methods for creating them. You learned how to alter tablespace availability status and `default storage` settings. Finally, we covered implementation of Oracle-Managed Files (OMF) with respect to tablespace management.

Two-Minute Drill

- ■ Understand how tablespaces and datafiles relate to one another. A tablespace can have many datafiles, but each datafile can associate with only one tablespace.

- ■ At database creation, there is one tablespace—SYSTEM. In Oracle9i, it is possible to create a default temporary tablespace for the database and an UNDOTBS tablespaces as well.

■ All other tablespaces are created with the `create tablespace` command.

■ There are two methods Oracle uses for free space management in a tablespace. Dictionary-managed tablespaces have all their free space information stored and managed via the Oracle data dictionary. Locally managed tablespaces have all their free space information stored and managed in the datafile headers of all tablespace datafiles.

■ The DBA should *not* place all database objects into that tablespace, because often their storage needs conflict with each other. Instead, the DBA should create multiple tablespaces for the different segments available on the database and place those objects into those tablespaces.

■ The SMON process handles periodic coalescence of noncontiguous free space in dictionary-managed tablespaces into larger, contiguous blocks of free space. No coalescence takes place in locally managed tablespaces, however.

■ Permanent segments store data in permanent database objects, such as tables.

■ Temporary segments store data in temporary segments, generated whenever Oracle performs a disk sort.

■ Temporary tablespaces differ from permanent tablespaces in that only temporary segments can be stored in them. In contrast, permanent tablespaces can house both permanent and temporary segments. However, for practical purposes you learned about in the chapter, temporary segments should be kept out of permanent tablespaces.

■ Tablespaces are brought online by Oracle automatically after they are created by default.

■ In Oracle9*i*, all tablespaces use local extent management by default unless you specify otherwise at tablespace creation time.

■ Temporary tablespaces should use local extent management because of performance reasons.

■ A new memory area called the sort extent pool manages how user processes allocate extents for disk sorts in temporary tablespaces.

■ SMON handles deallocation of temporary segments in permanent tablespaces when the transaction no longer needs them.

■ You cannot create permanent database objects, such as tables, in temporary tablespaces. You also cannot convert permanent tablespaces into temporary ones unless there are no permanent objects in the permanent tablespace.

- You can get information about temporary segments and sort segments from the DBA_SEGMENTS, V$SORT_SEGMENT, V$SESSION, and V$SORT_USAGE dictionary views.

- A sort segment exists in the temporary tablespace for as long as the instance is available. All users share the sort segment.

- The size of extents in the temporary tablespace should be set to a multiple of SORT_AREA_SIZE, plus one additional block for the segment header, in order to maximize disk sort performance.

- Know what dictionary views are used to find information about storage structures, including DBA_SEGMENTS, DBA_TABLESPACES, DBA_TS_QUOTAS, V$TABLESPACE, DBA_EXTENTS, DBA_FREE_SPACE, and DBA_FREE_SPACE_COALESCED.

- You can change the availability status of tablespaces using the `alter tablespace` command. Review the chapter to understand all the different statuses available.

- You can use the Oracle-Managed Files (OMF) feature in conjunction with tablespace management. When OMF is used, you do not need to specify the name or location of datafiles related to the tablespaces you want to create.

Fill-in-the-Blank Questions

1. The Oracle background process that handles periodic coalescence of free space in a tablespace is _____.

2. The status of a tablespace as soon as it is created is _____.

3. This tablespace cannot be brought offline as long as the database is open: _____.

4. You should configure temporary segments/extents to be a multiple of this `init.ora` parameter value: _____.

Chapter Questions

1. **The keyword that prevents you from creating a table in a tablespace marked for use when you run `select order by` statements on millions of rows of output is which of the following choices?**

   A. `lifespan`

   B. `permanent`

   C. `online`

   D. `offline`

   E. `temporary`

   F. `read only`

2. **When no storage options are specified in a `create table` command, what does Oracle use in order to configure the object's storage allocation?**

   A. The default options specified for the user in the tablespace

   B. The default options specified for the table in the tablespace

   C. The default options specified for the user in the database

   D. The default options specified for the table in the database

3. **To determine the space allocated for temporary segments, the DBA can access which of the following views?**

   A. DBA_TABLESPACES

   B. DBA_TABLES

   C. DBA_SEGMENTS

   D. DBA_FREE_SPACE

4. The process that most directly causes fragmentation in a tablespace storing temporary segments because it deallocates segments used for disk sorts is which of the following choices?

   A. Server

   B. DBWR

   C. SMON

   D. LGWR

5. Which of the following choices best describes the methodology for sizing extents for the sort segments on your Oracle database?

   A. DB_BLOCK_SIZE + 6

   B. X * SORT_AREA_SIZE + DB_BLOCK_SIZE

   C. (avg_row_size - init_row_size) * 100 / avg_row_size

   D. 100 - pctfree - (*avg_row_size* * 100) / avail_data_space

6. Each of the following choices identifies an event in a series of events that are run from SQL*Plus. If A is the first event and D is the last event, which of the following choices identifies the event that will cause an error?

   A. create tablespace TB01 datafile '/oracle/tb01.dbf' default storage

   B. (initial 10K next 10K pctincrease 0 minextents 4 maxextents 20) temporary;

   C. create table my_tab (my_col varchar2(10)) tablespace TB01;

   D. alter tablespace TB01 permanent;

   E. create table my_tab (my_col varchar2(10)) tablespace TB02;

7. You are trying to determine how many disk sorts are happening on the database right now. Which of the following dictionary tables would you use to find that information?

   A. V$SESSION

   B. V$SYSSTAT

   C. DBA_SEGMENTS

   D. V$SORT_USAGE

Fill-in-the-Blank Answers

1. SMON

2. Online

3. SYSTEM

4. SORT_AREA_SIZE

Answers to Chapter Questions

1. E. `temporary`

Explanation   Oracle enforces the intended use of a temporary tablespace through the use of the `temporary` keyword. There is no `lifespan` keyword, although the concept of a life span is very important in understanding tablespace fragmentation, eliminating choice A. Choices C, D, and F are incorrect because the tablespace availability status is not the factor that is being tested in this situation. Finally, although there is a difference between permanent and temporary tables, `permanent` is not an actual keyword used anywhere in the definition of your tablespace.

2. B.   The default options specified for the table in the tablespace

Explanation   All `default storage` parameters for table objects are specified as part of the tablespace creation statement. A default tablespace can be named for a user on username creation, along with a maximum amount of storage in a tablespace for all objects created by the user. However, there are no `default storage` parameters on a table-by-table basis either in the database or for a user. Refer to the discussion of tablespace creation.

3. C.   DBA_SEGMENTS

Explanation   Choices A and D are incorrect because they are not actual views in the data dictionary. Choice B is incorrect because DBA_TABLES only lists information about the tables in the database, not the temporary segments created as part of a sort operation. Refer to the discussion of viewing storage information in Oracle.

4. C.   SMON

Explanation   The SMON process automatically drops temporary segments from the permanent tablespace as soon as they are no longer needed by the transaction. The server process can only retrieve data from disk, eliminating choice A. DBWR handles writing data changes to disk, but does not drop the temporary segment, eliminating choice B. Choice D is also incorrect because LGWR handles writing redo log entries to disk, as explained in Chapter 7.

> **5.** B.   X * SORT_AREA_SIZE + DB_BLOCK_SIZE

Explanation   If the data to be sorted was any smaller than the init*sid*.ora parameter SORT_AREA_SIZE, then the sort would take place in memory. Thus, you can be sure that all disk sorts will write data at least as great as SORT_AREA_SIZE to disk, so you should size your sort segment to be a multiple of that parameter. Because the sort segment will need a header block, adding in DB_BLOCK_SIZE is required to make the extra room for the header. Choices C and D are formulas for determining pctfree and pctused, respectively, so they are wrong. Choice A is used to determine the number of undo segments your database needs, making that one wrong as well.

> **6.** B.   create table my_tab (my_col varchar2(10))
>   tablespace TB01;

Explanation   Because tablespace TB01 is temporary, you cannot create a permanent object like a table in it, making choice B correct. Incidentally, if the tablespace created in choice A had been permanent, then choice C would have been the right answer because an error occurs when you try to convert a permanent tablespace into a temporary one when the tablespace contains a permanent object. Choice D could be correct in that scenario, too, because your MY_TAB table would already exist.

> **7.** D.   V$SORT_USAGE

Explanation   The V$SORT_USAGE view shows the sessions that are using sort segments in your database. Although you may want to join that data with the data in choice A, V$SESSION, to see the username corresponding with the session, V$SESSION by itself gives no indication about current disk sorts. V$SESSTAT or DBA_SEGMENTS do not either, eliminating those choices as well.

CHAPTER
13

Storage Structures
and Undo Data

n this chapter, you will learn about and demonstrate knowledge in the following areas:

- Storage structures and relationships
- Managing undo data

As a DBA, part of your daily job function is to create database objects. This is especially true for database administrators who manage development and test databases. However, even DBAs working on production systems will find that a good deal of their time is spent exploring the depths of setting up database objects. In this chapter, you will cover what you need to know about the underlying storage structures like segments and extents that house database objects like tables and indexes in Oracle. You will also learn about undo segments, which are important data structures used for managing transactions and read-consistency in Oracle. The contents of this chapter lay the foundation for management of tables, indexes, and integrity constraints, which are topics covered in Chapter 5. The information covered in this chapter comprises about 14 percent of material tested on the OCP DBA Fundamentals I exam.

Storage Structures and Relationships

In this section, you will cover the following topics concerning storage structures and relationships:

- Different segment types and their uses
- Using block space utilization parameters
- Obtaining information about storage structures
- Criteria for separating segments

The storage of database objects in Oracle can often become a cantankerous matter, because each of the different types of database objects has its own storage needs and typical behavior. What's more, the behavior of one type of database object often interferes with the behavior of other objects in the database. As the Oracle DBA, your job is to make sure that all objects "play well together." To help you with OCP and in being a DBA, this section will discuss the different segment types and their uses. You'll also learn how to control Oracle's use of extents, the management of space at the block level, where to go for information about your database storage allocation, and how to locate segments by considering fragmentation and lifespan.

TIP

Refer to the discussion titled "Describing the Logical Structure of the Database" listed as a subtopic for the "Storage Structures and Relationships" section, which is covered in Chapter 3. The OCP Candidate Guide for the Oracle9i DBA track has the same discussion topic listed for both sections. For brevity's sake, we'll only cover it once.

Different Segment Types and Their Uses

For a quick review, the logical structure of your database consists of the following components: tablespaces, segments, and extents. Tablespaces are logical structures that house Oracle database objects and are comprised of one or more datafiles. Segments are collections of physical data blocks that are used for housing the data in database objects (for example, a table). When Oracle runs out of room in the segment used for housing data in that object, Oracle acquires another set of physical data blocks to house the data being added. This next set of physical data blocks is called an extent.

In the previous chapter, we said that different types of objects need different types of tablespaces to store them. In contrast, Oracle usually creates a database with only one tablespace—the SYSTEM tablespace. This tablespace should only be used for housing Oracle data dictionary and SYSTEM undo segments. Oracle9i permits you to create undo and temporary tablespaces when you create the database, so at a minimum, in addition to the SYSTEM tablespace, you will have separate tablespaces for your tables, indexes, undo segments, and temporary segments.

In order to understand the different types of tablespaces (and why it is a bad idea to ever try to store all your database objects in the SYSTEM tablespace), you must understand the different types of objects that a tablespace may store. Every database object, such as tables or undo segments, ultimately consists of segments and extents. For this reason, the discussion focuses on the different types of segments available on the Oracle database and how they are used.

Table Segments and Their Usage

The first type of segment is the table segment. Each segment contains data blocks that store the row data for that table. The rate at which the table fills and grows is determined by the type of data that table will support. For example, if a table supports an application component that accepts large volumes of data insertions (sales order entries for a popular brand of wine, for example), the segments that comprise that table will fill at a regular pace and rarely, if ever, reduce in size. Therefore, the DBA managing the tablespace that stores that segment will want to plan for regular growth. If, however, this table is designed for storing a small amount of validation data, the size requirements of the table may be a bit more static. In this case, the DBA may want to focus more on ensuring that the entire table fits comfortably into one segment, reducing the potential fragmentation that extent allocation could cause. Still another factor to consider when planning table segments is whether or not you intend to use parallel processing on your Oracle database. Under those circumstances, you would actually want your table divided into several segments and extents, or even to use partitioning. We'll consider this topic in more detail shortly.

Index Segments and Their Usage

Another type of segment is the index segment. As with table segments, index segment growth is moderated by the type of role the index supports in the database. If the table to which the index is associated is designed for volume transactions (as in the wine example mentioned previously), the index also should be planned for growth. However, the index will almost invariably be smaller than the tables in your database, because it only houses one or a few columns from the table in an easy-to-search format, along with the ROWID information for the associated rows from the table.

What does an index consist of exactly? An index consists of a list of entries for a particular column (the indexed column) that can be easily searched for the values stored in the column. Corresponding to each value is the ROWID for the table row that contains that column value. The principle behind index growth is the same as the growth of the corresponding table. If an index is associated with a table that rarely changes, the size of the index may be relatively static. However, if the index is associated with a table that experiences high `insert` activity, then plan the index for growth as well. Again, however, if you plan to use parallel processing in your database, you might actually want your index data stored in a few segments or even to use partitioning. Again, we'll discuss the criteria for separating index segments shortly.

Undo Segments and Their Usage

Undo segments are different from the table and index segments just discussed. Undo segments store data changes from transactions to provide read consistency and transaction concurrency. The segments used to store data for tables and indexes are generally for ongoing use, meaning that once data is added to a table or index segment, it generally stays there for a while. Undo segments aren't like that. Instead, once a user process has made its database changes and `commits` the transaction, the space in the undo segment that held that user's data is released for reuse in support of another user's transaction. Oracle's undo segment architecture is designed to allow the undo segment to reuse that space. Usually, an undo segment has some extents allocated to it at all times to store uncommitted transaction information.

As the number of uncommitted transactions rises and falls, so, too, does the amount of space used in the undo segment. Where possible, the undo segment will try to place uncommitted transaction data into an extent that it already has allocated to it. For example, if an undo segment consists of five extents, and the entire initial extent contains old data from committed transactions, the undo segment will reuse that extent to store data from new or existing uncommitted transactions once it fills the fifth extent. However, if the undo segment fills the fifth extent with data from a long uncommitted transaction, and the first extent still has data from uncommitted transactions in it, the undo segment will need to allocate a new extent. Various long- and short-running transactions on your Oracle database can cause undo segments to allocate and deallocate dozens of extents over and over again throughout the day, which can adversely affect the growth of other database objects because of tablespace fragmentation. Thus, it is wise to keep undo segments by themselves, in their own undo tablespace.

TIP
You can create an undo tablespace when you issue the `create database` *command by including the* `undo tablespace` *name* `datafile` `'filename'` `size` *number*`[K|M]` *clause in that command. If you don't create an undo tablespace when you create the database, you should create one later using the* `create tablespace` *command.*

Temporary Segments and Their Usage

Next, consider the temporary segment. True to its name, the temporary segment is allocated to store temporary data for a user transaction that cannot all be stored in memory. One popular use for temporary segments in user processes is for sorting data into a requested order. These segments are allocated on-the-fly and dismissed when their services are no longer required. Their space utilization is marked by short periods of high storage need followed by periods of no storage need. Because you have no idea when a temporary segment could come in and use all the available space in a tablespace, you can't make an adequate plan to accommodate the growth of other database objects—you really need to keep temporary segments in their own tablespace as separate from other database objects as possible.

TIP
You can create a default temporary tablespace along with your Oracle database using the default temporary tablespace *clause in the* create database *command. If you don't create a temporary tablespace when you issue the* create database *command, you should create them later using the* create default temporary tablespace *command.*

Beyond the Basics: LOB, Cluster, and IOT Segments

The final types of segments that may be used in your Oracle database are LOB segments, cluster segments, and IOT segments. LOB stands for large object, and a large object in Oracle will use a special type of segment to house its data. If your database uses large objects frequently, you may want to create a separate tablespace to hold these objects. Otherwise, don't bother to create the extra tablespace.

You may have heard of clustered tables—a physical grouping of two or more tables in the same segment around a common index. Cluster segments support the use of clusters on the database. The sizing of cluster segments and planning for their growth is complex and should be performed carefully, as each segment will essentially be storing data from two different tables in each block.

Finally, IOT stands for index-organized table, in which essentially the entire table is stored within the structure. This was historically reserved only for use by indexes. Obviously, these segments have storage needs that are similar to indexes. However, your use of cluster and IOT segments will probably be so limited that you don't need to worry about any potential conflict between these objects and your other database objects.

A Note about Database Tools

Database administrative tools like Oracle Enterprise Manager operate based on a set of tables, indexes, and other database objects that collect data about your database. This set of database objects is often called a *repository*. Although the segments that house repository objects are the same as those segments that house your data, you should create a separate tablespace to store repository objects for several reasons. One reason is that this will keep a logical division between your organization's data and the tool's data. Another reason is that, although it is not likely, the repository may have a table or other object with the same name as an object in your database, causing a conflict. By using a special TOOLS tablespace to store objects used by your database administrative tools, you will ease your own efforts later.

Why Separate Segments into Different Tablespaces?

In order to answer that question, let's consider the fragmentation potential for the different segments (and thus tablespaces) you may store in your database. This will help you understand why it is so important to store these different types of segments in different tablespaces. First, consider the following question: What makes fragmentation happen? A tablespace gets fragmented when objects stored in the tablespace are truncated or dropped and then re-created (or, for undo segments, when extents the object has acquired are deallocated). The amount of time a segment or extent will stay allocated to a database object is known as its *lifespan*. The more frequently an extent is deallocated, the shorter the extent's lifespan. The shorter the lifespan, the more fragmented your tablespace can become. The SMON background process continuously looks for smaller fragments of free space left over by `truncate` or `drop` operations, and pieces or coalesces them together to create larger chunks of free space.

Now, consider the potential for tablespace fragmentation on different tablespaces. The SYSTEM tablespace houses the system undo segment and the data dictionary. Oracle manages its SYSTEM tablespace effectively, and extents have a long lifespan, so you are likely to see very little or no fragmentation in this tablespace. Your TOOLS tablespace will likely have little fragmentation, because you won't (and shouldn't) typically go into your TOOLS tablespace and manage things yourself—your best bet is to let the administrative tool manage the repository itself. Again, extents have a long lifespan.

The next two tablespaces to consider are DATA and INDEX. The amount of fragmentation that may happen with these tablespaces will depend completely on how often you truncate or drop tables. In your production system, you may never, or hardly ever, do this, so extents will have a long lifespan, and fragmentation may be low. In development, however, you may do this all the time, potentially making extent lifespan very short and fragmentation in the tablespace very high. You are your own best judge for interpreting fragmentation for these tablespaces, which is based on how long or short the extent lifespan is in those systems.

The other two types of tablespaces, UNDOTBS for undo segments and TEMPORARY for temporary segments (you can have more than one tablespace for sorting and temporary segments), will experience high to very high fragmentation. This is true in the UNDOTBS tablespace because undo segments have potentially a very short lifespan, and Oracle can allocate and deallocate extents as necessitated by long-running transactions. In the next chapter, you will learn more about undo segment extent allocation and deallocation. Finally, the lifespan of segments and extents in the TEMPORARY tablespace is incredibly short. Temporary segments are used to handle sort operations (a sort might be caused by issuing a `select  ...  order  by` statement) that manipulate too much data to be stored in memory. Oracle automatically allocates the space when needed. Once the sort operation is finished, Oracle again automatically deallocates the space. Thus, by definition of usage and lifespan, the TEMPORARY tablespace will have the highest amount of fragmentation of any tablespace on your database.

TIP
Extent lifespan and tablespace fragmentation are inversely proportional—the shorter the lifespan, the higher the potential for tablespace fragmentation.

Thus, although the SYSTEM tablespace can store any database object, it is not recommended that you put objects in it other than the dictionary objects and the system undo segment. To avoid problems with your database, you will need to prepare a few other tablespaces to store types of segments. By placing these objects in other databases designed to fit their storage needs, the DBA prevents a number of potential storage problems.

Creating the Necessary Tablespaces for Housing Different Segments

One of your first database activities should be to create separate tablespaces to store tables, indexes, undo segments, temporary segments, and segments associated with database administrative tools such as Oracle Enterprise Manager. The tablespaces necessary for your Oracle database can be created with statements like the following:

```
CREATE TABLESPACE UNDOTBS datafile '/u05/oradata/oracle/undo01.dbf'
SIZE 300M EXTENT MANAGEMENT LOCAL ONLINE;

CREATE TABLESPACE data datafile '/u06/oradata/oracle/data01.dbf'
SIZE 300M EXTENT MANAGEMENT LOCAL ONLINE;

CREATE TABLESPACE index datafile '/u07/oradata/oracle/index01.dbf'
SIZE 300M EXTENT MANAGEMENT LOCAL ONLINE;

CREATE TABLESPACE tools datafile '/u08/oradata/oracle/tools01.dbf'
SIZE 300M EXTENT MANAGEMENT LOCAL ONLINE;

CREATE temporary TABLESPACE temp tempfile '/u09/oradata/oracle/temp01.dbf'
SIZE 300M EXTENT MANAGEMENT LOCAL online;
```

Each of these different types of database objects has its own unique behavior, and sometimes the behavior of one type of object conflicts with another. The section on storage structures and relationships helped you learn more about the various types of segments that exist in Oracle and why it is important to put them in their own tablespaces. When identifying default storage parameters for these tablespaces, you should attempt to set parameters that work well for the type of database object that will be stored in this tablespace, or simply use uniform extent allocation, which is the default allocation type in Oracle9i. You don't need to specify default storage in your `create tablespace` commands in Oracle9i because of this fact. We covered this feature in Chapter 3 and also in the next discussion.

For Review

1. Be sure you can identify the types of segments available for storing database objects.

2. Know that it is important not to store all the segments in your Oracle database inside the SYSTEM tablespace. Oracle9i offers clauses in the `create database` statement such as `default temporary tablespace` and undo tablespace that permit you to create tablespaces specifically for temporary and undo segments when you create your database. This is used to prevent Oracle from dumping these segments into the SYSTEM tablespace, which should be used only to house data dictionary and SYSTEM undo segments.

3. You can also create the different tablespaces you will need for separating different types of segments by using the `create tablespace` command, as we showed by example in the discussion.

4. Be able to distinguish the following types of segments in an Oracle database and describe why they should be stored in their own tablespaces: DATA, INDEX, UNDOTBS, TEMP, and TOOLS.

Exercises

1. **You are configuring your Oracle database to handle different types of segments. Which of the following statements is true regarding the separation of segments and extents?**

A. A segment used for housing different types of data in Oracle is comprised of data blocks, making most types of segments fundamentally the same; thus, they can all be placed in the SYSTEM tablespace to minimize DBA time and effort.

B. A segment used for housing table data will likely be referenced immediately after Oracle accesses the segment housing associated index data; thus, it is desirable to house table and index segments in separate tablespaces.

C. A segment used for housing temporary data can be frequently allocated and deallocated; thus, it should be housed in the same tablespace as that used by volatile table data, but separate from the SYSTEM tablespace.

D. The SYSTEM tablespace is used for housing SYSTEM undo segments, and because all undo segments have the same volatile nature, the SYSTEM tablespace is where you should house all undo segments in the Oracle database.

2. **Examine the following code block:**

```
create database mydb
controlfile reuse
character set US7ASCII
national character set US7ASCII
datafile '/u01/oradata/mydb/mydb01.dbf' size 400M
logfile group 1 ('/u02/oradata/mydb/redo01.log') size 10M,
        group 2 ('/u03/oradata/mydb/redo02.log') size 10M
default temporary tablespace temp
  tempfile '/u04/oradata/mydb/temp01.dbf' size 1024M
undo tablespace undotbs
 datafile '/u05/oradata/mydb/undo01.dbf' size 1024M
noarchivelog;
```

Which of the following choices identifies a tablespace that will not be created by the command shown in the previous code block?

A. SYSTEM

B. UNDOTBS

C. DATA

D. TEMP

3. **You are evaluating the placement of segments in tablespaces for the Oracle database. Which of the following segments has the shortest lifespan?**

A. Temporary segments

B. Undo segments

C. Index segments

D. Data dictionary segments

Answer Key
1. B. 2. C. 3. A.

Controlling the Use of Extents by Segments

Growth in a data segment is generally handled with extents. If the segment runs out of space to handle new record entries for the object, then the object will acquire an extent from the remaining free space in the tablespace. In general, a logical database object such as a table or index can have many extents, but all those extents (plus the original segment) must all be stored in the same tablespace. There are, however, some exceptions. For example, a table containing a column defined as a large object datatype (BLOB, CLOB, NCLOB) can store its nonLOB data in one tablespace while storing LOB data in a different tablespace. However, generally speaking, you should remember that most database objects will have all their extents stored in the same tablespace.

TIP
The fact that all extents for a database object should be stored in the same tablespace shouldn't be taken to mean that all extents for a database object will be stored in the same datafile. For example, a partitioned table may have its partitions or extents spread across datafiles on different disks to improve parallel processing performance. Oracle may also run out of room in one tablespace datafile and thus be forced to allocate an extent in another datafile. This fact is important to remember for OCP.

Uniform Space Allocation in Tablespaces

The default method for managing segment and extent size allocation in your tablespace in Oracle9i is uniform space allocation. To configure this option, you would use the `uniform size n[K|M]` keywords, where n is the size of the extent allocated in KB or MB, in place of `autoallocate`, when you issue the `create tablespace` command. When `uniform size` is specified, Oracle still manages all extent allocation and sizing automatically. The difference is that, when `uniform size` is specified, whatever you defined for n is the size Oracle uses for later extents allocated to the object in the tablespace, regardless of the settings of the other storage settings in the `create table` statement. Let's look at an example of creating a tablespace in which all extents will be sized by Oracle as 10KB:

```
SQL> create tablespace lmtab5 datafile
  2  'c:\oracle\oradata\orcl\lmtab501.dbf'
  3  size 10M reuse
  4  extent management local
  5  uniform size 10K online;
Tablespace created.
```

TIP
When uniform extent allocation is used, Oracle calculates the number of bits to use in the storage allocation bitmap as the number of uniformly sized extents that would fit in the tablespace. Otherwise, the number of bits used for the bitmap is the same as the number of blocks that would fit in the tablespace.

Explicitly Defined Object Storage and Locally Managed Tablespaces

When specified, Oracle always uses the value specified for `uniform size` when sizing extents in locally managed tablespaces. That said, you will see some conflicting information in your dictionary views when it comes to objects placed in locally managed tablespaces with uniform extent management if you explicitly ask for extents to be a different size than what Oracle wants to give you through automatic extent management. To demonstrate what I mean by this remark, let's create a table in the LMTAB5 tablespace:

```
SQL> create table mytab01
  2    (col1 number)
  3    tablespace lmtab5
  4    storage (initial 20K) online;
Table created.
```

Using the previous code in bold, I'm attempting to override the uniform extent management size in LMTAB5 for table MYTAB01 by specifying an initial extent size of 20KB with my own `storage` clause. Remember, Oracle is supposed to create every object in LMTAB5 with an extent size of 10KB. So, of course, Oracle ignored our attempted override of uniform storage management, right? Let's take a look at the DBA_TABLES view to see:

```
SQL> select table_name, initial_extent
  2  from dba_tables
  3  where table_name = 'MYTAB01';
TABLE_NAME INITIAL_EXTENT
---------- --------------
MYTAB01             20480
```

Wait a minute, I hear you say. Oracle's supposed to make the initial extent 10KB. So, why is DBA_TABLES telling us the initial extent is 20KB? This is strange behavior indeed. What's more, the same thing seems to happen when we use the `alter table allocate extent` command as well. Take a look:

```
SQL> alter table mytab01 allocate extent (size 30K);
Table altered.
SQL> select table_name, initial_extent, next_extent
  2  from dba_tables
  3  where table_name = 'MYTAB01';
TABLE_NAME INITIAL_EXTENT NEXT_EXTENT
---------- -------------- -----------
MYTAB01             20480       30720
```

Does this mean that Oracle's uniform extent management feature can be overridden by use of a `storage` clause when creating the table or by explicitly allocating extents of a larger size than that permitted by uniform extent management. No, not really. Take a look at the DBA_EXTENTS view to get a picture of what's really going on here:

```
SQL> select segment_name, extent_id, bytes
  2  from dba_extents
  3  where segment_name = 'MYTAB01';
SEGMENT_NA EXTENT_ID   BYTES
---------- ---------  -------
MYTAB01            0    10240
MYTAB01            1    10240
MYTAB01            2    10240
MYTAB01            3    10240
MYTAB01            4    10240
5 rows selected.
```

So, in reality, the data dictionary satisfies both your specified space allocation in the `storage` clause and in the `allocate extent` clause as well as its own rules about uniform extent sizes by simply allocating more extents of the same size. What do you think Oracle would do if we asked it to allocate an extent of 15KB in this context? Well, Oracle would simply allocate more space than you asked for by grabbing two more extents of 10KB each.

Extent Allocation in Dictionary-Managed Tablespaces

When you create a database object in a dictionary-managed tablespace, Oracle allocates it a single initial segment in the tablespace unless you specify otherwise, based on the database object's `storage` clause parameters if there are any. If the object creation command lacked a `storage` clause, then Oracle uses the `default storage` clause settings for the tablespace you place your object in. Usually, the object is initially created with only one segment of space allocated. As new rows are added to tables, the space of the segment is used to store that new data. When the segment storing the table data is full and more data must be added to the table, the table must allocate another extent to store that data in. Figure 13-1 illustrates an extent being acquired on an Oracle database.

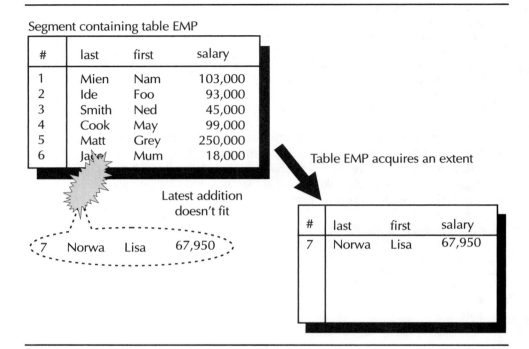

Segment containing table EMP

Table EMP acquires an extent

Latest addition doesn't fit

FIGURE 13-1. *Acquiring extents*

A new extent will be acquired for a database object only if there is no room in any of the object's current segments or extents for the new data. Once acquired, an extent will only be relinquished if the DBA truncates or drops and re-creates the table.

Acquiring Extents in Dictionary-Managed Tablespaces: An Example

The size of an acquired extent is based on the value specified for the next parameter inside the storage clause provided in the object creation clause. If the object is acquiring its third or greater extent, the size of the extent will equal next multiplied by pctincrease. This concept is a little tricky, so let's take a look at what we mean. Let's say you create a table called EMPLOYEE with the following command:

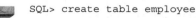

```
SQL> create table employee
  2  (empid number primary key,
  3   name varchar2(20),
```

```
   4   salary number)
   5   storage (initial 100K next 2K pctincrease 25
   6   minextents 1 maxextents 100)
   7   tablespace DATA;
Table created.
```

TIP

You'll learn more about table storage *clauses in the next chapter.*

Once you issue this command, Oracle immediately allocates a single segment 100KB in size inside the DATA tablespace. We don't know which datafile Oracle will place the segment into, just that it will be a datafile associated with the DATA tablespace. We know the initial segment will be 100KB in size because that's the value specified for the initial setting inside the storage clause. Now, let's pretend that a user adds several employees to the table, filling that initial segment. The initial segment is now full, so the next user who comes along to add an employee to the table will force Oracle to allocate another extent to the EMPLOYEE table. This extent will be allocated inside the DATA tablespace and will be 2KB in size. Again, we know the second extent will be 2KB in size because the next setting in the storage clause tells us so.

If you want to specify a different size for that next extent, you should issue the alter table storage (next *nextval*) statement before that next extent gets allocated, where *nextval* is the size of the next extent (in KB or MB). Oracle applies the value you specify for this setting to the next extent it acquires. The following statement gives an example:

```
SQL> ALTER TABLE employee STORAGE (NEXT 100K);
Table altered.
```

TIP

You'll learn more about altering table definitions in the next chapter.

Now, instead of allocating only 2KB for the next extent, Oracle allocates 100KB, so that the next extent is as big as the first one. Let's move on by pretending that the second user adds several employees such that the second extent is now full. What happens next? Well, Oracle has to do some calculating to determine how large to make the third extent. How do we know? We know because a value greater than zero was specified for the pctincrease setting. Whenever this happens, Oracle multiplies the value you specified for next in the storage clause by the percentage increase specified. Thus, because we specified 25 for the pctincrease setting and 100KB for `next` in our `storage` clause, Oracle will allocate 100KB×1.25, or 125KB, for the third extent.

Whenever Oracle allocates a new extent for an object where `pctincrease` is greater than zero, Oracle recalculates the value for `next` that is stored in the data dictionary record associated with this object. This could be dangerous because the size of subsequent extents allocated will increase exponentially. To understand what we mean by this, consider what will happen when Oracle allocates the fourth extent for the EMPLOYEE table. The size of the third extent was 125KB, so Oracle bases the size of the fourth extent on the size of the third extent, increased by the value specified for `pctincrease`. In other words, Oracle allocates 100KB×1.25×1.25, or 156.25KB, of space for the fourth extent. So you see, setting `pctincrease` to a value greater than zero is meant to slow down the extent allocation process for growing database objects by allocating progressively more space each time a new extent is required.

TIP
If you don't want your database objects to grow exponentially, set `pctincrease` *to zero in the* `storage` *clause when you first create the object. That way, all extents allocated will be the same size as the value you specified for* `next`.

Extents and Parallel Processing

If you don't use parallel processing on your Oracle database, you will get the best performance from a database object, such as a table or index, if all the data for that object is housed in only one segment or in a set of contiguous blocks. This is especially true when you use dictionary-managed tablespaces to house Oracle data and less true when when you use locally managed tablespaces to house Oracle data.

However, when you use parallel processing, you'll want your data stored in multiple extents (preferably spread across several disks), so that parallel processes accessing the same table won't contend with each other. If you use partitioned tables and the parallel query option, obviously you'll want to have as many different segments for your table as there are parallel I/O slave processes utilized by Oracle to search that table. Furthermore, certain trade-offs exist in deciding how much space to allocate, particularly for tables you know will grow quickly.

The Preallocation Balancing Act

Recall that in the `storage` clause defined for the EMPLOYEE table we created previously, we defined two other settings for this table. They were `minextents`, the number of extents Oracle allocates to the table when it's first created, and `maxextents`, the maximum number of extents Oracle will ever allocate for that object. Once Oracle has allocated the maximum number of extents you identified via the `maxextents` setting, that's it—the table cannot grow any larger (unless you change the value for `maxextents`, of course!).

Many inexperienced DBAs fall prey to the trap of preallocation. They want to preallocate as much space as possible to avoid problems later with hitting the limit set by `maxextents`. Sometimes that's a good thing—especially if you believe that users are going to fill the object with data quickly or if you need to keep all the data in one segment. However, there are a couple of drawbacks to be aware of. First, the host machine has limited space. Second, and more importantly, your database could suffer from poor backup performance because of the excessive time required to compress a tablespace containing mostly empty segments for storage on tape. A third drawback is also evident sometimes. If the tablespace has vast wastelands of empty segment space, then tables are placed far away from one another on disk. This could cause your database to experience the poor performance seen on databases with huge tables, even though your tables are mostly empty. On the other hand, don't fall victim to the miserly approach to storage allocation either. Every additional extent your database object has to allocate to store its information contributes to poorer performance on data queries and changes, although this problem is attributed mainly to the use of dictionary-managed tablespace and can be solved usually through the use of locally managed tablespaces. The trick, then, is to balance the following considerations:

- Using locally managed tablespaces instead of dictionary-managed tablespaces

- Leaving a generous percentage of additional space, both in the tablespace and the object's initial segment, to accommodate growth

- Planning disk purchases for the host machine or leaving extra space to add new tablespaces and datafiles in order to alleviate a space crunch

- If possible, setting up a monthly or quarterly maintenance schedule with your users so that you can have some downtime to reorganize your tablespaces to avert those potential sizing issues before they become headaches

For Review

1. Extents are allocated whenever a database object runs out of space for incoming data.

2. The size of an extent allocated depends on the storage settings defined when the object was created. This information comes either from the

`storage` clause in the object creation statement or from the `default` `storage` clause present on the tablespace the object is stored in.

3. Understand the use of uniform extent allocations in Oracle9i. Remember that uniform extent management is the default for locally managed temporary tablespaces, whereas automatic allocation is the default for locally managed permanent tablespaces.

4. Know what the `initial`, `next`, and `pctincrease` settings mean in the context of segments in dictionary-managed tablespaces. Pay particular attention to the exponential growth factor present whenever `pctincrease` is set to a value greater than zero.

5. Understand the balancing act required when considering how large to make your segments and extents. Too much preallocation leads to wasted space, whereas too little leads to too many extents. It's a tightrope that ultimately every DBA walks, and the right answer often depends on the needs of a particular system. For OCP, understand how to define these parameters, while for real life, you'll need a lot of experience with a particular system (or a lot of meetings with users to figure out how quickly they add data) before the numbers start seeming intuitive.

Exercises

1. **You create a locally managed tablespace with the following statement:**

```
SQL> create tablespace DATA datafile
  2    'c:\oracle\oradata\orcl\DATA01.dbf'
  3    size 150M reuse
  4    extent management local
  5    uniform size 500K online;
Tablespace created.
```

   After creating the tablespace, you create a table with the `initial` set to 100KB and `minextents` set to 3 in the `storage` clause. After the table is created, how much space will the table occupy in the tablespace?

   A. 100KB

   B. 300KB

   C. 500KB

   D. 1,500KB

2. **You want to create a locally managed tablespace for housing sort segments in Oracle. Which of the following statements would be appropriate for the purpose with respect to allocation of segments and extents?**

A. create temporary tablespace temp01 datafile
'/u01/oradata/orcl/temp01.dbf' size 100M extent
management local;

B. create temporary tablespace temp01 tempfile
'/u01/oradata/orcl/temp01.dbf' size 100M extent
management local;

C. create tablespace temp01 datafile
'/u01/oradata/orcl/temp01.dbf' size 100M extent
management local temporary;

D. create tablespace temp01 tempfile
'/u01/oradata/orcl/temp01.dbf' size 100M extent
management local temporary;

3. **You define a locally managed tablespace using the following syntax:**

```
SQL> create tablespace DATA datafile
  2   'c:\oracle\oradata\orcl\DATA01.dbf'
  3   size 150M reuse
  4   extent management local online;
Tablespace created.
```

**Which of the following choices indicates the storage allocation clause left
out but implied by Oracle when this tablespace was created?**

A. autoallocate

B. autoallocate size 1M

C. uniform

D. uniform size 1M

4. **You create a table with the following command:**

```
SQL> create table tester
  2   (col1 varchar2 primary key)
  3   tablespace testdata
  4   storage (initial 50M next 100M pctincrease 20
  5   minextents 1 maxextents 200);
```

**Which of the following choices indicates how large the fifth extent Oracle
allocates will be?**

A. 120MB

B. 144MB

C. 173MB

D. 207MB

5. A table was just created on your Oracle database with six extents allocated to it. Which of the following factors most likely caused the table to have so many extents allocated?

A. The value for `minextents` setting.

B. The value for `pctincrease` setting.

C. The value for `maxextents` setting.

D. By default, Oracle allocates six extents to all database objects.

Answer Key

1. D. This is because `minextents` tells Oracle to allocate three extents, and Oracle uses uniform storage allocation to determine how large to make the extents. 2. B. 3. A. 4. C. 5. A.

Using Block Space Utilization Parameters

In addition to overall storage allocation for extents on objects in the database, Oracle enables you to manage how the objects use the space inside each data block they are given. Space usage is determined at the block level with the `pctfree` and `pctused` options. By controlling space allocation at the block level, you can manage how a database object utilizes the space allocated to it more effectively according to the type of data change activity the object is likely to be subjected to. Database objects are subjected to data changes in different ways by different applications: for example, a database that supports high online transaction-processing (OLTP) activity where later data changes expand the size of existing rows by populating columns initially set to NULL when the row was added to the table need space preallocated at the block level to let the row grow. In contrast, a decision support system (DSS) such as a data warehouse will likely not see its data changed once rows are loaded for query access. In this case, you'll want to pack as much data into every block allocated to a row as possible.

Why do DBAs manage space allocation at the block level? Because the objects themselves are utilized differently by different application data manipulation language (DML) activities. For example, if a table experiences a high `update` activity that increases the size of rows in the table, the block space allocation for that database object should allow for additional growth per row. If data change activity on the object consists of a lot of `insert` statements entering rows mostly the same size, then the space usage goal within each block should be to place as many rows as possible into each block before allocating another one. This same approach may work if a table's size is static and rows are infrequently added to the table.

Leaving Extra Space for Row Growth: pctfree

The pctfree clause is specified at the database object level. It tells Oracle how much free space to leave in a block when that block initially gets populated with row data. This leftover space remains free in each block to accommodate the growth of existing rows in the block. For example, if a table has pctfree specified to be 10 percent, Oracle will stop adding new rows to the block when there is 10 percent free space left over in the block. That remaining space is used by existing rows when users set NULL columns to a non-NULL value.

You should use the following general approach when deciding how to set pctfree. If rows added to a table will be updated often and each update will add to the size in bytes of the row, then set pctfree to a high value. You'll see some examples of values that are considered high for pctfree in a moment. For now, understand that setting pctfree high prevents performance killers such as row migration (where Oracle moves an entire row to another block because the original block doesn't have the room to store it anymore). Conversely, if the rows in the block will not be updated frequently, or if the updates that will occur will not affect the size of each row, set the value for pctfree low on that database object.

TIP

A high value for pctfree is about 20 to 25, which means that 20 or 25 percent of space in a block is left free for later updates that might increase the size of an existing row in the block. Conversely, a low value for pctfree would be 4 or 5, which you might use for static or read-only tables.

Ongoing Management of Free Space in Blocks: pctused

The other option for managing free space in blocks is pctused. It is also defined at the database object level. The pctused option specifies the percent usage threshold by which Oracle will determine if it is acceptable to add new rows to a block. To understand what we mean, consider the situation where data is added to a table. As new rows are added, Oracle fills the block with inserted rows until reaching the cutoff set by pctfree. Later, as data is deleted from the table, that table's space utilization at the block level falls. When the space used in a data block falls below the threshold limit set by pctused, Oracle adds the block to a *freelist* maintained for that table. A freelist is a list of data blocks that are currently accepting new data rows.

When setting `pctused`, be mindful that Oracle incurs some performance overhead by marking a block free and adding it to a freelist for that database object. Thus, there is a trade-off inherent in specifying `pctused` that you should understand for OCP and beyond. You must temper your interest in managing space freed by row removal as efficiently as possible against that overhead incurred by each block. To prevent the block from making its way to the freelist when only one or two rows can even be added to the block, you should set the `pctused` option relatively low.

TIP

Unless you're really concerned about managing free space actively, don't set `pctused` higher than 40 or 50. A situation where you might be concerned about managing free space actively would be when you have very little free space on the disks in your host system.

Setting Actual Values for `pctfree` and `pctused`

These two options are defined at the database object level, and the values assigned must always be considered in tandem. You can specify a value for each option between 0 and 100. However, when determining values for `pctfree` and `pctused`, do not assign values for these space utilization options that exceed 100 when added together. In fact, you should not set values for these options that even approach 90, because this causes Oracle to spend more time managing space utilization than is necessary. The following bullets identify some values for `pctfree` and `pctused` that would likely be considered appropriate. Following each value is a description of the scenario in Oracle where this setting might be appropriate, along with an indication of whether this is considered a high or low value for either option:

- **`pctfree 5, pctused 40`**   Good for static or read-only tables, such as those loaded periodically for data warehouse and/or query-only applications

- **`pctfree 10, pctused 40`**   Good for all-around OLTP situations especially when existing rows won't be increased by update activity after the row is inserted

- **`pctfree 20, pctused 40`**   Good for OLTP activity where existing rows will be increased by updates after the row is inserted (20 is a high value for `pctfree`)

Setting `pctfree` and `pctused`: An Example

You'll learn more about storage options for creating database objects in later chapters. For now, to give you the opportunity to see `pctfree` and `pctused` in action, the following code block contains a `create table` statement with `pctfree` and `pctused` specified. Notice that these clauses are not defined as part of the `storage` clause—they are their own clauses in a `create table` command:

```
SQL> CREATE TABLE FAMILY
  2  ( NAME VARCHAR2(10) primary key,
  3    RELATIONSHIP VARCHAR2(10))
  4  storage (initial 100K next 100K
  5           pctincrease 0 minextents 1 maxextents 200)
  6  PCTFREE 20 PCTUSED 40;
Table created.
```

For Review

1. Understand the use of `pctfree` and `pctused` with respect to space management in a table.

2. The `pctfree` option tells Oracle how much space should be left over when new rows are added to a block in order to leave room for growth in existing rows.

3. The `pctused` option tells Oracle the space usage threshold below which Oracle should place a block on the table's freelist so new rows can be added to that block.

4. The values for these options are set in tandem when the database object is created, so that they never add up to a value close to 100.

Exercises

1. **User CAROLYN issues some statements in her SQL*Plus session against an Oracle database with a 4KB block size. The transcript from her session is shown in the following block:**

```
SQL> describe records
 Name                                    Null?    Type
 --------------------------------- -------- -----------
 RECORDNO                          NOT NULL NUMBER(4)
 RECNAME                                    VARCHAR2(10)
 RECDESC                                    VARCHAR2(4000)
 RECDATE                                    DATE
SQL> insert into records (recordno) values (1000);
```

```
1 row inserted.
SQL> select vsize(*) from records where recordno = 100;
VSIZE(*)
--------
      12
```

Later, another user populates the description for this record, which consists of a 100-word block of text. When Carolyn issues the `select vsize(*)` statement shown previously again, Oracle returns a value of 3,215. Which of the following choices identifies appropriate settings for `pctfree` and `pctused`?

- **A.** pctfree 5, pctused 80
- **B.** pctfree 10, pctused 50
- **C.** pctfree 15, pctused 20
- **D.** pctfree 80, pctused 5

2. You are configuring block space utilization on an Oracle table. Which of the following choices identifies block space utilization settings that are never appropriate under any circumstances?

- **A.** pctfree 5, pctused 90
- **B.** pctfree 15, pctused 80
- **C.** pctfree 20, pctused 70
- **D.** pctfree 10, pctused 40

Answer Key
1. D. **2.** B.

Obtaining Information about Storage Structures

You can determine storage information for database objects from many sources in the data dictionary. There are several data dictionary views associated with tracking information about structures for storage in the database, such as tablespaces, extents, and segments. In addition, there are dictionary views for the database objects that offer information about space utilization settings. The names of dictionary views are usually taken from the objects represented by the data in the dictionary view, preceded by classification on the scope of the data. Each segment has its own data dictionary view that displays the storage information. Assuming that you want to know the storage parameters set for all objects on the database, you may use the following views to determine storage information for the segment types already discussed:

- **DBA_SEGMENTS** This summary view contains all types of segments listed by the data dictionary views and their storage parameters.

- **DBA_TABLESPACES** You can use this view to see the default storage settings for the tablespaces in the database.

- **DBA_TS_QUOTAS** You can use this view to identify the tablespace quotas assigned for users to create objects in their default and temporary tablespaces.

- **V$TABLESPACE** This gives a simple listing of the tablespace number and name.

- **DBA_EXTENTS** You use this view to see the segment name, type, owner, name of tablespace storing the extent, ID for the extent, file ID storing the extent, starting block ID of the extent, total bytes, and blocks of the extent.

- **DBA_FREE_SPACE** This view identifies the location and amount of free space by tablespace name, file ID, starting block ID, bytes, and blocks.

- **DBA_FREE_SPACE_COALESCED** This view identifies the location of free space in a tablespace that has been coalesced by tablespace name, total extents, extents coalesced, and the percent of extents that are coalesced, as well as other information about the space in the tablespace that SMON has coalesced.

- **DBA_DATA_FILES** This view gives information about datafiles for every tablespace.

- **V$DATAFILE** This view gives information about datafiles for every tablespace.

TIP
Coalescing is the act of putting small chunks of free space in a tablespace, that are contiguous, and merging them into larger chunks of free space. The SMON process takes care of coalescing the tablespace on a regular basis. If you want to take care of coalescing the tablespace yourself, issue the `alter tablespace` *tblspc* `coalesce` *command. Also, when using locally managed tablespaces free space is monitored in datafile header bitmaps, so SMON doesn't need to coalesce.*

For Review

Know the different views in the data dictionary that give you information about storage.

Exercises

1. You need to find information about the total amount of space that has been allocated to a table in Oracle. Which of the following choices identifies a view you would look in?

   A. DBA_OBJECTS

   B. DBA_SEGMENTS

   C. DBA_EXTENTS

   D. DBA_FREE_SPACE_COALESCED

2. You want to determine the amount of space that has been allocated to the EMP table owned by SCOTT in Oracle, stored in tablespace DATA. Which of the following choices identifies the SQL statement you might use for this purpose?

   A. `select blocks from dba_tables where table_name = 'EMP' and owner = 'SCOTT';`

   B. `select sum(bytes) from dba_free_space where tablespace_name = 'DATA';`

   C. `select sum(bytes) from dba_extents where segment_name = 'EMP' and owner = 'SCOTT';`

   D. `select * from dba_objects where object_name = 'EMP' and owner = 'SCOTT';`

3. You want to identify the space utilization settings for tables owned by SMITHERS in Oracle. Which of the following SQL statements would be useful for this purpose?

   A. `select * from dba_objects where owner = 'SMITHERS';`

   B. `select * from dba_segments where owner = 'SMITHERS';`

   C. `select * from dba_extents where owner = 'SMITHERS';`

   D. `select * from dba_indexes where owner = 'SMITHERS';`

Answer Key

1. C. **2.** C. **3.** B.

Managing Undo Data

Oracle**9i**
and higher
 In this section, you will cover the following topics related to management of undo segments in Oracle9i:

- The purpose of undo segments

- Implementing automatic undo management

- Creating and configuring undo segments

- Dictionary views for undo data

Experienced Oracle DBAs may be familiar with the term "undo" in its prior form —rollback. Rollback segments have existed in Oracle for a long time as a resource that DBAs had to manage actively and manually. In Oracle9i, the database makes management of rollback segments much simpler than a mere name change might suggest. In addition to renaming rollback segments undo segments, Oracle9i offers several options for the simplified management of these occasionally problematic resources. This section will define the purpose of undo segments and the data they contain. It will also introduce you to implementing automatic undo segment management in Oracle9i. You will learn how to create and configure undo segments as well. Finally, you will cover where to look in the Oracle data dictionary for information about your undo segments.

TIP

If you're an experienced Oracle DBA and you're having trouble with the concept of undo segments, just substitute undo for rollback and you'll know exactly the role these objects handle!

The Purpose of Undo Segments

Often, the DBA spends part of any given day "fighting fires." Many times, these fires involve a group of database objects that in prior versions of the Oracle database were called rollback segments. In Oracle9i, these objects are referred to as undo segments. Undo segments store the old data value when a process is making changes to the data in a database. The undo segment stores data and block information, such as file and block IDs, for data from a table or index as that block existed before being modified. This copy of data changes made to the database is available to other users running queries until the user making changes `commits` his or her transaction. The undo segment stores the changes after the `commit` as well, but Oracle will eventually and systematically overwrite the data in an undo segment from committed transactions whenever a user process initiates a new transaction and therefore needs room in the undo segment to store data for its uncommitted changes. Undo segments serve three purposes:

- They provide transaction-level read consistency of data to all users in the database.

- They permit users to roll back, or discard, changes that have been made in a transaction in favor of the original version of that data.

- They provide transaction recovery in case the instance fails while a user is making a data change.

Undo segments are probably the most useful database objects in data processing, but they can be troublesome for DBAs to maintain. In prior versions of Oracle, you had to master the management of these fussy objects very quickly if you were going to survive as a DBA for long. However, Oracle9i has simplified administrative tasks related to undo segments greatly by automating many of the aspects of their management.

The contents of an undo segment are manifold. Each undo segment contains a table in the segment header. This table lists the transactions and users currently using this undo segment to store data changes for the purpose of read-consistency. Each undo segment also has several extents allocated to it. The extents store original versions of data from tables and indexes. Whenever a user issues an `update` or `delete` statement in Oracle, the server process writes the original version of the data being changed or removed to the undo segment. Later, if the user decides to roll back his or her transaction, Oracle can easily copy the old version of the data in the undo segment back into its proper place. Or, if the user decides to `commit` his or her transaction, Oracle simply leaves the original data in the undo segment. Later, the space in the undo segment can be reused for storing original data for another transaction that is needed by another user.

TIP
A new feature in Oracle9i called Flashback Query uses undo data stored in an undo segment to permit users to view data as it existed in the database at some point in the past.

Designing and administering undo segments manually is one of the most challenging tasks for DBAs. If the undo segments were not properly designed, users would experience the dreaded ORA-15555: Snapshot too old (rollback segment too small) error. This error message is misleading. This error could be caused not just due to small rollback segmetn but due to many other reasons. If this problem is not taken care you may face a situation where a batch process running for many hours had to be rerun just because it fails in the middle due to this error.

In order to understand and solve this problem one has to understand how Oracle supports read consistency. In a multi-user environment many transactions are writing or modifying rows. Before a transaction commits the changes it made, the changed data is visible to all statements within this transaction that is making the changes but not to other statements or transactions. Once committed the changes are visible to all subsequence transactions. Statements that began prior to the commit will continue to show the old data because those changes were not present at the start of this transaction. This is called Read Consistency.

How is this made possible by Oracle? We will consider two transactions - the changing transaction that is making the changes in the table and reading transaction that is reading the data that is being changed by changing transaction. As discussed before the changing transaction keeps the before-image of the data being changed in an undo segment. The reading transaction that started before the changing transaction committed the changes will read the before-image of the data from the undo segment. Once the changing transaction commits, the undo segments containing the before-image are marked free and can be used by any transaction or could be cleaned up due to shrinking of undo segment. If the reading transaction continues to exist and comes back to read the before-image data from the undo segment and finds it missing, it returns the 'ORA-1555' error message and rolls back all the changes it made since it started. This could be quite a disruption if this transaction was a long running one.

So what causes this to happen? It could be many reasons. It could be caused due to inadequate number of undo segments or inadequately sized undo segments or data buffer cache being too small or large and small transactions using the same undo segments or improperly sized optimal parameter (that could be shrinking too often) or sometimes committing too often in a transaction. One sure way of preventing this is making sure the undo tablespace is large enough, preventing too many shrinks (set larger Optimal value) and making sure the buffer cache has a high hit ratio. Oracle9i helps you prevent this situation by allowing you to specify how long to retain undo data after it is committed. The parameter is UNDO_RETENTION.

Oracle9i administers undo data in two ways—automatic undo management and manual undo management. For the purpose of passing the OCP DBA Fundamentals I exam, we'll look at how to implement both automatic undo management and manual management of undo segments. If you're an experienced DBA, rest assured —Oracle hasn't taken away your ability to configure undo segments manually.

Manual configuration of undo segments is still available in Oracle9i for backward compatibility. The OCP DBA Fundamentals Exam I may or may not test manual management of undo segments, so this book will cover how to manage undo segments automatically as well as manually.

For Review

1. Be sure you can define the threefold purpose of an undo segment in Oracle, including the usage of undo segments for read consistency, transaction recovery, and instance recovery.

2. Know the causes of the Snapshot too old error in Oracle.

Exercises

1. **You are administering the Oracle database. A user approaches you to inform you that he has just received the ORA-1555 error. Which of the following choices describes the reason this user has received the error?**

   A. The user remained connected overnight, and his connection has timed out.

   B. The user has queried a read-inconsistent view of data in the process of being changed by a long-running transaction.

   C. The OPTIMAL value of the undo segments is very small.

   D. The user's `drop table` command took too long, and the database needs time to acquiesce.

2. **A user is executing a transaction in an Oracle database. Which of the following choices correctly identifies all the statements that will generate undo information within the transaction?**

   A. `delete` statements only

   B. `insert` statements only

   C. `update` and `insert` statements only

   D. `delete` and `update` statements only

   E. `delete`, `insert`, and `update` statements only

Answer Key

1. C. 2. E.

Implementing Automatic Undo Management

Oracle**9i** and higher | Implementing automatic undo management is by far the easiest way to configure the management of undo segments in an Oracle database, especially for less-experienced DBAs. It is quick and easy, and it pushes the dirty work back on Oracle. Even if you're an experienced DBA, automatic undo management could be a good option to reduce the time you spend on mundane administrative tasks. This is because automatic undo management enables you to focus your attention on more interesting aspects of your work like strategic planning for data growth or architecture of new database systems just coming online. In addition, automatic undo management works well in Oracle systems that aren't transaction intensive, such as development or testing environments. Configuration and deployment of automatic undo management consists of three important steps:

1. You define an undo tablespace that Oracle can use for allocation and deallocation of undo segments.

2. You instruct Oracle to run in automatic undo management mode.

3. You instruct Oracle how long it should retain undo information in undo segments.

Step 1: Creating and Configuring Undo Segments

In order to use automatic undo management in an Oracle9i database, you must first create an undo tablespace. The undo tablespace houses undo segments, and it can be created in two different ways. You can create it when you create the database. The following code block shows an example of how to create an undo tablespace automatically during database creation in a Windows environment:

```
CREATE DATABASE DB1
CONTROLFILE REUSE
LOGFILE GROUP 1 ('C:\Oracle\oradata\DB1\redo01.log') SIZE 100K,
        GROUP 2 ('C:\Oracle\oradata\DB1\redo02.log') SIZE 100K,
        GROUP 3 ('C:\Oracle\oradata\DB1\redo03.log') SIZE 100K;
DATAFILE 'C:\Oracle\oradata\DB1\system01.dbf'
   SIZE 100M REUSE AUTOEXTEND ON NEXT 10240K MAXSIZE UNLIMITED
UNDO TABLESPACE UNDOTBS
   DATAFILE 'C:\Oracle\oradata\DB1\undotbs01.dbf'
   SIZE 50M REUSE AUTOEXTEND ON NEXT  5120K MAXSIZE UNLIMITED
NOARCHIVELOG
CHARACTER SET US7ASCII
;
```

Or, you can create the undo tablespace manually with the `create tablespace` command, as shown in the following code block:

```
SQL> CREATE UNDO TABLESPACE undotbs_2
  2  DATAFILE 'c:\oracle\oradata\DB1\undotbs2.dbf' SIZE 1M;
Tablespace created.
```

Step 2: Instruct Oracle to Run in Automatic Undo Management Mode

This step is accomplished by setting the UNDO_MANAGEMENT initialization parameter in your `init.ora` file. This parameter has two settings: MANUAL and AUTO. When set to MANUAL (this is the default setting when the UNDO_MANAGEMENT parameter isn't present in the `init.ora` file), then Oracle will permit you to manage undo segments manually, as you would have managed rollback segments in versions of Oracle prior to Oracle9i. To place the Oracle database into automatic undo management node, you set UNDO_MANAGEMENT to AUTO in the `init.ora` file, as shown in the following block:

```
UNDO_MANAGEMENT = AUTO
```

When a database is defined to run in automatic undo management mode, you have to have at least one undo tablespace created and online. If you have more than one undo tablespace in the tablespace, Oracle will use only one of them. You can explicitly specify which one to use by specifying it in the `init.ora` parameter UNDO_TABLESPACE.

```
UNDO_TABLESPACE = undotbs
```

This parameter can also be dynamically altered using the following command:

```
ALTER SYSTEM SET undo_tablespace = UNDOTBS;
```

Finally, a caveat: If you specify automatic undo management but provide no undo tablespace for Oracle to use, Oracle will not let your database start. So, for example, if you set UNDO_MANAGEMENT to AUTO but set UNDO_TABLESPACE to a tablespace that does not exist, then Oracle will issue the ORA-01092 error when you attempt to start up and open the database. The solution to this issue is to set the UNDO_TABLESPACE parameter to a valid undo tablespace in your database. Note, however, that if you actually have an undo tablespace available and have set UNDO_TABLESPACE to that tablespace at any point when the database was running before, Oracle will keep track of the setting for that parameter using the SPFILE feature. That way, if you simply omitted the UNDO_TABLESPACE parameter setting in `init.ora`, Oracle will still run normally. It is only when you incorrectly instruct Oracle to use an invalid tablespace that you will encounter this problem.

TIP
If you choose not to use automatic undo management, then you should ensure that you set the ROLLBACK_SEGMENTS parameter to bring named undo segments when the database starts. Otherwise, Oracle will only have the SYSTEM *undo segment in the* SYSTEM *tablespace online at database startup.*

Step 3: Instructing Oracle How Long to Retain Undo Data

One significant improvement with Oracle9i undo segments is the ability to retain prechange data in the undo segments for a specific period of time. This functionality works in conjunction with a new feature in Oracle9i called Flashback Query, which enables you to view old versions of your data after changes are committed for a specified period of time. With automatic undo management, you could specify how long you want to retain the committed undo information. The number of seconds to retain this data is specified in the `init.ora` parameter UNDO_RETENTION. This can also be dynamically changed using the `alter system set undo_retention = `*n* command, where *n* is the number in seconds that Oracle9i will retain the prechange original copy of data in an undo segment for Flashback Query. The default value for this parameter is 900.

Administering Undo Tablespaces

Even though undo data is a new concept in Oracle9i, the management of undo tablespace is same as any other tablespace. The undo tablespace can be altered using the `alter tablespace` command to add datafiles, rename datafiles, bring a datafile online, offline, or in backup mode. For full syntax of these actions, refer to the previous chapter on tablespaces and datafiles. Similarly, the `alter database` command can also be used to resize undo datafiles. An undo tablespace can also be dropped using a `drop tablespace` command but with a main restriction. An undo tablespace cannot be dropped while active transactions are using undo segments in it. This restriction is similar to the restriction on tablespaces containing active undo segments created manually. The following code block illustrates this:

```
SQL> drop tablespace undotbs_2;
drop tablespace undotbs_2
*
ERROR at line 1:ORA-30013: undo tablespace 'UNDOTBS_2' is currently in use
```

Oracle supports multiple undo tablespaces, but only one is used per instance. However, Oracle does let you switch from one undo tablespace to the other dynamically while the database is online and available to users. The following code block shows how this could be done. In this case, we move from using one undo tablespace to another in order to drop the other undo tablespace:

```
SQL> ALTER SYSTEM SET UNDO_TABLESPACE=undotbs;
System altered.
SQL> DROP TABLESPACE undotbs_2;
Tablespace dropped.
```

Creating the Undo Segments Themselves

If you're an experienced DBA, you might be asking yourself the question, "OK, so now I know how to create the undo tablespace, but how do I create the undo segments in Oracle9i?" The answer is, you don't. Oracle creates and manages all undo segments for you automatically as soon as the undo tablespace is created. Thus, when automatic undo management is enabled, you do not need to ensure that the undo segments are created or that they are online, the way you had to in earlier versions of Oracle. However, you can still manage undo segments manually if you like. The next discussion will cover how this is done. The OCP DBA Fundamentals I exam may or may not test manual management of undo segments, but it will definitely test automatic management of undo segments. Be sure you understand the fundamental difference in how undo segments are managed for Oracle9i, especially if you already have hands-on experience with the Oracle database from prior versions.

For Review

1. For automatic undo management, you must first create undo tablespaces in Oracle. Undo tablespaces can be created using the create undo tablespace command or by including the undo tablespace clause in the create database command.

2. Undo tablespaces can be altered using the alter tablespace or alter database commands to add datafiles, rename data files, and bring a datafile online, offline, or in backup mode. Undo tablespaces can also be dropped provided no active transactions are in them using the drop tablespace command.

3. To configure Oracle9i to run in automatic undo management mode, you must set the parameter UNDO_MANAGEMENT to AUTO in the init.ora file.

4. You can have more than one undo tablespace in your database, but only one will be used at a time per instance. If you have more than one undo tablespace, then the one to be used by the instance can be specified in the parameter UNDO_TABLESPACE. If you forget to set this parameter in your

`init.ora` file, it is still possible that Oracle will bring the correct undo tablespace online for you via the SPFILE feature in Oracle9i.

5. You also specify how long undo data should be kept available for Flashback Query by setting the UNDO_RETENTION initialization parameter.

6. Once the undo tablespace is created and automatic undo management is enabled, you do not have to actually create the undo segments themselves. Oracle9i creates them for you as soon as the undo tablespace is created. Moreover, Oracle brings the undo segments online automatically when the database starts.

Exercises

1. **You are configuring automatic undo management on your Oracle database. Which of the following choices indicates what you must do to handle the situation where more than one undo tablespace is available for storage of undo segments?**

   A. Set UNDO_MANAGEMENT to MANUAL in the `init.ora` file.

   B. Set UNDO_MANAGEMENT to AUTO in the `init.ora` file.

   C. Set UNDO_TABLESPACE to one of the tablespaces in the `init.ora` file.

   D. Set UNDO_TABLESPACE to both of the tablespaces in the `init.ora` file.

2. **The Oracle database with undo tablespaces UNDO_TBS1 and UNDO_TBS2 was opened with automatic undo management enabled for this database. In a prior session, the `alter system set undo_tablespace = UNDO_TBS1` command was issued. However, the appropriate parameter instructing Oracle as to which undo tablespace to use was omitted from `init.ora`. Which of the following choices correctly describes what happens when the first user connecting to Oracle initiates her first transaction?**

   A. The database will open, but only the system undo segment will be online.

   B. The database will open, but no undo segments will be online.

   C. The database will open and all undo segments in UNDO_TBS1 will be online.

   D. Oracle will return errors and the database will not open.

3. The Oracle database with undo tablespaces UNDO_TBS1 and UNDO_TBS2 was opened with automatic undo management enabled for this database. In a prior session, the `alter system set undo_tablespace = UNDO_TBS1` command was issued. In the `init.ora` file, the UNDO_TABLESPACE parameter was set to UNDOTBS1. Which of the following choices correctly describes what happens when the first user connecting to Oracle initiates her first transaction?

   A. The database will open, but only the system undo segment will be online.

   B. The database will open, but no undo segments will be online.

   C. The database will open and all undo segments in UNDO_TBS1 will be online.

   D. Oracle will return errors and the database will not open.

Answer Key
1. C. 2. C. 3. D.

Creating and Configuring Undo Segments Manually

Experienced DBAs might be wondering if they can still configure undo segments manually the way they configured rollback segments. The answer is emphatically yes! To understand undo segment manual configuration, let's start with a quick refresher on the types of undo segments. These objects can be broken into two categories: the system undo segment and non-SYSTEM undo segments. As you know, the system undo segment is housed by the SYSTEM tablespace and handles transactions made on objects in the SYSTEM tablespace. The other type of undo segments, non-SYSTEM undo segments, handles transactions made on data in non-SYSTEM tablespaces in the Oracle database. These non-SYSTEM undo segments are housed in a non-SYSTEM tablespace, such as the UNDOTBS tablespace. In order for Oracle to start when the database has one or more non-SYSTEM tablespaces, there must be at least one non-SYSTEM undo segment available for the instance to acquire outside the SYSTEM tablespace.

Non-SYSTEM undo segments come in two flavors: private and public undo segments. A *private* undo segment is one that is only acquired by an instance explicitly naming the undo segment to be acquired at startup via the ROLLBACK_SEGMENTS parameter in `initsid.ora`, or via the `alter rollback segment undo_seg online` statement issued manually by you, the DBA. *Public* undo segments are normally used when Oracle9i Real Application Clusters is running, but can also be used in a single instance. Public undo segments are acquired by Oracle automatically using a calculation of the TRANSACTIONS and the TRANSACTIONS_PER_ROLLBACK_SEGMENT init.ora parameters from a pool of undo segments available on the database.

How Transactions Use Undo Segments

Transactions occurring on the Oracle database need undo segments to store their uncommitted data changes. Transactions are assigned to undo segments in one of two ways. You can assign a transaction to an undo segment explicitly with the set transaction use rollback segment *undo_seg* statement. Or, if no undo segment is explicitly defined for the transaction, Oracle assigns the transaction to the undo segment that currently has the lightest transaction load, in round-robin fashion. Thus, more than one transaction can use the same undo segment, but each block in the undo segment houses data from one and only one transaction.

Undo segments are used as follows. An undo segment usually has several extents allocated to it at any given time, and these extents are used sequentially. After the database is started, the first transaction will be assigned to the first undo segment, and it will store its data changes in extent #1 of the undo segment. As the transaction progresses (a long-running batch process with thousands of update statements, let's say), it places more and more data into undo segment extent #1. An extent containing data from a transaction in progress is called an *active* extent. More and more transactions are starting on the database, and some of those other transactions may be assigned to this undo segment. Each transaction will fill extent #1 with more and more change data until the transactions commit.

If extent #1 fills with data changes before the transactions commit, the transactions will begin filling extent #2 with data. Transactions with data changes spilling over to a new extent are said to be performing a *extend*. A special marker called an undo segment *head* moves from extent #1 to extent #2 to indicate to the extent where new and existing transactions assigned to the undo segment can write their next data change. As soon as the transaction commits its data changes, the space in extent #1 used to store its data changes is no longer required. If extent #1 is filled with data change information from only committed transactions, extent #1 is considered *inactive*. Figure 13-2 displays this type of undo segment behavior.

To effectively use undo segment space, the undo segment allocates only a few extents, and those extents are reused often. The ideal operation of an undo segment with five extents is as follows: Transactions assigned to the undo segment should fill extent #5 a little after transactions with data changes in extent #1 commit. Thus, extent #1 becomes inactive just before transactions in extent #5 need to *wrap* into it. However, this behavior is not always possible. If a transaction goes on for a long time without committing data changes, it may eventually fill all extents in the undo segment. When this happens, the undo segment acquires extent #6, and wraps data changes from the current transaction into it. The undo segment head moves into

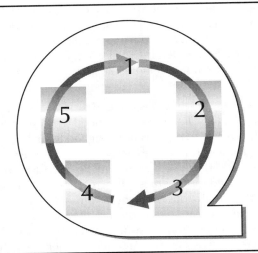

FIGURE 13-2. *Undo segment containing five reusable extents*

extent #6 as well. Figure 13-3 illustrates how Oracle obtains or allocates more extents for an undo segment.

If a transaction causes the undo segment to allocate the maximum number of extents for storing the long transaction's data changes—as determined by the maxextents storage option defined when the undo segment is created—the undo segment becomes enormously stretched out of shape. Oracle has an optimal option available in undo segment storage that permits undo segments to deallocate extents after long-running transactions cause them to acquire more extents than they really need. The optimal clause specifies the ideal size of the undo segment in KB or MB. This value tells Oracle the ideal number of extents the undo segment should maintain. If optimal is specified for an undo segment, that object will deallocate space when the undo segment head moves from one extent to another, if the current size of the undo segment exceeds optimal and if there are contiguous adjoining inactive extents. Figure 13-4 illustrates undo segment extent deallocation.

TIP
Extent deallocation as the result of optimal has nothing whatsoever to do with transactions committing on the database. The deallocation occurs when the undo segment head moves from one extent to another. Oracle does not deallocate extents currently in use (even if the total size exceeds optimal) and always attempts to deallocate the oldest inactive extents first.

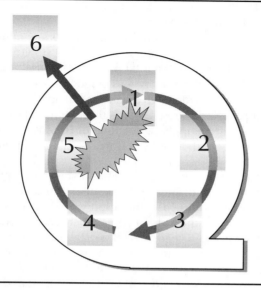

FIGURE 13-3. *How an undo segment acquires more extents*

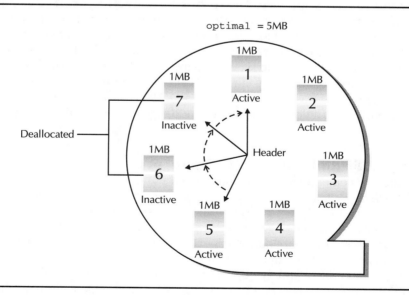

FIGURE 13-4. *Undo segment extent deallocation*

The Rule of Four to Plan Undo Segment Numbers for OLTP Systems

Oracle's recommended strategy for planning the appropriate number of undo segments for most online transaction-processing (OLTP) systems is called the *Rule of Four*, for easy recollection. Take the total number of transactions that will hit the database at any given time and divide by 4 to decide how many undo segments to create. Consider this example. You have a database that will be used for a small user rollout of an OLTP application. About 25 concurrent transactions will happen on the database at any given time. By applying the Rule of Four, you determine that about six undo segments are required. Shortly, you will see the additional calculation required for determining undo segment size.

Two exceptions exist to the Rule of Four. The first is, if the quotient is less than 4, round the result of the Rule of Four up to the nearest multiple of 4 and use that number of undo segments. In this case, the result would be rounded from 6 to 8. The second exception to the Rule of Four is that Oracle generally doesn't recommend more than 50 undo segments for a database, although that exception has faded somewhat in the face of massive database systems requiring more than 2,000 concurrent users. Thus, if the Rule of Four determines that more than 50 undo segments are needed, the DBA should start by allocating 50 and spend time monitoring the undo segment wait ratio to determine whether more should be added later.

Planning Undo Segment Numbers for Batch System Processing

When planning the number of undo segments required on the batch transaction-processing system, you need to make a small number of large undo segments available to support long-running processes that make several data changes. You should monitor the database to see how many transactions your batch processes execute concurrently and apply the Rule of Four to determine the number of undo segments needed, just as you would with an OLTP application. The next topic will demonstrate how to calculate the size of undo segments supporting both OLTP and batch transactions.

Sizing OLTP and Batch Undo Segments

There are two components to determining undo segment size, and the first is the overall size of the undo segment. The size of your undo segments, in turn, depends on two main factors: the type of DML statement used to perform the data change and the volume of data being processed. Different DML statements that change data require different amounts of data storage; the order from the least amount of data change information stored in an undo segment to greatest is `insert` (stores new ROWID in undo segment only), `update` (stores ROWID plus old column values), and `delete` (stores ROWID and all row/column data). Incidentally, data change information stored in an undo segment is called *undo*. So, if your transactions primarily `insert` data, your undo segments would be smaller than if your transactions primarily `delete` data.

The second component involved in undo segment size is the number of extents that will comprise the undo segment. Bigger is often better in determining the number of extents to have in your undo segment. By using more extents in the initial undo segment allocation—determined by the `minextents` storage option—you reduce the probability of your undo segment extending. Oracle recommends 20 (or more) extents as part of the initial undo segment allocation.

Creating Undo Segments with Appropriate Storage Settings

Undo segments are created with the `create rollback segment` statement. All extents in the undo segments of an Oracle database should be the same size. Commit this fact to memory—it's on the OCP exam in one form or another. To partially enforce this recommendation, Oracle disallows the use of `pctincrease` in the `create rollback segment` statement. (The `pctincrease` option is available for other objects, such as tables, to increase the size of subsequent extents that may be allocated to the object in order to reduce the overall number of extents allocated.) Sizes for undo segments and their included extents are determined by the options in the `storage` clause.

The following list of options is available for setting up undo segments:

- **`initial`**   The size in KB or MB of the initial undo segment extent.

- **`next`**   The size in KB or MB of the next undo segment extent to be allocated. Ensure that all extents are the same size by specifying `next` equal to `initial`.

- **`minextents`**   The minimum number of extents on the undo segment. The value for `minextents` should be 2 or greater.

- **`maxextents`**   The maximum number of extents the undo segment can acquire. Be sure to set this to a number and not to `unlimited`; this will prevent runaway transactions from using all your available tablespace. This is especially important if your UNDOTBS tablespace has datafiles using the `autoextend` feature.

- **`optimal`**   The total size in KB or MB of the undo segment, optimally. Assuming `initial` equals `next`, the value for `optimal` cannot be less than `initial` * `minextents`.

The following code block demonstrates the creation of a non-SYSTEM private undo segment in your database, according to the guidelines Oracle recommends. On OCP questions in this area, you should base your answers on the Oracle guidelines.

```
CREATE ROLLBACK SEGMENT rollseg01
TABLESPACE orgdbrbs
STORAGE ( INITIAL    10K
          NEXT       10K
          MINEXTENTS 20
          MAXEXTENTS 450
          OPTIMAL    300K );
```

TIP
*The previous command is designed for use with a
dictionary-managed tablespace.*

In the code block, notice the `public` keyword was not used. Undo segments
are private unless you create them with the `create public rollback
segment` command. After creating your undo segment, you must bring it online
so it will be available for user transactions. This is accomplished with the `alter
rollback segment` *undo_seg* `online` command. The number of undo
segments that can be brought online can be limited at instance startup by setting
MAX_ROLLBACK_SEGMENTS `init`*sid*`.ora` parameter to 1 plus the number of
non-SYSTEM undo segments you want available in Oracle.

TIP
*You can create undo segments using the Storage
Manager administrative utility in Oracle Enterprise
Manager, as well as from within SQL*Plus.*

Bringing Undo Segments Online at Instance Startup
Once you issue the `shutdown` command, any undo segments you created or
brought online while the database was up are now offline as well. They will only
be brought back online in two ways. The first is if you issue the `alter rollback
segment` *undo_seg* `online` command again for every undo segment you want
online.

The other way is through a multistep process engaged by Oracle at instance
startup. Oracle first acquires any undo segments at instance startup named by you
in the ROLLBACK_SEGMENTS `init`*sid*`.ora` parameter, specified as ROLLBACK_
SEGMENTS = (*rollseg01,rollseg02* . . .). Then, Oracle performs a calculation of the
undo segments required for the proper operation of the database, based on values
set for the TRANSACTIONS, TRANSACTIONS_PER_ROLLBACK_SEGMENT, and
`init`*sid*`.ora` parameters. The calculation performed is TRANSACTIONS /
TRANSACTIONS_PER_ROLLBACK_SEGMENT. Thus, if TRANSACTIONS is 146 and
TRANSACTIONS_PER_ROLLBACK_SEGMENT is 18, then Oracle knows it needs to
acquire eight undo segments. If eight undo segments were named, Oracle brings the

private undo segments online. If there weren't eight undo segments named, then Oracle attempts to acquire the difference from the pool of public undo segments available. If there are enough public undo segments available in the pool, Oracle acquires the difference and brings all its acquired undo segments online. Note, however, that the calculation step is required primarily for public undo segments where Oracle Parallel Server is being used.

TIP
If not enough public undo segments are available for Oracle to acquire, the Oracle instance will start, and the database will open anyway, with no errors reported in trace files or the ALERT log.

Maintaining Undo Segments Manually

Several statements are available in Oracle for maintaining undo segments. The first is the `alter rollback segment` statement. You have already seen this statement used to bring the undo segment online, as in `alter rollback segment` *undo_seg* `online`. You can bring an undo segment offline in this way also, with `alter rollback segment` *undo_seg* `offline`. However, you can only bring an undo segment offline if it contains no active extents supporting transactions with uncommitted data changes. This statement is used to change any option in the `storage` clause as well, except for the size of the `initial` extent. However, note that changing the `next` extent size will alter the size of the next extent the undo segment acquires, not the size of any extent the undo segment already has acquired, and furthermore, doing this is not recommended for reasons already explained.

```
ALTER ROLLBACK SEGMENT rollseg01
STORAGE ( MAXEXTENTS 200
          OPTIMAL    310K );
```

The `alter rollback segment` statement has one additional clause for you to use, and that clause is `shrink to`. This clause enables you to manually reduce the storage allocation of your undo segment to a size not less than that specified for `optimal` (if `optimal` is specified). As with `optimal`, Oracle will not reduce the size of the undo segment if extents over the size specified are still active. If no value is specified, Oracle will attempt to shrink the undo segment to the value specified for `optimal`. Finally, Oracle will ignore the `alter rollback segment` *undo_seg* `shrink [to` *x*`[K|M]]` statement if the value specified for *x* is greater than the current undo segment allocation. The following code block shows appropriate use of the `shrink to` clause:

```
ALTER ROLLBACK SEGMENT rollseg01 SHRINK;
ALTER ROLLBACK SEGMENT rollseg01 SHRINK TO 220K;
```

Finally, once brought offline, an undo segment can be dropped if you feel it is no longer needed, or if you need to re-create it with different `initial`, `next`, and `minextents` extent size settings. The statement used for this purpose is `drop rollback segment` *undo_seg*.

```
DROP ROLLBACK SEGMENT rollseg01;

CREATE ROLLBACK SEGMENT rollseg01
TABLESPACE orgdbrbs
STORAGE ( INITIAL      12K
          NEXT         12K
          MINEXTENTS 25
          MAXEXTENTS 400
          OPTIMAL      300K )
```

TIP

If you want to manage undo segments manually while Oracle9i is running in automatic undo management mode, then you must change the UNDO_SUPPRESS_ERRORS `init.ora` *parameter to true. This parameter is false by default, meaning that any manual attempt to manage undo segments while Oracle automatically manages them will result in errors.*

For Review

1. What happens to database performance if Oracle has to allocate extents to its undo segments frequently without giving them up? What storage option can be used to minimize this occurrence?

2. How are `minextents` and `maxextents` used in sizing undo segments? What is the Rule of Four? What rules can you apply to sizing undo segments on batch applications? Why is it important to use many extents in your undo segment?

3. How are extents of an undo segment deallocated?

4. Identify the options available for the undo segment storage clause, and describe their general use. How does Oracle attempt to enforce equal sizing of all extents in undo segments?

5. How are undo segments brought online after creation? At instance startup?

6. What storage option cannot be modified by the `alter rollback segment` statement? How might you manually make an undo segment unavailable for transaction usage, and what might prevent you from doing so?

7. What is the `shrink to` clause of the `alter rollback segment statement`, and how is it used? When is it appropriate (or possible) to eliminate an undo segment, and what statement is used to do it?

Exercises

I. **You are attempting to manage undo segments manually while automatic undo management is enabled on your system. Which of the following choices identifies what will happen when you issue the `alter rollback segment` command in this context?**

A. The undo segment will be altered as you requested.

B. The undo segment will be altered, but Oracle will issue warnings.

C. The undo segment will not be altered, and Oracle will issue errors.

D. The database will fail.

2. **You are attempting to manage undo segments manually while automatic undo management is enabled in your system. Which of the following choices identifies an appropriate method to configure Oracle to allow this situation to occur?**

A. Set UNDO_MANAGEMENT to AUTO.

B. Set UNDO_SUPRESS_ERRORS to FALSE.

C. Set UNDO_MANAGEMENT to MANUAL.

D. Set UNDO_RETENTION to 1,800.

3. **You have disabled automatic undo management on your Oracle database. Which of the following choices identifies the method that must be employed in order to ensure that undo segments are available for user processes?**

A. Set UNDO_TABLESPACE to the name of the undo tablespace.

B. Set ROLLBACK_SEGMENTS to a list of undo segments to bring online.

C. Bring the database online in read-only mode.

D. Nothing—Oracle will bring undo segments online automatically.

Answer Key
1. C. 2. C. 3. B.

Obtaining Information about Undo Data

Oracle has many dictionary and dynamic performance views both old and new to track undo statistics. Both the undo as well as the undo data dictionary views have to be used to obtain full information about the undo data. The following is a list of the views to be aware of:

- **DBA_ROLLBACK_SEGS** This is an existing view that displays the data about undo or undo segments such as the name of the undo segment, the tablespace they reside in, and their status.

- **DBA_UNDO_EXTENTS** This data dictionary view contains the information about the `commit` time for each extent in the undo tablespace.

- **V$UNDOSTAT** This view displays a histogram of statistical data to show the undo behavior. Each row in this view keeps statistics of undo segments in the instance for ten-minute intervals. This view can be used to estimate the amount of undo space required.

- **V$ROLLSTAT, V$ROLLNAME** These two are old views that display the dynamic performance information of the undo segments.

For Review

Be sure you can identify the dictionary and dynamic performance views available for managing undo segments in Oracle.

Exercises

1. **This view offers performance information for Oracle-managed undo segments in the database:** _____.

2. **This view offers a listing of undo segments created by Oracle for handling undo information:** _____.

Answer Key
1. V$UNDOSTAT. 2. DBA_UNDO_EXTENTS.

Chapter Summary

In this chapter, we covered information regarding the management of segments in the Oracle database and the use of undo segments. These two topics comprise approximately 14 percent of the contents of the Oracle9i OCP DBA Fundamentals I exam. You learned about the different types of segments used in Oracle databases, along with some analysis techniques you can use for understanding the fragmentation and lifespan of segments. This information is useful because it gives you the basis for separating different types of segments into different tablespaces. You also learned about how Oracle acquires new extents for database objects when the current extent is full. The particular importance of object storage settings with respect to the size of extents allocated was covered in some detail as well. You then learned about the use of undo segments in Oracle. We discussed how to manage undo segments using automatic undo management, as well as how to manage them manually. We wrapped up our coverage of undo segments by pointing you to where you can find more information about undo segments in Oracle in the data dictionary.

Two-Minute Drill

- Every database object in Oracle is stored in a segment. Because these segments support data in Oracle that are used for different purposes, you should keep the different segments in different tablespaces.

- Understand the inverse proportional relationship between the lifespan of extents and fragmentation in the tablespace—the shorter the lifespan, the higher the potential for fragmentation in the tablespace.

- Remember that the method by which you can control the allocation of extents by database objects is determined by the storage settings for a database object. These can either be set at the object level or inherited from the default settings for the tablespace. The storage settings are

  - `initial`   First segment in the object

  - `next`   Next segment allocated (not simply the second one in the object)

  - `pctincrease`   Percentage increase of next extent allocated over next value

  - `minextents`   Minimum number of extents allocated at object creation

  - `maxextents`   Maximum number of extents the object can allocate

- **pctfree** How much of each block stays free after `insert` for row `update`

- **pctused** Threshold that usage must fall below before a row is added

- Understand how Oracle enables the DBA to control space usage at the block level with `pctfree` and `pctused`.

- Know what dictionary views are used to find information about storage structures, including DBA_SEGMENTS, DBA_TABLESPACES, DBA_TS_QUOTAS, V$TABLESPACE, DBA_EXTENTS, DBA_FREE_SPACE, and DBA_FREE_SPACE_COALESCED.

- Undo segments used to be called rollback segments in prior versions of Oracle.

- Undo segments enable transaction processing to occur by storing the old version of data that has been changed but not committed by the users.

- Oracle9i offers a new feature for undo segments—automatic undo management. To use automatic undo management, you must execute the following steps:

    1. Create undo tablespaces either when you create the database using the `undo tablespace` clause or by using the `create undo tablespace` command.

    2. Set the UNDO_MANAGEMENT parameter to AUTO and the UNDO_TABLESPACE parameter to the undo tablespace you created.

    3. Set the UNDO_RETENTION parameter to the length of time you want to retain undo information in the segments in support of Flashback Query.

- You can also manage undo segments manually, as you did in previous versions of Oracle. If you do so, set UNDO_MANAGEMENT to MANUAL. You might also want to set UNDO_SUPPRESS_ERRORS to TRUE in order to avoid the chance that your database running in automatic undo management will return errors if you try to manage undo segments manually.

- If you decide to manage undo segments manually, make sure that undo segments consist of equally sized extents.

- The `pctincrease` option is not permitted on undo segments if you create them manually.

- Undo segments must be brought online in order to use them. Oracle will take care of this automatically if you use automatic undo management, but if you use manual undo management, you have to bring them online yourself.

■ An undo segment cannot be taken offline until all active transactions writing undo entries have completed. This same restriction applies to tablespaces containing active undo segments.

■ Entries are associated with transactions in the undo segment via the use of a system change number (SCN).

■ Specific private undo segments can be allocated at startup if they are specified in the ROLLBACK_SEGMENTS parameter in `initsid.ora` when you're using manual undo management.

■ Monitor performance in undo segments with V$ROLLSTAT and V$WAITSTAT when using manual undo management.

■ Know the new dictionary views in support of automatic undo management.

Fill-in-the-Blank Questions

1. The storage option for database objects that can cause exponential growth in the size of each extent acquired for a database object is
   _____.

2. The type of segment in an Oracle database that stores the original data in a record being changed by a user process is _____.

3. This type of database segment stores data for the duration of a disk sort: _____.

4. This initialization parameter is used for enabling automatic undo management in Oracle: _____.

5. The value set for this parameter determines whether the `alter rollback segment` command will encounter errors when automatic undo management is enabled in Oracle: _____.

Chapter Questions

1. **When determining the number of undo segments in a database, which of the following choices identifies a factor to consider?**

   A. Concurrent transactions

   B. Size of typical transactions

   C. Size of rows in table most frequently changed

   D. Number of anticipated disk sorts

2. **How many undo segments will be required if the value set for TRANSACTIONS is 20 and the value set for TRANSACTIONS_PER_ROLLBACK_SEGMENT is 4?**

   A. Two

   B. Four

   C. Eight

   D. Nine

3. **When an undo segment is created manually by you, its availability status is set to which of the following automatically by Oracle?**

   A. Online

   B. Pending online

   C. Offline

   D. Stale

4. **All of the following choices indicate a way to resolve the** ORA-1555 Snapshot too old (rollback segment too small) **error, except one. Which choice is it?**

   A. Create undo segments with a higher optimal value.

   B. Create undo segments with higher maxextents.

   C. Create undo segments with larger extent sizes.

   D. Create undo segments with higher minextents.

5. **You are managing transaction processing in Oracle. Entries in an undo segment are bound to a transaction by which of the following Oracle components?**

   A. Number of commit operations performed

   B. Number of rollback operations performed

   C. ROWID

   D. System change number

6. **You are managing segments in an Oracle table with storage settings of 100KB for** initial **and** next **when the table was first created, respectively, and** pctincrease **is set to 50. Which of the following choices identifies the size of the table after the fourth extent has been allocated?**

   A. 225KB

   B. 325KB

   C. 350KB

   D. 575KB

7. You are setting block space utilization parameters for a table in a data warehouse. The table is loaded weekly with data and then made available to users for query-only access. Which of the following choices identifies an appropriate setting for block space utilization?

   A. pctfree 5

   B. pctfree 40

   C. pctused 5

   D. pctused 40

8. You just added an undo tablespace to the database and now want to configure automatic undo management in your Oracle database. Which of the following parameters is required for configuring this feature?

   A. UNDO_MANAGEMENT

   B. UNDO_TABLESPACE

   C. UNDO_RETENTION

   D. UNDO_SUPPRESS_ERRORS

Fill-in-the-Blank Answers

1. `pctincrease`

2. Undo

3. Temporary

4. UNDO_MANAGEMENT

5. UNDO_SUPPRESS_ERRORS

Answers to Chapter Questions

1. A.   Concurrent transactions

Explanation   The number of concurrent transactions is used in part to determine the number of undo segments your database should have. Had the question asked for which choice played a role in determining the size of extents or total undo segment size, then choices B or C would have been correct. Because disk sorts have little to do with undo segments, under no circumstances should you have chosen D.

2. C.   Eight

Explanation   Refer to the Rule of Four in creating undo segments. Remember, the equation is TRANSACTIONS/TRANSACTIONS_PER_ROLLBACK_SEGMENT. In this case, the result is five. This is a special case in the Rule of Four, which gets rounded up to eight.

3. C.   Offline

Explanation   Once created, an undo segment status is offline and must be brought online in order to be used. Refer to the discussion of undo segments. In order to bring it online, you must issue the `alter rollback segment online` statement, eliminating choice A. Pending online is not a valid status for undo segments in Oracle, eliminating choice B. Stale is a valid status for redo logs, but not for undo segments, eliminating choice D.

4. B.   Create undo segments with higher `maxextents`.

Explanation   Refer to the discussion of indexes created in conjunction with integrity constraints.

5. D.   System change number

Explanation   SCNs are identifiers that group data-change statements together as one transaction both in undo segments and redo logs. The number of `commit` operations or `rollback` operations performed simply reduces the number of active transactions on the database, and thus the amount of active undo in an undo segment. Thus, choices A and B are incorrect. Finally, ROWIDs correspond to the location on disk of rows for a table and have little to do with grouping transactions, so choice C is incorrect.

6. D.   575KB

Explanation   The total amount of space allocated for this table is 575 because the first two extents are 100KB a piece, the third extent is 100KB×1.5, or 150KB, and the fourth is 100KB×1.5×1.5, or 225KB. Although choice A correctly identifies the size of the fourth extent, your careful reading of the chapter would tell you that the question is actually asking for the total size of the table after all four extents are allocated. Choice B indicates the total size of the first and fourth extent, whereas choice B indicates the total size of the second and third extent.

7. A.   `pctfree 5`

Explanation   Because this table is loaded periodically and then accessed by users for queries only, you know that you do not need to leave much space left over for row growth. Thus, you know that you must focus on `pctfree` rather than `pctused` because `pctfree` is used for managing row growth. Thus, choices C and D can be eliminated right away. Of the two, choice A is the most correct answer because it offers the lowest setting for `pctfree`.

8. A.   UNDO_MANAGEMENT

Explanation   In order to configure automatic undo management, you must set the UNDO_MANAGEMENT parameter in your `init.ora` file to AUTO. This is the only step required for initiating automatic undo management once the undo tablespace has been created because Oracle can figure out which tablespace to use if an undo tablespace exists; thus, choice B is incorrect. Choice C is incorrect because UNDO_RETENTION has a default value of 900. Finally, because you probably won't manage your undo segments manually when automatic undo management is enabled, you shouldn't need to change the setting for UNDO_SUPPRESS_ERRORS, making choice D incorrect.

CHAPTER
14

Managing
Database Objects

n this chapter, you will learn about and demonstrate knowledge in the following areas:

- Managing tables
- Managing indexes
- Managing data integrity

As a DBA, a big part of your daily job function is the creation and maintenance of database objects like tables and indexes. This is especially true for database administrators who manage development and test databases. Even DBAs working on production systems will find that at least some of their time is spent exploring the depths of setting up database objects. In this chapter, you will cover what you need to know for creating tables, indexes, and integrity constraints. Although there are other objects in Oracle, such as sequences, cluster tables, or index-organized tables (IOTs), tables and indexes are the core objects of most every Oracle database. Integrity constraints present a unique perspective on both tables and indexes. On one hand, constraints prevent bad data from entering your tables. On the other hand, sometimes integrity constraints use indexes as the underlying mechanism to support their activities. This chapter covers material that will comprise about 18 percent of the Oracle9i DBA Fundamentals I exam.

Managing Tables

In this section, you will cover the following topics related to managing tables:

- Various methods of storing data
- Distinguishing Oracle datatypes
- Extended and restricted ROWIDs
- Structure of a row
- Creating permanent and temporary tables
- Managing the storage structures in a table
- Reorganizing, truncating, and dropping tables
- Dropping columns in tables

Tables are used in Oracle for storing data. You already probably think of a table from a data perspective as an object similar to a spreadsheet insofar as a table has columns and rows for storing data. All information stored in a column will have the same datatype, whereas a row is considered a collection of single values defined for every column. This section will explore the table from an administrative perspective, as a collection of bits and bytes inside a file whose storage must be planned and managed carefully. We'll cover the different types of tables available in Oracle at a broad level, and also take a closer look at datatypes available in your Oracle database. You'll also take a long, hard look at ROWIDs, the mechanism Oracle uses for keeping track of where individual rows are stored in tables in files in databases. You'll look at the structure of a row and how to create tables in Oracle. Maintenance activities for tables will be covered as well.

Various Methods of Storing Data

Before beginning your exploration of tables in detail, consider the following question—how does a table differ from the data segments we already discussed in earlier chapters? After all, the data that users place in tables is actually stored in segments and extents inside datafiles. However, that's precisely what makes tables different—they offer a conceptual way to think of data inside a segment or extent that also enables us to reference that data, manipulate it, add new data, or even take data away. In other words, tables are the constructs that enable users to access the data that we as DBAs will think of as being stored in segments and extents.

Oracle supports various types of tables for storing user data in an Oracle segment. There are regular tables for housing permanent data and temporary tables for temporary data. Most DBAs will find that their organizational data needs are handled sufficiently with these two types of tables. However, there are also many exotic variations of tables that Oracle has introduced over the years, each of which serves an important niche purpose. These types of tables include partitioned tables, IOTs, and clustered tables. Let's now look at each of these table types in more detail.

Regular Tables

Regular tables are the most common types of table used storing the user data. When you execute the `create table` command, the default table that Oracle creates is a regular table. In keeping with E. F. Codd's original definition of tables in his landmark work on relational database theory, Oracle does not guarantee that row data will be stored in a particular order. This type of data storage is sometimes referred to as *heap-organized*, where data is stored in an unordered collection, or a heap. As you already know, order can be imposed later using various clauses in your SQL queries that you learned about for the OCP Oracle9i Introduction to SQL exam.

Temporary Tables

The users of Oracle who come to Oracle database administration from the world of Microsoft SQL Server might be familiar with the following concept. Suppose you want to create a complex report in which data must be run through a series of complex processing steps. To simplify processing, you believe it would be helpful to store data in an intermediate format using a table. The problem is that you don't want users to access that intermediate information during or after the report's execution, for fear of the confusion that may result. You could simply use a standard Oracle table, but then you have to remember to clean out the table when appropriate.

Oracle offers temporary tables as a means to enable you to create a table to retain session-private data for only the duration of the transaction or session. Although it doesn't necessarily offer functionality that isn't already available in Oracle using other means, the temporary table solves many annoying little problems associated with the alternative methods for you. First, because the data is only available to the session putting it there, there's no worry that other users will be able to see your data before you want them to. In addition, because the data stored in temporary tables is temporary in nature, there is no need for you to worry about eliminating the contents of the table when you don't need the data anymore. At the end of the transaction or session, the data will disappear, depending on how you define the temporary table.

TIP
Even though Oracle supports session privacy with respect to data in a temporary table, all temporary tables in Oracle are available for all current sessions to use, and the definition of the temporary table will continue to exist in the data dictionary even after its data gets eliminated.

Partitioned Tables

Partitioned tables are just like regular tables in Oracle except for an important small feature—they enable you to reference the individual segments that might support larger tables directly. The segment is not considered a separate database object, but rather it's considered a subobject that you happen to be able to reference directly. Partitioned tables give you more control over data distribution across multiple disks in the machine hosting the Oracle database. Every disk in a machine has a channel or hardware mechanism designed to facilitate access to that disk. However, that channel might not be able to provide enough bandwidth for many processes to access the disk fast enough to provide data for users during peak periods of activity.

This is where partitioning factors in. You can partition a large table that is accessed during peak periods and spread the data stored in that table across many disks. Because each disk spins independently and may have a channel available for direct access to it, partitioning supports a greater degree of parallel processing for busy databases than regular tables could allow. You might find partitioning used for the purposes of scaling extremely large tables, such as those found in data warehouses. In a partitioned table, data is stored in each partition according to a partition key, or column, that defines which range of row data goes into which partition. Each partition can then be stored in different tablespaces. Every partition in a table must have the same columns. There are several other facts about partitions that are worth knowing before you implement them, but because partitioning isn't a focus area for the OCP Oracle9i DBA core track, we won't spend a lot of time on this subject.

TIP

Several benefits are seen with partitions, including increased data availability and the potential for parallel data-change operations operating on different partitions simultaneously.

IOTs

In regular tables, data is stored in heap-organized fashion, which as you know means that data is not stored any in ordered way. Primary key indexes are typically associated with these tables in order to speed access to the unordered data in the table. These indexes are created in a B-tree structure, which is stored separately from the table. B-tree structure permits speedy retrieval of information stored within that structure.

Rather than storing data in an unstructured heap, Oracle stores data in index-organized tables in a B-tree index structure. The data is stored in the order of the primary key of the table. The rows in an index-organized table are not only sorted by their primary key values, but each row contains the primary key column values and other nonkey column values in it. There is no separate index structure to store the primary key in index-organized tables. This reduces storage overhead, especially for tables that don't have too many columns in them. Index-organized tables are particularly useful for data that is mostly retrieved based on primary key. An example of this sort of data would be a lookup table, where important terms are associated with short alphanumeric codes.

Cluster Table

Sometimes, you might have a set of tables that are all queried for data together at the same time. For example, an employee expense reimbursement system might contain two tables that are always being used together in a parent/child fashion. The parent table might contain key facts about each expense reimbursement request submitted by an employee. This table might store one row for each employee reimbursement request, containing column values defined for the employee's name or ID number, the expense request ID number, and the mailing address where the reimbursement check must be sent. The child table contains line items for each reimbursement request. For example, if the employee took a flight to Singapore for a trade show that lasted several days, the child table would store several rows, each corresponding to a particular expense (airfare, hotel, car, conference registration, meals, and so on), along with a charge-to account number for each expense.

A cluster might be handy in this business context because even though the data is stored as two separate tables, employees who want to see their particular expense reimbursement requests will almost invariably request data from both tables at the same time. Clusters enable you to store data from several tables inside a single segment so users can retrieve data from those two tables together very quickly. In order to store two or more tables together inside a cluster segment, the tables must all share at least one column in common. This column becomes the cluster key. Because clusters store related rows of different tables in the same physical data segments, it offers two benefits:

- The disk I/O is reduced and access time improves for joins of clustered tables.

- The common column(s) only needs to be stored once for all the tables grouped in a cluster.

TIP
Although it is a useful type of table, clusters work best when the data stored in them is primarily static or read-only. This is because the rows of one table stored in cluster segment blocks are laid out so that they are close to the associated rows from the other tables. If the size of a row increases too dramatically after Oracle performs the initial row layout in the cluster, then data could get shifted around inside the blocks of the cluster, negating the performance increase you might have otherwise enjoyed.

For Review

1. Regular tables in Oracle are great for general data storage needs. They are the most flexible type of database object in Oracle for storing data.

2. Temporary tables in Oracle are useful for housing intermediate datasets during complex processing for the duration of a transaction or session.

3. Partitioned tables in Oracle enable you to reference individual segments of data in a larger table directly, as though they were a miniature copy of the

table containing only a specific range of that table's data. These objects are handy for extremely large tables in data warehouses.

4. All the tables listed previously store data in a heap structure. To get at the data quickly, DBAs typically create indexes on the table. IOTs house data in an index structure to reduce storage overhead by not separating the table from the index. The result is that IOTs provide speedy lookups on their contents.

5. Usually, a segment houses information for only one table. However, clusters permit the storage of more than one table's data inside a single segment. This is useful for situations when users always access two or more tables together when attempting to access their data.

Exercises

1. **Your Oracle database stores data in a single table that is queried heavily by users of a data warehouse application. To speed parallel processing of data in that table, which of the following table variants might you consider switching to?**

   A. Temporary table

   B. Index-organized table

   C. Cluster table

   D. Partitioned table

2. **You have a long-running extract-transformation-load (ETL) batch process that performs extensive processing on several intermediate sets of data. At the end of processing, the intermediate sets must be eliminated in favor of the result set, which is then loaded directly into another table in the data warehouse. In order to facilitate that processing by providing a tabular disk storage mechanism, which of the following database objects might you use?**

   A. Temporary table

   B. Index-organized table

   C. Cluster table

   D. Standard Oracle table

3. **The rows inside three Oracle tables supporting a customer order entry system are frequently accessed together by means of a table join. Because**

data is always being added to the tables, you leave a lot of extra space inside each block to accommodate growth. Which of the following types of tables would be useful for storing the data in this context?

A. Temporary table

B. Index-organized table

C. Cluster table

D. Standard Oracle table

4. You are deploying some HIPAA-compliant healthcare applications supporting patient diagnosis and treatment. Every diagnosis is associated with a five-letter alphanumeric code that the application looks up dynamically as new patient records are entered. A sample of these codes is shown in the following block:

```
DIAGNOSIS     CODE
-----------   ----------------
Influenza     D43I2
Chicken Pox   R501F
Sore Throat   T40AS
```

Which of the following types of tables would work best for this application?

A. Temporary table

B. Index-organized table

C. Cluster table

D. Standard Oracle table

Answer Key
1. D. 2. A. 3. D. Remember, clusters work best when the data stored in the associated tables is static or read-only. 4. B.

Distinguishing Oracle Datatypes

Recall that each column in a table stores data of a particular datatype. Each row can contain values for columns of different datatypes, but each individual column can house data of only one datatype. Although Oracle offers many different datatypes that are useful for storing data, Oracle does not have as many different datatypes as you might be used to, particularly if you come to Oracle database administration from using single-user or department-level database products. For example, Oracle does not have a currency datatype because currency is nothing more than a number with a currency format mask. Thus, rather than bog users down with many different numeric datatypes, Oracle instead provides only one datatype for numbers, NUMBER, and a robust mechanism for applying whatever format masks you might deem appropriate to give your numbers meaning. Let's look at Oracle datatypes in more detail.

Oracle Scalar Datatypes

Oracle substantially reorganized the available datatypes between versions 7.3 and 8.0. There are two basic categories of datatypes in Oracle: built-in types and user-defined types. Within the built-in types, there are three basic classes of datatypes available: scalar, collection, and relationship datatypes. Within the user-defined types, the classes of datatypes you can define for your own application uses are endless. Let's look at the scalar datatypes in detail.

CHAR(L) and NCHAR(L)   These are fixed-length text string datatypes, where the data is stored with blanks padded out to the full width of the column (represented here by L). NCHAR is CHAR's NLS multibyte equivalent type. NLS stands for National Language Set, and it is used for making Oracle available in languages other than American English. Some world languages with large character sets (such as Japanese, Chinese, or Korean) or other substantial differences from English (such as being read from right to left, like Arabic or Hebrew) need multiple bytes to store one character. English, on the other hand, requires only one byte to store a character, such as the letter A. Both NCHAR and CHAR columns and variables can be up to 2,000 bytes in length in Oracle. In Oracle7, the limit was 255 bytes.

VARCHAR2(L) and NVARCHAR2(L)   These are variable-length text string datatypes, where data is stored using only the number of bytes required to store the actual value, which in turn can vary in length for each row. NVARCHAR2 is VARCHAR2's NLS multibyte equivalent type. (Actually, that's not quite correct: NCHAR and NVARCHAR2 are NLS datatypes that enable the storage of either fixed-width or variable-width character sets; you can also use them for nonmultibyte character sets, but that's not common. So, for all intents and purposes, NVARCHAR2 is VARCHAR2's NLS multibyte equivalent type.) These can be up to 4,000 bytes in length in Oracle.

NUMBER(L,P)   These are always stored as variable-length data, where one byte is used to store the exponent, one byte is used for every two significant digits of the number's mantissa, and one byte is used for negative numbers if the number of significant digits is less than 38 bytes.

TIP
A mantissa is the decimal part of a logarithm.
Oracle uses the logarithm of a number to store the
binary version of the number so that it takes up less
space.

DATE   This is stored as a fixed-length field of 7 bytes. The Oracle DATE format actually includes time as well as date, and this information is stored internally as a number. You can apply whatever formatting masks you need in order to render the date in the manner appropriate for your situation. By default, Oracle shows date information as DD-MON-YY, or a two-digit date, followed by a three-letter abbreviation for the month, followed by a two-digit year. Note that Oracle stores the date internally as a number that includes four-digit year references. The two-digit default representation of year information is just a formatting mask. You can change this format at the system or session level easily using the `alter [system|session] set nls_date_format = 'mask'` command, where an actual format mask is substituted for *mask*.

RAW(L)   This datatype holds a small amount of binary data. There are no conversions performed on raw data in Oracle. The raw data is simply stored as is. Oracle can house up to 2,000 bytes in a RAW column.

ROWID   This datatype is used to store ROWID information. A ROWID is a 10-byte string that identifies the location of row data in a datafile.

Comparing LONG, LONG RAW, and LOB Datatypes

Oracle can store very large amounts of information in columns using other scalar datatypes as well. There are several datatypes to be aware of, some of which are provided mainly for backward compatibility. The datatypes available in Oracle for storing very large amounts of data in a single column are listed as follows:

- **LONG**   Stores up to 2GB of text data.

- **LONG RAW**   Stores up to 2GB of binary data.

- **BLOB**   Stores up to 4GB binary data.

- **CLOB and NCLOB**   Store up to 4GB text data; NCLOB is a large fixed-width NLS datatype.

- **BFILE**   Stores up to 4GB unstructured data in operating system files.

Several key differences between LONG and LOB types make LOB types more versatile and helpful for large object management. First, there can be only one

LONG column in a table, because the LONG column data is stored *inline*, meaning that all data in the LONG column for each row in the table is stored in contiguous data blocks inside the segment used for storing the table's data. In contrast, there can be many LOB columns in a table, because when the LOB value is over 4,000 bytes, only a locator for the LOB type is stored inline with the table data—in other words, no LOB will ever require more than 4,000 bytes of space inline with other table data. The rest of the data in the LOB columns is stored in an overflow segment. Thus, `select` statements on LONG columns return the actual data, whereas the same statement on a LOB column returns only the locator. Oracle supports the use of the LOB types in object types except NCLOB, whereas LONG does not. LOBs can also be larger than LONGs—4GB for LOBs versus 2GB for LONGs. LOB data can also be accessed piecewise, whereas LONG access is sequential; only the entire value in the LONG column can be obtained, whereas parts of the LOB can be obtained.

Collection Datatypes

A collection is a gathering of like-defined elements. There are two collection types available in Oracle. The first is called a variable-length array (VARRAY). A VARRAY can be thought of as an ordered list of objects, all of the same datatype. The VARRAY is defined to have two special attributes (in addition to those attributes within the objects the VARRAY contains). These attributes are a *count* for the number of elements in the VARRAY and the *limit* for the maximum number of elements that can appear in a VARRAY. Although the VARRAY can have any number of elements, the limit must be predefined. Each element in the VARRAY has an index, which is a number corresponding to the position of the element in the array. Constraints and default values may not be created for elements in a VARRAY, and once the VARRAY is created, the user only refers to an individual element in a VARRAY with PL/SQL (although SQL can be used to access the entire VARRAY).

The other collection type is called the nested table and can be thought of as a table within a table. The nested table architecture is exceptionally suited for applications that have parent/child tables with referential integrity. A nested table is an unordered list of row records, each having the same structure. These rows are usually stored away from the table, with a reference pointer from the corresponding row in the parent table to the child table. Like VARRAYs, nested tables can have any number of elements, with the added bonus that you don't need to predetermine a maximum limit.

Reference and User-Defined Datatypes

Finally, consider the reference type and user-defined types. Developers can use the reference type to define a foreign key relationship between two objects. The reference type can reference all columns in the table for a particular row—it is a pointer to a particular object, not the object itself. User-defined types are abstract datatypes or compositions of existing scalar or other types that you can define to serve highly specialized purposes in Oracle. They are typically composed of scalar, collection, or other user-defined types.

For Review

1. There are two general categories for datatypes—built-in and user-defined. Within built-in types, you have scalar, reference, and collection datatypes. User-defined types are specialized composite datatypes you build for yourself using existing built-in types.

2. Be sure you can describe the difference between the LONG datatype and LOB datatypes available in Oracle for the storage of very large amounts of data in a single column. LOB types offer several advantages and are the preferred type for this purpose. The LONG type is provided for backward compatibility.

Exercises

1. **This datatype is capable of storing up to 2,000 bytes of character data, padded with trailing blank spaces to the entire width of the column: _____.**

2. **In Oracle, you can store up to _____(A)_____ bytes of data in a RAW column and up to 4,000 bytes in a _____(B)_____ column.**

3. **Internally, Oracle stores DATE information as a _____.**

4. **A ___(A)____ is a large object datatype capable of storing up to ____(B)____ GB of binary data. Similarly, a CLOB is a large object datatype capable of storing _____(C)_____ data.**

Answer Key
1. CHAR. **2.** (A) 2,000; (B) VARCHAR2. **3.** Number. **4.** (A) BLOB; (B) 4; (C) text.

Extended and Restricted ROWIDs

Recall that we mentioned the use of ROWIDs in Oracle for identifying the location of a row inside the database. ROWIDs are not addresses in memory or on disk; rather, they are identifiers that Oracle can use to compute the location of a row in a table. Locating a table row using the ROWID is the fastest way to find a row in a table. Although ROWID information can be queried like other columns in a table, a ROWID is not stored explicitly as a column value. When users add new rows to a database, Oracle generates a ROWID to identify that row's unique database location. The particular ROWID Oracle generates depends on a variety of factors, including

- The datafile storing the table that particular row is added to
- The segment corresponding to the object that the row will be stored in
- The block inside the segment that will house the row
- The slot or location inside an Oracle block that the row will be stored in

The previous bullets correspond to the components of information Oracle uses to generate a ROWID using Oracle's extended ROWID format that is 16 bytes in size and contains these four components. This format was introduced in Oracle 8.0.3 to overcome a limitation in the amount of space on disk that prior versions of Oracle were capable of addressing. In versions of Oracle after 8.0.3, Oracle uses 80 bits (10 bytes) for storage of an extended ROWID. The ROWID itself consists of four components: an object number (32 bits), a relative file number (10 bits), a block number (22 bits), and a row (slot) number (16 bits). Extended ROWIDs are displayed as 18-character representations of the location of data in the database, with each character represented in a base-64 format consisting of *A* through *Z*, *a* through *z*, zero through nine, +, and /. The first six characters correspond to the data object number, the next two are the relative file number, the next five are the block number, and the last three are the row number. With the use of extended ROWIDs, Oracle is capable of addressing rows in tables such that the database can grow to a virtually limitless size. The following code block demonstrates extended ROWID format:

```
SQL> select name, ROWID from employee;
NAME        ROWID
----------  ------------------
DURNAM      AAAA3kAAGAAAAGsAAA
BLANN       AAAA3kAAGAAAAGsAAB
```

The limitation we mentioned previously was due to the restricted ROWID format Oracle used in releases of the database software prior to Oracle 8.0.3. Historically, Oracle used a 6-byte format for ROWIDs that we now consider restricted because it does not store the object number for the table the row will be stored in. This format was acceptable in older versions of Oracle because at that time Oracle required all datafiles to have a unique file number within the database, regardless of the tablespace the file belonged to. In contrast, Oracle8i and later releases number datafiles relative to the tablespace they belong to. Restricted ROWIDs were displayed as 18 characters in base-16 format, where the first 8 characters represent the block number, characters 10 through 13 are the row number, and characters 15 through 18 are the (absolute) file number. Characters 9 and 14 are static separator characters.

With the added functionality provided by extended ROWIDs, you may wonder why Oracle bothers with restricted ROWIDs at all. Indeed, restricted ROWIDs are rarely used anymore, with one exception. Restricted ROWID format is still used to locate rows in nonpartitioned indexes for nonpartitioned tables where all index entries refer to rows within the same segment, thus eliminating any uncertainty about relative file numbers, because a segment can be stored in one and only one tablespace.

TIP
You might think it is silly, but here's how you can remember the components of Oracle ROWIDs. In Oracle7, the components are block ID, row number, and file number, which shorten to the acronym BRF. In Oracle9i, the components are object ID, block ID, row number, and relative file number, which shorten to OBRRF. To remember the acronyms, imagine how little dogs sound when they bark.

For Review

1. ROWIDs are addresses that point to the location of a row on disk with respect to a file, block, row number, and data object number.

2. Versions of Oracle prior to 8.0.3 use a restricted ROWID format. Current versions of Oracle still use this format for very limited purposes.

3. Starting with Oracle 8.0.3, Oracle also employs an extended ROWID format enabling the database to address more space on disk than previously allowed. This dramatically increases the amount of space an Oracle database can grow to.

Exercises

1. **You can query the ROWID of a row just as you would any other column (True/False).**

2. **The extended ROWID format uses a ROWID format __(A)__ bytes in size, where each symbol in the ROWID is in base-__(B)__ format.**

3. In contrast, the restricted ROWID format uses a ROWID format __(A)__ bytes in size, where each symbol in the ROWID is in base-__(B)__ format.

4. The primary difference between extended and restricted ROWID formats arises from the fact that earlier versions of Oracle required all datafile numbers to be _____(A)_____ in the database, whereas later versions of Oracle number datafiles _____(B)_____ to the tablespace the datafile is part of.

Answer Key

1. True. **2.** (A) 10; (B) 64. **3.** (A) 6; (B) 16. **4.** (A) unique; (B) relative.

Structure of Data Blocks and Rows

A cornerstone of storage management is Oracle's capability to enable you to manage the space in a data block. The size of a block is determined when you create the database by the DB_BLOCK_SIZE initialization parameter set for the instance at the time you create the database. Data block size is almost always a multiple of operating system block size. Usually, an operating system uses a block size of either 512 or 1,024 bytes. Oracle blocks are therefore a conglomeration of operating system blocks. An Oracle block can be anywhere from 2,048 to 16,384 bytes in size (even larger for some operating system platforms), with 8,192 bytes being a popular and common size for most Oracle databases. To understand more about data blocks, let's now explore their contents in more detail. There are several different components inside every data block in your Oracle database. Figure 14-1 illustrates block and row structure in Oracle. These components are divided loosely into the following areas:

- **Block header and directory information** Each block has a block header containing information about the block, including information about the table that owns the block and the row data the block contains.

- **Free space** This is the space reserved for growth of existing rows in the block and is determined by the pctfree setting used when the object was created.

- **Space occupied by existing rows** Every time a row is added to an object, Oracle places that row in the block. The amount of space available for rows to be added is determined by the setting for DB_BLOCK_SIZE, minus the space occupied by the block header, minus the space reserved by the setting for pctfree.

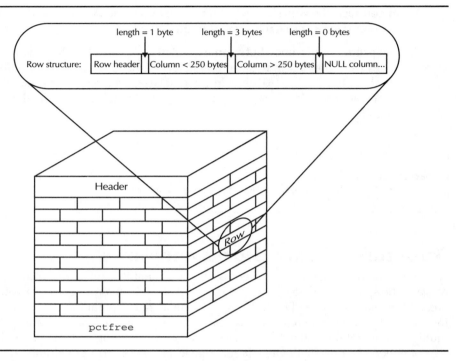

FIGURE 14-1. *The block and row structure in Oracle*

Looking at the Rows Themselves

Row data consists of the actual rows of each data table. Each row in a table has a row header. The *row header* stores the information about the number of columns in the row, chaining information, and the current lock status for the row. The row header is followed by actual row data. *Row data* consists of the actual rows of each data table. Row data is divided into columns, or column data. The *column data* for each row is stored in the order in which the columns were defined for the table. Additionally, a field indicating the *width* of the column is stored along with the non-NULL column data. If a column value is NULL for that row, no width field or column value will be stored in the block for that row column, and no bytes are used for the storage of NULL column values. Thus, you can see why we need to maintain some free space via pctfree for row growth. The column width field is 1 byte if the value for the column in this row is under 250 bytes, and it is 3 bytes if the value for the column in this row is 250 bytes or more. In both cases, Oracle stores a number identifying the width of the column value for this row only when the column value is not NULL.

For Review

1. Blocks consist of three components—a block header, row data, and leftover free space to accommodate existing row growth.

2. Rows themselves consist of a header, column data, and a field indicating the width of each column.

3. If no data is stored in the column for a particular row, Oracle doesn't waste any space in the block indicating that fact. Instead, nothing is stored there.

Exercises

1. **Every block in an Oracle database consists of a _____(A)_____, _____(B)_____, and _____(C)_____.**

2. **If a non-NULL value is stored for a column in a particular row, the width field will be __(A)__ byte(s) in size if the column value is less than 250 bytes wide, and __(B)__ byte(s) in size if the column value is 250 or more bytes wide.**

3. **A column value width field is not stored for a row with the value for the column is _____.**

Answer Key

1. (A) block header; (B) row data; (C) free space. **2.** (A) 1; (B) **3.** NULL.

Creating Permanent and Temporary Tables

Recall that for the OCP Oracle9i Introduction to SQL exam, you learned how to create permanent and temporary tables using the `create table` command. We're going to review how to do so here. However, we're also going to discuss how to manage storage considerations when doing so. Recall that in previous discussions of creating tablespaces, we discussed the use of the `default storage` clause. The settings in the `default storage` clause are applied to objects placed in that tablespace when the object itself gets created without a `storage` clause. In this discussion, we'll talk in more detail about the `storage` clause that can be defined for an object when it is created.

Creating Permanent Tables

Let's now look at creating permanent or regular tables in Oracle. You create a table in Oracle using the `create table` command. For this discussion, we'll assume you are placing your table into a dictionary-managed tablespace in order to cover the use of the `storage` clause. Later we'll discuss how locally managed tablespaces and uniform extent management factor into the `storage` clause you may define when creating your tables. The following code block shows an example of the `create table` command:

```
CREATE TABLE EMPLOYEE
(empid          NUMBER(10),
lastname        VARCHAR2(25),
firstname       VARCHAR2(25),
salary          NUMBER(10,4),
CONSTRAINT      pk_employee_01
PRIMARY KEY     (empid))
TABLESPACE data
PCTFREE    20   PCTUSED     50
INITRANS   1    MAXTRANS    255
NOCACHE         LOGGING
STORAGE ( INITIAL 100K   NEXT   150K
          MINEXTENTS 4   MAXEXTENTS   300
          PCTINCREASE 20 );
```

The `tablespace` keyword indicates which tablespace Oracle should create the table in. If you do not specify this clause, Oracle will put the table in the default tablespace you were assigned to when your userid was created. The next two clauses are for space utilization. Recall from an earlier discussion that the `pctfree` keyword specifies space that Oracle leaves free when inserting rows to accommodate growth later via updates. The `pctused` option specifies a threshold percentage of a block that the actual contents of row data must fall below before Oracle will consider the block free for new row inserts.

The next two space utilization clauses, `initrans` and `maxtrans`, control Oracle's capability to make concurrent updates to a data block. The `initrans` option specifies the initial number of transactions that can `update` the rows in a data block concurrently, whereas `maxtrans` specifies the maximum number of transactions that can `update` the rows in a data block concurrently. For the most part, the default values for each of these options should not be changed. For `initrans`, the default for tables is 1, while for clustered tables the default is 2. For `maxtrans`, the default for tables is 255.

The `nocache` clause specifies that Oracle should not make these blocks persistent in the buffer cache if a `select` statement on the table results in a full table scan. In this case, `select * from EMPLOYEE` would have Oracle load blocks into the buffer cache so that those blocks will not persist for very long. If you wanted the table to stay cached in the buffer cache when `select * from EMPLOYEE` was issued, you would specify the `cache` keyword instead. The default is `nocache`, which specifies that the blocks retrieved for this table are placed at the least recently used end of the LRU list in the buffer cache when a full table scan is performed.

The next clause, `logging`, tells Oracle to track table creation in the redo log so that in the event of disk failure, the table could be recovered. This is the default. However, this could be changed to `nologging` so that redo is not logged, which is handy in situations like the creation of the table and certain types of bulk data loads after which the DBA plans to take a backup after loading the data into Oracle will not be logged in the redo log file. Finally, you can specify `storage` clauses for table creation that will override the default storage settings of the tablespace you create the object in. The only tablespace default that your `storage` clause will not override is `minimum extent`.

Rules of Thumb about Table Storage for OCP

Observe the following rules of thumb when creating tables, and remember them for the OCP Oracle9i DBA Fundamentals I exam:

- Tables do not go in the same tablespace as undo segments, temporary segments, index segments, or into the SYSTEM tablespace.

- In order to make sure there is as little fragmentation in the tablespace as possible, have a collection of standard extent sizes that are complementary for your tables or use uniform extent allocation. This latter feature is used in Oracle9i by default, although Oracle will allocate multiple extents of uniform size in order to adhere to the allocation settings for `initial` or `next` in the `storage` clause of your `create table` command.

- Recall that the `cache` statement makes blocks read into the buffer cache via full table scans persist for much longer than they otherwise would. If you have a small lookup table accessed frequently, you may want to keep it in memory by specifying the `cache` clause or by issuing `alter table lookup_tblname` cache.

TIP

In Oracle9i, all tables are by default created as locally managed tables unlike pre-Oracle9i where tables were by default created dictionary-managed tables.

Creating Temporary Tables

Temporary tables are created with the `create global temporary table name ( tbldef ) on commit [delete|preserve] rows` statement. Your *tbldef* table definition can use any of the column or constraint definitions that a permanent table might, and associated temporary indexes will be generated in support of primary or unique keys. The data in a temporary table is stored in memory, inside the sort area. Thus, if more space is required, temporary segments in your temporary tablespace are used. When on commit delete rows is specified, the data in a temporary table (along with data in any associated index) is purged after the transaction completes. When on commit preserve rows is specified, rows will be stored in the table until the user who created the temporary table terminates the session. For that period, you can use the temporary table in the same way you would use any other table. If you do not specify an on commit clause, Oracle will use on commit delete rows by default. Let's look at an example where user SCOTT creates and uses a temporary table:

```
SQL> connect scott/tiger
Connected.
SQL> create global temporary table mytemptab
  2  (col1 number,
  3   col2 varchar2(30));
Table created.
SQL> insert into mytemptab values (1,'JUNK');
1 row created.
SQL> select * from mytemptab;
     COL1 COL2
--------- ----------------------------
        1 JUNK
SQL> commit;
Commit complete.
SQL> select * from mytemptab;
no rows selected
```

Now, let's look at the use of a temporary table where we want the data to persist for the duration of the session:

```
SQL> connect scott/tiger
Connected.
SQL> create global temporary table T_TABLE
  2  (col1 number,
  3   col2 varchar2(20))
  4  on commit preserve rows;
Table created.
SQL> insert into t_table values (1, 'JUNK');
1 row created.
SQL> select * from t_table;
     COL1 COL2
--------- --------------------
```

```
         1 JUNK
SQL> commit;
Commit complete.
SQL> select * from t_table;
     COL1 COL2
--------- -------------------
         1 JUNK
SQL> connect turner/ike
Connected.
SQL> connect scott/tiger
Connected.
SQL> select * from t_table;
no rows selected
```

Considerations When Using Temporary Tables

As I said a moment ago, other users can utilize the temporary table SCOTT created, too. They just won't see SCOTT's data. Likewise, SCOTT won't see their data. Furthermore, if SCOTT issues the truncate table MYTEMPTAB, only SCOTT's data will be removed. Other users' data will still be in the table. You may join the temporary table with permanent tables and create objects like views, indexes, and triggers that form object dependencies on the temporary table. However, no view can be created that contains a join between temporary and permanent tables. The create global temporary table statement does not log any redo, so temporary table data changes are not recoverable. However, data changes made to temporary tables will generate rollback information to enable Oracle to roll back the transaction and thus, the temporary table data, in the event the instance crashes. The TEMPORARY and DURATION columns in the DBA_TABLES view indicate whether a table is a temporary table and how long the data in the table will persist.

Temporary Tables and Storage

Oracle stores temporary table data in temporary segments in a temporary tablespace. Because temporary tablespace segment allocations are managed uniformly by Oracle, you typically do not need to worry about specifying a storage clause when creating your temporary tablespace. Instead, focus your attention as DBA on the question of whether or not the data in the temporary table should persist for the duration of a transaction or session.

For Review

1. Be sure you can create tables with appropriate storage settings in Oracle.

2. Be able to describe the concept underlying temporary tables in Oracle. Know the purposes they serve with respect to session-private storage of

information, global availability for all users, and retention of data for either the length of the transaction or the length of the session.

3. Understand how to create temporary tables in Oracle9i, including how to define the period of time the data in the temporary table will be retained. Know also where to find information about temporary tables in Oracle9i.

Exercises

1. **Your DATA tablespace is locally managed and uses uniform extent allocation. You issue the following statement:**

```
CREATE TABLE EMPLOYEE
(empid          NUMBER(10),
lastname        VARCHAR2(25),
firstname       VARCHAR2(25),
salary          NUMBER(10,4),
CONSTRAINT      pk_employee_01
PRIMARY KEY     (empid))
TABLESPACE data
PCTFREE     20  PCTUSED     50
INITRANS    1   MAXTRANS    255
NOCACHE         LOGGING
STORAGE ( INITIAL 100K   NEXT   150K
          MINEXTENTS 4  MAXEXTENTS   300
          PCTINCREASE 20 );
```

Which of the following statements is true about the table you just created?

A. The table is created in the same tablespace where the temporary segments will be housed.

B. The first segment allocated for this table will be 100KB of contiguous blocks.

C. Redo information will be generated for the creation of this table.

D. When full table scans are issued on the EMPLOYEE table, blocks from the table will persist in the buffer cache for a long time after the statement executes.

2. **User FITZPATRICK creates a temporary table using the following statement:**

```
SQL> create global temporary table FITZTEMPTAB
  2  (name varchar2(10), value number, use_date date)
  3  on commit delete rows;
Table created
```

FITZPATRICK then informs users MCGILLICUDDY and OBRYAN of his temporary table. While each user is connected to Oracle9i and populating table FITZTEMPTAB, OBRYAN issues `truncate table FITZTEMPTAB`. Which of the following users had their records removed temporary table by this action?

A. FITZPATRICK only

B. OBRYAN only

C. OBRYAN and FITZPATRICK only

D. OBRYAN, FITZPATRICK, and MCGILLICUDDY

3. User FITZGERALD issues the following statement to the FITZTEMPTAB table created in the code shown in Question 1: `update fitztemptab set name = 'MYCHANGE' where value = 55`. Which of the following aspects of the database will Oracle definitely not utilize as part of this operation?

A. The sort area

B. The TEMP tablespace

C. The LGWR process

D. The rollback segment assigned to the transaction

4. User OBRYAN adds a record to FITZTEMPTAB, defined using the code block shown in Question 1. At what point will the data added to FITZTEMPTAB by OBRYAN be removed from the temporary table?

A. When FITZPATRICK `commits` the transaction

B. When OBRYAN `commits` the transaction

C. When OBRYAN logs off of Oracle9i

D. When FITZPATRICK issues `truncate table FITZTEMPTAB`

Answer Key
1. C. 2. B. 3. C. 4. B.

Managing Storage Structures in a Table

Recall from earlier chapters that Oracle allocates new extents for a table automatically when more data is added than the current allocation will hold. You can add more extents manually with the `alter table allocate extent (size num[K|M] datafile 'filename')` statement, where `num` is the size of the extent you want to allocate (subject to the tablespace limit set by `minimum extent`) and `filename` is the absolute path and filename of the datafile you want the extent stored in. Both the `size` and `datafile` clauses are optional. If `size` is not used, Oracle uses the size specified in the `next` storage option for the table. If `datafile` is excluded, Oracle manages placement itself. You would use this command to control the distribution of extents before performing bulk data loads.

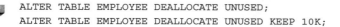

```
ALTER TABLE EMPLOYEE ALLOCATE EXTENT;
ALTER TABLE EMPLOYEE ALLOCATE EXTENT ( SIZE 200K );
ALTER TABLE EMPLOYEE ALLOCATE EXTENT
  (DATAFILE '/u10/oradata/oracle/data05.dbf' );
```

Table High-Water Marks and Unused Space

Now, consider how Oracle maintains knowledge about table size. A special marker called the *high-water mark* is used by Oracle to indicate the last block used to hold the table's data. As `insert` statements fill data blocks, Oracle moves the high-water mark farther and farther out to indicate the last block used. The high-water mark is stored in a table segment header and is used to determine where to stop reading blocks during full table scans. You can find the high-water mark for your table using the `unused_space( )` procedure from the DBMS_SPACE Oracle-supplied package or in the DBA_TABLES dictionary view after the `analyze` command has been run on your table. There is more information about `analyze` and the dictionary views housing table information later in this section.

Finally, if you want to eliminate the unused space allocated to your table, you can issue the `alter table tblname deallocate unused keep num [K|M]` statement, where `keep` is an optional clause that lets you retain `num` amount of the unused space. The `keep` clause specifies the number of bytes above the high-water mark that should be retained. If the command is used without the `keep` clause, the Oracle server will deallocate all unused space above the high-water mark. If the high-water mark is at an extent less than the value of `minextents`, the Oracle server will release extents above `minextents`.

```
ALTER TABLE EMPLOYEE DEALLOCATE UNUSED;
ALTER TABLE EMPLOYEE DEALLOCATE UNUSED KEEP 10K;
```

Row Migration and Chaining

If `pctfree` is too low for blocks in a table, `update` statements may increase the size of that row, only to find there is not enough room in the block to fit the change. Thus, Oracle has to move the row to another block in which it will fit. Row migration degrades performance when the server process attempts to locate the migrated row, only to find that the row is in another location.

Chaining is also detrimental to database performance. *Chaining* is when data for one row is stored in multiple blocks. This is a common side effect in tables with columns defined to be datatype LONG, because the LONG column data is stored inline with the rest of the table. The server process must piece together one row of data using multiple disk reads. In addition, there is performance degradation by DBWR when it has to perform multiple disk writes for only one row of data.

Analyzing Tables to Check Integrity and Migration

Typically, Oracle automatically handles validation of the structure of every data block used whenever the block is read into the buffer cache for user processes. However, there are two things you can do to validate the structural integrity of data blocks. The first is to use the `initsid.ora` parameter DB_BLOCK_CHECKSUM. Setting this parameter to TRUE makes the DBWR process calculate a checksum on every block it writes, regardless of tablespace, as a further measure to protecting the integrity of blocks in the database. In addition, Oracle calculates checksums for blocks written to the online redo logs as well. When this parameter is set to FALSE, the DBWR process calculates checksums only when writing blocks to the SYSTEM tablespace. The process of calculating checksums adds some overhead to normal database processing. You must balance that additional performance overhead with the need for ensuring that data blocks aren't corrupt.

The second method for checking integrity can be performed at any time using the `analyze table tblname validate structure` command. The optional `cascade` clause in this statement further validates the structure of blocks in indexes associated with the table. The `analyze` command is issued from SQL*Plus on one table at a time.

Using `analyze` to Detect Row Migration

The main use of the `analyze` command is determining performance statistics for cost-based optimization of how Oracle processes SQL statements. An added benefit of the `analyze` command is that it will also detect row migration on your table. There are two basic clauses for this command: `estimate statistics` and `compute statistics`. The former estimates statistics collection for the table based on a sample size of data that you can optionally specify with the `sample num [rows|percent]` clause. If you don't specify a `sample` clause, Oracle uses 1,064 rows. The `compute statistics` clause calculates statistics collection for the table based on every row in the table. Oracle suggests you use `estimate statistics` rather than `compute statistics` because the former is almost as accurate and takes less time.

Once statistics are generated, the CHAIN_CNT column in the DBA_TABLES dictionary view contains the number of chained and migrated rows estimated or found in the table. If you feel this number is high, you might want to save the table data, drop the table, re-create it, and reload the data to eliminate the problem. Remember, some chaining is to be expected, especially when your rows are wide (for example, if you have many VARCHAR2(4000) columns or a LONG column). Finally, if you want to validate integrity on an ongoing basis as part of a PL/SQL application, you can develop code that calls the `analyze_schema( )` procedures in the DBMS_UTILITY package or the `analyze_object` procedure in DBMS_DDL. The scope of these procedures should be self-evident.

TIP
The DBMS_STATS package can be used in place of the `analyze` command for gathering statistics. This package offers some advantages over the use of the `analyze` command, particularly when you want to save statistics and reuse those statistics in different databases.

Retrieving Data Dictionary Information about Tables

There are several data dictionary views available for obtaining information about tables. The views in the dictionary displaying this information base their content either on tables that exist in the database or on dynamic performance information about tables collected while the instance is running. The views you should remember for viewing table information include the following:

- **DBA_SEGMENTS** Gives information about the name, tablespace location, and owner of segments containing table data in Oracle

- **DBA_OBJECTS** Gives information about the object ID number used in part to determine ROWID for rows in the table, as well as the table creation timestamp for determining dependencies

- **DBA_TABLES** Gives information about all storage settings for the table, as well as the statistics collected as part of the `analyze` operation on that table

- **DBA_EXTENTS** Gives information about the number of extents allocated to a table, the datafiles in which they are stored, and how large each extent is

- **DBA_TAB_COLUMNS**   Gives information about every column in every table, including datatype, size, precision, column position in each row, and nullability

- **DBA_TAB_COMMENTS**   Gives comment information for every table, if any comment information is stored

- **DBA_COL_COMMENTS**   Gives comment information for every column in every table, if any comment information is stored

Because the possibilities for combining this data are vast, no example SQL statements will be shown here. Instead, consider the possible matchups. For example, if you wanted to determine whether an extremely large table was clumped in one datafile, you could query the DBA_EXTENTS view to find out. If you wanted to determine what rows were chained or migrated in your table, you could query the DBA_TABLES view to find out. If you were looking to see if there is a great deal of unused space in a table, you could query the DBA_TABLES view as well. Be aware that the columns you would query from DBA_TABLES in these cases will only be populated if `analyze` has been run on that table. If these columns are NULL, run `analyze` to tabulate the data you need.

For Review

1. Be sure you understand the process for manually allocating more extents to a table.

2. Know the name of the view can you use to find out the date/time a table was created and where you can look to see if there were rows chained or migrated in the table.

3. Be sure you understand what a high-water mark is and how it is set.

4. Understand what is meant by fragmentation. Fragmentation can manifest in many ways and row migration is one of the serious fragmentation problems.

Exercises

1. **Row migration in Oracle is detected using the _____ command.**

2. **Additional extents are allocated for a table using the _____ command.**

Answer Key
1. `analyze`. 2. `alter table allocate extent`.

Reorganizing, Truncating, and Dropping Tables

Moving a table into a different tablespace used to not be an easy task. To do so, you had to use the EXPORT tool to create a dump file containing the rows of the table, along with that table's definition. If there were indexes or constraints involved, you had to dump those objects to file using EXPORT, too. Generating the export dump was generally not too troublesome, but loading the table back into another tablespace via IMPORT might have been. You had to drop the table from the Oracle database after exporting it, and then you had to re-create the table in another tablespace. You then ran IMPORT with the IGNORE parameter set to Y so that IMPORT wouldn't fail when it saw that the table already existed. If you didn't perform this step, IMPORT would simply load the table right back into the tablespace it was stored in before. Worse, if that tablespace didn't exist, IMPORT would load the object into the default tablespace for the user you ran IMPORT as— which could have accidentally loaded the table into the SYSTEM tablespace if you weren't careful. You could have used SQL*Loader or the `create table as select` command with the `storage` and `tablespace` clauses explicitly defined instead, but both options would have required a long time to execute.

Relocating Tables in Oracle: Concept

Oracle now offers a great feature with respect to relocating and reorganizing tables. You can relocate a table to another tablespace or reorganize a table to resize the initial segment without the use of EXPORT and IMPORT and without the `create table as select` statement. Instead, these actions can be performed in Oracle through the use of the `move` option in the `alter table` command. The `alter table move` command supports the following clauses:

- **tablespace *name*** The `tablespace` clause enables you to identify the tablespace location where you want the table placed. If omitted, Oracle8*i* rebuilds the table in a new segment in the same tablespace.

- **storage (*storage_attributes*)** The `storage` clause enables you to reconfigure aspects of the table's storage, such as the `initial` extent or percentage increase of subsequent extents. If no `storage` clause is specified, then Oracle will re-create the table with the same storage attributes used when the table was initially created. Note that this aspect of table creation is useful only for placement in dictionary-managed tablespaces, not locally managed tablespaces.

- **logging or nologging** Use of the `logging` keyword explicitly states that you would like Oracle to write the changes made by `alter table move` to the online redo logs for recoverability purposes. This is the default behavior Oracle takes in this context. The `nologging` keyword is used to tell Oracle not to write the changes made by `alter table move` to the online redo log.

TIP

In Oracle Enterprise Edition, the `alter table move` *command also enables use of the* `online` *keyword to permit movement or reorganization of the table while the old version is still available for use.*

Relocating Tables in Oracle: Implementation

Now that we've explored the concepts underlying use of the `alter table move` command, let's explore how to use that command in action. The first example is where we move a table called WORK_TABLE from the USER_DATA tablespace to the LMTAB tablespace:

```
SQL> select owner, table_name, tablespace_name
  2  from dba_tables
  3  where table_name = 'WORK_TABLE';
OWNER       TABLE_NAME TABLESPACE_NAME
----------  ---------- ---------------
SCOTT       WORK_TABLE USER_DATA
SQL> alter table mytab move tablespace lmtab;
Table altered.
SQL> select owner, table_name, tablespace_name
  2  from dba_tables
  3  where table_name = 'WORK_TABLE';
OWNER       TABLE_NAME TABLESPACE_NAME
----------  ---------- ---------------
SCOTT       WORK_TABLE LMTAB
```

You can see where this command would be handy, especially for situations where a table must be moved out of the SYSTEM tablespace into a tablespace more appropriate for user-defined tables. However, although Oracle preserves the table's associated constraints, object privileges, and triggers when the table is moved from one tablespace to another, the `alter table name move tablespace tblspcname` command does not move any indexes associated with the table. Check out the following code block and you'll see what I mean:

```
SQL> create table TAB_W_INDEXES
  2  (col1 number primary key)
  3  tablespace system;
Table created.
```

```
SQL> select owner, table_name, index_name, tablespace_name
  2  from dba_indexes
  3  where table_name = 'TAB_W_INDEXES';
OWNER        TABLE_NAME       INDEX_NAME      TABLESPACE_NAME
----------   --------------   ------------    ---------------
SCOTT        TAB_W_INDEXES    SYS_C00953          SYSTEM
SQL> alter table tab_w_indexes
  2  move tablespace user_data;
Table altered.
SQL> select owner, table_name, index_name, tablespace_name
  2  from dba_indexes
  3  table_name = 'TAB_W_INDEXES';
OWNER        TABLE_NAME       INDEX_NAME      TABLESPACE_NAME
----------   --------------   ------------    ---------------
SCOTT        TAB_W_INDEXES    SYS_C00953          SYSTEM
```

The capabilities of this command far surpass similar functionality provided by the `create table as select` statement. Let's take a look at this functionality in action:

```
SQL> alter index sys_c00953 rebuild tablespace user_data;
Index altered.
SQL> select owner, table_name, index_name, tablespace_name
  2  from dba_indexes
  3  where table_name = 'TAB_W_INDEXES';
OWNER        TABLE_NAME       INDEX_NAME      TABLESPACE_NAME
----------   --------------   ------------    ---------------
SCOTT        TAB_W_INDEXES    SYS_C00953          USER_DATA
```

> **TIP**
> *Just like creating a table in a locally managed tablespace, these parameters will show up in DBA_TABLES, but may not be in effect. You should check the actual size of the extents, listed in the BYTES or BLOCKS in the DBA_EXTENTS view.*

Finally, let's look at the situation where we use the `alter table move` clause to reorganize an existing table in its original tablespace. Remember, Oracle places the table in a new segment within the original tablespace in order to rebuild the storage allocation according to your specifications. The following code block illustrates this usage:

```
SQL> alter table tab_w_indexes
  2  move storage (initial 20K next 20K);
```

```
Table altered.
SQL> select owner, table_name, initial_extent, next_extent
  2  from dba_tables
  3  where table_name = 'TAB_W_INDEXES';
OWNER        TABLE_NAME     INITIAL_EXTENT NEXT_EXTENT
----------   -------------  -------------- -----------
SCOTT        TAB_W_INDEXES          20480       20480
```

TIP

If you are performing reorganization on a large table and want to improve performance on the operation, you can also specify the nologging *keyword as part of the* alter table *move command. You will improve performance because the changes made by Oracle8i will not be written to the online redo log, but beware—the changes will not be recoverable later.*

Space Considerations for Relocating Tables

The operation of the alter table *name* move statement requires enough space for two copies of the table to exist in Oracle8i until the operation completes and Oracle8i can drop the table. During the period of moving the table, users can still issue select statements to see data in the table, but they cannot make any changes to data in the table.

Truncating and Dropping Tables

Now, consider a favorite tidbit from the archives of Oracle minutiae. You issue a delete statement on a table with many hundreds of thousands or millions of rows and commit it. Feeling smug with your accomplishment, you issue a select count(*) statement. A few minutes later, you get your count of zero rows. What happened? Oracle didn't reset the high-water mark after the delete statement, and what's more, it never does! To get rid of the extents allocated that are now empty and reset the high-water mark while still preserving the table definition, the truncate table command (with optional drop storage clause) is used. Note that this is a data definition language (DDL) operation, not data manipulation language (DML), meaning that once the table is truncated, you cannot issue a rollback command to magically get the data back. Recall also that any change made to minextents after table creation will now be applied to the table, unless you specify the optional reuse storage clause, which preserves the current storage allocation and does not reset the high-water mark. A final word of note—any associated indexes will also be truncated, and any optional drop storage or reuse storage clauses will also be applied to associated indexes.

```
TRUNCATE TABLE EMPLOYEE;
TRUNCATE TABLE EMPLOYEE DROP STORAGE;
TRUNCATE TABLE EMPLOYEE REUSE STORAGE;
```

TIP
Here's an interesting fact about truncate table
*that may or may not find its way to OCP Exam.
Despite your inability to* rollback *a table
truncation, Oracle does acquire a rollback segment
for the job. Why? Because if you terminate the*
truncate table *command, or if some failure
occurs, the rollback segment stores the changes
made for the duration of the truncate operation to
enable crash recovery.*

Finally, to rid yourself of the table entirely and give all allocated space back to
the tablespace, issue the drop table statement. There is an optional clause you
must include to handle other tables that may have defined referential integrity
constraints into this table: the cascade constraints clause. The following code
block demonstrates this command:

```
DROP TABLE EMPLOYEE;
DROP TABLE EMPLOYEE CASCADE CONSTRAINTS;
```

For Review

1. Know the statement that is used for moving a table to another tablespace.
    Understand how is this statement similar in function to the create table
    as select statement.

2. Understand the limitation to alter table move with respect to movement of
    supporting indexes. Be sure you know that the alter index rebuild
    tablespace command can be used for moving the associated indexes.

3. Be sure you know the space considerations involved in relocating or
    reorganizing a table, and also be sure you know the trade-offs inherent in
    use of the nologging keyword in the alter table move command.

Exercises

1. **You need to move table EMP from the DATA tablespace to the
    LARGE_DATA tablespace. This table was created with a unique constraint
    on the GOVT_ID column, with the associated index placed in the IDX
    tablespace. You want to move this index to the LARGE_INDX tablespace as**

well. Which of the following commands can be used for moving the corresponding index on the GOVT_ID column to the appropriate tablespace?

A. `alter index myidx rebuild tablespace large_index;`

B. `alter table emp move tablespace large_data index tablespace large_index;`

C. `alter table emp move tablespace large_index;`

D. `alter index myidx move tablespace large_index;`

2. You move the EMP table from the DATA tablespace to the LARGE_DATA tablespace. Which of the following statements about Oracle behavior regarding corresponding objects in this context is not true?

A. The object privileges granted to users on this table are preserved through the move.

B. A new segment in the LARGE_DATA tablespace now houses EMP's data.

C. Code for the triggers associated with the table is moved from the DATA tablespace to the LARGE_DATA tablespace.

D. The associated primary key continues to enforce uniqueness on the key column through the move.

3. You issue the following statement in Oracle: `alter table EMP move storage (initial 50K next 100K) nologging.` Which of the following statements made about this command is not true?

A. Table EMP has been moved to a new segment.

B. Table EMP has been moved to a new tablespace.

C. The change to table EMP was made without acquiring the redo allocation latch.

D. The change to table EMP will not be recoverable.

Answer Key

1. A. 2. C. Trigger code is stored in dictionary tables in the SYSTEM tablespace. 3. B.

Dropping Unused Columns from Tables

Try to envision the following scenario in versions of Oracle prior to Oracle9i. You have a table called EMPLOYEE that stores employee data. One of the columns stored a text string corresponding to the name of the subsidiary company the employee worked within. A reorganization of the company takes place where all subsidiary companies are now consolidated within the parent company, making it unnecessary to store subsidiary information as its own column. If you wanted to eliminate the unnecessary column, you would have to dump the contents of the table to a flat file, drop the table, re-create the table without the subsidiary column, and use SQL*Loader to reload the table records to your newly created table. Depending on how many employees there were in your company, this process could take a long time. Alternately, you could use Pro*C instead of SQL*Loader to load the records into the table more quickly using array fetches, but there would still be several steps involved in executing this task. You would likely need some downtime in order to accomplish the task as well.

Dropping Unused Columns: Concept

Instead of requiring that you execute this potentially arduous task, Oracle9i permits you to drop unused columns from tables simply by using the `alter table` command. There are two ways to drop a column in Oracle9i. The first is a logical method that removes no data but otherwise behaves as if the column has been removed. This option is known as marking the column as unused. The second is physically removing the column from the table. Let's look at the concepts behind each in more detail.

Marking a Column Unused   Users of the table cannot see an unused column. Information about the unused column does not appear in the output of the `describe table` command, nor can you query data in an unused column. Marking a column as unused is like deleting a column logically because the data is still in the table, but it cannot be used. The syntax for marking a column as unused is `alter table` *name* `set unused column` *colname*. To see which tables have unused columns, you can query the dictionary view in Oracle9i known as DBA_UNUSED_COL_TABS, and all tables with unused columns will be listed. The COUNT column in that view indicates how many unused columns there are for each table. If you wanted to drop the columns after marking them unused, you could use the `alter table` *name* `drop unused column` statement instead. Marking a column as unused and then using the `alter table` *name* `drop unused column` statement is useful because it enables you to take away column access quickly and immediately. Later on, during a DBA maintenance weekend or after business hours, you can then remove the column with `alter table` *name* `drop unused column` to reclaim the space.

Physically Removing the Column   The other method for dropping a table column is through the use of the `alter table` *name* `drop column` *colname* statement. This statement actually removes all data from the column and eliminates the column from the table definition. This operation may take more time to complete than marking the column as unused because Oracle has to go through all blocks of the table and actually remove the column data in order to reclaim the space used by that column.

Dropping Columns in Oracle9i: Implementation

Let's take a look at some examples where you drop columns in Oracle9i using the `alter table` statement. The first example instructs Oracle to ignore the column by using the `set unused column` clause. In this situation, no information is removed from the table column. Oracle simply pretends the column isn't there. Later, we can remove the column using the `drop unused columns` clause. Both steps are shown in the following block:

```
SQL> alter table employee set unused column subsidiary;
Table altered.
SQL> alter table employee drop unused columns;
Table altered.
```

The second option is to remove the column and all contents entirely from the table immediately. This statement is shown in the following block:

```
SQL> alter table employee drop column subsidiary;
Table altered.
```

Other Syntax for Removing Columns

There are a few optional clauses for the `alter table` *name* `drop column` *colname* statement, which are all added on after *colname* in the statement:

- **`cascade constraints`**   Any foreign keys referring to the column to be dropped, or any constraints on the column itself, will be eliminated along with the column.

- **`invalidate`**   Any objects related to the table whose column is being dropped will be marked invalid. Recall that objects that relate to a table in this fashion include PL/SQL blocks that refer to a table, triggers, and views.

- **`checkpoint num`**   This enables you to reduce the amount of space used in a rollback segment by having Oracle9i perform a checkpoint every *num* number of rows. For the duration of the `alter table drop column` operation, the table shows a status of INVALID. If the operation terminates abnormally (if, for example, the session or instance crashed), Oracle would be able to roll back only to the most recent checkpoint and the table would remain in an INVALID state. However, you can resume the removal of the column after instance recovery is made or when you reconnect using the `alter table` *name* `drop columns continue` statement.

For Review

1. Be sure you know how to add columns using the `alter table` statement with the `add` clause.

2. Know how to modify column datatype definition using the `alter table` statement with the `modify` clause.

3. Understand both uses of the alter table command for dropping columns— one using the `set unused column` and `drop unused columns` syntax and the other with the `drop column` syntax.

Exercises

1. **You just issued the following statement:** `alter table sales drop column profit`. **Which of the following choices identifies when the column will actually be removed from Oracle?**

   A. Immediately following statement execution

   B. After the `alter table drop unused columns` command is issued

   C. After the `alter table set unused column` command is issued

   D. After the `alter table modify` command is issued

2. **The Acme Sales Company reorganizes to consolidate its entire sales force into one region, eliminating the need for a SALES_REGION column. You issue the following statement in Oracle9i:** `alter table sales set unused column sales_region`. **At what point will data actually be removed from the table?**

   A. When the `alter table sales drop unused columns` statement is issued.

   B. When the `alter table sales set unused column sales_region` statement finishes executing.

C. When you dump the contents of the table to flat file, re-create the table without the SALES_REGION column, and reload the data using SQL*Loader.

D. Never—a column is only removed when you use the `alter table sales drop column sales_region` statement.

3. **You want to determine how many columns in the EMPLOYEE table are marked unused for later removal. Which of the following methods would be appropriate for the purpose?**

   A. Querying the DBA_TABLES view

   B. Using the `describe` command

   C. Querying the DBA_UNUSED_COLS view

   D. Querying the DBA_UNUSED_COL_TABS view

Answer Key
1. A. 2. A. 3. C.

Managing Indexes

In this section, you will cover the following topics on managing indexes:

- Different index types and their use
- Creating B-tree and bitmap indexes
- Reorganizing indexes
- Dropping indexes
- Getting index information from the data dictionary
- Monitoring use of an index

Tables can grow quite large, and when they do, it becomes difficult for users to quickly find the data they need. For this reason, Oracle offers indexes as a method of speeding database performance when accessing tables with a lot of data. Oracle provides different types of indexes for different uses, and you will learn about them here. You will also learn about the specific procedures for creating B-tree and bitmap indexes and what sorts of situations may cause you to choose one over the other. The methods used to reorganize and drop indexes are shown here as well. Finally, you will learn where to look in the data dictionary for information about your indexes and how to monitor the use of an index.

Different Index Types and Their Uses

An index in Oracle can be compared to the card catalog in a library. When you want to find a book, you go to the card catalog (or computer) and look up the book under author, title, or subject. When you find the card for that book, it lists the location of the book in the library according to a classification system. Looking for a book in this way reduces the time you spend looking for a book on fly-fishing in the section where autobiographies are kept. Oracle indexes work the same way. You find row data that matches your search criteria in the index first, and then use the ROWID for that row from the index to get the entire row quickly from the table.

Several criteria are used to determine what kind of index you're looking at. The first criterion is how many columns the index has. *Simple* indexes contain only one column of data through which you can search plus the ROWID of the corresponding row in the table. *Composite* indexes store more than one column of data for you to search plus the ROWID of the corresponding row in the table. You can put up to 32 columns in a composite index, but you may be restricted from including that many if the total size of all the columns you want in the index exceeds DB_BLOCK_SIZE / 3. Other criteria for identifying indexes are whether the indexed column(s) contains all unique (composite) values, whether an index is partitioned or nonpartitioned, and whether it is a traditional B-tree or a bitmap index, or whether the data in the index is stored in reverse order.

TIP
When composite indexes are in place on a table, Oracle will only use that index if the leading column(s) of the composite index are referenced in the where *clause of the query against the table.*

Oracle maintains indexes whenever user processes make data changes to tables. For example, if you `insert` a new row in a table, an associated entry is made in the index for that row's indexed column. That entry is not made to the last leaf block of the index, but, rather, the appropriate leaf block is located according to index sort order, and the entry is made there. The `pctfree` setting has no effect on the index except at the time of creation. When data is removed from the table, the corresponding index entry is marked for removal. Later, when all other rows corresponding to all index entries in the leaf node are removed, then and only then is the entire block purged of index entries. Thus, the structure of the index is preserved. An `update` statement that changes the value of a row's indexed column value is treated as a marked removal followed by an `insert`. Finally, index entries can be added to a block even past the `pctfree` threshold.

Nonpartitioned B-Tree Indexes

The B-tree index is the traditional indexing mechanism used in Oracle. It stores data in a treelike fashion, as displayed in Figure 14-2. At the base of the index is the *root node*, which is an entry point for your search for data in the index. The root node contains pointers to other nodes at the next level in the index. Depending on the value you seek, you will be pointed in one of many directions. The next level in the index consists of *branch nodes*, which are similar to the root node in that they, too, contain pointers to the next level of nodes in the index. Again, depending on the value you seek, you will be pointed in one of many directions. Branch nodes point to the highest level of the index: the *leaf nodes*. In this highest level, *index entries* contain indexed column values and the corresponding ROWIDs of rows storing those column values. Each leaf node is linked to both the leaf node on its left and on its right, in order to make it possible to search up and down through a range of entries in the index.

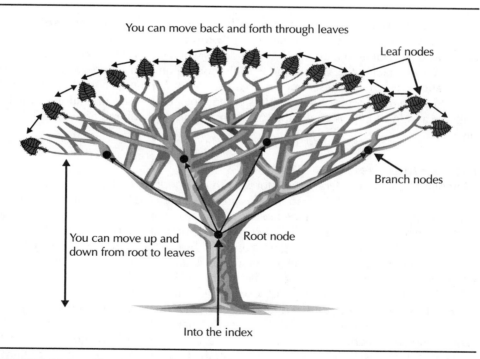

FIGURE 14-2. *The B-tree index structure*

Within a single index entry, there are several elements, some of which have already been covered. The first is the *index entry header*, containing the number of columns in the entry. Following that, the entry stores the values for the column(s) in the index. Preceding each column value is a length byte that follows the same rules that length bytes follow in row entries. Finally, the index entry stores the ROWID. No length byte is needed for this value because all ROWIDs are the same length.

There are a few special cases of data stored in index entries that you should understand:

■ If the index is nonunique and several rows contain the same value for the column, then each row with that value will have its own index entry to store each unique ROWID.

■ If a row has a NULL value for the column(s) being indexed, there will be no corresponding index entry for that row.

■ For nonpartitioned indexes only, because the index stores data for only one table and because all tables can be stored in only one tablespace, the object ID number is not required to locate the row from the index. Thus, nonpartitioned B-tree indexes use restricted ROWIDs to point to row data.

B-tree indexes are used most commonly to improve performance on `select` statements using columns of unique or mostly distinct values. It is relatively easy and quick for Oracle to maintain B-tree indexes when data is changed in an indexed column, too, making this type of index useful for online transaction-processing applications. However, these indexes do a bad job of finding data quickly on `select` statements with `where` clauses containing comparison operations joined with `or` and in situations where the values in the indexed column are not very distinct.

Bitmap Indexes

Although all indexes in Oracle are stored with the root-branch-leaf structure illustrated in Figure 14-2, bitmap indexes are conceptualized differently. Instead of storing entries for each row in the table, the bitmap index stores an entry containing each distinct value, the start and end ROWIDs to indicate the range of ROWIDs in this table, and a long binary string with as many bits as there are rows in the table.

For example, say you are looking at a representation of a bitmap index for a table such as the one in Figure 14-3. The APPLE_TYPE column indexed has only three distinct values. The bitmap index would have three entries, as you see in the figure. The start and end restricted ROWIDs for the object are also shown, so that you know what the potential ROWID range is. Finally, you see a binary string representing a bitmap. A position will be set to 1 for the entry if the column for that row contains the associated value; otherwise, the bit is set to 0. If an entry contains a bit set to 1, the corresponding bit in every other entry will always be set to 0.

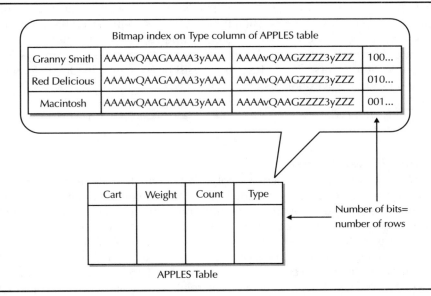

FIGURE 14-3. *A logical representation of a bitmap index*

Actually, this binary entry is also compressed, which means you cannot see the bitmap with 0 and 1, but this is how the information is represented internally.

Bitmap indexes improve performance in situations where you `select` data from a column whose values are repeated often, as is the case with employee status (for example, active, LOA, or retired). They also improve performance on `select` statements with multiple `where` conditions joined by `or`.

Bitmap indexes improve performance where data in the column is not distinct and is infrequently or never changed. By the same token, it is a somewhat arduous process to change data in that column. This is because changing the value of a column stored in a bitmap index requires Oracle to lock the entire segment storing the bitmap index to make the change. Locking occurs to the whole bitmap index. In other words, when changes are made to the key column in the table, bitmaps must be modified. This results in locking of the relevant bitmap segments.

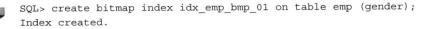

```
SQL> create bitmap index idx_emp_bmp_01 on table emp (gender);
Index created.
```

Reverse-Key Indexes

Finally, consider the use of reverse-key indexes. This type of index is the same as a regular B-tree index except for one thing—the data from the column being indexed is stored in reverse order. Thus, if the column value in a table of first names is

JASON, the reverse-key index column will be NOSAJ. Typically, users see the most benefit from reverse-key indexes when their `select` statements contain `where` clauses that use equality comparisons, such as `where X = 5`, but not in situations where range comparisons are used, such as `where X between 4 and 6`. The value or benefit to reverse-key indexes is to assist performance in Oracle Real Application Cluster environments.

```
SQL> create index idx_emp_rev_01 on table emp (lastname) reverse;
Index created.
```

Function-Based Indexes

The function-based index is a new type of index in Oracle8i that is designed to improve query performance by making it possible to define an index that works when your `where` clause contains operations on columns. Traditional B-tree indexes won't be used when your `where` clause contains columns that participate in functions or operations. For example, suppose you have table EMP with four columns: EMPID, LASTNAME, FIRSTNAME, and SALARY. The SALARY column has a B-tree index on it. However, if you issue the `select * from EMP where (SALARY*1.08) > 63000` statement, the relational database management system (RDBMS) ignores the index, performing a full table scan instead. Function-based indexes are designed to be used in situations like this one, where your SQL statements contain such operations in their `where` clauses. The following code block shows a function-based index defined:

```
CREATE INDEX idx_emp_func_01
ON emp(SALARY*1.08);
```

By using function-based indexes like this one, you can optimize the performance of queries containing function operations on columns in the `where` clause, like the query shown previously. As long as the function you specify is repeatable, you can create a function-based index around it. A repeatable function is one whose result will never change for the same set of input data. For example, 2 + 2 will always equal 4, and will never change one day so that it equals 5. Thus, the addition operation is repeatable. To enable the use of function-based indexes, you must issue two `alter session` statements, as follows:

```
SQL> alter session set query_rewrite_enabled = true;
Session altered.
SQL> alter session set query_rewrite_integrity=trusted;
Session altered.
```

TIP
Bitmap indexes can also be function-based indexes.
Function-based indexes can also be partitioned.

Descending Indexes

Another new type of index instituted in Oracle8i and later is the descending index. Recall that the `order by` clause is used in SQL statements to impose sort order on data returned from the database to make it more readable. Oracle does not typically store data in any particular order, a common practice in relational database systems. However, a B-tree index does store information in a particular order. In versions of Oracle before Oracle8i, the order used by B-tree indexes has been ascending order, ordered from the lowest column value to the highest.

In Oracle8i and later, you can now categorize data in a B-tree index in descending order as well. This feature can be useful in applications where sorting operations are required in conflicting ways. For example, say you have the EMP table with four columns: EMPID, LASTNAME, SALARY, and DEPT. As part of a departmental performance comparison, you may have to query this table by department code in ascending order and salary in descending order, using the following query:

```
SQL> select dept, salary, empid, lastname
  2  from emp
  3  order by dept asc, salary desc;
```

If the EMP table is large, then prior versions of Oracle may have required enormous amounts of sort space to obtain DEPT data in one sort order and SALARY data in another. Descending indexes can be used to change that. For example, you could define separate, simple indexes for DEPT and SALARY data, where the DEPT data used the traditional ascending method in its B-tree index, while the SALARY column used descending order in the index. To create the simple indexes, you could use the following code block:

```
-- Regular ascending index
CREATE INDEX emp_dept_idx_01
ON EMP(DEPT);

-- Descending index
CREATE INDEX emp_sal_idx_01
ON EMP(SALARY DESC);
```

Different sort orders can be specified for columns in a composite index as well. Using the previous example, you could define a composite index containing two columns with different sort orders specified for each column, such as the index definition shown in the following code block:

```
CREATE INDEX emp_dep_sal_idx_01
ON EMP(dept ASC, salary DESC);
```

TIP
You can also combine function-based indexes with descending-index features to create function-based descending indexes. Descending indexes can also be partitioned.

For Review

1. Be sure you know what a unique index is and how it compares with a nonunique index. Know the differences between composite and simple indexes, as well as the differences between B-tree and bitmap index structure.

2. Know what the other types of indexes are in Oracle, including descending indexes, function-based indexes, reverse-key indexes, and so on.

Exercises

1. **Your Oracle EMPLOYEE table contains many unique values in the FIRSTNAME column. You want to index that column to take advantage of this fact in query access. Which of the following indexes might you use?**

   A. Bitmap index

   B. Function-based index

   C. Simple B-tree index

   D. Composite B-tree index

2. **You want to employ bitmap indexes in your Oracle database. Which of the following statements is true regarding bitmap indexes?**

   A. Bitmap indexes are useful where a table column contains few unique values, and those values are changed frequently.

   B. Bitmap indexes are useful where a table column contains many unique values, and those values are changed frequently.

C. Bitmap indexes are useful where a table column contains few unique values, and those values are changed infrequently.

D. Bitmap indexes are useful where a table column contains many unique values, and those values are changed infrequently.

Answer Key
1. C. 2. C.

Creating B-Tree and Bitmap Indexes

The `create index` statement is used to create all types of indexes. To define special types of indexes, you must include various keywords, such as `create unique index` for indexes on columns that enforce uniqueness of every element of data or `create bitmap index` for creating bitmap indexes. The following code block shows the statement for creating a unique B-tree index. The statement also includes options for data storage and creation:

```
CREATE UNIQUE INDEX employee_lastname_indx_01
ON employee (lastname ASC)
TABLESPACE INDEXES
PCTFREE 12
INITRANS 2 MAXTRANS 255
LOGGING
NOSORT
STORAGE ( INITIAL 900K
          NEXT 1800K
          MINEXTENTS 1
          MAXEXTENTS 200
          PCTINCREASE 0 );
```

There are several items in the storage definition that should look familiar, such as `pctfree`, `tablespace`, `logging`, and the items in the `storage` clause. Other than `pctfree`, these options have the same use as they do in `create table` statements. Oracle uses `pctfree` only during the creation of the index to reserve space for index entries that may need to be inserted into the same index block.

There are a few other items that may look unfamiliar, such as `unique`, `asc`, and `nosort`. You specify `unique` when you want the index to enforce uniqueness for values in the column. The `asc` keyword indicates ascending order for this column in the index, and `desc` (descending) can be substituted for this clause.

The `nosort` keyword is for when you have loaded your table data in the proper sort order on the column you are indexing. In this case, it would mean that you have loaded data into the EMPLOYEE table sorted in ascending order on the LASTNAME column. By specifying `nosort`, Oracle will skip the sort ordinarily used in creating the index, thereby increasing performance on your `create index` statement. You might use this option if your operating system offered a procedure for sorting that was more efficient than Oracle's. Finally, `pctused` is not used in index definitions. Because all items in an index must be in the right order for the index to work, Oracle must put an index entry into a block, no matter what. Thus, `pctused` is not used.

You can create bitmap indexes with several storage specifications as well, but remember that they are used to improve search performance for low-cardinality columns, so bitmap indexes may not be unique. The following code block creates a bitmap index:

```
CREATE BITMAP INDEX employee_lastname_indx_01
ON employee (lastname)
TABLESPACE ORGDBIDX
PCTFREE 12
INITRANS 2 MAXTRANS 255
LOGGING
NOSORT
STORAGE ( INITIAL 900K
         NEXT 1800K
         MINEXTENTS 1
         MAXEXTENTS 200
         PCTINCREASE 0 );
```

The performance of commands that use bitmap indexes is heavily influenced by an area of memory specified by the CREATE_BITMAP_AREA_SIZE init*sid*.ora parameter. This area determines how much memory will be used for storing bitmap segments. You need more space for this purpose if the column on which you are creating the bitmap index has high cardinality. For a bitmap index, high cardinality might mean a dozen or so unique values out of 500,000 (as opposed to B-tree indexes, for which high cardinality might mean 490,000 unique values out of 500,000). So, in this situation, you might stick with the Oracle default setting of 8MB for your CREATE_BITMAP_AREA_SIZE initialization parameter.

An example of low cardinality for a column would be having two distinct values in the entire table, as is the case for a column indicating whether an employee is male or female. In this case, you might size your initialization parameter considerably lower than the Oracle default, perhaps around 750KB.

Sizing and Other Index-Creation Issues

Searching a large table without the benefit of an index takes a long time because a full table scan must be performed. Indexes are designed to improve search performance. Unlike full table scans, whose performance worsens as the table grows larger, the performance of table searches that use indexes gets exponentially better as the index (and associated table) gets larger and larger. In fact, on a list containing 1 million elements, a binary search tree algorithm similar to the one used in a B-tree index finds any element in the list within 20 tries—in reality, the B-tree algorithm is actually far more efficient.

However, there is a price for all this speed, which is paid in the additional disk space required to store the index and the overhead required to maintain it when DML operations are performed on the table. To minimize the trade-off, you must weigh the storage cost of adding an index to the database against the performance gained by having the index available for searching the table. The performance improvement achieved by using an index is exponential over the performance of a full table scan, but there is no value in the index if it is never used by the application. You should also consider the volatility of the data in the table before creating an index. If the data in the indexed column changes regularly, you might want to index a more static column.

Also, consider how you are sizing `pctfree` for your index. Oracle only uses `pctfree` to determine free space when the index is first created. After that, the space is fair game, because Oracle has to keep all the items in the index in order. So, after creation, Oracle will put index records in a block right down to the last bit of space available. To determine the best value for `pctfree` on your index, consider the following. If the values in the column you are indexing increase sequentially, such as column values generated by sequences, you can size `pctfree` as low as 2 or 3. If not, you should calculate `pctfree` based on row-count forecasts for growth over a certain time period (12 months, for example) with the following formula: $((max\_\#\_rows\_in\_period - initial\_\#\_rows\_in\_period) / max\_\#\_rows\_in\_period) \times 100$.

For Review

1. Be sure you can describe the settings that can and cannot be used in a storage clause for an index and know the reason why this is the case.

2. Know that you cannot create unique bitmap indexes—this is a contradiction in terms. Also, understand how Oracle uses the SORT_BITMAP_AREA_SIZE parameter with respect for creating bitmap indexes.

Exercises

1. **You are defining the storage allocation settings for an index. Which of the following choices identifies an aspect of index storage allocation that is not present for tables?**

   A. `pctfree`

   B. `pctincrease`

   C. `pctused`

   D. `initial`

2. **You plan to use the text file shown in the following code block as the source for loading data into the EMPLOYEE table:**

   ```
   0193 FLOM        BETSY
   4302 BUTTERWORTH LORNA
   6302 GUPTA       RAJIV
   1201 FLOM        TOM
   ```

   Which of the following choices identifies a method that you could use when creating an index on the LASTNAME column that would improve performance without sacrificing recoverability?

   A. Create the index before loading the table with low `storage` clause settings.

   B. Use the `nosort` keyword when creating the index after loading the table.

   C. Use the `nologging` keyword when creating the index after loading the table.

   D. Create the index before loading the table with high `storage` clause settings.

Answer Key
1. C. 2. B.

Reorganizing Indexes

Reorganizing indexes is handled with the alter index statement. The alter index statement is useful for redefining storage options, such as next, pctincrease, maxextents, initrans, or maxtrans. You can also use the alter index statement to change the pctfree value for new blocks in new extents allocated by your index. You can also add extents manually to an index much like you do for tables, with the alter index allocate extent statement, specifying size and datafile optionally. You can also rid yourself of unused space below the index high-water mark with the alter index deallocate unused statement, optionally reserving a little extra space with the keep clause.

Another option for reorganizing your index is to rebuild it. This operation enables you to create a new index using the data from the old one, resulting in fewer table reads while rebuilding, tidier space management in the index, and better overall performance. This operation is accomplished with the alter index idxname rebuild tablespace tblspcname statement. The tablespace clause in this statement also moves the index to the tablespace named, which is handy for situations where you want to accomplish this task easily. All the storage options you can specify in a create index statement can be applied to alter index rebuild as well. You would rebuild an index in situations where you want to move the index to another tablespace or when many rows have been deleted from the table, causing index entries to be removed as well. Queries can continue to use the existing index while the new index is being built.

TIP
You can use the analyze index validate structure *command as you would with tables to check for block corruption. The INDEX_STATS dictionary view shows you the number of index entries in leaf nodes in the LF_ROWS column compared to the number of deleted entries in the DEL_LF_FOWS column. Oracle recommends that if the number of deleted entries is over 30 percent, you should rebuild the index.*

Building or Rebuilding Indexes Online

Indexes are maintained by Oracle behind the scenes whenever you make a change to data on the indexed column in the table. As time goes on, the values in an indexed column may change such that Oracle has to rearrange the contents of the index to make room for the new values in the indexed column. If enough column values are changed over that time to skew the overall number of elements in the index from the configuration Oracle initially made when it created the index, the index may become stale. A stale index does a poor job of retrieving data quickly, which causes users to notice degraded performance when running their queries even though the statement execution plan shows that the index is being used.

You can rebuild indexes in order to correct index staleness using the `alter index rebuild` statement. In order to rebuild the index, Oracle places a DML lock on the base table whose index is about to be rebuilt. During the time Oracle holds this DML lock, you cannot make any changes to data in the base table. Thus, if you had to build or rebuild an index for any reason, you usually had to plan when you would perform the maintenance operation around the needs of users needing to make changes to the tables. If the table being indexed was both large and had to be available to users, downtime at night or over the weekend was required, because Oracle had to prevent DML operations to data in the table while building or rebuilding the index. However, for e-business applications requiring 24×7 availability, downtime is simply not possible.

Oracle provides a method for building or rebuilding indexes using less-restrictive locking mechanisms. This less-restrictive locking method permits other users to make changes to data in the table while you continue to build or rebuild the index. These changes are also recorded in the new or rebuilt index as well. Oracle performs the work for an online index rebuild in the following way. First, Oracle obtains locks on the table for a very short time to define the structure of the index and to update the data dictionary. This step is illustrated in Figure 14-4. During this time, the table and the index are not available for data queries or changes.

When the first step is complete, Oracle releases the lock required to obtain index structure, and users can once again make data changes to the table. The index as it currently exists is made available for queries only, while Oracle starts rebuilding a copy of the index. Oracle simultaneously maintains a small copy of the

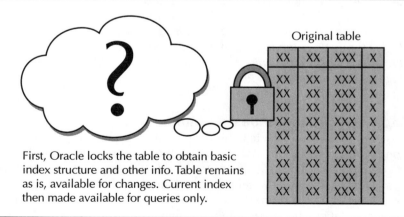

First, Oracle locks the table to obtain basic index structure and other info. Table remains as is, available for changes. Current index then made available for queries only.

Original table

FIGURE 14-4. *The first step of rebuilding indexes online*

index called a *journal table*. This journal table is built exclusively for housing new information added to the table column. This step is illustrated in Figure 14-5.

Next, Oracle incorporates new data added to the table column previously stored in the smaller index copy into the larger index copy. An even smaller copy of the index exists for capturing any new data added to the table during the time that the other copy is added to the index being rebuilt. Once changes from the small copy are added to the rebuilt index, Oracle begins incorporating the new data found in the even smaller copy. Oracle then repeats the process, creating the smallest copy of the index for housing the few new records added while Oracle incorporated new data from the smaller copy, as shown in Figure 14-6.

This process cannot continue forever, so after Oracle integrates the changes from the smaller copy, it locks a few rows of the table at a time, so that no users can change data. The smallest index copy is then incorporated into the index being rebuilt. When finished, Oracle discards the original index in favor of the rebuilt version, releases all locks, and users are once again given access to the table. This is shown in Figure 14-7.

Building or Rebuilding Indexes Online: Syntax

To build an index on a table while continuing to leave the table online and available for user changes in this fashion, you can use the `create index` *name* `on` `table(`*columns*`)` `online` statement. To rebuild an existing index, you can use the `alter index` *name* `rebuild online` statement. The following code block shows the use of the `online rebuild` command in a SQL*Plus session:

```
SQL> alter index idx_emp_01 rebuild online;
Index altered.
```

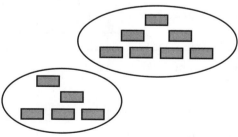

Next, Oracle starts building a new index, while simultaneously maintaining a smaller index for new information added to the table after the rebuild operation started.

Original table

XX	XX	XXX	X
XX	XX	XXX	X
XX	XX	XXX	X
XX	XX	XXX	X
XX	XX	XXX	X
XX	XX	XXX	X
XX	XX	XXX	X
XX	XX	XXX	X
XX	XX	XXX	X
XX	XX	XXX	X
XX	XX	XXX	X

FIGURE 14-5. *The second step of rebuilding indexes online*

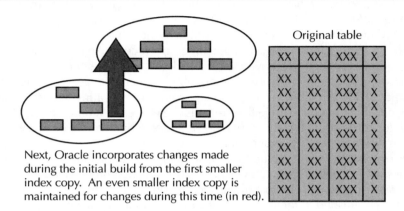

Next, Oracle incorporates changes made during the initial build from the first smaller index copy. An even smaller index copy is maintained for changes during this time (in red).

Original table

FIGURE 14-6. *The third step of rebuilding indexes online*

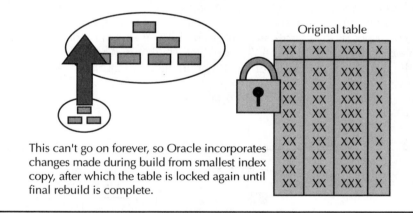

This can't go on forever, so Oracle incorporates changes made during build from smallest index copy, after which the table is locked again until final rebuild is complete.

Original table

FIGURE 14-7. *The final step in rebuilding indexes online*

TIP
Depending on the size of the table being indexed and how much data is changed by users while the index is being rebuilt, the online rebuild *operation could take a long time to complete. Unfortunately, there is little that can be done to tune*

the process. That's just one of the trade-offs you have to make when you want 24×7 data availability. You can minimize impact on end users by scheduling the `online rebuild` *during off-peak times.*

Building or Rebuilding Indexes Online: Restrictions

You cannot use this method for building or rebuilding any kinds of bitmap or cluster indexes. This method works mainly for B-tree indexes and their variants, such as function-based, descending, and reverse-key indexes, and for partitioned indexes. You also cannot use this indexing method on secondary indexes in IOTs.

For Review

1. Be sure you know what situations you would want to rebuild an index and the statement for doing so. Know what storage parameters cannot be changed as part of the `alter index` command as well.

2. Know what the usage of the INDEX_STATS dictionary table is and how it relates to the `analyze` command.

3. Be sure you can describe the process in which indexes are built or rebuilt by default. Understand why this operation requires downtime. Know how this operation can be performed online in Oracle.

4. Be sure you can identify the syntax used to rebuild an index online. Know the performance implications and other restrictions for doing so as well.

Exercises

1. **You want to rebuild an index in Oracle. Which of the following choices identifies the reason why rebuilding indexes online is possible in Oracle?**

    A. Less restrictive locks on underlying base tables

    B. More restrictive locks on the index rebuild

    C. Use of a standby database for temporary storage

    D. Use of a temporary table for temporary storage

2. You are examining use of rebuilding indexes online for your 24×7 Oracle database. Which of the following choices identifies an index that cannot be rebuilt online?

   A. Partitioned B-tree indexes

   B. Bitmap indexes

   C. Reverse key indexes

   D. Secondary IOT indexes

Answer Key
1. A. 2. D.

Dropping Indexes

What happens when you want to expand your index to include more columns or to get rid of columns? Can you use `alter index` for that? Unfortunately, the answer is no. You must drop and re-create the index to modify column definitions or change column order from ascending to descending (or vice versa). This is accomplished with the `drop index idxname` statement.

   You may want to get rid of an index that is used only for specific purposes on an irregular basis, especially if the table has other indexes and volatile data. You may also want to drop an index if you are about to perform a large load of table data, perhaps preceded by purging all data in the table. In this way, your data load runs faster, and the index created later is fresh and well organized. You may have to re-create your index if it has a status of INVALID in the DBA_OBJECTS view, or if you know the index is corrupt from running DBVERIFY on the tablespace housing the index or the `analyze` command on the index itself.

For Review

Know why you might want to drop an index and how to do so.

Exercises

   1. The statement for dropping an index is _____.

Answer Key
1. drop index.

Getting Index Information from the Data Dictionary

You may find yourself looking for information about your indexes, and the Oracle data dictionary can help. The DBA_INDEXES view offers a great deal of information about indexes, such as the type of index (normal or bitmap), its current status (valid, invalid, and others), and whether the index enforces uniqueness or not. You also get information about which table is associated with the index. Another view that contains information about the columns that are stored in an index is called DBA_IND_COLUMNS. The most valuable piece of information this view can give you (in addition to telling you which columns are indexed) is the order in which the columns of the index appear. This is a crucial factor in determining whether the index will improve performance in selecting data from a table. For example, if you were to issue select * from EMPLOYEE where LASTNAME = 'SMITH' and a composite index existed in which LASTNAME was the first column in the index order, then that index would improve performance. However, if the index listed FIRSTNAME as the first column, then the index would not help. Figure 14-8 illustrates this concept.

Finally, a note on finding information about reverse-key indexes. You might notice, if you have reverse-key indexes in your database, that there is no information in the DBA_INDEXES view telling you specifically that the index is reverse key. To see this information, you must execute a specialized query that uses a SYS-owned table called IND$, as well as the DBA_OBJECTS view. The following code block shows the query:

```
SELECT object_name FROM dba_objects
WHERE object_id IN (SELECT obj#
FROM ind$
WHERE BITAND(property,4) = 4);
```

For Review

1. Identify some dictionary views and tables that contain information about indexes.

2. Understand the significance of column position in a composite index and where you can look in the data dictionary to find this information.

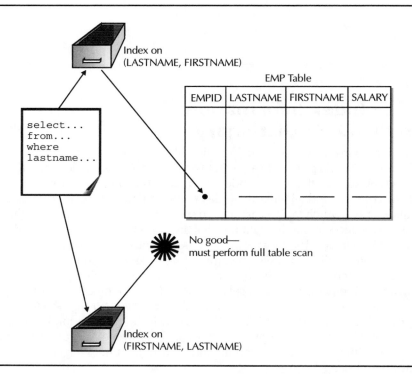

FIGURE 14-8. *The effect of column position in composite indexes*

Exercises

1. This is the view you would look into in order to determine the columns on a table that have been indexed: _____.

2. This is the view you would use to determine what indexes exist for certain tables: _____.

Answer Key
1. DBA_IND_COLUMNS. 2. DBA_INDEXES.

Monitoring Use of Indexes

As said repeatedly, the purpose of indexes is to speed performance in users' ability to access data in a large table. However, an index isn't doing its job if no one uses the index. In order to make sure your users are utilizing the indexes you've generated, Oracle provides a means of monitoring indexes to determine if they are being used or not used. Although you might be tempted to provide as many indexes as possible to improve performance in as many query situations as possible, each index you create takes up space that could have been used for other purposes. Even though disk space isn't very expensive anymore, if you determine that an index is not being used, then you can drop that index, eliminating unnecessary statement overhead, if only to make room for a new index that stands a better chance of being utilized.

Oracle's mechanism for monitoring disk usage is activated with the `alter index` *name* `monitoring usage` command, where *name* is the name of the index you intend to monitor. You then let users access the Oracle database for a while. During this time, Oracle gathers information about which indexes are used and which aren't. For accuracy purposes, try to ensure that usage of the Oracle database during this period realistically reflects typical use of the database. For example, you wouldn't want to monitor index disk usage from late on a Friday evening to early Saturday morning if you knew that most of your users would be at home during that time and that no batch processes would be running either. Later, you issue the `alter index` *name* `nomonitoring usage` statement to have Oracle stop monitoring index usage.

Once Oracle's done with gathering the usage statistics, you can look in the V$OBJECT_USAGE dynamic performance view to figure out whether your index is being employed by users in a meaningful way. Records for every index that has been monitored during the life of the instance will be kept in this view, listed by the name of the index and its associated table. As soon as you start monitoring the index for the first time, a corresponding record is added to V$OBJECT_USAGE. Subsequent attempts to monitor the index will not add new records to V$OBJECT_USAGE, but the MONITORING column will contain YES for this index whenever monitoring is turned on for the index and any previous monitoring information for that index in V$OBJECT_USAGE will be cleared and reset. This view also contains a column called USED. Possible values for this column include YES or NO, making its interpretation fairly easy as well. If the index was used during the monitoring period, Oracle lists YES; otherwise, Oracle lists NO. The view also contains the start and stop times of the monitoring period.

TIP
You must be logged into Oracle as the user owning the index in order to see index statistics in the V$OBJECT_USAGE. For example, if the index being monitored is owned by SCOTT and you log in as SYS to query V$OBJECT_USAGE, you won't see info for SCOTT's index.

Monitoring Object Usage: Scenario

The USED column in V$OBJECT_USAGE only changes when the index being monitored has been used, so it is worth noting when indexes are used and when they are not. For this scenario, we'll employ the standard DEPT table owned by that ever-popular Oracle user, our old friend SCOTT. SCOTT is concerned that the index on the DEPTNO column in the DEPT table, PK_DEPT, is not being utilized effectively by other users in Oracle, so he logs into the database and starts monitoring the PK_DEPT index. He also queries the V$OBJECT_USAGE table to make sure everything is in place for Oracle to start monitoring use of the index. These activities are shown in the following code:

```
SQL> connect scott/tiger
Connected.
SQL> alter index pk_dept monitoring usage;
Index altered.
SQL> select * from v$object_usage;
INDEX_NAME      TABLE_NAME      MONI USED START_MONITORING END_MONITORING
--------------  --------------  ---- ---- ---------------- --------------
PK_DEPT         DEPT            YES  NO   10/21/2001 13:21
```

At this point, SCOTT is convinced that index monitoring is turned on. The SYSTEM user then logs into Oracle9i and issues the following query on the DEPT table:

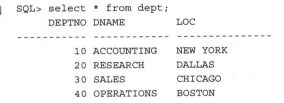

```
SQL> select * from dept;
    DEPTNO DNAME          LOC
---------- -------------- ---------------
        10 ACCOUNTING     NEW YORK
        20 RESEARCH       DALLAS
        30 SALES          CHICAGO
        40 OPERATIONS     BOSTON
```

Later, SCOTT queries the V$OBJECT_USAGE view again to see how things have progressed:

```
INDEX_NAME     TABLE_NAME      MONI USED START_MONITORING END_MONITORING
-------------- --------------- ---- ---- ---------------- --------------
PK_DEPT        DEPT            YES  NO   10/21/2001 13:21
```

"But how can that be?" I hear you saying. SYSTEM logged in and queried the DEPT table, yet Oracle tells us that the index on the DEPTNO column isn't being used. That's exactly how it should be, because SYSTEM didn't query the DEPT table based on the contents of the DEPTNO table—SYSTEM simply asked for all the data, which resulted in Oracle executing a full table scan to retrieve all data from the DEPT table. Had SYSTEM issued `select * from dept where deptno = 10` instead, SCOTT would have seen the following output:

```
INDEX_NAME     TABLE_NAME      MONI USED START_MONITORING END_MONITORING
-------------- --------------- ---- ---- ---------------- --------------
PK_DEPT        DEPT            YES  YES  10/21/2001 13:21
```

For Review

1. Know how to use the `alter index monitoring usage` and `alter index nomonitoring usage` command, and that the purpose these commands serve is to enable you to detect whether an index is being used in the database.

2. Understand the contents of the V$OBJECT_USAGE view. It is populated with records pertaining to indexes being monitored only after that index is being monitored for the first time. The record will persist after monitoring is turned off, and later attempts to monitor that index's usage will clear and reset values from the previous attempt.

3. Generally speaking, understand when indexes will and will not be used in a database. An index will likely be used when the indexed column is referenced in a `where` clause. An index will not be used when the query has no `where` clause or references columns that aren't indexed.

Exercises

1. **Use the following information to answer the question. You have a table called ODDS_AND_EVENS containing two columns: THE_NAME and THE_NUMBER. The column THE_NUMBER has an index on it. Your users issue the following query on this table: `select * from ODDS_AND_EVENS where mod(THE_NUMBER,2) = 0`. What sort of index on the column THE_NUMBER will be used in support of executing the previous query?**

A. Bitmap index

B. B-tree index

C. Function-based index

D. Descending index

2. **You issue the `alter index my_idx monitor usage` command on your Oracle database. This is the second time you've monitored this index since creating your database, and the instance has been shut down only once since the last time you monitored this index. Which of the following statements is true regarding the contents of the V$OBJECT_USAGE view?**

   A. V$OBJECT_USAGE will be populated with a new record corresponding to MY_IDX when the previous command is issued.

   B. V$OBJECT_USAGE will be populated with a second record corresponding to MY_IDX when the previous command is issued.

   C. The information in the existing MY_IDX record in V$OBJECT_USAGE will be cleared and reset when the previous command is issued.

   D. The information in the existing MY_IDX record in V$OBJECT_USAGE will be cleared but not reset when the previous command is issued.

3. **You terminate monitoring the MY_IDX index after monitoring its use for several hours. Which of the following statements is correct regarding V$OBJECT_USAGE in this context?**

   A. Oracle removes the record corresponding to MY_IDX from V$OBJECT_USAGE.

   B. Oracle fills in the END_MONITORING column in the record corresponding to MY_IDX in the V$OBJECT_USAGE view.

   C. Oracle fills in the USED column in the record corresponding to MY_IDX in the V$OBJECT_USAGE view.

   D. Oracle clears all values in the record corresponding to MY_IDX in the V$OBJECT_USAGE view.

Answer Key
1. C. **2.** A. **3.** B.

Managing Data Integrity

In this section, you will cover the following topics related to managing data integrity constraints:

- Implementing data integrity constraints
- Maintaining integrity constraints
- Obtaining constraint information from Oracle

The goal of an integrity constraint is to enforce business rules of some kind. For example, in an organization that wants to be sure every employee has a last name, there are three ways to accomplish the goal. The one most commonly employed in Oracle databases is using a declarative integrity constraint. The LASTNAME column of the EMPLOYEE table can have a not NULL constraint that prevents any row of information from being added without that LASTNAME column populated. The popularity of integrity constraints relates to the fact that they are easy to define and use, they execute quickly, and they are highly flexible. This section explains how to use, maintain, and manage your integrity constraints in Oracle.

Implementing Data Integrity Constraints

As you should recall from taking the Oracle9i OCP Introduction to SQL exam, there are five types of declarative integrity constraints in Oracle: primary keys, foreign keys, unique keys, check constraints, and not NULL constraints. Each will be described here to refresh your memory.

Primary Keys

The primary key of a database table is the unique identifier for that table that distinguishes each row in the table from all other rows. A primary key constraint consists of two data integrity rules for the column declared as the primary key. First, every value in the primary key column must be unique in the table. Second, no value in the column declared to be the primary key can be NULL. Primary keys are the backbone of the table. You should choose the primary key for a table carefully. The column or columns defined to be the primary key should reflect the most important piece of information that is unique about each row of the table.

Foreign Keys

The creation of a foreign key constraint from one table to another defines a special relationship between the two tables that is often referred to as a parent/child relationship, as illustrated in Figure 14-9. The parent table is the one referred to by the foreign key, whereas the child table is the table that actually contains the foreign

EMP—parent table

empid	empname	salary
1	Smith	105,000
2	Jones	56,000
3	Kamil	78,00
4	Doody	18,000

BANK_ACCOUNT—child table

Bankacct	ABA_rtng#	empid
0304060	595849235-090348	3
1374843	34874754	3
2342356	987234085	4
8543858	48594393	1

Foreign-key relationship

FIGURE 14-9. *Creating parent/child table relationships using foreign keys*

key. The DBA should ensure that foreign keys on one table refer only to primary keys on other tables. Unlike primary key constraints, a foreign key constraint on a column does not prevent user processes from setting the value in the foreign key column of the child table to NULL. In cases where the column is NULL, there will be no referential integrity check between the child and the parent.

Unique Constraints

Like the primary key, a unique constraint ensures that values in the column on which the unique constraint is defined are not duplicated by other rows. In addition, the unique constraint is the only type of constraint other than the primary key constraint that has an associated index created with it when the constraint is named.

Not NULL Constraints

NULL cannot be specified as the value for a column on which the not NULL constraint is applied. Often, the DBA will define this constraint in conjunction with another constraint. For example, the not NULL constraint can be used with a foreign key constraint to force validation of column data against a valid value table.

Check Constraints

Check constraints enable the DBA to specify a set of valid values for a column, which Oracle will check automatically when a row is inserted with a non-NULL value for that column. This constraint is limited to hard-coded valid values only. In other words, a check constraint cannot look up its valid values anywhere, nor can it perform any type of SQL or PL/SQL operation as part of its definition.

TIP

Primary keys and unique keys are created with an associated unique index. This index preserves uniqueness in the column(s) and also facilitates high-performance searches on the table whenever the primary key is named in the where *clause.*

Creating an Integrity Constraint

Constraint definitions are handled at the table-definition level, either in a create table or alter table statement. Whenever a constraint is created, it is enabled automatically unless a condition exists on the table that violates the constraint. If the constraint condition is violated, Oracle will create the constraint with disabled status and the rows that violated the constraint are optionally written to a special location. Alternatively, you can specify your constraint to be disabled on creation with the disable clause or force the constraint to be created and enabled by not validating the data with the novalidate clause. Some general guidelines for creating constraints are as follows:

- Put indexes associated with constraints in a tablespace separate from table data.

- Disable constraints before loading tables with lots of row data, and then reenable the constraints afterward.

- Make constraints deferrable when using self-referencing foreign key constraints.

Creating Primary Keys and Not NULL Constraints

The primary key is defined with the constraint clause. A name should be given to the primary key in order to name the associated index. The type of constraint is defined on the next line; it will either be a primary key, foreign key, unique, or check constraint. For indexes associated with primary and unique keys, the tablespace used for storing the index is named in the using tablespace clause. You should specify a separate tablespace for indexes and the tables, for performance reasons. The code block here illustrates the creation of a table with constraints defined:

```
CREATE TABLE emp
( empid        NUMBER        NOT NULL,
  empname      VARCHAR2(30)  NOT NULL,
  salary       NUMBER        NOT NULL,
  CONSTRAINT pk_emp_01
  PRIMARY KEY (empid)
  NOT DEFERRABLE
  USING INDEX TABLESPACE indexes_01 DISABLE)
TABLESPACE data_01;
```

The preceding example displays a create table statement defining constraints after the columns are named. This is called *out-of-line* constraint definition because the constraints are after the columns. You must do this if you plan to use two or more columns in your primary or unique keys. A different way to use create table with inline constraint definitions is shown here, but remember that if you use inline constraint definition, your constraint can only apply to the column it is inline with. Also, remember that not NULL constraints must always be defined inline.

```
CREATE TABLE emp
( empid        NUMBER
  CONSTRAINT pk_emp_01
  PRIMARY KEY NOT DEFERRABLE
  USING INDEX TABLESPACE indexes_01 ENABLE NOVALIDATE,
  empname      VARCHAR2(30)  NOT NULL,
  salary       NUMBER        NOT NULL )
TABLESPACE data_01;
```

Creating Foreign Keys

A foreign key is also defined in the create table or alter table statement. The foreign key in one table refers to the primary key in another, which is sometimes called the parent key. Another clause, on delete cascade, is purely optional. When included, it tells Oracle that if any deletion is performed on EMP that causes a bank account to be orphaned, the corresponding row in BANK_ACCOUNT with the same value for EMPID will also be deleted. Typically, this relationship is desirable because the BANK_ACCOUNT table is the child of the EMP table. If the on delete cascade option is not included, then deletion of a record from EMP that has a corresponding child record in BANK_ACCOUNT with the EMPID defined will not be allowed. Additionally, in order to link two columns via a foreign key constraint, the names do not have to be the same, but the datatype for each column must be identical.

```
CREATE TABLE bank_account
(bank_acct       VARCHAR2(40)       NOT NULL,
 aba_rtng_no     VARCHAR2(40)       NOT NULL,
 empid           NUMBER             NOT NULL,
 CONSTRAINT pk_bank_account_01
 PRIMARY KEY (bank_acct)
 USING INDEX TABLESPACE indexes_01,
 CONSTRAINT fk_bank_account_01
 FOREIGN KEY (empid) REFERENCES (emp.empid)
 ON DELETE CASCADE)
TABLESPACE data_01;
```

TIP
In order for a foreign key to reference a column in the parent table, the datatypes of both columns must be identical.

Creating Unique and Check Constraints

Defining a unique constraint is handled as follows. Suppose the DBA decides to track telephone numbers in addition to all the other data tracked in EMP. The `alter table` statement can be issued against the database to make the change. As with a primary key, an index is created for the purpose of verifying uniqueness on the column. That index is identified with the name given to the constraint.

```
alter table emp
add (home_phone varchar2(10)
constraint ux_emp_01 unique
using index tablespace indexes_01);
```

The final constraint considered is the check constraint. The fictitious company using the EMP and BANK_ACCOUNT tables places a salary cap on all employees of $110,000 per year. In order to mirror that policy, the DBA issues the following `alter table` statement, and the constraint takes effect as soon as the statement is issued. If a row exists in the table whose column value violates the check constraint, the constraint remains disabled.

```
ALTER TABLE emp
ADD CONSTRAINT ck_emp_01
CHECK (salary < 110000);
```

Constraint Deferability

Oracle furthers the success of declarative integrity constraints with new features for their use. The first change made to the declarative integrity constraints in the Oracle database is the differentiation between deferred and immediate constraints. *Immediate* constraints are those integrity constraints that are enforced immediately, as soon as the statement is executed. If the user attempts to enter data that violates the constraint, Oracle signals an error and the statement is rolled back. Up until Oracle8i, all declarative integrity constraints in the database were immediate constraints. However, Oracle8i and later releases also offer the DBA an option to defer database integrity checking. *Deferred* integrity constraints are those that are not enforced until the user attempts to commit the transaction. If, at that time, the data entered by statements violates an integrity constraint, Oracle will signal an error and roll back the entire transaction.

The user can defer any and all constraints that are deferrable during the entire session using the alter session set constraints=deferred statement. Alternatively, the user can defer named or all constraints for a specific transaction, using the set constraint *name* deferred or set constraint all deferred. This form of lazy evaluation temporarily enables data to enter the database that violates integrity constraints. For example, in Oracle7, there was no way to insert data into a child table for which there wasn't also data in the parent. In Oracle8i, the user can conduct the insert on the child table before inserting data into the parent simply by deferring the foreign key constraint. The user may also set constraints for immediate enforcement, using the set constraint *name* immediate or set constraint all immediate statement. You can define constraints as either deferrable or not deferrable, and either initially deferred or initially immediate. These attributes can be different for each constraint. You specify them with keywords in the constraint clause, as described next.

Deferrable or Not Deferrable   The definition of a constraint determines whether the constraint is deferrable by users. Two factors play into that determination. The first is the overall deferability of the constraint. If a constraint is created with the deferrable keyword, the constraint is deferrable by user processes until the time the transaction is committed. In contrast, if the constraint is created with the not deferrable keywords, then user process statements will always be bound by the integrity constraint. The not deferrable status is the default for the constraint. If a constraint has been created with the not deferrable status, then the alter session and set statements for deferring integrity constraints, mentioned previously, cannot be used.

Initially Deferred or Initially Immediate   The second factor is the default behavior of the constraint. The first option is to have the constraint deferred, defined with the initially deferred keyword. This option and the not deferrable keyword option described previously are mutually exclusive. The other option is to have the integrity constraint enforced unless explicitly deferred by the user process, which is specified by the initially immediate keywords.

```
CREATE TABLE employees
(empid      NUMBER(10)      NOT NULL,
 name       VARCHAR2(40)    NOT NULL,
 salary     NUMBER(10)      NOT NULL,
 CONSTRAINT pk_employees_01
 PRIMARY KEY (empid) NOT DEFERRABLE);
```

TIP

If you do not include an indication about whether the constraint can be deferrable, Oracle will assume the constraint cannot be deferrable. Later attempts to issue alter table modify constraint name deferrable *will return an error. To make the constraint deferrable, you will have to drop and re-create the constraint.*

For Review

1. Understand what declarative data integrity means, and be sure you can name the five types of integrity constraints used on the Oracle database. Know how to use the alter table command or create table command to generate constraints.

2. Be sure you remember that Oracle creates indexes in support of primary keys and unique constraints in the database.

3. Remember that when defining foreign key constraints between two columns in two different tables, those two columns must be defined with the exact same datatype. The column names do not have to be the same, however.

Exercises

1. **You implement an integrity constraint in an Oracle database using the following command:** alter table EMP add constraint PK_EMP_01 primary key (EMPNO). **Which of the following statements is true about the constraint you just added?**

   A. The constraint will cause Oracle to generate a bitmap index to support its activities.

   B. The constraint will reference back to the primary key in another table for valid values.

C. The constraint will be created but will remain disabled unless all values in the EMPNO column are unique and not NULL.

D. The constraint will enforce uniqueness, but NULL values will be permitted.

2. **You create a table with the following command:**

```
CREATE TABLE employees
(empid      NUMBER(10)      NOT NULL,
 name       VARCHAR2(40)    NOT NULL,
 salary     NUMBER(10)      NOT NULL,
 CONSTRAINT pk_employees_01
 PRIMARY KEY (empid) NOT DEFERRABLE);
```

Several rows are then added to the table. Which of the following choices indicates a statement that if issued, will result in Oracle returning an error?

A. `alter table employees disable novalidate pk_employees_01;`

B. `alter table employees modify constraint pk_employees_01 deferrable;`

C. `alter employees enable novalidate pk_employees_01;`

D. `alter employees enable validate pk_employees_01;`

Answer Key
1. C. 2. B.

Maintaining Integrity Constraints

Historically, there have been two basic statuses for the integrity constraints: `enable` and `disable`. In more recent versions of Oracle, the database offers variations on the theme. For example, the `enable` status has been modified to include an `enable validate` status, whereby the current contents of the constrained column are checked for violations. Another status for integrity constraints, `enable novalidate`, enables Oracle to enforce the constraint on new data entering the table (enabling), but not on data that already exists on the table (no validating). These statuses can be used by issuing the `alter table` *table_name* `enable novalidate constraint` *constraint_name* statement or `alter table` *name* `enable validate constraint` *constraint_name* statement.

Also, Oracle can support unique constraints being enforced with nonunique indexes. The columns indexed as part of the unique constraint should be the first columns in the nonunique index, but as long as those columns are the leading columns of the index, they may appear in any order. Other columns can also be present in the index to make it nonunique. This feature speeds the process of enabling primary key or unique constraints on the table. The nonunique index supporting the unique or primary key constraint cannot be dropped.

TIP

In Oracle8i and later releases, there is a fourth status for integrity constraints called DISABLE VALIDATE. *If a constraint is in this state, any modification of the constrained columns is not allowed. In addition, the index on the constraint is dropped and the constraint is disabled. That is useful for a unique constraint; the* DISABLE VALIDATE *state enables you to load data efficiently from a nonpartitioned table into a partitioned table using the* EXCHANGE PARTITION *option of the* alter table *command.*

Constraints perform their intended operation when enabled, but do not operate when they're disabled. The alter table *tblname* enable constraint command enables a constraint. You can use the optional validate or novalidate keywords to have Oracle validate or not validate data currently in the constrained column for compliance with the constraint. Using validate means Oracle will check the data according to the rules of the constraint. If Oracle finds that the data does not meet the constraint's criteria, Oracle will not enable the constraint. Using novalidate causes Oracle to enable the constraint automatically without checking data, but users may later have trouble committing their changes if the changes contain data that violates the deferred constraint.

```
ALTER TABLE emp ENABLE NOVALIDATE CONSTRAINT pk_emp_01;
ALTER TABLE emp ENABLE VALIDATE CONSTRAINT pk_emp_01;
ALTER TABLE emp ENABLE CONSTRAINT pk_emp_01;  -- automatic validate
```

Disabling a constraint is much simpler—just use the alter table *tblname* disable constraint command. If you want to remove a constraint from the table, use the alter table *tblname* drop constraint statement. If you want to remove a table from your database that is referenced by foreign keys in other tables, use the drop table *tblname* cascade constraints statement.

```
ALTER TABLE emp DISABLE CONSTRAINT pk_emp_01;
ALTER TABLE emp DROP CONSTRAINT ux_emp_01;
DROP TABLE emp CASCADE CONSTRAINTS;
```

TIP
When using novalidate *to enable or*
deferrable *to defer a primary or unique key,*
your associated index must be nonunique to store
the potential violator records for a short time while
the transaction remains uncommitted.

Using the EXCEPTIONS Table

The only foolproof way to create a constraint without experiencing violations on constraint creation is to create the constraint before any data is inserted. Otherwise, you must know how to manage violations using the EXCEPTIONS table, which is created by running a script provided with the Oracle software distribution called utlexcpt.sql. This file is usually found in the rdbms/admin subdirectory under the Oracle software home directory. You can alternatively use a table you name yourself, so long as the columns are the same as those created by the utlexcpt.sql script for the EXCEPTIONS table. This table contains a column for the ROWID of the row that violated the constraint and the name of the constraint it violated. In the case of constraints that are not named explicitly (such as not NULL), the constraint name listed is the one that was automatically created by Oracle at the time the constraint was created. The exceptions into clause also helps to identify those rows that violate the constraint you are trying to enable.

The following code block demonstrates a constraint violation being caused and then resolved using the EXCEPTIONS table. First, you create the problem:

```
SQL> truncate table exceptions;
Table truncated.
SQL> alter table emp disable constraint ux_emp_01;
Table altered.
SQL> desc emp
 Name                            Null?    Type
 ------------------------------- -------- ----
 EMPID                           NOT NULL NUMBER
 EMPNAME                         NOT NULL VARCHAR2(30)
 SALARY                          NOT NULL NUMBER
 HOME_PHONE                               VARCHAR2(10)
SQL> insert into emp (empid, empname, salary, home_phone)
  2  values (3049394,'FERRIS',110000,'1234567890');
1 row created.
SQL> insert into emp (empid, empname, salary, home_phone)
```

```
  2   values(40294932,'BLIBBER',50000,'1234567890');
1 row created.
SQL> commit;
Commit complete.
SQL> alter table emp enable validate constraint ux_emp_01
  2   exceptions into exceptions;
alter table emp enable validate constraint ux_emp_01
*
ERROR at line 1:
ORA-02299: cannot enable (SYS.UX_EMP_01) - duplicate keys found
```

Once you come up against a problem like this, you can use the EXCEPTIONS table to resolve it. Note that EXCEPTIONS shows you every row that violates the constraint. You could easily have simply deleted the offending data as well, and then added it after enabling the constraint:

```
SQL> select rowid, home_phone from emp
  2   where rowid in (select row_id from exceptions);
ROWID              HOME_PHONE
------------------ ----------
AAAA89AAGAAACJKAAA 1234567890
AAAA89AAGAAACJKAAB 1234567890
SQL> update emp set home_phone = NULL where rowid =
  2   chartorowid('AAAA89AAGAAACJKAAB');
1 row updated.
SQL> commit;
Commit complete.
SQL> select * from emp;
    EMPID EMPNAME                                SALARY HOME_PHONE
--------- ------------------------------- ---------- ----------
  3049394 FERRIS                                 110000 1234567890
 40294932 BLIBBER                                  50000
SQL> alter table emp enable validate constraint ux_emp_01;
Table altered.
SQL> truncate table EXCEPTIONS;
Table truncated.
```

TIP
Remember to clean up the EXCEPTIONS table before and after you use it to avoid being confused by rows violating constraints from different tables.

For Review

1. Understand that whether Oracle enforces the constraints on a table depends on whether those constraints are enabled or not. If a constraint is enabled, Oracle validates incoming data. If not enabled, Oracle does not validate incoming data.

2. You can use the `validate` and `novalidate` keywords to determine whether or not Oracle will check the existing data in a table for violations.

Exercises

1. **You are managing integrity constraints in Oracle. Which of the following choices identifies the command you would use if you wanted to disable a primary key integrity constraint?**

   A. `alter table`

   B. `alter constraint`

   C. `alter index`

   D. `alter system`

2. **You want to determine what rows in a table violate an integrity constraint you are trying to enable. Which of the following scripts would you use to generate the database objects supporting this activity?**

   A. `utlfile.sql`

   B. `utlxplan.sql`

   C. `catalog.sql`

   D. `utlexcpt.sql`

Answer Key
1. A. 2. D.

Obtaining Constraint Information from Oracle

There are several ways to access information about constraints. Many of the data dictionary views present various angles on the constraints. Although each of the views listed are prefixed with DBA_, the views are also available in the ALL_ or

USER_ versions, with data limited in the following ways. ALL_ views correspond to the data objects, privileges, and so on that are available to the user who executes the query, whereas the USER_ views correspond to the data objects, privileges, and so on that were created by the user.

DBA_CONSTRAINTS

This view lists detailed information about all constraints in the system. The constraint name and owner of the constraint are listed, along with the type of constraint it is, the status, and the referenced column name and owner for the parent key, if the constraint is a foreign key constraint. One weakness lies in this view—if trying to look up the name of the parent table for the foreign key constraint, the DBA must try to find the table whose primary key is the same as the column specified for the referenced column name. Some important or new columns in this view for Oracle9i include the following:

- **CONSTRAINT_TYPE**   Displays *p* for primary key, *r* for foreign key, *c* for check constraints (including checks to see if data is not NULL), and *u* for unique constraints

- **SEARCH_CONDITION**   Displays the check constraint criteria

- **R_OWNER**   Displays the owner of the referenced table, if the constraint is foreign key

- **R_CONSTRAINT_NAME**   Displays the name of the primary key in the referenced table if the constraint is foreign key

- **GENERATED**   Indicates whether the constraint name was defined by the user creating a table or if Oracle generated it

- **BAD**   Indicates whether the check constraint contains a reference to two-digit years, a problem for millennium compliance

DBA_CONS_COLUMNS

This view lists detailed information about every column associated with a constraint. The view includes the name of the constraint and the associated table, as well as the name of the column in the constraint. If the constraint is composed of multiple columns, as can be the case in primary key, unique, and foreign key constraints, the position or order of the columns is specified by a 1, 2, 3, . . . *n* value in the POSITION column of this view. Knowing the position of a column is especially useful in tuning SQL queries to use composite indexes when there is an index corresponding to the constraint.

For Review

Know where you would look in the data dictionary to find out whether a constraint's status is enabled or disabled and where to determine what columns have integrity constraints on them.

Exercises

1. This is the view you would use to determine whether a constraint existed on a particular column in Oracle tables: _____.

2. This is the view you would use in order to determine the constraints associated with a particular table in Oracle: _____.

Answer Key
1. DBA_CONS_COLUMNS. 2. DBA_CONSTRAINTS.

Chapter Summary

We covered a lot of ground in this chapter with respect to preparation for the OCP DBA Fundamentals 1 exam. In this chapter, we started off by covering a lot of information about the administrative aspects of managing tables in an Oracle database. You learned about various types of tables and the relative advantages and disadvantages of each for storing data in your Oracle database. You reviewed the different datatypes available in Oracle as well. We covered the purpose and structure of restricted and extended ROWIDs, along with a brief history of each in the Oracle database. From there, we went on to discuss the internal structure of blocks in Oracle, along with the structure of row data inside those blocks. You also learned how to create regular and temporary tables from an administrative perspective. The management of storage structures (that is, segments and extents) within tables was discussed at length as well. You learned how to maintain tables, including table reorganization, truncation, and removal, along with how to drop unused columns. From there, we moved on to cover indexes in Oracle. You learned the administrative aspects of indexes, such as how to create, maintain, rebuild online, and drop indexes. You learned how to find out whether an index is being used and where to look in the data dictionary for information about indexes. Finally, we discussed integrity constraints in Oracle. You learned how to create them, manage them, and find information about them in your data dictionary.

Two-Minute Drill

- There are four types of tables: regular tables, partitioned tables, cluster tables, and index-organized tables.

- There are two categories of datatypes: user-defined and built-in.

- There are three classes of built-in types: scalar, collection, and relationship types.

- The regular-size scalar types include CHAR, NCHAR, VARCHAR2, NVARCHAR2, DATE, RAW, ROWID, and NUMBER.

- The large-size scalar types include LONG and LONG RAW from Oracle7, and CLOB, NCLOB, BLOB, and BFILE.

- The collection types include VARRAY, which is a variable-length array, and TABLE, which is a nested table type.

- The relationship type is REF, and it is a pointer to other data in another table.

- Collection and relationship types require the object option installed on your Oracle database.

- To remember the components of a ROWID, think of the BRF and OBRRF acronyms (and a little dog barking).

- Remember how to use each of the options for defining storage and table creation. They are as follows:

  - **initial** First segment in the table

  - **next** Next segment allocated (not simply the second one in the table)

  - **pctincrease** Percentage increase of next extent allocated over next value

  - **minextents** Minimum number of extents allocated at table creation

  - **maxextents** Maximum number of extents the object can allocate

  - **pctfree** How much of each block stays free after `insert` for row `update`

  - **pctused** Threshold that usage must fall below before a row is added

  - **initrans** Number of concurrent changes that can happen per block

  - **maxtrans** Maximum number of transactions that can perform the same function

- ■ **logging/nologging** Whether Oracle will store redo for the `create table` statement

- ■ **cache/nocache** Whether Oracle lets blocks stay in the buffer cache after full table scans

■ Row migration is when an `update` makes a row too large to store in its original block.

■ Chaining is when a row is broken up and stored in many blocks. Both require multiple disk reads/writes to retrieve/store, and therefore, are bad for performance.

■ Indexes are used to improve performance on database objects in Oracle. The types of indexes in Oracle are bitmap, B-tree, descending, function-based, and reverse-key.

■ Bitmap indexes are best used for improving performance on columns containing static values with low cardinality or few unique values in the column.

■ B-tree indexes are best used for improving performance on columns containing values with high cardinality.

■ The decision to create an index should weigh the performance gain of using the index against the performance overhead produced when DML statements change index data.

■ The `pctused` parameter is not available for indexes, because every index block is always available for data changes as the result of Oracle needing to keep data in order in an index.

■ DBA_INDEXES and DBA_IND_COLUMNS are dictionary views that store information about indexes.

■ Data integrity constraints are declared in the Oracle database as part of the table definition.

■ There are five types of integrity constraints:

- ■ **Primary key** Identifies each row in the table as unique

- ■ **Foreign key** Develops referential integrity between two tables

- ■ **Unique** Forces each non-NULL value in the column to be unique

- ■ **Not NULL** Forces each value in the column to be not NULL

- ■ **Check** Validates each entry into the column against a set of valid value constants

- There are different constraint states in Oracle, including deferrable constraints or nondeferrable constraints.

- In addition, a constraint can be enabled on a table without validating existing data in the constrained column using the `enable novalidate` clause.

- Oracle uses unique indexes to enforce unique and primary key constraints when those constraints are not deferrable. If the constraints are deferrable, then Oracle uses nonunique indexes for those constraints.

- When a constraint is created, every row in the table is validated against the constraint restriction.

- The EXCEPTIONS table stores rows that violate the integrity constraint created for a table.

- The EXCEPTIONS table can be created by running the `utlexcpt.sql` script.

- The DBA_CONSTRAINTS and DBA_CONS_COLUMNS data dictionary views display information about the constraints of a database.

- Constraints can be enabled or disabled. If enabled, constraints will be enforced. If disabled, constraints will not be enforced.

Fill-in-the-Blank Questions

1. The keyword used in order to cause a table DDL operation not to log any redo log entry: _____.

2. The datatype that allows for up to 4GB of text data to be stored in a table column: _____.

3. A term used to describe what Oracle must do when users attempt to add more data to an existing row in the database, but the block housing the row has no room for the row to grow: _____.

4. The scope of availability used whenever defining temporary tables in Oracle: _____.

5. A type of index that would store a listing of numbers from highest to lowest, rather than from lowest to highest: _____.

6. A block space clause that is not relevant for defining indexes: _____.

7. A declarative integrity constraint that prevents duplicate values from entering a column: _____.

8. A dictionary view that contains a listing of all columns that are part of declarative integrity constraints: _____.

Chapter Questions

1. You want to compute statistics for cost-based optimization on all rows in your EMPLOYEE table using Oracle default settings. Which of the following choices contains the statement you will use?

   A. `analyze table EMPLOYEE validate structure;`

   B. `analyze table EMPLOYEE compute statistics;`

   C. `analyze table EMPLOYEE estimate statistics;`

   D. `analyze table EMPLOYEE estimate statistics sample 10 percent;`

2. The DBA suspects there is some chaining and row migration occurring on the database. Which of the following choices indicates a way to detect it?

   A. `select CHAIN_CNT from DBA_SEGMENTS`

   B. `select CHAIN_CNT from DBA_TABLES`

C. `select CHAIN_CNT from DBA_OBJECTS`

D. `select CHAIN_CNT from DBA_EXTENTS`

3. Which of the following datatypes are used in situations where you want an ordered set of data elements, where every element is the same datatype, and where you predefine the number of elements that will appear in the set?

   A. REF

   B. TABLE

   C. CLOB

   D. VARRAY

4. Using the `nologging` clause when issuing `create table as select` has effects described by which of the following choices?

   A. Slows performance in creating the table

   B. Ensures recoverability of the table creation

   C. Improves performance in creating the table

   D. Makes blocks read into memory during full table scans persistent

5. The largest size a table has ever reached is identified by which of the following items stored in the segment header for the table?

   A. ROWID

   B. High-water mark

   C. Session address

   D. None of the above

6. The DBA is designing the data model for an application. Which of the following statements is not true about primary keys?

   A. A primary key cannot be NULL.

   B. Individual or composite column values combining to form the primary key must be unique.

   C. Each column value in a primary key corresponds to a primary key value in another table.

D. A primary key identifies the uniqueness of that row in the table.

E. An associated index is created with a primary key.

7. **In working with developers of an application, the DBA might use the POSITION column in DBA_CONS_COLUMNS for which of the following purposes?**

A. To indicate the position of the constraint on disk

B. To relate to the hierarchical position of the table in the data model

C. To improve the scalability of the Oracle database

D. To identify the position of the column in a composite index

8. **The DBA is evaluating what type of index to use in an application. Bitmap indexes improve database performance in which of the following situations?**

A. `select` statements on a column indicating employee status, which has only four unique values for 50,000 rows

B. `update` statements where the indexed column is being changed

C. `delete` statements where only one or two rows are removed at a time

D. `insert` statements where several hundred rows are added at once

9. **The DBA is developing an index creation script. Which of the following choices best explains the reason why indexes do not permit the definition of the `pctused` storage option?**

A. Indexes have a preset `pctused` setting of 25.

B. Oracle must keep index entries in order, so index blocks are always being updated.

C. Indexes are not altered unless they are re-created.

D. Indexes will not be modified after the `pctfree` threshold is crossed.

10. **The DBA is designing an architecture to support a large document-scanning and cross-referencing system used for housing policy manuals. The architecture will involve several tables that will house in excess of 30,000,000 rows. Which of the following table designs would be most appropriate for this architecture?**

A. Partitioned tables

B. Index-organized tables

C. Clustered tables

D. Regular tables

11. **In order to design a table that enforces uniqueness on a column, which three of the following choices are appropriate?**

A. Unique constraint

B. Bitmap index

C. Primary key

D. Foreign key

E. Not NULL constraint

F. Partitioned index

G. Unique index

H. Check constraint

12. **In designing a database architecture that maximizes performance on database `select` statements, each of the following would enhance performance except _____.**

A. Using indexes on columns frequently used in `where` clauses

B. Using bitmap indexes on frequently updated columns

C. Putting indexes in a separate tablespace from tables on a different disk resource

D. Designing index-organized tables around `select` statements used in the application

13. **When attempting to reenable the primary key after a data load, the DBA receives the following error: "ORA-02299: cannot enable (SYS.UX_EMP_01) - duplicate keys found." Where might the DBA look to see what rows caused the violation?**

A. DBA_CONS_COLUMNS

B. DBA_CONSTRAINTS

    C. DBA_CLU_COLUMNS

    D. EXCEPTIONS

14. **The DBA notices that the system-generated indexes associated with integrity constraints in the Oracle database have been defined to be nonunique. Which of the following choices accurately describes the reason for this?**

    A. Nondeferrable primary key constraints

    B. Deferrable unique constraints

    C. Internal error

    D. Incomplete data load

Fill-in-the-Blank Answers

1. `nologging`

2. CLOB

3. Migration

4. GLOBAL

5. Descending

6. `pctused`

7. Unique

8. DBA_CONS_COLUMNS

Answers to Chapter Questions

1. B. `analyze table EMPLOYEE compute statistics;`

Explanation   The tip-off in this question is that you are being asked to compute statistics for all rows in the table. In this situation, you would never estimate, because you are processing all rows in the table, not just some of them. Thus, choices C and D are both incorrect. Also, because the `validate structure` clause only verifies structural integrity of data blocks, choice A is also incorrect.

2. B. `select CHAIN_CNT from DBA_TABLES`

Explanation   The CHAIN_CNT column is found in the DBA_TABLES dictionary view, making choice B correct. The trick of this question is identifying not where the data comes from, for it obviously comes from the CHAIN_CNT column, which is populated by the `analyze` command. The trick is knowing where to look in the dictionary for information. Before taking OCP Exam 2, be sure you go through each of the dictionary views identified in this chapter and run the `describe` command on them to get a feel for which columns show up where.

3. D. VARRAY

Explanation   The content in the question, namely that you want an ordered set of data elements, where every element is the same datatype, and where you predefine the number of elements that will appear in the set, describes the features available in a VARRAY. A nested table is not correct because the nested table is an unordered set, eliminating choice B. Choice A, REF, is a relationship type that stores a pointer to data, not data itself, and is therefore wrong. Finally, a CLOB is a text large object, eliminating choice C.

4. C. Improves performance in creating the table

Explanation Because `nologging` causes the `create table as select` statement to not generate any redo information, performance is improved somewhat for the overall operation. This is the logical opposite of choice A, and given these other facts, choice A is wrong. Choice B is also wrong because disabling redo generation means your operation is not recoverable. Finally, choice D is wrong because the `cache` option is used to make blocks read into memory for full table scans persistent, not `nologging`.

5. B. High-water mark

Explanation ROWID information is simply a locator for rows in a table. It does nothing to determine the size of that table. Thus, choice A is incorrect. Choice C is incorrect because the session address is dynamic information about the user processes currently connected to Oracle. This has nothing to do with the size of any table anywhere in the database. Because choice B is correct, choice D is logically wrong as well.

6. C. Each column value in a primary key corresponds to a primary key value in another table.

Explanation All other statements made about primary keys are true. They must be not NULL and unique in order to enable them to represent each row uniquely in the table. An associated index is also created with a primary key. Refer to the discussion of primary keys as part of integrity constraints.

7. D. To identify the position of a column in a composite index

Explanation Constraints are stored with the data definition of a table, without regard to the value stored in POSITION. Therefore, choice A is incorrect. POSITION also has nothing to do with parent/child hierarchies in the data model or with scalability, thereby eliminating choices B and C. Refer to the discussion on using dictionary views to examine constraints.

8. A. `select` statements on a column indicating employee status, which has only four unique values for 50,000 rows

Explanation Bitmap indexes are designed to improve performance on a table whose column contains relatively static data of low cardinality. This means there are very few unique values in a large pool of rows. Four unique values out of 50,000 definitely qualify. Choice B is incorrect because of the point made about the column values being relatively static. Because it is a relatively processor-intensive activity to change a value in a bitmap index, you should use bitmap indexes mainly on column values that are static.

9. B.   Oracle must keep index entries in order, so index blocks are always
being updated.

Explanation   Recall from the discussion of how an index works that in order for
Oracle to maintain the index order, all blocks are always available for update. Thus,
choice B is the correct answer to this question. Besides, there is no default `pctused`
value for indexes.

10. A.   Partitioned tables

Explanation   30,000,000 rows is a lot of data to manage in an ordinary table. Thus,
you should eliminate choice D immediately. A smart DBA will want to maximize
data availability by ensuring that the table is partitioned and that the partitions are
spread across multiple drives to make it possible to use parallel processing.
Although IOTs are designed for text scanning, they also cannot be partitioned,
making them a poor candidate for storing this much data. Thus, eliminate choice B.
Finally, because no mention of table joins is made, you have no reason to choose
choice C.

11. A, C, and G.   Unique constraint, primary key, unique index

Explanation   Unique indexes enforce uniqueness of values in a column or
columns. They are used by Oracle as the underlying logic for primary keys and
unique keys as well. This fact makes A, C, and G the correct answers. Choices D
and E are eliminated because neither of these declarative integrity constraints have
unique indexes nor any other mechanism to support uniqueness. Bitmap indexes
cannot be unique either, eliminating choice B.

12. B.   Using bitmap indexes on frequently updated columns

Explanation   Bitmap indexes should never be used on columns that are frequently
updated, because those changes are very costly in terms of maintaining the index.
Using indexes on columns frequently used in `where` clauses, putting indexes in a
separate tablespace from tables on a different disk resource, and designing index-
organized tables around `select` statements used in the application are all good
methods for performance enhancement.

13. D.   EXCEPTIONS

Explanation   When a constraint fails upon being enabled, you would not look in
the data dictionary at all. This fact eliminates choices A, B, and C. Instead, you look
in the EXCEPTIONS table. Recall that the `exceptions into EXCEPTIONS`
clause in the `alter table enable constraint` statement enables you to put
the offending records into the EXCEPTIONS table for review and correction later.

14. B.   Deferrable unique constraints

Explanation   The entire rationale behind the situation described in this question, namely that the system-generated indexes associated with integrity constraints in the Oracle database have been defined to be nonunique, is completely a product of deferrable integrity constraints. Because the constraint is deferrable, the index cannot be unique, because it must accept new record input for the duration of the transaction. The user's attempted `commit` causes the transaction to roll back if the constraints are not met.

CHAPTER
15

Managing Database Users

In this chapter, you will learn about and demonstrate knowledge in the following areas:

■ Managing users

■ Managing password security and resources

■ Managing privileges

■ Managing roles

This chapter focuses on the functionality Oracle provides for limiting database access. There are several different aspects to limiting database use. In many larger organizations, you may find that a security administrator handles security—the functionality provided by Oracle for security might not be handled by the DBA at all. As the resident expert on Oracle software, it helps to familiarize yourself with this subject in order to better manage the Oracle database. Bear in mind that this discussion will use the terms *DBA* and *security administrator* interchangeably and that the main reason it is covered here is that there will be questions about security on the OCP Exam 2. Approximately 16 percent of the content of this exam focuses on database security.

Managing Users

In this section, you will cover the following topics related to managing users:

■ Creating new database users

■ Altering and dropping existing users

■ Monitoring information about existing users

The safest database is one with no users—but take away the users, and there's little reason to have a database! This section of the chapter focuses on the prudent creation of users in Oracle. You will learn the basic syntax for user creation and how to avoid problems with user creation. We're covering this section before discussing password security and resources because inherent in the discussion of password security and resources is an understanding of how to create users. Thus, it makes sense to talk about user creation first.

Creating New Database Users

One of your primary tasks early on in the creation of a new database is adding new users. However, user creation is an ongoing task. As users enter and leave the organization, so too must you keep track of access to the database granted to those

users. When using Oracle's own database authentication method, new users are
created with the `create user` statement:

```
CREATE USER spanky
IDENTIFIED BY first01
DEFAULT TABLESPACE users_01
TEMPORARY TABLESPACE temp_01
QUOTA 10M ON users_01
PROFILE app_developer
PASSWORD EXPIRE
ACCOUNT UNLOCK;
```

This statement highlights several items of information that comprise the syntax
and semantics of user creation, and these areas will be covered in the following
subtopics:

create user

This is the user's name in Oracle. If you're using operating system authentication
to enable users to access the database, then the usernames should by default be
preceded with OPS$. In no other case is it recommended that a username contain
a nonalphanumeric character, although both _ and # are permitted characters in
usernames. The name should also start with a letter. On single-byte character sets,
the name can be from 1 to 30 characters long, while on multibyte character sets, the
name of a user must be limited to 30 bytes. In addition, the name should contain
one single-byte character according to Oracle recommendations. The username is
not case sensitive and cannot be a reserved word.

identified by

This is the user's Oracle database password. This item should contain at least three
characters, and preferably six or more. Generally, it is recommended that users
change their password once they know their username is created. Oracle enforces
this with the `password expire` clause. Users should change their passwords to
something that is not a word or a name that preferably contains a numeric character
somewhere in it. As is the case with the username, the password can be a maximum
length of 30 bytes and cannot be a reserved word. If operating system authentication
is being used, you would use the keywords `identified externally`. This is the
only aspect of a user's ID in Oracle that the user is allowed to change with the
`alter user` command.

default tablespace

Tablespace management is a crucial task in Oracle. The `default tablespace`
names the location where the user's database objects are created by default. This

clause plays an important role in protecting the integrity of the SYSTEM tablespace. If no `default tablespace` is named for a user, objects that the user creates may be placed in the SYSTEM tablespace. Recall that SYSTEM contains many database objects, such as the data dictionary and the SYSTEM rollback segment, that are critical to database use. Users should not be allowed to create their database objects in the SYSTEM tablespace.

temporary tablespace

As you may recollect from the discussions on creating databases early in this book, Oracle9i enables you to create a *default temporary tablespace* either during the creation of the database or altering it using the `create temporary tablespace` command. By creating default temporary tablespaces, you need not specify the `temporary tablespace` clause for every user created. You can, however, assign users to a different temporary tablespace than the default temporary tablespace for all users, using the `temporary tablespace` option in the `create user` or `alter user` commands.

NOTE

If a default temporary tablespace is not defined and if `temporary tablespace` *is not explicitly specified by the DBA when the username is created, the location for all temporary segments for that user will be the SYSTEM tablespace. SYSTEM, as you already know, is a valuable resource that should not be used for user object storage.*

quota

A `quota` is a limit on the amount of space the user's database objects can occupy within the tablespace. If a user attempts to create a database object that exceeds that user's `quota` for that tablespace, then the object creation script will fail. A `quota` can be specified either in kilobytes (KB) or megabytes (MB). A `quota` clause should be issued separately for every tablespace other than the temporary tablespace on which the user will have access to create database objects. If you want a user to have the ability to use all the space in a tablespace, `quota unlimited on` *tblspcname* can be specified.

TIP

Users need `quotas` *on tablespaces to create database objects only. They do not need a* `quota` *on a tablespace to* `update`, `insert`, *or* `delete` *data in an existing object in the tablespace, so long*

as they do have the appropriate privilege on the
object for data being inserted, updated, or deleted.

profile

`profiles` are a bundled set of resource-usage parameters that the DBA can set in order to limit the user's overall host machine utilization. A driving idea behind their use is that many end users of the system only need a certain amount of the host machine's capacity during their session. To reduce the chance that one user could affect the overall database performance with, say, a poorly formulated ad hoc report that drags the database to its knees, you may assign profiles for each user that limit the amount of time they can spend on the system.

password expire

This clause enforces the requirement that a user change his or her password on first logging into Oracle. This extra level of password security guarantees that not even you, the DBA, will know a user's password. If this clause is not included, the user will not have to change the password on first logging into Oracle.

account unlock

This is the default for the user accounts created. It means that the user's account is available for use immediately. The DBA can prevent users from using their accounts by specifying `account lock` instead.

Creating an Operating System Authenticated User

An Oracle database user can be authenticated at various levels—by Oracle itself, by an operating system, or by a remote service. We already discussed in the previous section how to create Oracle users authenticated by Oracle. The following command shows how to create a user authenticated by an operating system:

```
CREATE USER sam
   IDENTIFIED EXTERNALLY
   DEFAULT TABLESPACE users;
```

   The previous command creates a user called SAM who will be authenticated by the operating system. This means the user SAM must have an operating system account on the machine the Oracle is executing, and once logged into the machine, the user SAM should give the following command to log into the database:

```
sqlplus /
```

Before creating an operating system-authenticated user, the OS_AUTHENT_PREFIX initialization parameter has to be defined. This parameter specifies the format of the username of operating system-authenticated users. This value defaults to OPS$ to make it backward compatible, but it can now be defined as a NULL as follows:

```
OS_AUTHENT_PREFIX = ""
```

To permit operating system-authenticated users to log into Oracle from a remote machine, you can set the REMOTE_OS_AUTHENT parameter to TRUE. Doing so specifies that the user can be authenticated by a remote operating system. The default value of this parameter if FALSE. However, be aware that using this parameter opens a security hole in the database, whereby operating system-authenticated users on rogue systems may be able to gain access to your Oracle database.

Guidelines for User-Account Management

The following list identifies several new guidelines to follow when managing user accounts. In many cases, these items are new for Oracle8i and enhance the management of user accounts:

- Use a standard password for user creation, such as `123abc` or `first1`, and use `password expire` to force users to change this password to something else the first time they log into Oracle.

- Avoid operating system authentication unless all your users will access Oracle while connected directly to the machine hosting your database (this second part is also not advised).

- Always create a default temporary tablespace. Then you don't have to worry about assigning one during user creation. But in case you don't have a default temporary tablespace, be sure to always assign `temporary tablespace` and `default tablespace` to users with the ability to create database objects, such as developers.

- Give few users `quota unlimited`. Although it's annoying to have users asking for more space, it's even more annoying to reorganize tablespaces carelessly filled with database objects.

- Become familiar with the user-account management and other host machine limits that can be set via profiles. These new features take Oracle user-account management to new levels of security.

For Review

1. Understand how to set up new users in Oracle using the `create user` command. Know each of the components of that statement as well. In particular, pay attention to the `default tablespace` and `temporary tablespace` clauses.

2. Be aware of the clauses that force users to change their password regularly and after they first login.

Exercises

1. The following tablespace information was taken from an Oracle database:

```
SQL> select tablespace_name, contents from dba_tablespaces;
TABLESPACE_NAME     CONTENTS
------------------  --------------
SYSTEM              PERMANENT
DATA                PERMANENT
INDEXES             PERMANENT
UNDOTBS             UNDO
TEMP                TEMPORARY
USERS               PERMANENT
```

   You create a user in this database with the following command: `create user serena identified by tranquill`. Which of the following choices identifies the location where Oracle will place SERENA's data required for disk sorts?

   A. SYSTEM

   B. DATA

   C. TEMP

   D. UNDOTBS

2. The security administrator for YourCo., a Fortune 500 user of Oracle database software, has issued a mandate that all users in the organization must have a password that no one, not even the DBA, must know. User BETTYBOOP just joined the firm today, and your job as DBA is to create her a new user ID on the Oracle database. Which of the following `create user` clauses would you use to ensure that BETTYBOOP has to change her password the first time she logs into Oracle?

   A. `identified by`

   B. `quota`

    C. `password expire`

    D. `account unlock`

3. **The following tablespace information was taken from your Oracle database:**

```
SQL> select tablespace_name, contents from dba_tablespaces;
TABLESPACE_NAME     CONTENTS
------------------  -------------
SYSTEM              PERMANENT
DATA                PERMANENT
INDEXES             PERMANENT
UNDOTBS             UNDO
TEMP                TEMPORARY
USERS               PERMANENT
```

    You create a user in this database with the following command: `create user serena identified by tranquill`. Which of the following choices identifies the location where Oracle will place SERENA's new table that she creates with the `create table mytab (col1 number primary key)` command?

    A. SYSTEM

    B. DATA

    C. TEMP

    D. UNDOTBS

Answer Key

1. C. SYSTEM is not used because this database has a default temporary tablespace. **2.** C. **3.** A. If no `default tablespace` clause is included in a `create user` command, tables and indexes for that user are placed in the SYSTEM tablespace if no `tablespace` clause is included in the `object creation` command.

Altering and Dropping Existing Users

Once a user is created, there are a few reasons you'll need to modify that user. One is to expire the password if a user forgets it, so that the next time the user logs in, the password can be changed by the user. The `alter user identified by` statement is used to change the user's password:

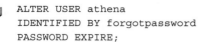

```
ALTER USER athena
IDENTIFIED BY forgotpassword
PASSWORD EXPIRE;
```

TIP
Users themselves can also issue the alter user
identified *by command to change their own
passwords. However, this is the only aspect of a
user's ID that the user can change.*

In certain situations, as the result of user profiles, a user's account may become locked. This may occur if the user forgot his or her password and tried to log in using a bad password too many times. To unlock a user's account while also making it possible for the user to change the password, the following alter user statement can be used:

```
ALTER USER athena
IDENTIFIED BY forgotpassword
ACCOUNT UNLOCK
PASSWORD EXPIRE;
```

TIP
*You'll learn more about account locking in the
password management section later in this chapter.*

Other situations abound. In an attempt to prevent misuse, you may want to lock an account that has been used many times unsuccessfully to gain access to Oracle with the following statement:

```
ALTER USER athena
ACCOUNT LOCK;
```

TIP
*You should remember that changes to passwords,
account lock status, or password expiration are
applied only to subsequent user sessions, not the
current one.*

Changing User Tablespace Allocation
You may want to reorganize tablespaces to distribute the input/output (I/O) load and make more effective use of the hardware running Oracle. Perhaps this effort involves dropping some tablespaces and creating new ones. If the DBA wants to change a user's default tablespace, the alter user default tablespace statement can be used. As explained earlier, this change is good for preserving the integrity of the SYSTEM tablespace. Only newly created objects will be affected by this statement.

Existing objects created in other tablespaces by that user will continue to reside in those tablespaces until they are dropped. Additionally, if the user specifies a tablespace in which to place a database object, that specification will override the default tablespace.

```
ALTER USER spanky
DEFAULT TABLESPACE overflow_tabspc01;
```

By the same token, you may want to reorganize the tablespace used for disk sorts as you move from permanent tablespaces to temporary tablespaces, and this is done using `alter user temporary tablespace`. Only the DBA can make these changes; the users cannot change their own temporary or default tablespaces.

```
ALTER USER spanky
TEMPORARY TABLESPACE temp_overflow_01;
```

TIP
You only need to specify the `temporary` `tablespace` *clause for users if no default temporary tablespace exists for the database, or if you want to assign users to a temporary tablespace other than the default temporary tablespace for the database.*

A tablespace accessible to the user at user creation can have a quota placed on it. A quota can be altered by the DBA with the `alter user quota` statement. For example, the DBA may want to reduce the quota on the USERS_01 tablespace from 10MB to 5MB for user SPANKY. If the user has already created over 5MB worth of database objects in the tablespace, no further data can be added to those objects and no new objects can be created. Only the DBA can change a user's tablespace quota; the users cannot change their own quotas.

```
ALTER USER spanky
QUOTA 5M ON users_01;
```

TIP
Specifying `quota 0` *on SYSTEM for a user will prevent him or her from creating any object in the SYSTEM tablespace, even if that user still has his or her* `default tablespace` *set to SYSTEM. However, this restriction does not include the creation of packages, stored procedures, and functions.*

Aspects of User Accounts Changeable by Users

All aspects of the user's account covered already are the components that can be modified by the DBA. However, the aspects of the account that can be changed by the actual user are far more limited. A situation may arise in regular database use where a user wants to change his or her password. This is accomplished with the following:

```
ALTER USER athena
IDENTIFIED BY mynewpassword;
```

TIP

Except for altering the password, the user can change nothing about his or her own user account, except in certain situations where the alter any user *privilege has been granted to that user.*

Dropping User Accounts

As users come and go, their access should be modified to reflect their departure. To drop a user from the database, you execute the drop user statement. If a user has created database objects, the user cannot be dropped until the objects are dropped as well. In order to drop the user and all related database objects in one fell swoop, Oracle provides the cascade option.

```
DROP USER spanky CASCADE;
```

TIP

If you want to remove a user but assign his or her table(s) to another user, you should use the EXPORT tool to dump the user's table(s), and then use IMPORT with the FROMUSER and TOUSER parameters to import the tables as that other user.

For Review

1. Understand how to use the alter user statement to change a user's ID configuration. Also, be aware that the only aspect of a user's ID that can be changed with the alter user statement that cannot also be set with the create user statement is the default role clause. We'll discuss roles in more detail later in this chapter.

2. Users can only change their own passwords. All other aspects of changing a person's user ID must be completed by you, the DBA.

Exercises

1. User BETTYBOOP logs onto Oracle. Which of the following statements can she herself execute to change an aspect of her own user ID?

   A. `alter user bettyboop identified by boop2edoop;`

   B. `alter user bettyboop default tablespace users;`

   C. `alter user bettyboop quota 100M on tablespace SYSTEM;`

   D. `alter user bettyboop default role none;`

2. User BOBSMITH has been asked to leave YourCo. The department director asks you to drop his user ID from the Oracle database. In your analysis, you discover that BOBSMITH has about 60 tables in his schema, all of which are housed in the USERS tablespace, along with tables for many other users. Which of the following choices identifies the command that will eliminate BOBSMITH's user and schema contents in the fewest number of steps?

   A. Issue `drop table` for all 60 tables and then `drop user bobsmith;`.

   B. Issue `spool genscrpt.sql`, followed by `select 'drop table ' || table_name || ';' from dba_tables where owner = 'BOBSMITH'` to generate a script, then issue `@genscrpt`, and then `drop user BOBSMITH`.

   C. Issue the `drop user bobsmith cascade` command.

   D. Issue the `drop tablespace users including contents` command.

3. You issue the following command in Oracle: `alter user JOSEPHINE default tablespace SYSTEM quota 0 on SYSTEM`. Assuming JOSEPHINE has the appropriate privileges to do so, which of the following commands will JOSEPHINE not be able to issue as a result of this action?

   A. `create table mytab (col1 number primary key);`

   B. `create procedure myproc begin null; end;`

   C. `create function myfunc return null begin null; end;`

   D. `create table mytab2 (col1 number primary key) tablespace data;`

Answer Key
1. A. 2. C. 3. A.

Monitoring Information about Existing Users

As the DBA, you may periodically want to monitor information about users. Several data dictionary views may be used for the purpose of obtaining information about users. Some information you may want to collect includes default and temporary tablespace information, objects created by that user, and what the current account status for that user account is. The following data dictionary views can be used to determine this information:

- **DBA_USERS**   Contains the username, Oracle-generated ID number, encrypted password, default and temporary tablespace information, and user profile that was specified in the ID creation statements or any alteration that may have followed. Also, the view offers ACCOUNT_STATUS, which may be locked, open, or expired; LOCK_DATE, which is the date on which the account was locked (NULL for open accounts); and EXPIRY_DATE, which is the date for account expiration.

- **DBA_OBJECTS**   Contains the specific information about every object in the database. The DBA can determine which objects belong to which users by using the OWNER column of this view.

- **DBA_SEGMENTS**   Similar to DBA_OBJECTS. Contains information about various segments (tables, indexes, and so on) created by users, where they reside, and their space allocation information.

- **DBA_TS_QUOTAS**   Names all users and any tablespace quotas that have been created for them.

TIP
A value of -1 in MAX_BYTES or MAX_BLOCKS means that the user has an unlimited space quota for that tablespace.

For Review

1. Know the views you might use to find information about users in your Oracle database: DBA_USERS and DBA_TS_QUOTAS.

2. Understand where to look in the data dictionary for information about where a user's database objects may reside: DBA_OBJECTS and DBA_SEGMENTS.

Exercises

1. You issue the following command in Oracle, and Oracle responds with the following information:

```
SQL> select username, tablespace_name, max_bytes from dba_ts_quotas
  2  where username = 'CAPTAINCRUNCH';
USERNAME        TABLESPACE_NAME  MAX_BYTES
-------------   ---------------  ----------
CAPTAINCRUNCH SYSTEM            1048576
CAPTAINCRUNCH DATA              -1
CAPTAINCRUNCH TEMP              -1
CAPTAINCRUNCH INDEXES          10485760
```

Which of the following choices correctly describes an aspect of CAPTAINCRUNCH's tablespace allocation quota?

A. CAPTAINCRUNCH can allocate up to 1MB worth of space in the SYSTEM tablespace for procedure source code.

B. CAPTAINCRUNCH can perform disk sorts that generate enough temporary segments to fill the TEMP tablespace.

C. CAPTAINCRUNCH can allocate up to 10MB of storage in the DATA tablespace.

D. CAPTAINCRUNCH can allocate up to 1MB of storage in the INDEXES tablespace.

2. You issue the following command in Oracle, and Oracle responds by providing the following information:

```
SQL> select * from dba_users where username = 'SYS';
USERNAME                                USER_ID PASSWORD
----------------     -----------------------------   ----------------
ACCOUNT_STATUS       LOCK_DATE                       EXPIRY_DATE
----------------     -----------------------------   ----------------
DEFAULT_TABLESPACE TEMPORARY_TABLESPACE              CREATED
----------------     -----------------------------   ----------------
PROFILE              INITIAL_RSRC_CONSUMER_GROUP     EXTERNAL_NAME
----------------     -----------------------------   ----------------
SYS                                          0 D4C5016086B2DC6A
OPEN
SYSTEM               TEMP                            06-JUN-01
DEFAULT              SYS_GROUP
```

Which of the following statements is true regarding the user information shown previously?

A. No user may log into Oracle as SYS.

B. If SYS creates a table without specifying a `tablespace` clause, the table will be placed into the TEMP tablespace.

C. The password for the SYS user on this database is D4C5016086B2DC6A.

D. If SYS performs a disk sort, the temporary segments will be placed in the TEMP tablespace.

3. **You are attempting to find information in the DBA_USERS view about a given username. Which of the following informational components about the SYS user cannot be found in the DBA_USERS view?**

A. Default role

B. Default tablespace

C. Default temporary tablespace

D. Default profile

Answer Key
1. B. 2. D. 3. A.

Managing Password Security and Resources

In this section, you will cover the following topics related to managing resource use:

- Controlling resource use with profiles
- Administering profiles
- Managing passwords using profiles
- Obtaining profile information from the data dictionary

Profiles are objects in the Oracle database that limit a user's ability to utilize the resources of the system hosting the Oracle database. In other words, if you wanted to restrict a group of users from abusing the central processing unit (CPU) utilization on the machine hosting the Oracle database, you would use profiles in order to do so. Oracle's use of the host machine on behalf of certain users can be managed by creating specific user profiles to correspond to the amount of activity anticipated by typical transactions generated by those different types of users. The principle of user profiles is not to force the user off the system every time an artificially low resource-usage threshold is exceeded. Rather, resource-usage thresholds should enable the users to do everything they need to on the Oracle database, while also limiting unwanted or unacceptable use. If users make a mistake, or try to do something that hurts database performance, profiles can stop them short, helping to reduce problems. Let's now explore how to use profiles in the Oracle database.

Controlling Resource Use with Profiles

The main purpose behind user profiles is to control the use of host system resources by the Oracle database with respect to the user. Before proceeding into a full-fledged discussion of profiles, however, you must make a change to your `init.ora` file so that Oracle will enforce host system resource limits set in profiles. To use resource limits, you must first change the RESOURCE_LIMIT `init.ora` parameter to TRUE on your Oracle database. To enable resource restrictions to be used in conjunction with profiles on the current database session, you can also issue the following statement:

```
ALTER SYSTEM
SET RESOURCE_LIMIT = TRUE;
```

Once resource limits are enabled, there are three different aspects of resource usage and limitation to consider when setting up profiles. This discussion will cover all three. They are session-level resource limits for individuals, call-level resource limits, and the assignment of resource cost to enable composite limits.

Setting Individual Resource Limits: Session Level

The following resource-usage areas can have limits assigned for them within the profiles you create. If a session-level resource limit is exceeded, the user gets an error and the session is terminated automatically. At the session level, the resource limits are as follows:

- **sessions_per_user** The number of sessions a user can open concurrently with the Oracle database.

- **cpu_per_session** The maximum allowed CPU time in $1/100$ seconds that a user can utilize in one session.

- **logical_reads_per_session** The maximum number of disk I/O block reads that can be executed in support of the user processing in one session.

- **idle_time** The time in minutes that a user can issue no commands before Oracle times out his or her session.

- **connect_time** The total amount of time in minutes that a user can be connected to the database.

- **private_sga** The amount of private memory in KB or MB that can be allocated to a user for private storage. This is only used when MTS is in use on your Oracle database.

TIP
You'll see examples of profiles with these limits set in the next discussion.

Individual Resource Limits: Call Level

At the call level, the resource-usage areas can have limits assigned for them within the profiles you create. If the user exceeds the call-level usage limits he or she has been assigned, the SQL statement that produced the error is terminated, any transaction changes *made only by the offending statement* are rolled back, previous statements remain intact, and the user remains connected to Oracle. Call-level usage limits are identified as follows:

- **logical_reads_per_call** The maximum number of disk I/O block reads that can be executed in support of the user's processing in one session.

- **cpu_per_call** The maximum allowed CPU time in $\frac{1}{100}$ seconds that any individual operation in a user session can use.

TIP
You'll see examples of profiles with these limits set in the next discussion.

Setting Composite Limits and Resource Costs

In some cases, you may find individual resource limits inflexible. The alternative is setting composite limits on the principle of resource cost. Resource cost is an arbitrary number that reflects the relative value of that resource based on the host machine's capabilities. For example, on a host machine with few CPUs and many disk controllers, you might consider `cpu_per_session` more valuable than `logical_reads_per_session`. The statement used for assigning a resource cost is `alter resource cost`. Resource costs only apply to the `cpu_per_session`, `logical_reads_per_session`, `connect_time`, and `private_sga` resources. The default value for each resource cost is zero. Resource costs are not necessarily monetary costs. Cost is specified as an abstract unit value, not a monetary resource price. For example, setting the resource cost of CPU cycles per session equal to 1.5 does not mean that each CPU cycle costs a user process $1.50 to run.

```
ALTER RESOURCE COST
CPU_PER_SESSION 10
LOGICAL_READS_PER_SESSION 2
PRIVATE_SGA 6
CONNECT_TIME 1;
```

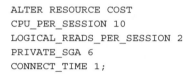

TIP
You'll see an example of a profile with composite limits set in the next discussion.

Resource Consumer Groups and Host System Resource Management

In Oracle8i, Oracle introduced a new feature for host system resource management —the use of resource consumer groups. This feature uses built-in PL/SQL procedures and functions to control the use of host system resources by users. Although not tested extensively on the OCP DBA Fundamentals I exam, it's worth taking some time to explore this feature on your own. For more information, consult the database resource management section of the Oracle9i Database Administrators Guide that comes as part of your Oracle Generic Documentation.

For Review

1. Know that you must set the RESOURCE_LIMIT initialization parameter before Oracle will enforce resource limits according to your profile settings.

2. Be sure you can identify the different levels of host system resource settings: session-level, call-level, and composite limits. To set composite limits, you use the `alter resource cost` command to define cost values for resources.

Exercises

1. You want to use composite resource limits in the Oracle database. Which of the following commands must be issued so that composite resources are assigned a value for composite limits?

   A. `alter system`

   B. `alter resource cost`

   C. `alter profile`

   D. `alter user`

2. You issue the following command in the Oracle database: `alter system set resource_limit = true;`. Which of the following statements describes the purpose this command serves?

   A. This command is meant to set composite resource limit costs in your Oracle database.

   B. This command is meant to enable the use of profiles to limit host system resource utilization.

   C. This command is meant to create profiles for use in Oracle.

   D. This command is meant to assign users to profiles in Oracle.

3. You are defining resource limits for use with profiles. Which of the following is not a resource limit that can be set in conjunction with composite limits on your Oracle database?

   A. IDLE_TIME

   B. CPU_PER_SESSION

   C. PRIVATE_SGA

   D. CONNECT_TIME

Answer Key
1. B. 2. B. 3. A.

Administering Profiles

Profiles are assigned to users with the `create user` or `alter user` command. You've already seen some examples of the `create user` command in previous discussions. A special user profile exists in Oracle at database creation called DEFAULT. If you do not assign a profile to a user with the `profile` clause in the `create user` statement, Oracle assigns the DEFAULT profile to that user automatically. The DEFAULT profile isn't very restrictive of host system resources; in fact, DEFAULT gives users unlimited use of all resources definable in the database. You might create a user profile that has some host system usage restrictions on it, such as the one in the following code block:

```
CREATE PROFILE developer LIMIT
SESSIONS_PER_USER 1
CPU_PER_SESSION 10000
CPU_PER_CALL 20
CONNECT_TIME 240
IDLE_TIME 20
LOGICAL_READS_PER_SESSION 50000
LOGICAL_READS_PER_CALL 400
PRIVATE_SGA 1024;
```

This code block is a good example of using profiles to set *individual resource limits*. You don't need to define limits for all available resources, because any resources not explicitly assigned limits when you create a profile will be assigned the default value for that limit, specified in the DEFAULT profile. Thus, if you change the value for a resource limit in the DEFAULT profile, you may be making changes to other profiles on your system as well. Once profiles are created, they are assigned to users with the `profile` clause in either the `create user` or `alter user` statement. The following code block contains some examples of each statement:

```
CREATE USER spanky
IDENTIFIED BY orange#tabby
TEMPORARY TABLESPACE temp_01
QUOTA 5M ON temp_01
PROFILE developer;

ALTER USER athena
PROFILE developer;
```

Altering and Dropping Profiles

Once created, you can alter the host system resource limit settings in your profile using the `alter profile` command. Changing a user profile may be required if user profiles in the database rely on default values set in the DEFAULT profile. For example, if the resource limit `cpu_per_session` in DEFAULT is changed from `unlimited` to 20,000, then `cpu_per_session` in any user profile that didn't explicitly set one for itself will also be affected. You may not want this to happen, but only by explicitly setting its own value for `cpu_per_session` will the profile not depend on the DEFAULT profile for the `cpu_per_session` limit. You issue the following statement to change a resource limit in a profile:

```
ALTER PROFILE developer LIMIT
CPU_PER_SESSION UNLIMITED;
```

TIP
Any option in any profile can be changed at any time; however, the change will not take effect for users assigned to that profile until the user logs out and logs back in.

If you want to drop a user profile from the database, do so by executing the `drop profile` statement. A question you might have is, what happens if you try to drop a profile that has already been assigned to users? Well, in that case, you must use the `drop profile cascade` command. After issuing the `drop profile cascade` command, Oracle switches users assigned to the dropped profile back to the DEFAULT profile instead. For obvious reasons, the DEFAULT profile cannot be dropped. Let's look at an example of the `drop profile` command to understand the syntax:

```
DROP PROFILE developer CASCADE;
```

TIP
To gather information about how users are utilizing the host machine in database sessions to set resource limits properly, use the `audit session` *command. You'll learn more about auditing in a later discussion. Resource limits you can gather information for include* `connect_time,` `logical_reads_per_session,` *and* `logical_reads_per_call.`

Creating Profiles with Composite Limits Set
Once resource costs are set, you assign composite limits to your users. Composite limits restrict database use by specifying a limit of how much a host machine resource can be used per session. Each time the session uses a resource, Oracle

tallies the total resource use for that session. When the session hits the `composite_limit`, the session is terminated. Profiles are altered to include a `composite_limit` with the `alter profile` statement.

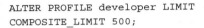

```
ALTER PROFILE developer LIMIT
COMPOSITE_LIMIT 500;
```

For Review

1. Be sure you understand the basic purpose behind profiles. They prevent misuse of underlying host system resources by setting limits on those resources at the user level.

2. Know the purpose of the DEFAULT profile. It is assigned to users when you do not specify a `profile` clause in the `create user` command. It isn't very restrictive, however—all host resource-usage limits are set to `unlimited`.

3. You create profiles with the `create profile` command. If you don't set an aspect of host system limits in your profile, Oracle defaults that host system limit to whatever setting is present for that limit in the DEFAULT profile.

4. If you drop a profile that has been assigned to a user, you must use the `cascade` option in the `drop profile` command. Oracle switches the user back to the DEFAULT profile in this situation.

Exercises

1. **The following output was taken from a session with your Oracle database:**

```
SQL> select username, profile from dba_users;
USERNAME        PROFILE
--------------  --------------
SYS             SYS_PROFILE
SYSTEM          SYS_PROFILE
MARYANN         DATA_ADMIN
MARYSUE         DEVELOPER
MARYJANE        MANAGER
```

If you issue the `drop profile DATA_ADMIN cascade` command, which of the following profiles will MARYANN be assigned to?

A. DEVELOPER

B. MANAGER

C. SYS_PROFILE

D. DEFAULT

2. **You create a profile using the following command:**

```
CREATE PROFILE myprofile LIMIT
SESSIONS_PER_USER 1
CPU_PER_CALL 20
CONNECT_TIME 240
IDLE_TIME 20
PRIVATE_SGA 1024;
```

Which of the following choices best identifies how Oracle will determine what the value for the CPU_PER_SESSION limit will be?

A. Oracle uses the same value as CPU_PER_CALL from this `create profile` command.

B. Oracle uses the value for CPU_PER_SESSION from the SYS_PROFILE profile.

C. Oracle uses the value for CPU_PER_SESSION from the DEFAULT profile.

D. Oracle sets CPU_PER_SESSION to `unlimited`.

3. **You have created three profiles on your Oracle database at YourCo., a Fortune 500 user of Oracle database software: DEVELOPER for your Oracle developers, MANAGEMENT for IT managers, and ORACLE_USERS for the end users of your Oracle database. BETTYBOOP's first day at YourCo. is today, and your job is to create a user ID for her. You issue the following in Oracle: `create user bettyboop identified by changeme password expire account unlock`. Which of the following choices identify the resource profile BETTYBOOP will be assigned?**

A. DEVELOPER

B. ORACLE_USERS

C. MANAGEMENT

D. DEFAULT

E. None—no `profile` clause was specified in the `create user` command.

Answer Key

1. D. 2. C. 3. D.

Administering Passwords Using Profiles

We've already hinted that advanced password management features are available in Oracle through the use of profiles. These features include *account locking, password aging and expiration, password history*, and *password complexity requirements*. These features are designed to make it harder than ever to hack the Oracle database as an authorized user without knowing the user's password. This protects the integrity of assigned usernames as well as the overall data integrity of the Oracle database.

Though not required to enable password management, the DBA can run the utlpwdmg.sql script as SYS to support the functionality of password management. This script can be found in the rdbms/admin subdirectory under the Oracle software home directory. This script makes some additions to the DEFAULT profile, identified earlier in the chapter, for use with password management. When the password management script is run, all default password management settings defined in the DEFAULT profile are enforced at all times on the Oracle database. This is unlike other resource limits, which still require that RESOURCE_LIMIT be set to TRUE before the instance starts.

Account Management

Account locking enables Oracle to lock out an account when users attempt to log into the database unsuccessfully on several attempts. The maximum number of failed attempts is defined per user or by group. The number of failed attempts is specified by the DBA or security officer in ways that will be defined shortly, and the failed attempts are tracked by Oracle such that if the user fails to log into the database in the specified number of tries, Oracle locks out the user automatically. In addition, a time period for automatic user lockout can be defined such that the failed login attempt counter will reset after that time period, and the user may try to log into the database again. Alternatively, automatic lockout can be permanent, disabled only by the security administrator or DBA. User accounts can also be locked manually if the security administrator or DBA so desires. In this situation, the only way to unlock the account is manually. The following command shows how to set the parameters for account locking:

```
ALTER PROFILE default LIMIT
  FAILED_LOGIN_ATTEMPTS 3
  PASSWORD_LOCK_TIME unlimited;
```

In the previous example, the FAILED_LOGIN_ATTEMPTS setting defines the number of failed login attempts before the account is locked out. In this case, we've set this option to 3, meaning that after three failed attempts at logging, Oracle locks the user's account automatically. The other option, PASSWORD_LOCK_TIME, indicates the number of days the account is locked after three failed login attempts. In this case, we've specified that the user account stays locked indefinitely, until we, as DBAs, investigate the situation and unlock the account manually.

Password Aging and Rotation

A password can also be aged in the Oracle database. The DBA or security administrator can set a password to have a maximum lifetime in the Oracle database. Once a threshold time period passes, the user must change his or her password or be unable to access the Oracle database. A grace period can be defined, during which the user must change the password. If the time of the grace period passes and the user doesn't change the password, the account is then locked and only the security administrator can unlock it. A useful technique for creating new users is to create them with expired passwords, such that the user enters the grace period on first login and must change the password during that time.

A potential problem arises when users are forced to change their passwords. Sometimes users try to "fool" the system by changing the expired password to something else and then immediately changing the password back. To prevent this, Oracle8i supports a password history feature that keeps track of recently used passwords and disallows their use for a specified amount of time or number of changes. The interval is defined within the user profile, and information on how to set it will be presented shortly. The following is some sample code to implement password aging and rotation:

```
ALTER PROFILE default LIMIT
  PASSWORD_LIFE_TIME 60
  PASSWORD_GRACE_TIME 10
  PASSWORD_REUSE_TIME 1800
  PASSWORD_REUSE_MAX 0;
```

The PASSWORD_LIFE_TIME parameter defines the lifetime of the password in days after which the password will expire. The PASSWORD_GRACE_TIME parameter defines the grace period in days for changing the password after the first successful login once the password has expired. The PASSWORD_REUSE_TIME parameter specifies the maximum number of days before the user can reuse a previous password. Finally, the PASSWORD_REUSE_MAX parameter specifies the maximum number of times a previous password can be reused.

Password Complexity Verification

Finally, and perhaps most important to the integrity of an Oracle user's account, there is the feature of password complexity verification. There are many commonly accepted practices in creating a password, such as making sure it has a certain character length, that it is not a proper name or word in the dictionary, that it is not all numbers or all characters, and so on. Too often, however, users don't heed these mandates and create passwords that are easy to decode using any of a number of products available for decoding encrypted password information.

To prevent users from unwittingly subverting the security of the database, Oracle supports the automatic verification of password complexity with the use of a

PL/SQL function that can be applied during user or group profile creation to prevent users from creating passwords of insufficient complexity. The checks provided by the default function include making sure the minimum password length is four characters and is not the same as the username. Also, the password must contain at least one letter, number, and punctuation character, and the password must be different from the previous password defined by at least three characters.

If this level of complexity verification provided by the given PL/SQL function is not high enough, a PL/SQL function of sufficient complexity may be defined by the organization, and be subject to certain restrictions. The overall call syntax must conform to the details in the following code listing. In addition, the new routine must be assigned as the password verification routine in the user's profile or the DEFAULT profile. In the `create profile` statement, the following must be present: `password_verify_function user_pwcmplx_fname`, where `user_pwcmplx_fname` is the name of the user-defined password complexity function. Some other constraints on the definition of this function include that an appropriate error must be returned if the routine raises an exception or if the verification routine becomes invalid, and that the verification function will be owned by SYS and used in system context. The call to the PL/SQL complexity verification function must conform to the following parameter-passing and return-value requirements:

```
USER_PWCMPLX_FNAME
( user_id_parm      IN VARCHAR2,
  new_passwd_parm   IN VARCHAR2,
  old_passwd_parm   IN VARCHAR2
) RETURN BOOLEAN;
```

To show the coding used in a password complexity function, the following example is offered. This example is a simplified and modified block of code similar to the password verification function provided with Oracle. The function will check three things: that the new password is not the same as the username, that the new password is six characters long, and that the new password is not the same as the old one. When the DBA creates a username, the verification process is called to determine whether the password is appropriate. If the function returns TRUE, the DBA will be able to create the username. If not, the user creation will fail. This example is designed to give you some groundwork for coding your own password complexity function; bear in mind, however, that the function in the following listing is greatly simplified for example purposes only:

```
CREATE OR REPLACE FUNCTION my_pwver (
x_user     IN   VARCHAR2,
x_new_pw   IN   VARCHAR2,
x_old_pw   IN   VARCHAR2
```

```
)RETURN BOOLEAN IS
BEGIN
   IF LENGTH(x_new_pw) < 6 THEN
     RAISE_APPLICATION_ERROR(-20001, 'New password too short.');
   ELSIF x_new_pw = x_user THEN
     RAISE_APPLICATION_ERROR(-20002, 'New password same as username');
   ELSIF x_new_pw = x_old_pw THEN
     RAISE_APPLICATION_ERROR(-20003, 'New password same as old');
   ELSE
     RETURN(TRUE);
   END IF;
END;
```

The function itself can be defined in the profile as follows:

```
ALTER PROFILE default LIMIT
   PASSWORD_VERIFY_FUNCTION my_pwver;
```

Password Management Resource Limits in the DEFAULT Profile

After the `utlpwdmg.sql` script is run, default values will be specified for several password-management resource limits. An explanation of each option is listed in this section. The default value for each of these settings is `unlimited` or NULL.

- **failed_login_attempts**   The number of unsuccessful attempts at login a user can make before the account locks

- **password_life_time**   The number of days a password will remain active

- **password_reuse_time**   The number of days before the password can be reused

- **password_reuse_max**   The number of times the password must be changed before one can be reused

- **password_lock_time**   The number of days after which Oracle will unlock a user account that is locked automatically when the user exceeds `failed_login_attempts`

- **password_grace_time**   The number of days during which an expired password must be changed by the user or else Oracle permanently locks the account

- **password_verify_function**   The function used for password complexity verification

Using Password Settings for Profiles: Example
Following is a sample code of creating a new profile with all of the previous password parameters:

```
CREATE PROFILE tmp_profile LIMIT
  FAILED_LOGIN_ATTEMPTS 3
  PASSWORD_LOCK_TIME unlimited
  PASSWORD_LIFE_TIME 30
  PASSWORD_REUSE_TIME 30
  PASSWORD_VERIFY_FUNCTION my_pwver
  PASSWORD_GRACE_TIME 5;
```

For Review

1. Understand the account management features available in Oracle. You can lock and unlock user accounts using this feature.

2. Be sure you can identify the password aging and rotation features available in Oracle. You can specify it so that Oracle does not enable the reuse of passwords for a period of time, and that Oracle forces users to change their passwords periodically.

3. Know how Oracle manages password complexity verification in the database, and be sure you can describe the use of PL/SQL functions for this purpose.

Exercises

1. You create a profile using the following code block:

```
CREATE PROFILE tmp_profile LIMIT
  FAILED_LOGIN_ATTEMPTS 3
  PASSWORD_LOCK_TIME unlimited
  PASSWORD_LIFE_TIME 30
  PASSWORD_REUSE_TIME 180
  PASSWORD_VERIFY_FUNCTION my_pwver
  PASSWORD_GRACE_TIME 5;
```

Which of the following choices identifies a true statement about the profile you just created?

A. After three failed login attempts, a user assigned this profile will have to wait three days before trying to log into Oracle again.

B. After 180 days, a user assigned this profile can reuse his or her password.

    C. A user assigned this profile must change his or her password every 30 minutes.

    D. A user has up to five minutes to specify a password the first time he or she logs in before Oracle automatically locks the account.

2. **You plan to run the `utlpwmg.sql` script as part of managing passwords. Which of the following directory locations can this script be found in?**

    A. `$ORACLE_HOME/dbs`

    B. `$ORACLE_HOME/sqlplus/admin`

    C. `$ORACLE_HOME/rdbms/admin`

    D. `$ORACLE_HOME/network/admin`

3. **You want to set up password management features in your Oracle database such that users may never reuse a password and that a user has three days to change his or her default password the first time he or she logs into Oracle before the account gets locked. Which of the following choices identifies the statement you will use for this purpose?**

    A. `alter profile default limit failed_login_attempts 3 password_reuse_time unlimited;`

    B. `alter profile default limit password_grace_time 3 password_reuse_limit unlimited;`

    C. `alter profile default limit failed_login_attempts 3 password_grace_time unlimited;`

    D. `alter profile default limit password_reuse_time 3 failed_login_attempts unlimited;`

Answer Key
1. B. 2. C. 3. B.

Obtaining Profile Information from the Data Dictionary

The following dictionary views offer information about the resource-usage limits defined for profiles and about the profiles that have been assigned to users:

- **DBA_PROFILES** Contains specific information about the resource-usage parameters specified in conjunction with each profile.

- **RESOURCE_COST** Identifies all resources in the database and their corresponding cost, as defined by the DBA. Cost determines a resource's relative importance of use.

- **USER_RESOURCE_LIMITS** Identifies the system resource limits for individual users, as determined by the profile assigned to the users.

- **DBA_USERS** Offers information about the profile assigned to a user, current account status, lock date, and password expiry date.

TIP
Spend a little time on your Oracle database gaining familiarity with the contents of each of these dictionary views before taking the Oracle9i DBA Fundamentals I exam.

For Review

1. The profile assigned to a user can be found in the DBA_USERS view.

2. Resource cost and resource limit settings can be found in the RESOURCE_COST and USER_RESOURCE_LIMITS views, respectively.

3. The DBA_PROFILES view is handy for finding the resource settings in a particular profile.

Exercises

1. **You are administering profiles on your Oracle database. Which of the following queries would you use in order to determine which resource limits were in effect for user SALLY if you didn't know which profile SALLY was assigned?**

   A. `select resource_name, limit from dba_profiles where profile = (select profile from dba_users where username = 'SALLY');`

   B. `select resource_name, limit from dba_profiles where profile = (select profile from dba_users where user_id = 'SALLY');`

   C. `select resource_name, unit_cost from resource_cost where resource_name in (select resource_name from`

```
dba_profiles where profile = (select profile from
dba_users where username = 'SALLY'));
```

D. `select resource_name, unit_cost from resource_cost`
`where resource_name in (select resource_name from`
`dba_profiles where profile = (select profile from`
`dba_users where user_id = 'SALLY''));`

2. **You are attempting to determine which profiles have resource settings that do not impose limits on user resource utilization. Which of the following queries would be the most useful for this purpose?**

   A. `select profile from dba_profiles where profile =`
   `(select username from dba_users where profile =`
   `'UNLIMITED');`

   B. `select profile from dba_profiles where limit =`
   `(select unit_cost from resource_cost where`
   `resource_name = 'CPU_PER_SESSION');`

   C. `select profile from dba_profiles where limit =`
   `'UNLIMITED';`

   D. `select distinct profile from dba_profiles where`
   `limit = 'UNLIMITED';`

Answer Key

1. A. 2. D. The question asks for the query most useful for this purpose. The query in choice C is hard to read because the output lists the profile name once for every resource limit set to `unlimited` and is therefore less useful than the query in choice D.

Managing Privileges

In this section, you will cover the following topics related to managing privileges:

- Identifying system and object privileges
- Granting and revoking privileges
- Identifying audit capabilities

All access in an Oracle database requires database privileges. Access to connect to the database, the objects the user is permitted to see, and the objects the user is allowed to create are all controlled by privileges. Use of every database object and system resource is governed by privileges. There are privileges required to create objects, to access objects, to change data within tables, to execute stored procedures, to create users, and so on. Because access to every object is governed by privileges, security in the Oracle database is highly flexible in terms of which objects are available to which users.

Identifying System and Object Privileges

There are two categories of privileges, and the first is *system privileges*. System privileges control the creation and maintenance of many database objects, such as rollback segments, synonyms, tables, and triggers. Additionally, the ability to use the `analyze` command and the Oracle database `audit` capability is governed by system privileges. The other category is object privileges. These privileges govern a user's ability to manipulate database objects owned by other users in the database.

System Privileges Identified

Generally speaking, there are several subcategories of system privileges that relate to each object. Those categories determine the scope of ability that the privilege grantee will have. The classes or categories of system privileges are listed here. In the following subtopics, the privilege itself gives you the ability to perform the action against your own database objects, whereas the `any` keyword refers to the ability to perform the action against any database object of that type in Oracle.

Admin Functions   These privileges relate to activities typically reserved for and performed by the DBA. Privileges include `alter system`, `audit system`, `audit any`, `alter database`, `analyze any`, `SYSDBA`, `SYSOPER`, and `grant any privilege`. You must have the `create session` privilege to connect to Oracle. More information about `SYSDBA` and `SYSOPER` privileges and the activities they permit you to do will be discussed in the section "The `SYSDBA` and `SYSOPER` Privileges" later in this chapter.

Database Access   These privileges control who accesses the database, when they can access it, and what they can do regarding management of their own session. Privileges include `create session`, `alter session`, and `restricted session`.

Tablespaces   You already know that tablespaces are disk resources used to store database objects. These privileges determine who can maintain these disk resources. These privileges are typically reserved for DBAs. Privileges include `create tablespace`, `alter tablespace`, `manage tablespace`, `drop tablespace`, and `unlimited tablespace`. Note that you cannot grant `unlimited tablespace` to a role. More information on roles appears in the next section.

Users   These privileges are used to manage users on the Oracle database. Typically, these privileges are reserved for DBAs or security administrators. Privileges include `create user`, `become user`, `alter user`, and `drop user`.

Undo Segments   You already know that rollback segments are disk resources that make aspects of transaction processing possible. The privileges include `create rollback segment`, `alter rollback segment`, and `drop rollback segment`. Note that you only need these privileges if you plan to administer undo segments manually. If you plan to use automatic undo management, no users need to be granted these privileges.

Tables   You already know that tables store data in the Oracle database. These privileges govern which users can create and maintain tables. The privileges include `create table`, `create any table`, `alter any table`, `backup any table`, `drop any table`, `lock any table`, `comment any table`, `select any table`, `insert any table`, `update any table`, and `delete any table`. The `create table` or `create any table` privilege also enables you to drop the table. The `create table` privilege also bestows the ability to create indexes on the table and run the `analyze` command on the table. To be able to truncate a table, you must have the `drop any table` privilege granted to you.

Clusters   You already know that clusters are used to store tables commonly used together in close physical proximity on disk. The privileges include `create cluster`, `create any cluster`, `alter any cluster`, and `drop any cluster`. The `create cluster` and `create any cluster` privileges also enable you to alter and drop those clusters.

Indexes   You already know that indexes are used to improve SQL statement performance on tables containing lots of row data. The privileges include `create any index`, `alter any index`, and `drop any index`. You should note that there is no `create index` system privilege. The `create table` privilege also enables you to alter and drop indexes that you own and that are associated with the table.

Synonyms   A synonym is a database object that enables you to reference another object by a different name. A public synonym means that the synonym is available to every user in the database for the same purpose. The privileges include `create synonym`, `create any synonym`, `drop any synonym`, `create public synonym`, and `drop public synonym`. The `create synonym` privilege also enables you to alter and drop synonyms that you own.

Views   You already know that a view is an object containing a SQL statement that behaves like a table in Oracle, except that it stores no data. The privileges include `create view`, `create any view`, and `drop any view`. The `create view` privilege also enables you to alter and drop views that you own.

Sequences   You already know that a sequence is an object in Oracle that generates numbers according to rules you can define. Privileges include `create sequence`, `create any sequence`, `alter any sequence`, `drop any sequence`, and `select any sequence`. The `create sequence` privilege also enables you to drop sequences that you own.

Database Links   Database links are objects in Oracle that, within your session connected to one database, enable you to reference tables in another Oracle database without making a separate connection. A public database link is one available to all users in Oracle, whereas a private database link is one that only the owner can use. Privileges include `create database link`, `create public database link`, and `drop public database link`. The `create database link` privilege also enables you to drop private database links that you own.

Roles   Roles are objects that can be used for simplified privilege management. You create a role, grant privileges to it, and then grant the role to users. Privileges include `create role`, `drop any role`, `grant any role`, and `alter any role`.

Transactions   These privileges are for resolving in-doubt, distributed transactions being processed on the Oracle database. Privileges include `force transaction` and `force any transaction`.

PL/SQL   You have already been introduced to the different PL/SQL blocks available in Oracle. These privileges enable you to create, run, and manage those different types of blocks. The privileges include `create procedure`, `create any procedure`, `alter any procedure`, `drop any procedure`, and `execute any procedure`. The `create procedure` privilege also enables you to alter and drop PL/SQL blocks that you own.

Triggers   You know that triggers are PL/SQL blocks in Oracle that execute when a specified DML activity occurs on the table to which the trigger is associated. Privileges include `create trigger`, `create any trigger`, `alter any trigger`, and `drop any trigger`. The `create trigger` privilege also enables you to alter and drop triggers that you own.

Profiles   You know that profiles are objects in Oracle that enable you to impose limits on resources for users in the machine hosting Oracle. Privileges include `create profile`, `alter profile`, `drop profile`, and `alter resource cost`.

Snapshots and Materialized Views   Snapshots are objects in Oracle that enable you to replicate data from a table in one database to a copy of the table in another. Privileges include `create snapshot`, `create any snapshot`, `alter any snapshot`, and `drop any snapshot`.

Directories   Directories in Oracle are objects that refer to directories on the machine hosting the Oracle database. They are used to identify a directory that contains objects Oracle keeps track of that are external to Oracle, such as objects of the BFILE type. Privileges include `create any directory` and `drop any directory`.

Types   Types in Oracle correspond to user-defined types you can create in the Oracle8i Objects Option. Privileges include `create type`, `create any type`, `alter any type`, `drop any type`, and `execute any type`. The `create type` privilege also enables you to alter and drop types that you own.

Libraries   A library is an object that enables you to reference a set of procedures external to Oracle. Currently, only C procedures are supported. Privileges include `create library`, `create any library`, `alter any library`, `drop any library`, and `execute any library`.

The SYSDBA and SYSOPER Privileges

In the beginning of this book, we introduced the system privileges SYSDBA and SYSOPER when discussing authentication using a password file. The SYSDBA privilege is usually assigned to DBA accounts and SYSOPER to database operator accounts. Only users who are assigned these privileges may log into the database using a password file with unrestricted privileges and perform operations on database and database objects. The SYSOPER privilege enables the user assigned this privilege to do the following:

- STARTUP, SHUTDOWN

- ALTER DATABASE OPEN | MOUNT

- ALTER DATABASE BACKUP CONTROLFILE

- RECOVER DATABASE

- ALTER DATABASE ARCHIVELOG

The SYSDBA privilege enables the user assigned this privilege to do the following:

- Receive all SYSOPER privileges

- CREATE DATABASE

- ALTER DATABASE [BEGIN|END] BACKUP
- RESTRICTED SESSION
- RECOVER DATABASE

System Privilege Restrictions

Oracle provides an option to prevent regular database users from accessing the base tables that make up the data dictionary. Users with UPDATE ANY TABLE should be able to update the base tables of the data dictionary and by doing so they could jeopardize the integrity of entire database. To prevent such mishaps, Oracle provides an initialization parameter O7_DICTIONARY_ACCESSIBILITY as a dictionary protection mechanism. If the dictionary protection is enabled by setting O7_DICTIONARY_ACCESSIBILITY to FALSE, then access to objects in SYS schema (containing the data dictionary base tables) is restricted to users who connect as SYSDBA and the SYS user itself. Users with system privileges providing access to ANY SCHEMA will not be allowed access to SYS schema objects. This prevents non-DBA users from accessing the base tables that make up the data dictionary views and from modifying them. By default, this parameter is set to FALSE. By setting this parameter to TRUE, the users whose system privilege enables access to objects in any schema are also given access to SYS schema objects.

Identifying Object Privileges

The other category of privileges granted on the Oracle database is the set of *object privileges*. Object privileges permit the owner of database objects, such as tables, to administer access to those objects according to the following types of access. The eight types of object privileges are as follows:

- **select** Permits the grantee of this object privilege to access the data in a table, sequence, view, or snapshot.

- **insert** Permits the grantee of this object privilege to insert data into a table or, in some cases, a view.

- **update** Permits the grantee of this object privilege to update data into a table or view.

- **delete** Permits the grantee of this object privilege to delete data from a table or view.

- **alter** Permits the grantee of this object privilege to alter the definition of a table or sequence *only*. The alter privileges on all other database objects are considered system privileges.

■   **index**   Permits the grantee of this object privilege to create an index on a table already defined.

■   **references**   Permits the grantee to `create` or `alter` a table in order to create a foreign key constraint against data in the referenced table.

■   **execute**   Permits the grantee to run a stored procedure or function.

TIP
A trick to being able to distinguish whether something is a system or object privilege is as follows. Because there are only eight object privileges, memorize them. If you see a privilege that is not one of the eight object privileges, it is a system privilege.

For Review

1. Be sure you can distinguish system privileges from object privileges in Oracle. The easiest way to do so is to memorize the object privileges, and assume everything else is a system privilege.

2. Know the purpose of the SYSDBA and SYSOPER privileges. These superuser privileges give users the ability to perform administrative tasks on the database.

Exercises

1. **You need to allow users on the Oracle database to create indexes on a table owned by user SCOTT. Which of the following choices identifies the appropriate means for doing so?**

A. Grant the `create table` system privilege to users who need to create those indexes.

B. Grant the `create index` system privilege to users who need to create those indexes.

C. Grant the `references` object privilege on the table to users who need to create those indexes.

D. Grant the `index` object privilege on the table to users who need to create those indexes.

2. **You grant the SYSDBA privilege to a user of the Oracle database. Which of the following abilities does this privilege bestow upon its grantee?**

   A. Ability to query all tables in Oracle

   B. Ability to grant the SYSDBA privilege to others

   C. Ability to back up the database

   D. Ability to delete information from any table in Oracle

Answer Key
1. D. 2. C.

Granting and Revoking Privileges

Giving system and object privileges to users is done with the grant command. System privileges are first given to the SYS and SYSTEM users, and to any other user with the grant any privilege permission. As other users are created, they must be given privileges, based on their needs, with the grant command. For example, executing the following grant statements provides the ability to create a table to user SPANKY and object privileges on another table in the database:

```
GRANT CREATE TABLE TO spanky;                    -- system
GRANT SELECT, UPDATE ON athena.emp TO spanky;    -- object
```

TIP
To grant object privileges to others, you must own the database object, or you must have been given the object privilege with grant option.

In addition to granting object privileges on database objects, privileges can also be granted on columns within the database object. The privileges that can be administered on the column level are the insert, update, and references privileges. However, the grantor of column privileges must be careful when administering them in order to avoid problems—particularly with the insert privilege. If a user has the insert privilege on several columns in a table but not all columns, the privilege administrator must ensure that no columns in the table that do not have the insert privilege granted are not NULL columns.

Consider the following example. Table EMP has two columns: NAME and EMPID. Both columns have not NULL constraints on them. The insert access is granted for the EMPID column to SPANKY, but not the NAME column. When SPANKY attempts to `insert` an EMPID into the table, Oracle generates a NULL for the NAME column, and then produces an error stating that the user cannot `insert` a not NULL value into the NAME column because the column has a not NULL constraint on it. Administration of `update` and `insert` object privileges at the column level must be handled carefully, whereas using the `references` privilege on a column level seems to be more straightforward.

Some special conditions relate to the use of the `execute` privilege. If a user has the ability to execute a stored procedure owned by another user, and the procedure accesses some tables, the object privileges required to access those tables must be granted *to the owner of the procedure,* and not the user to whom `execute` privileges were granted. What's more, the privileges must be granted directly to the user, not through a role. When a user executes a stored procedure, the user is able to use whatever privileges are required to execute the procedure. For example, `execute` privileges are given to SPANKY on procedure `process_deposit( )` owned by ATHENA, and this procedure performs an update on the BANK_ACCOUNT table using an `update` privilege granted to ATHENA. SPANKY will be able to perform that `update` on BANK_ACCOUNT via the `process_deposit( )` procedure even though the `update` privilege is not granted to SPANKY. However, SPANKY will *not* be able to issue an `update` statement on table BANK_ACCOUNT from SQL*Plus, because the appropriate privilege was not granted to SPANKY directly.

Giving Administrative Ability along with Privileges

At the end of execution for the two statements shown at the beginning of the discussion, SPANKY will have the ability to execute the `create table` command in her user schema and to `select` and `update` row data on the EMP table in ATHENA's schema. However, SPANKY can't give these privileges to others, nor can she relinquish them without the help of the DBA. In order to give user SPANKY some additional power to administer to other users the privileges granted to her, the owner of the object can execute the following queries:

```
GRANT CREATE TABLE TO spanky WITH ADMIN OPTION; -- system privileges
GRANT SELECT, UPDATE ON emp TO SPANKY WITH GRANT OPTION; -- object
privileges
```

The `with admin option` clause gives SPANKY the ability to give or take away the system privilege to others. Additionally, it gives SPANKY the ability to make other users administrators of that same privilege. Finally, if a role is granted to SPANKY `with admin option`, SPANKY can alter the role or even remove it. The `with grant option` clause for object privileges gives SPANKY the same kind of ability as `with admin option` for system privileges. SPANKY can `select` and update data from EMP, and can give that ability to others as well. Only privileges given with grant option or with admin option can be administered by the grantee. Additionally, there is a consolidated method for granting object privileges using the keyword all. Note that all in this context is not a privilege; it is merely a specification for all object privileges for the database object.

```
GRANT ALL ON emp TO spanky;
```

Revoking System Privileges from Users

There may also come a time when users must have privileges revoked as well. This task is accomplished with the revoke command. Revoking the create table privilege also takes away any administrative ability given along with the privilege or role. No additional syntax is necessary for revoking either a system privilege granted with admin option or an object privilege granted with grant option.

```
REVOKE CREATE TABLE FROM spanky;
REVOKE SELECT, UPDATE ON emp FROM spanky;
```

In the same way, roles can be revoked from users, even if the user created the role and thus has the admin option. The ability to revoke any role comes from the grant any role privilege, whereas the ability to grant or revoke certain system privileges comes from being granted the privilege with the admin option. When a system privilege is revoked, there are no cascading events that take place along with it. Thus, if SPANKY created several tables while possessing the create table privilege, those tables are not removed when the privilege is revoked. Only the drop table command will remove the tables.

TIP
Understand the following scenario completely before continuing: User X has a system privilege granted to her, with admin option. User X then grants the privilege to user Y, with the administrative privileges. User Y does the same for user Z. Then X revokes the privilege from user Y. User Z will still have the privilege. Why? Because there is no cascading effect to revoking system privileges other than the fact that the user no longer has the privilege.

Revoking Object Privileges from Users

When an object privilege is revoked, there are some cascading events. For example, if you have the update privilege on SPANKY's EMP table and SPANKY revokes it, then you will not be able to change records in the table. However, the rows you've already changed don't get magically transformed back the way they were before. There are several considerations to make when revoking object privileges. For instance, if a privilege has been granted on two individual columns, the privilege cannot be revoked on only one column—the privilege must be revoked entirely and then regranted, if appropriate, on the individual column. Also, if the user has been given the `references` privilege and used it to create a foreign key constraint to another table, then there is some cascading that must take place in order to complete the revocation of the `references` privilege.

```
REVOKE REFERENCES ON emp FROM spanky CASCADE CONSTRAINTS;
```

In this example, not only is the privilege to create referential integrity revoked, but any instances where that referential integrity was used on the database are also revoked. If a foreign key constraint was created on the EMP table by user SPANKY, and the prior statement was issued without the `cascade constraints` clause, then the `revoke` statement will fail.

TIP
Understand this fact sequence before proceeding. User X grants user Y an object privilege, with grant option, *and user Y then grants the same privilege to user Z. When user X revokes the object privilege user Y, user Z will also have that privilege revoked. This is because Oracle cascades the revocation of object privileges.*

Open to the Public
Another aspect of privileges and access to the database involves a special user on the database. This user is called PUBLIC. If a system privilege, object privilege, or role is granted to the PUBLIC user, then every user in the database has that privilege. Typically, it is not advised that the DBA should grant many privileges or roles to PUBLIC, because if the privilege or role ever needs to be revoked, then every stored package, procedure, or function will need to be recompiled.

Dictionary Information on Privileges
To display privileges associated with users and roles, you can use the following views:

- **DBA_SYS_PRIVS**   Shows all system privileges associated with this user.
- **DBA_TAB_PRIVS**   Shows all object privileges associated with this user.
- **SESSION_PRIVS**   Shows all privileges available in this session for this user.

You can find information about system privileges granted to all users in the DBA_SYS_PRIVS view and the privileges available to you as the current user in the session using the SESSION_PRIVS dictionary view. You can also find information about the object privileges granted in the database with the DBA_TAB_PRIVS and DBA_COL_PRIVS dictionary views.

For Review

1. Know how to give system and object privileges to users and how to take them away as well. Also, understand which clauses are required for giving the ability to administrate other users' ability to have a privilege for both system and object privileges.

2. Understand the role of the PUBLIC user in Oracle. When privileges are given to PUBLIC, every user has the privilege.

3. Know where to look in the data dictionary for information about privileges granted to users in Oracle.

Exercises

1. User MARYANN has the `create table` privilege granted to her from IMADBA with the following command: `grant create table to maryann with admin option`. MARYANN then grants the privilege to GILLIGAN. IMADBA finds out and issues the `revoke create table from maryann` command. Which of the following statements is true regarding MARYANN, GILLIGAN, and IMADBA?

    A. IMADBA and GILLIGAN have the privilege, but MARYANN does not.

    B. IMADBA and MARYANN have the privilege, but GILLIGAN does not.

    C. IMADBA has the privilege, but GILLIGAN and MARYANN do not.

    D. IMADBA, GILLIGAN, and MARYANN all have the privilege.

2. User MARYANN has the `select` privilege granted on the EMPLOYEE table to her from IMADBA with the following command: `grant select on EMPLOYEE to maryann with grant option`. MARYANN then grants the privilege to GILLIGAN. IMADBA finds out and issues the `revoke select on EMPLOYEE from maryann` command. Which of the following statements is true regarding MARYANN, GILLIGAN, and IMADBA?

    A. IMADBA and GILLIGAN have the privilege, but MARYANN does not.

    B. IMADBA and MARYANN have the privilege, but GILLIGAN does not.

    C. IMADBA has the privilege, but GILLIGAN and MARYANN do not.

    D. IMADBA, GILLIGAN, and MARYANN all have the privilege.

3. **You would like to know which system privileges have been granted to user GINGER. Which of the following queries would be useful for this purpose?**

    A. `select privilege from dba_tab_privs where grantee = 'GINGER';`

    B. `select privilege from dba_sys_privs where grantee = 'GINGER';`

    C. `select privilege from session_privs where grantee = 'GINGER';`

    D. `select grantor from dba_sys_privs where grantee = 'GINGER';`

Answer Key
1. A. 2. C. 3. B.

Identifying Audit Capabilities

Securing the database against inappropriate activity is only one part of the total security package Oracle offers the DBA or security administrator of an Oracle database. The other major component of the Oracle security architecture is the ability to monitor database activity to uncover suspicious or inappropriate use. Oracle provides this functionality via the use of database auditing. This section will cover differentiating between database and value-based auditing, using database auditing, using the data dictionary to monitor auditing options, and viewing and managing audit results.

 TIP
Auditing your database requires a good deal of additional space allocated to the SYSTEM tablespace for storing the audit data generated.

Several things about your database are always audited. They include privileged operations that DBAs typically perform, such as starting and stopping the instance and logins, as `sysdba` or as `sysoper`. You can find information about these activities in the ALERT log on your database, along with information about log switches, checkpoints, and tablespaces taken offline or put online.

You can also configure systemwide auditing with the AUDIT_TRAIL init*sid*.ora parameter. Valid values for this parameter include DB (TRUE), operating system (FALSE), or NONE. DB indicates that the database architecture will be used to store audit records. You can alternately specify TRUE for AUDIT_TRAIL to accomplish the same result DB gives. Operating system indicates that the audit trail will be stored externally to Oracle, using some component of the operating system. You can alternately specify FALSE for AUDIT_TRAIL to accomplish the same result operating system gives. Finally, NONE indicates that no database auditing will be conducted at all. After changing the value set for this parameter, the instance must be shut down and started again.

Database and Value-Based Auditing

There is a difference between *database auditing* and *value-based auditing*. Database auditing pertains to audits on database object access, user session activity, startup, shutdown, and other database activity. The information about these database events is stored in the audit trail, and the information can then be used to monitor potentially damaging activities, such as rows being removed from tables. The data can also be used by the DBA for statistical analysis of database performance over time. Value-based auditing pertains to audits on actual column/row values that are changed as the result of database activity. The Oracle audit trail does not track value-based audit information, so instead you must develop triggers, tables, PL/SQL code, or client applications that handle this level of auditing in the database.

A good example of value-based auditing in a package delivery application would be to track status changes on existing deliveries from the time the order is received to the time it is delivered. Customers can then call in or access the system via the Web to find out the package delivery status. Each time the package reaches a certain milestone, such as "picked up at local office" or "signed over to recipient," the delivery status is updated and a historical record is made of the old status, the time of status change, and the username of the person making the change. However, as you might imagine, value-based auditing is specific to an application. Thus, the DBA will focus much of his or her time managing database auditing with Oracle's audit features.

TIP
*When AUDIT_TRAIL is set to operating system, your audit trail information will be stored in the directory named by your AUDIT_FILE_DEST init*sid*.ora file, which is set to the rdbms/audit directory under your Oracle software home directory by default. When AUDIT_TRAIL is set to DB, your audit trail information is stored in the AUD$ table owned by SYS.*

Using Database Auditing

A database audit is most effective when the DBA or security administrator knows what he or she is looking for. The best way to conduct a database audit is to start the audit with a general idea about what may be occurring on the database. Once the goals are established, set the audit to monitor those aspects of database use and review the results to either confirm or disprove the hypothesis.

Why must an audit be conducted this way? Database auditing generates lots of information about database access. If the DBA tries to audit everything, the important facts would get mixed into a great deal of unnecessary detail. With a good idea about the general activity that seems suspicious as well as knowledge of the types of statements or related objects on the database that should be looked at, the DBA can save a lot of time sorting through excess detail later.

Using the Audit Command for Privilege or Statement Audits

You do not need to set the AUDIT_TRAIL init.ora parameter in order to use the audit SQL command to set up the auditing options you want to use. You can set auditing features to monitor database activities including starting, stopping, and connecting to the database. Or you can set up audits on statements involving the creation or removal of database objects. Additionally, you can set up audits on direct database use, such as table updates or inserts.

The general syntax for setting up auditing on statements or system privileges is as follows. State the name of the statement (such as update) or system privilege (such as create table) that will be audited. Then state which users will be monitored, either by username, by session, or by access. Finally, state whether or not the audit should record successful or unsuccessful executions of the activity in question. The following code block shows an example of an audit statement:

```
AUDIT CREATE TABLE, ALTER TABLE, DROP TABLE
BY spanky
WHENEVER SUCCESSFUL;
```

The following statement demonstrates how you can record the data-change operations that happen on particular tables:

```
AUDIT UPDATE, DELETE
ON spanky.cat_toys
BY ACCESS
WHENEVER NOT SUCCESSFUL;
```

Consider some other unique features in the audit syntax. The person setting up audits need not name particular users on which to monitor activity. Rather, the activities of this sort can be monitored every time the statement is issued with the by access clause. Additionally, when the not successful option is specified, audit records are generated only when the command executed is unsuccessful. The omission of clauses from the audit syntax causes audit to default to the widest scope permitted by the omission. For example, an audit can be conducted on all inserts on table PRODUCTS, regardless of user and completion status, by omitting the by and whenever clauses:

```
AUDIT INSERT ON products;
```

You can use the default option of the audit command to specify auditing options for objects that have not yet been created. Once you have established these default auditing options, any subsequently created object is automatically audited with those options. The following code block demonstrates use of the default keyword:

```
AUDIT INSERT
ON DEFAULT
WHENEVER SUCCESSFUL;
```

Using the audit Command for Object Audits

Any privilege that can be granted can also be audited. However, because there are more than 100 system and object privileges that can be granted on the Oracle database, the creation of an audit statement can be an excessively long task. As an alternative to naming each and every privilege that goes along with a database object, Oracle enables the administrator to specify the name of an object to audit, and Oracle will audit all privileged operations. Instead of listing all privileged operations related to the type of object that would be audited, the security administrator could name the type of object and achieve the desired result.

```
AUDIT TABLE
BY spanky
WHENEVER SUCCESSFUL;
```

Finally, the person setting up auditing can also specify that audit records are to be compiled by session. This means that audit will record data for audited activities in every session, as opposed to by access. Eliminating the when successful clause tells audit to record every table creation, alteration, or drop activity for every session that connects to the database, regardless of whether or not they were successful.

```
AUDIT TABLE
BY SESSION;
```

Using Audit Definition Shortcuts

There are other options available to consolidate the specification of database activities into one easy command for auditing. These commands are listed in the following:

- **connect**   Audits the user connections to the database. It can be substituted with `session` for the same effect. `connect` audits the login and logout activities of every database user.

- **resource**   Audits detailed information related to the activities typically performed by an application developer or a development DBA, such as creating tables, views, clusters, links, stored procedures, and rollback segments.

- **dba**   Audits activities related to "true" database administration, including the creation of users and roles, and granting system privileges and system audits.

- **all**   Is the equivalent of an on/off switch, where all database activities are monitored and recorded.

TIP
A PL/SQL procedure or SQL statement may reference several different objects or statements being audited. Thus, many audit trail entries can be produced by one single statement.

Disabling Audit Configuration

There are two methods used to disable auditing. The first method is to change the initialization parameter AUDIT_TRAIL to NONE or FALSE. On database shutdown and restart, this option will disable the audit functionality on the Oracle database. Note, however, that because you don't need to set AUDIT_TRAIL in order to use the SQL `audit` command, the other option used for changing the activities that `audit` will record is called `noaudit`. This option can be executed in two ways. The first is used to turn off selective areas that are currently being audited.

```
NOAUDIT INSERT ON application.products;
```

In some cases, however, the person conducting the audit may want to shut off all auditing processes going on and simply start auditing over again. Perhaps the auditor has lost track of which audits were occurring on the database. This statement can be further modified to limit turning off auditing to a particular database object.

```
NOAUDIT ALL;
NOAUDIT ALL PRIVILEGES;
NOAUDIT ALL ON application.products;
```

Finally, Remember to Protect the Audit Information!
Above all else in handling database audits for inappropriate activity is the importance of protecting the evidence. The DBA must ensure that no user can remove records from the audit logs undetected. Therefore, a key step in auditing is to audit the audit trail. This step might include write-protecting the $ORACLE_HOME/rdbms/audit directory using operating system commands (such as chmod in UNIX), and it might also include monitoring the removal of data from the SYS.AUD$ table, as demonstrated in the following code block:

```
AUDIT delete ON sys.aud$;
```

Viewing Enabled Auditing Options
The following views offer information about the enabled audit options configured in the Oracle database:

- **DBA_OBJ_AUDIT_OPTS**   A list of auditing options for views, tables, and other database objects

- **DBA_PRIV_AUDIT_OPTS**   A list of auditing options for all privileges on the database

- **DBA_STMT_AUDIT_OPTS**   A list of auditing options for all statements executed on the database

- **ALL_DEF_AUDIT_OPTS**   A list of all default options for auditing database objects

Retrieving and Maintaining Auditing Information
The following data dictionary views are used to find results from audits currently taking place in the Oracle database. These views are created by the cataudit.sql script found in rdbms/admin off the Oracle software home directory. This script is run automatically at database creation by the catalog.sql script. Some additional audit information is stored in the ALERT log, as explained earlier, and more audit information will be stored in an operating system file if operating system auditing is used:

- **DBA_AUDIT_EXISTS**   A list of audit entries generated by the exists option of the audit command

- **DBA_AUDIT_OBJECT**   A list of audit entries generated for object audits

- **DBA_AUDIT_SESSION**   A list of audit entries generated by session connects and disconnects

- **DBA_AUDIT_STATEMENT**   A list of audit entries generated by statement options of the `audit` command

- **DBA_AUDIT_TRAIL**   A list of all entries in the AUD$ table collected by the `audit` command

Managing Audit Information

Once created, all audit information will stay in the AUD$ table owned by SYS. In cases where several auditing options are used to gather information about database activity, the AUD$ table can grow to be large. In order to preserve the integrity of other tables and views in the data dictionary, and to preserve overall space in the SYSTEM tablespace (where all data dictionary objects are stored), the DBA or security administrator must periodically remove data from the AUD$ table, either by deleting or by archiving and then removing the records. Additionally, in the event that audit records on an Oracle database are being kept to determine whether there is suspicious activity, the security administrator must take additional steps to ensure that the data in the AUD$ table is protected from tampering.

TIP

You may want to move the AUD$ table outside the SYSTEM tablespace because of the volatile and high-growth nature of audit data. To do so, create another table with AUD$ data, using the `alter table move tablespace` *statement. Next, drop AUD$ and rename your other table to AUD$. Next, create one index on the new AUD$ table on the SESSIONID and SES$TID columns in the new tablespace (storing the index outside of the SYSTEM tablespace, of course). Finally, grant* `delete` *on the new AUD$ table to DELETE_CATALOG_ROLE.*

In order to prevent a problem with storing too much audit data, the general guideline in conducting database audits is to record enough information to accomplish the auditing goal without storing a lot of unnecessary information. The amount of information that will be gathered by the auditing process is related to the number of options being audited and the frequency of audit collection (namely, `by username`, `by access`, and `by session`). What if problems occur because too much information is collected? To remove records from AUD$, a user with the `delete any table` privilege, the SYS user, or a user to whom SYS has granted `delete` access to AUD$ must log onto the system and remove records from AUD$. Before doing so, however, it is generally advisable for archiving purposes to make a copy of the records being deleted. This task can be accomplished by copying all records from AUD$ to another table defined with the same columns as AUD$, spooling a `select` statement of all data in AUD$ to a flat file, or using EXPORT to place all AUD$ records into a database dump file. After this step is complete, all or part of the data in the AUD$ table can be removed using either `delete from AUD$` or `truncate table AUD$`. But remember to protect the audit trail using methods already outlined.

For Review

1. Understand the purpose served by auditing in the database and the difference between database auditing and value-based auditing.

2. Know that the auditing feature in Oracle is enabled using the `audit` command.

3. Know that all audit records are stored in the SYS.AUD$ dictionary base table in Oracle, and that there are many dictionary views that give you information from this table.

4. Auditing generates a lot of information being stored in the SYSTEM tablespace. If you plan to use this feature, it's best that you know what you're looking for first, rather than set up auditing haphazardly and have a lot of extraneous audit information fill your SYSTEM tablespace.

Exercises

1. **Auditing on the database is configured using this command:**
   _____.

2. **When auditing is enabled, records are placed in the _____(A)_____ table owned by user _____(B)_____. This table can be found in the _____(C)_____ tablespace.**

3. **To set up auditing in Oracle, the _____(A)_____ initialization parameter must be set to _____(B)_____.**

Answer Key
1. `audit`. 2. (A) AUD$; (B) SYS; (C) SYSTEM. 3. (A) AUDIT_TRAIL; (B) TRUE.

Managing Roles

In this section, you will cover the following points on managing roles:

- Creating and modifying roles
- Controlling the availability of roles
- Removing roles
- Using predefined roles
- Displaying role information from the data dictionary

Roles take some of the complexity out of administrating user privileges. A role in the database can be thought of as a virtual user. The database object and system privileges that are required to perform a group of user functions are gathered together and granted to the role, which then can be granted directly to the users. In this section, you will learn how to create and change roles, control their availability, remove roles, use roles that are predefined in Oracle, and display information about roles from the data dictionary.

Creating and Modifying Roles

As users add more objects to the database, privilege management can become a nightmare. This is where roles come in. Roles are named logical groupings of privileges that can be administered more easily than the individual privileges. Roles are created on databases in the following manner. The DBA determines which types of users exist on the database and which privileges on the database can be logically grouped together.

Creating Roles

In order to create a role that will support user privilege management, one of the following statements can be executed. Once the role is created, there are no privileges assigned to it until you explicitly grant privileges to the role. The following statement can be used to create a role in Oracle:

```
CREATE ROLE cat_priv;
```

This statement creates a role named `cat_priv`. The following code block shows a variant of the `create role` command, where we explicitly state that this role does not require a password in order to be enabled for the user. This is the default behavior for roles in Oracle.

```
CREATE ROLE cat_priv NOT IDENTIFIED;
```

The following statement shows a role created in your database called `cat_priv`. This time, we set up the role to require the user to supply a password whenever the role is to be enabled for use. This role must be enabled by the user before the privileges associated with the role can be utilized. Let's take a look at the statement now:

```
CREATE ROLE cat_priv IDENTIFIED BY meow;
```

Granting Roles

Once created, roles must have privileges granted to them. Privileges are granted to roles in the following manner. At the same time that the DBA determines the resource use of various classes of users on the database, the DBA may also want to determine which object and system privileges each class of user will require. Instead of granting the privileges directly to users on an individual basis, however, the DBA can grant the privileges to the roles, which then can be granted to several users more easily.

```
GRANT SELECT, INSERT, UPDATE ON cat_food TO cat_privs;
GRANT SELECT, INSERT, UPDATE ON litter_box TO cat_privs;
GRANT SELECT ON fav_sleeping_spots TO cat_privs;
```

Roles enable dynamic privilege management as well. If several users already have a role granted to them, and you create a new table and grant `select` privileges on it to the role, then all the users who have the role will be able to `select` data from your table. Once granted, the ability to use the privileges granted via the role is immediate. Roles can be granted to other roles as well. However, you should take care not to grant a role to itself (even via another role) or else Oracle will return an error.

Granting Roles to Users

Once you've created a role and granted some privileges to it, you must then grant the role to a user. This allows the user to have access to the privileges the role is meant to manage. You give the role to a user with the `grant` command and take it away with the `revoke` command. The following code block shows how to `grant` a role to a user:

```
GRANT cat_privs TO spanky;
```

Passwords and Roles

Using a password to authenticate users of a role is optional. If used, however, the password provides an extra level of security over the authentication process at database login. For heightened security when using roles with passwords, set the role authenticated by a password to be a nondefault role for that user. That way, if the user tries to execute a privilege granted via the role, he or she will first have to supply the role's password. Like users, roles have no owner, nor are they part of a schema. The name of a role must be unique among all roles and users of a database.

Altering Roles

Later on, you may want to change a role using the `alter role` command. All items that are definable in `create role` are also definable using `alter role`, as shown in the following code block:

```
ALTER ROLE role_name NOT IDENTIFIED;
ALTER ROLE role_name IDENTIFIED BY role_password;
```

Administrative Ability and Roles

By default, only the user who creates the role has administrative privileges over that role, including the ability to grant that role to other users. Other users can, of course, grant privileges to the role—so long as they are permitted to grant those privileges. However, like privileges, roles can be granted with an administrative ability to users. This is accomplished using the `grant rolename to username with admin option`, the same option as that used for granting administrative abilities with system privileges.

For Review

1. Understand what a role is conceptually. To use roles, you must first create a role and then grant privileges to it. Then you can consolidate the granting of those privileges to the users by simply granting the role to that user.

2. Roles can be created to enforce password authentication. When password authentication is used, the user must supply the password in order to use privileges associated with the password-authenticated role. Passwords on roles are optional in Oracle.

3. By default, the owner of the role has the ability to grant that role to others. However, roles can be granted to users along with the administrative ability over that role using the `grant rolename to username with admin option` command.

Exercises

1. **You create a role in Oracle called DEVELOPER and then grant it to user SKIP. SKIP then logs into the Oracle database. You then grant the `create table` privilege to your DEVELOPER role. Which of the following statements best describes SKIP's ability to create tables in Oracle?**

   A. SKIP can create tables the next time he logs into Oracle.

   B. SKIP can create tables immediately after you grant that privilege to the role.

   C. SKIP must own the role in order to create tables with it.

   D. SKIP cannot create tables in Oracle without having the role given to him as a default role.

2. **You want to use roles in Oracle to manage privileges. Which of the following choices correctly describes the sequence of events required in order for users to employ roles successfully in using privileges?**

   A. Create the role, grant privileges to the role, grant the role to users, and users enable the role.

   B. Create the role, users enable the role, grant privileges to the role, and grant the role to users.

   C. Grant privileges to the role, create the role, grant the role to users, and users enable the role.

   D. Users enable the role, create the role, grant the role to users, and grant privileges to the role.

Answer Key
1. B. 2. A.

Controlling Availability of Roles

A user may have several roles granted when he or she logs on. By default, all the roles assigned to a user are enabled at logon without the need of a password. Some, all, or none of these roles can be set as a default role, which means that the privileges given via the role will be available automatically when the user logs on to Oracle. There is no limit to the number of roles that can be granted to a user;

however, if there are privileges granted to a user through a nondefault role, the user may have to switch default roles in order to use those privileges.

All roles granted to a user are default roles initially. You can change which roles are default roles after granting the role to the user with the `alter user` statement. The `alter user default role all` statement sets all roles granted to SPANKY to be the default role. Other options available for specifying user roles include physically listing one or more roles that are to be the default, or specifying all roles except for the ones named using `all except (role_name [,...])` or none.

 `ALTER USER spanky DEFAULT ROLE ALL;`

The previous statement sets all roles granted to user SPANKY as default roles. The following statement sets the ORG_USER and ORG_DEVELOPER roles as default roles for user SPANKY:

`ALTER USER spanky DEFAULT ROLE org_user, org_developer;`

In the previous statement, the roles ORG_USER and ORG_DEVELOPER are assigned as the default roles, and the rest of the granted roles are not default roles for the user SPANKY. The following statement makes the ORG_MGR role the only nondefault role SPANKY has:

`ALTER USER spanky DEFAULT ROLE ALL EXCEPT (org_mgr);`

The following statement makes it so that SPANKY has no default role set up at login. The only privileges that the user SPANKY has at login will be those privileges assigned directly to the user.

`ALTER USER spanky DEFAULT ROLE NONE;`

TIP
Note that `default role` *is only an option used for the* `alter user` *statement. You do not define a default role in* `create user` *because no roles have been granted to the user yet. Keep in mind the default roles are subsets of roles granted to the user that are enabled automatically when the user logs into Oracle.*

Enabling or Disabling Roles

When a user logs in, the user's default roles are automatically activated. However, it is possible to enable and disable roles that are not default roles using the `set role` command. Those roles enabled or disabled using the `set role` command will apply as long as the user session is active. Once the user exits from the session and logs back into Oracle, only the default roles will again be active. The following code block shows an example of the `set role` command:

```
SET ROLE cat_privs;
```

Note that, if the `cat_privs` role requires a password, you must supply the password when you enable the role using the `set role` command. The following code block shows this syntax:

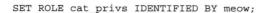

```
SET ROLE cat_privs IDENTIFIED BY meow;
```

TIP
You can also enable many roles at once (so long as none of the roles requires a password) using the `set role all` *command. You can also exclude certain roles from being enabled using the* `set role all except role_name` *command. Additionally, you can disable all roles granted to you using the* `set role none` *command.*

The DBMS_SESSION package contains a procedure called `set_role( )`, which is equivalent to the `set role` statement. It can enable or disable roles for a user and can be issued from Oracle forms, reports, anonymous blocks, or any other tool that enables PL/SQL, except for stored PL/SQL functions, procedures, and packages. Finally, note that enabling or disabling a role using the `set role` command does not change whether or not the role is a default role for this user. Only the `alter user default role` command issued by the DBA can change whether the role is a default role for the user.

For Review

1. Roles granted to users are considered default roles unless you specify otherwise. You make or do not make a role a default role using the `alter user username default role rolename` command.

2. When a user logs into Oracle, he or she will be able to use all privileges assigned to him or her directly and via default roles.

3. Assigning a role as a nondefault role to a user adds a level of security, especially when the nondefault role has a password. In this case, users must employ the `set role rolename identified by password` command in order to enable use of the role.

4. Setting a role in the way shown previously does not make the role a default role—it merely enables the role for the current session. The user will have to use the set role command in order to enable those role-given privileges again.

Exercises

1. The following output shows a listing of roles granted to user KENNY:

```
GRANTEE   GRANTED_ROLE     ADM DEF
--------  ---------------  --- ---
KENNY     APP_DEVELOPER    NO  NO
KENNY     POWER_USER       NO  YES
```

The create table privilege is granted to KENNY via the APP_DEVELOPER role. Which of the following statements best describes what happens when KENNY attempts to issue the create table mytab (col1 number primary key) tablespace data1 command?

A. Oracle will return an error indicating KENNY's quota on tablespace DATA1 was exceeded.

B. Oracle will return an error indicating that KENNY lacks sufficient privileges to perform this task.

C. Oracle will return an error indicating that he needs to enable the POWER_USER role.

D. Oracle performs the task successfully.

2. Review the following transcript from a SQL*Plus session:

```
SQL> connect scott/tiger
Connected.
SQL> create user smithers identified by mort1;
User created.
SQL> create role user_role identified by useme;
Role created.
SQL> grant all on scott.emp to user_role;
Grant succeeded.
SQL> grant user_role to smithers;
Grant succeeded.
SQL> grant create session to smithers;
Grant succeeded.
SQL> alter user smithers default role none;
User altered.
SQL> connect smithers/mort1
Connected.
SQL> select * from scott.emp;
```

Which of the following choices describes the command that SMITHERS will need to issue in order to see the contents of the EMP table as requested in the session transcript?

A. None—the `select` statement will execute successfully.

B. `connect smithers/useme`

C. `set role user_role identified by useme;`

D. `alter user smithers default role user_role;`

Answer Key
1. B. 2. C.

Removing Roles

Another way to restrict role use is to revoke the role from the user. This is accomplished with the `revoke` command in the same way that a privilege is revoked. The effect is immediate—the user will no longer be able to use privileges associated with the role. You can drop a role to restrict its use as well. You don't need to revoke the role from users before dropping it—Oracle handles that task for you. However, you must have the `drop any role` privilege or have been granted the role `with admin option` in order to drop it.

```
REVOKE cat_privs FROM spanky;
DROP ROLE cat_privs;
```

TIP
In order to drop a role, you must have been granted the role `with admin option` *or have a* DROP ANY ROLE *system privilege.*

For Review

1. Know that the `revoke` command is used for taking roles away from other users, and that the `drop role` command is used for removing roles from the database.

2. Roles needn't be revoked from all grantees before they are dropped, so long as you have permission to drop the role.

Exercises

1. You remove a role from the database using the _____(A)_____ command (two words). You (need to/need not) revoke the role from grantees before dropping the role from the database.

2. A role can be removed from the database either by the user who _____(A)_____ the role or by a user with the _____(B)_____ privilege (three words).

Answer Key

1. (A) `drop role`; need not. **2.** (A) created (owns also acceptable); (B) `drop any role`.

Using Predefined Roles

There are some special roles available to the users of a database. The roles available at database creation from Oracle7 onward include the CONNECT, RESOURCE, DBA, EXP_FULL_DATABASE, and IMP_FULL_DATABASE roles. Additionally, Oracle8i adds the DELETE_CATALOG_ROLE, EXECUTE_CATALOG_ROLE, and SELECT_CATALOG_ROLE roles to the mix and much more. The use of each role is described in the following list:

- **CONNECT**   Enables the user extensive development abilities within his or her own user schema, including the ability to use `create table`, `create cluster, create session, create view, create sequence`, and more. The privileges associated with this role are platform-specific, and therefore the role can contain a different number of privileges, but typically the role never enables the creation of stored procedures.

- **RESOURCE**   Enables the user moderate development abilities within his or her own user schema, such as the ability to execute `create table`, `create cluster, create trigger`, and `create procedure`. The privileges associated with this role are platform-specific, and therefore the role can contain a different number of privileges.

- **DBA**   Enables the user to administer and use all system privileges.

- **EXP_FULL_DATABASE**   Enables the user to export every object in the database using the EXPORT utility.

- **IMP_FULL_DATABASE**   Enables the user to import every object from an export dump file using the IMPORT utility.

- **DELETE_CATALOG_ROLE** Extends delete privileges on SYS-owned dictionary tables in response to the new restriction on delete any table privileges that prevent grantees from removing rows from SYS-owned dictionary tables.

- **EXECUTE_CATALOG_ROLE** Enables the user to receive execute privileges on any SYS-owned package supplied with the Oracle software.

- **SELECT_CATALOG_ROLE** Enables the user to select data from any SYS-owned dictionary table or view.

Using Other Predefined Roles

Other optional, predefined roles are available in Oracle and are usually defined by the DBA using SQL scripts provided with the database. For example, AQ_ADMINISTRATOR_ROLE and AQ_USER_ROLE are created by the dbmsaqad.sql script. These roles are used with the advanced queuing feature in the Oracle database. Other roles you might find on your database include PLUSTRACE, which is created by running the plustrce.sql script for setup of the autotrace feature in SQL*Plus.

For Review

1. Understand the predefined roles in Oracle. CONNECT, RESOURCE, and DBA are very popular for giving users the ability to get started quickly. However, you should be careful when using these roles because they may give far more privileges to users than you care to offer them.

2. Know the purpose behind the catalog roles. These roles give users the ability to see data in the data dictionary. You don't always need to grant these roles to end users in order for the user to see certain dictionary views, but in the event a user cannot see an object in the data dictionary, the catalog roles will give the user that ability.

Exercises

1. The _____ role is useful for database administrators because it grants all the administrative privileges one needs to act as the database administrator.

2. The _____ role enables users to export the contents of an Oracle database.

3. The _____ role enables users to query the data dictionary.

Answer Key
1. DBA. 2. EXP_FULL_DATABASE. 3. SELECT_CATALOG_ROLE.

Displaying Role Information from the Data Dictionary

You can find information about the roles created in your Oracle database in the data dictionary. The following bullets list the various views available for finding information about your created roles:

- **DBA_ROLES**   Names all the roles created on the database and whether a password is required to use each role.

- **DBA_ROLE_PRIVS**   Names all users and the roles granted to them in the database.

- **ROLE_ROLE_PRIVS**   Identifies all the roles and the roles that are granted to them in the database.

- **DBA_SYS_PRIVS**   Identifies all the role and user grantees and the granted system privileges to those roles and users.

- **ROLE_SYS_PRIVS**   Identifies all the system privileges granted only to roles in Oracle.

- **ROLE_TAB_PRIVS**   Identifies all the object privileges granted only to roles in Oracle.

- **SESSION_ROLES**   Identifies all the roles available in the current session of Oracle.

Fine-Grained Access Control

Fine-grained access control enables you to implement security policies with functions and then associate those security policies with tables or views. The database server automatically enforces those security policies. You can use different policies for select, insert, update, and delete. You can also use security policies only where you need them (for example, on salary information). Finally, you can use more than one policy for each table, including building on top of base policies in packaged applications.

The function or package that implements the security policy you create returns a predicate (a where condition). This predicate controls access as set out by the policy. Rewritten queries are fully optimized and sharable. The PL/SQL package

DBMS_RLS enables you to administer your security policies. Using this package, you can add, drop, enable, disable, and refresh the policies you create.

For Review

1. The DBA_ROLES view shows you all the roles in your Oracle database. ROLE_TAB_PRIVS and ROLE_SYS_PRIVS show all object and system privileges granted to roles in Oracle.

2. DBA_ROLE_PRIVS shows roles granted to users in Oracle, whereas ROLE_ROLE_PRIVS shows you the roles granted to other roles in Oracle.

3. The SESSION_ROLES view shows all current roles active in a user's session.

Exercises

1. To determine which roles are active in your session, you can look in the _____ dictionary view.

2. To determine which system privileges have been granted to a role, use the _____(A)_____ view. To determine which object privileges have been granted to a role, use the _____(B)_____ view.

3. To determine the roles available in the database, use the _____ view.

Answer Key
1. SESSION_ROLES. 2. (A) DBA_SYS_PRIVS; (B) DBA_TAB_PRIVS. 3. DBA_ROLES.

Chapter Summary

This chapter covered the fundamentals you need to understand about users, profiles, privileges, and roles for the OCP Oracle9*i* DBA Fundamentals I exam. We discussed the creation of users and the management of created users in Oracle. You learned how to create users, maintain them, and where to look for more information. You also learned about profiles, Oracle's tool for the management of underlying host system resources accessed via Oracle by end users. We discussed how to create profiles and assign users to them. The special topic of composite resources was defined and discussed as well.

We also covered system and object privileges in Oracle. You learned that every action available on the Oracle database is governed by a privilege. You learned what system privileges were and how they differ from object privileges. You also learned how to grant and revoke privileges, with or without administrative ability. We discussed the audit capabilities available in Oracle for detecting misuse of the database as well.

Finally, we covered the particular importance that roles play in Oracle. You learned that roles act as a clearinghouse for granting privileges more efficiently, especially when there are many database objects and many users of an Oracle system. You learned how to create roles, grant privileges to roles, and how to grant roles to users. You learned the difference between a default role and a nondefault role, and how to use the `alter user default role` command to set up a user's default roles. You learned that the privileges given to users via nondefault roles are not available until users issue the `set role` command, which adds an extra layer of protection and security, especially when password-authenticated roles are used. We covered how to drop roles, use predefined roles, and where to find information about roles in the data dictionary as well. All in all, this chapter covered 16 percent of the materials tested on the OCP Oracle9i DBA Fundamentals I exam.

Two-Minute Drill

- New database users are created with the `create user` statement.

- A new user can have the following items configured by the `create user` statement:

  - Password

  - Default tablespace for database objects

  - Temporary tablespace

  - Quotas on tablespaces

  - User profile

  - Account lock status

  - Whether the user must specify a new password on first logging on

- User definitions can be altered with the `alter user` statement and dropped with the `drop user` statement. Users can issue the `alter user` statement only to change their password and default roles.

- Information about a database user can be found in the following data dictionary views:

  - DBA_USERS

  - DBA_PROFILES

- DBA_TS_QUOTAS
- DBA_OBJECTS
- DBA_ROLE_PRIVS
- DBA_TAB_PRIVS
- DBA_SYS_PRIVS

- Users in operating system-authenticated database environments generally have their usernames preceded by OPS$ at user-creation time.

- User profiles help to limit resource usage on the Oracle database.

- The DBA must set the RESOURCE_LIMIT parameter to TRUE in order to use user profiles.

- The resources that can be limited via profiles include the following:

  - Sessions connected per user at one time
  - CPU time per call
  - CPU time per session
  - Disk I/O per call
  - Disk I/O per session
  - Connection time
  - Idle time
  - Private memory (only for MTS)
  - Composite limit

- Profiles should be created for every type or class of user. Each parameter has a resource limit set for it in a user profile, which can then be assigned to users based on their processing needs.

- Oracle installs a special profile granted to a user if no other profile is defined. This special profile is called DEFAULT, and all values in the profile are set to `unlimited`.

- Any parameter not explicitly set in another user profile defaults in value to the value specified for that parameter in DEFAULT.

- New Oracle8i features in password administration are also available:

  - `failed_login_attempts` The number of unsuccessful attempts at login a user can make before the account locks. The default is three.

- **password_life_time** The number of days a password will remain active. The default is 60.

- **password_reuse_time** The number of days before the password can be reused. The default is 1,800 (approximately five years).

- **password_reuse_max** The number of times the password must be changed before one can be reused. The default is `unlimited`.

- **password_lock_time** The number of days after which Oracle will unlock a user account locked automatically when the user exceeds `failed_login_attempts`. The default is 1/1,440 (one minute).

- **password_grace_time** The number of days during which an expired password must be changed by the user or else Oracle permanently locks the account. The default is 10.

- **password_verify_function** The function used for password complexity verification. The default function is called `verify_function( )`.

- Database privileges govern access for performing every permitted activity in the Oracle database.

- There are two categories of database privileges: system privileges and object privileges.

- System privileges enable the creation of every object on the database, along with the ability to execute many commands and connect to the database.

- Object privileges enable access to data within database objects.

- There are three basic classes of system privileges for some database objects: `create`, `alter`, and `drop`. These privileges give the grantee the power to create database objects in their own user schema.

- Some exceptions exist to the preceding rule. The `alter table` privilege is an object privilege, while the `alter rollback segment` privilege is a system privilege. The `create index` privilege is an object privilege as well.

- Three oddball privileges are `grant`, `audit`, and `analyze`. These privileges apply to the creation of all database objects and to running powerful commands in Oracle.

- The `any` modifier gives the user extra power to create objects or run commands on any object in the user schema.

■ The final system privilege of interest is the `restricted session` privilege, which enables the user to connect to a database in `restricted session` mode.

■ Object privileges give the user access to place, remove, change, or view data in a table or one column in a table, as well as to alter the definition of a table, create an index on a table, and develop foreign key constraints.

■ When system privileges are revoked, the objects a user has created will still exist.

■ A system privilege can be granted using `with admin option` to enable the grantee to administer others' ability to use the privilege.

■ When object privileges are revoked, the data placed or modified in a table will still exist, but you will not be able to perform the action allowed by the privilege anymore.

■ An object privilege can be granted using `with grant option` to another user in order to make him or her an administrator of the privilege.

■ The `grant option` cannot be used when granting a privilege to a role.

■ Roles are used to bundle privileges together and to enable or disable them automatically.

■ A user can create objects and then grant the nongrantable object privileges to the role, which then can be granted to as many users require it.

■ There are roles created by Oracle when the software is installed:

   ■ **CONNECT** Can connect to the database and create clusters, links, sequences, tables, views, and synonyms. This role is good for table schema owners and development DBAs.

   ■ **RESOURCE** Can connect to the database and create clusters, sequences, tables, triggers, and stored procedures. This role is good for application developers. It also has unlimited tablespace.

   ■ **DBA** Can use any system privilege using `with admin option`.

   ■ **EXP_FULL_DATABASE** Can export all database objects to an export dump file.

   ■ **IMP_FULL_DATABASE** Can import all database objects from an export dump file to the database.

   ■ **DELETE_CATALOG_ROLE** Extends `delete` privileges on SYS-owned dictionary tables in response to the new restriction on `delete any` `table` privileges that prevent grantees from removing rows from SYS-owned dictionary tables.

■ **EXECUTE_CATALOG_ROLE**   Enables the grantee to have `execute` privileges on any SYS-owned package supplied with the Oracle software.

■ **SELECT_CATALOG_ROLE**   Enables the grantee to `select` data from any SYS-owned dictionary table or view.

■ Roles can have passwords assigned to them to provide security for the use of certain privileges.

■ Users can alter their own roles in a database session. Each role requires 4 bytes of space in the Program Global Area (PGA) in order to be used. The amount of space each user requires in the PGA can be limited with the MAX_ENABLED_ROLES initialization parameter.

■ When a privilege is granted to the user PUBLIC, every user in the database can use the privilege. However, when a privilege is revoked from PUBLIC, every stored procedure, function, or package in the database must be recompiled.

■ Auditing the database can be done either to detect inappropriate activity or to store an archive of database activity.

■ Auditing can collect large amounts of information. In order to minimize the amount of searching, the person conducting the audit should limit the auditing of database activities to where he or she thinks a problem lies.

■ Any activity on the database can be audited either by naming the privilege or by naming an object in the database.

■ The activities of one or more users can be singled out for audit, or every access to an object or privilege, or every session on the database, can have their activities audited.

■ Audits can monitor successful activities surrounding a privilege, unsuccessful activities, or both.

■ In every database audit, starting and stopping the instance, as well as every connection established by a user with DBA privileges as granted by `SYSDBA` and `SYSOPER`, are monitored regardless of any other activities being audited.

■ Audit data is stored in the data dictionary in the AUD$ table, which is owned by SYS.

- Several dictionary views exist for seeing data in the AUD$ table. The main ones are as follows:
  - DBA_AUDIT_EXISTS
  - DBA_AUDIT_OBJECT
  - DBA_AUDIT_SESSION
  - DBA_AUDIT_STATEMENT
  - DBA_AUDIT_TRAIL

- If auditing is in place and monitoring session connections, and if the AUD$ table fills, no more users can connect to the database until the AUD$ table is (archived and) emptied.

- The AUD$ table should be audited, whenever in use, to detect any tampering of its data.

Fill-in-the-Blank Questions

1. The name of the table in Oracle where audit data is stored:

    _____.

2. The name of the Oracle-defined role that lets you execute all Oracle-supplied packages: _____.

3. The Oracle database object that facilitates use of advanced Oracle password management features: _____.

4. Use of this object privilege enables you to define a foreign-key relationship:

    _____.

5. The name of the profile created for you by Oracle when you first create a database: _____.

Chapter Questions

1. **The DBA is considering restricting her users' use of the host machine via the Oracle database. If the DBA wants to use resource costs to limit resource usage, the first thing she must do is which of the following?**

    A. Change the value of RESOURCE_LIMIT to TRUE.

    B. Change the value of `composite_limit` in the user profile to 0.

    C. Change the value of `composite_limit` in the DEFAULT profile to 0.

    D. Change the value of the resource costs for the resources to be limited.

2. **The owner of a database table is eliminating some foreign key dependencies from the Oracle database prior to the removal of some tables. When revoking the `references` privilege, the DBA must use which option to ensure success?**

    A. `with admin option`

    B. `with grant option`

    C. `cascade constraints`

    D. `trailing nullcols`

3. **The DBA is using operating system authentication for his Oracle database. He is creating a user for that database. Which line of the following statement will produce an error?**

   A. `create user OPS$ELLISON`

   B. `identified externally`

   C. `default tablespace USERS_01`

   D. `default role CONNECT;`

   E. There are no errors in this statement.

4. **The DBA is about to enable auditing on the Oracle database in an attempt to discover some suspicious database activity. Audit trail information is stored in which of the following database object names?**

   A. SYS.SOURCE$

   B. SYS.AUD$

   C. DBA_SOURCE

   D. DBA_AUDIT_TRAIL

5. **The creator of a role is granted which of the following privileges with respect to the role she has just created?**

   A. `grant any privilege`

   B. `create any role`

   C. `with admin option`

   D. `with grant option`

   E. `sysdba`

6. **In order to find out how many database objects a user has created, which view would the DBA query in the Oracle data dictionary?**

   A. DBA_USERS

   B. DBA_OBJECTS

   C. DBA_TS_QUOTAS

   D. DBA_TAB_PRIVS

7. **The DBA is considering which settings to use for profiles in the Oracle database. Upon database creation, the value of the CONNECT_TIME parameter in the DEFAULT profile is set to which of the following choices?**

   A. 1

   B. 10

   C. 300

   D. `unlimited`

   E. None—the DEFAULT profile hasn't been created yet.

8. **A user cannot change aspects of his or her account configuration with the exception of one item. Which of the following choices identifies an area of the user's account that the user can change himself or herself using an `alter user` statement?**

   A. `identified by`

   B. `default tablespace`

   C. `temporary tablespace`

   D. `quota on`

   E. `profile`

   F. `default role`

9. **The DBA is considering implementing controls to limit the amount of host machine resources a user can exploit while connected to the Oracle database. Which of the following choices accurately describes a resource cost?**

   A. A monetary cost for using a database resource

   B. A monetary cost for using a privilege

   C. An integer value representing the importance of the resource

   D. An integer value representing the dollar cost for using the resource

10. **The DBA gets a production emergency support call from a user trying to connect to Oracle, saying that the database won't let her connect and that the audit log is full. Which of the following choices accurately describes what is happening on the Oracle database?**

A. The database is up and running.

B. The AUD$ table has been filled and `session` is being audited.

C. Restricted session has been disabled.

D. Operating system authentication is being used.

11. **The DBA needs to keep track of when the database is started due to a reported problem with Oracle being available after the host machine reboots. When auditing instance startup, the audit records are placed in which of the following locations?**

A. SYS.AUD$

B. DBA_AUDIT_TRAIL

C. ARCHIVE_DUMP_DEST

D. AUDIT_FILE_DEST

12. **In determining resource costs for defining user profiles, the DBA will assign a resource a high-resource cost to indicate which of the following?**

A. A less expensive resource

B. A lower amount of resource used per minute

C. A more expensive resource

D. A higher amount of resource used per minute

Fill-in-the-Blank Answers

1. SYS.AUD$

2. EXECUTE_CATALOG_ROLE

3. Profiles

4. References

5. DEFAULT

Answers to Chapter Questions

1. A.   Change the value of RESOURCE_LIMIT to TRUE.

Explanation   In order for any value set for a resource cost to be effective, and in order to use any user profile, the RESOURCE_LIMIT initialization parameter must be set to TRUE. Refer to the discussion of user profiles.

2. C.   cascade constraints

Explanation   If a foreign key constraint is defined as the result of a references privilege being granted, then in order to revoke the references privilege, the cascade constraints option must be used. Choices A and B are incorrect because admin option and grant option relate to the granting of system and object privileges, respectively, while this question is asking about the revocation of an object privilege. Choice D is incorrect because trailing nullcols refers to an option in the SQL*Loader control file covered in the next chapter. Refer to the discussion of administering object privileges.

3. D.   default role CONNECT

Explanation   Although a user profile can be specified as part of a user-creation statement, the individual options specified in a user profile cannot be. Therefore, the user-creation statement will error out on line D. This is because no privileges or roles have been granted to the user yet. After creating the user and granting some privileges and/or roles to him or her, you can issue the alter user default role statement. Refer to the section on user creation.

4. B.   SYS.AUD$

Explanation   AUD$ holds all audit trail records. It is owned by user SYS. Choice A is incorrect because SOURCE$ contains source code for all stored procedures, functions, and packages. Choices C and D are dictionary views that provide access to the underlying data dictionary tables named in choices A and B. Although they enable viewing of the data, the views themselves store nothing because they are views. Refer to the discussion of auditing.

5. D. `with grant option`

Explanation   Choice D is the correct answer because it is the appropriate administrative clause offered to the creator of a role in Oracle. The creator of a role can do anything he or she wants to with the role, including remove it. Choice C is incorrect because `with admin option` refers to the administrative clause for system privileges. Choices A, B, and E are incorrect because no privileges are given to a role on creation. Refer to the discussion of roles and the `with grant option`.

6. B.   DBA_OBJECTS

Explanation   The DBA_OBJECTS view lists all objects that are in the Oracle database as well as the owners of those objects. Choice A is incorrect because DBA_USERS contains the actual user-creation information, such as the encrypted password, default and temp tablespace, user profile, and default role. Choice C is incorrect because DBA_TS_QUOTAS identifies all the tablespace quotas that have been named for the user. Choice D is incorrect because DBA_TAB_PRIVS names all the table object privileges that have been granted and to whom they have been given. Refer to the discussion of monitoring information about existing users.

7. D.   `unlimited`

Explanation   All resource limits in the DEFAULT user profile created when Oracle is installed are set to `unlimited`. You can change them later using the `alter profile` command. Refer to the discussion of the DEFAULT profile in the managing resource-usage discussion.

8. A.   `identified by`

Explanation   There is only one user-creation option that the created user can modify. All others are managed either by a security administrator or the DBA. Although users can change the current role from the roles currently granted to them using the `set role` statement, they cannot issue the `alter user` statement to get the same result. Refer to the discussion of user creation.

9. C.   An integer value representing the importance of the resource

Explanation   The resource cost is an integer that measures the relative importance of a resource to the DBA. Its value is completely arbitrary and has nothing to do with money. Therefore, choices A, B, and D are all incorrect. Refer to the discussion of assessing resource costs in the section on user profiles.

10. B. The AUD$ table has been filled and `session` is being audited.

Explanation If user connections are being audited and the AUD$ table fills, no user can connect until the AUD$ table is cleared. Choice A is incorrect because the database is open for everyone's use when it is up and running. By the same token, choice C is incorrect as well, because when a restricted session is disabled, the database is open for general access. Choice D is incorrect because operating system authentication is simply another means of verifying user passwords; it doesn't cut users off from accessing the database. Refer to the discussion of managing the audit trail.

11. D. AUDIT_FILE_DEST

Explanation This is a difficult question. For instance, upon startup, `audit` places the information collected in this action into a special file that is placed where background process trace files are written. The location where background processes place their trace files is identified at instance startup with the AUDIT_FILE_DEST initialization parameter. Because the database has not started yet, the AUD$ table cannot be the location to which instance startup information is written, eliminating choice A. Because DBA_AUDIT_TRAIL is a view on AUD$, choice B is wrong, too. Choice C is the location where archive logs are written, which is closer to the spirit of the answer, but still not correct. Refer to the discussion of auditing system-level database activity.

12. C. A more expensive resource

Explanation The higher the value set for resource cost, the more valued the resource is to the database system, increasing its relative "expense." Choice A is incorrect because the exact opposite is true. Choices B and D are incorrect because, although the DBA can track resource use on a per-minute basis, there is no value added by doing so—nor does doing so indicate the relative expense of using the resource.

PART
IV

OCA Oracle9i
DBA Fundamentals I
Practice Exams

CHAPTER
16

OCA Database Administration Fundamentals I

he OCP Oracle9*i* DBA Fundamentals I exam in the Oracle DBA track covers concepts and practices regarding routine Oracle database administration. To pass this exam, you need to demonstrate an understanding of the features available in Oracle for administering your database objects and the overall database itself. In more recent editions of this exam, the focus has included understanding the use of automatic undo management, Oracle-Managed Files (OMF), and other new Oracle9*i* features. In addition, you should also be sure you understand use of National Language Support (NLS) for language control.

IMPORTANT
Do not take any of these practice exams until you have reviewed the contents of Appendix A, "Globalization Support." Although this is not a big topic, there are sure to be a few questions about globalization support on the OCP DBA Fundamentals I exam!

Practice Exam I

1. **Automatic archiving of redo information is enabled, and all redo logs are found on the same disk resource. Which background processes may conflict with one another's operation?**

   A. SMON and LGWR

   B. ARCH and RECO

   C. PMON and DBWR

   D. ARCH and LGWR

2. **You are adding redo logs to the Oracle database. Creating a new redo log adds information to which of the following Oracle resources?**

   A. Shared pool

   B. Control file

   C. SGA

   D. PGA

3. You need to find where the data dictionary tables are stored in your Oracle database. The tables that store information about the Oracle database—such as table names, users, and online undo segments—are found in which of the following tablespaces?

   A. SYSTEM

   B. TEMP

   C. UNDOTBS

   D. INDEX

4. You are performing the steps that will create your Oracle data dictionary. The objects in the Oracle data dictionary are part of which of the following schemas?

   A. SYSTEM

   B. SYS

   C. PUBLIC

   D. SCOTT

5. As the DBA, you are attempting to limit users' misuse of Oracle's capability to use host machine resources. Which of the following features of the Oracle database is useful for this purpose?

   A. Undo segments

   B. Roles

   C. Profiles

   D. Parameter files

6. You have identified a table in the database that is experiencing severe row chaining. Which of the following choices best identifies a way to correct the problem?

   A. Increase pctused.

   B. Increase pctfree.

   C. Increase pctincrease.

   D. Increase next.

7. Which of the following choices best identifies the Oracle feature enabling you to save multiple online copies of redo information on several disks to prevent problems with media failure?

   A. Multiplexing

   B. Archiving

   C. Redoing

   D. Logging

8. You have a database with thousands of tables and users. Managing complex databases with many objects and users is best handled with which of the following access methods?

   A. Granting privileges to profiles directly

   B. Granting privileges to users directly

   C. Use of profiles

   D. Granting privileges to roles directly

9. You are attempting to increase the checkpoint interval on your database. Each of the following choices will affect the duration and/or frequency of checkpoints, except one. Which is it?

   A. Size of redo logs

   B. Number of datafiles

   C. LOG_CHECKPOINT_INTERVAL

   D. LOG_CHECKPOINT_TIMEOUT

10. As the result of configuring an area of the Oracle database, the Oracle RDBMS has been spending more time managing the space utilization of blocks on a high transaction volume OLTP system. Which of the following choices identifies a potential cause for this behavior?

   A. High pctfree

   B. High pctused

   C. Low pctfree

   D. Low pctused

11. You intend to prevent excessive host machine processing by user SPANKY on the database. Which of the following choices indicates the step you must take in order for this to be possible in the current instance?

A. Issue grant LIMITER to SPANKY, where LIMITER is a profile.

B. Issue grant LIMITER to SPANKY, where LIMITER is a role.

C. Issue alter user SPANKY PROFILE LIMITER, where LIMITER is a profile.

D. Issue alter user SPANKY PROFILE LIMITER, where LIMITER is a role.

12. Your application regularly issues the following statement:

```
SELECT * FROM BANK_ACCT
WHERE ACCT_BALANCE BETWEEN 1000 AND 100000;
```

Which of the following database objects would be inappropriate for use with this statement?

A. Materialized views

B. Indexes

C. Index-organized tables

D. Hash clusters

13. The DBA needs to reorganize a tablespace. Which of the following privileges will be used in order to log into Oracle while the database is open, but not available to other users?

A. create session

B. restricted session

C. connect

D. mount

14. You are trying to alter the initial segment size given to a table in a dictionary-managed tablespace. Which of the following keywords would be used as part of this process?

A. drop table

B. alter table

C. resize

D. coalesce

15. You are in the process of creating users in the database. Which of the following clauses in a `create user` statement prevents a user's disk sorts from conflicting with dictionary objects?

    A. `identified by`

    B. `temporary tablespace`

    C. `default tablespace`

    D. `default role`

16. In order to enable remote administration of users and tablespaces on an Oracle database, which of the following types of files must exist in the database?

    A. Password file

    B. Initialization file

    C. Datafile

    D. Control file

    E. Nothing—`SYSDBA` privileges are not required for these actions.

17. All of the following choices identify a component of Oracle's redo architecture, except one. Which of the following is not a direct component of Oracle's redo mechanism when the database is in `archivelog` mode?

    A. DBW0

    B. Redo log buffer

    C. LGWR

    D. Online redo log

    E. CKPT

    F. Archive redo logs

18. Examine the following statement:

```
CREATE TABLE SPANKY.EMPLOYEE
(empid          NUMBER(10),
lastname        VARCHAR2(25),
firstname       VARCHAR2(25),
salary          NUMBER(10,4),
CONSTRAINT      pk_employee_01
PRIMARY KEY     (empid))
```

```
TABLESPACE orgdbdata
EXTENT MANAGEMENT DICTIONARY
PCTFREE    20  PCTUSED    50
INITRANS   1   MAXTRANS   255
NOCACHE        LOGGING
INITIAL 100K  NEXT  150K
MINEXTENTS 4  MAXEXTENTS  300
PCTINCREASE 20 );
```

What is wrong with this statement?

A. The primary key is declared improperly.

B. Both the index and data from the table must be stored in the same tablespace.

C. The statement will not succeed because a not NULL constraint is needed on the EMPID column.

D. The statement will succeed, but no data will be inserted.

E. The storage clause is improperly defined.

19. **User ANN has `insert` privilege on the EMP table `with grant option`. ANN grants the `insert` privilege to SIMON. What is the most immediate effect of the DBA revoking ANN's privilege?**

A. ANN's records will be removed from table EMP.

B. ANN will continue to have the ability to add records to EMP.

C. SIMON will not be able to add records to the EMP table anymore.

D. The DBA's ability to add records to EMP will be revoked.

20. **You have a table and you are trying to determine appropriate `pctfree` and `pctused` values for it. The initial insert of new data into the table will leave most of its large columns NULL, to be filled in later by subsequent updates. Records are never removed. What is the appropriate value combination for `pctfree` and `pctused`?**

A. pctused = 99, pctfree = 1

B. pctused = 40, pctfree = 30

C. pctused = 40, pctfree = 10

D. pctused = 80, pctfree = 10

21. You are configuring your index to be stored in a tablespace. Which of the following storage parameters are not appropriate for indexes?

    A. OPTIMAL

    B. INITIAL

    C. PCTINCREASE

    D. NEXT

22. You need to manage some configuration for new and existing users. Which of the following clauses are available in `alter user` statements but not in `create user` statements?

    A. `identified by`

    B. `temporary tablespace`

    C. `profile`

    D. `default role`

    E. `account lock`

    F. `password expire`

23. When you arrive at work in the morning, you have messages from several users complaining that they have received the following error when they tried logging into Oracle with their new user ID and password:

    ```
    Error accessing PRODUCT_USER_PROFILE
    Warning:  Product user profile information not loaded!
    ```

    What do you need to do in order to solve the problem?

    A. Run pupbld.sql as SYSTEM.

    B. Do a shutdown abort.

    C. Drop and re-create the users.

    D. Drop and re-create the database.

24. During regular database operation, which background process will take smaller blocks of free space in a dictionary-managed tablespace and move things around to make bigger pieces of free space?

    A. DBW0

    B. LGWR

    C. ARCH

    D. SMON

    E. PMON

25. You are designing the physical database layout on your host machine. What is the relationship between tablespaces and datafiles in the Oracle database?

    A. One tablespace has only one datafile.

    B. Many tablespaces can share one datafile.

    C. One tablespace can have many datafiles.

    D. One datafile can contain many tablespaces.

26. In order to set resource cost high on CPU time, and low on the overall time a user spends connected to Oracle, which of the following would be appropriate?

    A. Increase value of COMPOSITE_LIMIT.

    B. Increase value on CPU_PER_SESSION, and decrease value on CONNECT_TIME.

    C. Decrease value on CPU_PER_SESSION, and increase value on LOGICAL_READS_PER_SESSION.

    D. Set PRIVATE_SGA to UNLIMITED.

27. You are attempting to take the UNDOTBS01 tablespace offline when using manually managed undo segments and receive the following error: ORA-01546 - cannot take tablespace offline. What might be causing the problem?

    A. A table has too many extents allocated to it.

    B. Your `init.ora` file is unavailable.

    C. An uncommitted transaction is still in progress.

    D. The online redo log is being archived.

28. You are analyzing how Oracle processes user statements. SQL and PL/SQL parse information is stored in which of the following database memory areas?

A. Library cache

B. Row cache

C. Dictionary cache

D. Large area

E. Buffer cache

29. Information in the buffer cache is saved back to disk in each of the following situations except one. In which situation does this not occur?

A. When a timeout occurs

B. When a log switch occurs

C. When the shared pool is flushed

D. When a checkpoint occurs

30. You want to set up password management on your Oracle database. Which of the following choices indicates what you should do to view an example for setting up a password management function?

A. Set RESOURCE_LIMIT to TRUE.

B. Run utlpwmg.sql.

C. Drop the DEFAULT profile.

D. Run catproc.sql.

31. Inspect the following transcript from user ATHENA's session:

```
SQL>  create table obobobo (bobobo varchar2(3))
  2>    tablespace rman;
create table obobobo (bobobo varchar2(3))
*
ERROR at line 1:
ORA-01536: space quota exceeded for tablespace 'RMAN'
```

Where can the DBA look to find out information to solve this problem?

A. Looking in the DBA_TS_QUOTAS dictionary view

B. Looking in the DBA_USERS view

    C. Looking in the DBA_TAB_COLUMNS view

    D. Looking in the DBA_TABLESPACES view

32. **The DBA issues the following statement:**

```
CREATE USER DBADMIN
IDENTIFIED BY DBADMIN;
```

    What profile will user DBADMIN have?

    A. DEFAULT

    B. None

    C. CONNECT

    D. DBA

33. **You have several profiles in your database, each with various values set to make users stay on the database for various periods of time. Where would you look to find information about the appropriate profile to assign a user who should connect for only very short periods of time?**

    A. DBA_USERS

    B. DBA_PROFILES

    C. RESOURCE_COST

    D. RESOURCE_LIMIT

34. **You have finished creating your new database and have run scripts to create the data dictionary views. Which of the following choices identifies what you need to do next to create Oracle-supplied packages?**

    A. `catproc.sql`

    B. `catalog.sql`

    C. `utlpwdmg.sql`

    D. `utllockt.sql`

35. You are trying to strengthen security on your database. Which of the following Oracle resources supports password-authenticated security over and above the abilities a user might be granted in accessing an application?

   A. Profiles

   B. Tables

   C. Undo segments

   D. Roles

36. A disk crashes that contains the only copies of all four of your online redo log files. How would you alter your Oracle database to prevent this from causing much damage in the future?

   A. Change the CONTROL_FILES parameter in the `init.ora` file.

   B. Use the `alter database add LOGFILE GROUP 5;`.

   C. Create multiple members for each of your four groups and place them on different disks.

   D. Set LOG_BLOCK_CHECKSUM in the `init.ora` file.

37. A table has a primary key that has been disabled. Upon reenabling it, the DBA discovers that users have entered duplicate records into the table. Which of the following database objects might play a role in rectifying the situation?

   A. EXCEPTIONS

   B. DBA_TABLES

   C. USER_TAB_COLUMNS

   D. AUD$

38. After creating a new user for your Oracle database, a user still complains she cannot log in because of insufficient privileges errors. Which of the following actions should you take?

   A. Grant create table privileges to the user.

   B. Reset the user's password.

   C. Grant the CONNECT role to the user.

   D. Unlock the user's account.

39. **On an Oracle server installation, which of the following reorganizations of your indexes would be appropriate in order to improve performance of queries on tables containing all words in the dictionary starting with the letter *s*?**

    A. Convert your B-tree index to a bitmap index.

    B. Convert your bitmap index to a B-tree index.

    C. Convert your B-tree index to a reverse-key index.

    D. Convert your reverse-key index to a B-tree index.

40. **You plan to store large blocks of text in your table. You want the column to be large enough to store about ten sentences. The column must also be fixed width. Which of the following datatypes are most appropriate?**

    A. CLOB

    B. LONG

    C. VARCHAR2

    D. CHAR

41. **You have enabled an audit in your database using the following statement:**

    ```
    AUDIT UPDATE, DELETE
    ON spanky.cat_toys
    BY ACCESS
    WHENEVER NOT SUCCESSFUL;
    ```

    Which choice best explains how Oracle will audit data?

    A. Successful `insert` statements on CAT_TOYS performed by SPANKY will be recorded.

    B. Unsuccessful `update` and `delete` statements performed by any user on CAT_TOYS will be recorded.

    C. Unsuccessful `update` and `delete` statements performed by user ACCESS on CAT_TOYS will be recorded.

    D. Unsuccessful `update` and `delete` statements performed by SPANKY on any table will be recorded.

42. **The primary key of the EMP table has three columns: EMPID, LASTNAME, and FIRSTNAME. You issue the following `select` statement:**

```
SELECT * FROM EMP
WHERE LASTNAME = 'HARRIS'
AND FIRSTNAME = 'BILLI'
AND EMPID = '5069493';
```

    What dictionary view could you use to verify the order of leading columns in the index associated with the primary key?

    A. DBA_IND_COLUMNS

    B. DBA_TAB_COLUMNS

    C. DBA_INDEXES

    D. DBA_CLU_COLUMNS

43. **You issue the following statement:**

```
DROP PROFILE LTD_PROGRAMMER;
```

    The LTD_PROGRAMMER profile was granted to several users on the Oracle database. What happens to those users?

    A. The users who had the LTD_PROGRAMMER profile can no longer log in to Oracle.

    B. The users who had the LTD_PROGRAMMER profile now have the DEFAULT profile.

    C. The users who had the LTD_PROGRAMMER profile now have no profile.

    D. Nothing—You cannot drop a profile that has been granted to users.

44. **You want to reduce the number of extents a segment will allocate as part of table growth. Each of the following choices indicates an action that will do so, except one. Which is it?**

    A. Running EXPORT with the COMPRESS parameter set to Y

    B. Increasing the value set for `pctused` on the table

    C. Increasing the value set for `pctincrease` on the table

    D. Increasing the value set for `next` on the table

45. You are planning which segments to place in which tablespaces. Which of the following segment types usually has the lowest turnover in the Oracle database?

A. Undo segments

B. Table segments

C. Temporary segments

D. SYSTEM segments

46. You issue the shutdown command at 3 P.M. on a Friday. Two hours later, the database is still in the process of shutting down. Which of the following options did you most likely use in order to shut down the database?

A. `shutdown abort`

B. `shutdown immediate`

C. `shutdown transactional`

D. `shutdown normal`

47. The user is selecting data from the Oracle database. Which of the following processes handles obtaining data from Oracle for that user?

A. The user process obtains information on its own.

B. The DBW0 process obtains information for the user.

C. The server process obtains information for the user.

D. The listener process obtains information for the user.

48. The result of select count(*) from DBA_TABLES where TABLESPACE_NAME _ 'MY_TBLSPC' is listed as follows:

```
COUNT(*)
----------------
150
```

You then issue the `drop tablespace MY_TBLSPC` command. What happens next?

A. The `drop tablespace` command succeeds.

B. The `drop tablespace` command fails because you didn't include the cascade constraints option.

   C. The `drop tablespace` command fails because you didn't include the including contents option.

   D. You cannot drop a tablespace after creating it.

49. **After starting SQL*Plus in line mode, you issue the `shutdown immediate` command. What will most likely happen next?**

   A. The database shuts down.

   B. The database does not shut down because users have to disconnect.

   C. SQL*Plus returns an error saying you need to connect to Oracle first.

   D. Nothing happens. SQL*Plus is not a line-mode tool.

50. **You need to view the initialization parameter settings for your Oracle database. Which of the following choices does not identify a method you can use to obtain values set for your initialization parameters?**

   A. Issue `select * from DBA_PARAMETERS;` from SQL*Plus.

   B. Issue `select * from V$PARAMETER;` from SQL*Plus.

   C. Issue `show parameters` from SQL*Plus.

   D. Use OEM Instance Manager.

51. **You issue the following statement in Oracle:**

```
CREATE UNIQUE BITMAP INDEX employee_lastname_indx_01
ON employee (lastname ASC)
TABLESPACE ORGDBIDX
PCTFREE 12
INITRANS 2 MAXTRANS 255
LOGGING
NOSORT
STORAGE ( INITIAL 900K
NEXT 1800K
MINEXTENTS 1
MAXEXTENTS 200
PCTINCREASE 0 );
```

What is wrong with this statement for dictionary-managed tablespaces?

   A. You cannot use the `nosort` keyword in creating an index.

   B. Bitmap indexes cannot be unique.

C. The `tablespace` clause must be omitted.

D. You should omit the `asc` keyword.

52. **You manage database access privileges with roles where possible. You have granted the SELECT_MY_TABLE role to another role called EMP_DEVELOPER. To view information about other roles that may be granted to EMP_DEVELOPER, which of the following dictionary views are appropriate?**

    A. DBA_ROLE_PRIVS

    B. DBA_TAB_PRIVS

    C. USER_SYS_PRIVS

    D. ROLE_ROLE_PRIVS

53. **Your current session displays date information in the following format: 10-FEB-1999:10:15AM. Which of the following statements most likely produced this result?**

    A. alter session set NLS_DATE_FORMAT = 'DD-MON-YYYY:HH:MIAM';

    B. alter session set NLS_DATE_FORMAT = 'DD-MON-YY:HH24:MI';

    C. alter session set NLS_DATE_FORMAT = 'DD-MON-YY:HH:MIAM';

    D. alter session set NLS_DATE_FORMAT = 'DD-MON-YYYY:HH24:MI';

54. **You need to set up auditing in an order entry and product shipment application so that when the ORDER_STATUS column in the ORDERS table changes to *SHIPPED*, a record is placed in a special table associated with a part of the application that gives sales representatives a daily list of customers to call on a follow-up to make sure the customer is satisfied with the order. Which of the following choices represents the best way to perform this auditing?**

    A. Statement auditing

    B. Object auditing

    C. Audit by access

    D. Value-based auditing

55. You are in the process of granting several permissions to a role. Which of the following privileges is not a system privilege?

  A. analyze any

  B. index

  C. create rollback segment

  D. create synonym

56. When sizing temporary tablespaces, you should try where possible to make the default INITIAL storage setting for the temporary tablespace a multiple of which of the following initialization parameters?

  A. LOG_BUFFER

  B. DB_BLOCK_BUFFERS

  C. SORT_AREA_SIZE

  D. SHARED_POOL_SIZE

57. When you issue the `commit` statement in your session, which of the following things will not occur?

  A. Acquired row or table locks are released.

  B. Cached data is saved immediately to disk.

  C. Acquired undo segment locks are released.

  D. Redo entry generated for committed transaction.

58. You are processing an `update` statement. At what point in SQL statement processing is the data change actually made to block buffers?

  A. When the cursor is opened

  B. When the statement is parsed

  C. When data is fetched from the cursor

  D. When the statement is executed

59. You are defining storage for various segment types in the Oracle database. Which of the following is not a valid type of segment in Oracle?

  A. Data segment

  B. Undo segment

    C. Temporary segment

    D. Sequence segment

60. You need to identify the remaining free space in a tablespace. From which of the following views would you get this information most easily?

    A. DBA_TABLESPACES

    B. DBA_FREE_SPACE

    C. V$TABLESPACE

    D. DBA_EXTENTS

Practice Exam 2

I. **If you wanted to find the name and location of your control files, you could find that information in each of the following locations except one. Which is it?**

   A. V$CONTROLFILE_RECORD_SECTION

   B. V$CONTROLFILE

   C. V$PARAMETER

   D. init.ora file

2. **You are planning the storage requirements for your database. Which of the following is an effect of maintaining a high pctfree for a table?**

   A. Oracle will manage filling data blocks with new records more actively.

   B. Oracle will manage filling data blocks with new records less actively.

   C. Oracle will leave more space free in data blocks for existing records.

   D. Oracle will leave less space free in data blocks for existing records.

3. **The DBA has a table created with the following statement:**

```
CREATE TABLE EMPL
(EMPID NUMBER(10),
LASTNAME VARCHAR2(40),
RESUME LONG RAW);
The DBA attempts to issue the following statement:
ALTER TABLE EMPL
ADD ( PERF_APPRAISE LONG);
```

   What happens?

   A. The statement succeeds.

   B. The statement succeeds, but column is added as VARCHAR2.

   C. The statement fails.

   D. The statement adds a DISABLED constraint.

4. **User ANN has insert privilege on the EMP table. What is the most immediate effect of the DBA revoking ANN's privilege?**

   A. ANN's records will be removed from the database.

   B. ANN will not have the ability to create tables.

    C. ANN will not be able to access the database anymore.

    D. Users to which ANN granted `insert` privileges will not be able to `insert`.

5. **If you wished to make it so that every user in Oracle could have only one connection to the database at a time, which of the following choices identifies how you would do it?**

    A. Set LICENSE_MAX_SESSIONS = 1 in `init.ora`.

    B. Set SESSIONS_PER_USER in the DEFAULT profile to 1.

    C. Set IDLE_TIME in the DEFAULT profile to 1.

    D. Set SESSIONS_PER_USER = 2 in `init.ora`.

6. **Records from the data dictionary information are stored in which of the following database memory areas?**

    A. Library cache

    B. Row cache

    C. Session UGA

    D. Buffer cache

7. **Which of the following choices correctly describes the difference between a data load via the conventional path and the direct path?**

    A. One runs faster than the other.

    B. A conventional path data load bypasses most of the Oracle RDBMS, whereas a direct path data load is a high-speed version of the SQL `insert`.

    C. A direct path data load bypasses most of the Oracle RDBMS, whereas a conventional path data load is a high-speed version of the SQL `insert`.

    D. The conventional path runs when the `conventional` command-line parameter is set to TRUE.

8. **The location of indexes in a database and the size of those indexes is information that can be found in which of the following dictionary views?**

    A. DBA_TS_QUOTAS

    B. DBA_OBJECTS

C. DBA_SEGMENTS

D. DBA_INDEXES

9. You have a long-running process you want to assign to a specific undo segment brought online for that express purpose. You are not using automatic undo management. What statement can be used for this task?

   A. `alter database`

   B. `set transaction`

   C. `alter rollback segment`

   D. `alter table`

10. In a situation where no multiplexing of redo logs takes place, what happens when Oracle cannot read data from the online redo log group for archiving?

    A. Nothing happens.

    B. Oracle will automatically switch redo logs when detected.

    C. Oracle eventually won't allow new records to be added to the database.

    D. The instance crashes.

11. All except one of the following will alter the number of checkpoints that occur in one hour on the database. Which is it?

    A. Decreasing tablespace size

    B. Decreasing size of redo log members

    C. Setting LOG_CHECKPOINT_INTERVAL greater than the size of the redo log file

    D. Setting LOG_CHECKPOINT_TIMEOUT to zero

12. You are defining profile areas on your Oracle database. Which of the following profile areas can be used to control the resource usage for the other four?

    A. LOGICAL_READS_PER_SESSION

    B. CONNECT_TIME

    C. COMPOSITE_LIMIT

    D. CPU_PER_SESSION

    E. PRIVATE_SGA

13. User ANN has the `create any table` privilege with administrative abilities on that privilege. Which of the following statements shows how to revoke the administrative component from ANN without limiting her overall ability to create tables?

    A. `revoke admin option from create any table;`

    B. `revoke admin option from create any table; then grant create any table to ANN;`

    C. `revoke create any table from ANN; then grant create any table to ANN;`

    D. `revoke create any table from ANN with admin option; then grant create any table to ANN;`

14. The DBA is defining a default role for users. Which of the following is not an acceptable method for defining a default role?

    A. `alter user default role all;`

    B. `alter user default role all except ROLE_1;`

    C. `alter user default role none;`

    D. `alter user default role none except ROLE_1;`

15. You issue the following statement from SQL*Plus: `startup mount`. Where does Oracle obtain values for starting the instance?

    A. From your `init.ora` file

    B. From Oracle default values

    C. From the default settings for the tablespace

    D. From the default settings in your redo log file

16. You are analyzing the components of the redo log mechanisms in your Oracle database. Which of the following purposes does the CKPT process serve?

    A. Writes dirty buffers to disk

    B. Writes current redo log number to datafile headers

C. Writes redo log information to disk

D. Reads information into memory for users

17. **You are architecting the database to be used in a production OLTP environment. Which of the following choices best illustrates why you should multiplex online redo logs?**

A. To take advantage of the increase in storage space

B. To avoid degraded redo log performance

C. To reduce dependency on the redo log buffer

D. To prevent users from waiting if a redo log member cannot be archived

18. **You are configuring some new profiles for your database. Which of the following is not an area that you can specify a resource profile limit on?**

A. LOGICAL_READS_PER_SESSION

B. CONNECT_TIME

C. LOGICAL_WRITES_PER_SESSION

D. IDLE_TIME

19. **You are attempting to clear an unarchived redo log file. In order to manually enact a log switch, which of the following statements is appropriate?**

A. `alter database`

B. `alter system`

C. `alter user`

D. `alter redo log`

20. **Which of the following clauses is available in `alter user` statements but not in `create user` statements?**

A. `identified by`

B. `temporary tablespace`

C. `profile`

D. `default role`

21. **Which of the following choices lists an alter user option that can be executed by the user himself?**

A. `default tablespace`

B. `identified by`

C. `temporary tablespace`

D. `profile`

22. **In order to set a limit on the combined resource usage for users, which of the following statements would be appropriate?**

A. `alter profile default limit COMPOSITE_LIMIT 3500;`

B. `RESOURCE_COST=TRUE`

C. Set `CPU_PER_SESSION = 100` in DEFAULT profile.

D. Set `LICENSE_MAX_SESSIONS = 1` in `init.ora`.

23. **To allocate another role to a user, which command is most appropriate?**

A. `alter user`

B. `alter database`

C. `alter system`

D. `grant`

24. **Which of the following operations does not require Oracle to store information in an undo segment as part of the transaction?**

A. `insert`

B. `select`

C. `update`

D. `delete`

25. **You have enabled dedicated servers to be used on your Oracle database system. Where in the Oracle database is session information when dedicated servers are being used?**

A. In the PGA

B. In the shared pool

C. In the buffer cache

D. In the redo log buffer

E. Large area

26. **Which of the following clauses in a `create user` statement restricts the number of tables a user can add to a tablespace?**

    A. `quota on`

    B. `default tablespace`

    C. `profile`

    D. `identified by`

27. **You have a block space utilization identified by the following values: `pctfree 25, pctused 30`. Which of the following choices best describes the block management on your database?**

    A. Little free space left for `updates` and space left free by `deletes` actively filled in by Oracle

    B. Little free space left for `updates` and space left free by `deletes` not actively filled in by Oracle

    C. Much free space left for `updates` and space left free by `deletes` actively filled in by Oracle

    D. Much free space left for `updates` and space left free by `deletes` not actively filled in by Oracle

28. **You are defining the path a user process takes to get information out of the Oracle database. Which of the following purposes does the process labeled D009 serve?**

    A. Writes dirty buffers to disk

    B. Writes current redo log number to datafile headers

    C. Dispatches user process access to a shared server

    D. Writes redo log entries to disk

29. **You are considering using the MTS architecture on the Oracle database. Where in the Oracle database is session information stored when shared servers are being used?**

    A. In the PGA

    B. In the shared pool

    C. In the buffer cache

    D. In the redo log buffer

    E. Large area

30. The DBA executes the following statement:

```
CREATE OR REPLACE VIEW MY_VW AS
SELECT EMPID, LASTNAME, FIRSTNAME,
TO_CHAR(SALARY) AS SALARY FROM EMP;
```

If the SALARY column in the EMP table is datatype NUMBER(10), what will the datatype of the SALARY column be in MY_VW when the DBA queries the data dictionary?

    A. ROWID

    B. NUMBER

    C. DATE

    D. VARCHAR2

31. You have defined your national language on the Oracle database to be English, and the text data in some tables contains German characters. In order to ensure that you can list this text data in ascending alphabetical order according to German syntax, while still ensuring the language on the database is English, which of the following parameters could be set?

    A. NLS_DATE_FORMAT

    B. NLS_RULE

    C. NLS_TERRITORY

    D. NLS_SORT

32. When choosing a character set and national character set, which of the following factors should not enter into consideration?

    A. Your character set must either be US7ASCII or a superset of it.

    B. Your national character set and character set should be closely related where possible.

    C. You can use varying-length multibyte character sets as both character sets on your database.

    D. Oracle supports only English-like languages as its character set for entering SQL and PL/SQL commands.

33. You are working for the United Nations as an Oracle DBA. You maintain databases in multiple countries in multiple languages. To determine the date conventions for a database in a particular country, you might use which of the following database views?

    A. V$NLS_PARAMETERS

    B. NLS_DATE_FORMAT

    C. DBA_DATES

    D. V$NLS_VALID_VALUES

34. You are running Oracle in America in support of a financial analysis project for the government of Egypt. In order to produce reports that display monetary amounts as Egyptian pounds, rather than dollars, which of the following initialization parameters would be useful?

    A. NLS_SORT

    B. NLS_CURRENCY

    C. NLS_LANG

    D. NLS_DATE_FORMAT

35. You are trying to find the ALERT file on a host machine for a database you have never administered before. Which of the following initialization parameters is used to identify the location of the ALERT file?

    A. BACKGROUND_DUMP_DEST

    B. USER_DUMP_DEST

    C. LOG_ARCHIVE_DEST

    D. CORE_DUMP_DEST

36. You issue the `alter tablespace read only` command against an Oracle database. Which of the following choices best describes what happens next?

    A. Oracle immediately puts the tablespace into read-only mode.

    B. Oracle puts the tablespace into read-only mode after the last user logs off.

C. Oracle puts the tablespace into read-only mode after the last prior transaction against that tablespace commits while preventing subsequent DML until the change happens.

D. Oracle returns an error.

37. You are using locally managed tablespaces in Oracle. Which of the following choices best describes the way Oracle implements this feature in the database?

A. Using a bitmap in the space header segment

B. Using the data dictionary on the local database

C. Using a flat file in the local directory storing the datafile

D. Using the data dictionary in a distributed database

38. You are configuring Oracle's large pool feature. Which of the following choices best describes information that gets stored in the large pool if one is defined for your database?

A. Parse trees for SQL statements

B. Session memory for MTS configuration

C. Session memory for dedicated server configuration

D. Block buffer overflow

39. You need to remove a column from the database. Which of the following choices best identifies how to do so if your objective is to quickly execute the task without necessarily freeing up space in your tablespace?

A. alter table drop column

B. alter table set unused column

C. alter table modify column

D. truncate table

40. When generating global temporary tables, which of the following places in your Oracle database is the actual data used by your temporary table stored in?

    A. PGA

    B. Buffer cache

    C. SYSTEM tablespace

    D. RBS tablespace

41. You are using SQL*Loader to insert data into your database quickly. Which of the following features enables you to define a row of data in your datafile to begin at a point other than the beginning of a line?

    A. `fields separated by`

    B. `fields terminated by`

    C. `trailing nullcols`

    D. `recseparator`

42. You are rebuilding indexes in Oracle. Which of the following activities cannot be combined with rebuilding your index in an Oracle database, but must instead be performed as a separate operation?

    A. Estimate statistics.

    B. Compute statistics.

    C. Move the index to another tablespace.

    D. Rebuild online.

43. You want to maintain multiple archive log destinations in Oracle. Which of the following parameters can be used to indicate how many ARCH processes Oracle needs to run in order to manage storage of archive logs to multiple destinations?

    A. LOG_ARCHIVE_PROCESSES

    B. LOG_ARCHIVE_MAX_PROCESSES

    C. LOG_ARCHIVE_MIN_SUCCEED_DEST

    D. LOG_ARCHIVE_START

44. **You have installed Oracle and used the Database Configuration Assistant to create a database in a Windows environment. Where would you find the datafiles for the database that you just created?**

    A. %ORACLE_BASE%\admin

    B. %ORACLE_BASE%\rdbms\admin

    C. %ORACLE_BASE%\database

    D. %ORACLE_BASE%\oradata

45. **You issue the following statement on an Oracle database where DB_BLOCK_SIZE is 4KB:**

```
CREATE TABLESPACE orgdbindex
DATAFILE '/oracle/disk_8/index01.dbf'
SIZE 300M
EXTENT MANAGEMENT LOCAL
UNIFORM SIZE 100K
ONLINE;
```

How many blocks will each bit represent in the bitmap area of the locally managed datafiles?

    A. 25

    B. 50

    C. 80

    D. 250

46. **You have assigned three tables to the keep pool. How should you determine the appropriate size for your keep pool?**

    A. Based on the size of your shared pool

    B. Based on the number of blocks in the table only

    C. Based on the number of blocks in the table plus the number of blocks in associated indexes

    D. Based on the number of blocks in associated indexes only

    E. None of the above

47. **A DBA in Germany needs to ensure that both the German mark and the Euro will be supported in the latest currency conversion application. Which of the following NLS parameters will work best for this purpose?**

    A. NLS_TERRITORY

    B. NLS_LANG

    C. NLS_COMP

    D. NLS_DUAL_CURRENCY

48. **The user attempts to `insert` data into a column that would violate a nondeferrable constraint. The user has issued the `alter session set constraints = deferred` statement. What happens on `insert`?**

    A. The `insert` succeeds at the time it is issued, but the transaction will roll back later.

    B. The `insert` fails at the time it is issued and the transaction will end.

    C. The `insert` succeeds at the time it is issued and the transaction will not roll back later.

    D. The `insert` fails at the time it is issued, but the transaction will continue.

49. **The value stored in an index for a column is '596849'. The DBA then issues the `alter index reverse` statement. What does the data in the index now look like?**

    A. '596849'

    B. '849596'

    C. '948695'

    D. '695948'

50. **The best choice for decreasing size requirements for tables that need only be accessed via the primary key is which of the following?**

    A. Create more indexes on the table.

    B. Create an index-organized table to store the data.

    C. Drop the primary key.

    D. Increase the `pctfree` value set for table blocks.

51. While administering passwords on an Oracle database, you discover that users are simply reusing older passwords whenever their current password expires. If you wanted to prevent the reuse of passwords for a three-year period, which of the following choices identifies a profile-related method you might use to do so?

A. Set password_reuse_time to 3.

B. Set password_reuse_time to 39.

C. Set password_reuse_time to 339.

D. Set password_reuse_time to 1095.

E. Set password_reuse_time to 3195.

52. You issue the following statement in Oracle:

```
grant create table to STARSKY with admin option;
```

After which, user STARSKY issues the following statement in Oracle:

```
grant create table to HUTCH;
```

You discover STARSKY's actions and act in the following way:

```
revoke create table from STARSKY;
```

Which of the following choices correctly describes the result?

A. HUTCH can no longer create tables, but you can.

B. STARSKY can no longer create tables, but HUTCH can.

C. You and STARSKY can no longer create tables, but HUTCH can.

D. You and HUTCH can no longer create tables, but STARSKY can.

53. You grant a nondefault password-protected role to a user that permits the user to act as an application superuser with respect to adding records to certain tables. Which of the following choices best identifies the way the grantee might use to exercise the privileges granted to him or her with this role?

A. The user issues the appropriate DML commands.

B. The user issues the `alter user` command, then issues the DML commands.

C. The user issues the `set role` command, then issues the DML commands.

D. The user requires DBA intervention to exercise these privileges.

54. **You are about to alter the size of a tablespace. Which of the following choices identifies a constraint on performing this operation if the intended size of the tablespace is larger than the tablespace's current size?**

    A. Presence of objects in the datafile resized

    B. Availability of space on disk where datafiles are added

    C. Whether AUTOEXTEND is in use on datafiles for the tablespace

    D. Availability of space in memory for temporary storage of blocks in tablespace

55. **Developers are complaining that after a few minutes of querying the database, their session disconnects abruptly. Which of the following choices does not identify a potential cause for the disconnection?**

    A. The DEVELOPER profile shows a value of 230,000 for COMPOSITE_LIMIT.

    B. The DBA is issuing the `alter system kill session` command repeatedly.

    C. The DEFAULT profile shows a value of 100 for CPU_PER_SESSION.

    D. The USERS profile shows a value of 500 for CONNECT_TIME.

56. **You are granting roles to users on an Oracle database. Which of the following roles is not predefined when the Oracle database is created?**

    A. CREATE_CATALOG_ROLE

    B. SELECT_CATALOG_ROLE

    C. EXP_FULL_DATABASE

    D. IMP_FULL_DATABASE

57. **You are managing a 24×7 database environment and need to rebuild an index online. Which of the following choices best identifies the factor you will need to consider when determining the time to execute the `online rebuild`?**

    A. Availability for downtime

    B. Performance

    C. System idleness

    D. Batch processing

58. You are concerned about row chaining as a performance degrader on your Oracle database environment. Which of the following Oracle resources cannot be used to determine how many rows are chained on a table in your database?

   A. The `analyze` command

   B. The DBMS_DDL package

   C. The DBMS_UTILITY package

   D. The `alter tablespace coalesce` command

59. You attempt to issue the `alter tablespace move datafile` command in the Oracle database. Which of the following choices indicates a step that must take place after this command is issued?

   A. Physically move the datafile to the new location.

   B. Bring the tablespace offline.

   C. Bring the tablespace online.

   D. Execute IMPORT to load the new metadata.

60. You create a user on your Oracle database with the following command:

```
create user GIANT identified by GREEN;
```

You then issue the following query:

```
SQL> select password from dba_users where username = 'GIANT';
PASSWORD
-----------------------------
C55278B93918BF29
```

You then issue the following statement:

```
alter user GIANT identified by "C55278B93918BF29";
```

Which of the following choices best describes what GIANT's password is now set to?

   A. GREEN

   B. C55278B93918BF29

   C. This question is irrelevant because GIANT can't connect without `create session` privileges.

   D. This question is irrelevant because GIANT's account was locked by default.

Practice Exam 3

I. **You are configuring the use of servers in your Oracle database. Which of the following statements describes what happens after the listener process detects a user attempting to connect to Oracle when dedicated servers are being used?**

   A. The listener spawns a new server process.

   B. The listener passes the request to a dispatcher.

   C. The listener passes the request to LGWR.

   D. The listener passes the request to DBW0.

2. **A user issues a `select` command against the Oracle database. Which of the following choices describes a step that Oracle will execute in support of this statement?**

   A. Acquire locks on table queried.

   B. Generate redo for statement.

   C. Fetch data from disk into memory.

   D. Write changes to disk.

3. **A user issues an `insert` statement against the Oracle database. Which of the following choices describes a step that Oracle will execute in support of this statement?**

   A. Make changes to data block in memory.

   B. Parse statement if parse tree already exists in shared pool.

   C. Write changed records to undo segment.

   D. Write redo for transaction to datafile.

4. **You are implementing Oracle in your organization. Which of the following identifies a feature of Optimal Flexible Architecture?**

   A. OFA lumps software, database, and administrative files into one area so they are easy for DBAs to locate.

   B. Use of OFA enables DBAs to define their own filesystem layouts using proprietary naming conventions in order to facilitate management of Oracle databases.

    C. Use of OFA reduces support headaches by standardizing filesystem layouts for all Oracle installations.

    D. OFA lumps all database objects like tables and indexes into one tablespace so they are easy for DBAs to manage.

5. You are creating a password file in Oracle. Which of the following choices identifies how you will specify this command if you want your password file named orapwdORCL.pwd, located in /u01/app/oracle/database, to enable up to 100 other DBAs to connect and administer the database?

    A. `orapwd directory=/u01/app/oracle/database`
       `file5orapwdORCL.pwd`

    B. `orapwd file=/u01/app/oracle/database/orapwdORCL.pwd`
       `password=oracle entries=100`

    C. `orapwd file=/u01/app/oracle/database/orapwdORCL.pwd`
       `entries=100`

    D. `orapwd file=orapwdORCL.pwd password=oracle`
       `entries=100`

6. You are managing the Oracle database. Which of the following choices correctly identifies when Oracle reads the contents of the `init.ora` file?

    A. When the instance is started

    B. When the database is mounted

    C. When the database is opened

    D. When the database is closed

7. You issue the following command in Oracle: `create tablespace BOB_TBS datafile "bob01.dbf" size 2M;`. Later queries against the database reveal that the tablespace is located in the /u01/oradata/oracle directory. Which of the following choices identifies how Oracle likely determined what directory to place bob01.dbf in?

    A. DB_CREATE_FILE_DEST

    B. DB_CREATE_ONLINE_LOG_1

    C. DB_CREATE_ONLINE_LOG_2

    D. The directory is an operating system-specific default value in Oracle that can neither be specified manually nor changed.

8. You have configured OMF on your Oracle database system. After careful analysis, you determine that a tablespace must be removed from the database. Which of the following choices identifies how OMF can assist you in this task?

   A. OMF will automatically update the data dictionary to remove reference to the tablespace datafiles.

   B. OMF will automatically remove the underlying datafiles from the host environment.

   C. OMF will tell Oracle to automatically stop using the datafiles associated with the tablespace.

   D. None of the above choices identify the functionality provided by OMF.

9. Choose the appropriate choice to complete the following statement: If you want to use OMF to handle specifying the location of your online redo logs, then you must specify at least _____ destinations for Oracle to use through the definition of OMF-related `init.ora` parameters.

   A. One

   B. Two

   C. Three

   D. Four

10. You are administering an instance of your Oracle database. Which of the following choices identifies a command that can be used to tell Oracle to temporarily cease database operations?

    A. `startup nomount`

    B. `alter database open read only`

    C. `alter system suspend`

    D. `alter system resume`

11. You need to shut down the Oracle database on short notice. Which of the following choices indicates the command you would use if you were prepared to let Oracle execute instance recovery the next time the database was opened?

    A. `shutdown abort`

    B. `shutdown transactional`

C. shutdown normal

D. shutdown immediate

12. The following excerpt of a trace file was taken from an Oracle database:

```
Tue Jul 18 17:04:33 2000
alter database dismount
Completed: alter database dismount
archiving is disabled
Dump file c:\Oracle\admin\orcl\bdump\orclALRT.LOG
Tue Jul 18 17:05:00 2000
ORACLE V9.0.1.0.0 - Production vsnsta=0
vsnsql=d vsnxtr=3
Windows NT V4.10, OS V192.0, CPU type 586
Starting up ORACLE RDBMS Version: 9.0.1.0.0.
System parameters with non-default values:
  processes              = 59
  shared_pool_size       = 15728640
  java_pool_size         = 20971520
  disk_asynch_io         = FALSE
  control_files          = c:\Oracle\ORADATA\orcl\control01.ctl,
c:\Oracle\ORADATA\orcl\control02.ctl
  db_block_buffers       = 200
  db_block_size          = 2048
  compatible             = 9.0.1.0.0
  log_buffer             = 8192
  log_checkpoint_interval  = 10000
  log_checkpoint_timeout   = 0
```

Which of the following choices identifies the most likely name for that trace file?

A. orclDBW0.trc

B. orclLGWR.trc

C. orclALRT.trc

D. orcl13095.trc

13. You are preparing to create an Oracle database. Which of the following parameters must be changed in your init.ora file in order to create a new database that will not interfere with any existing databases on the machine hosting Oracle when you've copied the init.ora file from one of those other databases for use in this one?

A. CONTROL_FILES

B. DB_BLOCK_SIZE

    C. DB_DOMAIN

    D. SHARED_POOL_SIZE

14. **You are using the Database Configuration Assistant to configure your Oracle database. Which of the following terms pertains to the creation of an object from which creation of other databases can be based?**

    A. Clone

    B. Copy

    C. Template

    D. Terminal

15. **You have just created an Oracle database using the `create database` command. To which of the following tablespaces will any datafile identified as part of the `datafile` clause for the `create database` command belong?**

    A. DATA

    B. INDEX

    C. UNDOTBS

    D. SYSTEM

16. **You are about to create your Oracle data dictionary for use with the database. Which of the following users would you connect to the database as for this purpose in Oracle9i and later releases?**

    A. SYSTEM

    B. OUTLN

    C. INTERNAL

    D. SYS

17. **You are identifying dictionary objects in the Oracle database. Which of the following is a view in the data dictionary?**

    A. V$DATABASE

    B. DBA_TABLES

    C. SYS.AUD$

    D. EMP

18. Use the following code block to answer this question:

```
TEXT
---------------------------------------------
declare
  x varchar2(10);
begin
  x := 'hello world';
  dbms_output.put_line(x);
end;
```

Which of the following views might this data?

A. DBA_ERRORS

B. DBA_SOURCE

C. DBA_VIEWS

D. DBA_TRIGGERS

19. Use the following code block to answer this question:

```
SQL> select text from DBA_views where view_name =
  2  'DBA_TABLES';
TEXT
----------------------------------------------------------------

select u.name, o.name,
       decode(bitand(t.property, 4194400), 0, ts.name, null),
```

Which of the following choices identifies a formatting command that can be used for displaying the rest of the output?

A. set long 9999

B. column text format a9999

C. set long 50

D. column text format a50

20. Your attempts to start the Oracle database have failed. After looking in the appropriate location, you ascertain the value for the CONTROL_FILES parameter to be set to /u01/oradata/orcl/control01.ctl. Which of the following choices identifies the likely next step you would take to troubleshoot the problem?

A. Verify the actual directory location of your control file.

B. Check the hardware to see if the memory card is defective.

    C. Verify the actual directory location of your SYSTEM datafile.

    D. Check to see if you have created two redo logs.

21. **Examine the following excerpt from an init.ora file:**

```
DB_CREATE_ONLINE_LOG_DEST_1 = /u01/oradata/db1
DB_CREATE_ONLINE_LOG_DEST_2 = /u02/oradata/db1
DB_CREATE_ONLINE_LOG_DEST_3 = /u03/oradata/db1
DB_CREATE_FILE_DEST = /u04/oradata/db1
```

Which of the following choices does *not* identify the location where Oracle will place you control file when the database gets created?

    A. /u01/oradata/db1

    B. /u02/oradata/db1

    C. /u03/oradata/db1

    D. /u04/oradata/db1

22. **You are using OMF in conjunction with management of your Oracle database control file. Which of the following choices identifies an aspect of control file management that Oracle handles regardless of whether OMF is used or not?**

    A. Placement of the control file in the appropriate directory

    B. Multiplexing control files to multiple destinations

    C. Updates to the contents of the control file when new tablespaces are added

    D. Assigning values automatically to the CONTROL_FILES parameter

23. **You are implementing control file multiplexing. Which of the following choices identifies the method you can use in order to generate the control file copies that Oracle will maintain?**

    A. Issue alter database backup controlfile to *filename*.

    B. Make a copy of the control file with the database shut down.

    C. Issue alter database backup controlfile to trace.

    D. Make a copy of the control file with the database still running.

24. **You are analyzing the redo log structure of your Oracle database. Which of the following choices identifies the name of the background process**

that writes changes from online redo logs to archived copies in support of a database running in ARCHIVELOG mode?

A. LGWR

B. CKPT

C. DBW0

D. ARC0

25. **You have implemented OMF for redo log management. Which of the following choices reflects a log filename that might be employed when OMF is enabled?**

A. `log01.log`

B. `logORCL01.log`

C. `1_2.log`

D. `ora_1_asdf1234.log`

26. **You issue the following statement on the Oracle database:**

```
create tablespace tbs_temp
datafile '/u05/oradata/oracle/tbs_temp01.dbf' size 600M
extent management dictionary online;
```

Which of the following choices correctly describes the tablespace you just created?

A. You created a locally managed temporary tablespace.

B. You created a dictionary-managed temporary tablespace.

C. You created a locally managed permanent tablespace.

D. You created a dictionary-managed permanent tablespace.

27. **You are creating tablespaces in Oracle. Which of the following keywords or clauses permits the datafiles of a tablespace to grow automatically in order to accommodate data growth?**

A. `default storage`

B. `extent management`

C. `autoextend`

D. `datafile`

28. You want to configure space allocation in temporary tablespaces. Which of the following choices identifies a feature in Oracle that, when implemented, will force the tablespace segment allocations to all be the same size regardless of storage allocations defined on objects placed in the tablespace?

    A. `default storage`

    B. `storage`

    C. `uniform extent management`

    D. `autoextend`

29. You are about to drop a tablespace. Which of the following statements can be used for dropping tablespaces that contain parent tables in foreign key relationships?

    A. `alter database datafile offline drop`

    B. `alter tablespace offline immediate`

    C. `drop tablespace cascade constraints`

    D. `drop tablespace including contents`

30. You alter a tablespace's `default storage` settings in the Oracle database to increase the size of initial extents. Which of the following choices identifies when the change will take effect for tables that already exist in that tablespace?

    A. The change takes effect immediately.

    B. The change takes effect when data is added to the table.

    C. The change takes effect when data is removed from the table.

    D. The change will not take effect for existing tables.

31. You are implementing OMF on your Oracle database. When OMF is enabled, Oracle manages creation and removal of datafiles from the host system for which of the following tablespaces?

    A. SYSTEM tablespace only

    B. UNDO tablespace only

    C. TEMP tablespace only

    D. All tablespaces in the database

32. Examine the following code block:

```
create database mydb
controlfile reuse
character set US7ASCII
national character set US7ASCII
datafile '/u01/oradata/mydb/mydb01.dbf' size 400M
logfile group 1 ('/u02/oradata/mydb/redo01.log') size 10M,
        group 2 ('/u03/oradata/mydb/redo02.log') size 10M
default temporary tablespace temp
  tempfile '/u04/oradata/mydb/temp01.dbf' size 1024M
undo tablespace undotbs
 datafile '/u05/oradata/mydb/undo01.dbf' size 1024M
noarchivelog;
```

Which of the following choices identifies a tablespace that will not be created by the command shown in the previous code block?

A. SYSTEM

B. UNDOTBS

C. DATA

D. TEMP

33. You create a locally managed tablespace with the following statement:

```
SQL> create tablespace DATA datafile
  2  'c:\oracle\oradata\orcl\DATA01.dbf'
  3  size 150M reuse
  4  extent management local
  5  uniform size 500K online;
Tablespace created.
```

After creating the tablespace, you create a table with the `initial` set to 100KB and `minextents` set to 3 in the `storage` clause. After the table is created, how much space will the table occupy in the tablespace?

A. 100KB

B. 300KB

C. 500KB

D. 1,500KB

34. **You want to create a locally managed tablespace for housing sort segments in Oracle. Which of the following statements would be appropriate for the purpose with respect to allocation of segments and extents?**

    A. `create temporary tablespace temp01 datafile '/u01/oradata/orcl/temp01.dbf' size 100M extent management local;`

    B. `create temporary tablespace temp01 tempfile '/u01/oradata/orcl/temp01.dbf' size 100M extent management local;`

    C. `create tablespace temp01 datafile '/u01/oradata/orcl/temp01.dbf' size 100M extent management local temporary;`

    D. `create tablespace temp01 tempfile '/u01/oradata/orcl/temp01.dbf' size 100M extent management local temporary;`

35. **You define a locally managed tablespace using the following syntax:**

    ```
    SQL> create tablespace DATA datafile
       2   'c:\oracle\oradata\orcl\DATA01.dbf'
       3   size 150M reuse
       4   extent management local online;
    Tablespace created.
    ```

    Which of the following choices indicates the `storage allocation` clause left out but implied by Oracle when this tablespace was created?

    A. `autoallocate`

    B. `autoallocate size 1M`

    C. `uniform`

    D. `uniform size 1M`

36. **A table was just created on your Oracle database with six extents allocated to it. Which of the following factors most likely caused the table to have so many extents allocated?**

    A. The value for `minextents` setting

    B. The value for `pctincrease` setting

    C. The value for `maxextents` setting

    D. By default, Oracle allocates six extents to all database objects.

37. **You want to determine the amount of space that has been allocated to the EMP table owned by SCOTT in Oracle, which is stored in tablespace DATA. Which of the following choices identifies the SQL statement you might use for this purpose?**

A. `select blocks from dba_tables where table_name 5 'EMP' and owner 5 'SCOTT';`

B. `select sum(bytes) from dba_free_space where tablespace_name 5 'DATA';`

C. `select sum(bytes) from dba_extents where segment_name 5 'EMP' and owner 5 'SCOTT';`

D. `select * from dba_objects where object_name 5 'EMP' and owner 5 'SCOTT';`

38. **You are administering the Oracle database. A user approaches you to inform you that he has just received the ORA-15555 error. Which of the following choices describes the reason this user has received the error?**

A. The user remained connected overnight, and his connection has timed out.

B. The user has queried a read-inconsistent view of data in the process of being changed by a long-running transaction.

C. The user's long-running transaction has taken so long that space for undo information has been exhausted.

D. The user's `drop table` command took too long, and the database needs time to quiesce.

39. **The Oracle database with undo tablespaces UNDO_TBS1 and UNDO_TBS2 was opened with undo management enabled for this database. In a prior session, the `alter system set undo_tablespace _ UNDO_TBS1` command was issued. However, the appropriate parameter instructing Oracle which undo tablespace to use was omitted from `init.ora`. Which of the following choices correctly describes what happens when the first user connecting to Oracle initiates her first transaction?**

A. The database will open, but only the system undo segment will be online.

B. The database will open, but no undo segments will be online.

C. The database will open and all undo segments in UNDO_TBS1 will be online.

D. Oracle will return errors and the database will not open.

40. The Oracle database with undo tablespaces UNDO_TBS1 and UNDO_TBS2 was opened with undo management enabled for this database. In a prior session, the `alter system set undo_tablespace _ UNDO_TBS1` command was issued. In the `init.ora` file, the UNDO_TABLESPACE parameter was set to UNDOTBS1. Which of the following choices correctly describes what happens when the first user connecting to Oracle initiates her first transaction?

A. The database will open, but only the system undo segment will be online.

B. The database will open, but no undo segments will be online.

C. The database will open and all undo segments in UNDO_TBS1 will be online.

D. Oracle will return errors and the database will not open.

41. You are attempting to manage undo segments manually while automatic undo management is enabled in your system. Which of the following choices identifies an appropriate method to configure Oracle to enable this situation to occur?

A. Set UNDO_MANAGEMENT to AUTO.

B. Set UNDO_SUPRESS_ERRORS to FALSE.

C. Set UNDO_MANAGEMENT to MANUAL.

D. Set UNDO_RETENTION to 1800.

42. The rows inside three Oracle tables supporting a customer order entry system are frequently accessed together by means of a table join. Because data is always being added to the tables, you leave a lot of extra space inside each block to accommodate growth. Which of the following types of tables would be useful for storing the data in this context?

A. Temporary table

B. Index-organized table

C. Cluster table

D. Standard Oracle table

43. Your DATA tablespace is locally managed and uses uniform extent allocation. You issue the following statement:

```
CREATE TABLE EMPLOYEE
(empid          NUMBER(10),
lastname        VARCHAR2(25),
firstname       VARCHAR2(25),
salary          NUMBER(10,4),
CONSTRAINT      pk_employee_01
PRIMARY KEY     (empid))
TABLESPACE data
PCTFREE    20  PCTUSED    50
INITRANS   1   MAXTRANS   255
NOCACHE        LOGGING
STORAGE ( INITIAL 100K  NEXT  150K
          MINEXTENTS 4  MAXEXTENTS  300
          PCTINCREASE 20 );
```

Which of the following statements is true about the table you just created?

A. The table is created in the same tablespace as temporary segments will be housed.

B. The first segment allocated for this table will be 100KB of contiguous blocks.

C. Redo information will be generated for the creation of this table.

D. When full table scans are issued on the EMPLOYEE table, blocks from the table will persist in the buffer cache for a long time after the statement executes.

44. User FITZPATRICK creates a temporary table using the following statement:

```
SQL> create global temporary table FITZTEMPTAB
  2  (name varchar2(10), value number, use_date date)
  3  on commit delete rows;
Table created
```

FITZPATRICK then informs users MCGILLICUDDY and OBRYAN of his temporary table. While each user is connected to Oracle and populating table FITZTEMPTAB, OBRYAN issues truncate table FITZTEMPTAB. Which of the following users had his or her records removed temporary table by this action?

A. FITZPATRICK only

B. OBRYAN only

C. OBRYAN and FITZPATRICK only

D. OBRYAN, FITZPATRICK and MCGILLICUDDY

45. User OBRYAN adds a record to FITZTEMPTAB, defined using the code block shown in the previous question. At what point will the data added to FITZTEMPTAB by OBRYAN be removed from the temporary table?

A. When FITZPATRICK commits the transaction

B. When OBRYAN commits the transaction

C. When OBRYAN logs off of Oracle

D. When FITZPATRICK issues truncate table FITZTEMPTAB

46. You just issued the following statement: alter table sales drop column profit. Which of the following choices identifies when the column will actually be removed from Oracle?

A. Immediately following statement execution

B. After the alter table drop unused columns command is issued

C. After the alter table set unused column command is issued

D. After the alter table modify command is issued

47. You wish to determine how many columns in the EMPLOYEE table are marked unused for later removal. Which of the following methods would be appropriate for the purpose?

A. Querying the DBA_TABLES view

B. Using the describe command

C. Querying the DBA_UNUSED_COLS view

D. Querying the DBA_UNUSED_COL_TABS view

48. You want to rebuild an index in Oracle. Which of the following choices identifies the reason why rebuilding indexes online is possible in Oracle?

A. Less restrictive locks on underlying base tables

B. More restrictive locks on the index rebuilt

C. Use of a standby database for temporary storage

D. Use of a temporary table for temporary storage

49. **You terminate monitoring the MY_IDX index after monitoring its use for several hours. Which of the following statements is correct regarding V$OBJECT_USAGE in this context?**

    A. Oracle removes the record corresponding to MY_IDX from V$OBJECT_USAGE.

    B. Oracle fills in the END_MONITORING column in the record corresponding to MY_IDX in the V$OBJECT_USAGE view.

    C. Oracle fills in the USED column in the record corresponding to MY_IDX in the V$OBJECT_USAGE view.

    D. Oracle clears all values in the record corresponding to MY_IDX in the V$OBJECT_USAGE view.

50. **You implement an integrity constraint in an Oracle database using the following command:** `alter table EMP add constraint PK_EMP_01 primary key (EMPNO)`. **Which of the following statements is true about the constraint you just added?**

    A. The constraint will cause Oracle to generate a bitmap index to support its activities.

    B. The constraint will reference back to the primary key in another table for valid values.

    C. The constraint will not be created unless all values in the EMPNO column are unique and not NULL.

    D. The constraint will enforce uniqueness, but NULL values will be permitted.

51. **The following tablespace information was taken from your Oracle database:**

```
SQL> select tablespace_name, contents from dba_tablespaces;
TABLESPACE_NAME     CONTENTS
------------------  ------------
SYSTEM              PERMANENT
DATA                PERMANENT
INDEXES             PERMANENT
UNDOTBS             UNDO
TEMP                TEMPORARY
USERS               PERMANENT
```

You create a user in this database with the following command: `create user serena identified by tranquill`. **Which of the following**

choices identifies the location where Oracle will place SERENAs new table that she creates with the `create table mytab (coll number primary key)` command?

A. SYSTEM

B. DATA

C. TEMP

D. UNDOTBS

52. You issue the following command in Oracle: `alter user JOSEPHINE default tablespace SYSTEM quota 0 on SYSTEM`. Assuming JOSEPHINE has the appropriate privileges to do so, which of the following commands will JOSEPHINE not be able to issue as a result of this action?

A. `create table mytab (coll number primary key);`

B. `create procedure myproc begin null; end;`

C. `create function myfunc return null begin null; end;`

D. `create table mytab2 (coll number primary key) tablespace data;`

53. You issue the following command in Oracle, and Oracle responds by providing the following information:

```
SQL> select * from dba_users where username = 'SYS';
USERNAME                             USER_ID PASSWORD
------------------ ----------------------------- ----------------
ACCOUNT_STATUS     LOCK_DATE                     EXPIRY_DATE
------------------ ----------------------------- ----------------
DEFAULT_TABLESPACE TEMPORARY_TABLESPACE          CREATED
------------------ ----------------------------- ----------------
PROFILE            INITIAL_RSRC_CONSUMER_GROUP   EXTERNAL_NAME
------------------ ----------------------------- ----------------
SYS                                            0 D4C5016086B2DC6A
OPEN
SYSTEM             TEMP                          06-JUN-01
DEFAULT            SYS_GROUP
```

Which of the following statements is true regarding the user information shown previously?

A. No user may log into Oracle as SYS.

B. If SYS creates a table without specifying a `tablespace` clause, the table will be placed into the TEMP tablespace.

C. The password for the SYS user on this database is D4C5016086B2DC6A.

D. If SYS performs a disk sort, the temporary segments will be placed in the TEMP tablespace.

54. **You want to use composite resource limits in the Oracle database. Which of the following commands must be issued so that composite resources are assigned a value for composite limits?**

A. `alter system`

B. `alter resource cost`

C. `alter profile`

D. `alter user`

55. **You are defining resource limits for use with profiles. Which of the following is not a resource limit that can be set in conjunction with composite limits on your Oracle database?**

A. IDLE_TIME

B. CPU_PER_SESSION

C. PRIVATE_SGA

D. CONNECT_TIME

56. **You create a profile using the following command:**

```
CREATE PROFILE myprofile LIMIT
SESSIONS_PER_USER 1
CPU_PER_CALL 20
CONNECT_TIME 240
IDLE_TIME 20
PRIVATE_SGA 1024;
```

Which of the following choices best identifies how Oracle will determine what the value for the CPU_PER_SESSION limit will be?

A. Oracle uses the same value as CPU_PER_CALL from this `create profile` command.

B. Oracle uses the value for CPU_PER_SESSION from the SYS_PROFILE profile.

C. Oracle uses the value for CPU_PER_SESSION from the DEFAULT profile.

D. Oracle sets CPU_PER_SESSION to unlimited.

57. You create a profile using the following code block:

```
CREATE PROFILE tmp_profile LIMIT
   FAILED_LOGIN_ATTEMPTS 3
   PASSWORD_LOCK_TIME unlimited
   PASSWORD_LIFE_TIME 30
   PASSWORD_REUSE_TIME 180
   PASSWORD_VERIFY_FUNCTION my_pwver
   PASSWORD_GRACE_TIME 5;
```

Which of the following choices identifies a true statement about the profile you just created?

A. After three failed login attempts, a user assigned this profile will have to wait three days before trying to login to Oracle again.

B. After 180 days, a user assigned this profile can reuse his or her password.

C. A user assigned this profile must change his or her password every 30 minutes.

D. A user has up to five minutes to specify a password the first time he or she logs in before Oracle automatically locks the account.

58. You want to set up password management features in your Oracle database such that users may never reuse a password and that a user has three days to change his or her default password the first time he or she logs into Oracle before the account gets locked. Which of the following choices identifies the statement you will use for this purpose?

A. `alter profile default limit failed_login_attempts 3 password_reuse_time unlimited;`

B. `alter profile default limit password_grace_time 3 password_reuse_limit unlimited;`

C. `alter profile default limit failed_login_attempts 3 password_grace_time unlimited;`

D. `alter profile default limit password_reuse_time 3 failed_login_attempts unlimited;`

59. You are attempting to determine which profiles have resource settings that do not impose limits on user resource utilization. Which of the following queries would be the most useful for this purpose?

A. `select profile from dba_profiles where profile = (select username from dba_users where profile = 'UNLIMITED');`

B. `select profile from dba_profiles where limit = (select unit_cost from resource_cost where resource_name = 'CPU_PER_SESSION');`

C. `select profile from dba_profiles where limit = 'UNLIMITED';`

D. `select distinct profile from dba_profiles where limit = 'UNLIMITED';`

60. You grant the SYSDBA privilege to a user of the Oracle database. Which of the following abilities does this privilege bestow upon its grantee?

A. Ability to query all tables in Oracle

B. Ability to grant the SYSDBA privilege to others

C. Ability to back up the database

D. Ability to delete information from any table in Oracle

Answers to Practice Exam I

I. D. ARCH and LGWR

Explanation The ARCH and LGWR processes may have a tendency to conflict with one another when log switches occur because both processes will attempt to access the same disk resources at the same time during this operation. Choice A is incorrect because SMON handles instance recovery and tablespace coalescence, while LGWR writes redo information from memory to disk. These two processes should not conflict because datafiles and redo log files won't usually be on the same disk, and there is little overlap between the two functions. Choice B is incorrect because the RECO process handles transaction recovery between distributed systems and will not usually interfere with ARCH's archiving of redo logs. Choice C is incorrect because PMON handles process recovery when user processes fail while DBWR handles writing dirty buffers to disk—two functions that normally will not cause I/O or other types of contention. **(Topic 7.3)**

2. B. Control file

Explanation Creating a new redo log on your Oracle database adds information to the control file. The shared pool is incorrect because information is added to that resource when SQL or PL/SQL statements are issued by users against Oracle. The SGA is a superset of the shared pool making it wrong as well. A Program Global Area (PGA) is a memory region containing data and control information for a single process. **(Topic 6.1)**

3. A. SYSTEM

Explanation Using standard tablespace naming conventions, the SYSTEM tablespace contains all Oracle data dictionary objects. TEMP is incorrect because it identifies the temporary tablespace, which is designed to hold temporary segments for disk sorts. RBS is also incorrect because that tablespace is designed to store undo segments. Finally, the INDEX tablespace is incorrect because that nomenclature is used to identify the tablespace that holds indexes. **(Topic 5.1)**

4. B. SYS

Explanation Objects in the Oracle data dictionary are part of the SYS schema. Although the SYSTEM user owns some important database objects, the dictionary views and their underlying tables are not one of them, making that choice incorrect. The PUBLIC user is more of an alias for granting access for various things to many users, not so much a user in and of itself, thus making that choice incorrect as well. Finally, user SCOTT is commonly found in training Oracle databases, but its existence is by no means guaranteed—nor will it ever own objects as critical as the data dictionary. **(Topic 5.1)**

5. C.   Profiles

Explanation   Profiles are appropriately used for the purpose of limiting a user's ability to manipulate host machine resources, making it the correct answer. Undo segments provide transaction-level read consistency, but do not limit usage of the host machine in any substantial way, making this choice incorrect. Roles limit the user's ability to perform actions based on the privileges granted to those roles, but because the user may need a certain type of access and may be able to properly handle that access using appropriate methods, this choice is incorrect because you have no accurate way to limit resource usage using roles. Finally, parameter files such as `init.ora` may contain settings that limit resource usage, perhaps through limiting the number of users that may connect at any one time, but this answer is incorrect because `init.ora` parameters will do little to restrict a user's misuse of host machine resources once connected. **(Topic 14.3)**

6. B.   Increase `pctfree`

Explanation   Actually, although `pctfree` isn't the complete solution, it will reduce chaining for future records added to the table. `pctused` is not a component in the solution because that parameter simply reduces the frequency a data block will spend on a freelist. Changing the value set for `pctincrease` or `next` may decrease the number of extents a table will allocate if that table is growing fast, but this parametric change does little to nothing about chaining at the block level, making both those answers incomplete and incorrect. **(Topic 9.3)**

7. A.   Multiplexing

Explanation   The term *multiplexing* is the correct answer because that term refers to having online copies (as opposed to archives) of redo logs. These logs are then spread across several disks to reduce I/O bottlenecks. Archiving is incorrect because this choice means that the copy of the redo log information made will not be available online. Neither redoing nor logging accurately describes what the question asks for. **(Topic 7.4)**

8. D.   Granting privileges to roles directly

Explanation   The choice mentioning the use of roles is the correct answer. You would first grant the privileges to roles, and then give the roles to users. Profiles are not used for granting or revoking privileges or access; they are used instead for limiting host machine processing, making those two choices incorrect. Also, granting privileges directly to users is the support nightmare you are trying to avoid. **(Topic 17.1)**

9. B.   Number of datafiles

Explanation   The size of redo logs can have an effect on checkpoint intervals, because larger redo logs usually mean less frequent log switches. Fewer log switches mean fewer checkpoints. The number of datafiles will affect the duration of a checkpoint, because although the CKPT process has to write checkpoint sequence information to each datafile header (and more datafiles means more headers), this is not a time-consuming activity and happens in parallel with other activities occurring during a checkpoint. Finally, the two init.ora parameters identified in this question have a direct correlation on the frequency of checkpoints. **(Topic 7.3)**

10. B.   High `pctused`

Explanation   A high setting for `pctused` will make Oracle fill data blocks with new records when comparatively fewer records are deleted from the block. In contrast, a low setting for `pctused` causes Oracle to fill data blocks only after many records have been deleted from the block. `pctused` identifies the threshold for Oracle to return a block to a freelist for addition of new records. Lowering `pctused` will make Oracle manage its block space utilization less actively, whereas `pctfree` simply indicates how much space should be left over for updates that make records grow. **(Topic 9.3)**

11. C.   Issue `alter user SPANKY PROFILE LIMITER`, where `LIMITER` is a profile.

Explanation   The correct method for limiting Oracle's use of the host machine on SPANKY's behalf is with a profile, not a role, eliminating half the choices right there. The next aspect to consider is how to properly assign a profile to a user. This is accomplished with an `alter user` statement, not a `grant`, making the choice indicating a `grant` statement where `LIMITER` is a profile incorrect. **(Topic 14.3)**

12. D.   Hash clusters

Explanation   Range operations do not perform well when the data is stored in a cluster. Though it is more efficient in general to use comparison operations instead of range operations, normal tables will work fine with range operations, making that choice incorrect. Indexes can process range operations just fine as well, making that choice incorrect. So can index-organized tables, which makes that choice incorrect. **(Topic 12.1)**

13. B.   `restricted session`

Explanation   The DBA needs the `restricted session` privilege to make the database open but not available for users. The DBA could simply revoke the `create session` privilege from all users and simply leave the database open, but this task may require issuing several `revoke` commands, followed by the same number of grants later. It's easier to use restricted session. The CONNECT role is similar to create session in that create session is granted to CONNECT, which is then often granted to users. There is no such thing as a mount privilege. **(Topic 16.1)**

14. A.   drop table

Explanation   You cannot alter or resize the initial extent on your table using the alter table command, making that choice incorrect. Nor can you use the resize or coalesce keywords, as these are used as part of tablespace operations. Your only alternative is to drop and re-create the table using different storage settings. **(Topic 11.2)**

15. B.   temporary tablespace

Explanation   By assigning a temporary tablespace other than SYSTEM, the DBA reduces the possibility that a user will interfere with the overall operation of the Oracle database when disk sorts are performed by users. The identified by clause is incorrect because that is where the password is assigned, not disk usage. The default tablespace is also incorrect even though that clause is used to define disk usage because the disk usage is for creating permanent objects, not temporary ones. Finally, the default role clause is only available in alter user statements, not create user statements, and is used to change the permissions available to the user. **(Topic 15.1)**

16. E.   Nothing—SYSDBA privileges are not required for these actions.

Explanation   The correct answer is nothing. Because the DBA does not plan to use remote administration for startup, shutdown, backup, or recovery, there is no need for a password file. Instead, the DBA can simply connect in normal mode using the SYS or other privileged account to create and administer users and tablespaces. **(Topic 2.4)**

17. A.   DBW0

Explanation   DBWR, although affected by the transaction logging mechanism— particularly during log switches and checkpoints—is not an actual part of Oracle's transaction logging mechanism. The redo log buffer, LGWR, CKPT, and archive/online redo logs are all part of the operation of Oracle's transaction logging mechanism. **(Topic 7.1)**

18. E.   The storage clause is improperly defined.

Explanation   The correct answer to this question is that the storage clause is improperly defined. Instead of simply naming the different storage parameters loose in the statement, you must bundle them into a storage clause, which is denoted with the `storage` keyword and set inside parentheses. The primary key is declared properly, so there are no problems on that end. You never need to put index and table data in the same tablespace, and in fact there are compelling reasons not to do so, making that choice wrong as well. Finally, you do not need to define a separate not NULL constraint on the EMPID column because the primary-key index will handle it for you. For reasons of a malformed `storage` clause, the `create table` `statement` will not succeed, making that choice incorrect as well. **(Topic 11.1)**

19. C. SIMON will not be able to add records to the EMP table anymore.

Explanation When object privileges given `with grant option` are revoked from a user who has given them to other users, Oracle cascades the revocation. So, not only will ANN lose the ability to add records to EMP (making the choice stating she can continue to add records to EMP incorrect), but SIMON loses the ability as well, making that the correct answer. The DBA does not lose the ability to add records to EMP, because she is the person revoking privileges. ANN's records will stay in the EMP table, even though she cannot add new ones either, making that choice incorrect as well. **(Topic 16.2)**

20. B. `pctused = 40`, `pctfree = 30`

Explanation The choice where `pctused` is 99 and `pctfree` is 1 should be discarded immediately because you should never set the space allocation options in a way that the two equal 100 added together. Because rows are never removed, you can set `pctused` relatively low. This leaves you with the two choices where `pctused` is 40. Next, consider row growth. The rows in this table are going to grow substantially, which means you need a higher `pctfree` than just 10 percent. Remember, the largest columns are going to be NULL on initial insert and then populated later. To avoid row migration, you are best off choosing `pctused = 40`, `pctfree = 30`. **(Topic 9.3)**

21. A. OPTIMAL

Explanation The OPTIMAL `storage` clause is used primarily for storing undo segments in Oracle. You do not use it for any other database object. All the rest, namely INITIAL, PCTINCREASE, and NEXT, are valid for use. Be aware that you do not have to configure this aspect of undo segments if you use automatic undo management in Oracle. **(Topic 10.3)**

22. D. `default role`

Explanation You do not use the `default role` clause in `create user` statements. It is part of the `alter user` syntax because when a user is created, the user doesn't have any roles granted to it yet. `identified by` is for password definition, and is part of the `create user` statement. `temporary tablespace` keeps the user's disk sorts out of the SYSTEM tablespace and is part of the create user statement. profile, account unlock, and password expire are all aspects of a robust create user statement, and therefore all these choices are incorrect. **(Topic 17.2)**

23. A.   Run pupbld.sql as SYSTEM.

Explanation   In this situation, Oracle needs user profile information to be generated for the users. In the error output for this message, Oracle will instruct you abort what is needed to resolve the issue, which is to run pupbld.sql to build the product user profile information. You do not need to shut down the database with the abort option—moreover, you shouldn't, because that will require a database recovery. Dropping and re-creating the users will not help either—they will get the same error ten minutes later when they try logging on again. Finally, you shouldn't waste your time dropping and re-creating the database. **(Topic 4.3)**

24. D.   SMON

Explanation   SMON coalesces free space in a tablespace on a regular basis, as well as manages instance recovery after instance failure. You will learn more about instance recovery in Practice Exam 3. LGWR is wrong because that process simply handles writing log information from memory to disk. ARCH handles copying online redo logs to archive destinations and is also wrong. DBWR is incorrect because it only performs writes of data blocks from buffer cache to disk, and PMON is wrong because it handles process recovery—something you will cover on the OCP DBA Fundamentals II exam. **(Topic 8.1)**

25. C.   One tablespace can have many datafiles.

Explanation   A tablespace is a collection of one or more datafiles residing on your host machine that Oracle treats as one logical area for storing data. This fact eliminates the choice that says one tablespace has only one datafile. Also, the two other choices basically state the same thing—that one datafile can contain many tablespaces—and this is just not true. **(Topic 8.1)**

26. B.   Increase value on CPU_PER_SESSION and decrease value on CONNECT_TIME.

Explanation   The correct answer is increase value on CPU_PER_SESSION, and decrease value on CONNECT_TIME. This makes resource costs for CPU time higher, and connection time lower. The COMPOSITE_LIMIT increase is too imprecise— remember, one of the resource costs is increasing, while the other is decreasing. Increasing COMPOSITE_LIMIT will only increase a user's ability to use host system resources. PRIVATE_SGA has nothing to do with CPU time or connection time, and therefore is incorrect. **(Topic 14.2)**

27. C.   An uncommitted transaction is still in progress.

Explanation   The first thing to look at in this situation is the tablespace name: UNDOTBS01. Oracle recommends having different tablespaces for different purposes. A tablespace containing the string *RBS* or *UNDOTBS* will most likely contain undo segments. In addition, if one of the undo segments is online and in use (indicated by a session having a lock on it), you will get the ORA-01546 error when you try to take the tablespace offline. A tablespace containing overextended tables can be taken offline, so that answer is incorrect. The init.ora file being unavailable has no impact on taking a tablespace offline, but it might interfere with restarting your Oracle database. Although in some situations you might see performance degradation because of an online redo log being archived, this will not interfere with taking a tablespace offline. **(Topic 10.2)**

28. A.   Library cache

Explanation   The library cache, sometimes referred to as the shared SQL area, stores parse and execution plan information for SQL and PL/SQL statements running on your database. The row and dictionary caches are one in the same and store data dictionary information for quick retrieval, and thus are incorrect. The large pool allocation heap is used in multithreaded server (MTS) systems for session memory, by parallel execution for message buffers, and by backup processes for disk I/O buffers. Finally, the buffer cache stores data blocks for quicker retrieval by server processes, and is also incorrect. **(Topic 1.1)**

29. C.   When the shared pool is flushed

Explanation   The data in the buffer cache will not be saved to disk when you flush the shared pool. You flush the shared pool with the `alter system flush shared_pool` command. Items in the buffer cache are saved to disk when a timeout occurs and when a checkpoint occurs. Because a checkpoint happens at every log switch, buffer cache information is saved to disk when a log switch occurs, too. **(Topic 7.3)**

30. B.   Run `utlpwmg.sql`.

Explanation   Running `utlpwmg.sql` is a step you accomplish for setting up password management on your Oracle database. Unlike other areas of resource limitation, you do not need to set the RESOURCE_LIMIT parameter to TRUE, making that choice incorrect. You should also not drop the DEFAULT profile beforehand. Creating a password verification function is optional, because Oracle provides you with one in the software release. **(Topic 14.1)**

31. A.   Looking in the DBA_TS_QUOTAS dictionary view

Explanation   The DBA_TS_QUOTAS view contains quota information for users and tablespaces. This is the DBA's best bet in identifying what ATHENA's limits are and how they could be set differently. DBA_USERS only identifies default and temporary tablespaces for ATHENA, which isn't useful because the create table statement identifies its own tablespace storage. DBA_TAB_COLUMNS won't even have information about this table or anything related to tablespace quotas, because it lists the columns in every table on the database. The DBA_TABLESPACES choice is a good distractor. To avoid choosing the wrong answer, you need to be sure you are familiar with the use of dictionary views like this one. **(Topic 15.3)**

32. A.   DEFAULT

Explanation   All users are assigned the DEFAULT profile if none is identified in the create user statement. CONNECT and RESOURCE are both roles, so those choices are incorrect. Although there is no profile clause in this statement, it would be incorrect to assume that no profile gets assigned to the user because of it. **(Topic 15.1)**

33. B.   DBA_PROFILES

Explanation   DBA_PROFILES is the dictionary view where you can find information about profiles and the resource settings associated with them. The DBA_USERS view is incorrect because it only identifies what profile is assigned to a user. RESOURCE_COST is incorrect because it only identifies the relative cost assigned to those resources that can be lumped together using resource costing. RESOURCE_LIMIT is incorrect because it is not a view—it is an initialization parameter that must be set in order to use profiles. **(Topic 14.4)**

34. A.   catproc.sql

Explanation   The catproc.sql script must be run after running catalog.sql to create your Oracle-supplied packages. utlpwdmg.sql is a script you run later to add password management, whereas utllockt.sql is a script you also run later to detect whether there are lock-wait events on your database. **(Topic 4.3)**

35. D.   Roles

Explanation   Roles permit you to configure password authentication to limit the use of the privileges they bestow. This is accomplished with the identified by clause—the same as in the create or alter user statements. Profiles don't require passwords, nor do tables or undo segments, unless you count the password you supplied to log in to the database. **(Topic 17.2)**

36. C.   Create multiple members for each of your four groups and place them on different disks.

Explanation   To solve this problem, you must create multiple members for each of your four groups and place them on different disks. The init.ora file has nothing whatsoever to do with multiplexing online redo logs, so you can eliminate those choices. Finally, although adding groups improves some situations, you are not looking for more redo logs—you are looking for more members in each log. **(Topic 7.4)**

37. A.   EXCEPTIONS

Explanation   The EXCEPTIONS table can be used by the DBA to identify ROWIDs for rows with duplicate primary keys. The DBA_TABLES view is not going to help, because you don't need to know the table, tablespace, or storage information to enable or fix a primary key. USER_TAB_COLUMNS is also of limited value. Finally, AUD$ is no good because that's where audit records are stored. You might be able to find the folks who did it, but that isn't going to solve the problem. **(Topic 13.1)**

38. C.   Grant the CONNECT role to the user.

Explanation   The appropriate resolution is to somehow enable the user to create a session with Oracle. This is done in two ways: either by granting create session privileges or by granting the CONNECT role, which has the create session privilege granted to it. Unlocking the user's account won't help because he or she hasn't even gotten to the point where they can successfully connect yet, while resetting the user's password and granting create table privileges are both incorrect for roughly the same reason. **(Topic 17.5)**

39. C.   Convert your B-tree index to a reverse-key index.

Explanation   Oracle recommends using reverse-key indexes in situations where the leading significant figures of a number or characters in a string are not unique enough to provide the lead-in differentiation required for making an index perform better. If the reverse-key index choices had not been present, the B-tree index choices would have been more correct—making for strong distractors. Any conversion between bitmap and B-tree indexes is unnecessary and detrimental because bitmap and B-tree indexes improve query performance in exactly opposite situations. **(Topic 12.3)**

40. D.   CHAR

Explanation   The CHAR datatype is the most appropriate for this given situation because you want to store data in a fixed-width column. That means the column will contain extra blanks to the full, declared size of the column. VARCHAR, CLOB, and LONG do not let you do this, because they are variable-width column datatypes. Also, ten sentences of text are probably not more than 2,000 characters, the limit for CHAR datatypes in Oracle8. **(Topic 11.2)**

   41. B.   Unsuccessful `update` and `delete` statements performed by any user on CAT_TOYS will be recorded.

Explanation   The correct answer is unsuccessful `update` and `delete` statements performed by any user on CAT_TOYS will be recorded. Auditing data change activities `by access` causes Oracle to write one record for each audited statement; in comparison to this, `by session` causes Oracle to write a single record for all SQL statements of the same type issued in the same session. The `whenever not successful` clause means only unsuccessful statements will be recorded. Finally, only the CAT_TOYS table will be audited. **(Topic 16.3)**

   42. A.   DBA_IND_COLUMNS

Explanation   You would look in the DBA_IND_COLUMNS to see what the column order for the primary-key index was. The DBA_TAB_COLUMNS will only tell you what columns are in the table. The DBA_INDEXES table will give you structural information about the index, but not its contents. The DBA_CLU_COLUMNS view will only obtain information about clustered columns. **(Topic 12.5)**

   43. D.   Nothing—you cannot drop a profile that has been granted to users.

Explanation   The correct answer is nothing. You cannot drop a profile that has been granted to users without specifying the `cascade` option. That option is missing from the statement you issued, so nothing happens. Had you included the `cascade` option, users who had the LTD_PROGRAMMER profile might now have the DEFAULT profile, so watch out for distractors like that one. Otherwise, all other statements are incorrect. **(Topic 14.2)**

   44. B.   Increasing the value set for `pctused` on the table

Explanation   You can increase the values set for `pctincrease` and `next` using the `alter table` statement to reduce the number of extents a segment will allocate as part of table growth. If you wanted, you could reorganize the table using EXPORT with the COMPRESS option. However, you couldn't use `pctused` to perform this task. **(Topic 9.3)**

   45. D.   SYSTEM segments

Explanation   SYSTEM object segments typically have the lowest turnover of all database segments in Oracle. This is because SYSTEM tables are never dropped and re-created, or truncated (AUD$ table notwithstanding). Undo segments frequently allocate and deallocate extents, as do temporary segments. User-defined tables usually have more volatility than SYSTEM-owned objects. **(Topic 9.5)**

46. D. `shutdown normal`

Explanation You most likely used the `shutdown normal` option to turn off the Oracle database. `shutdown normal` will not end existing sessions; instead, it will wait for users to finish their work and disconnect, but it will not allow others to log in after the `shutdown` command is issued. `shutdown immediate` would have forced user transactions to roll back and disconnected them at the time the statement was issued, whereas `shutdown abort` would simply end database operation, terminating all uncommitted transactions in progress. `shutdown transactional` is a new option that enables users already connected to complete their current transaction, but after that disconnects them in order to speed database shutdown. **(Topic 3.3)**

47. C. The server process obtains information for the user.

Explanation Information is obtained for user processes by means of the server process. DBW0 is incorrect because that process writes data to disk, not from disk into memory. The user process certainly doesn't do this work on its own, and the listener process doesn't actually obtain data from disk for the user either. **(Topic 1.2)**

48. C. The `drop tablespace` command fails because you didn't include the `including contents` option.

Explanation In this situation, the `drop tablespace` command fails because you didn't include the `including contents` option. To drop the tablespace, you must issue `drop tablespace by_tblspc including contents`. There may be some problem with `cascading constraints`, but you don't have enough information to declare this the correct answer, so it's wrong. Obviously, the `drop tablespace` command does not succeed. Finally, you must certainly drop a tablespace after creating it. **(Topic 8.5)**

49. C. SQL*Plus returns an error saying you need to connect to Oracle first.

Explanation After starting SQL*Plus and before you start doing anything substantial with it, you must connect to Oracle as a privileged user. If you don't connect as a privileged user but try performing privileged activities anyway, SQL*Plus returns errors. The database will not shut down until after you issue `shutdown immediate` while connected to Oracle, but once issued, Oracle will disconnect users forcibly and also roll back their transactions. Finally, SQL*Plus most certainly is a command-line mode tool. **(Topic 2.1)**

50. A.   Issue `select * from DBA_PARAMETERS;` from SQL*Plus.

Explanation   The `select * from DBA_PARAMETERS` statement yields nothing because DBA_PARAMETERS is not a valid dictionary view in Oracle. The V$PARAMETER view is appropriate for this purpose, as is the `show parameters` command in SQL*Plus. Finally, Instance Manager will show you initialization parameters in a GUI display. **(Topic 3.1)**

51. B.   Bitmap indexes cannot be unique.

Explanation   When you issue this statement, Oracle will give you a syntax error, stating it was looking for the `index` keyword after unique instead of the `bitmap` keyword. Thus, you cannot create bitmap indexes as unique indexes. You certainly can use the `nosort`, `tablespace`, and `asc` keywords in this statement, and in this statement they are all used correctly. However, the `unique bitmap` bit makes it invalid, and Oracle will give you an error. **(Topic 12.2)**

52. D.   ROLE_ROLE_PRIVS

Explanation   ROLE_ROLE_PRIVS is the correct answer because it displays all the roles and the roles granted to the roles. DBA_ROLE_PRIVS shows only users who have roles granted to them. DBA_TAB_PRIVS shows the users with object privileges granted to them. The USER_SYS_PRIVS view shows only those system privileges granted to you, the user connected to Oracle. **(Topic 17.5)**

53. A.   `alter session set NLS_DATE_FORMAT = 'DD-MON-YYYY:HH:MIAM';`

Explanation   Because all the statements are roughly the same, you must look carefully at the syntax in order to know what the correct answer is. The proper date format is 'DD-MON-YYYY:HH:MIAM', which obtains you the result 10-FEB-1999:10:15AM. DD-MON-YY:HH24:MI gives you a result of 10-FEB-99:10:15, so it is incorrect, while DD-MON-YY:HH:MIAM gives you 10-FEB-99:10:15AM, which is also incorrect. Finally, DD-MON-YYYY:HH24:MI gives you a result of 10-MON-1999:10:15, which is still incorrect. **(Topic 18.2)**

54. D.   Value-based auditing

Explanation   Value-based auditing best describes this situation. Statement auditing is not right because you don't want to audit every statement—only those that change a particular column to a particular value. Triggers will work best for this situation. You don't want to audit every access on the ORDERS table either, so object auditing is out. Finally, many different users might have the ability to change order status in several different phases of the order entry and shipment process, so audit by access isn't necessarily appropriate. Value-based auditing is auditing done by triggers or programmatically to detect when specific values change to specific other values. **(Topic 16.3)**

55. B. index

Explanation Of the privileges mentioned, only the index privilege is an object privilege. The rest are system privileges. One way to ensure that you understand the difference between system and object privileges is to remember that object privileges give access to objects, whereas system privileges let you create objects. In this case, however, even this basic principle of Oracle privileges is violated in concept because even though the index privilege lets you create indexes off of tables, it is still an object privilege. Thus, the best way to distinguish object privileges from system privileges is simply to memorize the object privileges (there are less than a dozen of them) and simply assume everything else is a system privilege. **(Topic 16.1)**

56. C. SORT_AREA_SIZE

Explanation Your INITIAL default storage setting for the temporary tablespace should be some multiple of SORT_AREA_SIZE because this ensures a relationship between the area in memory used for sorts and the utilization of disk space for that purpose when you run out of space in memory. LOG_BUFFER is the size of the redo log buffer and has little to do with disk sorts. DB_BLOCK_BUFFERS is the number of buffers that constitutes the buffer cache, and again there is little relationship between the buffer cache and disk sorts. Finally, SHARED_POOL_SIZE is exactly that—the size of the shared pool—which, again, has little to do with disk sorts. **(Topic 8.6)**

57. B. Cached data is saved immediately to disk.

Explanation Oracle divorces transaction activity from disk I/O by having a database writer process handle writing changes to disk. This activity doesn't necessarily happen immediately, and completion of the commit doesn't depend on it happening. All the other activities, such as releasing locks on tables, rows, or undo segments, do happen, however, and a commit statement generates a redo entry. **(Topic 1.1)**

58. D. When the statement is executed

Explanation Data changes are made at the time Oracle actually executes the statement. Opening and parsing the statement all occur before the statement is executed, so the data change hasn't occurred yet. update statements do not have data to fetch from a cursor the way `select` statements do, so there is no `fetch` activity in a DML statement like an `update`. **(Topic 1.1)**

59. D.   Sequence segment

Explanation_Sequences are not physically stored in a tablespace as database objects. Rather, their definition is stored in the data dictionary and in memory, and called upon when values from the sequence are required. All the other choices identify valid types of segments in Oracle. **(Topic 9.2)**

60. B.   DBA_FREE_SPACE

Explanation   If you only wanted to know how much of a particular tablespace was free, you would use the DBA_FREE_SPACE view. DBA_TABLESPACES AND DBA_EXTENTS will tell you the total allocation for the tablespace and the total amount of space allocated for objects in that tablespace, respectively, and although you could calculate the free space from those two amounts, it is far easier to select the appropriate value from DBA_FREE_SPACE. V$TABLESPACE will only give you the tablespace name and number for the tablespace on the database. **(Topic 9.4)**

Answers to Practice Exam 2

1. A.   V$CONTROLFILE_RECORD_SECTION

Explanation   Information about the name and location of your control files can be found in the two database views V$CONTROLFILE and V$PARAMETER, and in the `init.ora` file. However, the V$CONTROLFILE_RECORD_SECTION will not tell you your control file locations. **(Topic 6.2)**

2. C.   Oracle will leave more space free in data blocks for existing records.

Explanation   By keeping `pctfree` high, Oracle will leave more space free in database blocks for existing records to grow via later `updates`. `pctused` is the storage option that dictates how Oracle manages filling data blocks on tables more or less actively, so those choices should be easily eliminated. **(Topic 9.3)**

3. C.   The statement fails.

Explanation   The `alter table` statement will fail because you cannot have more than one column in an Oracle table with a LONG datatype. You can, however, have multiple LOB type columns in the same table in Oracle8 and Oracle. Oracle is not programmed to create the LONG column for you using a different datatype. **(Topic 11.1)**

4. D.   Users to which ANN granted `insert` privileges will not be able to insert.

Explanation_Though it doesn't say whether or not ANN had the `grant option` on this object privilege, the choice stating that users to which ANN granted `insert` privileges will not be able to `insert` is the only thing that truly happens when the DBA revokes `insert` privileges from ANN. So long as the DBA didn't revoke ANN's `create session` privilege (nothing in the question points to this conclusion), ANN can still connect. Records for a user are never removed when an object privilege is revoked either. Finally, nothing in the question pointed to the conclusion that ANN was ever able to create tables, so discard that choice as well. **(Topic 16.2)**

5. B.   Set SESSIONS_PER_USER in the DEFAULT profile to 1.

Explanation   The best way to handle the job the question indicates is to make an adjustment to the user profile, not the `init.ora` file, eliminating two choices right there. After that, it's simply a matter of choosing the profile limit that looks the best. In this case, SESSIONS_PER_USER looks more like something that would limit user sessions in Oracle, more so than IDLE_TIME would. **(Topic 14.2)**

6. B.   Row cache

Explanation   Data dictionary records are kept in a memory area of the shared pool. This is to improve overall performance of the Oracle database by keeping frequently accessed areas of the dictionary in memory. The library cache is where SQL statement parse trees are stored, not dictionary information. The shared area cache is a vague term, and thus has no real meaning. The buffer cache stores recently used information from SQL statements that didn't use the data dictionary. Finally, the redo log buffer stores redo information for nondata dictionary changes. **(Topic 1.1)**

7. C.   A direct path data load bypasses most of the Oracle RDBMS, whereas a conventional path data load is a high-speed version of the SQL `insert`.

Explanation   The most accurate description of why these two paths differ is that the direct path data load bypasses most of the Oracle RDBMS, whereas a conventional path data load is a high-speed version of the SQL `insert`. Simply saying one is faster than the other doesn't really get to the heart of the matter. The other statements are technically invalid. **(Topic 1.1)**

8. C.   DBA_SEGMENTS

Explanation   DBA_SEGMENTS is the most useful view for the purpose of finding the location of indexes in a tablespace or datafile, and the amount of space used by those indexes. DBA_TS_QUOTAS will give you information about how much space a user's objects can use in a tablespace, but that's about it. DBA_OBJECTS will tell you when the object was created, but not how big it is. DBA_INDEXES will give you information about storage configuration, but not actual storage allocation. **(Topic 12.5)**

9. B. `set transaction`

Explanation The `set transaction` statement is used to assign transactions to specific undo segments. Though not typically recommended, this can be a useful technique, particularly if you have one or two long-running batch processes and specific large undo segments that are usually offline but brought online to handle this specific need. `alter database` will not assign a transaction to a undo segment, nor will `alter table`, so those choices are wrong. Finally, you must avoid the obvious distractor in `alter rollback segment`—the question clearly indicates that the undo segment is *already* online. **(Topic 10.3)**

10. C. Oracle eventually won't allow new records to be added to the database.

Explanation In this situation, Oracle eventually won't allow new records to be added to the database, and the entire database will go into a prolonged wait state until the redo log is cleared. So, something will happen, and Oracle will not switch to a new redo log automatically. However, the instance does not crash, either—it simply freezes and won't allow changes to be made or new users to connect. **(Topic 7.4)**

11. A. Decreasing tablespace size

Explanation All choices affect the number of checkpoints on the database, except for decreasing tablespace size. Smaller redo logs cause log switches to occur more frequently, making for more frequent checkpoints. Setting LOG_CHECKPOINT_TIMEOUT to zero makes checkpoints happen less frequently, as does setting LOG_CHECKPOINT_INTERVAL greater than the size of the redo log file. However, checkpoints have nothing to do with the size of your database's tablespaces. **(Topic 8.3)**

12. C. COMPOSITE_LIMIT

Explanation In this question, you must read the choices carefully, and understand what is being asked. The real question here is whether you understand resource costs and composite limits. Each of the choices other than COMPOSITE_LIMIT can be rolled up into COMPOSITE_LIMIT with the use of resource costing. Only the resources available for profiles can be included as part of a composite limit. **(Topic 14.2)**

13. C. `revoke create any table from ANN;` then `grant create any table to ANN;`

Explanation In a `revoke` command, you don't refer to the `admin option` at all. However, when you `revoke` a privilege that was granted with administrative capability, the entire privilege along with administrative capability is removed. As such, you must `grant` the privilege back to the user without administrative privileges in order for the user to continue using the privilege. **(Topic 16.2)**

14. D. `alter user default role none except ROLE_1;`

Explanation You may use the `except` keyword in your `alter user default role` command, but only if the `all` keyword is also used. The `none` keyword in this command must be used by itself, which makes the choice that says `alter user default role none except ROLE_1;` a bad statement, and thus the correct answer. **(Topic 17.2)**

15. A. From your `init.ora` file

Explanation Oracle will always prefer to use your `init.ora` file to determine startup settings. You can get away without specifying the absolute path of your `init.ora` file for the PFILE parameter if you have a copy of the `init.ora` file for this database stored in the DBS directory under $ORACLE_HOME in UNIX (DATABASE directory in NT). If no `init.ora` file is found and if a location is not specified using PFILE, Oracle will not mount or open your database, but will use some internal default settings to start an idle instance. Tablespace default settings have no function in database startup, and anything regarding initialization parameters is read from the redo log file. **(Topic 3.3)**

16. B. Writes current redo log number to datafile headers

Explanation The CKPT process handles two things in Oracle: it signals to DBWR that dirty buffers must be written to disk, and it also writes log sequence numbers to datafile headers and the control file. It does not, however, write dirty buffers to disk —DBWR does that. It also doesn't write redo log information to disk, only LGWR does that. Finally, it does not read data from disk into memory for user processes— the server process performs this task. **(Topic 7.3)**

17. D. To prevent users from waiting if a redo log member cannot be archived

Explanation The choice identifying the reason for multiplexing redo logs as to prevent users from waiting if a redo log member cannot be archived is probably the best answer. You do not have enough information to tell if there is an increase in storage space on your host machine; besides, multiplexing is also supposed to prevent I/O bottlenecks between the ARCH and LGWR processes—which improves redo log performance, not degrades it. However, in some cases, such as when two redo log members are on the same disk, you might see some performance degradation associated with double-writes to disk. Finally, there will always be a dependency on the redo log buffer, because users write their redo entries there instead of directly to disk. **(Topic 7.1)**

18. C.   LOGICAL_WRITES_PER_SESSION

Explanation   Each of the following choices indicates an appropriate resource profile, except for LOGICAL_WRITES_PER_SESSION. LOGICAL_READS_PER_SESSION is the number of reads to the buffer cache that are permitted in the session before Oracle must terminate. CONNECT_TIME defines a hard timeout for connections to the database before Oracle closes the session. IDLE_TIME is another timeout that defines how long a session can be connected while doing no work. All these parameters indicate settings within a resource profile. So, because LOGICAL_WRITES_PER_SESSION is not a real resource profile setting, that choice is the correct answer. **(Topic 14.2)**

19. B.   `alter system`

Explanation   The `alter system switch logfile` statement is used to manually switch a log file. `alter database` is not used, nor is `alter user`, nor is `alter redo log`, which incidentally isn't even a real SQL statement. **(Topic 7.3)**

20. D.   `default role`

Explanation   You cannot use the `default role` clause in the `create user` statement, because no roles have been granted to the user yet. This is an interesting little fact to keep in mind about the `create user` statement that may find its way onto your OCP exam. Other than that, assigning a `temporary tablespace`, password with `identified by`, or a user profile, are all fair game. **(Topic 17.2)**

21. B.   `identified by`

Explanation   Of the choices given, only the `identified by` clause indicates a clause that can be issued in the `alter user` statement by the users themselves. All the rest are managed by the DBA. This is, of course, true in the absence of the user being granted the `alter any user system` privilege, but there is no indication in the question that should cause you to believe that the user has the `alter any user` privilege. **(Topic 15.2)**

22. A. `alter profile default limit COMPOSITE_LIMIT 3500;`

Explanation To perform the action indicated in the question, you would use the `alter profile default limit COMPOSITE_LIMIT 3500;` statement. RESOURCE_COST is not an appropriate `init.ora` parameter; instead, you would use RESOURCE_LIMITS. You wouldn't in fact need to make a change to a licensing parameter in the `init.ora` file at all. Finally, changing a resource limit for the profile doesn't alter its cost or its composite limit. **(Topic 14.3)**

23. D. `grant`

Explanation Giving a role to a user is the same process as giving a privilege to a user—it also is handled with the same command, `grant alter user` may be used to switch the default role later, but not until the role is actually granted. Because we are only working with one user, there is no need for a systemwide or databasewide alteration. **(Topic 16.2)**

24. B. `select`

Explanation Because undo segments are allocated for all transactional statements, all the DML statements will force the user to acquire an undo segment. However, no undo segment gets allocated when the `select` statement is issued, making that the correct answer. **(Topic 1.1)**

25. A. In the PGA

Explanation When dedicated servers are in use, session information is stored in the PGA for the session. If MTS was in place, the shared pool would have been the correct answer. Session information is never stored in the buffer cache or redo log buffer. **(Topic 1.1)**

26. A. `quota on`

Explanation The `quota on` clause in a `create user` statement will limit the amount of space the user can allocate in a tablespace with his or her own tables. It will usually not, however, impose consistent limits on the amount of data a user can add to his or her own or another user's tables `default tablespace`, `profile`, and `identified by` have nothing to do with tablespace space allocation. **(Topic 15.1)**

27. D. Much free space left for `updates` and space left free by deletes not actively filled in by Oracle

Explanation A high `pctfree` value (25 is fairly high) will leave much free space for `updates` to increase the size of each row, while a low value for `pctused` (30 is low) means that space left free by table `delete` operations will not return the block to a freelist quickly. Little free space left for updates, and space left free by deletes actively filled in by Oracle means that `pctused` is high (60 to 70) and `pctfree` is low (5 to 10). Little free space left for `updates`, and space left free by `deletes` not actively filled in by Oracle means that `pctfree` is low (5 to 10) and `pctused` is low (20 to 30). Much free space left for `updates`, and space left free by `deletes` actively filled in by Oracle means that `pctfree` is high (20 to 30) and `pctused` is high (60 to 70). **(Topic 9.3)**

28. C.   Dispatches user process access to a shared server

Explanation   DNNN, where NNN is a three-digit number (009 in this case), indicates a dispatcher process, which is a process that runs in the MTS making that choice the correct answer. DBWR writes dirty buffers to disk, making that choice incorrect, whereas CKPT writes the current redo log number to datafile headers during checkpoints and log switches, making that choice incorrect. The LGWR process writes redo log entries to disk. **(Topic 1.2)**

29. B.   In the shared pool

Explanation   When MTS is in use, session information is stored in the shared pool. Only when dedicated servers are being used will Oracle store session information in the PGA, making that choice incorrect. Session information is never stored in the buffer cache, redo log buffer, or large area. **(Topic 1.2)**

30. D.   VARCHAR2

Explanation   Views adopt the datatype of the columns from the base tables they select from, as long as there are no data conversion functions present in the view. In this case, the underlying column is a number, but there is also a TO_CHAR operation on that column, making the resulting datatype in the view a VARCHAR2. **(Topic 11.2)**

31. D.   NLS_SORT

Explanation   The NLS_SORT parameter enables you to define overriding sort order according to a language other than the national language set for the database. NLS_DATE_FORMAT is not use here, because that simply identifies the date format. NLS_RULE is an invalid national language set variable. One potential distractor in this situation is the NLS_LANG variable, which is used to define the language set the database will use. NLS_LANG consists of `language_territory.charset` and therefore it can implicitly influence the sorting, while NLS_TERRITORY helps Oracle identify the peculiarities of the geographical location the database runs in. **(Topic 18.4)**

32. C.   You can use varying-length multibyte character sets as both character sets on your database.

Explanation   You can *not* use varying-length multibyte character sets as both character sets on your database, so the choice stating you can shouldn't enter into consideration when choosing character set and national character set for your database. Other than that, you should consider making your character set US7ASCII or a superset of it (although the national character set can be whatever you choose), your national character set and character set should be closely related where possible, and Oracle supports only English-like languages as its character set for entering SQL and PL/SQL commands. **(Topic 18.1)**

33. A.   V$NLS_PARAMETERS

Explanation   The view you might use for this purpose is V$NLS_PARAMETERS. NLS_DATE_FORMAT is actually an initialization parameter, not a view, so you should be able to eliminate that one immediately as a choice. DBA_DATES is not a real view, so you should be able to eliminate that as choices as well. This leaves you with V$NLS_VALID_VALUES. You should investigate the database views supporting language specifications before taking OCP Exam 2. **(Topic 18.5)**

34. B.   NLS_CURRENCY

Explanation   The NLS_CURRENCY parameter could be set in your database to indicate the currency symbol is not $. NLS_SORT enables you to alter the default sort order in support of other languages. NLS_LANG is the parameter that indicates to Oracle the national language for this database, whereas NLS_DATE_FORMAT is used to indicate the date display characteristics. **(Topic 18.3)**

35. A.   BACKGROUND_DUMP_DEST

Explanation   You can find your ALERT file in the directory specified by the BACKGROUND_DUMP_DEST initialization parameter because the ALERT file is similar in behavior to a background process trace file that tracks—except that it tracks systemwide events, not just events occurring for one background process. USER_DUMP_DEST is used to identify the location for user trace files from user sessions. LOG_ARCHIVE_DEST is used to identify where Oracle places archived redo logs. CORE_DUMP_DEST is where Oracle places core dump files from failed processes. **(Topic 3.1)**

36. C.   Oracle puts the tablespace into read-only mode after the last transaction against that tablespace commits while preventing subsequent DML until the change happens.

Explanation   Only after the last transaction commits does Oracle put the tablespace into read-only mode. The tablespace cannot be put into read-only mode before a transaction against data in that tablespace commits due to the locks on mutating database objects held by the incomplete transaction. This point eliminates choice A. Oracle does not need to wait until the users all log off, however—Oracle can change tablespace status after the transaction commits, eliminating choice B. Finally, choice D is incorrect because Oracle returning an error is the behavior Oracle demonstrated in versions prior to Oracle. **(Topic 8.5)**

37. A.   Using a bitmap in the space header segment

Explanation   The principle behind locally managed tablespaces is that the space management is handled using a bitmap stored in the datafile header rather than by storing available space information in the data dictionary. Thus, choice B is incorrect. The locality of the database into which the information is stored is not relevant, either, so choice D is also incorrect. Finally, choice C is incorrect because Oracle does not store information integral to the operation of your database in a flat file, due to complex recovery issues inherent in doing so. **(Topic 8.2)**

38. B.   Session memory for MTS configuration

Explanation   The large pool, when configured, will be used by Oracle to store session memory for MTS configuration. This relieves the burden on the shared pool to store this information when MTS is in use, leaving more room for SQL parse trees. Only the shared pool may be used for storing SQL parse trees, so choice A is incorrect. Choice C is also incorrect because session memory in the dedicated server configuration is always stored in a private area seen only by that process. Finally, choice D is incorrect because the buffer cache is used for storing all block buffers, and there is no real concept of *overflow* with respect to this memory area. **(Topic 1.1)**

39. B. `alter table set unused column`

Explanation   The `alter table set unused column` command marks a column as being unused in the table without actually removing any data from the column or table. The operation executes quickly because the only change actually made is to the data dictionary in the Oracle database. The `alter table drop column` command is more extensive and long-running, but also removes the actual data from the table, thus freeing up space, so choice A is incorrect. Choice C is used for changing the datatype definition of a column and is incorrect. Choice D deallocates all storage for a table, leaving only the definition intact, which is also incorrect. **(Topic 11.8)**

40. A. PGA

Explanation   Data in temporary tables in Oracle is stored in the sort area, and the sort area is a part of your PGA. Because the table is temporary, there is no way for Oracle to store the data either in your buffer cache or in any tablespace other than TEMP. Thus, choices B, C, and D are all incorrect. The reason temporary table data might be stored in your TEMP tablespace is because the temporary table data might fill your sort area. In this situation, Oracle behaves as every version of Oracle behaved, and puts overflow in the temporary tablespace used for disk sorts.
(Topic 1.1)

41. D. `recseparator`

Explanation   The `recseparator` keyword in your SQL*Loader control file enables you to define a character other than "newline" that separates records. Thus, multiple rows of data can be stored on one line, or a single line of data can be found spanning multiple lines. Choice A is incorrect because the `fields separated by` clause defines the column separation delimiter, not the line delimiter. The `fields terminated by` clause defines a character to be found when SQL*Loader reaches the end of a column, making choice B incorrect as well. Finally, `trailing nullcols` identifies to SQL*Loader that, if additional columns are found in the table for which there are no records in the load file, then SQL*Loader will place a NULL value for that column. Thus, choice C is incorrect.
(Topic 1.1)

42. A. Estimate statistics.

Explanation   You can compute statistics, but not estimate statistics, on Oracle indexes when you rebuild them. Thus, choice A is correct, and choice B is incorrect. The `rebuild` clause does enable you to rebuild in another tablespace as well by simply specifying the `tablespace` clause in the `alter index rebuild` command. This feature was actually implemented in Oracle8. Thus, choice C is incorrect as well. Finally, choice D indicates that the index can be rebuilt online, whereas users are still modifying data in the table. This is a new feature in Oracle, so choice D is incorrect. **(Topic 12.3)**

43. B. LOG_ARCHIVE_MAX_PROCESSES

Explanation   This question is tricky because one of the choices looks deceptively similar to the correct answer. Choice B is the correct name for the parameter used to define how many ARCH processes Oracle should run. Choice A does not identify an actual `init.ora` parameter, but looks like it *should* be right. It is important that you can distinguish the real from the imaginary on your OCP exam. Choice C is incorrect because although you can define how many archive destinations Oracle should maintain with LOG_ARCHIVE_MIN_SUCCEED_DEST, Oracle does not automatically start a specific number of ARCH processes based on the value for this parameter. Finally, choice D is incorrect because the LOG_ARCHIVE_START parameter merely tells Oracle that an ARCH process should be started at the time the instance is started, but by itself LOG_ARCHIVE_START tells Oracle to start only one ARCH process. **(Topic 7.4)**

44. D.   %ORACLE_BASE%\oradata

Explanation   Oracle significantly enhanced its support of the Oracle Flexible Architecture (OFA). Database Configuration Assistant now installs all Oracle datafiles under an oradata\<SID> directory within the software home tree in NT environments. In contrast, prior versions of Oracle would place all datafiles under the database directory, so choice C is incorrect for Oracle. Choice A is incorrect because only the admin components will be placed under the admin directory in the ORACLE_HOME tree. However, this is also an OFA-compliant way to set up the Oracle environment, so it is also important to understand. Finally, choice B is incorrect because Oracle-supplied DBA scripts are found in the rdbms\admin area. **(Topic 2.3)**

45. A.   25

Explanation   The bits in the local-management bitmap in each datafile will either represent one block or many blocks. The bit will represent many blocks only if UNIFORM SIZE is used, in which case the number of blocks represented by one bit equals the number of blocks in each extent. In this case, the block size is 4KB, while the uniform extent size is 100KB, meaning that each extent contains, and each bit represents, 25 blocks. **(Topic 8.1)**

46. C.   Based on the number of blocks in the table plus blocks in associated indexes

Explanation   When sizing the keep pool, ensure that there is enough room for the entire table plus all associated indexes. If one or the other is omitted, you may size the keep pool too small and lose blocks, resulting in I/O operations later to read either table or index data back into memory. You wouldn't base the size of the keep pool on anything from your shared pool. **(Topic 1.1)**

47. D.   NLS_DUAL_CURRENCY

Explanation   NLS_DUAL_CURRENCY is used for EU countries supporting two currencies so that dual currencies can be identified in the database. NLS_TERRITORY may identify their national currency, but not necessarily the euro, eliminating choice A. The NLS_LANG parameter is used to identify the national language, but not the currency, making choice B incorrect. NLS_COMP is used for enhanced comparison operations, not to support dual currencies, eliminating choice C. **(Topic 18.5)**

48. D. The insert fails at the time it is issued, but the transaction will continue.

Explanation A nondeferrable constraint cannot be deferred by the alter session set constraints=deferred statement. Therefore, the insert statement will fail. However, statement failure does not cause a transaction to fail. Therefore, choice D is correct. **(Topic 13.1)**

49. C. '948695'

Explanation A reverse key index reverses the values stored in the index for high-speed search purposes. Given the value by the question, choice C is correct because the choice presents the indexed value reversed. Choices A, B, and D are thus logically incorrect for this same reason as well. **(Topic 12.1)**

50. B. Create an index-organized table to store the data.

Explanation Index-organized tables take less space to store than a comparable table-plus-primary-key setup. Because the table will only be accessed via the primary key, there is no need for additional indexes. Furthermore, for storage reasons, the DBA won't want to create more indexes, eliminating choice A. Choice C is incorrect because dropping the primary key will reduce storage but has the unwanted effect of making data difficult to access. Choice D is incorrect because increasing pctfree makes a table require more storage to store the same number of rows. Review the discussion of index-organized tables. **(Topic 11.1)**

51. D. Set password_reuse_time to 1095

Explanation The password_reuse_time profile option represents the number of *days* that must pass before a password can be reused. Because you want to restrict reuse to a three-year period, you will set password_reuse_time to the number of days in three years, which is 1,095 (assuming no leap year in that three-year period). Choices A and B are both incorrect, because the values used represent the restriction as a number of years and months, respectively. Choices C and E are incorrect because they are meaningless values designed to distract you from the real answer. **(Topic 14.1)**

52. B. STARSKY can no longer create tables, but HUTCH can.

Explanation Because the create table privilege was revoked from STARSKY, that user will no longer be able to perform the task given by the privilege. However, unlike object privileges, system privileges are not revoked from privilege grantees when the grantor loses the privilege. Thus, HUTCH keeps the ability to create tables even when STARSKY loses it, making choice A incorrect. You do not lose the privilege in any of the actions shown in the question, which eliminates choices C and D. **(Topic 16.2)**

53. C.   The user issues the set role command, and then issues the DML commands.

Explanation   Because the user has been granted the nondefault role, that user must issue the set role command to activate the role so he or she can use the privileges associated with that role. The user cannot simply issue the commands, because the role is not a default one for the user, making choice A incorrect. However, the solution is not to make this role a default role for the user, as indicated by choice C with the alter user statement (using the default role clause). For one, the user cannot issue this command on himself or herself—he or she would require DBA intervention. For another, because the application superuser privileges are meant to be nondefault privileges, making this role a default role would defeat the purpose of password protection on the role itself. **(Topic 17.2)**

54. B.   Availability of space on disk where datafiles are added

Explanation   To increase the size of a tablespace, you must have additional disk space Oracle can use to store its datafiles. You do not need to use autoextend in order to increase the size of a tablespace, however, making choice C incorrect. Choice A is also incorrect because that consideration is a factor only when reducing the size of a tablespace. Finally, choice D is incorrect because block information is not stored in memory in support of increasing the size of a tablespace. **(Topic 8.3)**

55. A.   The DEVELOPER profile shows a value of 230,000 for COMPOSITE_LIMIT.

Explanation   A value of 230,000 for COMPOSITE_LIMIT is pretty high, and can most likely accommodate a few minutes' worth of queries from developers. This is the only choice that is not a potential culprit for the problem. Choice B is suspect because developers would be disconnected if the DBA manually killed their sessions. Choice C is also a problem because a low value for CPU_PER_SESSION (measured in $1/100$ seconds) means that developers would be allotted absurdly low CPU time when connected to process their queries. Finally, choice D is a problem because a connection time of ten minutes as measured by CONNECT_TIME would kick the developers off the system after a few minutes, as indicated by the question. **(Topic 14.3)**

56. A.   CREATE_CATALOG_ROLE

Explanation   Of the choices given, only CREATE_CATALOG_ROLE is a role not created automatically when the Oracle database is created. SELECT_CATALOG_ROLE gives the user access to dictionary information, making choice B incorrect. EXP_FULL_DATABASE enables the user to export every database object using the EXPORT utility, making choice C incorrect. Finally, choice D is incorrect because IMP_FULL_DATABASE enables the user to import the entire contents of an export dump file into the database. **(Topic 17.4)**

57. B.   Performance

Explanation   Even though index rebuilds can take place online in Oracle, you still have to consider the performance degradation inherent in the overhead required to rebuild the index online. This question is a challenging one because choices B, C, and D are all interrelated. Although the best performance will be experienced when the system is most idle, choice C is not the right answer because it identifies a course of action to take, not a factor to consider in determining the course of action. Choice D is also wrong, because system idleness is determined as a combination between user activity and batch processing. Finally, choice A is incorrect because in a 24×7 environment, no downtime is permitted. **(Topic 12.3)**

58. D.   The `alter tablespace coalesce` command

Explanation   Although the `alter table coalesce` command can be used to coalesce small chunks of free space into larger ones by SMON, this command does little about row chaining or migration at the table level in the Oracle database. Choice A is wrong because `analyze` populates the CHAIN_CNT column in DBA_TABLES, which tells the DBA how many rows are chained in the table of the database. Choice B is wrong because DBMS_DDL contains a procedure that analyzes objects for cost-based optimization. Choice C is also wrong because DBMS_UTILITY contains a procedure that analyzes every object in a user's schema for cost-based optimization. **(Topic 8.5)**

59. C.   Bring the tablespace online.

Explanation   Once you issue the `alter tablespace move datafile` command, you can then bring the tablespace online, provided the file appears where you told Oracle it would appear with the command from the question. Remember, alter tablespace only updates the Oracle data dictionary and control file with the new filesystem location information. Oracle does not actually move the file for you. You would take the tablespace offline before issuing the alter tablespace move datafile command, and you would also move the file first, making choices B and A incorrect, respectively. Finally, use of IMPORT as indicated in choice D is appropriate for transportable tablespaces, a subject not tested by this question. **(Topic 8.5)**

60. B. C55278B93918BF29

Explanation   Oracle always sets a password to whatever string literal you assign using the `alter user identified by` command. Enclosing the data shown in DBA_USERS for password information in double quotes does not circumvent Oracle's security measures for not showing a password in plaintext in the data dictionary, so choice A is wrong. Also, although GIANT cannot connect until `create session` is granted to the user, this fact itself is irrelevant because the question asks about the password, not connectivity status, making choice C incorrect as well. Finally, Oracle does not lock new user accounts by default, so choice D is also wrong. **(Topic 15.2)**

Answers to Practice Exam 3

1. A.   The listener spawns a new server process.

Explanation   When dedicated servers are in use in Oracle, the listener will spawn a new dedicated server for every user process that contacts the listener to establish service with Oracle. Because MTS is not in use, choice B is wrong because no dispatcher process will be running on the Oracle database. Oracle background processes do not communicate with server processes directly, so choices C and D are incorrect as well. **(Topic 1.2)**

2. C.   Fetch data from disk into memory.

Explanation   The only step Oracle will execute in support of a user query from the choices given is fetching data from disk into memory. Choices A, B, and D are all incorrect because they indicate steps Oracle will execute in support of data change commands such as `insert`, `update`, and `delete`, but not in support of queries. **(Topic 1.1)**

3. A.   Make changes to data block in memory.

Explanation   When users issue `insert` statements in Oracle, the server process always makes the changes in memory, not on disk. So, choice A is correct. Choice B is incorrect because Oracle would never parse a statement if the parse tree for an identical statement already exists in the shared pool. Choice C is incorrect because undo information is only written for `update` or `delete` statements. Finally, choice D is incorrect because redo for a transaction is never written to the datafile, it is written to the online redo log. **(Topic 1.1)**

4. C.   Use of OFA reduces support headaches by standardizing filesystem layouts for all Oracle installations.

Explanation   Choice C correctly describes a cornerstone of OFA-compliant infrastructures in that the filesystem layout of Oracle files is standardized for easy location. Choice A is incorrect because OFA distributes software, database, and administrative filesystem components into different areas so that they are easy to find and don't conflict with one another from an I/O perspective. Choice B is incorrect because enabling DBAs to arrive at their own filesystem layouts using proprietary naming conventions leads to nonstandard Oracle installations and is the antithesis of OFA. Choice D is incorrect because OFA separates database objects into different tablespaces based on I/O requirements. **(Topic 2.3)**

5. B.   `orapwd file=/u01/app/oracle/database/orapwdORCL.pwd password=oracle entries=100`

Explanation   Your call to the ORAPWD utility must include reference to all three parameters: FILE, PASSWORD, and ENTRIES. Further, your reference to the password filename you want to create must include its absolute path specification unless you want Oracle to write the password file in the current directory. Choice B alone conforms to these requirements. Choices A and C are both missing reference to the PASSWORD parameter, whereas choice D incorrectly places the password file in the current directory rather than the one specified by the question. **(Topic 2.4)**

6. A.   When the instance is started

Explanation   Oracle reads the contents of your `init.ora` file whenever the instance is started. Choices B and C are both incorrect because by the time the database is mounted and opened, the instance has already been started and the initialization parameter file has been read into memory. Finally, Oracle never reads the parameter file when the database is closed, making choice D incorrect as well. **(Topic 3.3)**

7. A.   DB_CREATE_FILE_DEST

Explanation   The Oracle-managed files feature in Oracle9i specifies that datafiles will be created in the directory identified by the parameter named in choice A. Choices B and C are both incorrect because those locations are used for writing redo logs and control files when OMF is in use. Finally, choice D is incorrect because these directory locations are most definitely controlled by you, the DBA, when you manually specify settings for the parameters identified in choices A, B, and C in this question. **(Topic 3.2)**

8. B.   OMF will automatically remove the underlying datafiles from the host environment.

Explanation   Choice B correctly identifies the primary feature OMF offers DBAs. Choices A and C are both incorrect because they specify functionality that is standard within Oracle when a tablespace that uses particular datafiles is dropped from the Oracle database. Finally, choices B and D are mutually exclusive, making choice D incorrect by virtue of choice B's correctness. **(Topic 3.2)**

9. B.   Two

Explanation   OMF will try to multiplex online redo logs if you use it for generating your redo log files. Multiplexing requires that at least two different locations are specified for the appropriate OMF parameters. Thus, all other choices are incorrect. **(Topic 3.2)**

10. C.   `alter system suspend`

Explanation   The `alter system suspend` command is useful for periodic acquiescing of host system I/O resources, particularly when high-speed disk mirror or synchronization mechanisms are in place on the I/O devices supporting Oracle database files. Choice D shows how to continue Oracle database operation after the `alter system suspend` command has been issued, and therefore that choice is incorrect. Choice A indicates a command you would use when you only wanted to start the Oracle instance, making that choice incorrect. Finally, choice B is incorrect because making the database read only does not cease database operations temporarily. **(Topic 3.3)**

11. A.   `shutdown abort`

Explanation   The `shutdown abort` command lets you stop your Oracle database from operating on short notice, and requires that instance recovery be performed the next time the database is started. Choice B is incorrect because the `shutdown transactional` command stops the database from operating after the current transactions are ended by the user process, which may not take place on short notice if the transactions are long-running. Choice C is incorrect because the `shutdown normal` command only stops the database from operating after the last user logs off Oracle, which may not happen on short notice. Finally, choice D is incorrect because even though the `shutdown immediate` command closes the database after rolling back current transactions, the rollback activity itself may take a long time. **(Topic 3.3)**

12. C. `orclALRT.trc`

Explanation The contents of the trace file clearly indicate that this file is the alert log for the database. You can glean this fact from observing that the trace file contents include initialization parameter settings and startup/shutdown times for the database. Choice A is incorrect because the contents of this trace file give you no indication that an error occurred with the DBW0 process. Choice B is incorrect for the same reason, insofar as you have no indication of a failure with the LGWR process. Finally, no user process information is present in this trace file, meaning that it cannot be a user process trace file as the name of the file in choice D would indicate, making that choice incorrect as well. **(Topic 3.4)**

13. A. CONTROL_FILES

Explanation If you do not change the setting for CONTROL_FILES in the parameter file before you create a new database, there is a chance Oracle will use the control files specified by this parameter, which correspond to another database. This could lead to problems with your other database, making choice A the correct answer. Choice B is incorrect because two databases on the same host system can have the same database block size. Choice C is incorrect because you can have two Oracle databases in the same domain when both databases are hosted on the same machine. Choice D is incorrect because the shared pool size for two databases on the same host can be the same, so long as there is enough memory for both databases' SGAs. **(Topic 3.1)**

14. C. Template

Explanation A template is a relatively new component supported by the Oracle Database Creation Assistant. This component permits the creation of many databases from a generic specification you define. Choices A and B are incorrect because clone and copy refer to the creation of another database from the actual datafiles of an original database. Finally, choice D is incorrect because a terminal is a process or machine that enables you access to a minicomputer or mainframe. **(Topic 4.2)**

15. D. SYSTEM

Explanation Any datafile named as part of the `datafile` clause of your `create database` command will belong to the SYSTEM tablespace. Although you can create undo tablespaces for your database with the `create database` command, choice C is incorrect because the creation of an undo tablespace is defined using the `undo tablespace` clause in the `create database` command. Choices A and B are incorrect because DATA and INDEX tablespaces cannot be created in the `create database` command. **(Topic 4.3)**

16. D.   SYS

Explanation   The internal user has been rendered obsolete in Oracle8i and later database releases, so because you need a privileged connection to Oracle to create the data dictionary, you need to use the SYS user as identified in choice D. Choices A and B both indicate users who do not have sufficient privileges to create the data dictionary. **(Topic 4.1)**

17. B.   DBA_TABLES

Explanation   The views prefixed with DBA_, USER_, or ALL_ are considered part of the Oracle data dictionary, along with a select list of other views. Choice A is incorrect because V$ views are considered dynamic performance views and as such aren't part of the data dictionary. Choice C is incorrect because SYS.AUD$ is a base table in Oracle, from which dictionary views can be derived. Finally, the EMP table is a sample table that is not associated with the data dictionary in any way. **(Topic 5.1)**

18. B.   DBA_SOURCE

Explanation   The output in this question is clearly a PL/SQL block, the source code for which can be found in the DBA_SOURCE dictionary view. Choice A is incorrect because DBA_ERRORS is a dictionary view you might employ as part of the PL/SQL compilation process to identify syntax errors in your PL/SQL code. Choice C is incorrect because DBA_VIEWS contains information about the views in your Oracle database, not PL/SQL code. Finally, choice D is incorrect because the source code shown contains no evidence that it is associated with a trigger. **(Topic 5.3)**

19. A.   set long 9999

Explanation   Because the contents of the TEXT column in DBA_VIEWS is cut off before the entire output of that column was displayed, chances are good that there is some problem in the way columns of LONG datatype are set to display in SQL*Plus. Choice A is correct because it defines a nice large value for LONG column width, as opposed to choice C, which only supports 50 characters. Choices B and D are both incorrect because they configure the width of a column called TEXT in VARCHAR2 or CHAR datatype format, which is not the case for this TEXT column, which is of LONG datatype. **(Topic 5.2)**

20. A.   Verify the actual directory location of your control file.

Explanation   Because you have very little information in this question, your only option is to follow the logical sequence of events starting with what little information you have. This question starts by explaining the value specified for the CONTROL_FILES parameter. Because you also know that Oracle must open your control files as part of the instance startup process, the next logical step is to determine if the control files are found where Oracle expects to find them. Choice B is incorrect because you have no information that would indicate a problem with real memory. Choices C and D are incorrect because we haven't even started the instance yet, so its too early to expect problems with datafiles or online redo logs. **(Topic 6.1)**

    21. D. `/u04/oradata/db1`

Explanation When you specify the DB_CREATE_ONLINE_LOG_DEST_n parameters, Oracle places control files in each of the locations you define for those parameters. Otherwise, Oracle would have used the DB_CREATE_FILE_DEST parameter in determining where to place the control files. Thus, you know that a control file will be placed in the directories identified by choices A, B, and C, but not in the directory indicated by choice D. **(Topic 6.4)**

    22. C. Updates to the contents of the control file when new tablespaces are added

Explanation Even when you don't use OMF, Oracle still updates the contents of your control file whenever a new tablespace is added to your database. This is the default functionality for supporting Oracle filesystem layout that Oracle provides. Choice A is incorrect because Oracle will expect you to determine where the control files are located using the CONTROL_FILES parameter in lieu of OMF. Choice B is incorrect because Oracle will only multiplex your control files when you specify multiple directory and file locations for the CONTROL_FILES parameter. Finally, choice D is incorrect because you, not Oracle, must specify values for CONTROL_FILES in the parameter file. **(Topic 6.4)**

    23. B. Make a copy of the control file with the database shut down.

Explanation When multiplexing control files, you should make a copy of the control file when the database is shut down and move that copy to the appropriate location given by the CONTROL_FILES parameter so that Oracle will maintain the multiplexed copy. Choices A and D are incorrect because they both indicate that the database should be open during control file copying, which of course it shouldn't. Finally, choice C indicates how to create a script for recreating your control file if it should be lost, which isn't relevant to this discussion. **(Topic 6.3)**

    24. D. ARC0

Explanation The archiver process will make a copy of your online redo log file in the appropriate archiving destination whenever LGWR fills the current log. Choice A is incorrect because LGWR will not make this archived copy for you. The CKPT process will also not copy an online log to its archiving destination, making choice B incorrect. Finally, the DBW0 process copies dirty buffers to datafiles, and has little if anything to do with archiving filled redo logs, making choice C incorrect as well. **(Topic 7.1)**

25. D. `ora_1_asdf1234.log`

Explanation The filename specified in choice D indicates a filename Oracle might use for creating a redo log when OMF is used. Choices A, B, and C do not follow the OMF naming convention we described in this text, and therefore could not be the correct answers to this question. **(Topic 7.5)**

26. D. You created a dictionary-managed permanent tablespace.

Explanation Although its name would indicate that temporary data might be stored in this tablespace, the `temporary` or `tempfile` keywords were not used in defining the tablespace, making it impossible for Oracle to create this tablespace as a temporary tablespace. Choices A and C are incorrect because the keywords `extent management local` were not used, meaning that this tablespace could not be a locally managed tablespace. The keywords `extent management dictionary` were used, however, meaning that this is a dictionary-managed tablespace. Choice B is incorrect however, because the tablespace is not a temporary tablespace, as you already know. **(Topic 8.2)**

27. C. `autoextend`

Explanation The `autoextend` keyword indicates a clause in which you can define whether a datafile extends automatically in support of tablespace growth. Choice A is incorrect because the `default storage` clause indicates default settings for segments and extents of objects placed into this tablespace when no `storage` clause was specified in creating that object. Choice B is incorrect because the `extent management` clause is a clause used for defining whether the tablespace free space allocation will be locally managed or dictionary managed. Finally, choice D is incorrect because the `datafile` clause is used when creating tablespaces to identify the name of a datafile to create in support of this tablespace. **(Topic 8.2)**

28. C. `uniform extent allocation`

Explanation The `uniform extent allocation` clause identifies that segments allocated in this tablespace will all be the same size, as requested by the question. Choice A is incorrect because segment and extent allocation specified by `default storage` clauses will be optional and only implemented when the object placed in that tablespace has no `storage` clause of its own. Choice B is incorrect because the storage clause is defined on a database object placed in the tablespace to configure how segments and extents will be allocated to that object. Choice D is incorrect because the autoextend clause is used for determining whether a datafile can grow beyond its original size automatically in support of tablespace growth. **(Topic 8.3)**

29. C. drop tablespace cascade constraints

Explanation   The cascade constraints clause in the drop tablespace command is used for ensuring that any constraints between objects inside and outside this tablespace will be severed. Choice A is incorrect because you wouldn't ordinarily drop just the datafile in the context of this question. Choice B is incorrect because simply taking the tablespace offline will not remove the contraints between objects inside and outside this tablespace. Finally, though the including contents clause would be included in the drop tablespace command whenever you wanted to drop a nonempty tablespace, this clause alone won't drop the constraints between objects inside and outside this tablespace being dropped. **(Topic 8.5)**

30. D.   The change will not take effect for existing tables.

Explanation   You can change default storage settings for initial extents all you want, but the change will never take effect for existing tables in Oracle. Because choice D is the correct answer, and because the other choices are mutually exclusive, choices A, B, and C are all incorrect. **(Topic 8.6)**

31. D.   All tablespaces in the database

Explanation   When OMF is enabled for your database, Oracle will handle the creation and removal of datafiles associated with every tablespace in your Oracle database. This is a handy aspect of OMF that will help you minimize the storage allocation of space on your host system. Choices A, B, and C all indicate that OMF is somehow limited to managing datafile removal for only a specific tablespace, which, of course, isn't the case. Therefore, each of those choices is incorrect. **(Topic 8.7)**

32. C.   DATA

Explanation   Of the choices given, only the DATA tablespace will not be created by the Oracle when the create database command given by the question is issued. Choice A is incorrect because the SYSTEM tablespace is always created by Oracle when a database is created. Choice B is incorrect because the UNDOTBS tablespace will be created by this create database command due to the presence of the undo tablespace clause. **(Topic 10.2)**

33. D.   1,500KB

Explanation   Even though you specify a storage allocation of 300KB in the `storage` clause of your `create table` statement, Oracle uses the uniform extent management configuration of 500KB set when the tablespace was created. Further, since you specified three extents with the `minextents` option in the `table storage` clause, Oracle allocates three extents of size 500KB each, for a total of 1,500KB. Thus, choice D is the correct answer, and choices A, B, and C are incorrect. **(Topic 11.6)**

34. B.   `create temporary tablespace temp01 tempfile`
    `'/u01/oradata/orcl/temp01.dbf' size 100M extent`
    `management local;`

Explanation   Choice B presents the best option for creating the temporary tablespace. Although choice C is also technically correct, the syntax in choice B follows newer conventions established by Oracle. Choices A and D are both incorrect and will result in errors if issued against an Oracle database. **(Topic 8.4)**

35. A.   `autoallocate`

Explanation   The `autoallocate` clause was left out but implied in Oracle. This is the default functionality for tablespaces in the Oracle database. Choices B, C, and D all indicate clauses that must be explicitly stated in order for Oracle to use them. **(Topic 8.2)**

36. A.   The value for the `minextents` setting.

Explanation   When more than one extent is allocated to a database table on creation, chances are the table was created with `minextents` set to a value greater than one in the `storage` clause when the object was created. Oracle would never create a database table with more than one extent by default, so choice D is incorrect. Choices B and C both indicate storage settings that have no bearing on the initial number of extents allocated to a table, so they are both incorrect as well. **(Topic 8.6)**

37. C.   `select sum(bytes) from dba_extents where`
    `segment_name = 'EMP' and owner = 'SCOTT';`

Explanation   The statement for choice C indicates a query that would give you the total space allocation for the EMP table owned by SCOTT in your Oracle database. You use the `sum( )` function because there will be more than one entry in the DBA_EXTENTS view if more than one extent is allocated to that table. Choice A is incorrect because DBA_TABLES will not give you the information you need. Choice B is incorrect because DBA_FREE_SPACE contains free space information, whereas you are looking for allocated space information. Finally, choice D is incorrect because the DBA_OBJECTS view will not give you the information you need. **(Topic 9.4)**

38. C. The user's long-running transaction has taken so long that space for undo information has been exhausted.

Explanation   Although the ORA-01555 error will affect other users in the way listed for choice B, choice C is the correct answer because the user running the long-running transaction will actually receive the ORA-01555 error. Choices A and D are not related to the "snapshot too old" error, and therefore can be disregarded. **(Topic 10.1)**

39. C. The database will open and all undo segments in UNDO_TBS1 will be online.

Explanation   Choice C is correct due to the SPFILE feature in Oracle, which remembers the setting made with the `alter system` command from your previous instance's execution. Choices A and B are incorrect, although this was the old functionality prior to Oracle9*i* when the ROLLBACK_SEGMENTS parameter wasn't set. Finally, choice D is incorrect as well because the database definitely will open and undo segments will be online. **(Topic 10.2)**

40. D. Oracle will return errors and the database will not open.

Explanation   Because your `init.ora` file contained an incorrect setting, Oracle mistakenly attempted to open the UNDOTBS1 undo tablespace when in fact the name of that tablespace was UNDO_TBS1. Oracle returns errors and the database will remain mounted but will not open. Choices A, B, and C are all incorrect because the database will be unable to open. The SPFILE feature is no good here because `init.ora` overrides it with the erroneous undo tablespace name. **(Topic 10.2)**

41. C. Set UNDO_MANAGEMENT to MANUAL.

Explanation   Your only correct option in this situation is to turn off automatic undo management. Choice B would have been the right answer if it indicated you were switching UNDO_SUPRESS_ERRORS to TRUE, but it is not the correct answer as it currently stands. Choice A indicates turning on automatic undo management, which is what caused the error in the first place. Finally, choice D is incorrect because UNDO_RETENTION has no bearing on the matter asked in the question. **(Topic 10.2)**

42. D.   Standard Oracle table

Explanation   Although choice C initially might seem like the right answer, notice that the question states that this table experiences frequent data change activity—the bane of a cluster table's existence. Thus, you must use standard tables, and choice D is correct. Choice A is also incorrect because nothing in the question indicates that you need the functionality offered by temporary tables. Finally, choice B is incorrect because nothing in the question indicates the need for an IOT. **(Topic 11.1)**

43. C.   Redo information will be generated for the creation of this table.

Explanation   Of the choices given, the only statement that can be made accurately about the table created in this question is choice C—redo will be generated because the logging keyword was present in the create table command. Choice A is incorrect because you have no information that would indicate this table is being placed in a temporary tablespace. Choice B is incorrect because the uniform extent allocation of the DATA tablespace will likely override whatever settings are made in the storage clause of the create table command given. Finally, choice D is incorrect because the nocache keyword in the create table command given ensures that blocks read into the SGA as part of full table scans will be purged by Oracle quickly. **(Topic 11.5)**

44. B.   OBRYAN only

Explanation   Data in a temporary table is session-private; OBRYAN therefore can remove only his own data using the truncate command. Thus, choices indicating other users will also have their data eliminated are incorrect. **(Topic 11.5)**

45. B.   When OBRYAN commits the transaction

Explanation   This temporary table was defined to retain records until the end of a user's transaction. Thus, when OBRYAN ends his current transaction, Oracle removes OBRYAN's data from the temporary table. All other choices indicate wrong answers because they either refer to users other than OBRYAN or to a scenario other than the end of OBRYAN's transaction. **(Topic 11.5)**

46. A.   Immediately following statement execution

Explanation   Once the alter table drop column statement is issued, Oracle removes the column from the table immediately. Choices B, C, and D are all incorrect because they indicate that the column will be removed at some later point when another command is issued, which is not the case for the alter table drop column command shown in the question. **(Topic 11.8)**

47. D.   Querying the DBA_UNUSED_COL_TABS view

Explanation   The DBA_UNUSED_COL_TABS view contains a listing of unused columns and tables that contain unused columns. Choice C is incorrect because it refers to the wrong dictionary view name. Choices A and B are both incorrect because they refer to methods you cannot use to find a listing of unused columns. **(Topic 11.8)**

48. A.   Less restrictive locks on underlying base tables

Explanation   Oracle reduced restrictions on the locks used for rebuilding indexes online in Oracle to permit that functionality. Choice B is incorrect because more restrictive locks would reduce the likelihood that online index rebuilds would be possible. Choice C is incorrect because standby databases are not involved in this process. Finally, choice D is incorrect because temporary tables are not involved in the process, either. **(Topic 12.3)**

49. B.   Oracle fills in the END_MONITORING column in the record corresponding to MY_IDX in the V$OBJECT_USAGE view.

Explanation   Because you terminated monitoring on this index, Oracle notes the date and time you did so in the corresponding record from V$OBJECT_USAGE. Oracle would only change the value in the USED column if someone used the index while monitoring was enabled, so choice C is incorrect. Choice A is incorrect because Oracle doesn't remove records from V$OBJECT_USAGE until the next time the instance is restarted. Finally, choice D is incorrect because the values for the record corresponding to MY_IDX in V$OBJECT_USAGE were cleared when monitoring was started. **(Topic 12.6)**

50. C.   The index will not be created unless all values in the EMPNO column are unique and not NULL.

Explanation   The only statement that is true from the choices given is choice C. Choice A is incorrect because the constraint uses a B-tree index, not a bitmap index. Choice B is incorrect because foreign keys in tables typically reference back to primary keys in other tables. Finally, choice D is incorrect because NULL values are not permitted in primary keys. **(Topic 13.1)**

51. A.   SYSTEM

Explanation   SERENA's tables will be placed in the SYSTEM tablespace unless you specify another default tablespace using the appropriate clause in the `create user` command. Choice B is incorrect because the table didn't contain reference to the DATA tablespace, nor is that tablespace the default for this user. Choice C is incorrect because the TEMP tablespace will be used for housing temporary segments but not permanent segments for this user. Finally, choice D is incorrect because the UNDOTBS tablespace will be used for housing undo segments not data segments. **(Topic 15.1)**

52. A. `create table mytab (coll number primary key);`

Explanation   Because JOSEPHINE has no space quota allotment in her default tablespace, she will not be able to issue the statement given in choice A. This restriction does not apply to space allocation in dictionary tables, however, so the statements indicated in choices B and C can both be issued by JOSEPHINE. Finally, choice D is incorrect because JOSEPHINE places that table created in the DATA tablespace, which is outside the realm of the question being asked. **(Topic 15.1)**

53. D.   If SYS performs a disk sort, the temporary segments will be placed in the TEMP tablespace.

Explanation   Of the statements given, only the statement for choice D is true. Choice A is incorrect because we have no information about SYS's actual password or account lock status that would indicate that no user can log in as SYS. Choice B is incorrect because if SYS creates a table without specifying the `tablespace` clause, the table will be placed in SYSTEM according to the dictionary info given. Finally, choice C is incorrect because the statement indicates the encrypted password value, not the actual value. **(Topic 8.4)**

54. B.   `alter resource cost`

Explanation   The command indicated in choice B is the one that must be issued in order to assign resource costs to resources in order for composite limits to work. Choice A is incorrect because the `alter system` command cannot be used for changing resource allocation costs. Choice C is incorrect for this reason as well, although you can set the value for COMPOSITE_LIMIT with the command shown in that choice. Finally, choice D is incorrect because the `alter user` command is used for assigning a profile to a user, not for explicit allocation of resource costs. **(Topic 14.3)**

55. A.   IDLE_TIME

Explanation   Idle time is not a resource that can be managed via composite limits. All other choices are incorrect because they indicate resource allocations that can be managed using the composite limit feature in Oracle resource profiles. **(Topic 14.3)**

56. C.   Oracle uses the value for CPU_PER_SESSION from the DEFAULT profile.

Explanation If a value for a profile resource is not set when the profile is created, Oracle uses the setting found in the DEFAULT profile. Thus, choice C is correct. Choice A is incorrect because Oracle doesn't use settings for other resources in order to set CPU_PER_SESSION. There is no SYS_PROFILE in Oracle unless you create that profile manually, and even then Oracle won't use it for anything other than resource management for users you assign that profile to. Thus, choice B is incorrect. Finally, choice D is incorrect because although Oracle might set CPU_PER_SESSION to UNLIMITED if that is what the resource setting is in the DEFAULT profile, if you've changed that setting in DEFAULT profile, Oracle will use the value you changed it to instead. **(Topic 14.2)**

    57. B.   After 180 days, a user assigned this profile can reuse his or her password.

Explanation Of the choices given, only choice B indicates a true statement that can be made about this profile. Choice A is incorrect because the PASSWORD_LOCK_TIME setting is unlimited, not three days. Choice C is incorrect because a PASSWORD_LIFE_TIME setting of 30 means 30 days, not 30 minutes. Finally, choice D is incorrect because PASSWORD_GRACE_TIME indicates how many days a user has to login to Oracle to change their password for the first time. **(Topic 14.1)**

    58. B. `alter profile default limit password_grace_time 3`
        `password_reuse_limit unlimited;`

Explanation The question asks for the statement that will bar reuse of passwords and give the user three days to login to change his/her password for the first time, and choice B accommodates that request nicely. The PASSWORD_REUSE_LIMIT setting restricts reuse of passwords. That fact alone makes it easy to eliminate choices C and D. You know that PASSWORD_GRACE_TIME forces users to log in within a certain period of time to change their passwords for the first time or else the account gets locked. In contrast, FAILED_LOGIN_ATTEMPTS simply locks the account after the prescribed number of failed attempts to log in, eliminating choice A. **(Topic 14.1)**

    59. D. `select distinct profile from dba_profiles where`
        `limit = 'UNLIMITED';`

Explanation Each row in DBA_PROFILES indicates a resource setting for a profile, meaning that a single profile might have numerous rows in DBA_PROFILES. Thus, you would use the `distinct` keyword to limit output to only one row per profile, making choice D correct. Choice C would have been right if the `distinct` keyword was used. Choices A and B do not query the data in that dictionary view with the appropriate search criteria, making both choices incorrect. **(Topic 14.1)**

60. C.   Ability to back up the database

Explanation   Although the `SYSDBA` privilege is quite powerful, it is not omniscient, especially when it comes to object privileges. For this reason, choices A and D are incorrect. Additionally, because no information about granting administrative ability along with the privilege was indicated by the question, you can eliminate choice B as well. **(Topic 15.1)**

APPENDIX
A

Globalization Support

his appendix discusses Oracle's Globalization Support Architecture. This feature enables you to deploy Oracle in languages other than English. This topic comprises only 3 percent of the actual test material on the OCP DBA Fundamentals I exam. In Oracle8i and before, Oracle's Globalization Support capabilities were referred to as National Language Support (NLS) features. NLS is now a subset of Globalization Support. In this section, you will cover the following points on using NLS in Oracle:

- Choosing a database and a national character set for a database

- Specifying language-dependent behavior

- Using different types of NLS parameters

- Obtaining information about NLS settings

Oracle supports many different language-encoding schemes in order to produce a product that is usable worldwide. There are four different classes supported, including single-byte character sets (both 7-bit and 8-bit), varying-width multibyte character sets, fixed-width multibyte character sets, and Unicode character sets. You may be familiar with the single-byte character set US7ASCII, the 7-bit ASCII character set used in the United States. It uses single byte to store a character and so can represent 128 characters. Several 8-bit character sets are used throughout Europe to represent the characters found in those languages, in addition to those used in English. WE8ISO8859P1 is the Western European 8-bit International Organization for Standardization (ISO) standard character set and is widely used. Unlike US7ASCII, which uses 7 bits to represent a character, it uses 8 bits to represent a character and so can represent 256 characters instead.

Oracle uses varying- and fixed-width character sets to support languages like Japanese, Chinese, Korean, and other languages that use complex characters to represent language, and for Arabic and Hebrew, which add the complexity of being read from right to left. Unicode is a standard for encoding all characters usable in computers, including all characters in all languages, plus specialized print media, math, and computer characters. In this section, you will learn about choices in character sets for the database—how to specify NLS behavior in different scenarios, NLS parameters, NLS usage, and what influence language-dependent application behavior may have.

The database character set is defined during the database creation using the `character set` clause in the `create database` command. There are few options to change the character set after the database is created. The database character set can only be changed if the new character set is a superset of the existing character set. This is for the obvious reason that the existing character set of the database should be represented in the new character set. If this condition is met, then the character set can be changed by using the command `alter database` `character set`. If not, then a full export of the database, recreating the database with a new character set, and then a full import of the database should take care of it.

Choosing a Database and a National Character Set for a Database

Two character sets can be defined for your database: the *database character set* and the *national character set*. Both database and national character sets are defined when you create your database. The database character set is used for Oracle SQL and PL/SQL source-code storage, whereas the national character set is used to represent your table data. SQL and PL/SQL must be stored in a language containing all characters in U.S. 7-bit ASCII or EBCDIC, whichever is supported by your host machine. So, even if you speak Korean and want to store Korean in your database, you still need to know enough English to type in the SQL and PL/SQL commands.

The national character set is specified at the time of database creation using the clause `national character set`. If this is not specified, then Oracle defaults it to the database character set. Some special conditions apply to national character sets and text or large object variables. The CLOB, CHAR, and VARCHAR2 datatypes can store database character sets, and each has national character set equivalents, called NCLOB, NCHAR, and NVARCHAR2, respectively. The LONG datatype can only store character sets that are allowed to be database character sets. The client or user machines can have a different character set from the database character set. This is achieved by setting the environment variable. Make sure that the database character set is a superset of the client character set.

Varying-Width Multibyte Character Sets

In a varying-width character set, a multibyte character set is represented by one or more bytes per character. The value of the most significant bit is used to indicate if a byte represents a single byte or is part of a series of bytes representing a character.

Fixed-Width Multibyte Character Sets

Fixed-width character sets provide support similar to multibyte character sets, except that the format is a fixed number of bytes for each character.

Note also that the terms fixed length and varying length have different meanings for CHAR and VARCHAR2 datatypes than fixed width and variable width in the CHAR and NCHAR or VARCHAR2 and NVARCHAR2 context. In the first case, fixed width means that the data stored in a CHAR(3) will always be three characters long, even if you specify only one character of data. The one character will be padded with two extra spaces. VARCHAR2 columns will not be padded with extra blanks, so the same one character of data in a VARCHAR2(3) column will be only one character long. In the second case, fixed and varying width refer to the number of bytes used to store each character in the string.

The Need for National Character Sets

It is not possible to use a fixed-width multibyte character set as the database character set; it can only be used as the national character set. The data types NCHAR, NVARCHAR2, and NCLOB are provided to declare columns as variants of the basic types CHAR, VARCHAR2, and CLOB to note that they are stored using the national character set and not the database character set.

TIP
Your database and national character sets should be closely related for best results. Also, the trade-off between fixed-width and varying-width character sets is that fixed-width sets permit better performance in string operations, such as length( ) *and* substr( )*, but varying-width sets are better for managing space.*

For Review

1. Compare fixed-length and varying-length datatypes to fixed-width and varying-width multibyte character sets. What is meant by each?

2. Compare database and national character sets. What is meant and permitted by each?

Specifying Language-Dependent Behavior

There are several different areas where language-dependent behavior can be specified. Specifying these NLS parameters changes the default values that are based on the database and national character set defined. These parameters can be changed in the following ways:

- **By specifying the parameter in the database initialization file on the server** These settings have no effect on the client side, but only on the server behavior.

  ```
  NLS_TERRITORY = "CZECH REPUBLIC"
  ```

- **By specifying NLS as an environment variable on the client** This defines the behavior of the client and overrides the default values set for the session in the initialization parameter file. The following is an example of setting NLS as an environment variable in a UNIX system:

  ```
  # export NLS_SORT=FRENCH
  ```

■   **At a session level by using the `alter session` command**

```
alter session set NLS_DATE_LANGUAGE = FRENCH;
```

■   **By specifying certain SQL functions**

```
TO_CHAR(hiredate, 'YYYY-MM-DD', 'NLS_DATE_LANGUAGE = FRENCH'))
```

The NLS parameters defined in SQL functions have the highest priority, followed by parameters specified in the `alter session` command, followed by the environment variable, followed by the initialization parameter, and finally followed by the lowest priority—the database default parameters.

NLS Parameters

The following is a list of some NLS parameters and their specifications:

■   **NLS_LANGUAGE**   Indicates the language for error messages, the names of days and months, and the symbols for 12-hour time of day and calendar era; this parameter also defines the sort mechanism Oracle will use.

■   **NLS_DATE_LANGUAGE**   Changes the language for day and month names, and other language components of date information.

■   **NLS_SORT**   Changes the sort mechanism Oracle uses; for example, you can override the default sort order of the national character set to use the sort order of another character set.

■   **NLS_TERRITORY**   Indicates the numbering for day of the week, default date format, currency symbols, and decimal symbol.

■   **NLS_CURRENCY**   Identifies a new currency symbol.

■   **NLS_ISO_CURRENCY**   Identifies a new territory whose ISO currency symbol should be used.

■   **NLS_DATE_FORMAT**   Identifies a new date format.

■   **NLS_NUMERIC_CHARACTERS**   Identifies a new decimal (0.00) and group (0,000) separator.

NLS_LANG overrides default NLS settings for the user, using the following format: *language_territory.characterset*. Altering NLS parameters within the session is accomplished in two ways: either by using the `alter session set` *parm_name = value* command, where *parm_name* is the name of the NLS parameter and *value* is what you want to set the parameter to; or, you can use the set_nls( ) procedure in the DBMS_SESSION package, which accepts two values: *parm_name* and *value*.

For Review

1. Identify two ways to change NLS parameters in your session.

2. Identify the parameter that changes the format of information in the DATE datatype.

Obtaining Information about Globalization Support Usage

You can get NLS information from your database in two ways: information about your data in various NLS formats and information about the general NLS setup for your database. The first set of information can be obtained through the standard SQL functions to_char( ), to_number( ), and to_date( ). These functions accept various NLS parameters and return information based on the NLS parameter you gave them.

In addition, several NLS functions are available that utilize the NLS_SORT parameter. The following code block shows output from a table with NLS parameters used to assist in providing meaningful formatting in a simple report. For this example, note the use of L, G, and D as the local currency, group or thousands, and decimal separator character markers in your formatting mask:

```
SQL> select year,
to_char(gnp,'L9G999G999G999D99','NLS_NUMERIC_CHARACTERS='''.,$''')
  2> as GNP
  3> from us_gnp;
    YEAR GNP
--------- ---------------------------
    1997         $5,948,399,939.34
    1998         $6,043,345,223.34
    1999         $6,143,545,453.80
```

TIP
Experiment with the order of characters specified for the previous NLS_NUMERIC_CHARACTERS init*sid*.ora *parameter, and see what happens with your output. The appropriate order for specifying them is* D, G, L, *and* C *(which represents the local ISO currency symbol, such as USD for U.S. dollars).*

Dictionary Views Containing NLS Parameters

In addition to the V$PARAMETER view, you can find information about settings for your NLS parameters in Oracle by looking at several different views, which are in the following list:

- **NLS_DATABASE_PARAMETERS**   All NLS databasewide parameters are stored in this view.

- **NLS_INSTANCE_PARAMETERS**   All NLS instancewide parameters are stored in this view.

- **NLS_SESSION_PARAMETERS**   All NLS parameters for the active session are stored in this view.

- **V$NLS_PARAMETERS**   This is a superset of the previous three views.

- **V$NLS_VALID_VALUES**   This is a listing of all valid values for all parameters.

For Review

1. Identify the view that contains all NLS parameters for your instance, session, and database.

2. Identify a way you might use an NLS parameter in a SQL conversion function. In what other ways might this be a useful feature in Oracle?

Index

Symbols

&
   lexical substitution variables, 172
   specifying column values before
      query processing, 167
* wildcard variable, 124
—, comments, 172
/, slash command, 166
@ command, executing scripts, 170
@@ command, executing scripts from
      scripts, 170
[ ], system variable abbreviations, 174
{ }, system variable values, 174

A

Abs( ) function, 69, 77
Accept command, prompting for input
      data, 171
access controls, fine grained, 863

accounts
   locking, 811, 826
   management, 808
   unlock option, 807
   user changeable options, 813
acquired extents, dictionary managed
      tablespaces, 676–677
Add_months( ) function, 82
adding
   columns to tables, 220
   rows to tables, 260–261
admin function system privileges, 834
admin option
   privileges, 841
   roles, 855
administration, OEM, 518
Administrative authentication, 509
Administrative privileges, 359
aging passwords, 827
ALERT log file, 540, 560

aliases, 48
  columns, 33
  tables, 101, 136
ALL data dictionary views, 576
ALL_TABLES data dictionary view, 579
allocating space
  tablespaces, 811–812, 816
  temporary segments, 640
  temporary tablespaces, 642
allocation, extents, 675
alter object privilege, 357, 838
alter role identified by statement, 367
alter sequence statements, 338
Alter system command, 558
alter table allocate extent
    statement, 740
Alter table move command, 745
alter table statements, 219
Alter user default role command, 368
alter user identified by statement, 810
alter user quota statement, 812
alter user statement, 865
alter view statements, 337
altering user profiles, 822
ambiguous table joins, 101
Analyze table tblname validate
    structure command, 741
And keyword, 63
ANSI/ISO
  cross joins, 106
  join syntax, 103–104
  outer joins, 112–113
answers to practice exam 1,
    439–450, 936–948
answers to practice exam 2,
    452–464, 949–962
answers to practice exam 3,
    464–478, 963–977
Append command, 44
architecture, OEM, 518
architecture, 484

archive modes, changing, 603
ARCHIVELOG mode, 602–604
arithmetic functions, 69, 77–78
arithmetic operations, table data, 29
Arraysize command, 174
As keyword, 34
ascending sort order, 57
asterisk, wildcard variable, 124
auditing, 869
  databases, 845–847
  objects, 848
  shortcuts, 849
  disabling, 849
  managing data, 851
  protecting data, 850
  value based, 846
  viewing options, 850
authentication
  host based, 349
  password file, 513
  users, 807
Autocommit immediate command, 74
autoextending tablespaces, 638
automatic definitions, runtime
    variables, 169
automatic undo, 693–694, 697
Autotrace traceonly command, 174
availability, control files, 595
Avg( ) function, 123

B

background processes, 15
backups, control files, 600
base tables, 574
  complex views, 306
  views, 294
batch processing, undo segments, 702
BFILE datatypes, 726
bitmap indexes, 324, 338, 756–757

BLOB datatypes, 215, 726
block space utilization parameters, 682
blocks, 625
   free space, 683–685
   utilization parameters, 682–683
Break command, 184
B-tree indexes, 323, 326–327, 338,
     755–756, 761–762
buffer cache, 13, 485
building indexes online, 766, 769

C

call level resource limits, 819
Cartesian products, 102, 106, 136
cascading effects of revoking
     privileges, 361–362
case translators, 74–75
Ceil( ) function, 70, 77
chaining, 741
changing tablespace status, 645–646
CHAR datatype, 27, 213, 725
character functions, 74–75
Chartorowid( ) function, 86
check constraint, 231, 779, 782
checkpoints, 497, 605–607
child tables, foreign keys, 99
clauses
   exists, 147
   group by, 126–128
   having, 133–134
   order by, 56, 129
   where, 61–62
Clear buffer command, 44
CLOB datatypes, 215, 726
closing databases, 559
cluster segments, 668
cluster system privileges, 835
cluster tables, 721–722
Cmdsep command, 174

collections, 727
Colsep command, 175
Column datatypes, 27
Column format heading
     command, 182
columns
   aliases, 33
   concatenation, 34
   constraints, 232
     group functions, 122–125
     prefixing with table name, 29
   data, 732
   dropping, 750–751
   marking unused, 750
   removing, 751–752
   tables
     adding, 220
     comments, 226
     datatypes, 220–221
     deleting, 222
commands
   SQL*Plus, 43–46
   writing in scripts, 41–42
comments, 172, 226
Commit command, 280
commit statements, 557
comparison operations, 90
comparison operators, 63–66
Compatibility command, 175
complex views, 305–306, 336
complexity verification, passwords,
     827–828
components
   OEM, 516
   Oracle databases, 11
composite indexes, 754
composite limits, 823
composite primary keys, 234
composite resource limits, 819
Compute command, 184
Concat command, 175

concatenating columns, 34
Concatenation operator, 34
configuration assistants, 500
configuring OMF, 527
CONNECT role, 370, 861
connecting subqueries to parent
    queries, 146
connections, databases, 21
console, OEM, 518
constraints, 228, 232, 249–250,
    784–786
  accessing data, 789
  check, 231, 782
  data integrity, 778–779
  deferability, 243–245, 782
  disabling, 239, 786
  enabling, 240
  foreign key, 229, 235, 781
  immediate, 782, 785
  indexes, 237
  integrity, 238, 785
  not NULL, 231, 780
  primary key, 232, 780
  removing, 242
  unique, 231, 236, 782
  viewability, 301
  violations, 240–241
control files, 585–588, 591, 595, 598
  backups, 600
  content data, 596
  granular data, 597
  multiplexing, 599
  names, 595
  OMF
    management, 592–593
    naming conventions, 594
  recreating, 588–590
CONTROL_FILES parameter, 546, 586
conversion functions, 86
Convert( ) function, 87
Copycommit command, 175

Copytypecheck command, 175
correcting statements, 38
correlated subqueries, 147
Count( ) function, 123
Count(expr) function, 123
Count(rowid) function, 123
Create database command, 553
create database statements, 554
Create global temporary table
    command, 206
create index statement, 761
Create public synonym command, 339
create sequence statements, 315
create table as select statements, 207
Create table command, 205, 734
create user option, 805
create user statement, 865
create view statement, 293, 337
creating databases, 543–544, 550–552
cross joins, 106
cross tabulations, 131–132
cube operations, 131
CURRVAL column, 337
customizing SQL*Plus
    environment, 173

D

data blocks, 731
data dictionaries, 570
  base tables, 574
  queries, 581, 584
    constraints, 583
  user-accessible views, 574
data dictionary views, 571–574,
    580–581, 686
  ALL_TABLES, 579
  auditing, 850
  constraints, 789
  DBA_IND_COLUMNS, 583
  DBA_INDEXES, 582

DBA_USERS, 582
indexes, 771
monitoring users, 815
privileges, 843
profile resource limits, 831
roles, 863
scope, 575
tables, 742
temporary segments, 642–643
temporary tablespaces, 644
topics, 576–578
undo data, 708
USER_TABLES, 575
data integrity constraints, 778–779
data position, insert statements,
    262–263
DATA tablespace, 669
data
  deleting from databases, 270
  limiting return, 62
  merging in tables, 273–275
  sorting with order by clause, 56–59
database access privileges, 353, 834
database access roles
  predefined, 370
  privileges, 367
  revoking, 369
database administrative tools, 500
database auditing, 845–847
Database Configuration Assistant,
    500, 549
  creating databases, 550
  templates, 550
database link system privileges, 836
Database objects, 314
database operation modes, 535
database passwords, 805
database privileges, 833
databases
  arithmetic functions, 69, 77–78
  authentication, 349

bitmap indexes, 324
B-tree indexes, 323–327
character functions, 74
columns
  aliases, 33
  concatenation, 34
complex views, 305–306
composite primary keys, 234
connections, 21
constraints
  check, 231
  disabling, 239
  enabling, 240
  foreign keys, 229, 235
  integrity, 238
  not NULL, 231, 236
  primary keys, 229, 232–233
  removing, 242
  unique, 231, 236
  violations, 240
conversion functions, 86–87
creating, 543
date arithmetic, 84
date formatting, 87
date functions, 81
decode( ) function, 73
deleting data, 270
developing apps, 17
DUAL table, 30
flat file, 7
function-based indexes, 327
hierarchical queries, 295
indexes, 237, 322
  deleting, 328
limiting return data, 61
list functions, 70
locks, 284
manual creation, 552
multiple comparisons, 63
NULL values, 31
operator precedence, 30

parent tables
  dropping, 242
privileges, 348
read only, 535
read consistency, 283
relational, 7
security, passwords, 355
sequences
  dropping, 321
  gaps, 321
  modifying definitions, 319
  referencing, 318
  sequences, 315
simple views, 294
  changing table data, 297
  restrictions, 298
single-row functions, 67
sorting data, order by clause, 56
starting automatically, 535
tables
  adding columns, 220
  arithmetic operations, 29
  column datatypes, 220
  column default values, 217
  comments, 226
database tables
  constraint deferability, 243
  creating with other table data, 207
  creating, 202
  datatypes, 211
  deleting, 224
  displaying data, 98
  dropping columns, 222
  editing, 219
  naming, 208
  pseudocolumns, 216
  records, 26
  renaming, 225
  schema, 28
  truncating, 225
database temporary tables, 206–207

database text functions, 68, 74
database updatable join views, 306
database users
  administrative privileges, 359
  creating, 348
  object privileges, 357
  PUBLIC privileges, 358
  retrieving user data, 350
  revoking privileges, 352
  system privileges, 351–354
database viewability constraints, 301
database views
  base tables, 294
  modifying, 310
  read-only clauses, 302
  removing, 312
  views, 292
datafiles, 14, 625
  tablespaces
    OMF, 653
    relocating, 649–650
datatypes, 724–725
  BLOB, 215
  CLOB, 215
  collections, 727
  column, 27
  Date, 215
  LONG RAW, 215
  LONG, 215
  NCLOB, 215
  NUMBER, 214
  RAW, 215
  reference, 727
  ROWID, 216
  scalar, 725
  table columns, 220
  text, 213
  user defined, 727
date arithmetic, 84
DATE datatype, 27, 215, 726
date formatting, 87

date functions, 81–83
date, limiting return, 61–62
DB_BLOCK_CHECKSUM
    parameter, 741
DB_BLOCK_SIZE parameter, 545
DB_CACHE_SIZE parameter, 546
DB_DOMAIN parameter, 545
DB_NAME parameter, 545
DBA data dictionary views, 576
DBA role, 370, 861
DBA_CONS_COLUMNS view, 790
DBA_CONSTRAINTS view, 789
DBA_DATA_FILES view, 687
DBA_EXTENTS view, 687
DBA_FREE_SPACE view, 687
DBA_FREE_SPACE_COALESCED
    view, 687
DBA_IND_COLUMNS data dictionary
    view, 583
DBA_INDEXES data dictionary
    view, 582
DBA_SEGMENTS view, 687
DBA_TABLESPACES view, 687
DBA_TS_QUOTAS view, 687
DBA_USERS data dictionary view, 582
DBWO (database writer process),
    496, 557
Decode( ) function, 71–73
Default keyword, setting column
    values, 269
default profiles, 822, 829
default roles, 856–857
default storage options,
    tablespaces, 635
default tablespace option, 805
default temporary tablespaces, 628
default values, table columns, 217
deferability of constraints, 243
deferred constraints, 782
defining runtime variables
    automatically, 169

definitions, sequences, modifying, 319
Del command, 44
delete object privilege, 357, 838
delete statements, 271, 286
DELETE_CATALOG role, 862
deleting
    constraints, 242
    database data, 270
    indexes, 328
    parent tables, 242
    sequences, 321
    table columns, 222
    tables, 224
    views, 312
descending indexes, 759
descending sort order, 57
Describe command, 203
Describe depth command, 175
detail tables, foreign keys, 99
developing database apps,
    PL/SQL, 17–18
diagnostic file monitoring, 539
dictionary-managed tablespaces,
    acquired extents, 675–677
dictionary views
    displaying privileges, 355
    roles, 370
dictionary-managed tablespaces, 625
directory PL/SQL privileges, 837
dirty buffers, 496
disabling
    auditing, 849
    constraints, 239, 786
disabling roles, 857
disk components, Oracle
    control files, 14
    datafiles, 14
    parameter files, 15
    password files, 14
Dispatcher processes, 491
Dispatcher, 488

displaying data from tables, 98
Distinct keyword, 32
double dashes, comments, 172
drop user statement, 813
drop view statements, 337
dropping
    columns, 750
    indexes, 771
    parent tables, 242
    sequences, 321
    tables, 747
        columns, 222
    users, 810, 813, 822
DUAL table, 30, 48
dynamic performance views,
        578–579, 596

E

Echo command, 176
Edit command, 40, 49
Editfile command, 176
editing
    row data, 267
    statements, 40
    tables, 219
    views, 310
Embedded command, 176
enabling constraints, 240
enabling roles, 857
entering variables, SQL*Plus, 165–167
equality operations, table joins, 104
equijoins, 103, 136
error messages, 39
Escape command, 176
EXCEPTIONS table, 787–788
excluding data via having clause, 133
execute object privilege, 839
execute privileges, 357
execute statements, 495
EXECUTE_CATALOG role, 862

executing select statements, 25
exists clauses, subqueries, 146
Exit command, 46
EXP_FULL_DATABASE role, 861
explicit default values, tables, 266
extended ROWIDs, 729–730
extents, 624
    allocation, 675
    parallel processing, 678
    segments, 673–674
    uniform management, 674

F

Feedback command, 176
fields. *See* columns.
fine grained access control, 863
Flagger command, 176
flat file databases, 7, 10
Floor( ) function, 70, 77
Flush command, 176
flushing redo buffer, 602
foreign keys, 99, 135
    constraints, 229, 235, 779–781
formatting dates, 87
free space, blocks, 683–685
frequency, checkpoints, 605–606
From clauses, subqueries, 162
From keyword, 48
full outer joins, 114
function-based indexes, 327–328, 758
functions
    arithmetic, 69
    avg( ), 123
    conversion, 86
    count( ), 123
    count(expr), 123
    count(rowid), 123
    date, 81
    decode( ), 71

group, 122
    ignoring NULL values, 125
list, 70
max( ), 124
min( ), 124
nvl( ), 31, 125
select statements, 73
single-row, 67
subqueries, 148
sum( ), 124
text, 68

G

gaps in sequences, 321
Get command, 42
global scope, 147
Grant command, 339
granting privileges, 840
granting roles, 854
granular data, control files, 597
Greatest( ) function, 70
Group by clauses, 126–128, 137
    having clauses, 133
    order by clauses, 129
group functions, 122–125
    ignoring NULL values, 125
    subqueries, 148
grouping functions, 137
guidelines for creating indexes, 329
guidelines for privileges, 363

H

Having clauses, 133–134, 152
Heading command, 177
Headsep command, 177
Hextoraw( ) function, 87
hierarchical queries, 295
high water marks, tables, 740

host authentication, 349
host system resource management, 820

I

identified by option, 805
immediate constraints, 782
IMP_FULL_DATABASE role, 861
improving output readability, 181–186
index object privilege, 357, 839
index privileges, 353
index segments, 666
INDEX tablespace, 669
indexes, 9, 237, 250, 322, 338, 753,
        760, 765, 776–777
    system privileges, 835
    bitmap, 324, 756–757
    B-tree, 323, 326–327, 755–756,
        761–762
    building, 769
    deleting, 328
    descending, 759
    dropping, 771
    function based, 327–328, 758
    monitoring use, 773
    online rebuilding, 766
    reorganizing, 765
    reverse key, 758
    sizing, 763
    types, 754
index-organized tables, 721
individual resource limits, 822
Initcap( ) function, 68
initialization parameter file, 521–524
initialization parameters
    OMF, 528–529
    operating system authentication, 512
initrans option, 734
inline views, 162–163, 191–192
Input command, 44
input data, prompting for, 171

insert object privilege, 357, 838
insert statements, 260, 286
   nonexplicit columns, 262
   populating tables with other table
      data, 264
   position of data, 262
installation log, 505
installing software, 503
Instance command, 177
instance parameters, 558
instances, 484
   managing, 521
   shutting down, 536
   starting, 531
Instr( ) function, 68
integrity constraints, 238, 248, 265,
      780, 785
   data changes, 269
   deleting data, 272
integrity of tables, 741
IOTs (index-organized tables),
      668, 721
iterative programming language, 23

J–K

join conditions, merge command, 276
joins, 116–117
   ANSI/ISO syntax, 103
   natural, 105
   outer, 109–112
   self, 118–120
   tables, 99, 107–108, 121
      Cartesian products, 102
      equality operations, 104
      full outer, 114
      select statements, 100
   where clauses, 115

keywords
   and, 63
   as, 34
   distinct, 32
   or, 63

L

large pool, SGA, 13
Last_day( ) function, 82
Least( ) function, 70
Length( ) function, 68
lexical substitution variables, 167
LGWR (log writer process), 497
library PL/SQL privileges, 837
Linesize command, 177
links, 135
List command, 43
list functions, 70
Listener processes, 490
LOB segments, 668
Loboffset command, 177
local scope, 147
locally managed tablespaces, 625
locally managed temporary
      tablespaces, 641
locking accounts, 811, 826
locks, 284
log buffer, SGA, 13
log files, 540, 601
log switches, 605
LOG_BUFFER parameter, 546
logging clause, 735
Long command, 177
LONG datatypes, 215, 726
LONG RAW datatypes, 215, 726
Longchunksize command, 177
Lower( ) function, 68
Lpad( ) function, 68, 74

M

managing
  audit data, 851
  instances, 521
  privileges, 833
  resources, 817
  roles, 853
  tables, 718, 723–724
manual database creation, 552
manual undo segment
     maintenance, 705
marking unused columns, 750
master tables, primary keys, 99
materialized PL/SQL privileges, 837
Max( ) function, 124
maxtrans option, 734
members, redo log files, 609
memory areas, SGA, 14
memory, Oracle databases, 11
Merge command, 274
merging data in tables, 273–276
Min( ) function, 124
Mod( ) function, 70
modifiable join views, 306
modifying
  roles, 853
  row data, 267
  views, 310
monitoring
  diagnostic files, 539
  index use, 773
  object use, 774
  user data, 815
Months_between( ) function, 82
MTS (multithreaded server), 488
multicolumn subqueries,
    156–157, 191
multiple comparisons, 63–66

multiple tables, displaying data, 98
multiplexing control files, 599
multiplexing redo log files, 608
multirow subqueries, 152, 191

N

names, control files, 595
naming tables, 208
natural joins, 105
NCHAR datatypes, 725
NCLOB datatypes, 215, 726
N-dimensional cross tabulations, 131
nested tables, 727
nesting select statements within select
    statements, 144
Network Configuration Assistant, 500
New_time( ) function, 82–84
Newpage command, 177
Next_day( ) function, 82
NEXTVAL column, 337
NOARCHIVELOG mode, 602–604
nocache clause, 734
nonpartitioned B-tree indexes, 756
Not NULL constraint, 231, 236,
    779–780
Null command, 177
NULL values, 31, 48
  ignoring by group functions, 125
  rows, 732
  subqueries, 158–160
NUMBER datatype, 27, 214, 725
number functions, 77
Number string command, 45
Numformat command, 178
Numwidth command, 178
NVARCHAR2 datatypes, 725
Nvl( ) function, 31, 48, 125, 159

O

object auditing, 848
object privileges, 357–358, 838
    cascading effects of revocation, 361
    revoking, 360, 842
objects, database, 314
objects, monitoring use, 774
OEM, 501
    administration, 518
    architecture, 518
    components, 516
    Console, 518
OFA (Optimal Flexible Architecture),
    506–507, 545
OLAP
    cube operations, 131
    rollup operations, 130
OMF (Oracle-Managed Files), 652
    configuring, 527
    control file management, 592–593
    initialization parameters, 528
    redo log files, 611
    tablespace datafiles, 653
    tempfiles, 653
on commit delete rows option, 736
on commit preserve rows option, 736
online index rebuilding, 766
online redo log files, 611–612
online redo log groups, 554
online redo logs, 601
online undo segments, 704
operating system authentication,
    510–512
operations
    cube, 131
    rollup, 130
operator precedence, 30
operators
    comparison, 63
    concatenation, 34
    outer join, 111

Or keyword, 63
Oracle architecture, 484
Oracle databases, 7–11
Oracle DBA Studio, 501
Oracle Migration Assistant, 500
Oracle server, 15, 500, 556
Oracle
    starting, 532
    stopping, 537
ORDBMS, 15
Order by clause, 56, 90, 129
OUI (Oracle Universal Installer),
    502, 557
outer join operator, 111
outer joins, 109–113
outer tables, 136
output, improving readability, 181–186

P

Pagesize command, 178
parallel processing, extents, 678
parameter files, 15, 545
parameters, block space
    utilization, 682
parent queries, 146
parent tables
    dropping, 242
    primary keys, 99
parse statements, 495
parsing, 9
partitioned tables, 720
password expire option, 807
password file authentication, 509
password file default locations, 514
password files, 14
password management resource
    limits, 829
password security, 817
passwords, 355, 373, 810
    aging, 827
    complexity verification, 827–828

databases, 805
profiles, 826, 830
roles, 854
Pause command, 178
pctfree clause, 683–685
pctused option, 683–685
permanent segments, tablespaces, 632
permanent tables, 733
permanent tablespaces,
        627, 633, 636, 640
PGA (Program Global Area), 487
PL/SQL
    developing database apps, 17
    privileges, 836
position of data, insert statements, 262
preallocation, tablespaces, 678
precedence of operators, 30
predefined roles, 370, 861
prefixing columns with table
        names, 29
primary key constraints, 778
primary keys, 99
    composite, 234
    constraint, 229
private synonyms, 332
privilege auditing, 847
privileges, 833, 844, 867–868
    admin option, 841
    administrative, 359
    create table, 205
    granting, 840
    object, 357–360, 838, 842
    PL/SQL, 836
    PUBLIC, 358
    revoking, 352, 840
    roles, 367, 854
    SYSDBA, 837
    SYSOPER, 837
    system, 351, 834, 836, 842
    usage guidelines, 363
    viewing, 355

procedural programming language, 23
PROCESSES parameter, 547
processes
    background, 15
    listener, 490
    server, 487
processing
    commit statements, 497
    DML statements, 495
    queries, 493
profile option, 807
profile PL/SQL privileges, 836
profiles, 822, 830
    altering, 822
    composite limits, 823
    default, 822
    password, 826, 830
    resource limits, 866
    resource usage, 818, 831–832
prompting for Input data accept
        command, 171
protecting audit data, 850
pseudocolumns, tables, 216
PUBLIC privileges, 358
Public synonyms, 333
PUBLIC users, privileges, 843

Q

queries
    data dictionaries, 581–584
    hierarchical, 295
    processing, 493
    top-N, 163
quota option, 806

R

RAW datatypes, 215, 726
Rawtohex( ) function, 87
RDBMS (relational database
        management system), 8, 493

read only clauses, views, 302
read only databases, 535
read only online tablespaces, 646
readability of output, 181
read consistency, databases, 283
rebuilding indexes online, 766, 769
records, tables, 26
recreating control files, 588–590
Recsep command, 178
Recsepchar command, 178
redo information log buffer, 13
redo log buffer, 487
redo log files, 601–602, 610
   adding or removing, 609
   members, 609
   multiplexing, 608
   OMF management, 611
   renaming, 609
redo log groups, 554
redo logs, 14
reference datatypes, 727
references object privilege, 839
references privileges, 357
referencing sequences, 318
referential integrity, 249
regular tables, 719, 733
relational databases, 7–10
relationships, storage structures, 664
relocating tables, 744–746
relocating tablespace datafiles, 649
REMOTE_OS_AUTHENT
   parameter, 808
removing
   columns, 751
   constraints, 242
   roles, 860
   indexes, 328
   views, 312
Rename command, 225
renaming redo log files, 609
renaming tables, 225

reorganizing indexes, 765
repositories, 668
request queue, 491
resource consumer groups, 820
resource limit profiles, 866
resource management, 817
   call level limits, 819
   composite limits, 819
   profiles, 818, 831–832
   session level limits, 818
RESOURCE role, 370, 861
response files, 505
restricted ROWIDs, 729
restrictions
   online index rebuilding, 769
   simple views, 298
   system privileges, 838
retaining undo data, 695
return data
   limiting, 61
   sorting with order by clause, 56
reverse key indexes, 758
Revoke command, 339
revoking object privileges, 842
revoking privileges, 352, 360–362, 840
revoking roles, 860
revoking system privileges, 842
role privileges, 354
role system privileges, 836
roles, 853, 858–859, 869
   admin option, 855
   creating, 853
   defaults, 856
   dictionary views, 370
   disabling, 857
   enabling, 857
   modifying, 853
   passwords, 854
   predefined, 370, 861
   privileges, 854
   revoking, 369, 860

Rollback command, 280
rollbacks, 631
rollup operations, 130
Round( ) function, 70, 77
row level locks, 284
row migration, 741–743
ROWID datatypes, 216, 726
ROWIDs, 728
  extended, 729–730
  restricted, 729
Rowidtochar( ) function, 86
rows, 731
  chaining, 741
  data, 732
  NULL values, 732
  tables
    adding, 260
    editing data, 267
Rpad( ) function, 68, 74
Rule of Four, undo segments, 702
Run command, 45
runtime variables, 165, 169, 192

S

Save command, 46
Savepoint command, 280
savepoints, 283
saving SQL*Plus customized
      settings, 188
scalar datatypes, 725
scalar subqueries, 151
schema ownership, 331
schema transparency, 333
schema, 28
scope, data dictionary views, 575
scope, 147
scripts, 41, 187–188
security, 372
  passwords, 355, 817
  users, creating, 348

segments, 624
  cluster, 668
  extents, 673
  index, 666
  IOT, 668
  IOX, 668
  LOB, 668
  separating into tablespaces, 669
  table, 665
  tablespaces, 670
  temporary, 667
  undo, 666–667, 689–690, 693,
        696–698, 706–707
select object privilege, 357, 838
select statements
  correcting, 39
  distinct keyword, 32
  executing, 25
  functions, 73
  group by clauses, 126
  joining table data, 100
  nesting within select statements, 144
SELECT_CATALOG role, 862
self joins, 118–120, 136
sequence privileges, 354
sequence system privileges, 836
sequences, 315–318, 337
  dropping, 321
  gaps, 321
  modifying definitions, 319
  referencing, 318
server architecture, 485
server parameter file, 558
server processes, 487, 557
Serveroutput command, 178
servers, background processes, 15
session level resource limits, 818
sessions, 22
Set role command, 369
Set system_variable value
      command, 173

Set transaction command, 280
seven parameter file, 547
SGA (System Global Area), 11, 485
  buffer cache, 13
  large pool, 13
  log buffer, 13
  memory areas, 14
  shared pool, 13
shared pool, SGA, 13, 485
shared servers, 488
Shiftinout command, 179
shortcuts, auditing, 849
Showmode command, 179
shutdown abort option, 538
shutdown immediate option, 537
shutdown normal option, 537
shutdown transactional option, 538
shutting down instances, 536
Sign( ) function, 70, 78
silent mode, SQL*Plus, 26
simple indexes, 754
simple views, 294–296, 336
  changing table data, 297
  restrictions, 298
single-row functions, 67, 71, 88
single-row subqueries, 150, 191
sizing indexes, 763
sizing tablespaces, 637
sizing undo segments, 702
Slash command, 166
snapshot PL/SQL privileges, 837
software install, 503
sorting data with order by clause,
  56–59
space allocation, temporary
  tablespaces, 642
space management, tablespaces, 625
Spool command, 46
SQL (Structured Query Language), 8
  statements, 20
  writing statements, 20

Change command, 38
  commands, 43–46
SQL*Plus, 501
  customizing environment, 174
  editing statements, 40
  entering variables, 165
  improving output readability, 181
  saving customized settings, 188
  scripts, 187
  silent mode, 26
  writing commands in scripts, 41
SQL*Plus Worksheet, 518
Sqlblanklines command, 179
Sqlcase command, 179
Sqlcontinue command, 179
Sqlnumber command, 179
Sqlprefix command, 180
Sqlprompt command, 180
Sqlterminator command, 180
Sqrt( ) function, 70
Sqrt( ) function, 8
starting databases automatically, 535
starting databases, 559
starting instances, 531
starting Oracle, 532
startup force option, 534
startup mount option, 533
startup nomount option, 532
startup open option, 533
statement auditing, 847
statements
  alter role identified by, 367
  alter table, 219
  correcting, 38
  create sequence, 315
  create table as select, 207
  create view, 293
  editing, 40
  insert, 260
  select, executing, 25
  SQL, 20
  update, 268

status changes, tablespaces, 645
stopping Oracle, 537
storage rules, tables, 735
storage settings, tablespaces, 648
storage settings, undo segments, 703
storage structures, 664, 686
storage, temporary tables, 737
storing data in tables, 719–720
subqueries, 144–149, 154–156, 191
  correlated, 147
  exists clauses, 146
  from clauses, 162
  functions, 148
  having clauses, 152
  multicolumn, 156
  multirow, 152
  NULL values, 158
  nvl( ) function, 159
  parent queries, 146
  scalar, 151
  single row, 150
  update statements, 268
  with clauses, 153
Substr( ) function, 68, 75
Suffix command, 180
suggested tablespaces, 631
Sum( ) function, 124
synonym privileges, 353
synonym system privileges, 835
synonyms, 332–333, 339, 373
SYS user, 510
SYSDBA privilege, 837
SYSOPER privilege, 837
system privileges, 351–354, 834
  cascading effects of revocation, 360
  restrictions, 838
  revoking, 842
SYSTEM tablespace, 553, 627, 665, 669–670
SYSTEM user, 510
system variables, 173

T

Tab command, 180
table joins, 99, 116–117, 135
  Cartesian products, 102
  equality operations, 104
  select statements, 100
  where clauses, 115
table level locks, 284
table management, 718, 723–724
table privileges, 353
table segments, 665
table system privileges, 835
tables
  adding rows, 260
  aliases, 101
  arithmetic operations, 29
  BLOB datatype, 215
  CLOB datatype, 215
  cluster, 721–722
  columns
    adding, 220
    datatypes, 220
    default values, 217
    deleting, 222
    prefixing with table name, 29
    removing, 751
  data storage, 719–720
  deleting, 224
  dropping, 747–748
  DUAL, 30
  editing, 219
  equijoins, 103
  EXCEPTIONS, 787–788
  explicit default values, 266
  full outer joins, 114
  high water marks, 740
  indexes, 755
  integrity, 741
    constraints, 265, 269
  joins, 107
  LONG datatype, 215

LONG RAW datatype, 215
merging data, 273–276
naming, 208
natural joins, 105
NCLOB datatype, 215
nested, 727
NUMBER datatype, 214
outer joins, 109
parent, dropping, 242
partitioned, 720
permanent, 733
pseudocolumns, 216
RAW datatype, 215
records, 26
regular, 719
relocating, 744–746
renaming, 225
ROWID datatype, 216
rows
   editing data, 267
   migration, 741
schema, 28
self joins, 118
storage rules, 735
subqueries, 145
synonyms, 332
temporary, 206, 719–720, 736–739
text datatype, 213
truncating, 225, 747
unused space, 740
tablespace system privileges, 834
tablespaces, 624, 629–630, 639, 648,
      665, 671–672, 681, 805,
      809–810
allocation, 811–812, 816
creating, 631
DATA, 669
default storage options, 635
dictionary managed, 625
extent allocation, 675
housing permanent segments, 632
housing segments, 670

INDEX, 669
locally managed, 625
OMF datafiles, 653
Oracle9i limitations, 651
permanent, 627, 633, 636
preallocation, 678
quotas, 806
read-only online, 646
relocating datafiles, 649
sizing, 637
space management, 625
status changes, 645
storage settings, 648
suggested creations, 631
SYSTEM, 553, 627, 665, 669–670
temporary, 627, 633–636, 669
TOOLS, 669
undo, 695–696
UNDOTBS, 669
uniform space allocation, 673
tempfiles, temporary tablespaces, 653
templates, Database Configuration
      Assistant, 550
temporary segments, 640–641, 667
temporary tables, 206–207, 669,
      719–720, 735–739
temporary tablespace option, 806
temporary tablespace statement, 812
temporary tablespaces, 627–628,
      633–636, 640–641, 653
Termout command, 180
text datatypes, 213
text editors, 40
text functions, 68, 74
Time command, 180
Timing command, 180
To_char( ) function, 86–87
To_date( ) function, 86
To_multi_byte( ) function, 86
To_number( ) function, 86
To_single_byte( ) function, 86
TOOLS tablespace, 669

topics, data dictionary views, 576–578
top-N queries, inline views, 163
trace files, 539–540, 560
transaction controls, 279–282, 286
transaction privileges, 354
transaction system privileges, 836
transactions, 206
  undo segments, 699–700
  savepoints, 283
Translate( ) function, 87
trigger PL/SQL privileges, 836
Trim( ) function, 68
Trimout command, 180
Trimspool command, 180
Trunc( ) function, 70, 78
truncating tables, 225, 747
types PL/SQL privileges, 837
typos, correcting, 39

U

Undefine command, 170
Underline command, 182
undo segments, 666–667, 689–690,
    693, 696–698, 706–707
  system privileges, 835
  batch processing, 702
  manual maintenance, 705
  Rule of Four, 702
  sizing, 702
  storage settings, 703
  tablespaces, 695
  transactions, 699
undo
  automatic, 694, 697
  retaining data, 695
UNDO_MANAGEMENT
    parameter, 546
UNDO_TABLESPACE parameter, 546
UNDOTBS tablespace, 669

uniform extent management, 674
uniform space allocation, tables, 673
unique constraints, 231, 236, 779, 782
unused space, tables, 740
updatable join views, 306
update object privilege, 838
update statements, 286
  modifying column values, 268
  setting column values, default
    keyword, 269
  subqueries, 268
Upper( ) function, 68
user account management, 808
user authentication, 558
USER data dictionary views, 576
user defined datatypes, 727
user IDS, changing, 814
user privileges, 353
user profiles, altering, 822
user session info, 489
user system privileges, 835
user tablespace allocation, 811–812
USER_TABLES data dictionary
    view, 575
user-accessible views, 574
users
  account locking, 826
  changeable account options, 813
  composite limits, 823
  creating, 804
  default profiles, 822
  dropping, 810, 813
  monitoring data, 815
  object privileges, 357, 360, 842
  OS authentication, 807
  passwords, 355, 810–811, 827
  profiles, 807, 822, 826
  PUBLIC privileges, 358
  retrieving user data, 350
  revoking privileges, 352, 842

roles
  predefined, 370
  privileges, 367
  revoking, 369
  system privileges, 351
utilization parameters, blocks, 682–683

V

V$CONTROLFILE view, 595
V$CONTROLFILE_RECORD_SECTION
  view, 597
V$DATAFILE view, 687
V$TABLESPACE view, 687
value-based auditing, 846
values
  NULL, 31
  tables
    columns, default, 217
    explicit defaults, 266
VARCHAR datatype, 27
VARCHAR2 datatype, 213, 725
variable scope, 147, 191
variables
  entering, SQL*Plus, 165
  lexical substitution, 167
  runtime, 165, 169
  system, 173
VARRAYs, 727

Verify command, 181
verifying passwords, 828
view privileges, 354
view system privileges, 835
viewability constraints, 301
viewing privileges, 355
views, 292–293, 336
  base tables, 294
  complex, 305
  modifying, 310
  read-only clauses, 302
  removing, 312
  simple, 294
  updatable join, 306
violations of constraints, 240
Vsize( ) function, 70, 78

W

Where clauses, 61–62, 90
  delete statements, 271
  table joins, 115
width of columns, 732
wildcard variables, 124
With check option clauses, 337
With clauses, subqueries, 153
Wrap command, 183
writing commands in scripts, 41
writing SQL statements, 20

INTERNATIONAL CONTACT INFORMATION

AUSTRALIA
McGraw-Hill Book Company Australia Pty. Ltd.
TEL +61-2-9417-9899
FAX +61-2-9417-5687
http://www.mcgraw-hill.com.au
books-it_sydney@mcgraw-hill.com

CANADA
McGraw-Hill Ryerson Ltd.
TEL +905-430-5000
FAX +905-430-5020
http://www.mcgrawhill.ca

GREECE, MIDDLE EAST,
NORTHERN AFRICA
McGraw-Hill Hellas
TEL +30-1-656-0990-3-4
FAX +30-1-654-5525

MEXICO (Also serving Latin America)
McGraw-Hill Interamericana Editores S.A. de C.V.
TEL +525-117-1583
FAX +525-117-1589
http://www.mcgraw-hill.com.mx
fernando_castellanos@mcgraw-hill.com

SINGAPORE (Serving Asia)
McGraw-Hill Book Company
TEL +65-863-1580
FAX +65-862-3354
http://www.mcgraw-hill.com.sg
mghasia@mcgraw-hill.com

SOUTH AFRICA
McGraw-Hill South Africa
TEL +27-11-622-7512
FAX +27-11-622-9045
robyn_swanepoel@mcgraw-hill.com

UNITED KINGDOM & EUROPE
(Excluding Southern Europe)
McGraw-Hill Education Europe
TEL +44-1-628-502500
FAX +44-1-628-770224
http://www.mcgraw-hill.co.uk
computing_neurope@mcgraw-hill.com

ALL OTHER INQUIRIES Contact:
Osborne/McGraw-Hill
TEL +1-510-549-6600
FAX +1-510-883-7600
http://www.osborne.com
omg_international@mcgraw-hill.com

GET YOUR FREE SUBSCRIPTION TO ORACLE MAGAZINE

Oracle Magazine is essential gear for today's information technology professionals. Stay informed and increase your productivity with every issue of *Oracle Magazine*. Inside each free bimonthly issue you'll get:

- Up-to-date information on Oracle Database, E-Business Suite applications, Web development, and database technology and business trends
- Third-party news and announcements
- Technical articles on Oracle Products and operating environments
- Development and administration tips
- Real-world customer stories

Three easy ways to subscribe:

① Web

Visit our Web site at www.oracle.com/oraclemagazine. You'll find a subscription form there, plus much more!

② Fax

Complete the questionnaire on the back of this card and fax the questionnaire side only to +1.847.647.9735.

③ Mail

Complete the questionnaire on the back of this card and mail it to P.O. Box 1263, Skokie, IL 60076-8263

IF THERE ARE OTHER ORACLE USERS AT YOUR LOCATION WHO WOULD LIKE TO RECEIVE THEIR OWN SUBSCRIPTION TO ORACLE MAGAZINE, PLEASE PHOTOCOPY THIS FORM AND PASS IT ALONG.

Oracle Publishing

Oracle Corporation © 2002. All rights reserved. Oracle is a registered trademark of Oracle Corporation. All other names may be trademarks of their respective owners.

ORACLE®

FREE SUBSCRIPTION

O Yes, please send me a FREE subscription to *Oracle Magazine*   O **NO**

To receive a free subscription to *Oracle Magazine*, you must fill out the entire card, sign it, and date it (incomplete cards cannot be processed or acknowledged). You can also fax your application to +1.847.647.9735.
Or subscribe at our Web site at www.oracle.com/oraclemagazine/

O From time to time, Oracle Publishing allows our partners exclusive access to our e-mail addresses for special promotions and announcements. To be included in this program, please check this box.

O Oracle Publishing allows sharing of our mailing list with selected third parties. If you prefer your mailing address not to be included in this program, please check here. If at any time you would like to be removed from this mailing list, please contact Customer Service at +1.847.647.9630 or send an e-mail to oracle@halldata.com.

signature (required)   date

X

name   title

company   e-mail address

street/p.o. box

city/state/zip or postal code   telephone

country   fax

YOU MUST ANSWER ALL NINE QUESTIONS BELOW.

① WHAT IS THE PRIMARY BUSINESS ACTIVITY OF YOUR FIRM AT THIS LOCATION? (check one only)

- ☐ 01 Application Service Provider
- ☐ 02 Communications
- ☐ 03 Consulting, Training
- ☐ 04 Data Processing
- ☐ 05 Education
- ☐ 06 Engineering
- ☐ 07 Financial Services
- ☐ 08 Government (federal, local, state, other)
- ☐ 09 Government (military)
- ☐ 10 Health Care
- ☐ 11 Manufacturing (aerospace, defense)
- ☐ 12 Manufacturing (computer hardware)
- ☐ 13 Manufacturing (noncomputer)
- ☐ 14 Research & Development
- ☐ 15 Retailing, Wholesaling, Distribution
- ☐ 16 Software Development
- ☐ 17 Systems Integration, VAR, VAD, OEM
- ☐ 18 Transportation
- ☐ 19 Utilities (electric, gas, sanitation)
- ☐ 98 Other Business and Services

② WHICH OF THE FOLLOWING BEST DESCRIBES YOUR PRIMARY JOB FUNCTION? (check one only)

Corporate Management/Staff
- ☐ 01 Executive Management (President, Chair, CEO, CFO, Owner, Partner, Principal)
- ☐ 02 Finance/Administrative Management (VP/Director/ Manager/Controller, Purchasing, Administration)
- ☐ 03 Sales/Marketing Management (VP/Director/Manager)
- ☐ 04 Computer Systems/Operations Management (CIO/VP/Director/ Manager MIS, Operations)

IS/IT Staff
- ☐ 05 Systems Development/ Programming Management
- ☐ 06 Systems Development/ Programming Staff
- ☐ 07 Consulting
- ☐ 08 DBA/Systems Administrator
- ☐ 09 Education/Training
- ☐ 10 Technical Support Director/Manager
- ☐ 11 Other Technical Management/Staff
- ☐ 98 Other

③ WHAT IS YOUR CURRENT PRIMARY OPERATING PLATFORM? (select all that apply)

- ☐ 01 Digital Equipment UNIX
- ☐ 02 Digital Equipment VAX VMS
- ☐ 03 HP UNIX
- ☐ 04 IBM AIX
- ☐ 05 IBM UNIX
- ☐ 06 Java
- ☐ 07 Linux
- ☐ 08 Macintosh
- ☐ 09 MS-DOS
- ☐ 10 MVS
- ☐ 11 NetWare
- ☐ 12 Network Computing
- ☐ 13 OpenVMS
- ☐ 14 SCO UNIX
- ☐ 15 Sequent DYNIX/ptx
- ☐ 16 Sun Solaris/SunOS
- ☐ 17 SVR4
- ☐ 18 UnixWare
- ☐ 19 Windows
- ☐ 20 Windows NT
- ☐ 21 Other UNIX
- ☐ 98 Other
- 99 ☐ None of the above

④ DO YOU EVALUATE, SPECIFY, RECOMMEND, OR AUTHORIZE THE PURCHASE OF ANY OF THE FOLLOWING? (check all that apply)

- ☐ 01 Hardware
- ☐ 02 Software
- ☐ 03 Application Development Tools
- ☐ 04 Database Products
- ☐ 05 Internet or Intranet Products
- 99 ☐ None of the above

⑤ IN YOUR JOB, DO YOU USE OR PLAN TO PURCHASE ANY OF THE FOLLOWING PRODUCTS? (check all that apply)

Software
- ☐ 01 Business Graphics
- ☐ 02 CAD/CAE/CAM
- ☐ 03 CASE
- ☐ 04 Communications
- ☐ 05 Database Management
- ☐ 06 File Management
- ☐ 07 Finance
- ☐ 08 Java
- ☐ 09 Materials Resource Planning
- ☐ 10 Multimedia Authoring
- ☐ 11 Networking
- ☐ 12 Office Automation
- ☐ 13 Order Entry/Inventory Control
- ☐ 14 Programming
- ☐ 15 Project Management
- ☐ 16 Scientific and Engineering
- ☐ 17 Spreadsheets
- ☐ 18 Systems Management
- ☐ 19 Workflow

Hardware
- ☐ 20 Macintosh
- ☐ 21 Mainframe
- ☐ 22 Massively Parallel Processing
- ☐ 23 Minicomputer
- ☐ 24 PC
- ☐ 25 Network Computer
- ☐ 26 Symmetric Multiprocessing
- ☐ 27 Workstation

Peripherals
- ☐ 28 Bridges/Routers/Hubs/Gateways
- ☐ 29 CD-ROM Drives
- ☐ 30 Disk Drives/Subsystems
- ☐ 31 Modems
- ☐ 32 Tape Drives/Subsystems
- ☐ 33 Video Boards/Multimedia

Services
- ☐ 34 Application Service Provider
- ☐ 35 Consulting
- ☐ 36 Education/Training
- ☐ 37 Maintenance
- ☐ 38 Online Database Services
- ☐ 39 Support
- ☐ 40 Technology-Based Training
- ☐ 98 Other
- 99 ☐ None of the above

⑥ WHAT ORACLE PRODUCTS ARE IN USE AT YOUR SITE? (check all that apply)

Software
- ☐ 01 Oracle9i
- ☐ 02 Oracle9i Lite
- ☐ 03 Oracle8
- ☐ 04 Oracle8i
- ☐ 05 Oracle8i Lite
- ☐ 06 Oracle7
- ☐ 07 Oracle9i Application Server
- ☐ 08 Oracle9i Application Server Wireless
- ☐ 09 Oracle Data Mart Suites
- ☐ 10 Oracle Internet Commerce Server
- ☐ 11 Oracle interMedia
- ☐ 12 Oracle Lite
- ☐ 13 Oracle Payment Server
- ☐ 14 Oracle Video Server
- ☐ 15 Oracle Rdb

Tools
- ☐ 16 Oracle Darwin
- ☐ 17 Oracle Designer
- ☐ 18 Oracle Developer
- ☐ 19 Oracle Discoverer
- ☐ 20 Oracle Express
- ☐ 21 Oracle JDeveloper
- ☐ 22 Oracle Reports
- ☐ 23 Oracle Portal
- ☐ 24 Oracle Warehouse Builder
- ☐ 25 Oracle Workflow

Oracle E-Business Suite
- ☐ 26 Oracle Advanced Planning/Scheduling
- ☐ 27 Oracle Business Intelligence
- ☐ 28 Oracle E-Commerce
- ☐ 29 Oracle Exchange
- ☐ 30 Oracle Financials
- ☐ 31 Oracle Human Resources
- ☐ 32 Oracle Interaction Center
- ☐ 33 Oracle Internet Procurement
- ☐ 34 Oracle Manufacturing
- ☐ 35 Oracle Marketing
- ☐ 36 Oracle Order Management
- ☐ 37 Oracle Professional Services Automation
- ☐ 38 Oracle Projects
- ☐ 39 Oracle Sales
- ☐ 40 Oracle Service
- ☐ 41 Oracle Small Business Suite
- ☐ 42 Oracle Supply Chain Management
- ☐ 43 Oracle Travel Management
- ☐ 44 Oracle Treasury

Oracle Services
- ☐ 45 Oracle.com Online Services
- ☐ 46 Oracle Consulting
- ☐ 47 Oracle Education
- ☐ 48 Oracle Support
- ☐ 98 ther
- 99 ☐ None of the above

⑦ WHAT OTHER DATABASE PRODUCTS ARE IN USE AT YOUR SITE? (check all that apply)

- ☐ 01 Access
- ☐ 02 Baan
- ☐ 03 dbase
- ☐ 04 Gupta
- ☐ 05 IBM DB2
- ☐ 06 Informix
- ☐ 07 Ingres
- ☐ 08 Microsoft Access
- ☐ 09 Microsoft SQL Server
- ☐ 10 PeopleSoft
- ☐ 11 Progress
- ☐ 12 SAP
- ☐ 13 Sybase
- ☐ 14 VSAM
- ☐ 98 Other
- 99 ☐ None of the above

⑧ DURING THE NEXT 12 MONTHS, HOW MUCH DO YOU ANTICIPATE YOUR ORGANIZATION WILL SPEND ON COMPUTER HARDWARE, SOFTWARE, PERIPHERALS, AND SERVICES FOR YOUR LOCATION? (check only one)

- ☐ 01 Less than $10,000
- ☐ 02 $10,000 to $49,999
- ☐ 03 $50,000 to $99,999
- ☐ 04 $100,000 to $499,999
- ☐ 05 $500,000 to $999,999
- ☐ 06 $1,000,000 and over

⑨ WHAT IS YOUR COMPANY'S YEARLY SALES REVENUE? (please choose one)

- ☐ 01 $500,000,000 and above
- ☐ 02 $100,000,000 to $500,000,000
- ☐ 03 $50,000,000 to $100,000,000
- ☐ 04 $5,000,000 to $50,000,000
- ☐ 05 $1,000,000 to $5,000,000

123101

ORACLE® | CERTIFIED PROFESSIONAL

Get Certified Fast

Save 75% online and cut your learning time in half.

Looking to jump on the certification fast track? Oracle University s innovative learning methods ACCELERATE the certification process. What might take you 6 months of in-classroom training takes as little as 12 weeks with our online and CD-ROM-based learning methods. And you ll SAVE as much as 75% when you LEARN ONLINE, compared to our traditional training methods. Get the same high-quality material, at less than half the cost in time and money.

Oracle University. Knowledge from the people who know.

Become a certified professional. *Log on to www.oracle.com/education* today.

ORACLE®

About the BeachFrontQuizzer™ CD-ROM

BeachFrontQuizzer provides interactive certification exams to help you prepare for certification. With the enclosed CD, you can test your knowledge of the topics covered in this book with more than 175 multiple choice questions.

Installation

To install BeachFrontQuizzer:

1. **Insert the CD-ROM in your CD-ROM drive.**

2. **Follow the Setup steps in the displayed Installation Wizard. (When the Setup is finished, you may immediately begin using BeachFrontQuizzer.)**

3. **To begin using BeachFrontQuizzer, enter the 12-digit license key number of the exam you want to take:**

   120-007 Introduction to Oracle9i: SQL   360833394218
   120-031 Oracle9i Database: Fundamentals I   303437108175

Study Sessions

BeachFrontQuizzer tests your knowledge as you learn about new subjects through interactive quiz sessions. Study Session Questions are selected from a single database for each session, dependent on the subcategory selected and the number of times each question has been previously answered correctly. In this way, questions you have answered correctly are not repeated until you have answered all the new questions. Questions that you have missed previously will reappear in later sessions and keep coming back to haunt you until you get the question correct. In addition, you can track your progress by displaying the number of questions you have answered with the Historical Analysis option. You can reset the progress tracking by clicking the Clear History button. Each time a question is presented the answers are randomized so that you will not memorize a pattern or letter that goes with the question. You will start to memorize the correct answer that goes with the question instead.

Practice Exams

For advanced users, BeachFrontQuizzer also provides Simulated and Adaptive certification exams. Questions are chosen at random from the database. The Simulated Exam presents a specific number of questions directly related to the real exam. After you finish the exam, BeachFrontQuizzer displays your score and the passing score required for the test. You may display the exam results of this specific exam from this menu. You may review each question and display the correct answer.

NOTE
For further details of the feature functionality of this BeachFrontQuizzer software, consult the online instructions by choosing Contents from the BeachFrontQuizzer Help menu.

Technical Support

If you experience technical difficulties, please call (888) 992-3131. Outside the United States call (281) 992-3131. Or, you may e-mail bfquiz@swbell.net.

LICENSE AGREEMENT

THIS PRODUCT (THE "PRODUCT") CONTAINS PROPRIETARY SOFTWARE, DATA AND INFORMATION (INCLUDING DOCUMENTATION) OWNED BY THE McGRAW-HILL COMPANIES, INC. ("McGRAW-HILL") AND ITS LICENSORS. YOUR RIGHT TO USE THE PRODUCT IS GOVERNED BY THE TERMS AND CONDITIONS OF THIS AGREEMENT.

LICENSE: Throughout this License Agreement, "you" shall mean either the individual or the entity whose agent opens this package. You are granted a non-exclusive and non-transferable license to use the Product subject to the following terms:

(i) If you have licensed a single user version of the Product, the Product may only be used on a single computer (i.e., a single CPU). If you licensed and paid the fee applicable to a local area network or wide area network version of the Product, you are subject to the terms of the following subparagraph (ii).

(ii) If you have licensed a local area network version, you may use the Product on unlimited workstations located in one single building selected by you that is served by such local area network. If you have licensed a wide area network version, you may use the Product on unlimited workstations located in multiple buildings on the same site selected by you that is served by such wide area network; provided, however, that any building will not be considered located in the same site if it is more than five (5) miles away from any building included in such site. In addition, you may only use a local area or wide area network version of the Product on one single server. If you wish to use the Product on more than one server, you must obtain written authorization from McGraw-Hill and pay additional fees.

(iii) You may make one copy of the Product for back-up purposes only and you must maintain an accurate record as to the location of the back-up at all times.

COPYRIGHT; RESTRICTIONS ON USE AND TRANSFER: All rights (including copyright) in and to the Product are owned by McGraw-Hill and its licensors. You are the owner of the enclosed disc on which the Product is recorded. You may not use, copy, decompile, disassemble, reverse engineer, modify, reproduce, create derivative works, transmit, distribute, sublicense, store in a database or retrieval system of any kind, rent or transfer the Product, or any portion thereof, in any form or by any means (including electronically or otherwise) except as expressly provided for in this License Agreement. You must reproduce the copyright notices, trademark notices, legends and logos of McGraw-Hill and its licensors that appear on the Product on the back-up copy of the Product which you are permitted to make hereunder. All rights in the Product not expressly granted herein are reserved by McGraw-Hill and its licensors.

TERM: This License Agreement is effective until terminated. It will terminate if you fail to comply with any term or condition of this License Agreement. Upon termination, you are obligated to return to McGraw-Hill the Product together with all copies thereof and to purge all copies of the Product included in any and all servers and computer facilities.

DISCLAIMER OF WARRANTY: THE PRODUCT AND THE BACK-UP COPY ARE LICENSED "AS IS." McGRAW-HILL, ITS LICENSORS AND THE AUTHORS MAKE NO WARRANTIES, EXPRESS OR IMPLIED, AS TO THE RESULTS TO BE OBTAINED BY ANY PERSON OR ENTITY FROM USE OF THE PRODUCT, ANY INFORMATION OR DATA INCLUDED THEREIN AND/OR ANY TECHNICAL SUPPORT SERVICES PROVIDED HEREUNDER, IF ANY ("TECHNICAL SUPPORT SERVICES"). McGRAW-HILL, ITS LICENSORS AND THE AUTHORS MAKE NO EXPRESS OR IMPLIED WARRANTIES OF MERCHANTABILITY OR FITNESS FOR A PARTICULAR PURPOSE OR USE WITH RESPECT TO THE PRODUCT. McGRAW-HILL, ITS LICENSORS, AND THE AUTHORS MAKE NO GUARANTEE THAT YOU WILL PASS ANY CERTIFICATION EXAM WHATSOEVER BY USING THIS PRODUCT. NEITHER McGRAW-HILL, ANY OF ITS LICENSORS NOR THE AUTHORS WARRANT THAT THE FUNCTIONS CONTAINED IN THE PRODUCT WILL MEET YOUR REQUIREMENTS OR THAT THE OPERATION OF THE PRODUCT WILL BE UNINTERRUPTED OR ERROR FREE. YOU ASSUME THE ENTIRE RISK WITH RESPECT TO THE QUALITY AND PERFORMANCE OF THE PRODUCT.

LIMITED WARRANTY FOR DISC: To the original licensee only, McGraw-Hill warrants that the enclosed disc on which the Product is recorded is free from defects in materials and workmanship under normal use and service for a period of ninety (90) days from the date of purchase. In the event of a defect in the disc covered by the foregoing warranty, McGraw-Hill will replace the disc.

LIMITATION OF LIABILITY: NEITHER McGRAW-HILL, ITS LICENSORS NOR THE AUTHORS SHALL BE LIABLE FOR ANY INDIRECT, SPECIAL OR CONSEQUENTIAL DAMAGES, SUCH AS BUT NOT LIMITED TO, LOSS OF ANTICIPATED PROFITS OR BENEFITS, RESULTING FROM THE USE OR INABILITY TO USE THE PRODUCT EVEN IF ANY OF THEM HAS BEEN ADVISED OF THE POSSIBILITY OF SUCH DAMAGES. THIS LIMITATION OF LIABILITY SHALL APPLY TO ANY CLAIM OR CAUSE WHATSOEVER WHETHER SUCH CLAIM OR CAUSE ARISES IN CONTRACT, TORT, OR OTHERWISE. Some states do not allow the exclusion or limitation of indirect, special or consequential damages, so the above limitation may not apply to you.

U.S. GOVERNMENT RESTRICTED RIGHTS: Any software included in the Product is provided with restricted rights subject to subparagraphs (c), (1) and (2) of the Commercial Computer Software-Restricted Rights clause at 48 C.F.R. 52.227-19. The terms of this Agreement applicable to the use of the data in the Product are those under which the data are generally made available to the general public by McGraw-Hill. Except as provided herein, no reproduction, use, or disclosure rights are granted with respect to the data included in the Product and no right to modify or create derivative works from any such data is hereby granted.

GENERAL: This License Agreement constitutes the entire agreement between the parties relating to the Product. The terms of any Purchase Order shall have no effect on the terms of this License Agreement. Failure of McGraw-Hill to insist at any time on strict compliance with this License Agreement shall not constitute a waiver of any rights under this License Agreement. This License Agreement shall be construed and governed in accordance with the laws of the State of New York. If any provision of this License Agreement is held to be contrary to law, that provision will be enforced to the maximum extent permissible and the remaining provisions will remain in full force and effect.